CORRECTIONS & ERRATA

It has been brought to the attention of the publisher and author that certain information contained on pages 23, 24, 151, 321, 327 and 328 relating to the Webster Publishing Company, Ltd. is inaccurate. This information was obtained by the publisher and author from sources believed to have been reliable at the time.

We have determined that Webster Publishing Company, Ltd., the Webster Dictionary Company, Inc., and the G & C Merriam Company were involved in protracted civil litigation involving various allegations of infringement of certain rights. The parties have, however, settled the dispute and all litigation has ceased. All references to fines and selling imitations were based upon reports about civil litigation which were not accurate as to Webster Publishing Company, Ltd. Neither the publisher nor the author has any knowledge of any criminal fines or judgment against Webster Publishing Company, Ltd.

We are advised that Webster Publishing Company, Ltd. discontinued distribution of *The New American Encyclopedia* in 1979.

The publisher and author regret these errors and any inconvenience they may have caused.

ENCYCLOPEDIA BUYING GUIDE

ENCYCLOPEDIA BUYING GUIDE

A Consumer Guide to General Encyclopedias in Print

THIRD EDITION

Kenneth F. Kister

R. R. Bowker Company
New York & London, 1981

Our knowledge is the amassed thought and experience
of innumerable minds.

RALPH WALDO EMERSON
Letters and Social Aims

Published by R. R. Bowker Company
1180 Avenue of the Americas, New York, N.Y. 10036
Copyright © 1981 by Xerox Corporation
All rights reserved
International Standard Book Numbers   0-8352-1353-6 (hardbound)
                                     0-8352-1409-5 (paper)
International Standard Serial Number 0361-1094
Library of Congress Catalog Card Number 76-645701
Printed and bound in the United States of America

The author is grateful for permission to reprint the following from works held in
copyright:

Drawing by Dana Fradon. Reprinted with permission of The New Yorker Magazine, Inc. and Dana Fradon. © 1975.

"Encyclopedias and the Public Library: A National Survey" and the Professional
Reading review of *Purchasing an Encyclopedia: 12 Points to Consider*. Reprinted with permission from *Library Journal* April 15, 1979 and December 15,
1979. © 1979 by Xerox Corporation.

Letter from Ms. Rosalie Elespuru-Murphy to the editor of *RQ*. Reprinted from
RQ Summer 1980 with the permission of Ms. Elespuru-Murphy.

Contents

Preface

This edition of *Encyclopedia Buying Guide* reviews all general English-language encyclopedias published or distributed in the United States and Canada as of early 1981. The guide's coverage ranges from expensive multivolume sets for adults like *Collier's Encyclopedia* and the *New Encyclopaedia Britannica* to small one-volume items for children such as the *Junior Encyclopedia of General Knowledge*. In all, 36 in-print encyclopedias are closely and comparatively evaluated. Moreover, numerous discontinued titles that might be encountered on the secondhand or remainder market are described in Appendix A. The guide also provides pertinent consumer information, including a summary of laws and regulations affecting the merchandising of encyclopedic products and a suggested procedure for comparison shopping for encyclopedias. No other source covers the encyclopedia trade as thoroughly as *Encyclopedia Buying Guide*. The guide, which has become the standard work in this important area of reference publishing, is consulted by librarians, educators, publishers, booksellers, reviewers, journalists, and the general public for current, authoritative information about all-purpose encyclopedias.

Issued every three years, the *Buying Guide* is now in its third edition and continues the series originally entitled *General Encyclopedias in Print* (1963–1974). This edition reviews encyclopedias bearing 1980 copyright dates or earlier. In those instances when an encyclopedia has not been revised as recently as 1980 but remains in print (the *New American Encyclopedia* and the *Random House Encyclopedia* are examples), the latest printing or revision is reviewed. All encyclopedias, no matter what their dates, have been evaluated with the informational needs and developments of the early 1980s in mind.

A number of new features distinguish this edition of the *Buying Guide*. First, encyclopedias reviewed are now grouped in five size-user categories (e.g., "Multivolume Adult Encyclopedias") rather than arranged in a single alphabetical sequence as in previous editions. This new arrangement affords users a more convenient perspective on encyclopedias of similar size, purpose, and scope. Second, the trend toward computerized encyclopedias is briefly explored in the "Introducing Encyclopedias" portion of Part I. Third, the "Encyclopedias at a Glance" chart at the end of Part I is now printed on colored paper for easier access. Fourth, the new "Special Reports" feature (Part II) comprises two national surveys which offer users of the guide informed professional judgments by U.S. and Canadian librarians on the merits of specific encyclopedias. Fifth, the "Other Critical Opinions" section that concludes each review in the *Buying Guide* now provides digests of the major opinions cited. And finally, a roundup of general encyclopedias sold in the United Kingdom has been added to the guide's appended material (see Appendix C).

Information in the *Buying Guide* is current as of March 1981, the closing date for reporting new titles, price changes, review citations, etc. Responsibility for all descriptive matter and unattributed opinion ultimately rests with the author. Published reviews in sources like *American Reference Books Annual* and *Booklist* were naturally consulted, along with such standard reference guides as Bill Katz's two-volume *Introduction to Reference Work* (which treats encyclopedias in the first volume, *Basic Information Sources*) and Eugene P. Sheehy's *Guide to Reference Books*. The major critical input, however, is derived from original analysis of numerous articles in each encyclopedia by the author and five subject consultants commissioned by the R. R. Bowker Company. Much gratitude is due these consultants for their specialized knowledge and informative appraisals: Dr. John C. Briggs (Professor, Department of Marine Science, University of South Florida, St. Petersburg Campus); Dr. J. Michael Cupoli (Assistant Professor, Pediatrics Department, School of Medicine, University of South Florida, Tampa Campus); Dr. Silvio L. Gaggi (Associate Professor, Department of Humanities, University of South Florida, Tampa Campus); Clarice M. Ruder (Assistant Head, Special Collections Department, Tampa-Hillsborough Public Library, Fla.); and Dr. Donald C. Yelton (Free-lance Editorial Specialist, Watch Hill, R.I.).

Thanks are also due Dr. Norman Horrocks (Director, School of Library Service, Dalhousie University, Halifax, Nova Scotia) for his survey of Canadian public library attitudes toward general encyclopedias in that country.

From the outset, an advisory board of three distinguished librarians has overseen the planning and development of the *Buying Guide* project. These advisers furnished key ideas and invaluable feedback concerning the guide's organization, tone, and new features. The author is indebted to members of the board for their judicious and forthright counsel: Dr. Jack A. Clarke (Professor, Library School, University of Wisconsin, Madison); Allan J. Dyson (Librarian, University of California, Santa Cruz); and Eleanor Radwan (Head, General Reference Services, Mid-Manhattan Library, New York Public Library).

The author and his colleagues are obliged to the many encyclopedia publishers and distributors who actively assisted the *Buying Guide* project by providing review materials, price information, and a variety of factual data. This kind of cooperation on the part of the encyclopedia publishing community helps ensure the guide's dependability and usefulness as a consumer tool. By general agreement R. R. Bowker personnel had no hand in formulating the reviews in *Encyclopedia Buying Guide*, quite properly leaving this work to the author and his consultants.

KENNETH F. KISTER

How to Use This Book

ARRANGEMENT

Encyclopedia Buying Guide covers the world of encyclopedias step-by-step, proceeding from the general to the specific.

Part I discusses encyclopedias as a type of reference work, beginning with "Introducing Encyclopedias," which notes the purpose, history, and present status of general encyclopedias. The next section, "Selling Encyclopedias," explains how encyclopedias are normally merchandised and provides basic consumer protection information. Next, "Finding the Right Encyclopedia" furnishes a checklist of standard evaluative criteria (such as authority, reliability, recency, clarity, objectivity, and accessibility) used to determine the overall quality of any encyclopedia. This section also includes advice on comparison shopping for encyclopedias, often a frustrating business because, unlike most consumer products, encyclopedias are usually not sold in retail stores but must be purchased either through sales representatives who sell in the home or via direct mail order. Part I concludes with "Encyclopedias at a Glance," a comparative chart that itemizes factual information about all 36 encyclopedias in convenient tabular form. Note that the chart, which contains only raw quantitative data, is *not* intended as a final selection aid. Rather, the intention is to steer prospective consumers to those titles which, at least at first glance, appear to be reasonable candidates for purchase based on the simple criteria of size, price, and intended usership.

Part II comprises two special reports that reveal how a cross section of librarians—experts on reference materials—views the current crop of encyclopedias. The report by Ken Kister, author of *Encyclopedia Buying Guide,* presents the results of a national questionnaire survey of U.S. public librarians on encyclopedia use and the comparative effectiveness of individual titles. The report by Norman Horrocks, a leading North American library educator, offers similar survey data gathered from Canadian librarians. Like the chart in Part I, these reports are not intended as selection devices but they can provide consumers with pertinent overview information to help narrow the field to a manageable number of purchase possibilities.

Parts III–VII, the heart of the *Buying Guide,* consist of critical reviews of all in-print general English-language encyclopedias currently on the North American market. The detailed evaluations pinpoint each set's strengths and weaknesses in such decisive areas as accuracy, currency, and readability of articles, accessibility of contents, and quality of illustrations and bibliographies. The reviews, grouped alphabetically in five size-user categores (e.g., Part III is "Multivolume Adult Encyclopedias"), also evaluate each encyclopedia's physical format and special features (if any) and specify its most appropriate audience. A summary section digests the main critical points and concludes with a comparative note on competing encyclopedias of similar scope, usership, and price. For consumers who might want additional information, citations to other published opinions appear at the end of each review. Brief synopses of these opinions are provided as a matter of convenience, particularly for users of the *Buying Guide* who lack easy access to the sources cited.

Five appendixes and a title-subject index complete the *Buying Guide.* Appendix A describes general English-language encyclopedias discontinued during the past two decades. These out-of-print encyclopedias might be encountered in secondhand bookstores or as remainders in discount stores, and on occasion they are rebound and peddled as new works by fly-by-night operators. Appendix B identifies some popular almanacs and yearbooks that can inexpensively supplement a general encyclopedia, especially one beginning to show its age. Appendix C briefly notes those general encyclopedias currently available on the British market. Appendix D is an annotated list of books, articles, review journals, and nonprint items of potential interest to consumers, teachers, and students of encyclopedias. Appendix E is a comprehensive directory of North American encyclopedia publishers and distributors. Finally, the title-subject index cites all encyclopedic works discussed in the *Buying Guide* (including those in the appendixes) and provides references to the various topics covered in Parts I and II, such as secondhand encyclopedias and bias in encyclopedias.

To RECAP: *Encyclopedia Buying Guide* is a full consumer resource. For best results, read the introductory material (Part I) and "Special Reports" (Part II) prior to making any purchase decision. The "Encyclopedias at a Glance" chart (on colored paper at the end of Part I) will guide you to those several encyclopedias that seem to be sensible initial choices based on the fundamental determinants of size, reader suitability, and cost. Reviews should then be consulted for detailed critical information about each encyclopedia selected (Parts III–VII). Users of the guide simply seeking information about a particular encyclopedia can turn directly to the review, locating the title through the index.

METHODOLOGY

How were the criticisms in the *Buying Guide* formulated? What procedures were used to evaluate the encyclopedias? As noted in the preface, published reviews as well as commentaries in standard reference guides and texts were taken into account. For the most part, however, the *Buy-*

ing Guide's evaluations are based on close analysis of numerous topics in each encyclopedia. The topics, preselected by the author of the guide and analyzed by him and his corps of subject consultants, represent all fields of knowledge and cover types of information one might reasonably expect to find in a general encyclopedia.

The key topics checked in encyclopedias in both the adult and young adult categories are *Afghanistan, American Revolution, Atomic Energy Commission* (AEC), *Canada, child development, China, cults* (including religious sects), *diabetes, dinosaurs, estrogen, evolution* (biological), *Greenland, Warren Harding, homosexuality, hypnosis, Thomas Jefferson, mass transportation* (emphasis on *subways*), *motion pictures* (as an art form), *North American Indians, nuclear power, Nuclear Regulatory Commission* (NRC), *Georgia O'Keeffe, Paris, sharks, shock therapy, William Styron, suicide, tuberculosis, X rays,* and *Zimbabwe/Rhodesia*.

Children's encyclopedias, naturally less detailed and sophisticated than those intended for adults and older students, were checked for information on these topics: *Africa, baby/child, Canada, China, death, disease, evolution* (biological), *Greenland, Warren Harding, Thomas Jefferson, motion pictures, North American Indians, painting/drawing, Paris, psychology, religion, sharks, subways, suicide,* and *television*.

These topics were analyzed for *authority* (are the contributors and editors responsible for the material qualified?), *reliability* (is the material accurate?), *recency* (is the material reasonably up-to-date?), *objectivity* (is the material presented in a balanced, unbiased manner?), *clarity* (is the material written in a clear and readable style for the intended user?), and *accessibility* (can the material be easily retrieved?). In the course of these evaluations, each encyclopedia's *bibliographies* (lists of sources of further information), *graphics* (visual illustrations like diagrams, photographs, and maps), *physical format* (quality of print, page layout, paper, binding, and so forth), and *special features* (unique or unusual methods of presenting or organizing material, provision of supplementary volumes or learning aids, etc.) were appraised.

One other standard research technique—systematic random sampling— was used in the encyclopedia evaluation process. This method entails the methodical checking of every "kth" item. For instance, every fifth article in, say, the *C* volume of an encyclopedia might be read for clarity or every tenth index entry checked for accuracy. The author of the *Buying Guide* used random sampling extensively as a complement to in-depth analysis of specific topics.

EXCLUSIONS

Encyclopedia Buying Guide reviews all nonspecialized English-language encyclopedias in print in the United States and Canada. Specialized works like *Encyclopaedia Judaica,* the *New Catholic Encyclopedia,* the *Encyclopedia of World Literature in the 20th Century,* the *International Encyclopedia of the Social Sciences,* the *McGraw-Hill Encyclopedia of Science and Technology, Encyclopedia Canadiana,* and the *Great Soviet Encyclopedia* are excluded. These and many similar subject reference sources will eventually be reviewed in Bowker's forthcoming *Specialized Encyclopedias & Dictionaries,* a companion work to *Encyclopedia Buying Guide* and the author's *Dictionary Buying Guide* (R. R. Bowker, 1977), which systematically covers general English-language dictionaries and related wordbooks on the North American market.

PRICES AND OTHER DATA

Prices appear at the beginning of each review and in the "Encyclopedias at a Glance" chart at the end of Part I. Price information, current as of March 1981, was verified via questionnaire sent to the publishers and distributors. Lowest retail prices are quoted. Prices are also provided for schools and libraries (educational institutions normally receive a substantial discount). Users of the *Buying Guide* should understand that publishers and distributors may change their prices at any time. On the other hand, prices indicated in the guide should not vary markedly from those quoted by sales representatives. *Large price variations should be questioned.* If necessary, contact the publisher or distributor's home office (see Appendix E for addresses and telephone numbers).

Other encyclopedia data such as number of articles, words, illustrations, and contributors for each set usually represent estimates or actual counts furnished by the publisher or distributor. If the figures provided seem exaggerated or incorrect for any reason, the *Buying Guide* checks them by means of sample counts and, when necessary, makes appropriate changes. Cross-reference and index entry statistics, introduced in the last edition of the *Buying Guide,* have proved to be a useful comparative feature and hence are retained in this edition.

COMPARATIVE CROSS-REFERENCES

The reviews in *Encyclopedia Buying Guide* include numerous comparative references to encyclopedias of similar size, scope, purpose, arrangement, price, and intended readership. For example, in the "Arrangement and Accessibility" section of the *Random House Encyclopedia* review there is a comparative note about the *New Columbia Encyclopedia,* a major *Random House* competitor. And in the "Recency" section, *Random House* is compared with other important small-volume adult encyclopedias, including *New Columbia.* Unless otherwise stated, all comparative references in the *Buying Guide* are to encyclopedias reviewed in Parts III–VII. Comparative references therefore function as cross-references from one title to another.

I. GENERAL INFORMATION

Introducing Encyclopedias

The encyclopedia, like the wheel, is a simple yet very effective tool. And just as the wheel has played an instrumental role in human material progress over the centuries, the encyclopedia has proved to be an important vehicle for intellectual advancement.

The basic purpose of any general encyclopedia is to organize and summarize the most significant factual and theoretical knowledge available and, ultimately, to make that knowledge accessible (both physically and intellectually) to nonspecialists. François Guizot called the famous eighteenth-century French *Encyclopédie* a "vast intellectual bazaar where the results of all the works of the human spirit are offered to whosoever stops to satisfy his curiosity," a description that might apply to any great encyclopedia, ancient or modern. Encyclopedias, in short, aim to encompass and codify all that is worth knowing. In point of fact, the word *encyclopedia* comes to us from the Greek *enkýklios paideiā,* which translates variously as "circle of knowledge," "circle of learning," "complete system of learning," and "well-rounded education." The encyclopedia is (again like the wheel) an indispensable as well as inevitable tool of human development.

Encyclopedias have numerous uses, chief among which are to inform, to analyze, and to provide a frame of reference. General encyclopedias are thought of first and foremost as sources of facts, and they do offer basic factual information on literally thousands of subjects, from aardvarks and Henry Aaron to Zimbabwe and zucchini. Of equal importance, however, are the encyclopedia's comprehensive summaries of essential and often complex ideas from the constantly expanding store of universal knowledge. Any reputable encyclopedia for adults or older students will explain concisely, for example, how the human digestive system works, the role of nucleic acid in the genetic process, the main components of the New Criticism, how Art Deco differs from Art Nouveau, the political and economic tenets of Marxism, and the educational theories of Maria Montessori. The successful encyclopedia will render such subjects comprehensible to the literate layperson without sacrificing accuracy to oversimplification, which is not always an easy task.

Encyclopedias are a logical place to begin investigating any unfamiliar topic. By furnishing a succinct overview of the topic, the encyclopedia is able to orient the reader quickly and effectively. Likewise, encyclopedias normally provide practical information on everyday concerns like plumbing, gardening, medical problems, and games and hobbies; bibliographies, or lists, of selected materials for further information or study on a particular topic; and a great variety of visual aids such as photographs, drawings, art reproductions, instructional diagrams, charts, and maps.

Indeed, no other published work attempts as much or offers more than a well-made general encyclopedia. Small wonder that, along with dictionaries, encyclopedias are our most frequently consulted reference sources. No conscientious critic, however, would suggest that even our best encyclopedias are without flaws. Experienced users of encyclopedias are only too well aware that *no* encyclopedia is completely up-to-date, entirely reliable, totally objective, perfectly organized for maximum accessibility, or always a model of clarity. By virtue of their monumental goal—nothing short of embracing the world's most useful or important knowledge—even the most meticulously prepared encyclopedias leave something to be desired. As Robert Collison commented (in his article on encyclopedias in the *New Encyclopaedia Britannica*) on the attempt to make encyclopedias be all things to all people, "The effort has been magnificent, the results uncertain."

Whatever their imperfections, general encyclopedias can serve as a gateway to understanding the most profound or intricate knowledge human beings have yet produced. But users should be aware that encyclopedias are *not* substitutes for in-depth study and full mastery of a subject. Bill Katz, an authority on reference books, put it this way in his *Basic Information Sources* (McGraw-Hill, 3rd ed., 1978, p. 14): "To clear up a common misunderstanding, no general encyclopedia is a proper source for research. It is only a springboard." Encyclopedists do not conduct original research, nor do they normally base their text on primary sources. Rather, general encyclopedias are tertiary—that is, third-stage—compilations that usually extract their information and data from secondary sources such as trade books, popular journals, and current newspapers (which in turn draw upon primary accounts, original research, and the like). "It is wise to refer to encyclopedias for first guidance; it is priggish to disregard them," science historian George Sarton once wrote. But, he added, "It is foolish to depend too much on them."

HISTORICAL DEVELOPMENT OF ENCYCLOPEDIAS

Encyclopedias historically reflect the attitudes, needs, and capabilities of the society that produces them. For instance, most contemporary encyclopedists agree that recency of material is essential to a successful set. Likewise, most agree that visual illustrations are a vital part of any quality production. In earlier times, however, quite different standards prevailed. For good technological reasons, graphics have only recently come to be regarded as an integral part of the encyclopedic treatment. Similarly, the emphasis on up-to-dateness has become crucial only since the onset of the modern communications revolution. While the fundamental mission of the encyclopedia as an all-embracing source of knowledge has remained constant through the ages, the encyclopedia's style, format, contents, and intended audience have changed over the years in response to new social, political, and technical conditions.

The earliest encyclopedias, laboriously copied by hand, evolved in classical times as a means of classifying and systematizing what was then a comparatively small but growing body of knowledge accessible only to the learned few. For instance, Pliny the Elder's *Historia Naturalis* (A.D. 77), the most influential of the Roman encyclopedias and sometimes cited as the first known encyclopedia, organized ancient scientific scholarship into 37 books comprising some 2,500 chapters on such subjects as geography, physiology, zoology, botany, mineralogy, and medicine. Later, during the early Christian and medieval periods, church scholars and clerics compiled encyclopedias in an effort to interpret and codify existing knowledge in accordance with ecclesiastical doctrine. The theocentric monopoly of knowledge in the Middle Ages was based at least in part on the scarcity of parchment and the readily available services of monastic copyists. It is no accident that the influence of the Church began to decline with the advent of the printing press and its handmaiden, paper.

Mass printing fueled the Renaissance, a period marked by a return to classical learning as well as the beginnings of modern science. With the coming of the Industrial Revolution and resulting secularization of Western society, encyclopedias, now machine printed, became a prime means for keeping abreast of the new social and technical knowledge bubbling up everywhere in Europe. John Harris's *Lexicon Technicum* (1704), the first alphabetically arranged encyclopedia in English (despite its Latin title), and Ephraim Chambers's prestigious *Cyclopaedia* (1728) exemplified this trend in England. In France, long fertile ground for encyclopedias, such works also served as vehicles for the expression of new, frequently unpopular, and even heretical political and religious ideas generated by the Enlightenment. The outstanding examples are Pierre Bayle's *Dictionnaire Historique et Critique* (1697), which divided its contents into factual accounts and "remarks" (or opinions), and the justly celebrated *Encyclopédie* (1751—1772), a massive undertaking edited by the philosopher Denis Diderot and mathematician Jean le Rond d'Alembert. The *Encyclopédie,* though condemned by Pope Clement VIII and censored at various times by the French government, had an exhilarating effect on the intellectual and revolutionary thought of the day.

The 70-volume French *Encyclopédie,* initiated as a translation of Chambers's *Cyclopaedia* but ultimately a very different work, is especially notable in the history of encyclopedia-making for two reasons. First, the set extended coverage to the industrial trades and mechanical arts, heretofore considered inferior in the encyclopedic scheme of knowledge to the fine arts, religion and philosophy, and the natural sciences. Thus the *Encyclopédie,* which commanded the respect of savants everywhere, established the precedent for including the useful arts and other practical subjects within the purview of a general encyclopedia. Second, the *Encyclopédie* was the product of "une société de gens de lettres" (a society of scholars) that included some of the most distinguished thinkers of eighteenth-century France, including Voltaire, Rousseau, Turgot, Montesquieu, Quesnay, and Condorcet, along with editors Diderot and d'Alembert. Prior to the *Encyclopédie,* such works had been prepared by one person or, at most, several collaborators.

In retrospect, these developments seem entirely natural and logical. The Enlightenment, a time of great political and scientific ferment, witnessed major breakthroughs in medicine and technology, the emergence of the modern social and behavioral sciences, an awakening of working-class consciousness, and a massive yearning for a more egalitarian society, the latter culminating in the American and French revolutions. By the eighteenth century, the volume of essential knowledge had grown so large that no single individual, no matter how diligent or brilliant, could hope to master it all. In sum, Diderot's *Encyclopédie,* like all encyclopedias of consequence before or since, mirrored the intellectual conditions and aspirations of the people and times that created it. Significantly, the *Encyclopédie* also provided the impulse for the first edition of *Encyclopaedia Britannica* (1768—1771). For a fascinating scholarly account of the publishing history of the *Encyclopédie,* see Robert Darnton's *The Business of Enlightenment* (Harvard University Press, 1979).

During the nineteenth century, general encyclopedias took on most of the characteristics we associate with encyclopedias today. Their content and organization increasingly reflected the general growth of democratic ideals and institutions, particularly the movement toward universal public education and the concurrent need for easily accessible, readily digestible bits of information for the general public, including masses of schoolchildren. No longer was the general encyclopedia the preserve of sages, or clerics, or social philosophers. A famous German encyclopedia epitomized these developments. Friedrich Arnold Brockhaus's durable *Konversations-Lexikon* (first published in Germany during 1796–1811 with many successive editions) treated knowledge in short, fact-packed, up-to-date, accurate, popularly written articles. The success of *Brockhaus* (as the set is familiarly known) was contagious, and it exerted an enormous influence on encyclopedia-making throughout the nineteenth century. Most notably, *Brockhaus* served as the model for numerous other national encyclopedias, including *The Encyclopedia Americana,* first published between 1829 and 1833. Emphasis on popular knowledge and information, simplification of complex subject matter, attention to factual accuracy, use of specific entries, and a concern with up-to-dateness—all features of today's encyclopedias—are direct legacies of *Brockhaus.*

ENCYCLOPEDIAS IN THE TWENTIETH CENTURY

In response to the intellectual character and informational needs of the times, twentieth-century encyclopedists have adhered rather strictly to a well-defined set of qualitative standards that they believe produces the most utilitarian encyclopedias for the greatest number of potential users. Actually, at no other time in the long history of encyclopedia-making have the hallmarks of what constitutes a quality set been so clearly established and universally endorsed as they are today. All reputable contemporary encyclopedists strive, for instance, to be as objective as humanly possible in the treatment of sensitive or controversial subjects. No responsible encyclopedia editor in the 1980s would even consider publishing the sort of polemical articles Diderot and d'Alembert did in the *Encyclo-pédie,* simply because it is now agreed that the principal function of a general encyclopedia is to codify established knowledge as accurately and impartially as possible, not to instigate argumentation or promote contro-versial ideas. (A modern exception is the *Great Soviet Encyclopedia,* a major national work currently being published volume-by-volume from the Russian by Macmillan. Despite its monumental scholarship, the ency-clopedia reflects official Soviet political ideology and suffers from govern-ment censorship in some areas.) On the other hand, the practice of com-missioning distinguished contributors, as the editors of the *Encyclopédie* did, is now standard operating procedure in the encyclopedia business.

General agreement also exists that a good encyclopedia should provide selected bibliographies, and that at least the multivolume sets should have a separate index, complemented by cross-references throughout the text. Moreover, with some notable exceptions, encyclopedias today tend to-ward short articles and specific entries, à la *Brockhaus,* which lend them-selves to quick retrieval with the standard A–Z arrangement. Another common characteristic of present-day encyclopedias is simplicity of style and emphasis on straightforward (and usually bland) prose. Photographs, instructional drawings, and other visual aids frequently accompany the printed text. Visuals are now often printed in color, a recent development that has not only enhanced the attractiveness and informational capability of encyclopedias but vastly increased their production costs. There is also a strong tendency to include much popular and practical material on sports, hobbies, celebrities and newsworthy personalities, how-to-do-it topics, and the like. And in recent years the better sets have made a concerted effort to be more international (as opposed to Western) in perspective and treatment. Indeed, the appearance of the *New Encyclo-paedia Britannica* (15th ed.) in 1974, the first thorough overhaul of the *Britannica* in 45 years, set a new standard for world coverage of knowledge by a general encyclopedia.

Editorial procedures for achieving contemporary encyclopedia norms have likewise become firmly fixed. As noted earlier, recognized subject authorities are likely to be commissioned to write or authenticate articles, thereby ensuring a reasonable degree of accuracy and objectivity. Perma-nent editorial staffs, sometimes quite large, are maintained to produce general articles, perform routine updating chores, monitor areas where knowledge changes rapidly, assign topics to contributors, and edit com-missioned articles for such specifications as length, style, and readability. The larger encyclopedias are normally kept current by means of "continu-ous revision," a fairly recent but now securely entrenched technique that entails revising only a certain portion (about 10 percent) of a set's con-tents each year, thus eliminating the need for frequent costly new edi-tions. The major encyclopedia publishers also employ large promotion and sales forces, without which the editorial resources necessary to pro-duce a viable encyclopedia could not be maintained.

Obviously general encyclopedias today differ markedly from those of earlier times. Whereas once the emphasis was on long, scholarly treatises intended for the educated elite and later on the pathbreaking knowledge engendered by the Enlightenment, present-day encyclopedias are devoted largely to popular treatment of that knowledge and information deemed most useful or essential to what political analyst Ben J. Wattenberg has called "the first massive majority middle-class society in history." In a word, our encyclopedias have become democratized. And whereas encyclopedias were originally the products of a few learned men, they are now created by teams of specialists, men and women working together under the aegis of a large publishing house to make the ever-expanding universe of knowledge accessible to the general public. As Otto V. St. Whitelock rightly observed in his article "On the Making and Survival of Encyclopedias" (*Choice,* June 1967, p. 381), "The expansion of every field of knowledge has transformed the editorial process from an individual responsibility to a collective enterprise."

The upshot, unfortunately but predictably, is that today's encyclopedias too often cater to the lowest common intellectual denominator. In their desire to be all things to all consumers, our encyclopedias—like our automobiles—often look and sound much alike, at least on the surface. Similar objectives, standards, and methods have inevitably resulted in similar products. And in the competitive effort to make a profit, corners are sometimes cut and what at first glance looks like a quality product turns out to be a lemon on closer acquaintance. Even low quality encyclopedias can give the surface impression of respectability by, say, showing off some colorful visuals or listing a few Nobel Prize winners among the contributors. The trick for consumers, of course, is to determine which of the many look-alike encyclopedias on the market are works of genuine quality, and then which one in that group will best meet their informational needs at a reasonable price. But before making any hard-and-fast determinations about the qualitative worth of any particular title, it is helpful to have some idea of the multifarious problems that confront encyclopedists today.

ENCYCLOPEDIA WOES IN THE 1980s

"Publishing an encyclopedia is complicated far beyond the wildest nightmares of the fiction editor," once wrote Margaret G. Cook (in her *New Library Key,* H. W. Wilson, 2nd ed., 1963, p. 61). Not the least of the encyclopedia-maker's predicaments is keeping pace with new knowledge. This task has never been easy, but at the present time, because of what is popularly called the "knowledge explosion," it has reached nearly impossible dimensions. People in the business of estimates say that our knowledge is currently doubling every ten years or so. This exponential growth of knowledge threatens to submerge humankind in a torrent of paper, microforms, and computer printouts. For instance, one study suggests that approximately half-a-million pages of printed matter are currently added to our store of raw knowledge every minute. Another study concludes that it would take an average physician or trained medical researcher nearly 55 centuries just to read all the medical literature published in the year 1978 alone! The job of encyclopedia editors and their staffs is to sift through the sprawling, constantly accreting mass of published material in all areas, extract the relevant encyclopedic knowledge, and then organize and digest that knowledge in such a manner that it can be easily retrieved and understood by average readers. And because of the faster and faster pace of knowledge production, the job becomes proportionately more difficult every decade, every year, every day, indeed every minute. It is hardly an exaggeration, then, to suggest that making a quality general encyclopedia at this point in history requires not only much time, money, and endeavor, but also considerable courage and the possibility of more than a few nightmares.

Another vexing editorial problem encyclopedia-makers face in the 1980s is the paradoxical situation that, while knowledge is expanding at an astronomical rate, the world has shrunk, socioculturally speaking, to the size of a "global village," as Marshall McLuhan aptly put it some years ago. At the beginning of the last century, for example, Andrew Jackson fought the Battle of New Orleans on January 8, 1815, reputedly because he had not heard that the war had ended two weeks earlier with the signing of the Treaty of Ghent on December 24, 1814. But today, in the twinkling of an electron, people all over the world instantaneously know when a war or border conflict is over, who the new U.S. or Chinese leader is, where the latest natural disaster has struck, when a new gene has been mapped or a new planet discovered. No longer do encyclopedists have the luxury of time to contemplate their raw material, nor does geography limit the reaches of knowledge. The leisurely tempo and insular outlook of encyclopedias of earlier times have given way to demands for speedy and ecumenical treatment of new knowledge.

An analogous problem for today's encyclopedists concerns rapidly changing social attitudes and behavior. In recent times, perceptions about sex, race, women's rights, drug use, popular music, the environment, energy consumption, political morality, and life-styles in general have undergone dramatic and, in some cases, profound change in this country and, in fact, all over the world. Encyclopedia-makers must be attuned to, or at least aware of, such social changes and their consequences, which are frequently jarring and controversial. In the area of sexual behavior, for instance, the latest data indicate that over 50 percent of all women in the United States experience intercourse by age 18, and that 20 percent have had sexual relations by age 14. It is hardly unreasonable, therefore, to expect contemporary encyclopedias designed for young people between the ages of 12 and 18 to include forthright information about human reproduction, birth control, and parenthood. On the other hand, encyclopedia publishers feel pressure, real or imagined, to treat sex and childbirth in the old "birds-and-bees" manner. Some simply ignore the subject entirely. How an encyclopedia deals with topics involving rapidly changing social mores is the acid test of its makers' professional integrity and intellectual awareness.

Finding capable people to write for the encyclopedia is another obstacle editors confront. A logical source of qualified contributors is the academic community, but all too often encyclopedists find that academicians are unable to produce a coherent survey article on their specialty. Some professors apparently find it impossible to express themselves in terms that the general public can understand, while others simply cannot write. Nearly every experienced encyclopedia editor has a horror story about a distinguished scholar whose article finally ended up in the wastebasket. Compounding the problem of recruiting contributors who both know their subject and know how to express themselves in writing is the fact that writing for encyclopedias is not terribly lucrative. "We offer our contributors 10¢ a word, or about $50 for a 500-word article," revealed Frank Greenagel of the new *Academic American Encyclopedia* in an interview in *Wilson Library Bulletin* (March 1980, p. 438), "which isn't very much considering the difficulty of writing a really concise yet comprehensive and definitive encyclopedia article."

Encyclopedia-makers have yet other, albeit more mundane, problems arising from higher costs and declining sales and profits. Producing an encyclopedia of any consequence requires a heavy financial investment. Editors, editorial staffs, advisory boards, authoritative contributors, caption writers, marketing and sales personnel, proofreaders, indexers, printers, paper, color reproductions, computers, and operating facilities do not grow on trees in New York or Chicago (where most American encyclopedias are produced) or anywhere else for that matter. Moreover, as in all industries these days, inflation has driven encyclopedia production costs higher and higher each year. The 30-volume *New Encyclopaedia Britannica,* first issued in 1974, reputedly cost over $30 million. The small-volume *Random House Encyclopedia,* published in 1977, required an estimated $7 million for development alone, exclusive of production costs. And it took in the neighborhood of $25 million to produce the 21-volume *Academic American Encyclopedia* (1980), which is only about a third as large as the *Britannica* in terms of number of pages.

On the other side of the ledger, domestic encyclopedia sales and profits have sagged in recent years. One major reason for the downturn is what economic analysts call "bad demographics." In plain English, population trends show that fewer children are being born in the United States these days and, because families with children constitute a prime market for general encyclopedias, sales for the product show a corresponding decline. In point of fact, the U.S. birthrate has fallen drastically over the past 20 years, down from 3.7 children per family in 1957 to 1.8 in 1975. Even gloomier news for encyclopedia publishers is the fact that the number of families with *any* offspring has dropped even more sharply. More recent Census Bureau data confirm an almost unbroken decline in the fertility rate since the baby boom of the 1950s. In a *New York Times* article entitled "New Population Trends Transforming U.S." (February 6, 1977), Robert Reinhold noted, "It seems safe to assume that a country dominated by the old will need less baby food, toys, teachers, and maternity wards." The same logic applies, of course, to encyclopedias and related products, which have always appealed most strongly to house-

*"I can't put it into layman's language for you. I don't
know any layman's language."*

holds with youngsters in elementary and middle school. These "bad
demographic" trends show few signs of abating in the 1980s.

An equally important reason for the dismal encyclopedia sales-profit
picture in recent years has been the U.S consumer's growing disenchantment with traditional encyclopedia sales methods. As discussed more
fully in the next section of the *Buying Guide* ("Selling Encyclopedias"),
many consumers have become wary of door-to-door vendors, turned off
by their sometimes hard sell tactics. Encyclopedia sales representatives,
who in the past have used practically any means imaginable to gain entry
into people's homes and wring sales from reluctant buyers, have an especially bad reputation. Recent market research conducted on behalf of the
encyclopedia industry has underscored this point in no uncertain terms.
As a result, Grolier, one of the major U.S. encyclopedia publishers,
began selling its *New Book of Knowledge* by mail in 1978. Promotional
material for the mail-order set stressed that the *only* salesperson one
would ever see was the mail carrier. Likewise, the publisher of the *Academic American Encyclopedia*, the first entirely new multivolume general
English-language encyclopedia in well over a decade, has emphatically
rejected the door-to-door approach, opting instead to sell the set in department stores and major bookstores. Significantly, the *Academic
American*'s market research indicates a strong consumer preference for
in-store selling as opposed to in-home, or door-to-door, selling. It should
also be noted that during the 1970s, the Federal Trade Commission,
perhaps motivated by the aggressive consumerism advocated by Ralph
Nader and his protégés, cracked down hard on some of the major encyclopedia companies for flagrant sales malpractices. Indeed, when recently

commenting on the plight of the industry, a top executive of a large encyclopedia firm blurted out, "Consumerism is the basic problem."

A more subtle problem that hurts the encyclopedia business is negativism toward the product. Some people have the snobbish idea that encyclopedias are only for children or simpletons. They dismiss the notion that someone with a college degree or academic specialty might find a general encyclopedia a productive reference source. The reverse side of that attitude involves teacher bias against the use of encyclopedias by school students. Robert Ribble, a professor of education at the State University of New York at Brockport, has actually been quoted in a recent newspaper article ("Encyclopedia Purchase Merits Wise Shopping" by Patrick Boyle in the Rochester, N.Y., *Times-Union,* April 5, 1976) as stating that encyclopedias "can have a detrimental effect on the development of a child's ability to search and learn to use the full library," by teaching the child to take shortcuts. Perhaps encyclopedias should be made more obtuse and difficult to use, so that students will not be tempted by such "shortcuts." Ann Scarpellino, a children's librarian in New Jersey, makes the case for the encyclopedia in her article "School-Public Library Cooperation: Some Practical Approaches" (*U*N*A*B*A*S*H*E*D Librarian,* No. 32, 1979, p. 29): "An encyclopedia is, in itself, a small research library. Many librarians feel that asking anyone learning to do research to forego use of it is on a level with teaching someone to play tennis with the use of only the left hand." The real educational issue here, of course, goes well beyond encyclopedias per se. What will determine whether a child fully utilizes the library and its various resources is not use or nonuse of a particular type of reference work but the quality of instruction the student receives, the ingenuity of the assignment involved, and the student's own intellectual motivation and maturity. Nevertheless, the attitude toward encyclopedias expressed by Dr. Ribble is widespread among both U.S. and Canadian schoolteachers, as the Kister and Horrocks surveys of public library opinion reveal (see Part II of the *Buying Guide,* "Special Reports").

Adding to the encyclopedia industry's economic woes in recent years has been a decline in library funding at practically every level. Federal aid to education, which reached its zenith in the 1960s under the Johnson Great Society programs, was sharply curtailed during the next decade and shows few signs of rebounding in the early 1980s. Meanwhile, as school and public librarians are only too well aware, local communities have been increasingly reluctant to give schools and libraries all the funds they require, and in some places wholesale layoffs and painful budget cuts have occurred. Not only are residents burdened with rising tax rates, higher energy costs, and persistent inflation, but most tests and studies show that their children are not learning or reading as well as students did 10 or 20 years ago. For example, in 1980 the College Entrance Examination Board announced that average scores on the Scholastic Aptitude Test had declined for the *eighteenth* consecutive year. So, parents ask, why pour more and more money into schools, libraries, and educational resources? Although many library budgets for books and other materials continue to increase modestly each year, actual library buying power dropped over the past decade. The result, naturally enough, is fewer new books, magazines, films, and reference sources—including expensive new editions of encyclopedias.

In similar fashion, the average family now generally has less discretionary income than five or ten years ago. Increased expenditures for essentials such as food, housing, clothing, and transportation, coupled with high inflation, leave less for luxuries, which in many families include books and encyclopedias. A recent report by the Book Industry Study Group, Inc., entitled *Book Industry Trends—1977,* underscores this point, noting that a "new frugality" has developed among the book-buying public and that "the consumer increasingly views the book as a discretionary purchase" that must be rationalized within the context of one's overall budget.

All these diverse trends—increased encyclopedia production costs, reduced personal and library purchasing power, the declining number of children in the population, a negative image of encyclopedias fostered by intellectual snobbery and well-meaning but misplaced teacher disapproval, consumer dissatisfaction with deceptive encyclopedia sales practices, and the editorial rigors of making and maintaining a quality set in the late twentieth century—contribute to the current encyclopedia sales-profit slump. Only a flourishing business abroad, particularly in Europe but also in South America, the Middle East, and Asia, has saved some publishers from fiscal embarrassment (one firm, Grolier, Inc., has not been that fortunate).

The outlook, however, is not totally bleak. Good encyclopedias do continue to be produced, despite the formidable problems noted here. Most people who constantly need and use knowledge and information—teachers, librarians, students, various professionals, business executives, secretaries, et al.—recognize the potential value of encyclopedias. Moreover, many are quite prepared to pay what it costs to have a reliable, up-to-date set readily available in their classroom, library, study, or office. Parents who want their children to have every possible educational advantage also will often acquire an encyclopedia for use in the home. As a society we would be the worse for lack of such reference works. Over three centuries ago, Thomas Hobbes observed that knowledge is power. That observation remains valid today, but only so long as knowledge remains accessible and is not inundated or overwhelmed by its own irrepressible growth. Our best encyclopedias contribute significantly to harnessing essential knowledge so that it is within easy reach of those who need it. Admittedly, this is not the best of times for general encyclopedias as a type of reference work. But they have survived many changes throughout history, and there are current indications that general encyclopedias, notwithstanding their present difficulties, will be around in one form or another for some time to come.

COMPUTERIZED ENCYCLOPEDIAS AND OTHER NEW DEVELOPMENTS

Hardly a day goes by that we do not learn about some new marvel spawned by the computer. Thanks to microprocessors and advanced solid state electronics, there are now alarm clocks that say "Good morning" and ovens that count down the cooking time. About 70 percent of all long-distance telephone calls are currently relayed by microwave. More and more medical diagnoses are computer-assisted, as are financial transactions, travel reservations, and general record-keeping chores. At present there are a few hundred thousand computers operating in the world, but by 1984 it is estimated there will be some 20 million. Just as machines like bulldozers and forklifts can be viewed as extensions of human muscle, computers extend the human brain, performing calculations in a matter of seconds or minutes that would require a person days or even years to accomplish. The potential for computer development appears practically limitless at this time. "Computer power is growing exponentially; it has increased tenfold every eight years since 1946," according to Robert Jastrow, a top American scientist (see *Time*, February 20, 1978, p. 59). "Four generations of computer evolution—vacuum tubes, transistors, simple integrated circuits and today's miracle chips—followed one another in rapid succession." And Jastrow goes on to point out that the fifth generation of computers will be ready in the 1980s.

The computer revolution has already had an enormous impact on major segments of the knowledge industry. Publishers and book distributors have automated many of their internal operations; microcomputers are being used for a variety of instructional purposes in many schools; and librarians and information scientists are currently developing extensive computerized files that provide speedy access to bibliographic data of all kinds, including library holdings in every part of the country. Such advancements may be only the beginning of a profound change in the way we store, transmit, and retrieve information. Indeed, there are those who predict a "paperless" future (perhaps like those who foresaw the "horseless" carriage a century or more ago). Whether or not paper will eventually go the way of the workhorse is not yet known, but tentative efforts are now underway that give one pause. Consider, for instance, a new venture called The Source, a kind of electronic supermarket of information that delivers its contents directly to the home or office via telephone lines with a "smart" television set or video display unit acting as the receiver. Subscribers can call up the latest news from a major wire service, as well as stock market information, airline schedules, restaurant reviews, references to articles in the *New York Times,* miscellaneous facts from the *World Almanac,* and much, much more. The Source, which is available from Telecomputing Corporation of America, is fairly expensive at the present time—in early 1981 the initial hookup cost $100 and an hour of computer time between 7:00 A.M. and 6:00 P.M. $15, with the hourly rate reduced to $4.25 after 6:00 P.M.—but costs are expected to come down as subscribers go up. The truly important news, however, about computerized information services like The Source is not their interesting "menu" nor relatively high cost but their ability to deliver material electronically that heretofore was available only in print form.

The implications of such innovative developments have not escaped the notice of encyclopedia-makers. The possibility of marketing encyclopedic information electronically could help solve some of the industry's current economic problems by opening up potentially new markets while at the same time reducing or perhaps eliminating the need for in-home sales representatives. In the early stages of computer technology, encyclopedists tended to look upon automation with alarm. As Otto V. St. Whitelock put it in his *Choice* article on making encyclopedias (June 1967, p. 385), they feared being "replaced by mechanical monsters that will completely destroy their function." These apprehensions, of course, proved ill founded, and today general encyclopedia publishers are positioning themselves to offer their product via the computer through information vendors like The Source or any number of similar companies, such as OCLC, Inc., the New York Times Information Bank, Telidon of Canada, and CompuServe (a subsidiary of H. & R. Block). "You won't be buying an encyclopedia anymore," says Ivan Berger, an authority on new communications technology (quoted from a syndicated article by Paul Wilborn in the *Tampa* [Florida] *Tribune-Times,* October 12, 1980. "Instead, you'll be able to plug into the Britannica data bank—and have the charge added to your phone bill. That way, all the information will be up to date."

At this writing no general encyclopedia is widely available in electronic form. However, the *Academic American Encyclopedia,* a brand-new 21-volume work first published in 1980, is currently being offered on a limited experimental basis to subscribers in Columbus, Ohio, as part of a computerized home information service operated by OCLC, Inc., called "Channel 2000." And a tentative agreement has been reached to make the *Academic American* available via the New York Times Information Bank beginning in 1981. Publishers of *The World Book Encyclopedia* and *New Encyclopaedia Britannica* are also deep in negotiations to go online in the near future. Admittedly, problems remain to be solved before computerized encyclopedias become commonplace. The high cost of making accessible the entire contents of a work as large and complex as a multivolume encyclopedia is a particularly big stumbling block. As one senior encyclopedia editor told the *Buying Guide,* "Our encyclopedia will probably tell you who the youngest governor in the United States is, but to program the computer to deliver that information is both difficult and expensive." But such obstacles will be overcome, probably quite rapidly, and the general public may soon be trading in its heavy, bulky print sets for the latest electronic models. In the process, some well-known encyclopedias that have not been kept assiduously up-to-date in recent years (for example *The Encyclopedia Americana*) may well fall by the wayside. Certainly no sensible information vendor will invest in computerizing a stale encyclopedia.

There have been a number of other new developments in the encyclopedia world during the past several years of interest to consumers.

Doubtless the most significant event has been the publication in 1980 of the aforementioned *Academic American Encyclopedia,* the first entirely new multivolume English-language general encyclopedia since 1967. The *Academic American* claims attention not only because it is brand new, but as noted in the previous paragraph it is the first general encyclopedia to become available in an electronic format. Another interesting feature of the set is that it will be sold at retail only in department stores and bookstores, *not* in the home or door-to-door (the traditional method of marketing encyclopedias). Most knowledgeable encyclopedia people believe the *Academic American*'s in-store selling strategy will fail. Frank Greenagel, president of Aretê Publishing Company, the encyclopedia's publisher, has responded this way: "We're either going to crash and burn, or we're going to blow the hell out of this market" (see the *New York Times,* May 30, 1980). Aretê has also caused some controversy in the industry by its aggressive advertising, which features direct references to two major competitors, *The World Book Encyclopedia* and the *New Encyclopaedia Britannica.* Whatever the future might hold for it, the *Academic American Encyclopedia* is currently an exciting new enterprise that deserves close inspection by the encyclopedia buying public. The set is fully reviewed in Part III of the *Buying Guide* ("Multivolume Adult Encyclopedias").

Encyclopaedia Britannica, Inc., one of the major U.S. encyclopedia publishers, has been in the news recently on several fronts. In March 1980, Britannica lost an appeal to the Supreme Court to overturn a lower court ruling that upheld a finding against the company by the Federal Trade Commission (FTC) for deceptive sales practices. Immediately after the Supreme Court decision was announced, the company hired former congressman Wilbur Mills to lobby Congress to force the FTC to soften its stand on the Britannica matter. Later that year, in December, the FTC did indeed ease a key regulation pertaining to Britannica's sales practices. What role, if any, Mr. Mills played in this development is not known. (This issue is discussed further in the next section of the *Buying Guide,* "Selling Encyclopedias.")

In another Britannica move, Encyclopaedia Britannica Educational Corporation (a sister company) has prepared a new publication designed to improve access to the contents of the three-part *New Encyclopaedia Britannica* (15th ed., 1974+). Entitled *Library Guide to Encyclopaedia Britannica* and available only to schools and libraries, the single-volume work is an alphabetical "guide" (not index) to the contents of the 10-volume *Micropaedia* and 19-volume *Macropaedia.* The guide, issued in early 1981, contains some 240,000 citations, 20,000 cross-references, and comprehensive indexes to maps, pictures, and charts. Whether or not this publication will quiet the loud, often vituperative, complaints about the encyclopedia's controversial indexing system awaits the test of time. A thorough review of the *New Encyclopaedia Britannica* follows in Part III of the *Buying Guide* ("Multivolume Adult Encyclopedias"), including a full discussion of the index question under the subheading "Arrangement and Accessibility."

On the international front, Encyclopaedia Britannica, Inc., revealed in 1980 that a Chinese-language edition of the *Micropaedia* portion of the *New Encyclopaedia Britannica* will eventually be published in eight volumes. A cooperative project between Britannica and the Greater Encyclopedia of China Publishing House, the translated work should be ready for Chinese readers by 1983 or 1984 at a cost of approximately $150. As part of the agreement, Britannica has sales rights for the Chinese version outside China, thus opening up the possibility that interested U.S. and Canadian libraries will be able to acquire the set.

Another exciting encyclopedia translation project involves the Portuguese-language edition of *The World Book Encyclopedia*, entitled *Enciclopedia Delta Universal*. The 15-volume set, published in 1980 by Editora Delta in Rio de Janeiro, sells for the equivalent of $612 in Brazil. At the present time *Enciclopedia Delta Universal* is not available on the U.S. or Canadian market, but that situation could change in the future.

Closer to home, the highly regarded one-volume *New Columbia Encyclopedia* spawned a 24-volume supermarket edition, *The New Illustrated Columbia Encyclopedia*, in 1978. Distributed by Time-Life Books, the *New Illustrated Columbia* expands the original work by approximately 5,000 graphics, many of which are in color. Reviews of both titles follow in Parts III and IV of the *Buying Guide*.

Since the last edition of *Encyclopedia Buying Guide* (1978), eight general encyclopedias have gone out of print. None was a major work by any stretch of the imagination. The dated and unattractive *American Educator*, a 20-volume set for young adults, was completely outclassed by such fine titles as *Compton's Encyclopedia*, *Merit Students Encyclopedia*, and *The World Book Encyclopedia*. The 16-volume *Golden Book Encyclopedia*, last revised in 1969, suffered from both old age and mediocre quality. All the others were one-volume works, of which only the *Cadillac Modern Encyclopedia* and *Larousse Illustrated International Encyclopedia and Dictionary* had any substance. Unlamented are *The Great World Encyclopedia*, *Hamlyn Younger Children's Encyclopedia*, *My First Golden Encyclopedia*, and the *Quick Reference Encyclopedia*. Each of these titles is briefly reviewed in Appendix A of the *Buying Guide*, "Discontinued Encyclopedias 1960–1981."

Selling Encyclopedias

Until quite recently book publishing was considered an elite profession, a comfortable niche for serious people concerned as much with promoting good literature as making a decent living. Today, however, publishing in the United States is an aggressive, profit-conscious industry that logs well over $6 billion in annual sales. Still, in terms of dollar volume, book publishing in this country is a relatively small business as industries go. For instance, Americans spend 5 times as much on liquor and 20 times as much on clothing each year as they do on such items as books. One large corporation, American Telephone & Telegraph, actually reports annual *profits* that exceed publishing's total revenues. Comparatively speaking, U.S. book publishing is about the size of the processed peanut industry. People in the business, however, take some comfort in the presumption that books have a greater impact on our society than peanuts do.

Encyclopedia sales account for a surprisingly large share of the total publishing dollar. Although exact data are sometimes difficult to come by, available figures show that, of the $6.5 billion spent annually on books in the United States, approximately $400 million go for encyclopedias and related products, like yearbooks. This figure, currrent as of 1980, includes encyclopedias sold in the home, in supermarkets and discount stores, and to schools and libraries. U.S. encyclopedia companies also do a substantial amount of foreign business, perhaps as much as $250–$300 million a year. Altogether, encyclopedia sales constitute an estimated 10–12 percent of U.S. publishing's present trade here and abroad.

Despite this seemingly agreeable situation, encyclopedia publishers are not a happy lot these days. Sales of encyclopedic products have been in the doldrums in recent years, failing to keep pace with the book industry's overall growth, which has been steady but hardly spectacular, particularly in regard to unit sales. During the Great Society years of the 1960s, the encyclopedia business flourished, the *New York Times* reporting in an article headlined "Sales of Encyclopedias Advance Sharply" (October 6, 1967), "Sales are up, and so are profits. Eighty percent of the prospective market still has not been tapped, according to industry sources, and with the combination of the population explosion and the accent on education, the outlook for encyclopedias is considered bright." Today that prognosis has turned sour. The population boom has reversed course, and the current accent is more on tax revolt and the perils of inflation than new spending programs for education. For these and a host of other cogent reasons detailed in the preceding section of the *Buying Guide* ("Introducing Encyclopedias"), the domestic encyclopedia business has been in a prolonged slump for a number of years.

A robust international trade by the major U.S. encyclopedia publishers has helped offset the sluggish home market. Indeed, according to the best available estimates, foreign sales now account for about 40 percent of U.S. encyclopedia publishers' business annually. In the late 1960s this figure was only 30 percent, reflecting both the growth of overseas markets and the concurrent lackluster domestic sales picture. Industry insiders expect the world market for general encyclopedias to continue to expand in the foreseeable future. Not only have several U.S. companies established themselves in the United Kingdom and Western Europe, but hitherto less promising markets in the Middle East, Asia, and South America are becoming attractive. World Book-Childcraft International, Inc., for example, has developed a prosperous foreign trade with editorial offices in Europe, Asia, and Africa, as well as distributorship and copublishing arrangements in such countries as Brazil and Indonesia. In the case of Encyclopaedia Britannica, Inc., the overseas business has become so important to the firm's financial well-being that, in the opinion of encyclopedia critic Harvey Einbinder, *The New Encyclopaedia Britannica* deliberately sugarcoats the truth in some of its geographical and historical articles so that potential customers abroad will not be offended. "Political and social problems are treated cautiously. Controversial topics are covered superficially to avoid antagonizing national prejudices. This is natural," explains Einbinder, "because foreign schools and libraries are major overseas prospects for the *Britannica*. The purchasing policies of many of these institutions are controlled by officials who expect their country to be presented in a flattering light. Thus the essay on South Africa, which is an important English-speaking market, employs the term 'separate development' in discussing the government's racial policies. The word 'apartheid' is not used because South African officials now frown upon this term." (Quoted from Einbinder's "Politics and the New *Britannica*" in *The Nation*, March 22, 1975, p. 343.) On the other side of the coin, U.S. encyclopedia publishers can expect increased competition both at home and abroad from their foreign counterparts, particularly the British, who are also seeking to expand their share of the international market for English-language reference materials.

ENCYCLOPEDIA PUBLISHERS

Four large publishers and their affiliates currently dominate the U.S. encyclopedia scene. It is estimated that the Big Four—Encyclopaedia Britannica, Inc.; Grolier, Inc.; Macmillan Educational Company, Inc.; and World Book-Childcraft International, Inc.—control up to 95 percent of the in-home and school and library encyclopedia business in the United States. A dozen or so smaller firms compete for the remaining sliver of the market, of which the supermarket and discount store trade is the most lucrative. In the early 1980s, however, a newcomer to the encyclopedia industry, Aretê Publishing Company, Inc., will aggressively challenge the Big Four for a substantial share of the market with its entirely new *Academic American Encyclopedia,* an attractive multivolume set for older students and adults that reputedly cost $25 million to make. Aretê, a Dutch subsidiary, is well heeled and aims to compete head-to-head with the major publishers.

Among the Big Four, World Book-Childcraft International, Inc. (WBCI) is clearly the most successful in terms of sales, from the standpoint both of dollar volume and unit sales. Formerly Field Enterprises Educational Corporation (the company changed its name in 1977) and now a subsidiary of the Scott & Fetzer Company, WBCI currently accounts for a phenomenal 55–60 percent of all in-home encyclopedia sales in the United States with its two highly regarded sets, *The World Book Encyclopedia* and *Childcraft: The How and Why Library,* along with the various yearbooks that supplement them. Every year approximately 20 million individual volumes bearing the WBCI imprint are sold here and abroad. *World Book* sales alone average between 350,000 and 400,000 sets annually, making it the best-selling work of its kind anywhere. Overall, WBCI has revenues of about $200 million a year and is the acknowledged industry leader.

Encyclopaedia Britannica, Inc., blessed with a name that is practically synonymous with encyclopedias in the English-speaking world, runs second to WBCI in the area of sales. Britannica's mainstay, the *New Encyclopaedia Britannica,* retails for more than twice as much as WBCI's *World Book Encyclopedia,* but its current rate of sales (75,000–80,000 sets a year) is far below the *World Book* figure. Fortunately for the firm, sales of the *Britannica* have been stimulated in recent years by consumer interest in the innovative fifteenth edition, which first appeared in 1974 amid great hoopla. Formally titled *New Encyclopaedia Britannica* but popularly known as *Britannica 3* (because of its tripartite arrangement), the new edition represents the most radical revision ever undertaken of this famous encyclopedia, which traces its origins back to the eighteenth century and the monumental *Encyclopédie* of Diderot. Today the glow is off the "new" *Britannica,* but by all accounts it continues to do well in the marketplace, especially overseas. Encyclopaedia Britannica, Inc., also publishes *Compton's Encyclopedia, Britannica Junior Encyclopaedia,* and *Compton's Precyclopedia* (merchandised in some instances both in the United States and abroad under the title *The Young Children's Encyclopedia*). In addition, Encyclopaedia Britannica Educational Corporation (a sister company) distributes *The Random House Encyclopedia* in a special two-volume edition exclusively for schools and libraries. Prior to the 1974 publication of *Britannica 3,* Charles Swanson, Britannica's president, described sales as "depressed," and rumors swept the industry that some major properties were on the block, for instance *Compton's Encyclopedia.* Since 1975, however, the firm appears to have stabilized, currently averaging a healthy $70 million in sales a year.

Grolier, Inc., a dominant force in the reference book field in the 1950s and 1960s, has experienced very rocky financial going during the past decade. The firm's decline as a publisher of first importance has been due in part to the general malaise that has affected the domestic encyclopedia market since the Great Society years, in part to tougher government regulation of unscrupulous encyclopedia sales practices (which has hit Grolier as hard or harder than any of the other Big Four), in part to the company's foreign exchange losses, which have totaled millions of dollars, and in part to administrative myopia and mismanagement. The firm currently publishes *The Encyclopedia Americana*, the second largest English-language set on the market (behind the *New Encyclopaedia Britannica*), as well as the young adult *Encyclopedia International* and children's *New Book of Knowledge*. Numerous Grolier products have been discontinued in recent years, including the multivolume *Grolier Universal Encyclopedia* and *American Peoples Encyclopedia,* both victims of poor sales, negative reviews, and deteriorating quality (see Appendix A for descriptions of these and other discontinued encyclopedias). In the mid-1970s Grolier "restructured" its debt, which, in the words of one long-time encyclopedia executive, is "a fancy way of saying the banks now own Grolier." Indeed, knowledgeable people in the industry today wonder if this once powerful publisher can survive in the highly competitive encyclopedia environment of the 1980s.

Macmillan Educational Company, Inc. (formerly Macmillan Educational Corporation), a subsidiary of Macmillan, Inc., is the smallest of the Big Four in terms of general encyclopedia sales, averaging under $40 million annually. The company publishes two multivolume sets, the adult *Collier's Encyclopedia* and the young adult *Merit Students Encyclopedia,* plus the usual yearbooks. Both encyclopedias are quality works of recent vintage that apparently have found greater sales acceptance thus far on the institutional level (schools and libraries) than on the more profitable in-home market.

Aside from the Big Four, there are several smaller reference book publishers that maintain full-time editorial and production staffs and compete vigorously for a reasonable share of the encyclopedia dollar. As noted earlier, the most formidable of these, at least in terms of promise, is the newly established Areté Publishing Company, Inc., an American subsidiary of the large Dutch publisher, Verenigde Nederlandse Uitgeversbedrijven (VNU). In 1980, Areté issued the *Academic American Encyclopedia,* the first completely new large-scale English-language general encyclopedia in over a decade. Frank Greenagel, Areté's president, has indicated that the company's goal is to capture roughly 10 percent of the American encyclopedia business with the new set by 1982. Another sizable operation is Funk & Wagnalls, Inc., publisher of the adult *Funk & Wagnalls New Encyclopedia* and *The Young Students Encyclopedia,* a children's set. Sold principally in supermarkets, the inexpensive but carefully maintained *Funk & Wagnalls New Encyclopedia* is especially successful in those areas of the United States and Canada where door-to-door encyclopedia salespeople are rarely if ever encountered. Finally, Standard Educational Corporation, a Chicago firm that dates back to 1909, publishes the *New Standard Encyclopedia,* an unpretentious set of

14 volumes modestly priced for general family use. Standard has the distinction of being the first encyclopedia publisher to use computers in its editorial process.

For a complete list of North American encyclopedia publishers and distributors and their addresses, see Appendix E of the *Buying Guide*. Similar information for major publishers and distributors in the United Kingdom is available in Appendix C.

ENCYCLOPEDIA SALES METHODS

Encyclopedias are merchandised in several ways. Some are sold via direct mail order, consumers responding to a circular or advertisement in a newspaper, magazine, or on television. Others are sold on a book-a-week basis in supermarkets and chain discount stores. Sales to libraries, schools, and other educational institutions (which account for approximately 10 percent of the total encyclopedia trade in the United States and Canada) are normally accomplished through commissioned sales representatives. Single-volume encyclopedias are usually sold as trade books—that is, over the counter in retail book and department stores. In addition, some publishers have recently begun experimenting with selling large multivolume sets through retail stores, most notably Aretê, which is utilizing selected stores as its sole method of retailing the new *Academic American Encyclopedia*. But unquestionably the most popular, practical, and effective means of selling large sets of encyclopedias at the retail level is in the consumer's home. In most instances, in-home selling means that the product cannot be acquired through normal retail channels but must be purchased directly from the publisher or authorized distributor through a commissioned representative. Because of the hefty price of most multivolume encyclopedias, in-home sales are customarily made on the subscription—or installment—basis. All the Big Four encyclopedia publishers rely heavily on the in-home subscription method of selling.

Direct selling in the home entails either door-to-door canvassing of neighborhoods by sales personnel or, more likely today, working by appointment from leads developed through referrals, mailing lists, telephone inquiries, consumer come-ons ("You can win a prize," "Get a free dictionary," etc.), and so on. Each company's approach to direct selling reflects the nature and composition of its sales organization. Encyclopaedia Britannica, Inc., for instance, maintains a sizable professional sales force that works mainly through leads generated by expensive television and popular magazine spot advertising prepared and paid for by the company. Britannica sales representatives in turn buy the leads from the company, reputedly at a cost of $17 each. World Book-Childcraft International, on the other hand, has a very large nationwide sales organization of some 100,000 people—housewives, teachers, retired people, and the like—who work at selling WBCI products on a part-time basis. WBCI and Britannica representatives are also often listed under "Encyclopedias" in the local Yellow Pages, particularly in larger metropolitan areas, another effective strategy for generating customer leads. But no matter how the sales operation is organized or leads are developed, the one constant in direct selling is the in-home sales presentation. Before such a presentation can take place, however, the sales representative must first get into the potential customer's home. It is at this crucial point in the sales scenario that some representatives and their companies have got into trouble in the past.

Knowledge is considerably more difficult to sell to the general public than, say, automobiles or toothpaste. One sales-wise observer once noted that encyclopedias are "sold, not bought." This dictum has never been truer than today, when profits and a major segment of the domestic encyclopedia market—households with school-age children—are declining. Moreover, inflation has cut into discretionary spending for such amenities as encyclopedias, and when the money is there, education-minded families are as likely today to invest in a home computer as a set of encyclopedias. Publishers of expensive multivolume sets of encyclopedias have also begun to feel the marketplace muscle of several small-volume works, particularly *The New Columbia Encyclopedia* and *The Random House Encyclopedia*, which sell for under $100 and can be readily acquired in bookstores. As in the automobile industry (with which encyclopedia publishing can be compared in many respects), the tendency toward compact models is evident. All these developments have prompted a scramble for the laggardly encyclopedia dollar. Again, as in the auto industry, competition for sales is fierce, sometimes cutthroat, especially among the Big Four. And as the 1980s get underway, the competitive juices have been stirred even more by the Aretê challenge in the form of the brand-new *Academic American Encyclopedia*.

The emphasis on sales, heightened by the fact that encyclopedia representatives normally work on commission, has led to some regrettable sales practices in the past, particularly in the area of direct, or in-home, selling. (Interestingly, the new *Academic American Encyclopedia* will be sold only in stores, not in homes.) The catalog of high-pressure tactics employed by encyclopedia salespeople ranges from mere gimmicks to get a foot in the consumer's door to brazen schemes that are unfair and deceptive—and often illegal. Examples involving so-called free or demonstration sets, prizes, discounts, research services, and questionnaire surveys are legion. An especially shameless practice has been to play on the aspirations of minorities and the disadvantaged, misrepresenting the encyclopedia as a surefire means of achieving social and educational betterment. Another widespread ploy is the suggestion that parents should buy an encyclopedia as tangible proof of concern for their children's intellectual well-being and future prospects. If you tell the salesperson that your oldest child is attending kindergarten, write Johnston and Trulock in their informative article "Buying an Encyclopedia" (*Consumers' Research Magazine*, February 1975, pp. 12+), the salesperson will "make you feel like a scoundrel for denying your offspring the right to grow up surrounded by the volumes of his [or her] knowledge-giving encyclopedia." False advertising may also be used to mislead or confuse the consumer. A blatant example involves full-page advertisements circulated in both the United States and Canada by a distributor of *The New American Encyclopedia* (the Webster Publishing Company, Ltd., of Toronto), which falsely claim that *Encyclopedia Buying Guide* rates the set "among the top encyclopedias in the world, regardless of price." What the *Buying Guide* actually said (and still says) about *The New American Encyclopedia* is quite different: "Overall, comparatively speaking, the set is a very shoddy piece of work that is certainly not worth the asking price."

CONSUMER PROTECTION DEVELOPMENTS

Prompted by consumer activists like Ralph Nader and Esther Peterson, Americans in the 1960s began to reject the worst forms of hucksterism. By the early 1970s, the consumer movement had become a full-fledged crusade against predatory business practices in all areas of the marketplace, including the smooth-talking encyclopedia representative who played fast and loose with the truth. As a result, a number of effective legal and legislative reforms came about under the banner of consumerism. Toward the end of the decade, however, the consumer movement seemed to lose its punch. In 1978, for instance, a *New York Times*-CBS News poll reported that 58 percent of those asked agreed that "the Government has gone too far in regulating business and interfering with the free enterprise system." Powerful business interests in Washington mounted a forceful campaign not only to squelch new consumer initiatives but to roll back previous gains. Nowhere was this development more evident than when in 1978 the 95th Congress decisively rejected a long-standing effort to create a strong, independent federal Consumer Protection Agency, or later in 1980 when Congress voted overwhelmingly to limit the consumer protection authority of the Federal Trade Commission (FTC) because, in the view of the business lobby, the agency had become "too quick to investigate and regulate." (Paradoxically, the FTC had been condemned for consumer inactivity only a decade before, ridiculed as "the little old lady on Pennsylvania Avenue" by a Ralph Nader study group in 1969.) On the encyclopedia front, Encyclopaedia Britannica, Inc., hired former congressman Wilbur Mills to lobby against FTC actions the company considers unfair and overly restrictive.

Despite the present antiregulatory mood in Congress, most of the achievements of the postwar consumer movement remain intact as we move into the 1980s. Regarding encyclopedia sales practices, three areas of consumer activity over the past decade stand out as major accomplishments: (1) FTC investigations into repeated charges of deception, misrepresentation, and fraud on the part of many encyclopedia companies, including three of the Big Four; (2) enactment of relevant consumer protection legislation at all levels of government as well as issuance of strict, detailed FTC regulations that have successfully clamped down on many noxious in-home and subscription selling practices; and (3) more than casual evidence that the encyclopedia companies themselves have finally ceased winking at dishonest sales tactics and are now serious about protecting consumers from at least the worst abuses of the past.

Federal Trade Commission Investigations

In the 1970s, the FTC, the U.S government regulatory agency charged with preventing (in the words of Lewis Engman, a former Commission chairman) "the free enterprise system from being stifled or fettered by monopoly or corrupted by unfair or deceptive trade practices," stepped up its consumer protection activities on a number of fronts, including questionable encyclopedia sales methods. Among the Big Four publishers, three—Britannica, Grolier, and Macmillan—were cited for violations after lengthy investigations. Only World Book-Childcraft International (formerly Field Enterprises Educational Corporation) received a clean bill of health. Some smaller publishers, like Standard Educational Corporation (which markets its *New Standard Encyclopedia* through various independent distributorships), also ran afoul of the FTC.

Early in the decade, the FTC issued a flurry of complaints against encyclopedia publishers. For instance, Macmillan and several subsidiary companies were cited in 1973 for product misrepresentation and deceptive billing procedures. Macmillan agreed to a cease-and-desist consent order—meaning the firm admitted to no law violation but consented to be held liable for any future conduct not in compliance with the order. Later, the FTC launched even more far-reaching investigations into encyclopedia sales practices under the auspices of the Magnuson-Moss Warranty-Federal Trade Commission Improvement Act of 1975. This landmark piece of consumer legislation permits the FTC to investigate and regulate whole industries rather than just individual companies, and it provides stringent penalties for those who knowingly disregard a cease-and-desist order.

The most significant cases to emerge from the FTC probes of the encyclopedia industry during the past decade involve Britannica and Grolier. Both companies ignored complaints issued by the agency in 1972, refusing to agree (as Macmillan did) to a cease-and-desist order. In time, both cases were heard by FTC administrative judges and, in each instance, the verdict went against the encyclopedia company. In the Britannica decision (1975), based on 27 days of formal hearings, the testimony of nearly a hundred witnesses, and more than a thousand exhibits, Judge Ernest G. Barnes found, among other things, that the firm's sales personnel used such ploys as pretending to deliver prizes or conduct educational surveys in order to gain entry into the homes of prospective customers. In the Grolier opinion (1976), which dealt with a complaint against Grolier, Inc., and 14 wholly-owned subsidiaries, Judge Theodor P. Von Brand found evidence of similar sales misrepresentations. In some instances, for example, Grolier salespeople "persuaded school officials to permit the dissemination of [promotional] materials without disclosing to such officials that they intended to follow up with sales presentations." The company "reinforced this impression in the case of parochial schools," observed Judge Von Brand in his decision, "by sending the materials home in a large envelope printed with a cross." On other occasions, Grolier representatives used false testimonials, going so far as to insinuate that Pope Paul endorsed one of the firm's sets.

In both these revealing FTC cases, the judge found that salespeople in the field often failed to identify themselves immediately as encyclopedia vendors. Thus both judges ordered that company sales representatives must henceforth present a card to all potential customers bearing the representative's name, the term "Encyclopedia Sales Representative," and the following statement in 10-point boldface type: "THE PURPOSE OF THIS REPRESENTATIVE'S CALL IS TO SOLICIT THE SALE OF ENCYCLOPEDIAS." Both judges also noted that company policy at the highest corporate echelons appeared to encourage or at least benignly tolerate deceptive sales practices at the door-to-door level. "Contrary to respondents' arguments, the findings of unlawful conduct which have been made herein are based on company documents, testimony of company officials, consumer testimony, and testimony of former sales representatives," wrote Judge Barnes in his Britannica ruling. In point of fact, "this decision is not based on a few isolated departures from company policy. There is no conflict in the record evidence; all evidence supports the findings of unlawful conduct, and almost every finding of fact is based upon company policy, or company-approved training, or company-condoned activities." Seldom if ever has such a severe rebuke been meted out to an encyclopedia publisher by a government official.

Britannica, arguing that it was the victim of discriminatory and unfair government regulation, appealed the Barnes decision to the full five-member commission, which unanimously upheld the judge. Britannica then took the case to the Seventh Circuit Court of Appeals in Chicago, where the company was again rebuffed. In a final effort to reverse the FTC and Judge Barnes, Britannica appealed the case to the U.S. Supreme Court, where on March 17, 1980, the justices voted 8–1 to let the lower court ruling stand. Britannica, however, currently refuses to let the matter rest. After losing in the courts, the company immediately hired Wilbur Mills, a former congressman and influential chairman of the House Ways and Means Committee, to persuade Congress to pressure the FTC to modify certain provisions of the original Barnes decision, particularly the irksome requirement that Britannica sales representatives must present an identification card to prospective in-home customers stating that the purpose of their visit is to sell encyclopedias. Exactly how effective Mr. Mills has been is not a matter of public record, but the FTC did inform the *Buying Guide* in November 1980 that certain changes regarding the card were being negotiated with Britannica. A month later the agency granted Britannica a one-year trial period in which the company's sales representatives could use a regular business card instead of the larger one prescribed by the FTC. Robert Blacher, director of the agency's Bureau of Consumer Affairs, indicated that Britannica will be obliged during the trial period to show that the business card approach is no longer being used in a deceptive manner. "If they fail to do that, then the order automatically will go back to the 3 inch by 5 inch card," Blacher said.

Laws and Regulations Governing Encyclopedia Sales

Modern consumer movements in the United States (specifically those during the Nader years and earlier during the reform era at the turn of the century) have induced passage of a number of important federal laws that affect encyclopedia sales practices in one way or another. In addition, the FTC has issued two regulations (which possess the force of law) expressly designed to correct direct-selling abuses. The most significant of these laws and regulations are described here in chronological order.

1. *The Federal Trade Commission Act.* Enacted in 1914 and subsequently amended over the years, this key legislation broadly prohibits "unfair methods of competition" and "unfair or deceptive acts or practices" in the conduct of business. The law, which created the FTC as a federal regulatory agency, is central to almost all legal actions involving encyclopedias, including the recent FTC investigations and cases discussed in the preceding paragraphs.

2. *The Truth-in-Lending Law.* Originally introduced in 1959, but not passed by Congress until 1968, the Truth-in-Lending Law is actually Title I of the Consumer Credit Protection Act. The lending provision, which is enforced by the FTC, requires that the seller inform consumers of all credit charges in plain language and no uncertain figures. The law specifically mandates that the seller must accurately state both the *total dollar cost* of any credit charges involved and the *annual percentage rate* of the total charge for credit. Most encyclopedia publishers, including the Big Four, sell their products on the installment basis. Contracts for such products must adhere to the Truth-in-Lending Law.

3. *FTC Trade Regulation Rule Concerning a "Cooling-off Period for Door-to-Door Sales."* As a quasi-judicial and quasi-legislative agency, the FTC is empowered to issue regulations that have the force of law. In 1972, the Commission proposed such a regulation, which would establish a fair period of time for consumers to cancel purchases made from door-to-door vendors. The regulation, which became effective in 1974, fixes a three-day "cooling-off" period during which the consumer may cancel any door-to-door purchase, lease, or rental of goods or services costing $25 or more, even though a contract has been signed. The buyer may cancel "any time prior to midnight of the third business day" after the date of the purchase. The seller *must* inform the buyer of this right to cancel in the contract. Furthermore, the seller must provide *two* copies of a "Notice of Cancellation" form that spells out in 10-point boldface type all the consumer's rights and obligations if the purchase should be canceled. To cancel, the consumer simply signs, dates, and mails one copy of this form to the seller within the specified three-day period. The second copy is for the consumer's files.

If the purchase is canceled, the seller must—within ten days—refund the consumer's money, return any goods or property accepted as trade-in, cancel and return all documents pertaining to the sale, and indicate when any merchandise left with the consumer will be claimed. Such goods must be returned to the seller "in substantially as good condition as when received." If, however, "the seller does not pick them [the goods] up within 20 days of the date on the cancellation notice, you may return or dispose of the goods without any further obligation." Consumers should be aware that certain types of door-to-door sales are not covered by this regulation, such as orders placed by telephone, by mail, or at the seller's address. For the full text of this basic consumer protection document, write to the Federal Trade Commission (Pennsylvania Ave. at Sixth St. NW, Washington, DC 20580) or contact your public library.

4. *FTC Trade Regulation Rule Concerning a "Use of Negative Option Plans by Sellers in Commerce."* Like the "Cooling-Off" rule, the Commission's "Negative Option" regulation became effective in 1974. The so-called negative option method of selling entails automatically mailing the next volume or "selection" of a subscription product to consumers— *unless* the seller is instructed not to send it. Books, magazines, and musical recordings are among the products sold in this manner. The FTC regulation does not prohibit negative option selling, but it does stipulate that consumers must have a minimum of ten days in which to accept or reject the selection, and that the seller must "clearly and conspicuously" inform consumers how to refuse the merchandise. Moreover, the seller must clearly instruct consumers how and where to return unsolicited items. The seller is also obliged to give full credit and guarantee postage for merchandise returned by consumers who indicated within the specified ten-day period they did not want it. The regulation evolved principally to correct widespread abuses of negative option selling by book and record clubs and magazine companies, but it also pertains to encyclopedia publishers who use negative option to sell mail-order encyclopedias and the annual yearbooks that normally accompany large multivolume sets.

5. *The Magnuson-Moss Warranty-Federal Trade Commission Improvement Act.* This far-reaching law (1975) deals in part with product warranties, which must now be clearly labeled "full" or "limited" and written in simple language devoid of legalese. But warranties are not mandatory for any consumer product, and encyclopedias of course do not carry them. Certain provisions of the Magnuson-Moss Act, however, directly affect the FTC's regulatory capabilities and clout—and that very much affects the encyclopedia industry and its consumers. Perhaps the most significant part of the law in this respect is Section 205, which provides strict penalties for companies knowingly engaged in unfair or deceptive dealings specifically covered by a cease-and-desist consent order. The statute also streamlines FTC administrative and investigative procedures, hitherto notoriously slow and cumbersome, thus permitting speedier action on new consumer protection investigations. Magnuson-Moss also allows the FTC to explore monopolistic and other unfair business practices on an industry-wide basis (whereas heretofore the Commission was restricted to investigating individual companies).

6. *The Equal Credit Opportunity Act.* This 1975 legislation prohibits credit discrimination on the basis of sex or marital status. Under the provisions of the Equal Credit Opportunity Act, the same standard of

creditworthiness must now be applied to, say, a single woman earning $15,000 a year and a single man earning the same amount. The law also guarantees married women the right to credit in their own names. Conversely, termination of credit or imposition of new conditions when separation, divorce, or death changes a consumer's marital status are forbidden. Encyclopedia publishers engaged in installment (or time payment) selling are obliged to extend credit in accordance with this statute.

7. *The Fair Credit Billing Act.* Like the Equal Credit Opportunity Act, this law was enacted in 1975. Concerned with resolving billing disputes and protecting consumers against unfair or heedless billing practices, the statute specifically requires that creditors must handle billing problems within 90 days upon receipt of a consumer inquiry or complaint. Creditors must also acknowledge such communications within 30 days and either furnish a corrected bill or explain why the original bill is correct as it stands. In addition, the legislation contains consumer safeguards against unwarranted dunning letters and creditor threats to release information potentially harmful to a person's credit rating. Past investigations by the FTC show that some encyclopedia companies have used billing procedures now illegal under the provisions of the Fair Credit Billing Act.

8. *The Fair Debt Collection Practices Act.* The first and only significant consumer protection legislation passed during the Carter administration, the Fair Debt Collection Practices Act of 1977 makes it a federal offense for debt collectors to harass, threaten, or abuse consumers. The law expressly prohibits dunning telephone calls prior to 8:00 A.M. and after 9:00 P.M., the use of foul or obscene language by debt collectors, and the publication of so-called shame lists. Another provision of the law stipulates that legal actions pertaining to nonpayment of debts must be filed where the debtor lives, not in some distant place. Moreover, if a consumer questions the validity or accuracy of the debt within 30 days, the collector must stop and verify the case information before proceeding further. Here again, FTC findings over the years indicate that some encyclopedia companies have engaged in abusive and unfair debt collection practices.

The Encyclopedia Industry and the New Consumer Reality

Of course no guarantee exists that reprehensible encyclopedia sales tactics on a large scale will not resume sometime in the future. A number of positive developments, however, have occurred within the industry during the past five or so years that encourage consumer protection advocates, including *Encyclopedia Buying Guide,* to believe that the most pernicious practices might be a thing of the past, save for the occasional rip-off by a fly-by-night operator. Certainly the aggressive FTC actions of the 1970s, coupled with the outpouring of much needed consumer protection legislation during the same period, have helped curb the worst selling abuses. But most heartening is unmistakable evidence that the encyclopedia publishers themselves, especially the Big Four that so thoroughly dominate the in-home market, are now convinced—finally—that they *must* clean up their sales act forthwith or face the real possibility that there might not be a viable in-home encyclopedia business left by the end of the 1980s.

At the beginning of the last decade, for instance, *Consumer Reports* noted in an article called "Encyclopedia Sales Fraud" (March 1971, pp. 172+) that Consumers Union had recently "received a number of complaints" about encyclopedia salespeople, "especially about representatives of Grolier, Inc." Four years later, however, Johnston and Trulock, writing in *Consumers' Research Magazine* ("Buying an Encyclopedia," February 1975, pp. 12+), were able to report fewer rather than more complaints, observing that a good many high-pressure encyclopedia salespeople "seem to have fallen by the wayside or gone into other enterprises. At least, one hears fewer complaints now." In 1977 and again in 1980, an FTC official in Washington confirmed this welcome trend, informing the *Buying Guide* that encyclopedia complaints, while still continuing, have dropped off noticeably in recent years.

Much of the credit for the improved record in the area of consumer complaints belongs to the major companies. World Book-Childcraft International, Inc. (formerly Field Enterprises Educational Corporation), the only one of the Big Four to avoid FTC action in the past decade, has had a tough and unambiguous voluntary "Code of Ethics" for years. The code, which all authorized WBCI sales representatives must sign and uphold, embodies the firm's credo: "Tell an honest story about an honest product." It expressly requires company representatives to identify themselves at the outset of a sales call. Moreover, the salesperson "always gives clear and accurate information regarding the Company's products, prices, services, credit terms, and policies and avoids the use of false, misleading, half-true, or exaggerated statements." The firm also has adopted a commendable "on approval" program that allows consumers to examine WBCI products for up to 30 days without obligation to purchase.

Encyclopaedia Britannica, Inc., and Grolier, Inc., have also instituted several effective consumer protection measures. Both companies, for example, now provide a "Cool Line" telephone service that receives and attempts to resolve customer complaints of any kind. Likewise, each publisher has developed an "Order Verification" system wherein a company employee not associated with the sales department contacts the consumer immediately after a sale to make sure that all terms of the contract are clearly understood, and that the sales representative acted in a responsible manner. Britannica, which voluntarily established a *four*-day "cooling-off" period prior to the FTC three-day regulation, also provides a 15-day "Satisfaction Guarantee" during which time a disgruntled consumer has the opportunity to return any purchase and obtain a full refund. Britannica's president, Charles Swanson, has been especially responsive to the new consumer reality. For instance, in a speech several years ago at a company sales meeting, Swanson observed, "When we come to the realization that consumer protection, both as legislation and—within reasonable limits—as agitation, is a legitimate aspect of the future that is here today, then we can stop reacting defensively to it, we can gain a genuine and full understanding of the reasons underlying it and the goals it seeks to attain, and we can live with it. Better than that, we can progress because of it." The Britannica executive who supplied the *Buying Guide* with the Swanson speech added that "the address was published as the lead article in our quarterly house organ, *Know*, where all employees once again were confronted with the fact that we mean business about good sales practices."

It would appear that the encyclopedia companies have at long last got the message—that deceptive sales practices will no longer be tolerated by the general public. Appropriately, Charles Swanson concluded his speech with this admonition: "Today, the consumer is king. His castle is his home. We are privileged to do business with him there. We offer him a product that is fit for a king. We dare not sell it like a knave." The *Buying Guide* will continue to monitor progress in the area of encyclopedia sales practices in future editions. In the meanwhile, some basic consumer advice—caveat emptor—is still in order.

CAVEAT EMPTOR, OR LET THE BUYER BEWARE

In 1963, John F. Kennedy proclaimed four essential consumer rights: the right to be heard, the right to a choice, the right to be protected against unsafe or defective products, and the right to a response to a legitimate complaint. Although the record now shows that unfair and deceptive encyclopedia dealings are on the wane, all the rights articulated by President Kennedy are not yet a reality in all encyclopedia sales transactions. Therefore, while mindful that most sales representatives are honest, hardworking, responsible, conscientious people who have no intention of misrepresenting their products or defrauding you in any way, be aware of these consumer "don'ts" when an encyclopedia vendor calls at your home:

Do *not* admit the salesperson unless and until proper credentials are produced, establishing the representative's name, company, and products. Reputable representatives of a reputable product will immediately identify themselves when they call, either on the telephone or at the door.

Do *not* hesitate to ask the salesperson to leave if later you discover any misrepresentation. If the vendor persists, call the police.

Do *not* fall for such timeworn gimmicks as "free" encyclopedias or yearbooks, "demonstration" sets, offers of "gifts" or "prizes" if you will sign on the dotted line, the "contest" or "questionnaire survey" routines, seemingly too-good-to-be-true "special discounts," or stories that you have been "specially selected by a computer." If the sales representative uses any of these or similar come-ons, terminate the conversation without delay.

Do *not* accept advertising claims or endorsements as the sole evidence of an encyclopedia's quality or worth. In some cases, promotion material contains exaggerations, distortions, or even outright lies. A particularly widespread practice is the use of undated excerpts from very old reviews that once praised the encyclopedia in question but now have no basis in fact. Consumers are advised to view all encyclopedia advertising with healthy skepticism.

Do *not* be pressured into making a purchase decision during or immediately after the sales presentation. *Do not buy in haste!* If you are interested in the particular encyclopedia being shown, ask the salesperson to leave the books with you for a week or two, so that you can properly examine the set at your leisure. If the salesperson or the publisher balks at this request, you are probably better off without that encyclopedia. (See the next section, "Finding the Right Encyclopedia," for tips about evaluating a set.)

Do *not* permit the sales representative to continue talking late into the night, when sales resistance is lowest for most people. A reputable salesperson will not attempt to keep you beyond 9:00 or 9:30 P.M. at the latest.

Do *not* accept oral promises as binding. They are not. Guarantees are valuable and enforceable only if they are in writing.

Do *not* sign a contract or any other papers without careful examination of the text. If you are unable to understand the language or all of the conditions, do *not* sign. Be sure that all credit charges are clearly indicated in accordance with the Truth-in-Lending Law.

Do *not* sign a blank contract. Likewise, do *not* sign a contract with blank spaces in the conditions.

Do *not* sign a contract for more than you can afford. Be certain that you understand *exactly* how much the encyclopedia and any other related products (like a yearbook or research service) will cost in toto, as well as the amount of each installment payment.

Consumers who heed this simple advice will not be cheated by the occasional overzealous or dishonest encyclopedia salesperson. But should you become the victim of product misrepresentation, misleading advertising, broken promises, credit discrimination, billing malpractices, abusive debt collection tactics, phony contests, or any other unfair or deceptive business dealings, promptly report the incident to your local Better Business Bureau, Chamber of Commerce, and municipal and/or county Consumer Affairs Office. Your telephone book or public library reference service will provide the necessary directory information. Time and energy permitting, you might want to report the case to these two national organizations:

1. *Federal Trade Commission* (Pennsylvania Ave. at Sixth St. NW, Washington, DC 20580; 202-655-4000). The FTC, established in 1914, is an independent federal administrative agency with broad and, as a result of the 1975 Magnuson-Moss Act, improved powers to deal with unfair and deceptive trade practices. But as noted previously in this section, the FTC's activist approach to consumer protection has recently incurred the displeasure of both Congress and the business lobby, resulting in some

congressional restrictions on the agency's regulatory discretion. Nevertheless, the FTC remains a strong and vital national force for consumer interests. Because the agency acts on behalf of the public interest and not individuals, it will not attempt to resolve your specific complaint. On the other hand, individual consumers—as well as business competitors, private consumer groups, and state and local agencies—are encouraged to report instances of alleged business malpractice. The FTC relies on such case information to initiate action against companies and industries suspected of law violations. *No formal application is required to make a complaint.* Simply state the pertinent facts of the case as clearly as you can, include copies of any documents or other evidence in your possession that support the complaint, and send them to the closest regional office of the FTC:

Room 1000
1718 Peachtree St. NW
Atlanta, GA 30309
404-881-4836

Room 1301
150 Causeway St.
Boston, MA 02114
617-223-6621

Suite 1437
55 E. Monroe St.
Chicago, IL 60603
312-353-4423

Suite 500
Mall Building
118 St. Clair Ave.
Cleveland, OH 44144
216-522-4207

Suite 2665
2001 Bryan St.
Dallas, TX 75201
214-729-0032

Suite 2900
1405 Curtis St.
Denver, CO 80202
303-837-2271

Room 13209
Federal Building
11000 Wilshire Blvd.
Los Angeles, CA 90024
213-824-7575

2243-EB, Federal Building
26 Federal Plaza
New York, NY 10007
212-264-1207

450 Golden Gate Ave.
Box 36005
San Francisco, CA 94102
415-556-1270

28th Floor
Federal Building
915 Second Ave.
Seattle, WA 98174
206-442-4655

2. *Direct Selling Association* (1730 M St. NW, Suite 610, Washington, DC 20036; 202-293-5760). DSA is a national voluntary trade association of more than 100 "personal selling" companies. The organization administers a strict code of ethics that requires member companies to conduct business in a fair and lawful manner and to take immediate action to correct any violations. The major encyclopedia firms are DSA members, along with the Southwestern Company, which sells its one-volume desk encyclopedia, *The Volume Library*, door-to-door. Consumers should report instances of improper sales practices directly to DSA if member companies are involved.

Finally, *Encyclopedia Buying Guide* (c/o R. R. Bowker Company, 1180 Ave. of the Americas, New York, NY 10036; 212-764-5100) welcomes information about encyclopedia sales encounters, good and bad, that readers feel are noteworthy for one reason or another.

Finding the Right Encyclopedia

An encyclopedia can cost as much as $950—more if a fancy binding or yearbooks are involved. Like any commercial product, encyclopedias vary in quality from excellent to poor. Some sets are more authoritative, more reliable, more up-to-date, better organized, more clearly written, better illustrated, and more sturdily bound—hence more useful and a better buy—than others. The decision to buy an encyclopedia, and then which one to buy, should be carefully considered, in terms not only of cost but of quality received. To buy a poor or mediocre encyclopedia merely because it is inexpensive is like buying a pair of shoes that are too small on the theory that the shoes are too good a deal to pass up. Misinformation, like footwear that does not fit, is no bargain at any price. Bear in mind also that there is no such thing as the "best" encyclopedia for everyone, just as there is no "best" automobile or detergent for everyone. The goal is to find that encyclopedia among the many on the market that is best for you.

But before deciding to buy an encyclopedia, consider whether *any* encyclopedia is actually needed. To repeat: do not be cajoled, pressured, or shamed into purchasing something as expensive as an encyclopedia if you really do not want or need one. The key consumer rule is and always has been this: *Any encyclopedia, no matter how fine it might be, is a poor investment if it is not used.* Specifically, before buying any new encyclopedia, consider the following questions.

Do the encyclopedias available at the local public and school libraries meet your reference needs and those of your family? It is entirely possible that library encyclopedias—publicly owned sets acquired with the help of your tax dollars—will be sufficient to meet most if not all your needs for encyclopedic information. Of course, this will depend on your particular circumstances. How frequently and how quickly do you and your family need access to such material? How important is the convenience of having an encyclopedia readily at hand? How far do you live from the library and what is the transportation situation? How well stocked is the local library and is it open at times when you usually need access to information?

Do teachers in the local schools discourage or prohibit student use of encyclopedias? As previously noted, a reliable general encyclopedia is often the most logical and intelligent source for certain types of information, particularly basic facts and overview material on unfamiliar or complicated subjects. Yet many teachers mindlessly insist that students not use encyclopedias in the course of their school work. This widespread and, frankly, strange approach to learning suggests a weak and inflexible teacher whose assignments are either inept or contrived or both. Some years ago the historian Richard B. Morris commented on this situation in his article "Adventures in the Reference Room" (*Wilson Library Bulletin,* January 1967, p. 498): "I know there are some teachers who try to keep their students out of the reference room. They often draw up an index of *Verboten* books, including the *Book Review Digest.* I don't feel this way at all. I think a student should be taught how to use the tools of the trade. . . . I see my responsibility as a teacher to encourage curiosity and suggest where it can be satisfied . . . , and I do not feel that reference books should be restricted." But whatever the merits of the issue, it is advisable to determine school policy on encyclopedia use by checking with the principal or superintendent prior to buying an encyclopedia intended primarily for your children.

Might a specialized encyclopedia better meet your reference needs? You should be aware that there are an enormous number of outstanding specialized, or subject, encyclopedias available, one or more of which could be a wiser long-term investment than a general encyclopedia, again depending upon your particular interests and needs. Specialized encyclopedias fall into three broad categories: (1) those that treat a particular field of knowledge, like the *Encyclopedia of World Art* or *Encyclopedia of Chemical Technology;* (2) those that cover a particular subject, like the new *Harvard Encyclopedia of American Ethnic Groups* or *Encyclopedia of Bioethics;* and (3) those that present knowledge from a particular point of view or national perspective, for instance *Encyclopaedia Judaica* or *Encyclopedia Canadiana.* As Bill Katz, the reference authority, has remarked in his *Basic Information Sources* (McGraw-Hill, 3rd ed., 1978, p. 137), "the punishing waves of new information have swamped the general encyclopedia, yet left in their wake excellent subject sets." The most important specialized encyclopedias and encyclopedic dictionaries are briefly noted in Eugene P. Sheehy's *Guide to Reference Books,* a standard source found in most libraries.

What about a secondhand encyclopedia? Occasionally the classified ads in local newspapers list used, or secondhand, encyclopedias for sale. Likewise, large bookstores in major cities sometimes have older sets available. In New York City, for instance, the Literary Mart Encyclopedia Agency (1261 Broadway, New York, NY 10001; 212-684-0588) and the Reference Book Center (175 Fifth Ave., New York, NY 10010; 212-677-2160) specialize in secondhand reference works, including major dictionary and encyclopedic sets. Catalogs are available upon request. Also, in the Northeast there is the Discount Encyclopedia Center (38 S. 19 St., Philadelphia, PA 19103; 215-561-5090) and the Buck-A-Book Shop (1440 Wareham St., Middleboro, MA 02346; 617-947-6869) and on the West Coast the Cherokee Book Shop (6607 Hollywood Blvd., Los Angeles, CA 90028; 213-463-6090).

Under the right circumstances, an older encyclopedia can be nearly as useful as a new, more expensive edition. If, say, your informational needs are principally in the area of history or the humanities (literature, philosophy, etc.), a used encyclopedia in good condition might be an excellent bargain. The Literary Mart, for example, recently listed a 1976 edition of *Merit Students Encyclopedia* for $200, whereas the current edition sells for more than twice that amount on the retail market. On the other hand, if you ordinarily look to the encyclopedia for scientific and technical information or current social and geographical data (where knowledge changes rapidly and up-to-date material is usually essential), a secondhand encyclopedia would be of little practical value. As a general rule, encyclopedias over five years old should be viewed with considerable caution and those more than ten years old avoided. (To determine a set's age, note the latest copyright date on the back of the title page in the first volume.) Prices of used encyclopedias will vary with age, condition, and demand, but normally a set depreciates in value between 15 and 20 percent the first year and about 10 percent each year thereafter. Shipping charges average about $25 for large multivolume sets. Finding a good secondhand encyclopedia is like finding a good used car—largely a matter of luck.

COMPARISON SHOPPING FOR ENCYCLOPEDIAS

If, after considering these questions, you decide that you do indeed want a new general encyclopedia (and there are many good reasons why you might so decide), the question then becomes which of the many titles on the market is best for you and your family, based on product quality, the needs and abilities of all who will be using the set, and the amount of money you can afford to spend. Most people make only one large encyclopedia purchase during their lifetime. Unlike automobiles, encyclopedias are not traded in on a new model every few years. For this reason, and because the total cost of an encyclopedia deal can run as high as $1,000 or more when everything (the yearbook, credit charges, etc.) is computed, shrewd consumers will weigh their encyclopedia purchase decisions as carefully as possible. Hence, the next step is comparison shopping.

But in the case of encyclopedias, comparison shopping is more easily said than done. When in the market for a stereo set or an automobile, you can go directly to various competing retail dealers at your convenience, talk with sales representatives, obtain any available promotional literature, and try out the makes and models that appeal. At some point, you will most likely discuss the merits of different makes with interested friends and family members. You may also seek out impartial product performance evaluations conducted and published by such independent organizations as the Consumer Union and Consumers' Research, Inc. Then, in your own good time, you can make a reasonably well-informed purchase decision based on this substantial and varied input. Not so with encyclopedias. As explained in the preceding section, "Selling Encyclopedias," encyclopedic products are not usually sold over the counter in retail stores (except for single-volume titles and the new multivolume *Academic American Encyclopedia,* which has opted to break the rules) but directly in the consumer's home or via mail order. As a result, the prospective buyer of an expensive large-scale encyclopedia has little if any opportunity to compare the various sets on the market.

Getting around this problem can be both frustrating and time-consuming. But comparison shopping, for all its bother, is well worth the effort, especially if you are thinking in terms of an encyclopedia in the $350–$950 range. To comparison shop for an encyclopedia, follow these steps:

Step 1: Consult the comparative chart, "Encyclopedias at a Glance," which follows at the end of Part I of the *Buying Guide*. Select several or more encyclopedias from the chart that, at least at first glance, seem to meet your basic requirements as far as size, price, and reader suitability are concerned.

Step 2: Read the reviews of these encyclopedias in Parts III–VII of the *Buying Guide*. You might also want to peruse the "Special Reports" (Part II), which offer the opinions of U.S. and Canadian librarians regarding the usefulness of individual encyclopedias. If none of the sets initially selected stands out as the best encyclopedia for you and your family, return to the chart and start the winnowing process over. When you have finally chosen two or three titles as likely purchase possibilities, go to the public library.

Step 3: Check to see if the library owns recent editions of the encyclopedias you have in mind. The latest date on the verso of the title page indicates the most recent revision. Critically examine each set, using the "Encyclopedia Evaluation Checklist" that immediately follows. Also, while at the library, read what other reviewing authorities have said about the encyclopedias. For your convenience, evaluations published in *American Reference Books Annual* (*ARBA*) and *Booklist* are cited and digested under "Other Critical Opinions" at the end of each review in the *Buying Guide*. Most libraries will have back files of *Booklist*, a periodical that includes lengthy reviews by the Reference and Subscription Books Review Committee of the American Library Association. Back volumes of *ARBA* will be less readily available, especially in smaller libraries. You might also want to talk with a reference librarian about the various encyclopedias you are considering.

Step 4: If the library does not have reasonably current editions of all the encyclopedias you are interested in, contact the publisher or distributor of each needed set (see Appendix E for directory information), requesting any available sales literature, including current price and edition information. At the same time, ask that the firm's area sales representative set up an appointment to call on you sometime in the near future—at your convenience.

Step 5: During the meeting with the salesperson, listen attentively to the sales presentation, but request (firmly if necessary) that a set of the encyclopedias be left with you for at least a week or, better, two weeks. Insist on having a full set. Under no circumstances accept or rely on a "demonstrator" or "prospectus" volume. Such volumes are often not entirely representative of the set as a whole, nor do they allow you to check the set's overall accessibility (index, cross-references, etc.). If, for any reason, the salesperson refuses your request for an examination set, write off that particular encyclopedia. At the present time, only World Book-Childcraft International, Inc., and Encyclopaedia Britannica, Inc., have stated policies on home examination of their products. An "on approval" guarantee provided by WBCI permits consumers to examine the product for 30 days without obligation to purchase. Britannica has a somewhat similar plan that provides for a 15-day "guarantee of satisfaction" or a complete refund.

Step 6: At your leisure, inspect each encyclopedia carefully. Ask the set questions and expect prompt, accurate answers. If, for instance, the encyclopedia cannot tell you what gene splicing is and how it works, or what the official language of Greenland is (it changed recently from Danish to a native Eskimo tongue), or how many popular and electoral votes President Reagan received in the 1980 election, the set is not performing well. By cross-examining the encyclopedia with questions based on your knowledge and interests, you can quite quickly discover its main strengths and weaknesses. As the British sage Dr. Samuel Johnson once said, "You do not have to eat the whole ox to find out that the meat is tough." Or to use a more familiar analogy, test-drive the encyclopedia, just as you would an automobile you were considering buying.

ENCYCLOPEDIA EVALUATION CHECKLIST

What specifically should one look for when judging the merits of an encyclopedia? The following list of evaluative criteria provides guidelines for determining the quality and utility of any general encyclopedia, no matter its size, price, or intended audience.

Purpose and Scope

What are the encyclopedia's stated aims? What do the editors and publisher claim for the work? For whom is the set designed? The introductory material, or front matter, should offer clear, succinct answers to these initial questions.

How extensive is the encyclopedia's coverage? Considering the set's announced objectives and intended usership, are subjects covered in sufficient depth, or is coverage superficial or capricious? Is a subject like Afghanistan treated in five pages or five lines? Are topics omitted that probably should be covered? For instance, is there an article on solar energy, Islam, Kabuki theater, water resources, Ronald Reagan, diabetes, mass transportation, Scientology, chess, condominium housing? Does the encyclopedia emphasize certain areas of knowledge over others, or is coverage among geography, history and biography, the arts and humanities, social and behavioral sciences, and physical and life sciences fairly well balanced? Is the scope of coverage international, or is the

United States the sole focus of attention? Does the work convey a world view of knowledge, or is its perspective limited to developments in the West? Does the encyclopedia favor concrete (or tangible) subjects over conceptual (or abstract) ones? The one-volume *New Columbia Encyclopedia,* for example, provides fine coverage of concrete topics like the Chickasaw Indians, Chihuahua (both the place in New Mexico and the breed of dog), and Lydia Maria Child (a nineteenth-century American abolitionist), but often neglects such concepts as child development and human growth.

No encyclopedia, of course, can be expected to cover everything or answer every question. In Marjorie Kinnan Rawlings's novel *The Sojourner,* the main character buys an encyclopedia and is "vaguely disappointed. Most of the information was strange and he read with absorption of the people and animals of other lands, of alien fruits and vegetation. But when he turned eagerly to learn about the stars, the planets, the cosmos, he did not find the things he was seeking. He had thought a book so large and thick would have some answers." This experience is commonplace among encyclopedia users and owners, both young and old, who have not yet learned that today the whole of knowledge is beyond any single mind or reference source. Hence, when evaluating the scope and coverage of an encyclopedia, keep in mind that such a work can only be an introduction and guide to the most important human achievements and discoveries.

History and Authority

Who made the encyclopedia? What is its history? Has the set achieved recognition through the years as a work of some substance, or is it a relatively new or undistinguished item? What is the reputation of the publisher? What credentials do the editors, advisers, and particularly the contributors bring to the work? Although computers might have set the type or assisted the indexing process, human beings still make encyclopedias and are responsible for their contents. It is reasonable therefore to ask who these people are. Reputable encyclopedias will identify their makers, usually listing them and their qualifications at the beginning of the first volume. Likewise, all but the shortest articles will be signed.

Often the consumer will not know offhand who is, and who is not, a recognized authority. A spot-check of standard biographical directories like *Who's Who in America* and *American Men and Women of Science* will soon provide some inkling of whether the encyclopedia is the work of hacks or reputable scholars. So-called big names, however, do not necessarily guarantee an encyclopedia's authority. In some cases, impressive contributors contribute very little except their impressive names. Encyclopedia editors also sometimes pad their list of contributors and advisers with the names of people who have made no real contribution to the preparation of the set. A good example of this can be found in the new *Academic American Encyclopedia.* Investigation by the *Buying Guide* has revealed that the *Academic American*'s 11-member Advisory Council (comprised mainly of librarians) had no part whatsoever in the encyclopedia's design or construction, yet the average consumer looking over the front matter will naturally assume that members of the council had some meaningful role in the making of the set. Why else would they be listed there? In his seminal article "On the Making and Survival of Encyclopedias" (*Choice*, June 1967, p. 382), Otto V. St. Whitelock has some pertinent advice for encyclopedists on the subject of contributors and advisers: "Encyclopedia readers are entitled to assume that the best thought has gone into the preparation of the articles, to rely upon their authority, and to expect more than a product of quick research in the company library by writers who are assigned topics according to editorial need. An encyclopedia bears a heavy, self-assumed obligation to its public and should never allow itself to become a refuge for ill-prepared amateurs and dilettantes."

Information about publishers' reputations is quite subjective and hence difficult to obtain. *Literary Market Place*, an annual Bowker directory, and Gale's *Book Publishers Directory* provide pertinent facts about U.S. publishers, such as the types of books published and the extent of the operation, which helps to separate the big firms from the little ones. But perhaps the best source of informed opinion about a publisher's standing is a knowledgeable librarian. A basic part of the librarian's job is distinguishing good publishers from bad. And, of course, the *Buying Guide* includes this type of information. Concerning "name" encyclopedias, a pamphlet written by the author of the *Buying Guide* entitled "Purchasing a General Encyclopedia" (American Library Association, 1969) offers this advice: "The prospective purchaser should . . . assume an attitude of healthy skepticism toward encyclopedia reputations, which are sometimes maintained more by high-powered advertising than by actual performance. A lesser-known encyclopedia might meet the individual needs of the purchaser as well as, or better than, one of the 'name' sets."

Reliability

Is the encyclopedia factually accurate? Is its interpretation of the facts reasonably in accord with responsible contemporary scholarship? An undertaking as immense and complicated as an encyclopedia is bound to contain some inaccuracies, no matter how conscientious or esteemed its makers and contributors. "There is no error so monstrous," Lord Acton once wrote, "that it fails to find defenders among the ablest men. Imagine a congress of eminent celebrities such as More, Bacon, Grotius, Pascal, Cromwell, Bossuet, Montesquieu, Jefferson, Napoleon, Pitt, etc. The result would be an Encyclopedia of Error."

A bit overstated perhaps, but the point is made. Some years ago, a physicist named Harvey Einbinder produced a book called *The Myth of the Britannica* (Grove Press, 1964), which exposed many errors of fact and interpretation in the most famous and highly regarded of all English-language encyclopedias. More recently, a Boston University administrator, Samuel McCracken, reported various mistakes in the latest edition of the *Britannica* (see "The Scandal of 'Britannica 3' " in *Commentary*,

February 1976, pp. 63+). For instance, the entry for Thomas Arundel, an archbishop of Canterbury who died in 1414, is illustrated with a portrait of Thomas Howard, who lived two centuries later. And the *Britannica* is not the only encyclopedia that contains misstatements. The 1980 edition of *The World Book Encyclopedia* says in one place in the "Kansas" article, "Terms for governor and other top state offices were increased from two years to four years, effective in 1974," but later states, "In 1972, Kansas voters approved a constitutional amendment that increased the terms of the governor and other chief state offices from two years to four years. The amendment took effect in 1975." Which is it, 1974 or 1975? The new *Academic American Encyclopedia* contains an uncomfortable number of errors of this kind. For example, the article "English Music" gives 1962 as the date of Benjamin Britten's *War Requiem*, whereas the article on Britten himself gives the date as 1961. The article "American Revolution" reports that the Continental Congress voted on July 4, 1776, to separate the American colonies from Great Britain, but actually that vote occurred on July 2 (on July 4 the Congress voted to adopt the Declaration of Independence, a statement justifying the July 2 action). And in the short article on Bob Dylan, the folk singer, the encyclopedia states, "His 'Blowin' in the Wind' became the anthem of the civil rights movement," an observation that will make those who sang "We Shall Overcome" wonder where Jonathan Kamin, the author of the article, was during the 1960s.

Such errors in an authoritative reference work are disturbing, but not unexpected. To repeat: no encyclopedia, no matter how carefully edited, is immune from error. No encyclopedia is perfect. What we can expect from a quality encyclopedia—one that has been prepared with care by knowledgeable, responsible people—is a *reasonable* level of reliability. In other words, a good encyclopedia can be relied upon to have its facts straight almost all the time. Mediocre and poor sets will err just often enough to make the user first uneasy and then distrustful. To evaluate an encyclopedia's reliability, again read several or more articles on subjects you know something about. Cross-examine, or interrogate, the set. How many states did Jimmy Carter win in the 1980 presidential election? Which ones? Where is geothermal energy used most successfully in the world today? What is the outlook for that form of energy? Is the *War Requiem* Benjamin Britten's most ambitious work? When was it first performed and by whom? What is the function of the liver? How does that organ work? What diseases are associated with the liver? Which dogs make good pets? Which ones are best with children? Ask questions for which you know the answers. At this point, too, you might enlist a relative, friend, or neighbor who has some specialized knowledge to read and evaluate an article or two. If the set is intended for children, have them read articles on topics of interest.

Recency

How current is the material in the encyclopedia? No encyclopedia can be completely up-to-date. There is simply too much new information and knowledge, accruing too rapidly, to be instantly accommodated by the encyclopedia format. A wholly new edition every year or so—even every ten years—is not economically feasible. But to meet the reference needs of users, encyclopedias must maintain a certain degree of currency. Editors employ two basic methods for keeping their multivolume sets reasonably up-to-date. Neither method is entirely satisfactory.

The first technique used to achieve an acceptable level of up-to-dateness is rather loftily called "continuous revision." Originally introduced by Britannica in the 1930s to keep the fourteenth edition of *Encyclopaedia Britannica* (1929–1973) relatively current, continuous revision simply means that only certain portions of the encyclopedia's text are revised each year. Roughly a minimum of 10 percent of the set should undergo *thorough* revision annually if the encyclopedia is to keep abreast of essential new knowledge and information. Encyclopedia advertising tends to ballyhoo the amount of annual revision, but there is no effective way to verify these claims, short of reading and comparing every article in successive editions. A "revised" article might have been completely rewritten or, as is more often the case, only a word or a sentence or a statistic has been changed or added. In any event, it is revision grist for the encyclopedia publicist's mill. Certainly the impression exists that revision claims are sometimes exaggerated. In one recent case, two publishers (World Book-Childcraft International and Aretê) strongly disputed each other's revision claims in their promotional literature.

On the subject of continuous revision, Bill Katz points out in his *Basic Information Sources* (McGraw-Hill, 3rd ed., 1978, pp. 138–139), "Primary attention is given to current news items, which by their very currency are more apt to be noticed by readers. Aspects of literature, philosophy, the social sciences, and even the sciences which are not likely to change drastically are usually skipped over in revision." In other words, an encyclopedia can be quite up-to-date in certain articles and equally obsolete in others. Sales performance during the previous year also frequently has a direct bearing on the amount of revision an encyclopedia receives. If the set has done well in the marketplace, more money is likely to be allocated for editorial revision (which means the set will remain competitive, which in turn means it will continue to be revised, and so on and on). As one industry executive once told the *Buying Guide* in private conversation, "The sales buck begets the revision buck." But when an encyclopedia begins to falter in terms of sales, revision tends to suffer, thus setting into motion a downward spiral that is difficult to reverse.

What makes continuous revision less than satisfactory from the consumer standpoint is the lack of any clear-cut means of determining or measuring the amount of revision that has occurred over a period of time. Many people, including some librarians and educators, naively assume that the latest copyright date on an encyclopedia offers a trustworthy guide to the recency of its contents. Not so. Just because an encyclopedia carries a current copyright date does not necessarily mean the set is up-to-date. *Consumers should know that the most recent date on the back of the title pages of any multivolume general encyclopedia represents only the latest PARTIAL revision* (unless, of course, the set is entirely new). Exactly how much of the text has been revised each year is questionable. As already noted, authorities recommend and responsible encyclopedists agree that approximately 10 percent of the set's total contents should be revised (or at least reviewed for revision) each year, so that the encyclopedia renews itself every decade. But—and this is the rub—legal requirements for copyrighting a "derivative work" such as a revised encyclopedia or dictionary are murky at best, and new copyright notices can be and are readily obtained on the basis of shockingly small amounts of new or revised material. The Copyright Office in Washington annually processes thousands and thousands of applications for copyright. In the case of derivative works, an examiner is responsible for making sure that the "material added to this work" statement in space 6 of the application is in accord with the facts. Due to the volume of work, however, the Copyright Office normally relies on the honesty of the applicant. Moreover, there are no explicit standards or requirements concerning the amount of revision necessary to obtain a new copyright, nor does the Copyright Office distinguish between major and minor revisions. The upshot for the consumer is this: *the latest copyright date on an encyclopedia cannot be accepted as a conclusive guide to the set's up-to-dateness.*

In the future, however, the term "continuous revision" will doubtless take on new meaning as encyclopedias, dictionaries, and similar reference sources become widely available in electronic (as opposed to print) form. The computerized encyclopedia, discussed in some detail in the "Introducing Encyclopedias" section of Part I, will dramatically speed up the revision process. New material and changes will be input into the encyclopedia directly at terminals linking the editorial staff and the set's contents in the computer memory, thus circumventing cumbersome and time-consuming printing, binding, and distribution operations. The advent of computerized encyclopedias will also induce a much greater rate of revision activity than heretofore. No longer will an encyclopedia owner (or subscriber) be satisfied with information on, say, Iran prepared before the overthrow of the Shah or the planet Saturn before the *Voyager I* mission. The technical capability for speedier revision will inevitably raise user expectations for improved currency. Encyclopedia publishers (like Grolier) that lack ample resources to compete in the new electronic environment run the risk of being unable to keep pace with both the new technology and anticipated user demands.

To determine the relative currency of an encyclopedia (print or electronic), check various articles on subjects where information is constantly changing, such as political and technical developments. Also look at articles in those areas like music and literature where knowledge is relatively static, or less prone to sudden or ostentatious change. If you are considering the purchase of a new edition of a title already owned (as librarians often do), make an effort to check the new version against the old. This procedure might help avoid the recent bad experience of Rosalie Elespuru-Murphy, reference librarian at Tompkins Cortland Community College, Dryden, N.Y. (reported in *RQ*, Summer 1980, p. 407): "We have lost all faith in the long-relied-upon integrity of Encyclopaedia Britannica since the publication of the 1979 edition. We wonder how many others have noticed they paid some $300+ for revisions so minor and unimportant they are almost impossible to find. I have taken time to check pages in the 1974 and 1979 editions for changes and updates. In volume after volume no revisions show; in a couple which I did find the changes are simply rewording of the same information."

The *Buying Guide* analyzes numerous selected topics for up-to-dateness in each encyclopedia reviewed. Representative topics are itemized in tabular form for comparable encyclopedias in the "Recency" section of each review. Consumers may want to check their findings against the *Buying Guide*'s research. In addition, the guide makes an effort to note revision trends in individual encyclopedias, based on comparative analysis of the current set under review and the set reviewed in the previous edition (in this case the 1980 and 1977 sets) as well as revision data provided by the publishers.

The other method encyclopedia-makers use to keep their sets up-to-date is publication of a yearbook, or annual record of significant events. Despite publisher claims to the contrary, these yearbooks rarely have a true or purposeful relationship to the parent set, aside from sharing a common title. Frequently overpriced and heavily promoted ("Only four cents a day"—or $12.95 a volume—or $130 over a ten-year period), encyclopedia yearbooks are enormously profitable, generating millions each year in sales for the major companies. Big press runs and automatic mailings, along with inflated prices, account for their high profitability.

Consumers who purchase a multivolume encyclopedia would do well to question the value of the companion yearbook. In its *Handbook of Buying for 1974,* Consumers' Research, Inc., specifically cautions encyclopedia buyers: "Never contract in advance for yearbooks, as these are little used by many purchasers. They are best purchased on a year-to-year basis." The *Buying Guide* agrees, but also suggests that a popular annual like *The Hammond Almanac of a Million Facts, Information Please Almanac,* or *The World Almanac* might better serve as an updating supplement to a general encyclopedia. Such almanacs, modestly priced and readily available in bookstores and at newsstands, often provide more useful information than the costlier encyclopedia yearbooks. Eight of these inexpensive almanacs are briefly described in Appendix B of the *Buying Guide.*

Objectivity

Is the encyclopedia unbiased in its presentation of religious, political, sexual, scientific, and racial subjects? Are there efforts to slant the facts or subtly influence the reader in areas of unresolved controversy, such as the Native American movement, homosexuality, hypnosis, nuclear power, pornography and obscenity, religious cults, and women's rights? Are controversial issues treated fairly with all sides of the question explained? Or are such issues ignored altogether, which is also a form of bias? Are contributors free from built-in bias? For instance, an article by an oil company executive on the energy crisis could not help but contain some bias, intended or not. Likewise, a government official may be overly protective of a particular agency or policy, as was J. Edgar Hoover, who used to prepare the FBI article for most of the major encyclopedias.

In an amusing little essay entitled "An Introduction to Omniscience" that appeared in *Bookletter* (September 16, 1974, p. 4), a now defunct newsletter published by Harper's Magazine Company, Stephen Brook reports on his brief but illuminating experience as an encyclopedia staffer in London. "The editor in chief was a fervent Roman Catholic, and he resolved to incorporate detailed biographies of all the lesser-known Early Church Fathers into our family encyclopedia." Brook, who left encyclopedia-making for trade publishing, concludes, "Objectivity is an illusion of the mechanical age. We rightly, we believe, confer more value on the profoundly perceived irrelevancy than on the casually recorded Fact. We parade invention as truth, experience as history." Of course he is right. There never has been, nor ever will be, a totally unprejudiced person or encyclopedia. The words of Livio C. Stecchini are instructive here: "Usually modern encyclopedias profess to be an expression of objective and impartial learning, but all the successful ones reflect a unifying ideology." (Quoted from Stecchini's "On Encyclopedias in Time and Space" in *American Behavioral Scientist,* September 1962, p. 4.) Nevertheless, modern encyclopedists almost always strive to be as evenhanded as humanly possible. More often their sins are of omission rather than commission. Rarely, for instance, do our encyclopedias delve too deeply into the "dark" side of Thomas Jefferson, apparently feeling that his ownership of slaves and illegitimate children by Sally Hemings, a black woman, have no historical standing. But those seeking the truth about the author of the Declaration of Independence and early American attitudes toward the race question surely would not agree.

To determine an encyclopedia's relative objectivity, check the set's treatment of controversial political ideas (e.g., Communism), religions (Scientology), sexual behavior (lesbianism), historical events (the Vietnam War), countries (Iran), organizations (the Ku Klux Klan), and people (Thomas Jefferson). Also scan the set for blatant sexist language and connotations, such as doctors always depicted as male, nurses always female.

Clarity and Reader Suitability

Is the encyclopedia clearly written? Is the style consistent throughout or does it vary from article to article? Are the articles presented in a reasonably interesting manner? Is the writing free from unexplained technical terminology and academic jargon? Most important, is the encyclopedia intelligible to those who will be using it?

Parents and teachers especially should be aware that many encyclopedias for young people are written to grade level—that is, the encyclopedia's articles on advanced topics like genetics and heredity will be written in a more sophisticated style requiring a higher level of reading comprehension than articles on such elementary subjects as, say, the states or snakes. Likewise, the better encyclopedias for young adults construct their articles on difficult topics to read from the simple to the complex. Hence, the article on oceanography or human reproduction will begin quite simply with the primary facts and then progressively become more complex in style as the complexity of the material increases. Sometimes called "pyramid" writing, this stylistic technique allows students of varying ages and educational levels to use the same encyclopedia productively. Users read a particular article only so far as their intellectual comprehension permits. Most encyclopedias intended for students also control their vocabulary by means of readability testing. Each article is checked by readability specialists to ensure that the text is comprehensible to readers at specified grade levels. Terminology found to be too advanced is either simplified or defined within the context of the article. *The World Book Encyclopedia* does an especially good job in this respect. For example, in the *World Book* article on glucose the following terms are italicized and then defined in context: *sucrose* (table sugar); *photosynthesis* (the food-making process); *monosaccharide* (sugar with a simple structure); *digested* (broken down into simple units); *intravenously* (injected directly into blood); and *conversion* (change).

Unfortunately, because they seek the widest possible market, encyclopedia publishers and their promotional departments have a bad habit of overstating claims concerning reader suitability. The *New Encyclopaedia Britannica,* for instance, is clearly an adult encyclopedia, but it continues to be advertised as "written in clear, readable language . . . the language of today . . . so that even the most complex subjects become much easier for your children to understand." The *Micropaedia* portion of the set is said to be "ideal for homework." There are indeed children who can and do use the new *Britannica* (the company has testimonials to prove it), but the vast majority in elementary and middle school will find the set, including the *Micropaedia,* beyond their normal reading comprehension. Significantly, because it *is* an adult encyclopedia, the *Britannica* is *not* written to grade level, does *not* employ the pyramid writing style, and is *not* vocabulary controlled by readability specialists. As Geoffrey Wolff wrote in his article "Britannica 3, History of" (*Atlantic,* June 1974, p. 47), making particular reference to Britannica salespeople, "Anyone who claims . . . that the set is suitable for schoolchildren too young to drive an automobile should be had up for perjury."

A realistic notion of the reading levels of everyone in your family is of utmost importance before buying an encyclopedia. If you are not a reading whiz, or if the children are not exceptional readers, accept the fact honestly and proceed from there. Many young people today have reading problems, as a multitude of national tests show. Moreover, estimates suggest that approximately 15 percent of children currently in school have some sort of mild learning disability, while another 3 to 5 percent have more severe problems. Another sad realization is that an astonishing number of adults will have difficulty comprehending an adult-level encyclopedia, or even one for children. Edward B. Fiske, education editor of the *New York Times,* recently reported, "Despite the country's long-standing commitment to universal literacy and the $70 billion a year that is poured into public schools in its pursuit, the fact is that millions of Americans—by some estimates as many as one of every five adults—do not possess the minimal reading, writing and calculating skills necessary to function in modern society" (*New York Times,* April 30, 1978). It is vital, therefore, that reading skills be appraised as stringently as possible prior to purchasing an encyclopedia. What is the use of an encyclopedia you and your family cannot read?

To evaluate an encyclopedia's clarity and reader suitability, read a number of articles on subjects about which you have little or no knowledge. Then ask yourself: *Do I understand what is being said?* Is the vocabulary on my level? Are unfamiliar, difficult, and technical terms satisfactorily explained? Have your children and others who will be using the encyclopedia do the same.

Arrangement and Accessibility

How is the encyclopedia organized? How easy is it to use? Is the arrangement of material sensible? Does it promote efficient retrieval of information? Specifically, is the encyclopedia arranged alphabetically or topically? If alphabetical, are the entries word-by-word (e.g., "Indian Ocean" precedes "Indiana") or letter-by-letter ("Indiana" precedes "Indian Ocean")? If topical, is the organization based on some logical plan or pattern? Are cross-references provided? How abundant are they? Are the articles short or long? For example, does the encyclopedia contain a specific article on the battles of Bull Run or is the topic covered within a broad treatment of the Civil War? Is there a detailed index? Is the index analytical? That is, are broad index entries like "Meteorology" made more specific by subentries (such as "Meteorology—Atmosphere," "Meteorology—Climate," "Meteorology—Hurricane," "Meteorology— Snow," "Meteorology—Stratosphere," "Meteorology—Weather Forecasting," and "Meteorology—Wind")?

The importance of an encyclopedia's index cannot be overestimated. A detailed, analytical index is an especially important requirement for encyclopedias that are arranged topically (or in a classified manner) and those that have adopted the broad-entry alphabetical approach (e.g., when Bull Run has no entry but is covered in an extended article on the Civil War). Oddly enough, however, encyclopedists have often resisted indexing their sets. *Encyclopaedia Britannica* had no index when it first appeared in 1768–1771, nor did its makers develop one until the middle of the nineteenth century, and only then because a competing work provided the impetus. Likewise, *The World Book Encyclopedia,* first published in 1917, managed without an index until the early 1970s, relying instead on an elaborate network of cross-references. And to this day the 14-volume *New Standard Encyclopedia* prefers to rely on specific entries and numerous cross-references in lieu of a comprehensive index, the editors arguing that the addition of an index would not measurably improve access to the encyclopedia's contents but would price the set out of the market. The *Buying Guide,* however, firmly believes that a multivolume general encyclopedia without a satisfactory index is an incomplete information resource. An encyclopedia without an index is like an automobile without a steering wheel: both devices are necessary to get to the final destination as dependably as possible.

Cross-references are also valuable finding devices, especially as complements to a detailed index. There are basically two types of cross-references, external and internal. External cross-references are those that appear as separate entries in the main alphabetical sequence—for example, "KING GEORGE'S WAR: see *French and Indian Wars.*" Internal cross-references are those found within or at the end of an article. They may be printed in small bold-faced capital letters (e.g., the text of the article "Naturalism" may refer to Henrik IBSEN, which signals the reader that additional information on Naturalism can be found in the Ibsen article), or they may be indicated by the use of *see* and *see also* labels or by the abbreviation *q.v.* (which stands for the Latin *quod vide,* or "which see"). Some encyclopedias also list "related subjects" at the end of selected articles.

Rabelais, the French satirist, once mused, "What harm in getting knowledge even from a sot, a pot, a fool, a mitten, or a slipper?" No harm at all—if the knowledge is reliable and easily obtained. The same can be said of an encyclopedia. If the set's knowledge is inaccurate, the knowledge is not worth retrieving. But if the knowledge is difficult or impossible to find, it matters little that the knowledge is reliable. To discover how an encyclopedia is arranged and how accessible its contents are, pose some questions: Who was Rabelais, when did he live, what are his principal works? When did the African nation of Zimbabwe become independent? How do computers operate? Then look for the answers. This approach will quickly tell you if the encyclopedia is conveniently arranged in an A–Z or topical format, if there are cross-references and how helpful they are, and if there is an index and how well it works.

Bibliographies

Does the encyclopedia include lists of materials for further study? Are the entries reasonably current? Are the most significant or best-known works cited? Are the works cited likely to be available in local libraries? Do the bibliographies include films, filmstrips, and other nonprint materials as well as books on such subjects as the human brain, nuclear energy, Thomas Jefferson, sharks, the metric system, and Zimbabwe? An encyclopedia is often only the first step in the information-gathering process, and the inclusion of selected bibliographies is designed to guide the user to other basic materials on the topic being investigated. Responsible encyclopedia-makers are keenly aware of the need for good bibliographies, as Frank Greenagel, the man behind the new *Academic American Encyclopedia,* was quick to point out in an interview with the *Buying Guide* in

Wilson Library Bulletin (March 1980, p. 439): "The encyclopedia will provide an overview and a jumping-off place. This is where bibliographies come in. We want to direct the student to the best, most readily accessible sources after they have read the encyclopedia article. They may include the definitive work on the subject, but only if it is accessible both physically *and* intellectually. We also include leading textbooks and books in paperback, although some encyclopedias exclude textbooks and paperbacks from their bibliographies. We want our bibliographies to be like a good professor—an adventuresome guide."

Located at the end of the articles or sometimes grouped together in the final volume of the set, bibliographies should at least be spot-checked for recency. Also, if time permits, several lists should be checked to determine if the most important titles on a particular subject are cited. For example, does the article "Existentialism" include references to William Barrett's indispensable *Irrational Man* and Walter Kaufmann's useful anthology *Existentialism from Dostoevsky to Sartre?* Does the article on parliamentary procedure cite the most recent edition of *Robert's Rules of Order?*

Graphics

Is the encyclopedia adequately illustrated? Encyclopedia-makers have long recognized the wisdom of the adage about a picture being worth a thousand words, and it is rare for a set today not to include both black-and-white and color photographs, line drawings, charts, graphs, art reproductions, maps, and the like. Do these visual aids help explain or clarify the written text, or are they simply page filler? Are the illustrations placed relatively near the text they supposedly complement? Are they of recent vintage? Do the illustrations normally have captions and, if so, are the captions informative? In the case of maps, are they sufficiently detailed? Are they up-to-date? Are they accurately drawn (or drawn to scale)? Are map legends and symbols clear? What kinds of maps are included—physical, political, distribution, historical, astronomical? Were they produced by a reputable cartographer? Are the maps indexed? Note that in some instances encyclopedias include an atlas, or collection of maps, in a separate volume or section.

Poorly reproduced or haphazardly chosen illustrations can mar the reference value of an otherwise adequate encyclopedia, as can the absence of graphics altogether. On balance, the visual quality of present-day encyclopedias far exceeds that of times past, due to superior modern graphics techniques and processes. Color, for instance, is comparatively new to encyclopedias, although its use has become practically mandatory today. A contemporary encyclopedia without abundant color reproductions and so on is likely to be viewed as a lackluster work, and so even the worst sets now sport glossy plates and shiny transparencies. The obligatory use of color, however, has helped drive encyclopedia production costs through the proverbial roof. In the words of one experienced editor, "Color in encyclopedia illustration is the tail that wags the dog."

To evaluate the quality and effectiveness of an encyclopedia's graphics, scan several volumes to see if the illustrative matter is clear, sharp, reasonably current, and properly related to the written text. Also determine if color is used for purposes of enhancing the informational content of the encyclopedia or simply to make it look pretty. For instance, pictures of birds or wild animals or reproductions of great paintings are of much greater value informationally if in color, but a diagram of how a fish respires or a photograph showing fencing positions can be just as effective in black-and-white. The quality of maps can be ascertained by looking up a town, city, river, mountain, or the like, known to you. It would also be wise to check a few recent place-name changes; for instance, Vietnam has been one country since 1976; Rhodesia became Zimbabwe in 1980.

Physical Format

Is the page makeup attractive and uncrowded? Is there sufficient space between headings and the general text? Do guide words appear at the top of each page? Is the print large and sharp enough to be read with ease? Are the margins wide enough, especially the inside ones (called gutters)? Is the paper of good grade and free from glare? Does the binding appear to be sturdy and durable? Is the binding washable, an especially important consideration if young children will be using the set? Does the encyclopedia employ the unit-letter system (meaning each letter of the alphabet is contained within a single volume), or the split-letter system (one letter ends and another begins within the same volume)? The value of the unit-letter approach is that each letter is conveniently in one volume, but it also means some volumes will be physically larger than others; on the other hand, the split-letter approach is less convenient but allows for uniform size of volumes. Do the volumes lie flat when open, so that they can be left on a desk, stand, or shelf top for ready consultation without springing shut? Overall, is the encyclopedia well made and pleasing to the eye?

Special Features

Does the encyclopedia include any features not normally found in comparable sets? Are such features useful or are they merely promotional gimmicks? As previously noted, general encyclopedias today tend to be rather similar in terms of purpose, coverage, and design, and many publishers feel the need to offer some unique or distinctive twist that might help set their encyclopedia apart from the competition. Such features range from including study guides and colorful information boxes throughout the text to appending special atlas and dictionary supplements. Provision of a free research service is another such feature. In the case of the *New Encyclopaedia Britannica* and *The Random House Encyclopedia*, the entire organization of the work might appropriately be viewed as a special feature. Identify and examine as many special features in the encyclopedia as you can, always questioning whether a particular feature actually improves the quality and utility of the set or whether it has been included because it makes good advertising copy.

Sales Information

How much does the encyclopedia cost? What is the lowest retail price?
The highest? Are educational institutions like schools and libraries accorded a discount and, if so, how much? Remarkably, inflation has not
affected encyclopedia prices as drastically as it has many other products.
Moreover, when compared with book prices generally (which have sky-
rocketed in recent years), good encyclopedias are a bargain. *Collier's
Encyclopedia,* for instance, sells for about $24 a volume at retail, whereas
numerous trade books with half the number of pages and far less substance cost as much or more.

Consumers should realize, however, that encyclopedia prices for the
same set can vary greatly, due to different bindings. The *same* encyclopedia in a so-called deluxe simulated leather binding might cost at least $100
more than the less elegant but equally durable buckram edition. In the
past, sales representatives have sometimes deliberately not mentioned the
availability of the lower-priced binding, at least not at first, in hopes of
selling the more costly set. Geoffrey Wolff, in an amusing "brief memoir"
in his *Atlantic* review (June 1974, p. 40) of the *New Encyclopaedia Britannica,* tells of hustling expensive morocco bindings one summer: "Hea-
ven," for a reference-book salesperson, "is called Full Morocco Terri-
tory." To repeat: during the saleperson's visit, ask for and get prices on
all available editions of the set. The lowest figure quoted should be the
same or very nearly the same as the one given in *Encyclopedia Buying
Guide* (which is updated every three years). Bear in mind that local and
state taxes can affect the final sales price as much as 10 percent, and that
all encyclopedia publishers charge for shipping and handling.

Prices may also be affected by "special offers" or "package deals"
involving additional encyclopedia products. Typically, the consumer is
offered a combination of items along with the encyclopedia, some of
which might be characterized as "free" or at a "discount." Be very wary
of such offers. If you must take a truckload of extras—atlases, dictionaries, bookcases, world globes, research services, teaching machines, yearbooks, literature anthologies, or whatever—just to get the encyclopedia
you want, forget it. Or better, write directly to the publisher (see Appendix E for directory information), explaining that all you want is the true
price of the encyclopedia. Odds are, given today's consumer climate, you
will get what you want. If all else fails, however, do not hesitate to
contact *Encyclopedia Buying Guide* (c/o R. R. Bowker Company, 1180
Ave. of the Americas, New York, NY 10036; 212-764-5100).

Summary

At this point, you have talked with encyclopedia sales representatives,
familiarized yourself with their promotional literature, read informed
critical evaluations of more than a few encyclopedias in Parts III–VII of
the *Buying Guide,* and examined firsthand two or more sets. *You are now
in a position to make an intelligent purchase decision.* First, summarize
your impressions of each encyclopedia's strengths and weaknesses in each

critical area (authority, reliability, recency, objectivity, and so forth). You might want to rate each category as excellent, good, fair, or poor, as the *Buying Guide* does in the summary section of each review. Second, compare the qualities of the two or three encyclopedias you have investigated, considering which best meets your informational needs for the least amount of money. Then, third and finally, make your selection.

Most consumers, of course, will not have the time nor the inclination to go through the detailed selection process suggested in "Finding the Right Encyclopedia," but the procedure is included here for those who are serious about the quality of their sources of knowledge and information, as well as concerned about getting the best return for their consumer dollar. For the many consumers who need critical material about encyclopedias currently on the market as quickly and painlessly as possible, the *Buying Guide* provides convenient digests and comparative summaries at the end of each review.

Other Critical Opinions

Obviously, the more critical input you have, the better informed your final decision will be, whether you use the selection process outlined in "Finding the Right Encyclopedia" or merely consult the summary section of the reviews. Time and energy permitting, you might want to look over the long reviews produced by the Reference and Subscription Books Review Committee of the American Library Association, which appear in the journal *Booklist,* and/or the much more compact notices found in *American Reference Books Annual* (*ARBA*). Brief synopses of the *Booklist* and *ARBA* reviews are provided at the end of the evaluations in Parts III–VII of the *Buying Guide.* Additional sources of critical information about encyclopedias can be found in Appendix D.

Encyclopedias at a Glance: A Comparative Chart

"Encyclopedias at a Glance" is a comparative chart that groups the 36 titles covered in *Encyclopedia Buying Guide* by five broad user categories: Adult—Multivolume; Adult—Small-Volume; Young Adult—Multivolume; Children—Multivolume; and Young Adult/Children—Small-Volume. Reader suitability is specified in the third column, followed by price, and then various statistics that provide a quantitative overview of each encyclopedia.

An additional function of the chart is to guide prospective consumers to those several or more encyclopedias that might best meet their particular reference needs, at least at first glance. After studying the chart and making some initial selections, users should consult the critical reviews that follow in Parts III–VII of the guide for a detailed description and evaluation of each set. For instance, after looking over the chart, a family of average means with two modestly bright children aged, say, 10 and 12 might want to have a closer look at *Compton's Encyclopedia, Encyclopedia International,* and *The World Book Encyclopedia,* the three least expensive sets in the multivolume young adult category. A careful reading of the reviews of these encyclopedias will result in either a tentative decision to go ahead and buy one of the sets or the judgment that none of the three is exactly what the family needs (in which case it's back to the chart).

SOME CAUTIONS ABOUT THE CHART

The chart is not intended as a final selection device. Always consult the reviews in Parts III–VII of the guide prior to making a final purchase decision. The *Buying Guide* also urges consumers to follow, when possible, the comparative shopping plan outlined in the preceding section, "Finding the Right Encyclopedia."

Quality and quantity are not the same. Merely because an encyclopedia has more words or more volumes or more illustrations than another does not necessarily make it a better work or a better investment.

User classifications and reader suitability designations should be viewed as flexible guidelines, not ironclad rules. Encyclopedists today design their products for the broadest possible audience and, by and large, they have been successful in this effort. It must be kept in mind, however, that

Title	Reader Suitability (age range)[1]	Lowest Retail Price	Vols.	Pages	Articles[2]	Words	Illustrations
Adult Multivolume							
Academic American Encyclopedia	12–GA	$400.00	21	9,728	28,500	9 mil	15,000
Collier's Encyclopedia	15–AA	579.50	24	19,000	25,000	21 mil	17,000
Encyclopedia Americana	15–AA	750.00	30	26,942	53,120	31 mil	21,505
Funk & Wagnalls New Encyclopedia	12–GA	77.83	27	12,976	25,000	9 mil	7,500
Harver World Encyclopedia	12–GA	375.50*	20	5,855	20,000	7.5 mil	16,000
New American Encyclopedia	12–GA	133.00	20	7,570	27,000	5.5 mil	9,000
New Caxton Encyclopedia	12–GA	599.50*	20	6,500	13,000	6 mil	17,300
New Encyclopaedia Britannica	15–AA	899.00	30	33,414	106,800	43 mil	23,300
New Illustrated Columbia Encyclopedia	15–AA	69.96	24	7,500	50,515	6.6 mil	5,000
New Standard Encyclopedia	12–GA	349.50	14	9,878	17,623	6.3 mil	12,200
Adult Small-Volume							
New Columbia Encyclopedia	15–AA	79.50	1	3,068	50,515	6.6 mil	407
New Lincoln Library Encyclopedia	12–GA	99.98	3	2,323	25,000	3.5 mil	1,200
Pears Cyclopaedia	15–AA	13.95	1	1,056	NA	1.2 mil	50
Random House Encyclopedia	12–GA	69.95	1 & 2	2,856	25,875	3 mil	13,800
University Desk Encyclopedia	12–GA	69.95	1	1,055	25,000	2 mil	3,000
Volume Library	12–GA	86.95	1	2,605	8,500	3.5 mil	2,000
Young Adult Multivolume							
Compton's Encyclopedia	9–18	419.00	26	11,100	45,000	8.6 mil	28,500
Encyclopedia International	9–18	288.80	20	11,935	29,830	9.5 mil	12,780
Merit Students Encyclopedia	9–18	579.50	20	12,000	21,800	9 mil	19,200
World Book Encyclopedia	9–18	399.00	22	14,280	20,000	10 mil	29,500
Children Multivolume							
Britannica Junior	7–14	199.50	15	8,000	4,100	5.3 mil	12,700
Childcraft	4–10	179.00	15	5,000	NA	750,000	6,700
Compton's Precyclopedia[4]	4–10	179.00	16	3,000	650	325,000	2,800
Illustrated Encyclopedia for Learning	7–12	49.95	12	1,536	4,500	291,000	6,000
New Book of Knowledge	7–14	360.00	20	10,500	9,326	6.8 mil	22,400
Oxford Junior Encyclopaedia	7–14	189.00	13	6,500	3,600	3.7 mil	6,100
Talking Cassette Encyclopedia	4–10	490.00	10	NA	100	100,000	None
Young Children's Encyclopedia[4]	4–10	74.50	16	2,700	650	300,000	2,500
Young Students Encyclopedia[5]	7–14	149.50	24	3,500	2,400	1.5 mil	4,400
Young Adult/Children Small-Volume							
Illustrated World Encyclopedia	7–14	19.95	1	1,619	7,300	2.5 mil	2,000
Junior Encyclopedia of General Knowledge	7–12	9.95	1	224	103	100,000	400
Junior Pears Encyclopaedia	7–14	11.95	1	704	NA	280,000	150
Nelson's Encyclopedia for Young Readers	7–14	34.95	2	973	2,000	350,000	1,300
Purnell's First Encyclopedia in Colour	7–12	6.95	1	125	300	50,000	500
Purnell's Pictorial Encyclopedia	7–12	19.95	1	192	88	75,000	550
Rand McNally's Children's Encyclopedia	7–12	4.95	1	61	NA	15,000	300

*Price to schools and libraries; not available at retail.

[1] GA (General Adult) requires reading skills at high school level; AA (Advanced Adult) requires reading skills at college level; 9–18 requires reading skills at junior high level and up; 7–14 requires reading skills at third grade level and up; 4–10 requires only beginning level reading skills.

Maps	Index Entries	Cross refs.	Contributors[3]	Publisher or Distributor	Title
1,100	250,000	67,000	2,250	Aretê	Academic American Encyclopedia
1,450	400,000	12,220	4,500	Macmillan	Collier's Encyclopedia
1,150	353,000	40,000	6,330	Grolier	Encyclopedia Americana
342	193,000	80,000	701	Funk & Wagnalls	Funk & Wagnalls New Encyclopedia
470	None	30,000	135	Marshall Cavendish	Harver World Encyclopedia
420	None	6,000	500	Webster	New American Encyclopedia
600	50,000	None	83	Purnell Reference Books	New Caxton Encyclopedia
1,080	225,000	83,100	4,300	Encyclopaedia Britannica	New Encyclopaedia Britannica
252	None	66,000	119	Time-Life	New Illustrated Columbia Encyclopedia
935	None	53,000	700	Standard Educational	New Standard Encyclopedia
252	None	66,000	119	Columbia University	New Columbia Encyclopedia
140	26,000	8,800	122	Frontier	New Lincoln Library Encyclopedia
36	900	150	Staff	Merrimack	Pears Cyclopaedia
100	None	20,000	500	Random House & Encyclopaedia Britannica	Random House Encyclopedia
350	None	35,000	68	Dutton	University Desk Encyclopedia
214	45,000	500	250	Southwestern	Volume Library
2,000	200,000	40,800	475	Compton	Compton's Encyclopedia
867	120,000	15,000	2,000	Grolier	Encyclopedia International
1,570	140,000	10,600	2,300	Macmillan	Merit Students Encyclopedia
2,350	150,000	100,000	3,300	World Book-Childcraft	World Book Encyclopedia
1,050	57,000	5,800	800	Encyclopaedia Britannica	Britannica Junior
None	20,000	None	Staff	World Book-Childcraft	Childcraft
20	800	500	150	Compton	Compton's Precyclopedia
425	None	None	13	Publishers Agency	Illustrated Encyclopedia for Learning
1,031	90,000	2,500	1,435	Grolier	New Book of Knowledge
150	35,000	2,000	1,050	Oxford	Oxford Junior Encyclopaedia
None	155	None	Staff	Troll	Talking Cassette Encyclopedia
20	None	500	150	Encyclopaedia Britannica	Young Children's Encyclopedia
335	15,000	10,000	39	Xerox Education & Funk & Wagnalls	Young Students Encyclopedia
158	None[6]	2,500	105	Bobley	Illustrated World Encyclopedia
11	1,100	None	13	Mayflower	Junior Encyclopedia of General Knowledge
10	None	100	Staff	Merrimack	Junior Pears Encyclopaedia
200	5,700	2,500	Staff	Thomas Nelson	Nelson's Encyclopedia for Young Readers
None	550	None	5	Pergamon	Purnell's First Encyclopedia in Colour
None	975	None	13	Pergamon	Purnell's Pictorial Encyclopedia
None	350	None	Staff	Rand McNally	Rand McNally's Children's Encyclopedia

[2]Not applicable: topical sections.   [3]Staff signifies staff produced.
[4]*Compton's Precyclopedia* and *The Young Children's Encyclopedia* are practically the same work (see reviews).
[5]There are two separate editions of *Young Students Encyclopedia*.
[6]Separate index available.

chronological age, particularly in children, often bears scant relationship to psychological age, reading ability, intellectual maturity, or educational motivation. Bright, inquisitive children of ten, for instance, whose reading comprehension is advanced for their age, might quite productively use an adult encyclopedia under certain circumstances, whereas apathetic high school students with poor reading skills would find an adult set well beyond their comprehension. Users of the chart should have a realistic notion of the reading capabilities of all who will be using the encyclopedia that is eventually selected.

Price information quoted in the chart, current at the time the guide went to press, is subject to change by the publisher or distributor at any time. But as noted elsewhere, prices obtained from sales representatives should not differ greatly from those given in the current "Encyclopedias at a Glance" chart. Large discrepancies should be questioned.

II. SPECIAL REPORTS

U.S. Public Librarians Rate the Encyclopedias: A Survey

In October 1978, a questionnaire on the use and effectiveness of general English-language encyclopedias was circulated to 100 U.S. public libraries of varying sizes in all parts of the country.[1] Seventy-seven libraries (77 percent) responded. This article reports the findings of that survey. The opinions of knowledgeable librarians concerning the relative merits of general encyclopedias are useful to both consumers and makers of such works.

Instructions accompanying the questionnaire asked "the most experienced general reference librarian(s)" on the library staff to complete the ten-question form, and suggested that "young adult and/or children's specialists might want to respond to those questions involving encyclopedias for young people." The questions are reproduced here as they appeared on the questionnaire. **Results** are expressed in actual numbers, not percentages (unless so indicated). **Comments,** which follow **Results** in questions 2–10, are selected verbatim opinions offered by the respondents. By agreement, respondents and their libraries will be anonymous.

1. At the present time, there are 37 general English-language encyclopedias for adults, students, and children on the U.S. market, including many one-volume works.[2] Please indicate the usefulness of each encyclopedia by circling the most appropriate designation:

A. Used *frequently;* in constant and heavy demand
B. Used *sometimes;* helpful but not in constant demand
C. Used *infrequently;* rarely consulted
D. No opinion/library does not own

Results

Title	A	B	C	D
American Educator Encyclopedia	0	3	4	70
Britannica Junior Encyclopaedia	3	22	24	28
Cadillac Modern Encyclopedia	0	6	7	64
Childcraft	7	21	15	34
Collier's Encyclopedia	28	34	8	7

Note: This report, written by the author of *Encyclopedia Buying Guide*, originally appeared in *Library Journal*, April 15, 1979, pp. 890–893.

Title	A	B	C	D
Compton's Encyclopedia	26	35	8	8
Compton's Precyclopedia	4	6	13	54
Encyclopedia Americana	66	9	0	2
Encyclopedia International	6	27	22	22
Funk & Wagnalls New Encyclopedia	0	2	9	66
Golden Book Encyclopedia	1	6	6	64
Great World Encyclopedia	0	0	2	75
Hamlyn Younger Children's Encyclopedia	0	0	1	76
Harver World Encyclopedia	0	1	3	73
Illustrated Encyclopedia for Learning	0	0	1	76
Illustrated World Encyclopedia	0	0	1	76
Larousse Illustrated International Encyclopedia & Dictionary	0	3	8	66
Lincoln Library	1	18	48	10
Merit Students Encyclopedia	16	27	14	20
My First Golden Encyclopedia	0	3	3	71
New American Encyclopedia	0	1	3	73
New Book of Knowledge	18	32	6	21
New Caxton Encyclopedia	1	5	10	61
New Columbia Encyclopedia	3	21	27	26
New Encyclopaedia Britannica	30	26	14	7
New Hutchinson 20th Century Encyclopedia	0	0	4	73
New Standard Encyclopedia	0	0	5	72
Oxford Junior Encyclopaedia	0	0	2	75
Purnell's First Encyclopedia	0	0	2	75
Quick Reference Encyclopedia	0	0	2	75
Rand McNally's Children's Encyclopedia	0	0	2	75
Random House Encyclopedia	2	15	19	41
University Desk Encyclopedia	0	0	1	76
Volume Library	0	0	1	76
World Book Encyclopedia	76	1	0	0
Young Children's Encyclopedia	0	1	1	75
Young Students Encyclopedia	1	3	3	70

Note: The new 21-volume *Academic American Encyclopedia* (1980) is not included in the survey, as it was not yet published when the survey was conducted.

2. Based on your experience, which encyclopedia among those listed above stands out as the most effective all-around general reference work? *Effective* meaning the work is reliable, easy to use, clearly written, and so forth.

Results. *The World Book Encyclopedia* was the overwhelming choice, named as the most effective encyclopedia on 56 (or 75 percent) of the questionnaires. *The Encyclopedia Americana* was cited as most effective on 25 questionnaires, followed by *Collier's Encyclopedia* (5) and *New Encyclopaedia Britannica* (2). No other titles were mentioned.

Comments. "*World Book* excellent for telephone reference work"; "No one encyclopedia is the 'best' "; "*World Book* as it is accessible to all ages"; "With adults, *Collier's* would be our choice. That choice would be different if *Britannica* had not changed its format"; "*World Book* is most used"; "A tie between *World Book* and *Americana*"; "*World Book*, but *Encyclopedia Americana* is a close second"; "*World Book* followed by *Britannica III*"; "*World Book* for general all-around use."

3. How do you rate the following major multivolume adult encyclopedias—*Collier's Encyclopedia, The Encyclopedia Americana,* and *New Encyclopaedia Britannica*—as effective sources of encyclopedic information? *Effective* again meaning the work is reliable, easy to use, clearly written, and so forth. 1 = most effective; 2 = next most effective; etc.

Results. *Americana* was rated most effective by a large majority of respondents (54), followed by *Collier's* (17) and *Britannica* (5). Conversely, *Britannica* was rated third, or least effective, by 50 respondents, followed by *Collier's* (20) and *Americana* (1). The complete comparative rating picture looks like this: *Americana* most effective—54; next most effective—20; third or least effective—1. *Collier's* most effective—17; next most effective—34; third or least effective—24. *Britannica* most effective—5; next most effective—20; third or least effective—50.

Comments. "*New Encyclopaedia Britannica* is not a good source for quick reference because the index is not specific enough"; "*Britannica's* information has considerably more depth than *Americana*'s, but the access to it is intimidating to most patrons"; "Would have rated 14th ed. of *Britannica* #1, but 15th ed. is NOT easy to use"; "New format of *Britannica* is extremely difficult to use—we still use the old edition"; " 'Old' *Britannica* would have been at the top of my list"; "All three are excellent. Constantly used to supplement one another. *Americana* and *Collier's* have slight edge because of convenience of indexes"; "Our librarians sharply divided over *New Encyclopaedia Britannica,* some think it's great, others don't like it"; "The *New Encyclopaedia Britannica* is not used by public—they find it, as does staff, very disappointing and patrons find it unhandy to use"; "I generally don't use *Britannica* and *Collier's* that often. I can usually find any information that requires an encyclopedia very easily in the *Americana*"; "*Britannica* has always been my first choice for credibility, but current format is difficult to use, also too scholarly for most"; "We swapped our latest old *Britannica* with the *New EB,* transferring the latter to circulating and the former to reference after experience demonstrated that the *New EB* is a reading course rather than a reference work"; "*Collier's* is the least intimidating encyclopedia of the three listed"; "The *New Ency. Britannica* is difficult to use, so that I refer to it only as a last resort"; "The former *Encyclopaedia Britannica* is much easier to use. While the *New Encyclopaedia Britannica* is full of information, the lack of a standard index makes it difficult and sometimes impossible to locate desired material."

4. How do you rate the following small-volume adult encyclopedias—*Cadillac Modern Encyclopedia, The Lincoln Library, The New Columbia*

Encyclopedia, The Random House Encyclopedia, The University Desk Encyclopedia, and *The Volume Library*—as effective sources of encyclopedic information? 1 = most effective; 2 = next most effective; etc.

Results. *New Columbia* was rated most effective by 29 respondents (or about 37 percent), followed by *Lincoln Library* (19 respondents), *Random House* (13), and *Cadillac Modern* (1). *University Desk* and *Volume Library* received very few ratings at all, and they were at the bottom end of the scale. The complete comparative rating picture for the three major small-volume encyclopedias looks like this: *New Columbia* most effective—29; second most effective—12; third most effective—4; fourth most effective—1. *Lincoln Library* most effective—19; second most effective—22; third most effective—11; fourth most effective—1. *Random House* most effective—13; second most effective—8; third most effective—10; fourth most effective—2.

Comments. "We have *Lincoln Library, New Columbia,* and *Random House* but do not use them often. We think they are better suited for home use"; "I don't really use these that often to fairly judge them. I have, however, found some biographical information in *Lincoln* that was unavailable elsewhere. I tend to go here for things as a final source"; "Infrequent use of all—evidently when in the library the public expects fuller treatment"; "The only one we own is *Lincoln Library* and I seldom use it"; "We use these so seldom, we feel unwilling to rate them"; "We do not really make much use of small-volume encyclopedias here. *Lincoln* is useful chiefly for its mathematical information"; "We seldom use one-volume encyclopedias in reference work. Do not own any of these but *Lincoln Library,* which is not used for reference work"; "We seldom use the one-volume works though they have good material when we do"; "We have never found any of the above useful. If it's not in large encyclopedia, it's not in small."

5. How do you rate the following young adult encyclopedias—*Compton's Encyclopedia, Encyclopedia International, Merit Students Encyclopedia,* and *The World Book Encyclopedia*—as effective sources of encyclopedic information? *Effective* again meaning the work is reliable, easy to use, clearly written, and so forth. 1 = most effective; 2 = next most effective; etc.

Results. *World Book* ran away from the field, being rated most effective by 71 respondents (over 90 percent), followed by scattered support for *Compton's* (5 respondents), *Merit Students* (4), and *International* (1). *Compton's* proved to be the clear second choice, with 35 respondents naming it second most effective, followed by *Merit Students* (24) and *International* (13). Fourth, or least, effective was *International* (27), followed by *Compton's* (9) and *Merit Students* (9). The complete comparative rating picture looks like this: *World Book* most effective—71; second most effective—3; third most effective—1; fourth or least effective—0. *Compton's* most effective—5; second most effective—35; third most effective—16; fourth or least effective—9. *Merit Students* most effective—4; second most effective—24; third most effective—15;

fourth or least effective—9. *International* most effective—1; second most effective—13; third most effective—15; fourth or least effective—27.

Comments. "*World Book* still the best. *Compton's* looks flashy but I find it often doesn't cover the subjects I need"; "By checking the physical appearance of these encyclopedias it is obvious that *World Book* receives the most use in all our agencies. Where the other encyclopedias will be in near mint condition, *World Book* is worn and tattered"; "We have never been very enthusiastic about *Compton's*. Refer to it when can't find something in *World Book* and usually don't find it in *Compton's*"; "*World Book* is outstanding for library reference work (telephone especially). It is the first work we reach for in answering general questions"; "*World Book* is by far the easiest and clearest and most used of all our encyclopedias"; "Teachers often make assignments with *World Book* in mind, so it is most used"; "*World Book* has been a long-time favorite. Good for students"; "*World Book* is the more well known and therefore young people use it first, but *Compton's* often gives more information"; "We go to *World Book* first, and it answers at least three-fourths of the time"; "*World Book* is outstanding. We often use it for adult reference as well as children's."

6. How do you rate the following multivolume children's encyclopedias—*Britannica Junior Encyclopaedia, The New Book of Knowledge,* and *The Young Students Encyclopedia*—as effective sources of encyclopedic information? 1 = most effective; 2 = next most effective; etc.

Results. *New Book of Knowledge* was rated most effective by over half of the respondents (41), followed by *Britannica Junior* (19). *Young Students,* which received no mention as most effective, was designated third, or least, effective by 15 respondents, followed by *Britannica Junior* (1) and *New Book of Knowledge* (1). The complete comparative rating picture looks like this: *New Book of Knowledge* most effective—41; second most effective—20; third or least effective—1. *Britannica Junior* most effective—19; second most effective—31; third or least effective—1. *Young Students* most effective—0; second most effective—1; third or least effective—15.

Comments. "Children do not use reference books much, prefer circulating material in our library"; "*Britannica Junior* has proven to be so inadequate that I seldom refer to it"; "We find *World Book* the most 'effective' encyclopedia in our work with children"; "*Britannica Junior* is improving but not yet as good"; "We consider *World Book* useful for grade 5 and up and is more useful than the three mentioned above"; "*World Book* is better"; "I'm impressed with *NBK, Britannica Junior* is lousy"; "At one time we had *Britannica Junior* but it was used infrequently."

7. In your community, do teachers sometimes prohibit, restrict, or discourage student use of general encyclopedias?
Results. Yes—66; No—11.
If *Yes,* what is your attitude toward this policy?

Results. Agree with—14; Disagree with—43; No opinion—9.

If *Disagree with,* have you contacted the school system, principal, or individual teacher(s) involved in an effort to change the policy?

Results. Yes—10; No—32.

Comments. "When the use of encyclopedias is restricted, the teacher is usually trying to encourage the students to use other types of reference materials"; "I really feel it is up to the individual teacher as far as what sources they want the students to use"; "Teachers sometimes are trying to broaden pupils' knowledge so they will realize there are books other than encyclopedias"; "We sometimes contact teachers if sufficient material is not available without using encyclopedias"; "I won't tell a teacher how to run his/her classes. I know for a fact, though, that a number of teachers will assign material to a class without knowing how extensive available material is or whether or not the assignment can be completed at all. Many of the assignments are outlandish"; "Sometimes encyclopedias are the only source of information"; "The choice is that of an individual teacher. It is not our place to interfere with an instructor's teaching methods. We leave it to the school librarian to instruct teachers"; "From time to time we make efforts to contact the schools and work more closely with teachers. These efforts have met great apathy and have had little success"; "The matter has been brought up at teacher/faculty meetings"; "Disagreement with teachers does not change their policy"; "Students should not be discouraged from using general encyclopedias, but they should be discouraged from over-reliance on them"; "We very often must start students with encyclopedias, even though they are not allowed to use encyclopedias in their bibliography"; "A divided issue among staff members"; "I have mixed feelings—when in a rushed situation, it would be easier to use a general encyclopedia. However, young people learn more about the library and sources found there by being forced to use other sources"; "It appears to be hopeless."

8. When patrons ask you for advice about buying a general encyclopedia, how do you normally respond? Do you refer the patron to sets in the library?

Results. Always—41; Sometimes—26; Never—4.

Do you refer the patron to reviews in such sources as *American Reference Books Annual (ARBA), Booklist,* and *Encyclopedia Buying Guide?*

Results. Always—66; Sometimes—8; Never—1.

Do you recommend your favorite encyclopedia?

Results. Always—2; Sometimes—20; Never—47.

Comments. "If asked for a definite answer I say what we use most frequently, but never say a favorite"; "Although I never tell a patron this, I really feel that individuals, unless very wealthy, have little business buying a multivolume set of encyclopedias"; "Suggest patron check subject he is familiar with in various encyclopedias and compare information, indexes, format, and illustrations"; "If asked which is most frequently used, we mention *World Book* but stress this may be habit rather than the merit of the set"; "Try to be impartial. Do suggest they look at sets in the library. Do answer if asked which we use most frequently. Do try to 'steer' if *Britannica* is being considered for elementary grade children"; "When patron is trying to decide between two sets that library owns, we may suggest coming in and looking over the two sets *in addition* to reading portions of review sources"; "Let patron make own choice, never make recommendation of favorite"; "Librarians should not express personal opinions in situations such as this, but should refer inquirer to printed sources and urge individual examination and comparison"; "We try to be impartial."

9. If you maintain a ready reference shelf or collection, which general encyclopedia (if any) is included in that select group of basic reference sources?

Results. *World Book Encyclopedia* was mentioned most frequently (29 respondents), followed by *Encyclopedia Americana* (11), *New Encyclopaedia Britannica* (6), *Collier's Encyclopedia* (5), *Lincoln Library* (3), *New Columbia Encyclopedia* (3), and *Random House Encyclopedia* (3). *Cadillac Modern Encyclopedia, Encyclopedia International, Merit Students Encyclopedia,* and the "Old" *Encyclopaedia Britannica* were each mentioned once.

Comments. "All encyclopedias are on reference shelf. Old ones circulate"; "All of our encyclopedias are together"; "None (no space) but circulate older sets"; "All reference encyclopedias are close at hand for use"; "None is kept at the desk but I usually use *World Book* or *Americana*"; "Both adult and children's encyclopedia shelves are located within 15 feet of the information desks."

10. Does your library have a formal or written encyclopedia replacement policy?

Results. Yes—20; No—57.

If Yes, briefly describe the policy.

Comments. "Replace at five year intervals"; "Rotation between departments. Each agency one new set every five years"; "Budget allowing, we buy new ones for reference department and transfer older ones to branches"; "All updated at least every five years, and more heavily used every two or three years, and older editions used in branch libraries"; "*World Book* is replaced every year, other sets are replaced every three or five years"; "We've drawn up a replacement schedule indicating which encyclopedias will be maintained for each section. We discard a set when it is five years old. Reference copies are usually one to three years old. Circulating sets are two–four years old"; "Encyclopedias are replaced on a rotating basis—nothing is purchased every year. *World Book* and *Americana* are purchased most frequently"; "When we have no budget difficulties, buy at least all new editions every two years."

CONCLUSIONS

Many conclusions might be drawn from this national survey of public library opinion about general encyclopedias. Perhaps the most interesting result to me, an encyclopedia critic, is the deep and widespread hostility (some of it quite vitriolic) expressed toward the *New Encyclopaedia Britannica* (15th ed., 1974–a), sometimes called *EB3* or *Britannica 3* because of its tripartite arrangement. Obviously, the good people of Britannica have not won the minds, let alone the hearts, of American public librarians. On the other hand, the affection for *The World Book Encyclopedia*, a longtime favorite among public librarians, continues unabated. And rightly so, as *World Book* continues to be, page-for-page, the best general encyclopedia available in English. The cool attitude toward one-volume encyclopedias, particularly the better ones like *The New Columbia Encyclopedia* and *The Random House Encyclopedia*, was unexpected. I was also mildly surprised at the lack of use of the few British sets available in the United States, especially *The New Caxton Encyclopedia*, which, though not a flawless production, has many virtues for American readers. Concerning the pervasive teacher bias against student use of encyclopedias (a nationwide phenomenon documented by this survey), it appears that public librarians do not approve of the situation but have not formulated an adequate response.

REFERENCES

1. A brief note on the survey's methodology is in order. The 100 libraries surveyed were selected by random sample from the *American Library Directory, 1976–77* within the following geographical and size parameters. As much as possible, all areas of the country were equally represented. At least one library in each state was surveyed. In the larger states as many as three libraries were surveyed. One-third (33) of the libraries included in the survey were classified as *small* (serving under 50,000 population), one-third (34) were *medium-sized* (serving 50,000–250,000 population), and one-third (33) were *large* (serving over 250,000 population). I am indebted to Jess Mullen of the Tampa-Hillsborough County (Fla.) Public Library for conducting the random sample. This procedure ensured an impartial selection process. I am also grateful to the 77 libraries and their librarians who responded to the survey. I should also note that the survey is an independent project initiated and conducted by the author of *Encyclopedia Buying Guide*. The survey is not sponsored or supported by any encyclopedia publisher, nor the R. R. Bowker Company.
2. Several librarians responding to Question 1 wondered why *Chambers's Encyclopaedia*, a well-known 15-volume British set, was not on the list of in-print encyclopedias. As explained in some detail in Appendix A of *Encyclopedia Buying Guide, Chambers's* has not been significantly revised since 1966 and is not generally available in this country, and in Britain it is said to be "virtually unobtainable."

Canadian Public Librarians Rate the Encyclopedias: A Survey

Norman Horrocks

In June 1980, a questionnaire on the use and effectiveness of general English-language encyclopedias was circulated to 75 Canadian public libraries in all parts of the country.[1] This was designed to be a companion survey to that reported on by Ken Kister for public libraries in the United States.[2] To quote from the Kister article,

> The opinions of knowledgeable librarians concerning the relative merits of general encyclopedias are useful to both consumers and makers of such works.

> Instructions accompanying the questionnaire asked "the most experienced general reference librarian(s)" on the library staff to complete the ten-question form, and suggested that "young adult and/or children's specialists might want to respond to those questions involving encyclopedias for young people." The questions are reproduced here as they appeared on the questionnaire. The results are expressed in actual numbers, not percentages (unless so indicated). Comments which follow the results in questions 2–10 are selected verbatim opinions offered by the respondents. By agreement, respondents and their libraries remain anonymous.

1. The following general English-language encyclopedias for adults, students, and children are currently available in Canada. Some of these are multivolumed and others one-volume works. Please indicate the usefulness of each encyclopedia by circling the most appropriate designation:
  A. Used *frequently;* in constant and heavy demand
  B. Used *sometimes;* helpful but not in constant demand
  C. Used *infrequently;* rarely consulted
  D. No opinion/library does not own

Note: This report, written by Dr. Norman Horrocks, director of the School of Library Service at Dalhousie University, Nova Scotia, Canada, was commissioned expressly for publication in *Encyclopedia Buying Guide.*

Title	A	B	C	D
American Educator Encyclopedia	0	0	0	55
Britannica Junior Encyclopaedia	1	17	5	30
Cadillac Modern Encyclopedia	2	3	2	49
Childcraft	4	7	7	38
Coles Concise Encyclopedia	1	5	5	45
Collier's Encyclopedia	16	18	7	16
Compton's Encyclopedia	1	18	10	1
Compton's Precyclopedia	2	1	4	47
Encyclopedia Americana	28	6	1	20
Encyclopedia International	2	16	6	30
Everyman's Encyclopedia	1	2	4	47
Funk & Wagnall's New Encyclopedia	0	3	2	46
Golden Book Encyclopedia	1	2	2	50
Great World Encyclopedia	0	0	2	52
Hamlyn Younger Children's Encyclopedia	0	0	2	52
Harver World Encyclopedia	0	0	0	54
Larousse Illustrated International Encyclopedia	1	5	9	46
Lincoln Library	2	6	18	30
Merit Students Encyclopedia	5	14	4	29
My First Golden Encyclopedia	0	1	2	51
New American Encyclopedia	1	4	2	47
New Book of Knowledge	13	17	2	24
New Caxton Encyclopedia	1	3	6	38
New Columbia Encyclopedia	6	7	11	27
New Encyclopaedia Britannica	27	12	2	11
New Hutchinson 20th Century Encyclopedia	1	2	0	51
New Standard Encyclopedia	0	1	1	52
Oxford Junior Encyclopedia	1	4	5	45
Purnell's First Encyclopedia	0	0	0	54
Quick Reference Encyclopedia	0	0	0	54
Rand McNally's Children's Encyclopedia	0	0	0	54
Random House Encyclopedia	1	3	15	37
University Desk Encyclopedia	0	0	0	54
Volume Library	0	0	0	54
World Book Encyclopedia	49	4	1	1

It should be noted that the multivolume *Encyclopedia Canadiana* is not included on the above list as it is a "national" rather than a "general" encyclopedia. It was written in by a few respondents as was the British *Chambers's Encyclopaedia,* which is excluded as being no longer in print. Also, the new *Academic American Encyclopedia* (1980) is excluded from the survey, as it was not yet available when the questionnaires were circulated. Although 57 questionnaires were returned, not all libraries responded to every question, which accounts for the occasional discrepancy in the tallies.

2. Based on your experience, which encyclopedia among those listed above stands out as the most effective all-around general reference work?

Effective meaning the work is reliable, easy to use, clearly written, and so forth.

Results. *World Book* was the clear leader, being cited 27 times in contrast to 10 mentions for both *New Encyclopaedia Britannica* and *Encyclopedia Americana. Collier's Encyclopedia* was cited twice and *Larousse Illustrated International* once.

3. How do you rate the following major multivolume adult encyclope-dias—*Collier's Encyclopedia, Encyclopedia Americana,* and *New Encyclopaedia Britannica*—as effective sources of encyclopedic information? Effective again meaning the work is reliable, easy to use, clearly written, and so forth. 1 = most effective; 2 = next most effective; etc.

Results. *Americana* was rated the most effective by 21 respondents with *Britannica* rated first by 14 and *Collier's* by 7. The complete comparative rating shows *Americana* most effective—21; next most effective—13; third or least effective—4. *Britannica* most effective—14; next most effective—19; third or least effective—11. *Collier's* most effective—7; next most effective—12; third or least effective—19.

Comments. *"Britannica* most comprehensive if less easy to use"; *"New Britannica* would be no. 1 if it still had a comprehensive index but the *Micropaedia* is not an adequate substitute. Also if our users were all fairly literate adults, instead of the general public (which includes a large proportion of high school students) it would be rated higher"; "Seems *New Britannica* has good information, but format a hin-drance—a good study plan, not reference source. Use "old" *Britannica* when subject appropriate"; "The old *Britannica* is very useful. The new *Britannica* less so"; "Usually go to *Britannica* first because the articles in the *Macropaedia* are quite thorough. Good definitions in *Micropaedia.* However, sometimes a shorter or more obscure topic isn't dealt with in *Britannica* but is in *Americana"; "*Although *New Encyclopaedia Britannica* is rated 2 in terms of reliability—it is cumbersome to use with its 2 complementary sets—*Macropaedia* and *Micropaedia"; "*Do not like *Britannica*'s *Macro* and *Micropedias.* Patrons often have to look back and forth between the 2 sections. Then also some items in previous *Britannica*s had an entry on their own—in new ed. material is scattered through several entries"; "For coverage and comprehensive-ness I prefer *Britannica* but *Americana* is easier to use"; "Arrangement of *Britannica* is confusing to layman"; "*Britannica* now too difficult to use for average person needing quick answer"; "Small print and new format of *New Britannica* make it difficult to use—nevertheless we refer to it constantly as it is authoritative"; *"Britannica* is good in content but *very* difficult to locate much of the information"; "In any comparison of this type the *New Encyclopaedia Britannica* will always show poorly. Its lack of a general comprehensive index is a major stumbling block"; "In rating the *Americana* ahead of the *Britannica,* ease of use and clear writing would be the most important factors. Students seem to find the *Britannica* more difficult to use. They appreciate the brevity of the *Americana* articles"; *"New Encyclopaedia Britannica* is most effective but harder to use. The *Encyclopedia Americana* is easier to use but not as detailed"; "Different encyclopedias have different 'personalities.' *Americana* is great for inf. about American states, cities, etc.; *Britannica* is good for historical information, bibliographies, etc."; "All our encyclopedias are used, depending on the inquiry and the specific needs of the user"; "Range of *Encyclopaedia Britannica* puts it slightly ahead of convenient organization of *Collier's Encyclopedia";* "The *New Encyclopaedia Britannica* seems to have been designed for home rather than library use. It is awkward to use."

4. How do you rate the following small-volume adult encyclopedias— *Cadillac Modern Encyclopedia, Lincoln Library, New Columbia Encyclopedia, Random House Encyclopedia, University Desk Encyclopedia,* and *Volume Library* as effective sources of encyclopedic information? 1 = most effective; 2 = next most effective, etc.

Results. Both the *New Columbia* and *Random House* were rated the most effective by 13 respondents each; an additional 9 libraries placed *New Columbia* second most effective whereas *Random House* was placed second by 5 libraries and fourth by one. The *Cadillac Modern* was rated second most effective by 2 respondents and third most effective by 7; *Lincoln Library* was rated the most effective by 2 respondents; third most effective by 3, and fourth most effective by 14; *University Desk* was mentioned by 1 respondent; *Volume Library* was not rated by any respondent.

Comments. "We have only the *New Columbia Encyclopedia* and it is rarely used"; "Library only owns *Random House* and it is used only occasionally"; "Seldom used. By consensus of ref. staff have not purchased or have removed most single or small-vol. general encyclopedias"; "Have only *Lincoln Library* of this group—seldom used"; "*Random House Encyclopedia* is excellent in terms of scope of diverse information, but major disadvantage is lack of index. Index would increase usage"; "Rarely used—entries usually too short"; "More suitable for home or office use—seldom used"; "One-volume general encyclopedias rarely used by reference staff"; "*Random* would be improved with an index replacing its contents list at beginning."

5. How do you rate the following young adult encyclopedias—*Compton's Encyclopedia, Encyclopedia International, Merit Students Encyclopedia,* and *World Book Encyclopedia*—as effective sources of encyclopedic information? Effective again meaning the work is reliable, easy to use, clearly written, and so forth. 1 = most effective; 2 = next most effective, etc.

Results. *World Book* was an overwhelming choice here with 43 respondents rating it the most effective with the only other ratings of "most effective" given to *International* and *Compton's* by 1 respondent each.

Opinion was divided almost equally between *Compton's* which was rated second most effective by 18, third most effective by 10, and fourth most effective by 1, and *Merit Students,* which was rated second most effective by 20 and third most effective by 10. In addition to its one rating as most effective, *International* was also rated second most effective by 5, third most effective by 7, and fourth most effective by 7. In addition to its 43 ratings as most effective, *World Book* was rated second most effective by 2.

Comments. "Encyclopedias are replaced with revised editions on a rotating basis. The most up-to-date are often also the most effective"; "These are all in the Children's Dept. (up to Grade 8 students), not 'Young Adult' section"; "*World Book* is the most used and the most effective"; "*World Book Encyclopedia* is used by both young adults and adults in our library"; "*World Book* very good for younger high school students, as well as adults wanting basic information. Illustrations very helpful"; "The students are used to *World Book* in school, prefer to use it; very difficult to get them to use others"; "We might reach different conclusions if our editions of these works were all the same vintage but when one title is considerably older than the others and is in fact shelved in secondary stacks, the comparison is slanted"; "*World Book* beats out all young adult encyclopedias for subjects covered, illustrations, updating, cross-referencing, etc."; "*World Book* most effective: others not in the race"; "*World Book* is the most fantastic encyclopedia"; "*World Book* is easy for children to use without assistance from adults. It has excellent photos and illustrations."

6. How do you rate the following multivolume children's encyclopedias— *Britannica Junior Encyclopaedia, New Book of Knowledge,* and *Young Students Encyclopedia*—as effective sources of encyclopedic information? 1 = most effective; 2 = next most effective, etc.

Results. *New Book of Knowledge* was rated a clear leader, being placed most effective by 27 respondents and next most effective by 12. *Britannica Junior* was rated most effective by 5 respondents, next most effective by 17, and third most effective by 5. *Young Students* was rated second most effective by 3 respondents and third most effective by 7.

Comments. "For North American coverage *New Book* is very effective"; "Much prefer *World Book*"; "Believe *World Book* accessible to quite young children and its material seems to 'fit' the 'young' questions; would put it 1. Encyclopedia format, in my opinion, of questionable value for very young"; "In considering the above questions, I think it is only fair to add that, because we are living in Canada, we consult *Canadiana* possibly as often as we do *World Book.* Also *Lands and Peoples* and *Peoples of the Earth* are frequently used. I think K. Kister should include these three sets in his *Encyclopedia Buying Guide*"; "In this institution high user levels have not permitted as much individual assistance as we would wish. The item given first place (*New Book of Knowledge*) is highly favoured by young people; the second (*Britannica Junior*) is seldom consulted unless directed by staff."

7. In your community, do teachers sometimes prohibit, restrict, or discourage student use of general encyclopedias?

　　Results. Yes—28; No—26.

If yes, what is your attitude toward this policy?

　　Results. Agree with—5; Disagree with—21; No opinion—2.

If disagree with, have you contacted the school system, principal, or individual teacher(s) involved in an effort to change the policy?

　　Results. Yes—6; No—17.

　　Comments. "Teachers want students to discover other reference books and they do not want encyclopedia articles copied verbatim, but I point out that libraries usually have some different encyclopedias compared to what schools have, that encyclopedias are good jumping off points . . . and that a library does not always have enough other sources when a whole class is doing an assignment"; "Letters are sent by Children's Coordinator explaining the problem and inviting him/her to seek out resources before giving assignments. Many teachers do not adequately prepare an assignment and are not aware that there may be little or no material available, other than in the general encyclopedias"; "I agree with the restrictions when they are intended to encourage students to read more widely on the subject"; "Not a major problem. Principals feel teachers have the right to limit sources. The problem being that in some cases the only info. we have is in an encyclopedia"; "I do not wish to pontificate to local teachers about the value of encyclopedias and dictionaries as a starting point for youngsters' research, but I almost always start with them myself when helping children with projects"; "The teachers are attempting to make the kids use research skills by using other books for their answers. Encycs. sometimes are an easy copout for a lazy student"; "Discussions with school librarians suggest the individual teacher must have the right to establish such a policy. Librarians, school or public, must 'live with' it"; "Sometimes the general encyclopedia is the only available source of information. In such cases restricting student use serves only to frustrate the search for knowledge and is counterproductive in that we've got the child in the library but our hands are tied in trying to assist. While it is possible to find grounds for teachers restricting student use of such materials there is more to be lost than gained. Intelligent librarians cannot but be hampered by such fiats"; "Ideal situation for students to obtain material from a variety of sources. This is impractical and unrealistic from viewpoint of library staff. Assignment frequently given to many classes at the same time"; "Students are not usually given instruction in what a general encyclopedia is, so that they refuse valuable material in more specialized reference works"; "When only info. available is in an encyclopedia we tell students to tell teacher and call us if there's any problem"; "I don't believe that judicious use of an encyclopedia lowers the students' likelihood of using other reference sources"; "I feel it is up to the individual teacher to decide"; "This problem has not occurred in our library. The teachers seem to encourage the use of our resources and are very cooperative when initiating their students to the public library."

8. When patrons ask you for advice about buying a general encyclopedia, how do you normally respond? Do you refer the patron to sets in the library?

Results. Always—25; Sometimes—18; Never—0.

Do you refer the patron to reviews in such sources as *American Reference Books Annual (ARBA), Booklist,* and *Encyclopedia Buying Guide?*

Results. Always—34; Sometimes—9; Never—1.

Do you recommend your favorite encyclopedia?

Results. Always—2; Sometimes—20; Never—18.

Comments. "I suggest the parent and child examine our collection and other local collections but also consider future use of the encyclopedia"; "We often get questions at Western Fair time when special deals on encyclopedia sets seem to abound. I emphasize the price; to check it against our information to make sure the patron is not getting taken. Also, the pressure—I stress that with libraries readily available in this city, a patron must not feel he has to purchase an encyclopedia set for the home"; "We avoid recommending a particular encyclopedia but will discuss which encyclopedias we have found useful for specific purposes"; "I usually refer the patrons to both review articles and sets in the library. I suggest that they come in and use the encyclopedias before buying one on its reputation alone"; "Often encourage them not to buy"; "The *Buying Guide* offers expert evaluation. The prospective buyer can make a judgment best by considering his/her needs and the price he/she is prepared to pay"; "We first caution all patrons that they are buying a set for the *right* reason—not because of pressure from salesmen, not for child's school homework (often not enough mat.), etc.—only if they would be in a habit of using it themselves. We caution them on 'currency' of the set"; "We make use of the *Encyclopedia Buying Guide* and explain the value of the sets we own"; "Honestly, we do not encourage patrons to buy their own encyclopedia because this would go against promoting the use of our own resources. Also the contents of the editions change too often and it makes encyclopedias expensive for a person who wishes to buy."

9. If you maintain a ready reference shelf or collection, which general encyclopedia (if any) is included in that selection of basic reference sources?

Results. *World Book* was mentioned the most, by 8 respondents, with *Britannica* mentioned by 6, *Americana* and *New Book of Knowledge* both receiving 5 mentions; *New Columbia* was mentioned by 4 respondents and *Random House, Compton's, Lincoln Library,* and *Collier's* were all mentioned once.

Comments. None.

10. Does your library have a formal or written encyclopedia replacement policy?

Results. Yes—7; No—47.

If yes, briefly describe the policy.

"Our goal is to have at least one if not two current, i.e., most recent, editions of encyclopedias available at all times"; "Acquisition of current editions of standard, comprehensive, general knowledge encyclopedias is on a rotating annual basis to maintain currency and to minimize strain on the book budget"; "Replace one a year, in order"; "Purchased on a rotating basis, one new set each year, all replaced every five years. No one-volume encyclopedias are purchased. When under budget restraints, preference given to *World Book* and *Britannica.*"

CONCLUSIONS

The conclusions to be drawn from this survey very largely confirm those found by Kister when he looked at the U.S. scene. As in the United States, there was lack of enthusiasm for the new *Britannica,* widespread support for the quality of *World Book,* and little said in favor of one-volume encyclopedias. There was much less discouragement of the use of encyclopedias by teachers than was shown in the U.S. survey (Question 7).

REFERENCES

1. The 75 libraries surveyed were selected by random sample from the *American Library Directory, 1976–77* within the following geographical and size parameters. As well as possible, all areas of the country were equally represented. At least one library in each province was surveyed. In the larger provinces as many as three libraries were surveyed. One-third (25) of the libraries included in the survey were classified as small (serving 5,000–25,000 population); one-third (25) were medium-sized (serving 25,000–150,000); and one-third (25) were large (serving 150,000 or more). The public libraries selected were in predominantly or virtually exclusively English-language communities. I am indebted to Ruth MacEachern of the Dalhousie University School of Library Service for conducting the random sample. This procedure insured an impartial selection process. I am also grateful to the 57 libraries and their librarians who responded to the survey. I should also note that the survey is an independent project initiated by the author of *Encyclopedia Buying Guide.* The survey is not sponsored or supported by any encyclopedia publisher, nor the R. R. Bowker Company.
2. Ken Kister, "Encyclopedias and the Public Library: A National Survey," *Library Journal* 104 (April 15, 1979): 890–893. Note that the Kister article is reprinted in the *Buying Guide* immediately preceding this report.

III. MULTIVOLUME ADULT ENCYCLOPEDIAS

Academic American Encyclopedia

Facts in Brief

Full Title: **Academic American Encyclopedia.** *Editors:* Sal J. Foderaro, Editor in Chief; Andrew C. Kimmens, Managing Editor. *Publisher:* Aretê Publishing Company, Inc. (a subsidiary of VNU America, Inc.), Princeton Forrestal Center, 101 College Rd. E., Princeton, NJ 08540. *Edition Reviewed:* First Edition, 1980 copyright.

Volumes: 21. *Pages:* 9,728. *Articles:* 28,500. *Words:* 9,000,000. *Illustrations:* 15,000. *Maps:* 1,000. *Index Entries:* 250,000. *Cross-references:* 67,000. *Contributors:* 2,250.

User Classification: Adult (Multivolume). *Reader Suitability:* Age 12 through General Adult. *Physical Size:* 8¼ × 10¼ in.; 26 cm. *LC:* 79-27430. *ISBN:* 0-933880-00-6. *Lowest Retail Price:* $400; to schools & libraries $389.

Purpose and Scope

The *Academic American Encyclopedia,* the first entirely new multivolume general English-language encyclopedia in over a decade, has been "created for students in junior high school, high school, or college and for the inquisitive adult" (preface). The encyclopedia's intentions are set forth in a straightforward manner in the preface: "Research has determined that such an audience wants an encyclopedia to fulfill four clearly defined objectives: (1) Students and adults expect an encylopedia to provide quick access to definitive factual information; (2) Both audiences also want to find a readily intelligible general overview of a subject that does not compel the reader to grasp intricate subtleties or wade through drawn-out historical analysis; (3) Among better students, and those who know how to approach a term paper, an encyclopedia is regarded as an excellent starting place for further research if it isolates key concepts, outlines the structure of the subject, and directs the reader to more specialized primary and secondary sources; and (4) Readers at all levels expect a reference work to help them visualize or recognize people, places, objects, and processes by means of maps, photographs, and drawings, many of which should be in full color." By and large, the makers of the *Academic American* have adhered faithfully to these general objectives.

The encyclopedia surveys the world's knowledge in 28,500 articles complemented by 16,000 graphics. The articles are normally quite specific (as opposed to broad). EXAMPLE: The *Academic American* covers the subject of motion pictures in a number of specific entries—"Animation"; "Cinematography"; "Documentary"; "Film, History of"; "Film Festivals"; and "Film Industry"—instead of treating the whole topic in one long, broad entry (as does, for instance, *The New Caxton Encyclopedia*, one of the *Academic American*'s chief competitors). This means articles in the *Academic American* are usually short, averaging 350 words in length, or roughly three articles per page. Articles of typical length in Volume 4 (C–CIV) include "Caligula, Roman Emperor"; "Caliphate"; "Callaghan, James"; "Callas, Maria"; "Calles, Plutarco Elias"; "Calorimeter"; "Calvinism"; "Cameo"; "Campbell, Alexander"; "Camping"; "Camus, Albert." Some articles, of course, are much briefer, consisting of only a paragraph or so (e.g., "California Bluebell"; "California Institute of Technology"; "Calisher, Hortense"; "Call of the Wild, The"; "Callicrates"). Others, however, are considerably longer than the average. EXAMPLES: "Calligraphy" covers four pages, "Cambrian Period" two pages, "Camera" four pages, "Canada" eleven pages, "Canada, History of" eight pages, "Cancer" nearly six pages, "Capitalism" a page and a half, "Cartoon" two pages, "Caste" more than a page.

Much information in the *Academic American* is conveyed via graphics (drawings, photographs, cartoons, art reproductions, maps, charts, bar graphs, and the like), which account for approximately a third of the encyclopedia's total text. Good examples of the importance of graphics to the encyclopedia's overall mission can be found in the articles "Film Industry"; "Indians, American"; "Nuclear Energy"; and "Subway." In each instance, the visual material is an integral part of the article as an information source. Captions also provide a significant amount of informative text, often summarizing a central theme or development in a sentence or two. EXAMPLES: The article "O'Keeffe, Georgia" is accompanied by a reproduction of O'Keeffe's *Black Iris;* the caption explains that the painting "demonstrates the American artist's unique style of delicately blended contour and sharp linear form." The article "Nuclear Physics" includes a photograph of Ernest Rutherford, who "holds the simple apparatus with which he achieved the first artificial nuclear transmutation in 1919. Under the impact of high-velocity alpha particles, nitrogen atoms were broken down to oxygen and hydrogen atoms." The value of such captions cannot be overestimated in a general encyclopedia, where studies show the reader's attention is normally first focused on the visual matter, then the captions, and lastly the general printed text.

Over 30 percent of the articles in the *Academic American* are biographies of people, both living and dead. Most of the biographical entries are very brief, averaging 150 words (or about ten lines), although length naturally varies with the prominence of the biographee, or person being described. Former President Jimmy Carter, for instance, receives a full page of coverage, whereas William Styron, the writer, is limited to 12 lines. Twentieth-century figures are accorded especially generous coverage by the *Academic American*, particularly in comparison with the set's main competitors (*Funk & Wagnalls New Encyclopedia, The New Caxton Encyclopedia, The New Illustrated Columbia Encyclopedia*, and *The New*

Standard Encyclopedia). As a rule, only the *Academic American* covers such contemporary personalities as Abbott and Costello, Lauren Bacall, F. Lee Bailey, Russell Baker, the Beach Boys, Yogi Berra, Francis Ford Coppola, Cream, Doris Day, Antal Dorati, Clint Eastwood, Bob Griese, the Jefferson Airplane, Al Pacino, Arthur Penn, and Fran Tarkenton. Biographies of these and many similar people or groups of celebrity status give the encyclopedia a trendy flavor, but the *Buying Guide* wonders if the space accorded, say, Brigitte Bardot or George Blanda might not have been better used for persons of more substance, such as François Bonvin (a notable nineteenth-century French painter), Hale Woodruff (a living black American artist of growing stature), or Alexander von Zemlinsky (a modern Viennese composer who has been called a "pivotal" musician of this century), none of whom is currently found in the *Academic American*.

Only 13 percent of the encyclopedia's text is devoted to geographical topics, a figure much lower than that expected in a substantial encyclopedia for adults and advanced students. (Most encyclopedias allot 20–25 percent or more of their space to place-names.) Generally speaking, however, the *Academic American* provides sufficient coverage of the countries, continents, and principal cities of the world, the states and provinces of North America, and important rivers, mountains, and other natural features. Nevertheless, this coverage is usually much less extensive than that found in competing encyclopedias of similar size and usership. For example, the *Academic American* devotes about five and a half pages to Florida, whereas *Funk & Wagnalls New Encyclopedia* and *The New Standard Encyclopedia* accord the state 14–15 pages. Only in the case of the somewhat smaller *New Illustrated Columbia Encyclopedia* and British *New Caxton Encyclopedia* does the *Academic American* compare favorably in terms of amount of geographical coverage. Where the set's limited coverage of place-names really shows is at the local level. Again using Florida as an example, the *Academic American* has no entries for such prominent localities as Boca Raton, Bradenton, Broward County, Clearwater, Dade County, Lake City, Lakeland, Palm Beach, and St. Petersburg (a city of over 200,000). Most major municipalities are included, but coverage is quite cursory; for instance, Miami receives a half a page, Jacksonville (the state's largest city) a fourth of a page, Tallahassee (the capital) 16 lines, Pensacola 14 lines, Orlando 12 lines. Lack of coverage, or minimal coverage, of many of the world's secondary places, particularly in North America, is one of the *Academic American*'s most conspicuous weaknesses.

The encyclopedia's subject coverage is reasonably well distributed among the major knowledge areas. The editors claim that the "list of entries (and their lengths) reflects the curriculum of American schools and universities" (preface), but there is no evidence that a detailed study of U.S. and/or Canadian curricula was undertaken, other than a perusal of representative textbooks. According to the editors, 36 percent of the set's space is devoted to the humanities and arts, 14 percent to the social and behavioral sciences, and 35 percent to science and technology (with the rest allocated to geography, sports, and general subjects). In all areas, the encyclopedia stresses contemporary practitioners, theories, events, and trends, while not neglecting historical developments. Literature, for example, is more than satisfactorily covered in longish survey articles (e.g., "Novel"; "Poetry"; "Short Story"; "Drama"; "Black American Literature"; "Canadian Literature"; "Danish Literature"; "Russian Literature") and much shorter articles on specific literary works (*"David Copperfield"; "Elmer Gantry"; "To Kill a Mockingbird"; "Tin Drum, The"; "Threepenny Opera, The"; "Tender Is the Night"*), individual characters from fiction ("Antigone"; "Tom Jones"; "Tom Sawyer"), and important writers (Margaret Atwood, Aleksandr Blok, Joan Didion, Lillian Hellman, H. L. Mencken, Romain Rolland, Cyril Tourneur, Kurt Vonnegut, Jr., William Butler Yeats).

In the area of sociology and anthropology, excellent survey coverage is accorded major ethnic groups (e.g., "Black Americans"; "Eskimo"; "Hispanic Americans"; "Indians, American"). Similarly, aspects of business and economics are well covered in such articles as "Data Processing"; "Deflation"; "Department Store"; "Depression of the 1930s"; "Direct Mail"; "Discount House"; "Discount Rate"; "Dollar"; and "Dollar Averaging." In history and political science, landmark decisions of the U.S. Supreme Court (e.g., *"Dennis* v. *United States"; "Mapp* v. *Ohio"; "University of California* v. *Bakke"*) and each amendment to the U.S. Constitution receive individual coverage. Major U.S. colleges and universities, like Antioch, Dartmouth, and Duke, are described in brief entries, but coverage is far from complete. For instance, the five-line description of Dickinson College in Pennsylvania makes no mention of the college's law school. State institutions of higher learning are sketchily covered in omnibus articles for each state. EXAMPLE: "South Dakota, State Universities and Colleges of." Likewise, key educational institutions abroad are identified in regional articles. EXAMPLES: "European Universities"; "Southeast Asian Universities."

Within the limits of the encyclopedia's size and objectives, scientific and technical subjects receive outstanding coverage. The various forms of plant and animal life, for example, are comprehensively treated in both extended survey articles (e.g., "Flower"; "Tree"; "Arthropod"; "Reptile"; "Bird"; "Mammal") and shorter entries on more specific flora and fauna (e.g., "Rose"; "Poplar"; "Dolphin"; "Shark"). Articles like "Animal Migration," "Biological Locomotion," "Carnivorous Plants," "Extragalactic Systems," "Hydrologic Cycle," "Ore Deposits," "Plant Distribution," and "Rockets and Missiles" are models of the encyclopedic form. All geological eras and periods have individual entries (e.g., "Cenozoic Era"; "Quaternary Period"), which augment "Geologic Time," an overview article. The encyclopedia also provides commendable coverage of medical topics, including articles on all important systems and parts of the human body, diseases and maladies, and various aspects of health care in general, such as *"Environmental Health," "Health-Care Systems," "Health Insurance,"* and *"Medical Instrumentation."*

The *Academic American*'s coverage is international in scope. EXAMPLES:

The article "Nuclear Energy" discusses developments in Great Britain, France, the Soviet Union, West Germany, and Japan, as well as the United States. In addition, the article includes a helpful chart showing worldwide distribution of nuclear reactors. The article "Film, History of" offers a concise survey of the motion picture art form around the world, concentrating on filmmaking in the United States, Europe, and, more recently, Asia. The article "Subway" covers underground transportation from Buenos Aires to Tokyo to Washington, D.C. The encyclopedia also furnishes metric measurements throughout, with English (or customary) equivalents given in parentheses. But if the *Academic American*'s scope is international, its emphasis is on Western society and particularly the United States. As the set's preface readily acknowledges, "A sympathetic awareness of non-Western cultures and alternative life-styles . . . need not interfere with an appreciation that a fuller explication of roots and traditions of our audience's dominant culture is appropriate."

Finally, compared with most encyclopedias of similar size and intended audience (e.g., *Funk & Wagnalls New Encyclopedia* and *The New Standard Encyclopedia*) as well as the better sets for young adult and family use (*Compton's Encyclopedia, Merit Students Encyclopedia,* and *The World Book Encyclopedia*), the *Academic American* stresses theoretical knowledge over practical, or how-to, information. For instance, the encyclopedia contains little or nothing on how to write a business letter (or letter-writing style), how to prepare a research paper, how to use a dictionary, how to copyright a book, how to proofread a manuscript, how to determine proper lighting levels, how to address government and religious officials, how to care for pets, how to remove difficult spots and stains, how to can food at home, or how to draw or prepare painting materials—all topics that are covered to some degree in the competing encyclopedias mentioned above. In this respect, the word *academic* in the *Academic American*'s title is used in its narrowest or most restrictive sense.

History and Authority

The *Academic American* first appeared in 1980 as a brand-new work. The publisher, Aretê Publishing Company, Inc., of Princeton, N.J., is a subsidiary of VNU America, Inc., a New York firm that is wholly owned by Verenigde Nederlandse Uitgeversbedrijven (VNU), a large Dutch publisher of books and newspapers with annual sales of 1.1 billion guilders (or nearly $600 million). In the early 1970s, VNU tentatively decided to enter the U.S. market, at first considering an English-language translation of its then new multivolume general encyclopedia entitled *Grote Spectrum Encyclopedie* (*Great Spectrum Encyclopedia*), which had been well received in the Netherlands. The translation idea, however, was eventually abandoned in favor of creating an entirely new encyclopedia for an English-speaking audience targeted principally at adult and student users in North America. Hence, in 1977 Aretê (a Greek word signifying excellence) was formed to produce and market the new work, to be called the *Academic American*

Encyclopedia, by 1980. VNU initially budgeted $6 million for the project but current estimates place the total cost of the first edition at more than $20 million (or 40 million guilders). Aretê, which is not scheduled to turn a profit until 1981, aspires to capture at least 10 percent of the U.S. and Canadian encyclopedia market by 1982.

By any reasonable standard, the *Academic American* is an authoritative encyclopedia. Aretê's president—and the moving force behind the set—is Dr. Frank L. Greenagel, a behavioral psychologist and former university professor. Immediately prior to heading Aretê, Dr. Greenagel served as a marketing executive in Litton Industries' publishing division. The set's editor in chief, Sal J. Foderaro, is an experienced hand who learned the encyclopedia business at Grolier working on *The Encyclopedia Americana* and the *Americana Annual* for many years. The managing editor, Dr. Andrew C. Kimmens, likewise brings a strong editorial background to the encyclopedia, having worked previously on a variety of reference book and textbook projects at such publishers as Prentice Hall and Random House. In all, a well-qualified professional staff of nearly 200, from senior editors to proofreaders and caption writers, labored for three-and-a-half pressure-filled years at Aretê's Princeton offices to have the encyclopedia ready by the 1980 deadline. According to unpublished material issued by Aretê for reviewers, a permanent staff of between 50 and 60 has been retained to work on future editions and the set's yearbooks, which will first appear in 1982. It should also be mentioned here that, although the *Academic American*'s editorial offices are located in Princeton, the encyclopedia has no connection, official or unofficial, with Princeton University.

An estimated 90 percent of the encyclopedia's 28,500 articles are the work of 2,250 outside contributors, mostly U.S. college and university professors. Occasionally the contributors are top people in their specialization (e.g., Carlos Baker on Ernest Hemingway), but in the main they are academicians who bring solid credentials to their work, even though they may not have national reputations in their fields. EXAMPLES: The article "China" is signed by Chuen-yan David Lai, associate professor of geography at the University of Victoria in British Columbia; "Dinosaur" by John H. Ostrom, professor of geology at Yale University; "Homosexuality" by Stephen P. McCary, director of psychological services at the Almeda Clinic in Houston; "Shark" by Perry and Claire Gilbert, directors of the Mote Marine Laboratory in Sarasota, Fla.; "Subway" by George M. Smerk, professor of transportation at Indiana University. Also noteworthy is the heavy representation of junior faculty among the contributors; publicity material furnished by the publisher explains, "In many cases younger scholars very much in the forefront of current research were selected in preference to more widely recognized names who made their major contributions a generation ago." The large majority of articles are signed, including all those of substantial length. In those instances when Aretê editors and the contributor could not agree on a final version, the article was referred to an outside authenticator, or reviewer, and the final draft carries the name of that person; for instance, "Maps and Mapmaking" is "Reviewed by Walter W. Ristow."

A 29-member Advisory Board of Editors assisted in the development of the encyclopedia. The board—which includes a number of distinguished names, such as Ashley Montagu (the anthropologist), John A. Garraty (editor of the prestigious *Dictionary of American Biography*), and Walter Terry (the dance critic)—"was involved at virtually every stage, from the preparation of the list of entries and the recruitment of other scholars to write for the encyclopedia, to the review of some of the basic or controversial articles" (preface). The front matter in Volume 1 also prominently lists an 11-member Advisory Council composed mainly of librarians. Nowhere is the function of this group explained. The inclusion of the list of librarians seems to suggest that librarians played an active part in the making of the set. Investigation by the *Buying Guide* has disclosed that the council had absolutely no role in the planning or preparation of the *Academic American*.

Additional background information on the history of the *Academic American* project can be found in the following articles, all of which will be readily available in almost any public or academic library: "The Making of the Academic American Encyclopedia: An Interview with the Publisher" by Ken Kister in *Wilson Library Bulletin* (March 1980, pp. 436–441); "Encyclopedia with New Twist" by N. R. Kleinfield in the *New York Times* (May 30, 1980, pp. 1–D+); and "New 21-Volume Encyclopedia Seeks Market Via Retail Outlets Only" by Daisy Maryles in *Publishers Weekly* (August 1, 1980, pp. 36+).

Reliability

The *Academic American* is, for the most part, a reliable encyclopedia. According to the encyclopedia's preface, "A large team of research editors—all specialists in their field—verified every fact, inference, and conclusion against primary and other authoritative sources in several of the world's largest libraries (Princeton, Columbia, New York, and Rutgers universities, as well as the New York Public Library). After this quality-control effort, edited copy had to clear several layers of senior editorial review before it was returned to the author for approval. Every article in the *Academic American Encyclopedia* has been subjected to multiple review to assure objectivity, balance, and accuracy." The *Buying Guide*'s independent analysis confirms that much care has been taken to achieve an encyclopedia distinguished by a high degree of accuracy. Careful study of articles on such test subjects as Afghanistan, Canada, child development, cults, diabetes, dinosaurs, estrogen, evolution, Greenland, homosexuality, mass transportation, motion pictures, North American Indians, nuclear power, Georgia O'Keeffe, Paris, rock music, sharks, shock therapy, William Styron, suicide, tuberculosis, X-rays, and Zimbabwe revealed no major errors of fact.

The encyclopedia, however, does contain an uncomfortable number of small inaccuracies, some of which might be attributable to first-edition jitters or the pressures of a very tight deadline (as noted earlier in this review under "History and Authority," the *Academic American* is entirely new and was produced in only three-and-a-half years, a very short time for a project of such magnitude). EXAMPLE: The article "Greenland" incorrectly identifies Danish as the country's official language; with the advent of home rule in 1979, Greenlandic, an Eskimo tongue, became Greenland's official language. EXAMPLE: The article "Britten, Benjamin" gives the date of his *War Requiem* as 1961, whereas "English Music" gives it as 1962. EXAMPLE: "Shark" informs, "Of the 100 or so unprovoked [shark] attacks that occur worldwide every year less than 35 are fatal"; in fact the statistics are more like 25 and 10 respectively. EXAMPLE: "Harding, Warren" reports that President Harding had no children when in fact he did have a child (though it was illegitimate). Likewise, the article on Thomas Jefferson fails to mention his several children by Sally Hemings, a black woman. EXAMPLE: "Indians, American" errs in asserting that beans were unknown in Europe prior to the discovery of America. EXAMPLE: "American Revolution" contains a distressing number of small but telling mistakes. A picture caption describing the Battle of Bunker Hill states that the British dislodged the colonists "after three unsuccessful charges," but specialized sources like the *Dictionary of American History* indicate the third charge was successful. In another picture caption, John Paul Jones's ship *Bonhomme Richard* is said to have "battered the larger *Serapis* into submission during a battle in the North Sea on June 23, 1779," but this battle actually took place on September 23 of that year, a fact accurately reported in the article "Jones, John Paul." The American capture of Montreal in 1775 is correctly noted on a map showing major events of the war as having occurred on November 13, but the article itself gives the date as November 10. In similar fashion, the date of the surrender of General Burgoyne at Saratoga is correctly given in the article as October 17, 1777, but incorrectly as October 7 in a picture caption on the following page. A serious lapse occurs in the caption for the reproduction of John Trumbull's painting *Surrender of General Burgoyne,* which mistakenly identifies Colonel Morgan of the Virginia Riflemen (in the white uniform) as General Gates, the American commander at Saratoga. It is to be hoped that such slips will be corrected in future editions.

Recency

As might be expected, the *Academic American,* an entirely new encyclopedia prepared during the late 1970s, is admirably up-to-date. Not only is the text as current as can be expected in a printed encyclopedia, but the choice of topics, language, and general tone reflect contemporary attitudes and concerns. The encyclopedia, for instance, carries an excellent two-page survey article on animals threatened with extinction ("Endangered Species"). There are articles of similar length and quality on the problems of the environment ("Environmental Health"; "Diseases, Occupational"; "Pollutants, Chemical"; "Pollution, Environmental"; "Pollution Control"). The subject of death is treated in an individual article ("Death and Dying"), part of which is devoted to understanding death psychologically. "Day-care Centers" is another individual entry, as is "Religious Cults," which includes coverage of such groups as the People's Temple, Hare Krishna, and the Unification Church of Sun Myung Moon. The problems of nuclear power, and specifically the 1979 accident at Harrisburg's Three Mile Island plant, are discussed at some length in the article "Nuclear Energy." "China" covers the so-called Gang of Four, among other recent topics, and includes (in parentheses) the new Pinyin spelling of Chinese names—under the new phonetic system Peking is Beijing and Teng Hsiao-p'ing becomes Deng Xiaoping. The map accompanying "Detroit" locates Renaissance Center, the city's glittering new convention complex. The article "Paris" likewise includes information about the Pompidou Center, the exciting but controversial art museum opened in 1978 and now *de rigueur* for tourists (and there is also a separate article on the Pompidou Center under "Beaubourg," its popular name).

To maintain the set's currency, the publisher promises a high rate of continuous revision. Specifically, Aretê plans to review from 10 percent (the minimum) to 20 percent (the maximum) of the encyclopedia's text each year, making changes, additions, and so forth as required. Toward this end, a permanent staff of between 50 and 60 has been retained. This core staff, which will work out of the company's editorial offices in Princeton, will be supplemented by outside free-lancers and consultants on a project basis. The task of keeping the *Academic American* as current as possible will also be assisted by the latest computer technology. The encyclopedia's text is completely machine-readable, which means that editorial revisions can be made directly at computer terminals, thus speeding the process considerably. Frank Greenagel, Aretê's president, discussed this operation in some detail in a recent interview with the author of the *Buying Guide* published in *Wilson Library Bulletin* (March 1980, p. 440): "As soon as an article has been cleared by the editorial staff, it goes to our video display terminals where it is entered, then stored and set into type. No word or article can appear in type unless it has gone through the computer. Hence the computer performs as an editorial control system. Nothing can be changed, even minor spelling or punctuation, unless proper procedures are followed. These are the computer's editorial and typesetting functions. It also gives us a full-page make-up system. In addition, we use it as a production control and planning device. In other words, the computer provides an enormous capability in a number of key operations, and in fact it will become even more useful as we begin revision."

A related development concerns Aretê's commitment to make the contents of the *Academic American* available to the general public in computerized form via information vendors like OCLC and the New York Times Information Bank. Merchandising the set in this manner will undoubtedly necessitate much greater revision activity than has hitherto been expected of a general encyclopedia, simply because users will not subscribe to an encyclopedia database that is not up-to-date. (For further information about the computerized version of the *Academic American*,

This Recency Table compares selected topics in the *Academic American* with those in other encyclopedias of similar size and intended usership.

Topic	Academic American	Funk & Wagnalls	New Caxton	New Standard
Afghanistan	Very current	Fairly current	Fairly current	Fairly current
Dinosaurs	Very current	Very current	Fairly current	Very current
Greenland	Very current	Not current	Not current	Very current
Thomas Jefferson	Fairly current	Fairly current	Not current	Fairly current
Mass Transportation/Subways	Very current	Fairly current	Very current	Fairly current
Nuclear Power	Very current	Not current	Fairly current	Not current
Paris	Very current	Not current	Very current	Not current
Sharks	Fairly current	Not current	Fairly current	Very current
Shock Therapy	Very current	Not current	Fairly current	Not current
Suicide	Fairly current	Not current	Not current*	Very current
Tuberculosis	Fairly current	Fairly current	Fairly current	Fairly current
Zimbabwe	Very current	Very current	Very current	Very current

*Topic not covered in encyclopedia.

see the "Arrangement and Accessibility" portion of this review and "Introducing Encyclopedias" in Part I of the *Buying Guide*.)

Like most other multivolume general encyclopedias, the *Academic American* will also offer annual supplements designed to update the basic set. According to Areté, the yearbooks will survey the major events of the past year and include a number of new or revised articles from the current edition of the encyclopedia. The publisher's announced intention is that the yearbooks "will be fully integrated with the structure of the encyclopedia to permit ease of use" (preface). The initial volume of the yearbook series is scheduled to appear in 1982 (covering the events of 1981).

Objectivity

The *Academic American*'s preface makes it clear that the editors strongly reject the idea of bias or partisan scholarship in their encyclopedia: "Scholars may differ among themselves even on questions that do not involve social policy. The aim of the *Academic American Encyclopedia* is to reflect those differences and to consider alternative theories or interpretation as well as opposing points of view." Even signed articles "cannot represent only a personal point of view," and large controversial issues "require a balanced treatment that, instead of avoiding all judgments, seeks to incorporate multiple perspectives and to tell who supports what position and why." The preface also notes that "a concerted effort has been made to produce an encyclopedia free of sexist language and attitudes."

These are not empty words. The makers of the *Academic American* have tried hard to keep bias, obvious and subtle, out of the set, and in most respects they have succeeded. The article on homosexuality, for instance, is careful to point out that "the causes of homosexuality remain obscure despite continued debate," which is followed by a list of commonly known theories. The article also observes, "Whatever the cause, it is increasingly becoming recognized that homosexuals can live as usefully, productively, and satisfactorily as heterosexuals." The article "Nuclear Energy" objectively describes how nuclear power works, the current role of that form of energy in the world today, what safety problems exist, and how and why the recent Three Mile Island accident happened. The article concludes with a brief statement summarizing the position of both proponents and opponents of further nuclear development. "Shock Therapy" recognizes the medical limitations of the treatment, noting that "its effect on schizophrenia is uncertain," and that its use in cases involving autistic children "has fallen into disrepute." "Divorce" informs that "the belief that high divorce rates produce social disorganization has not been proved," but goes on to point out that "divorce can be a devastating experience." Most other polemical topics—abortion, the Equal Rights Amendment, religious cults, the Vietnam War, Fidel Castro (his "social programs improved the daily lot of the poorest Cubans while at the same time antagonizing the middle-class business and professional people"), Ayatollah Khomeini, school busing, and the like—are treated as impartially as humanly possible.

In a few instances, however, the encyclopedia fails to cover all legitimate points of view. EXAMPLE: "Evolution," a substantial seven-page article, totally ignores the traditional Christian fundamentalist objections to the Darwinian theory of evolution (the famous Scopes—or monkey—trial is briefly covered in a separate article, but "Evolution" furnishes no cross-references to "Scopes Trial"); moreover, the current Christian movement to counter Darwinism, called Scientific Creationism, is not even mentioned in the encyclopedia. EXAMPLE: "Suicide" contains nothing on the question of the individual's right to suicide, an issue that has recently sparked much controversy in Western society, particularly the United States and Great Britain. In other cases, the encyclopedia does not include unwelcome facts about the lives of great historical personages. EXAMPLE: There is no reference to Thomas Jefferson's slave family and black mistress, Sally Hemings, in the article on Jefferson and elsewhere (even though the 1974 Fawn Brodie book *Thomas Jefferson: An Intimate History,* which introduced contemporary readers to Jefferson's controversial private life, is included in the Jefferson article's bibliography). Some encyclopedists might argue that such information lies outside the scope of a general reference work, but is it not pertinent to a better understanding of the man, his public policies, and his times? After all, it was none other than John Quincy Adams who wondered if Sally Hemings was the reason Thomas Jefferson, once a staunch abolitionist, suddenly lost his distaste for slavery after 1790. Students have a right to all the facts, pleasant or not.

Clarity and Reader Suitability

As noted at the outset of this review, the *Academic American* claims to be for junior high school, high school, and college students, as well as "inquisitive" adults. Junior high (or middle) school students, however, will usually find the encyclopedia's level and style of writing beyond their normal reading comprehension. Slower or less verbally inclined high school students and adults might also experience difficulty with the text. EXAMPLE: "Film, History of" is aimed squarely at the serious student and adult reader, as indicated by such statements as "[Film] is one of the few arts that is both spatial and temporal, intentionally manipulating both space and time. This synthesis has given rise to conflicting theories about film and its historical development." EXAMPLE: "Diabetes" makes no concession to those who might not understand such words as *multifactorial* and *etiologic:* "Most likely the causes are multifactorial, with genetic predisposition and environmental factors equally important. Viral infections, such as measles and encephalitis, are suspected etiologic factors." EXAMPLE: "Indians, American" will discourage younger and slower readers with terms like *xerophytic* and *anadromous.* EXAMPLE: "Hypnosis" is fine for the college student or interested adult but hardly the junior high student: "Hypnosis is therefore a state of mind the achievement of which depends more on the capacity of the individual to respond than on the induction process. It can lead to profound alterations in the individual's experience and may for a time profoundly affect memory as well as sensory modalities."

The encyclopedia's preface states that "technical terms generally are defined in the sentence in which they are used," which is not always true (unless one's definition of a technical term excludes words like *etiologic, anadromous,* and *modalities*). Although the style of the writing is almost always clear and serviceable, and jargon and unwarranted technical terminology have been kept to a minimum, there has been no systematic effort at vocabulary control, nor have the articles been tested for readability at various grade levels (as is done in encyclopedias for young adults). As a rule, the *Academic American* is best suited for serious high school and college students, along with well-educated adults. Others will be intimidated by the prose, which tends to be bookish, though they might find the visual material useful in certain instances.

Arrangement and Accessibility

The *Academic American* is arranged alphabetically, word-by-word ("Indian Ocean" precedes "Indiana"). The 32,000 specific entries include

3,500 external cross-references (e.g., "*Rhodesia.* See ZIMBABWE"; "*Cults.* See RELIGIOUS CULTS"). The set also includes 63,500 internal cross-references found within the text of the articles. These references are designated by words and phrases printed in SMALL CAPITAL LETTERS. EXAMPLE: The article "Harding, Warren G." informs, "Harding's administration is best known for the scandals associated with it. The most famous of these was the TEAPOT DOME affair," which signals the reader to turn to the article "Teapot Dome" for additional information. There are also occasional *See also* references at the end of an article, e.g., "Dinosaur" provides *See also* references to "Evolution"; "Fossil Record"; and "Prehistoric Animals."

The cross-references, both internal and external, normally lead the reader to related or additional material quickly and efficiently. In some cases, however, the cross-reference system breaks down. EXAMPLE: There is an external reference, "*Atomic Energy Commission:* see ENERGY, U.S. DEPARTMENT OF," but the article "Energy, U.S. Department of" does not mention the Atomic Energy Commission (AEC) by name, noting only that the new Department of Energy has "consolidated the activities of the Energy Research and Development Administration, the Federal Power Commission, the Federal Energy Administration, and some elements of other agencies." On the other hand, AEC *is* mentioned in the article "Nuclear Regulatory Commission" ("it was established in 1975 and replaced the Atomic Energy Commission"), but there is *no* cross-reference from AEC to the Nuclear Regulatory Commission (NRC). In another instance, NRC is mentioned in the article "Nuclear Energy," but there is no cross-reference to "Nuclear Regulatory Commission." EXAMPLE: The article "Sex Hormones" discusses steroids but fails to refer the reader to the article "Steroid." Likewise, "Steroid" discusses sex hormones but fails to provide a cross-reference to "Sex Hormones." EXAMPLE: The article "France" contains a subsection on education that covers the French school system in general terms, but no cross-reference is furnished to the article "European Universities," where individual institutions of higher learning in France are described.

The final volume of the encyclopedia comprises a large analytical index of approximately 250,000 entries. Prepared by a staff of 20 indexers under the direction of Barbara Preschel, who brings excellent professional credentials to the work, the index provides ready access to articles, facts, illustrations, maps, place-names, tables, and bibliographies found in the 20-volume A–Z portion of the set. As in all effective encyclopedia indexes, the broad entries are analyzed—that is, broken down into more specific subentries, so that even the smallest bits of information become easily retrievable. For instance, the index entry "Diabetes Mellitus" has 22 subentries, such as "acetone breath," "Best, Charles," "eye diseases," "gingivitis," "insulin," "metabolism," and "pregnancy and birth." This approach is in keeping with the comments made by Aretê's president, Frank Greenagel, in an interview with the *Buying Guide* (see *Wilson Library Bulletin,* March 1980, p. 441): "There's a lot of specific information in an encyclopedia, and you don't always know how users will approach it. So if you can design a way to access almost every conceivable bit, it becomes much more useful." The *Academic American*'s index also has several features not ordinarily found in encyclopedia indexes. Some index entries include lists of specific items as subentries. EXAMPLES: The entry "Hound" lists breeds recognized by the American Kennel Club, such as "Hound—borzoi." The entry "Medicine" lists winners of the Nobel Prize in medicine under the subentry "Nobel Prize," such as "Medicine—Nobel Prize—Arber, Werner." The entry "Folk Music" lists leading American folk musicians under the subentry "United States," such as "Folk Music—United States—Baez, Joan." Another helpful feature of the index is that entries for particular topics can serve as study guides or structured outlines. EXAMPLE: The index entry "Geology" indicates all the various fields and subdisciplines of geology under the subentry "Branches," such as "Geology—Branches—astrogeology." Yet another unusual feature is that place-names included on maps throughout the set are entered in the index (rather than in a separate gazetteer, which is the standard practice).

The *Academic American* is unquestionably a well-indexed encyclopedia. Not only does the index render the encyclopedia's contents readily accessible, but in comparison with competing works of similar size and usership, the set's index is second to none. Consider, for instance, the ratio of index entries to total words for encyclopedias in the intermediate adult group: the 9-million-word *Academic American* has some 250,000 index entries; the 9-million-word *Funk & Wagnalls New Encyclopedia* 193,000 index entries; the 7.5-million-word *Harver World Encyclopedia* no index at all; the 6.6-million-word *New Illustrated Columbia Encyclopedia* no index at all; the 6.3-million-word *New Standard Encyclopedia* no index at all; and the 6-million-word *New Caxton Encyclopedia* only 50,000 index entries. It should be realized, however, that the *Academic American*'s practice of including in its index every place-name on all the maps throughout the set tends to inflate the encyclopedia's index entry figure.

Thus far in this discussion of the *Academic American*'s arrangement and accessibility, only the printed set in 21 bound volumes has been considered. But in the near future the encyclopedia may well become generally available in electronic form via computer hookup in homes and libraries. When and if this happens, traditional questions about the set's arrangement will be irrelevant and those concerning accessibility quite different. The electronic version of the *Academic American* will not be arranged in alphabetical fashion, nor will access be achieved by consulting specific entries, cross-references, or an analytical index. No longer will readers manually handle individual volumes, simply because there will be no volumes to handle. Rather, the contents of the set will be stored on machine-readable tape and retrieved by giving the computer commands it is programmed to understand. The amount and type of information delivered will depend both on what information has been input into the encyclopedia database and on how the computer has been instructed to retrieve it. For instance, at the command for information about nuclear energy, a computer search could deliver all references on the subject in the database, no matter how tenuous or obscure (which would be expensive to program), or it could make only the main article on nuclear energy available, in which case much useful material might be overlooked (but the programming costs would be kept within reasonable limits).

Actually, the idea of the *Academic American* becoming widely available to the general public in a computerized format is not so farfetched. As already noted (see "Recency"), the encyclopedia's text has been completely machine-readable from the beginning. Because of this feature and the set's exceptional currency, the *Academic American* was selected to be tested as part of an experimental computerized home information service called "Channel 2000" offered by OCLC, Inc., in 1980 to 200 households and a university in Columbus, Ohio. The experiment utilized telephone lines to transmit information contained in a variety of databases, including a banking service and the encyclopedia. An ordinary television set equipped with a clip-on adapter displayed the information requested by users who instructed the computer by means of an attached numeric keyboard. The results of this experiment in instantaneous access to encyclopedic information have yet to be evaluated, but hopes were high at the outset. Said an OCLC representative, "In ten years, it is not inconceivable to imagine this service becoming available throughout the country. Aretê's computerized encyclopedia and all the information and knowledge it includes can be at your fingertips." Steps toward making this vision a reality were taken in early 1981 when the publisher of the *Academic American* reached a tentative agreement to make the contents of the encyclopedia available to subscribers of the New York Times Information Bank. (See "Introducing Encyclopedias" in Part I of the *Buying Guide* for additional comments on the future possibilities of computerized encyclopedias.)

Bibliographies

One of the glories of the *Academic American* is its fine bibliographies. As explained in the encyclopedia's preface, "Almost 13,000 entries (about 40 percent of the total) have accompanying bibliographies. The goal is to furnish a well-chosen list of standard and recently published works to which readers may turn for further information and additional development of particular points of view." The bibliographies, which are limited to works in English, include major textbooks, titles available in paperback, and occasionally periodical articles and recordings. In an interview with the *Buying Guide* (see *Wilson Library Bulletin*, March 1980, p. 439), Frank Greenagel, Aretê's president, further notes, "Our audience is largely students who are doing papers: The encyclopedia will provide an overview and a jumping-off place. This is where bibliographies come in. We want to direct the student to the best, most readily accessible sources after they have read the encyclopedia article. They may include the definitive work on the subject, but only if it is accessible both physically *and* intellectually. . . . We want our bibliographies to be like a good professor—an adventuresome guide."

With few exceptions, the editors have accomplished this difficult task admirably. Not only are the bibliographies plentiful, most of them appear to be intelligently selected. EXAMPLE: The article "Homosexuality" concludes with a bibliography of a dozen titles, all published in the 1970s except for Kinsey's classic studies on male and female sexuality. The latest work cited is Masters and Johnson's important *Homosexuality in Perspective* (1979). EXAMPLE: The ten-title bibliography at the end of "Jefferson, Thomas" includes both key older biographical studies and Fawn Brodie's more recent and indispensable *Thomas Jefferson: An Intimate History* (1974). EXAMPLE: "Nuclear Energy" has a bibliography of some 20 titles, all of which are quite current. In addition, there are works representing both sides of the ongoing nuclear power debate. EXAMPLE: The 14-title bibliography accompanying "Indians, American" necessarily omits many valuable older studies, but those included are all important references that will be helpful to serious students.

Graphics

Another outstanding feature of the *Academic American* is its clear, colorful, informative graphics. Approximately 15,000 photographs, art reproductions, drawings, diagrams, charts, and graphs complement the encyclopedia's printed text. There are also more than 1,000 maps. All told, a full third of the set's total space is devoted to visual material, a large majority of it in color. A background report prepared by Aretê for reviewers explains, "A generation raised on television has come to expect superior color graphics to help explain, expand, and support verbal concepts, stimulate the imagination, aid in recognition, and reinforce learning." To meet these expectations, Aretê commissioned some 5,000 original pieces of four-color art for the encyclopedia, utilizing artists who specialize in a particular subject, such as birds. With the exception of some basic tables and graphs and simple maps prepared in-house by staff artists, the rest of the graphics came from a large "illustration bank" in Europe created jointly by VNU (Aretê's parent company in the Netherlands) and the British firm Mitchell Beazley.

In almost all cases, the graphics are superb. The article "Indians, American," for instance, includes over 50 illustrations, plus four maps (two of them full-page). All are well selected and handsomely reproduced. The article "China" contains instructive photographs showing Chinese life in both urban and rural settings. "China, History of" is enhanced by reproductions of two period political cartoons that help illuminate crucial events in modern Chinese history in an interesting manner. The article "Camera" is heavily illustrated by cutaway drawings showing the parts of different types of cameras. It should be noted that cutaway illustrations are used throughout the set to explain how things work. See as examples the articles "Digestion, Human"; "Dome"; "Elevator"; "Elizabethan Playhouse"; "Intestine"; "Nuclear Energy"; "Pantheon"; "Plant"; and "Salyut." Note also that an enormous amount of text information is conveyed in picture captions (see "Purpose and Scope" for examples and a brief discussion of captions).

The maps are of equally high quality. Reputable cartographers, including Rand McNally and Donnelly Cartographic, prepared all the substantive maps exclusively for the *Academic American*. Basic map coverage for continents and countries varies from two-page spreads to maps of less than half a page, depending on the size and importance of the place, while North American states and provinces always have full-page maps. The principal (and often only) map for all these places combines coverage of both political and physical features. In some cases, however, thematic maps extend the coverage. EXAMPLE: In addition to a basic physical/political map, "Africa" contains small maps showing the continent's geology, climate, vegetation, precipitation, ethnic and tribal groups, population density, and natural resources. EXAMPLE: "Canada, History of" includes five maps depicting the country's historical development. There are also 46 specially created maps in the set that offer detailed coverage of major cities of the world, such as Chicago, Detroit, London, Mexico City, Moscow, New York, Paris, Rome, and Tokyo. Maps in the *Academic American* are drawn to scale but, like most encyclopedia maps, no attempt has been made to achieve consistency of scale; for instance, the map for China is scaled at 1:19,922,000 whereas Japan's is 1:10,615,000. One oddity concerning the encyclopedia's map coverage is the practice of listing map place-names in the general index (Volume 21) as opposed to a separate index, or gazetteer, on the reverse side of each map, which is the standard procedure. The latter is obviously more convenient for map users.

When comparing the quality of graphics in adult encyclopedias of intermediate size, the *Academic American* stands out as clearly superior to any of its competitors. *Funk & Wagnalls New Encyclopedia* is a drab affair compared with the *Academic American*. The same is true of the *New Standard Encyclopedia, The New Illustrated Columbia Encyclopedia*, and *The New American Encyclopedia*. Only *The New Caxton Encyclopedia*, a heavily illustrated British import, and perhaps the *Harver World Encyclopedia,* another Dutch venture into encyclopedia-making for North Americans, can begin to compare with the *Academic American* in terms of visual appeal. And when all is said and done, the *Academic American* is in a league by itself where graphics are concerned.

Physical Format

The encyclopedia comes in two bindings, both of which are good-looking and appear to be sturdy and reasonably durable. The consumer (or home) binding is maroon with gold lettering and black panels trimmed in gold. The library binding is blue with silver lettering and black panels trimmed in silver. The volumes lie flat when open for easy consultation. Inside, the attractive two-column page layout is often varied by graphics of different size and shape. Another feature that gives the page an inviting appearance is use of the so-called ragged right, where the right-hand margin of each column is not justified (that is, the end of each line of type is not in exact alignment with the others.) This simple but effective typographic technique not only improves the reading ease of the columns by reducing hyphenation and eliminating uneven spacing between words, but also gives the encyclopedia a contemporary look. The typeface itself, called Optima, is also fresh and legible. Guide words appear prominently at the top of every page, and article headings (in bold type with a dark rule, or line, underneath) and subheadings are easily distinguishable. The margins, while not excessively wide, are sufficient. The paper, 60-pound nonglare-surfaced stock, was chosen for its printing surface, which permits high quality reproduction of visual material. In sum, the *Academic American* is a well-made, physically appealing encyclopedia with a distinctly modern air.

Special Features

The *Academic American* boasts several special features. Perhaps the most striking difference between this set and other multivolume encyclopedias concerns the way they are merchandised. Unlike any other large set currently on the market, the *Academic American* is sold at retail exclusively in department stores and bookstores. The publisher has strictly ruled out in-home selling, the method used by all other major encyclopedia companies. (For more on Aretê's unique marketing approach, see the next section, "Sales Information.") Another potentially important special feature is the encyclopedia's technical capability to deliver its contents in electronic as well as print form. As already discussed, in 1980 the set was tested as part of an experimental computerized home information service, and some time in 1981 it will most likely become part of the highly respected New York Times Information Bank service. When and if computerized encyclopedias become generally available to the public, it is a good bet the *Academic American* will play a leading role. Already the set has the distinction of being a pioneer in this exciting new area of information service. (For more on this feature, see "Arrangement and Accessibility," as well as "Introducing Encyclopedias" in Part I of the *Buying Guide.*)

The encyclopedia has several other special features which, though not as dramatic as its unique sales strategy or computer capability, are nonetheless important. First, there are the set's many four-color illustrations specially commissioned for the work. As previously noted (see "Graphics"), these heavily captioned illustrations give the *Academic American* a visual flair not usually associated with general encyclopedias. Second, the set offers more articles with bibliographies (40 percent) than other general encyclopedias. Third, the encyclopedia includes pronunciation guides for about half its article headings. EXAMPLE: *Gary, Romain* [gah-ree´, roh-man´]. Fourth, the new Pinyin (or phonetic) system of transliteration is used in article headings involving Chinese proper names. The commonly known transcription, called Wade-Giles, is given first, followed by the Pinyin version. EXAMPLE: *Peking* (Beijing). And fifth, the use of creative typographic techniques like the ragged right column (see "Physical Format") gives the encyclopedia a clean, contemporary look.

Sales Information

The *Academic American* is sold to individual consumers exclusively through quality department stores and bookstores. Unlike other multivolume encyclopedias, it is *not* sold door-to-door or by appointment in the home. The purpose of this distinctive marketing approach is twofold: (1) it permits interested consumers to examine the encyclopedia in their own good time without feeling pressured to make a quick purchase decision, and (2) it avoids the "encyclopedia salesperson" stigma. At present (early 1981), selected stores in 11 major U.S. cities carry the *Academic American*, including Marshall Field's in Chicago, Sanger-Harris in Dallas, Hudson's in Detroit, Macy's Missouri in Kansas City, Horne's and Kaufmann's in Pittsburgh, and Stix, Baer & Fuller in St. Louis. Chain bookstores like B. Dalton's and Brentano's also stock the encyclopedia in some of their outlets, as do some independent bookstores around the country. In Florida, for instance, the encyclopedia is carried by Haslam's Book Store (St. Petersburg), Downtown Book Center (Miami), Paperback Place (Ft. Lauderdale), and Compact Books (Hollywood). The publisher intends to expand its retail outlets eventually to include many more market areas. Consumers interested in knowing where the *Academic American* is sold in their area can get that information by calling toll-free 800-257-5133. Also, consumers who want to acquire the encyclopedia but cannot get to a store where it is sold can order directly from the publisher using the same toll-free number.

The consumer binding (maroon and gold) sells for $400 plus tax, but a price increase is anticipated for some time in 1981. No other books or educational materials are sold in combination with the *Academic American*, nor does the price of the set include a research service or the like. Publication of a yearbook, however, will begin in 1982 (covering the events of 1981). At this time the yearbook is tentatively priced at $14.95. Educational institutions can purchase the library binding (blue and silver), which is reinforced for heavy use. The library binding currently sells for $389 to institutional customers, $425 to individuals. Independent sales representatives have been recruited to handle institutional sales, although librarians and educators can order the encyclopedia via the toll-free number noted in the preceding paragraph.

Consumers can expect promotional activity on behalf of the *Academic American* to be fast and furious during the next several years. The publisher is eager to gain a substantial share of the encyclopedia market, both in the United States and throughout the English-speaking world. (Note that the set is sold in the United Kingdom and British Commonwealth countries under the title *Macmillan Family Encyclopedia*.) To help achieve this goal, Aretê has initiated a hard-hitting advertising campaign with a budget estimated at $10 million. Already promotion for the *Academic American* has caused some controversy in the industry, particularly Aretê's use of comparative advertising that refers to competitors by name (the *Academic American* is said to be "More comprehensive than *World Book*, more comprehensible than *Britannica*"). Indeed, a battle royal appears to be shaping up between the brash new Aretê and longtime industry leaders. Veterans of the encyclopedia business, on the other hand, openly scoff at Aretê's idea that encyclopedias can be sold in stores. Says Larry Grinnel, a representative of Encyclopaedia Britannica, Inc., "I don't believe any multi-volume encyclopedia has been sold successfully from the shelf" (*Detroit Free Press*, August 20, 1980). From the consumer point of view, Aretê's aggressive promotion, comparative advertising, and unique sales strategy are welcome events. They should encourage a more critical approach to the business of buying an encyclopedia, and that can only benefit the consumer.

Summary

The *Academic American Encyclopedia* can be quickly summed up in this manner:

Scope: Good   Accessibility: Excellent
Authority: Good   Bibliographies: Excellent
Reliability: Good   Graphics: Excellent
Recency: Excellent   Physical Format: Excellent
Objectivity: Good   Special Features: Many
Clarity: Good   Price: Reasonable

To elaborate briefly, the *Academic American* is the first entirely new multivolume general encyclopedia in English to appear on the scene since 1967. Owned and financed by VNU, a major Dutch publisher, the encyclopedia was prepared in the United States between 1977 and 1980 by experienced editors and authoritative contributors, most of them Americans, at a cost reputed to be more than $20 million. The makers of the set say it is intended for readers at the junior high school level and up, but given the scholarly tone of many articles and lack of systematic vocabulary control, the encyclopedia seems best suited for serious high school students, college students, and well-educated adults.

The encyclopedia's coverage is international in scope, with a natural emphasis on Western society in general and the United States in particular. Subject coverage is reasonably well balanced, although scientific, technical, and medical topics receive especially generous attention. Conversely, some geographical topics, like secondary cities and rivers in North America, receive short shrift. There is also very little how-to information in the set, such as how to prepare a term paper. As might be expected of a new work, the encyclopedia's contents are usually quite current, reflecting the latest scholarship and research findings. Likewise, a stylish physical design and numerous colorful graphics give the set an attractive contemporary appearance. The graphics, which account for a full third of the total text, not only provide visual flair but significantly enhance the informational content of the encyclopedia. Other impressive features include bibliographies that are plentiful, up-to-date, and intelligently selected, and easy access to the set's contents, facilitated by an admirably detailed analytical index of nearly 250,000 entries. On the negative side, although the encyclopedia is usually reliable, a disquieting number of small errors and inconsistencies found their way into the first edition under review here.

The *Academic American* boasts a variety of special features, but two stand out. First, the encyclopedia, whose text is completely machine-readable, has recently been tested as part of an experimental computerized home information service, and there is every indication that in 1981 the *Academic American* will become part of the New York Times Information Bank service. The possibility, therefore, exists that sometime in the relatively near future the set's contents will be widely available to home users in electronic (as opposed to print) form. Such a development holds out the potential for revolutionary changes in the retrieval, use, and merchandising of encyclopedic information. Second, the encyclopedia is sold at retail *only* in department stores and bookstores, not in the home (the standard method of selling multivolume encyclopedias). Both these features distinguish the *Academic American* as an innovative, forward-looking encyclopedia with the wherewithal to become a major presence in the reference and information field in the 1980s.

The *Academic American* is an intermediate adult encyclopedia. Comparatively speaking, the set lacks the size and depth to compete with the three large adult titles, namely *Collier's Encyclopedia*, *The Encyclopedia Americana,* and the *New Encyclopaedia Britannica*. Nor can it successfully compete with the major young adult sets—*Compton's Encyclopedia, Merit Students Encyclopedia*, and *The World Book Encyclopedia*—which address a somewhat younger audience and offer such editorial features as systematic vocabulary control, readability testing, detailed curriculum orientation, and study guides, all of which the *Academic American* lacks. But when compared with other encyclopedias in the intermediate adult class, the *Academic American* is a standout. *Funk & Wagnalls New Encyclopedia* and *The New Illustrated Columbia Encyclopedia*, both supermarket sets, are inferior in practically every respect except price. The handsome *New Caxton Encyclopedia*, a British import, can challenge the *Academic American* in the area of graphics, but it costs $200 more and is vastly inferior in most other respects. The *New Standard Encyclopedia* compares well in terms of recency and price, but it lacks the *Academic American*'s superior accessibility, graphics, bibliographies, and physical design. The other two sets in the intermediate adult class—the *Harver World Encyclopedia* and *The New American Encyclopedia*—are aging works of no consequence.

Other Critical Opinions

At this writing, no other critical reviews of the *Academic American* have yet appeared. Major reviews will be cited in the next edition of the *Buying Guide*. There are, however, several informative journal articles available that describe the *Academic American* project prior to publication. Interested readers should have no trouble locating these articles in practically any public or academic library.

Kister, Ken. "The Making of the Academic American Encyclopedia: An Interview with the Publisher," *Wilson Library Bulletin,* March 1980, pp. 436–441. The author of *Encyclopedia Buying Guide* talks with Frank Greenagel, the moving force behind the *Academic American,* about how the set was developed and some of the problems encountered along the way.

Kleinfield, N. R. "Encyclopedia with New Twist," *New York Times,* May 30, 1980, pp. 1–D+. Kleinfield concentrates on the economics of encyclopedia publishing in this general article about the origins of the *Academic American.*

Maryles, Daisy. "New 21-Volume Encyclopedia Seeks Market Via Retail Outlets Only," *Publishers Weekly,* August 1, 1980, pp. 36+. As the title suggests, this piece deals with the encyclopedia's unique marketing strategy.

Wright, Helen K. "News in the Field: *Academic American Encyclopedia,*" *Booklist,* July 15, 1980, pp. 1689–1690. A simple descriptive profile of the new encyclopedia that manages to get some of the basic facts tangled. For instance, the author, an editor with the ALA Reference and Subscription Books Review Committee, confuses articles and entries, which are not the same thing.

Collier's Encyclopedia

Facts in Brief

Full Title: **Collier's Encyclopedia with Bibliography and Index.** *Editors:* William D. Halsey, Editorial Director; Emanuel Friedman, Editor in Chief. *Publisher:* Macmillan Educational Corporation, 866 Third Ave., New York, NY 10022. *Edition Reviewed:* 1980 copyright.

Volumes: 24. *Pages:* 19,000. *Articles:* 25,000. *Words:* 21,000,000. *Illustrations:* 17,000, *Maps:* 1,450. *Index Entries:* 400,000. *Cross-references:* 12,200. *Contributors:* 4,500.

User Classification: Adult (Multivolume). *Reader Suitability:* Age 15 through Advanced Adult. *Physical Size:* 8½ × 11 in.; 28 cm. *LC:* 79-89006. *ISBN:* 0-02-941-98. *Lowest Retail Price:* $579.50; to schools & libraries $467.

Purpose and Scope

Collier's Encyclopedia is one of only a few major American multivolume encyclopedias for adults to be launched in the twentieth century. The set's chief competitors—*The New Encyclopaedia Britannica* and *The Encyclopedia Americana*—date back to the eighteenth and nineteenth centuries respectively. Since its first edition (1949–1951), *Collier's* has aimed "to fill the needs of the most exacting school and home users" (preface). The encyclopedia's scope, again in the words of the editor's preface, covers "the essential content of the curricula of colleges and secondary schools, as well as the upper grades. The major areas of the physical sciences, life sciences, earth sciences, and social sciences, as well as the humanities, are presented comprehensively and in depth for the nonspecialist, but included, too, is the important information desired by the professional in the field."

Collier's, the most popularly written of the three major adult encyclopedias, favors the broad-entry approach. Articles range in length from a few lines to long essays of 80 or more pages. For instance, the article "Colorado Springs" is 21 lines long whereas "Canada" covers 82 pages. The article covering Thomas Hardy, the British novelist and poet, is three pages long. In addition to biographical information, the article provides fairly substantial critiques of Hardy's major novels, including *The Mayor of Casterbridge* and *Tess of the D'Urbervilles.* In a specific-entry encyclopedia, these critiques would have been separate entries. Articles average just under a page in length.

Collier's is the third largest general English-language encyclopedia currently on the market. As stated in the preface, the set comprehensively covers all the major areas of knowledge. Obviously, however, the coverage lacks the depth of that provided by *The New Encyclopaedia Britannica,* which is twice as large. Nor does *Collier's* provide the sort of special subject emphasis found in *The Encyclopedia Americana,* which is particularly strong in science and technology as well as North American history, biography, and geography. Rather, *Collier's* basic strength is its balanced coverage. Literature and the fine arts, religion and philosophy, the modern social and behavioral sciences, and the older natural sciences are all satisfactorily covered in light of their contemporary importance. The same is true of biographical and geographical subjects. In addition, the encyclopedia provides considerable practical information on such topics as forms of address, how to fish, identifying common wood grains, and how to recognize and treat common illnesses.

Like *The Encyclopedia Americana, Collier's* loosely emphasizes those subjects taught in U.S. and Canadian high schools, junior colleges, and colleges and universities at the undergraduate level. EXAMPLE: The article on Thomas Hardy mentioned above furnishes the reader with all the essential facts needed to begin a study of the writer and his works. The critiques of the various novels are presented in an interesting, incisive, and thoughtful manner, designed to stimulate the reader to further investigation. EXAMPLE: The 35-page article "Motion Pictures" is a mini-textbook on both artistic and technical aspects of the cinematographic art that might be used profitably at either the high school or college level.

Collier's is international in scope, but the coverage of foreign developments cannot compare with that customarily offered by *The New Encyclopaedia Britannica.* EXAMPLE: *Collier's* covers the subject of suicide in a few sentences in such articles as "Manic-Depressive Illness" and "Psychology," whereas *Britannica* (in the *Macropaedia*) provides considerable information about the phenomenon in societies all around the world.

Longer survey articles sometimes include glossaries of technical terms, a feature of great value for students. EXAMPLE: "Computer," a 19-page article, includes a list of some 60 terms commonly used in work with computers, such as *bit, chip, code, data, data bank, integrated circuit, memory, program, software, terminal.* Each term is briefly defined in language comprehensible to the layperson. Likewise, some articles include lists of famous people associated with the topic (e.g., "Television," "Tennis," "Theater"), and all the articles covering U.S. states and Canadian provinces conclude with brief biographies of prominent natives or residents. EXAMPLE: "Tennessee" includes such notables as William Gannaway ("Parson") Brownlow and Philip Lindsley. Other articles provide much summary information in chart form. EXAMPLE: "Textiles" has a four-page chart listing various characteristics of synthetic fibers like Dacron and Orlon. Articles covering plants and animals include scientific classifications. And during recent years, *Collier's* has added some 30,000 metric equivalents throughout the set.

History and Authority

The publisher, Macmillan Educational Corporation, is one of the four major encyclopedia publishers in the United States. The firm also publishes the *Merit Students Encyclopedia,* a relatively recent set for young adults that has gained a good reputation over the past decade. Macmillan likewise publishes several highly authoritative specialized encyclopedias, including the matchless *International Encyclopedia of the Social Sciences* and the *Encyclopedia of Philosophy.* And currently the company is embarked upon publication of the massive *Great Soviet Encyclopedia* in English translation, one of the most significant publishing events of recent years. Note that the company's name will change in 1981 to Macmillan Educational *Company.*

Collier's initially appeared in 20 volumes between 1949 and 1951. In 1962, the set was expanded to its present 24-volume size. During its 30 years of existence, *Collier's* has come to be recognized as a major reference work for students and adults. The set is found in most public, college, and secondary school libraries. From the beginning, *Collier's* has been marked by careful and intelligent editorial planning. Librarians and other knowledgeable professionals provided considerable input at the initial stages of the set's development. For instance, Louis Shores, a prominent authority on reference books, served as library consultant and advisory editor to the set as early as 1946. Dr. Shores served as *Collier's* editor in chief from the beginning until the 1970s when he retired from active editorial work. Currently, William D. Halsey is editorial director and Emanuel Friedman editor in chief. Both men are highly respected reference book editors with years of successful experience behind them. There is also a relatively small resident editorial staff of 22 people, some of whom hold advanced degrees in their area of specialization.

Two of the three advisory boards are comprised exclusively of important librarians here and abroad. The other board, concerned with curriculum orientation, lists two advisers, including the well-known educator B. Lamar Johnson. A "Classified List of Senior Editors and Advisers" is composed of 140 established scholars, the large majority of whom are Americans. Included are such impressive names as E. O. James (British authority on comparative religion), John Gassner (well-known Yale drama professor and critic), Richard B. Morris (U.S. historian), and A. L. Rowse (widely published Oxford historian). The approximately 4,500 contributors usually bring a high degree of authority to the encyclopedia. According to a recent review in *Booklist* (February 1, 1979, p. 884), well over a quarter of the contributors can be "located in major biographical directories." Since the 1977 edition (when the *Buying Guide* last reviewed *Collier's*), almost 3,000 new contributors have been added, such as John I. Alger (professor at West Point), J. A. Allan (lecturer at the University of London), Werner Baer (professor of economics, University of Illinois), Bernard Feld (English professor at the University of Alabama), Alan Holder (English professor at Hunter College), Torborg Lundell (professor of Germanic and Slavic languages at the University of

California at Santa Barbara), Kenneth R. Pelletier (professor of psychiatry at the University of California School of Medicine at San Francisco), Richard Painter Shryock (teaching assistant at Columbia University), Laurel L. Wilkening (professor of planetary science at the University of Arizona), and Gary A. Williams (professor of physics at the University of California at Los Angeles). As this small sample suggests, a large majority of new contributors to *Collier's* has been recruited from U.S. colleges and universities. In addition, a few new contributors are simply listed as organizations, such as the American Forest Institute. All individual contributors are fully identified, although some institutional affiliations are no longer current. Also, some contributors have been dead for quite some time. Approximately 90 percent of all articles in *Collier's* are signed with the full name of the contributor.

Reliability

Like its chief competitors (*The Encyclopedia Americana* and *The New Encyclopaedia Britannica*), *Collier's* is a generally reliable source of information. Errors of fact rarely occur and when they do they are usually insignificant. For instance, "Indians, American" states at the beginning of the article, "Today the Bureau of Indian Affairs, counting as Indians all to whom it provides services, reports an Indian population of nearly 400,000 in the United States, not including Alaska. The Bureau of the Census adds still another 50,000 who are not on tribal rolls, and a study by the University of Chicago boosted the estimate of all members of 'Indian communities' in the United States in 1950 to 610,000." Yet at the end of the article, it is noted that "in 1970 the total U.S. Indian population was 792,730." The inconsistency between American Indian population figures "today" and "in 1970" is obviously due to an editorial lapse at some point when the article was being revised. In fact, only in those cases where *Collier's* is not up-to-date (see "Recency") is the encyclopedia not entirely reliable.

Recency

From the beginning, *Collier's* has had a good record in the area of continuous revision. Like the other Macmillan general encyclopedia (*Merit Students Encyclopedia*), *Collier's* is revised within the following guidelines enunciated by William Halsey, editorial director: "Our policy and practice at Macmillan has been and continues to be that we will let the amount of additional material, altered material or updated material in a reference book reflect what we perceive to be the requirements imposed upon us by the events of the year and the needs of our users rather than by the mechanical limitations of the forms in which we print. As a practical matter, over a period of years, this has dictated a body of revision which is statistically very significant, particularly in the encyclopedias. The annual percentage has tended to range, as an average, slightly upwards of 20 percent of the pages. In fact, in order to handle

This Recency Table compares selected topics in *Collier's* with those in other encyclopedias of similar size and intended usership.

Topic	*Collier's*	*Encyclopedia Americana*	*New Encyclopaedia Britannica*
Afghanistan	Fairly current	Fairly current	Not current
Dinosaurs	Very current	Fairly current	Fairly current
Greenland	Not current	Not current	Not current
Thomas Jefferson	Not current	Not current	Not current
Mass Transportation/Subways	Very current	Fairly current	Not current
Nuclear Power	Fairly current	Not current	Not current
Paris	Very current	Fairly current	Not current
Sharks	Fairly current	Fairly current	Fairly current
Shock Therapy	Fairly current	Fairly current	Fairly current
Suicide	Not current	Not current	Not current
Tuberculosis	Very current	Not current	Fairly current
Zimbabwe	Very current	Very current	Not current

these pages *every* page in *every* work is considered by some qualified editorial person in *every* year" (*Booklist*, September 15, 1976, p. 210).

As with all large encyclopedias, however, some material in *Collier's* is inevitably dated. EXAMPLE: The article "Diabetes Mellitus" lacks information about the possibility of producing human insulin via gene splicing. EXAMPLE: The article "Greenland" is woefully out-of-date, containing nothing about the island's recent achievement of home rule. But in most instances, *Collier's* is reasonably current. Moreover, in the area of recency, *Collier's* is well out in front of its major competition, *The Encyclopedia Americana* and *The New Encyclopaedia Britannica*. Since 1977, when the *Buying Guide* last examined *Collier's*, a great many new articles have been added and many others have been either thoroughly or partially revised. For instance, the 1980 edition contains such new articles as "Art Deco"; "Brzezinski, Zbigniew"; "Child Abuse"; "Energy Resources"; "Freedom of Information Act"; "Inflation"; "Jogging"; "Laetrile"; "Nicklaus, Jack"; "Ozawa, Seiji"; "Rape"; "Solar Energy"; "Thatcher, Margaret"; and "Ventriloquism." Other articles have been completely rewritten, including "Castro, Fidel"; "Houston"; "Kissinger, Henry"; "Parapsychology"; "Psychoanalysis"; "Psychology"; "San Francisco"; "Solid State Science"; "Subway"; and "Tubman, Harriet." In all, the 1980 edition of *Collier's* includes 94 new entries, 34 thoroughly revised articles, 1,133 modestly revised articles, 195 new illustrations, and 2,849 pages of text that differ in some way from those in the previous edition. These statistics bear out editorial director Halsey's claim that the encyclopedia's annual revision rate is well above the minimum 10 percent figure expected of a viable multivolume set (at least when calculated on the basis of number of pages that show some new or altered material). The editors of *Collier's* deserve high marks for their responsible approach to continuous revision.

Macmillan also publishes an annual updating supplement entitled *Collier's Year Book.* This book, which also serves as a supplement to *Merit Students Encyclopedia,* bears no true relationship to either encyclopedia. The 1980 volume, for instance, begins with 12 lengthy articles on topics of general interest (e.g., "Accident at Three Mile Island"; "Albert Einstein 1879–1955"; "China"; "What Cure for Inflation?"), then reviews the previous year's events in some 300 alphabetically arranged topics (including such survey items as "Obituaries," "People in the News," and "Prizes and Awards"), and concludes with a chronology covering December 1978 to November 1979. There is also an index, which is fine except that it fails to index illustrations and their captions. For example, the article "Building and Construction Industries" includes a large photograph prominently headlined "Condominiums and Co-ops on the Rise," accompanied by an informative six-line caption. The index, however, makes no reference to this material under the heading "Condominiums" or any likely alternative. Available to owners of *Collier's* for $12.95, the *Year Book* is hardly an essential purchase.

Objectivity

Like its two major competitors, *Collier's* stresses objective treatment of controversial or sensitive subject matter. EXAMPLE: The article "Homosexuality" is a well-balanced treatment of the topic, covering such aspects as the legal situation, possible causes, and types of therapy. EXAMPLE: The article "Abortion" likewise discusses the current legal status of induced abortion, the various known procedures, and possible aftereffects. Opposition to the 1973 Supreme Court decision which legalized abortion in the United States is noted: "In the face of a concerted campaign by a well-organized and well-financed Right-to-Life movement, the legislatures of several states passed laws designed to prevent, or at least to limit or delay, implementation [of the court's decision]." What bias there is in *Collier's* stems from ignoring unpleasant or unwelcome information. The article on Thomas Jefferson, for instance, speaks glowingly of the man as "a devoted husband and father" and informs that he "was humorless but engaging, and particularly attractive to cultivated women." But nowhere in the article does the reader learn that Jefferson had a long and loving relationship with a black—and slave—woman that produced several illegitimate—and slave—children. Likewise, the article on Warren Harding ignores his illegitimate child by Nan Britton. The *Buying Guide* believes such information is an important part of the historical record, and therefore should be included in encyclopedias for adults and older students.

Clarity and Reader Suitability

As mentioned earlier, *Collier's* is the most popularly written of the three large adult sets. The style is dignified without being stuffy. Comprehension usually requires high school level reading skills, although some articles will be understandable to intelligent junior high school students. Ordinarily, however, the set will not be entirely useful until the student reaches the tenth or eleventh grade. The set's style, syntax, and vocabulary are most suitable for students at the junior college and university levels. EXAMPLE: The informative three-page article "Birth Control" begins in this manner: "The term birth control has at least three meanings. A usual and restricted meaning, found in common parlance and conforming to Margaret Sanger's idea when she invented the term 'birth control,' identifies it with contraception—that is, with all acts or methods that prevent sexual intercourse from leading to conception. A still more restricted meaning confines birth control solely to chemical and mechanical contraceptive devices or medicines. Technically and literally, however, the term has come to refer to any volitional behavior which affects the number of offspring." EXAMPLE: "Nuclear Fission" discusses the biological hazards of radioactive waste material in this manner: "Radioactive wastes can be dangerous to humans if the intensity of radiation is sufficient. This intensity is usually expressed in terms of roentgens (r). It has been found that a dose of I r measured at a particular point would cause tissues located at that point to absorb from 90 to 95 ergs of energy per gram. This is particularly true in biological tissue that contains elements of low atomic number." Bill Katz, in his authoritative *Basic Information Sources* (3rd ed., 1978, p. 158), observes that *Collier's* "never talks down to its readers." The examples here confirm that opinion.

Arrangement and Accessibility

Collier's is arranged alphabetically, letter-by-letter ("Indiana" precedes "Indian Ocean"). External cross-references are sometimes provided, such as *"People's Temple. See under* JONESTOWN." Too often, however, logical external cross-references are lacking. EXAMPLES: There are no references in the A–Z sequence from Zimbabwe to "Rhodesia"; from Atomic Energy Commission to "United States Atomic Energy Commission"; from cults to "Jonestown" or "Primitive Religion." Internal cross-references are also used quite sparingly, normally as *See also* references at the end of some articles. In some instances, the addition of internal cross-references would improve ready access to related material. For instance, the article "Birth Control" indicates that induced abortion is a form of birth control, but there are no cross-references to the article "Abortion." Likewise, "Abortion" provides no cross-reference to "Birth Control."

Access to the contents of the set is achieved principally through the very detailed general index in the final volume. Containing more than 400,000 entries, the index pinpoints even the most minute facts. It also includes references to illustrations, bibliographies, and maps. Because *Collier's* is a broad-entry encyclopedia, the index is an essential finding tool. For instance, as already noted, there is no article heading or external cross-reference for cults in the encyclopedia. The only way to find information on cults (or Zimbabwe, the Atomic Energy Commission, etc.) in *Collier's* is through the index. In the case of cults, there is an entry that refers the reader to "Primitive Religion" in Volume 19. In addition, there are three analytical references: "Cults—Brazil" (in Volume 4); "Cults—Castaneda, Carlos" (in Volume 5); and "Cults—People's Temple" (in Volume 13). In comparative terms, *Collier's* is clearly the best indexed of the three major adult encyclopedias, with *The Encyclopedia Americana* in second place. See the review of *The New Encyclopaedia Britannica* for detailed comparative examples of the indexing systems employed by *Collier's, Americana*, and *Britannica*.

Bibliographies

One of *Collier's* distinctive features is its bibliographies. Unlike other general encyclopedias, the set groups most of its references to further readings in the last volume, preceding the index. The approximately 11,500 titles are arranged by broad subjects and then further subdivided (e.g., Plant and Animal Life—Zoology—Entomology: Insects and Spiders). The titles listed usually represent the best available works on the topic. In addition, they are reasonably up-to-date and frequently annotated. The titles are listed in graded order (from simple to difficult) under each specific topic.

Ever since *Collier's* was first published some 30 years ago, encyclopedia critics have debated the merits of its separately grouped bibliographies. One criticism has been that the titles listed in Volume 24 are not directly related to the topics covered in the set. Defenders answer by noting that the bibliographies are referred to by subject in the index, the starting place for most searches in *Collier's*. Another criticism has been that the separate grouping is inconvenient, forcing the reader who wants references to further readings on a particular subject to consult an additional volume. The editors counter by pointing out that "the reader wishing an overview of related subjects would have to consult bibliographies widely scattered throughout many volumes" if the traditional method of listing bibliographies at the end of articles were followed. It is worth noting, however, that recently the editors have begun appending lists of suggested readings with major new articles, such as "Child Abuse." In some instances (e.g., "Abortion"), these lists are actually small bibliographic essays on the subject that are of enormous assistance to students.

In the final analysis, what is important is that *Collier's* bibliographies are carefully selected, generally up-to-date, helpfully annotated, and fully accessible through the general index. Moreover, almost all the titles listed are in print and might be expected to be located in any good public, school, or college library or through interlibrary loan. In comparison with other adult encyclopedias, *Collier's* provides more in terms of quality bibliographies than any other set, although other sets include more actual titles (for example, *The Encyclopedia Americana* lists about 100,000 further reading references, but many are dreadfully dated and/or inaccessible to students through libraries or bookstores).

Graphics

Collier's includes the usual range of illustrations, from photographs and reproductions of works of art to line drawings and diagrams. Except for numerous full-color, full-page plates found throughout the set, all illustrations are in black-and-white. In most instances, the lack of color does not materially affect the informational value of the illustrations, but occasionally it does. EXAMPLE: "Furniture" includes a three-quarter-page black-and-white photograph showing various types of wood used to make furniture. The last sentence of the caption reads: "Because of their beautiful grains and colors, the most desirable woods are the hardwoods, some of which are shown below." Obviously this illustration should be in color. EXAMPLE: The article on Vincent Van Gogh includes black-and-white reproductions of two of the artist's best-known paintings. Most students of art would agree that it is difficult to appreciate Van Gogh's work sans color reproduction. EXAMPLE: "Dinosaur" is capably illustrated with black-and-white drawings of the major dinosaur types. Unfortunately, the illustrations give the impression that all dinosaurs were gray or dark-skinned, which is not the case. Here, again, color would be helpful. It should be pointed out that the editors of *Collier's* are well aware of such deficiencies, and that a long-term effort to improve the situation will begin in 1981 with the addition of approximately 150 colorful new graphics to the set each year for the foreseeable future.

Lack of color is not the only problem with some of the encyclopedia's graphics. Now and then an illustration is poorly drawn or communicates little if any useful information. EXAMPLE: The drawing of the tiger shark accompanying "Shark" is a very poor representation. The placement of graphics could also be improved in some instances. EXAMPLE: In the article "Architecture," which is heavily illustrated, most major buildings mentioned in the text are accompanied by a photograph, but frequently the picture is on another page. And in other cases there are no illustrations where they are needed. EXAMPLE: The article on Georgia O'Keeffe, the American painter, reports that she is "famous for her lucid, almost geometrically composed desert landscapes and flower studies," but provides no reproduction of an O'Keeffe work.

For the most part, however, the illustrations are effective complements to the printed text. EXAMPLES: The drawings accompanying the article "Flight, Science and Art of" are valuable visual aids to understanding how airplanes actually work. "Nuclear Fission" is enhanced by a cutaway drawing of the nuclear power plant at Rowe, Massachusetts. "Indians, American," a substantial article of more than 50 pages, contains abundant and well-selected graphics, including photographs, drawings, art reproductions, and historical and thematic maps. In addition, the encyclopedia includes full-color plates of fish, flowers, and the like, which are usually instructive as well as attractive. There are also several color transparencies, including the frog and the human anatomy.

Collier's maps are excellent. Those for continents, major countries, and U.S. states were prepared by Rand McNally & Company. Numbering about 150, these maps are in full color and provide both political and physical information in good detail. Each map has its own geographical index. The remainder of the maps were drawn by staff cartographers. In black-and-white, they are mostly special-purpose and historical maps, such as those found in the article "Indians, American."

From a comparative standpoint, *Collier's* has the best graphics of the three advanced adult encyclopedias. *The Encyclopedia Americana* is visually drab and dated, whereas *The New Encyclopaedia Britannica* devotes relatively little space to illustrations.

Physical Format

The familiar black Fabrikoid binding with red panels and gold lettering is both attractive and sturdy. Rand McNally & Company prints and binds the encyclopedia. The opaque, glare-free paper is of excellent stock as well as easy on the eyes. Inside, the two-column page layout is clean and functional. The typefaces used are bold, legible, and modern in appearance. Large guide words appear at the top of every page, and the volumes lie entirely flat when open (for easy consultation). *Collier's* is not a flashy encyclopedia, but it is a well-made, neatly designed set of reference books.

Special Features

Sandwiched between the bibliographies and the index in the last volume is a 15-page Study Guide. Topically arranged (from Philosophy to Aviation and Space Travel), the guide directs students to appropriate articles on the subject in the encyclopedia. For instance, under Chemistry various articles are listed under the subtopic Laws of Chemistry ("Avogadro's Number," "Chemical Equation," "Chemical Kinetics and Equilibrium," "Equivalent Weight"). This type of topical guide is not unique (compare, for instance, the much more extensive *Propaedia* volume of *The New Encyclopaedia Britannica*), but it will be useful to students and teachers alike. The placement of the bibliographies might also be considered a special feature, in that they are segregated in the final volume rather than integrated throughout the text, which is the standard practice. (See "Bibliographies" for additional information.) Finally, *Collier's* furnishes pronunciations for key words in many article headings, particularly words and names that might be difficult for readers, such as the Greek sculptor Phidias. Pronunciations are based on the widely used system developed by the International Phonetic Association—for example, *Phidias* [fiˊdiəs]. Regrettably, only pronunciations are given for a person's last name, thus leaving the curious reader still wondering how to pronounce, say, Yitzhak Rabin's first name.

Sales Information

Collier's is sold in-home at the retail price of $579.50, plus shipping and handling charges and any state or local tax. The set is also available to educational institutions at $467, plus $10 for shipping, etc. Institutions ordering two or more sets pay $425 per unit. Also, schools and libraries are sometimes offered a "pre-publication" discount of approximately $50 if the latest edition is ordered prior to January 31 of that year. *Collier's* is available in only one binding, that being the black and red Fabrikoid already described (see "Physical Format").

Collier's is normally sold as part of an optional package deal that includes the *Collier's Year Book* (an updating supplement available to owners of the encyclopedia at $12.95 annually; see "Recency"), a reference service, a bookcase, and a choice of four selections from 15 available premiums. Premiums include such titles as *Junior Classics* (ten volumes), *First Steps* (a children's early learning program), *Everyday Library for Men* (six volumes), *Everyday Library for Women* (six volumes), and a four-volume medical encyclopedia. This package offer currently costs the consumer a grand total of $864.50.

Summary

Collier's Encyclopedia can be quickly summed up in this manner:

Scope: Excellent	Accessibility: Excellent
Authority: Excellent	Bibliographies: Excellent
Reliability: Excellent	Graphics: Good
Recency: Good	Physical Format: Good
Objectivity: Good	Special Features: Few
Clarity: Excellent	Price: Reasonable

To elaborate briefly, *Collier's* is of quite recent vintage, first published at the beginning of the 1950s. The encyclopedia seems especially young when compared with its chief competitors, *The New Encyclopaedia Britannica* and *The Encyclopedia Americana,* which date back to the eighteenth and nineteenth centuries respectively. But despite its relative newness, *Collier's* is now universally regarded a worthy competitor in the advanced adult category. *Collier's* is, above all else, a well-planned and well-executed encyclopedia. Its coverage of the major areas of knowledge reflects secondary school and college curricula, thus ensuring balanced attention to those subjects deemed important or essential by contemporary wisdom. Moreover, the set's treatment of these subjects is usually reliable, impartial, and up-to-date. *Collier's* is very well organized and easy to use, with access to the set's contents facilitated by an exceptionally large and thorough analytical index. The bibliographies, most of which are grouped together in the final volume, are outstanding. The maps are likewise of high quality, and the illustrations, though often lacking color and not always as helpful or informative as they might be, are an asset.

Consumers who want an advanced multivolume adult encyclopedia of 20 million words or more have three sets from which to choose: *Collier's Encyclopedia, The Encyclopedia Americana,* and *The New Encyclopaedia Britannica.* Each of these encyclopedias has its own particular strengths and weaknesses, and which is "best" is a matter of individual consumer needs and taste. From the comparative standpoint, *Collier's* is the smallest but also the least expensive of the three. It is the most readable and best indexed of the three, although *Americana* is a close second. Each set satisfactorily covers the major knowledge areas, but *Collier's* lacks the depth of *Britannica* (which is roughly twice as large as *Collier's*) and the special attention to American history, biography, and geography provided by *Americana. Collier's* is now clearly the most up-to-date of the three, thanks to its publisher's aggressive continuous revision program. *Britannica,* which revitalized itself with a completely new edition published in 1974, has skimped on revision since that time, and *Americana* is dreadfully dated in many areas. *Collier's* also leads the field in terms of graphics. Although its illustrations are usually not so fine as those found in such smaller (and newer) adult sets as the *Academic American Encyclopedia* and *The Random House Encyclopedia, Collier's* is visually superior to *Americana,* which is dark and dreary, and *Britannica,* which devotes most of its space to printed matter. *Britannica,* on the other hand, is the most scholarly of the three, and its list of contributors most impressive on an authority-by-authority basis, but all three encyclopedias are authoritative. *Britannica* is the most difficult to use and understand, whereas both *Collier's* and *Americana* are simple in construction and design. *Collier's* attention to revision, exceptionally thorough index, carefully prepared bibliographies, and clean layout are its best features, comparatively speaking. When all is said and done, the *Buying Guide* believes *Collier's* represents the best consumer value in the large multivolume adult class.

Other Critical Opinions

Booklist, February 1, 1979, pp. 884–886. Part of a series of reviews by the ALA Reference and Subscription Books Review Committee (RSBRC) entitled "Encyclopedias: A Survey and Buying Guide," this evaluation of *Collier's* is quite positive, although no final conclusions are offered. In its last regular review of *Collier's* (*Booklist,* June 1, 1973, pp. 913–916), RSBRC "recommended" the encyclopedia.

Katz, William A. *Basic Information Sources* (Vol. 1 of *Introduction to Reference Work,* 3rd ed., New York: McGraw-Hill, 1978), pp. 157–159. Katz, a professor of reference service, finds *Collier's* "a good set for anyone with an average to above-average vocabulary who does not require a sophisticated or a detailed explanation of complex matter."

Wynar, Bohdan S. *American Reference Books Annual,* 1979, pp. 33–34. This review notes that *Collier's* "is one of the most attractive encyclopedias on the market," and recommends the set "both for schools and home use."

Encyclopedia Americana

Facts in Brief

Full Title: **The Encyclopedia Americana.** *Editors:* Bernard S. Cayne, Editor in Chief; Alan H. Smith, Executive Editor; Eric E. Akerman, Art Director. *Publisher:* Americana Corporation (a subsidary of Grolier, Inc.), Sherman Turnpike, Danbury, CT 06816. *Former Title: The Americana* (1907–1912). *Edition Reviewed:* International Edition, 1980 copyright.

Volumes: 30. *Pages:* 26,942. *Articles:* 53,120. *Words:* 31,000,000. *Illustrations:* 21,505. *Maps:* 1,150. *Index Entries:* 353,000. *Cross-references:* 40,000. *Contributors:* 6,330.

User Classification: Adult (Multivolume). *Reader Suitability:* Age 15 through Advanced Adult. *Physical Size:* 7½ × 10¼ in.; 26 cm. *LC:* 79-55176. *ISBN:* 0-7172-0111-2. *Lowest Retail Price:* $750; to schools & libraries $499.

Purpose and Scope

The Encyclopedia Americana, the first important multivolume encyclopedia produced in the United States, originally appeared in 1829, based in part on the German *Konversations-Lexikon* (familiarly known as *Brockhaus*). The *Americana* is intended to "serve as a bridge between the worlds of the specialist and the general reader" (preface). The editors' preface also asserts that the encyclopedia's articles "communicate to a wide range of readers. Young students are able to find the information they are seeking—and to understand what they read. Teachers, librarians, and adults in other fields satisfy their reference needs without losing time trying to comprehend technicalities for which they have no specialized preparation." The *Americana* is the second largest general English-language encyclopedia in print. It dwarfs all other sets with the exception of *The New Encyclopaedia Britannica,* its chief rival (along with *Collier's Encyclopedia*) for preeminence among adult encyclopedias in the advanced category.

The *Americana* is a specific-entry encyclopedia, covering the universe of knowledge in articles that average about 600 words in length, or half a page. Articles range in size, however, from a brief paragraph to those that are nearly book length. The article on Canada, for instance, runs to well over 200 pages, and the China article comprises exactly 100 pages. Other major countries receive similar space, whereas nations of less prominence or size are accorded proportionately less coverage; for instance, Afghanistan is covered in 14 pages. The U.S. states and Canadian provinces average approximately 15 pages each. Most U.S. presidents are covered in three or four pages, although those of first rank (Washington, Jefferson, Lincoln, the two Roosevelts, et al.) receive eight or ten pages. In most instances, however, geographical and biographical subjects are covered in a paragraph or two.

The encyclopedia has long been known for its detailed coverage of U.S. and Canadian history, biography, geography, and organizations. This is still true, but only to a point. In recent years, the *Americana*'s emphasis on these topics has been systematically reduced during the course of a major revision effort (see "Recency"). There was a time, for example, when the set included an entry for virtually every town in the United States and Canada, as well as many minor place-names in the United Kingdom and Europe. Fairly small towns are still often included (e.g., New Cumberland, Pa., pop. 9,803; Bowmanville, Ontario, pop. 8,947; Melton Mowbray, England, pop. 19,932), but a great many have been dropped in recent years, apparently in response to criticism that the encyclopedia might be overly national or too provincial in perspective. For instance, the 1977 edition of *Americana* (the last reviewed by the *Buying Guide*) covered Ravenna, Ohio (pop. 11,780), but the 1980 edition does not. The same is true of people. EXAMPLES: The 1977 edition had entries for Sir David Kirke (an English merchant, 1596–1656), Percy Kirke (an English soldier, 1646–1691), Caroline Kirkland (an American author, 1801–1864), James H. Kirkland (an American educator, 1859–1939), John Thornton Kirkland (an American clergyman, 1770–1840), Joseph Kirkland (an American novelist, 1830–1894), and Samuel Kirkland (an American missionary, 1741–1808), whereas the 1980 edition does not. In fact, during the 1970s the editors of *Americana* reduced the total number of articles in the encyclopedia from about 60,000 to just over 50,000. The set's editorial focus today is on expanding international coverage while attempting not to sacrifice or slight its traditionally strong attention to U.S. and Canadian subjects, a very difficult juggling act indeed. The point should be made, however, that despite its name and origin as a national encyclopedia, the *Americana* has always been international in scope, if not emphasis.

Approximately 40 percent of the entries in the current edition are biographies. Another 20 percent cover geographical topics. Some effort is made to relate the set's evolving subject coverage to U.S. school curricula. According to a reviewing aid provided by the publisher, "The editors of the *Americana,* through their own research and with the guidance of curriculum consultants, maintain contact with the schools, with curriculum development, and with trends in education that are still in the experimental or pilot-school stage. As each year's revision is planned, consideration is given to the present and anticipated needs of the schools, and coverage is developed to meet these needs." In terms of subject coverage, the encyclopedia is not so well balanced as its major competitors, *Collier's Encyclopedia* and *The New Encyclopaedia Britannica*. The 1980 edition, for instance, contains nearly 15,000 articles in the general area of science and technology and fewer than 6,000 in the arts and humanities.

The *Americana* has long been known for its strong coverage of scientific, technical, and medical topics, a subject strength inherent in the set at the beginning and further developed during the long editorial reign of Frederick Converse Beach (see "History and Authority"). EXAMPLE: The articles "Diabetes" and "Tuberculosis" furnish clear, succinct information about the pathology, symptoms, diagnosis, and treatment of the diseases. These articles typify the *Americana*'s thorough attention to medical subjects. EXAMPLE: The 15-page article "Evolution" covers all the salient points concerning the scientific theory of evolution (although it neglects to mention various antievolutionist positions; see "Objectivity"). As with many of the encyclopedia's longer articles, there is a detailed table of contents at the beginning of "Evolution," a useful aid to the reader for quickly locating specific material within the article. EXAMPLE: The 25-page "Nuclear Energy" comprehensively surveys the development of nuclear power, providing solid explanations of nuclear fission and fusion and their practical applications. Some helpful black-and-white drawings accompany the text. EXAMPLE: The 25-page "Railroad" exemplifies the set's international approach to scientific and technical material. The article devotes approximately seven pages to U.S. railroad history, but concludes with a five-page survey of railroad systems around the world.

The editors of the 1980 edition under review here estimate that 14,500 articles pertain to the social and behavioral sciences, including geography. Topics in these subject areas are usually adequately covered, except for current developments. EXAMPLE: The short article "Cult" briefly defines the topic and refers interested readers to two additional articles, "Cargo Cults" and "Mystery Cults" (upon checking, the reader will find that no article entitled "Mystery Cults" exists). Coverage, however, is lacking for contemporary cult phenomena, such as the ill-fated People's Temple (even the article on Guyana, where the People's Temple tragedy occurred in 1978, fails to mention the cult or its community, Jonestown). EXAMPLE: Numerous short profiles of notable U.S. colleges and universities are included throughout the set, but sometimes the coverage is so dated as to be practically worthless. For instance, Wilson College, a private women's school in Chambersburg, Pa., is described as having an enrollment in excess of 600, when in fact the college nearly closed its doors recently for lack of students. For more on the *Americana*'s lack of up-to-date coverage, see "Recency."

In the area of the arts and humanities (where currency of material is not always as crucial), the encyclopedia's coverage is normally sufficient. Longer survey articles like "Drama," "Islam," "Logic," "Motion Picture," "Music," "Opera," "Painting," and "Philosophy" provide comprehensive overview treatment. On the other side of the coin, there are many brief, descriptive articles covering specific works of art, such as *"Madame Bovary"* (the novel), *"Death of a Salesman"* (the play), *"Barber of Seville"* (the opera), and *"Last Judgment"* (the paintings). In some instances, however, biographies of artists, writers, and the like lack current information (e.g., the article on William Styron). In other instances, coverage of artists and schools of art are incomplete for want of visual illustration. The article on the American painter Georgia O'Keeffe, for instance, describes the artist's work in this manner: "With such techniques, including the use of thin paint and clear colors to emphasize a feeling of mystical silence and space, she achieved an abstract, almost Oriental simplicity in her paintings." No reproduction of a representative O'Keeffe painting is furnished.

History and Authority

The publisher, the Americana Corporation, is a wholly-owned subsidiary of Grolier, Inc., one of the largest U.S. publishers of general encyclopedias. In addition to the *Americana,* the firm publishes *Encyclopedia International* (for young adults) and *The New Book of Knowledge* (for children). Grolier is also responsible for several major specialized reference sets, including the *Catholic Encyclopedia for School and Home* and *Encyclopedia Canadiana.* During the 1970s, Grolier suffered severe financial losses and is no longer the powerful publisher it once was. A gradual but unmistakable decline in the overall quality of Grolier products has been noticeable for some time now. For instance, *Encyclopedia Canadiana* (1957–1958) is sadly out-of-date, but Grolier recently informed the Canadian Library Association that the set will not be revised. (See "Selling Encyclopedias" in Part I of the *Buying Guide* for further information about Grolier.)

The *Americana* is Grolier's major publication. The set, which celebrated its 150th birthday in 1979, was originally issued in 13 volumes over a four-year period (1829–1833). The first editor was Francis Lieber, a German emigré who based the *Americana* on the seventh edition of the famous *Konversations-Lexikon* (or simply *Brockhaus* after its creator Friedrich Arnold Brockhaus). In the early twentieth century, the *Americana* expanded to 16 volumes under the editorship of Frederick Converse Beach. Beach also edited the magazine *Scientific American* at the time, and doubtless this connection accounts in large part for the encyclopedia's emphasis on science and technology then and now. The last completely new revision of the *Americana* occurred between 1918 and 1920, at which time the set expanded to its present 30 volumes.

The *Americana* today is edited by an experienced staff headed by Bernard S. Cayne, who, prior to accepting the top editorial post with the *Americana,* was a textbook editor at Ginn and Company and later an editor at Macmillan, where he worked on *Collier's Encyclopedia* and helped create *Merit Students Encyclopedia.* The relatively small resident editorial staff currently numbers 32 (up from 29 in 1977, when the *Buying Guide* last examined the *Americana*). There are also 51 advisory editors, eight of whom are Canadians by nationality or affiliation. The majority are professors and all bring good credentials to the encyclopedia. The *Americana* lists more contributors than any other encyclopedia in the English language. Many of the contributors are distinguished in their fields of expertise—Albert C. Baugh (philology), Dana L. Farnsworth (mental health), Sidney Hook (philosophy), C. Eric Lincoln (black studies), Lewis Mumford (social philosophy), Edward R. Murrow (journalism), C. F. Powell (physics), Edouard A. Stackpole (whaling), J. D. Watson (biology)—but many others are simply workaday professionals who have contributed one small article on a relatively minor subject. Many of the contributors are dead or no longer active. EXAMPLE: Zella D. Adams is listed as "Librarian, Public Library, West Palm Beach, Fla.," but Ms. Adams had not held that position for some time prior to her death a number of years ago. Some new contributors have been added in recent years, however, such as Charles W. Howe (professor of economics at the University of Colorado) and Alexander Rabinowitch (professor of history at Indiana University). Likewise, some contributors have been deleted from the list, such as F. N. Houser, Jr. (identified as the editor of a railroad magazine). All contributors are identified by their institutional connections and/or published works. All longer articles and some shorter ones are signed with the author's full name. Approximately 75 percent of the articles are signed.

Reliability

Any encyclopedia of the magnitude of the *Americana* (over 30 million words) will inevitably contain some errors of fact and questionable statements. EXAMPLE: The article "Biology" states, "In defining the branches of biology, such terms as botany, zoology, parasitology, protozoology, and the like have not been used because they are obsolescent." Really? But, on the whole, the set is reasonably accurate and dependable. Only when the material is dated—and that is all too frequently—is the *Americana* unreliable. For examples of obsolescence in the *Americana*, see the next section ("Recency").

Recency

Some articles in the *Americana* are reasonably current, but many others are clearly in need of revision. As mentioned earlier, the set has not been completely overhauled since 1918–1920, when it was enlarged to 30 volumes. In 1927, the editors introduced a two-pronged approach to continuous revision. First, the entire set is revised annually in those areas that require "urgent" attention, such as election data and significant political changes (e.g., Ronald Reagan's election as U.S. president and the Iranian revolution). Such revision is routine and minimal, as far as the amount of text is concerned. The other approach, carried out simultaneously, calls for a volume-by-volume rebuilding program extended over a period of years. Here the revision is systematic, fundamental, and thorough. All articles in the volume being revised are reviewed by the editors and appropriate subject advisers. Some articles are entirely rewritten, some are simply updated as required, others are dropped, and some new ones may be introduced. According to Wallace S. Murray, a longtime Grolier editorial presence, "In each year different particular volumes are completely reconstructed, with the editors free to change absolutely everything in them and to reorder and reorganize the knowledge within the alphabetical span of the volumes. Out of this rebuilding, an entirely new *Encyclopedia Americana* is emerging" (*Booklist,* September 15, 1976, p. 208).

The present cycle of "rebuilding" the *Americana* began in the late 1950s. Ten volumes, or a third of the set, were refashioned prior to 1969, and since that time 14 more volumes have undergone intensive revision. As of 1980 the rebuilt volumes are 1–17, 19, and 22–27. Also, some work has been done on Volume 18, and of course Volume 30 (the general index) is completely revised with each new edition. Much of the rebuilding activity has centered on eliminating biographies of relatively obscure people born prior to 1900. For example, Volume 23, one of the latest of *Americana*'s reconstructed volumes, no longer covers Frederick William Robertson (an English clergyman, 1816–1853), James Robertson (an American pioneer, 1742–1814), James Robertson (a British governor of New York, 1720–1788), James Robertson (a Canadian clergyman, 1839–1902), James Burton Robertson (an English historian, 1800–1877), James Craigie Robertson (a Scottish clergyman, 1813–1882), James Wilson Robertson (a Canadian educator, 1857–1930), John Mackinnon Robertson (a British author and legislator, 1856–1933), John Ross Robertson (a Canadian journalist, 1841–1918), Morgan Robertson (an American writer about the sea, 1861–1915), Thomas William Robertson (an English actor and dramatist, 1829–1871), William Robertson (a Scottish historian, 1721–1793), William H. Robertson (an American judge and politician, 1823–1898), and Sir William (Robert) Robertson (a British soldier, 1860–1933). In fact, the *only* person in the current edition of the *Americana* with the surname Robertson is Oscar (an American basketball player, 1938–). In addition, coverage of many small U.S. and Canadian towns has fallen victim to the so-called rebuilding program.

This approach to revision has inherent problems that far transcend the loss of many personal names and place-names. Specifically, some of the material in the volumes that have not yet been thoroughly revised is dreadfully dated. EXAMPLE: The article "Oceanography" (Volume 20) is current only as of the late 1960s, and much pathbreaking work has occurred in this important field during the past decade. EXAMPLE: "Nuclear Energy" (also Volume 20) not only fails to discuss the traumatic accident at Harrisburg's Three Mile Island nuclear facility, the article informs that nuclear power plants are subject to regulation by the Atomic Energy Commission (which ceased to exist years ago). The article also cites Atomic Energy Commission studies that are simply obsolete today: "The projections indicate that about 60% of the electrical needs in the year 2000 will be met by nuclear reactors. The AEC expects that fast breeder reactors will account for about 30% of the nuclear power generation capacity in 2000, and that high-temperature gas-cooled reactors will account for about 10%." EXAMPLE: Many articles covering smaller places in the unrevised volumes provide population data from the 1960s and even the 1950s.

What is even more regrettable about this situation is that those volumes that were rebuilt prior to 1969 are now beginning to show distinct signs of

This Recency Table compares selected topics in the *Americana* with those in other encyclopedias of similar size and intended usership.

Topic	Encyclopedia Americana	Collier's	New Encyclopaedia Britannica
Afghanistan	Fairly current	Fairly current	Not current
Dinosaurs	Fairly current	Very current	Fairly current
Greenland	Not current	Not current	Not current
Thomas Jefferson	Not current	Not current	Not current
Mass Transportation/Subways	Fairly current	Very current	Not current
Nuclear Power	Not current	Fairly current	Not current
Paris	Fairly current	Very current	Not current
Sharks	Fairly current	Fairly current	Fairly current
Shock Therapy	Fairly current	Fairly current	Fairly current
Suicide	Not current	Not current	Not current
Tuberculosis	Not current	Very current	Fairly current
Zimbabwe	Very current	Very current	Not current

old age. EXAMPLE: The article "Child Development" (Volume 6), in a discussion of human intelligence within the context of the heredity-environment debate, informs that "correlations between the IQ scores of both identical and fraternal twins, raised apart, provided a relatively sound test that tended to support the genetic point of view." Nowhere, however, does the reader learn that such findings have been discredited by recent revelations that the late Sir Cyril Burt, the British psychologist responsible for much of the research on intelligence in twins, used fraudulent methods and data to "prove" his preconceived notions. Indeed, Burt went so far as to create his own coauthors and research assistants. Also, the article "Burt, Sir Cyril Lodovic" contains no hint of Burt's questionable behavior. EXAMPLE: "Indian, American" (Volume 15) furnishes dated population figures and estimates. The article also fails to discuss the militancy among Native Americans in the late 1960s and 1970s. EXAMPLE: "Greenland" (Volume 13) fails to include information about the island's new home rule, achieved from Denmark in 1979 (although discussions about home rule date back to 1975). In fact, the *Americana* offers no information about Greenland after 1951. EXAMPLE: "China" (Volume 6) states that the Wade-Giles system of rendering Chinese characters into the Roman alphabet is preferred by the Chinese government, and that the Pinyin system is "used as a form of writing only on a limited scale." Actually, since January 1, 1979, the Chinese have used Pinyin for all news reports and official documents sent abroad. As a result, the United Nations, the U.S.Board on Geographic Names, and major elements of the English-language press have adopted the Pinyin system.

Also troubling is the encyclopedia's rate of annual continuous revision, which consistently falls well below the minimum standard of 10 percent. The 1980 edition, for instance, offers 1,200 "new or revised" articles out of a total of more than 50,000 articles— or an annual revision rate of 2.5 percent. Calculated another way, the 1980 edition includes 2,200 "revised or reset" pages, including the 900-page index in Volume 30, out of a total of 27,000 pages—or an annual revision rate of 8 percent. On a more long-term basis, the publisher reports that 5,800 articles (of the 50,000+ total) were new or revised during the four-year period 1977–1980, which amounts to an annual revision rate of under 2 percent.

It should be apparent to any objective and independent critic that the *Americana* is sorely in need of a complete revision. Obviously, the piecemeal approach to updating a very large encyclopedia that has not been overhauled from top to bottom since the 1920s is no longer feasible. Richard T. Jameson's observation in *Film Comment* (July–August 1976, p. 60) might be made about the whole set: "The *Americana*'s entries on Motion Pictures in general . . . are virtually dated artifacts in themselves."

Like practically all multivolume encyclopedias, the *Americana* is supplemented by a yearbook. Entitled the *Americana Annual*, it has been published continuously since 1923 and is said to be "similar to the encyclopedia in format and arrangement." This is true, but there is no real relationship between *Encyclopedia Americana* and the *Americana Annual*, save that they share the same name. The *Annual* is useful as a record of the year's events. As an updating tool, however, its value is negligible.

Objectivity

"My wish has been not to obtrude opinions," said Francis Lieber in 1829, "but to furnish facts." The *Americana* has remained true, over the years, to its first editor's desire for impartial treatment of knowledge, no matter how controversial or sensitive the subject matter. To as great a degree as perhaps any other major adult encyclopedia, the *Americana* presents all legitimate points of view where controversy exists. Examples of this emphasis on balanced treatment are found in such articles as "Abortion," "Communism," "Islam," "Homosexuality," "Equal Rights Amendment," and "Disarmament." Inevitably, however, some bias does occur. EXAMPLE: The article "Sex Education" is written by a proponent (Mary S. Calderone, Executive Director, SIECUS—The Sex Information and Education Council of the United States) of sex education courses in the public schools. The various arguments against such instruction are not even mentioned in the article. Conversely, SIECUS materials are prominently cited and the overall tone is propagandistic. EXAMPLE: "Evolution" begins by stating that "the only scientifically tenable explanation of organic diversity and of adaptedness is the theory of evolution." At no point in the article are fundamentalist Christian objections to evolutionary theory mentioned, nor is any attention given to the notions embodied in the current movement known as Scientific Creationism.

Clarity and Reader Suitability

From the beginning, the *Americana* has stressed stylistic clarity, directness, and simplicity. The editors' stated goal of serving as "a bridge between the worlds of the specialist and the general reader" is skillfully accomplished in most instances. Even technical subject matter is usually made comprehensible to students and adults reading at the eleventh and twelfth grade levels. Efforts are made not to "write down" to *Americana* readers.

Like most general adult encyclopedias, the *Americana* claims to be understandable to average readers at the middle school level. Often such claims are exaggerated, and the *Americana*'s is no exception. Isolated articles might be suitable for students with junior high school reading skills, but the articles are not written to grade level, nor is the vocabulary tested and controlled as it is in the better sets for young adults (i.e., *The World Book Encyclopedia, Merit Students Encyclopedia,* and *Compton's Encyclopedia*). Indeed, the overall syntax (sentence structure) and vocabulary customarily require a much higher level of reading sophistication. The following excerpt from the article "Dinosaur" is fairly typical of the *Americana*'s style: "Why the dinosaurs and other groups, such as the flying reptiles and ichthyosaurs, became extinct while other groups, such as snakes, turtles, tortoises, crocodiles, and birds, continued to live and flourish is not completely understood. It is known that the disappearance of dinosaurs was not caused by epidemic disease, catastrophe, or the destruction of dinosaur eggs by the rapidly evolving mammals, but it was probably caused by physical conditions around that part of the beginning of the Upper Cretaceous period known as the Cenomanian."

Arrangement and Accessibility

The encyclopedia is arranged alphabetically, word-by-word ("Indian Ocean" precedes "Indiana"). Access is enhanced by the set's emphasis on specific entries. Cross-references are generously provided throughout, appearing as external references in the A–Z sequence (e.g., "*Greyhound Racing.* See DOG RACING") and as internal *See* and *See also* references within and at the end of articles. EXAMPLE: At the end of the article "Shock Therapy" there is a reference to "Electroshock Therapy," a related article. In some instances, however, the internal references are blind, or false. EXAMPLE: Among the many references at the end of "Philosophy" is "Freedom of the Will," but the interested reader will find no article in the encyclopedia under that title. Altogether, the *Americana* furnishes some 40,000 cross-references, most of them true.

Since 1943, the encyclopedia has provided a comprehensive index. The index to the 1980 edition, found in Volume 30, comprises more than 353,000 entries, many of them analytical in nature. Only *Collier's Encyclopedia* offers a larger general index among all the general encyclopedias currently in print. Compared with *The New Encyclopaedia Britannica*'s index (the *Micropaedia),* the *Americana*'s index is much, much easier to use and unquestionably more effective. This does not mean, however, that the *Americana* index is without flaws. EXAMPLE: The index entry "Cult" refers the reader to the basic article "Cult" in Volume 8, and gives one analytical reference to "Cult—Roman religion" in Volume 23. No analytical reference, however, is given for the article "Hare Krishna," a contemporary religious cult. See the review of *The New Encyclopaedia Britannica* for detailed comparative examples of the indexing systems employed by the *Americana, Collier's,* and *Britannica.*

Bibliographies

All major articles, as well as many shorter ones, have lists of further readings. In most instances the bibliographies are carefully selected references to the best or most important works available on a particular subject. Efforts have been made to provide citations to both general and specialist materials. In keeping with the *Americana*'s emphasis on objectivity, bibliographies usually include works that represent different points of view if the subject matter happens to be controversial. Like *Collier's Encyclopedia,* the *Americana* attempts to include references to books that might normally be found in most well-stocked public and school libraries. The problem with many of the bibliographies is the same one that plagues the encyclopedia as a whole—lack of currency. EXAMPLE: The bibliography appended to "Afghanistan" is scandalously out-of-date, offering several works published in the nineteenth century and a 1936 item entitled *Afghanistan: A Brief Survey.* EXAMPLE: The bibliography with "Indian, American" has no entry later than 1968, and the multivolume *Handbook of Middle American Indians,* completed in 1971, is cited as an open entry (1964–   ). EXAMPLE: The bibliography with "Child Development" includes only titles published in the 1950s and 1960s. No entry is more current than 1967. In all, the *Americana* provides more than 10,000 bibliographies in which over 100,000 individual titles are cited.

Graphics

Of the 21,000-plus illustrations in the *Americana,* over half (13,500) are photographs, most in black-and-white. The remainder of the illustrations are drawings, diagrams, charts, and graphs. With rare exceptions, the illustrations enhance or clarify the written text. Like so much of the *Americana,* the graphics are practical and functional, rather than exciting or spectacular. Only about 5 percent of the graphics are in color (usually page-long color plates), and sometimes they are quite dated. The article "Paris," for instance, includes an archaic photograph of Les Halles Centrales, the central food market, which has not existed for over a decade (it was moved near Orly ten miles away in 1969).

The maps are of reasonably good quality. The well-known cartographical firm of C. S. Hammond & Company has provided some 450 full-color maps covering the world's continents, major countries, all U.S. states, and Canadian provinces. These maps are fully indexed. In addition, many smaller black-and-white locator and special-purpose maps appear throughout the set. The *Americana* provides fewer city layout maps than either *Collier's* or the *Britannica*. In general, however, the *Americana*'s maps are equal to *Collier's* and superior to the *Britannica*'s.

Physical Format

The *Americana* is sturdily bound in red Lexotone with black panels and gold lettering and stamping. A likeness of the American eagle appears on the front of each volume. The lettering on the spine is bold and easy to read even at some distance. Inside, the two-column page layout is dull and functional rather than attractive. The eight-point Times Roman type is legible. Guide words are normally provided at the top of the page, except when illustrations interfere, which is too often. The glare-free paper is of satisfactory quality and durability, and the volumes lie flat when open for easy consultation. Overall, the *Americana* is a drab encyclopedia whose physical format is utilitarian in both appearance and construction.

Special Features

There are several special features that deserve mention. Each century of the Christian era (e.g., "First Century") has its own article. These articles survey each century's developments on an international and interdisciplinary basis, providing the interested student with an excellent historical perspective. Another useful feature is the provision of the full text of some important historical documents, such as the Atlantic Charter, the Emancipation Proclamation, and Washington's Farewell Address. Also helpful, particularly to students, are the many glossaries of technical terms included with articles where a specialized vocabulary is essential, such as "Archaeology," "Architecture," "Astronomy," "Atom," "Automobile." It is puzzling, however, why other articles on similar subjects lack such glossaries, such as "Anthropology," "Art," "Astronautics," "Atmosphere." Finally, pronunciations are given for most terms, personal names, and place-names. EXAMPLES: *Mao Tse-tung* [mou dzə-do͞ong]; *Tuberculosis* [to͞o-bər-kyə-lō´sis].

Sales Information

The *Americana,* like its major competitors, is sold in-home on the subscription, or installment, basis. Only one binding is available to retail customers, that being the red Lexotone already described (see "Physical Format"). The set sells for $750 (up from $550 three years ago), plus shipping, handling, and any tax. A blue Sturdite binding, reinforced for very heavy use, is sold to schools and libraries at $499, plus the usual added charges. The publisher reports that the *Americana* is currently not sold as part of any package offer involving other reference titles, research services, bookcases, or the like. However, a yearbook, entitled the *Americana Annual* (see "Recency"), is available to owners of the encyclopedia at $14 per volume.

Summary

The Encyclopedia Americana can be quickly summed up in this manner:

Scope: Good	Accessibility: Good
Authority: Good	Bibliographies: Fair
Reliability: Good	Graphics: Fair
Recency: Poor	Physical Format: Good
Objectivity: Good	Special Features: Few
Clarity: Excellent	Price: High

To elaborate briefly, the *Americana* is now over a century and a half old, having celebrated its sesquicentennial in 1979. It is the second largest encyclopedia in the English language. Moreover, it was the first encyclopedia of national importance to be published in the United States. The current edition is usually reliable, easy to use, and reasonably authoritative, although Grolier is no longer the publisher it once was. Except in rare instances, the set's contents are presented in a clear, direct, and relatively simple manner. Most articles will be comprehensible to the average high school student in the junior or senior year, as well as college students and literate adults. Despite its name and origin as a national encyclopedia, the *Americana* is international in scope. Its subject strengths, however, still lie in its detailed coverage of North American history, place-names, and people, as well as scientific and technical achievements. No other general encyclopedia offers as much geographical and biographical information about the United States and Canada as does the *Americana*, although the breadth of this coverage is systematically being reduced at the present time. In point of fact, the number of articles in the encyclopedia has shrunk from 60,000 to just over 50,000 during the past ten or so years. The set's greatest weakness is lack of up-to-dateness. No completely new edition of the *Americana* has appeared in 60 years. The volume-by-volume "rebuilding," or revision, program has resulted in an encyclopedia that is often sadly dated. In addition, the rate of annual continuous revision has not met even minimum standards in recent years. An entirely new edition of the *Americana* is urgently required.

An advanced adult encyclopedia is not for everyone. Adults with modest informational needs will ordinarily be better off with a smaller, less expensive adult set (such as the new and very attractive *Academic American Encyclopedia* or the bargain-priced *Funk & Wagnalls New Encyclopedia)* or one of the three fine young adult sets available (*Compton's Encyclopedia, Merit Students Encyclopedia,* and *The World Book Encyclopedia*). Consumers with relatively young children will, again, find the young adult or larger children's sets more appropriate. But for those people who seriously need access to as wide a range of reliable general knowledge and information as possible (high school students planning to go to college, college students, professional people, inquisitive laypeople, and so on), only the advanced adult encyclopedia will fully meet their needs. Here the choice is limited to three sets: *Collier's Encyclopedia, The Encyclopedia Americana,* and *The New Encyclopaedia Britannica.*

Each of these three large encyclopedias has its own particular strengths and weaknesses, and which is "best" is a matter of individual consumer needs and taste. Libraries of any consequence will stock all three. From the comparative standpoint, the *Americana* is smaller than *Britannica* but larger than *Collier's.* Likewise, *Americana* costs less than *Britannica* but more than *Collier's.* *Americana* is readable and well indexed, but *Collier's* holds the edge in both these areas (*Britannica* is quite erudite in tone and poorly indexed). *Collier's* also is visually superior to *Americana,* which is dark and dreary, and *Britannica,* which devotes most of its space to printed matter. Each encyclopedia satisfactorily covers the major knowledge areas, but *Americana* lacks the balanced coverage of *Collier's* and the depth of *Britannica* (which is roughly 25 percent larger than *Americana*), except where American history, biography, and geography are concerned. *Collier's* is now clearly the most up-to-date of the three sets, thanks to its aggressive continuous revision program. *Americana* is often badly dated, especially in those volumes that have not been thoroughly and systematically revised (or "rebuilt") in many years. *Britannica,* which revitalized itself with a completely new edition published in 1974, has skimped on revision since that time. *Britannica* is the most scholarly of the three, and its list of contributors is most impressive on an authority-by-authority basis, but all three encyclopedias are authoritative. *Britannica* is the most difficult to use and understand, whereas both *Americana* and *Collier's* are simple in construction and design. *Americana*'s detailed index, strong coverage of U.S. topics, and clear treatment of material are its best features, comparatively speaking. But when all is said and done, the *Buying Guide* believes *Collier's* represents the best consumer value in the advanced adult class.

Other Critical Opinions

Booklist, February 1, 1979, pp. 886–889. Part of a series of reviews by the ALA Reference and Subscription Books Review Committee (RSBRC) entitled "Encyclopedias: A Survey and Buying Guide," this evaluation of the *Americana* (1975 edition) is critical of the set's coverage of the humanities, its currency in many areas, and its alleged fragmentation of knowledge. No final conclusions are offered, however. In its last regular review of the *Americana* (*Booklist,* July 1, 1976, pp. 1541–1544), RSBRC "recommended" the encyclopedia.

Katz, William A. *Basic Information Sources* (Vol. 1 of *Introduction to Reference Work,* 3rd ed., New York: McGraw-Hill, 1978), p. 156. Katz, a professor of reference service, notes that "in technical and social areas the lack of a total revision is sometimes evident [but] on balance, the set is reliable for its timeliness." He also points out that the *Americana* is "a basic set in almost all libraries."

Wynar, Bohdan S. *American Reference Books Annual*, 1977, pp. 40–44. Wynar, an experienced reference book reviewer and editor, generally commends the encyclopedia for its balanced coverage and authoritative treatment of general knowledge, and its "strong emphasis on American-oriented topics."

Funk & Wagnalls New Encyclopedia

Facts in Brief

Full Title: **Funk & Wagnalls New Encyclopedia.** *Editors:* Leon L. Bram, Editorial Director; Robert S. Phillips, Editor; Norma H. Dickey, Executive Editor. *Publisher:* Funk & Wagnalls, Inc., 666 Fifth Ave., New York, NY 10019. *Distributor to Schools & Libraries:* Quality Books, Inc., 400 Anthony Trail, Northbrook, IL 60062. *Former Titles: Funk & Wagnalls Standard Reference Encyclopedia* (1959–1971); *Universal Standard Encyclopedia* (1954–1958); *New Funk & Wagnalls Encyclopedia* (1949–1952); *Funk & Wagnalls New Standard Encyclopedia of Universal Knowledge* (1931–1948); *Funk & Wagnalls Standard Encyclopedia* (1912–1930). *Edition Reviewed:* Regency Edition, Spring 1980 (copyright 1979).

Volumes: 27 (including 2-volume index and bibliography). *Pages:* 12,976. *Articles:* 25,000. *Words:* 9,000,000. *Illustrations:* 7,500. *Maps:* 342. *Index Entries:* 193,000. *Cross-references:* 80,000. *Contributors:* 701.

User Classification: Adult (Multivolume). *Reader Suitability:* Age 12 through General Adult. *Physical Size:* 6½ × 9¼ in.; 24 cm. *LC:* 72-170933. *ISBN: 0-8343-0033-8. Lowest Retail Price:* Volume 1, $0.09; Volumes 2–27, $2.99 each = $77.83 the set; to schools & libraries $139.50 (price includes 3 yearbooks).

Purpose and Scope

Funk & Wagnalls New Encyclopedia is an inexpensive multivolume work for home and student use sold principally in supermarkets on a book-a-week basis. The overriding goal of the set's makers is to provide a reliable, easy-to-use, reasonably up-to-date, objective, and comprehensive encyclopedia that is "priced low enough to be within the reach of the general public" and will be "of value for every member of the family." The preface also notes that *Funk & Wagnalls* "has been concisely written in nontechnical language equally suited to the student or the casual reader interested in a date, a person, an event, or a place."

As the set's vital statistics indicate, *Funk & Wagnalls* is a middle-sized adult encyclopedia. Its articles tend to be brief, specific, and factual, usually devoid of extensive historical or interpretative background information. The articles average approximately half a page (or 360 words) in length, but are frequently shorter. This observation is especially true of biographical and geographical topics, which account for roughly 50 percent of the encyclopedia's 25,000 articles. The world's major historical figures and places, however, receive extended coverage. EXAMPLES: The U.S. presidents are accorded from one to four pages, depending on the individual's historical importance; for instance, George Washington has four pages whereas Warren Harding has one. Napoleon Bonaparte is covered in three-and-a-half pages, Charles de Gaulle in a page and a half, William Shakespeare in more than three pages (plus four pages of color plates), and Alfred Lord Tennyson in just under a page and a half. The article "Canada" runs to 32 pages, including numerous photographs and a two-page map with two more pages devoted to a map index. Following this survey article are more specific entries covering Canadian art and literature. By comparison, "Greenland" is dealt with in three pages, including several photographs but no map.

Subject coverage emphasizes the natural and technical sciences, including lengthy survey articles on individual fields of study (e.g., agriculture, astronomy, botany, calculus, chemistry, engineering, geometry, geophysics, medicine, meteorology, surgery, zoology) and short, specific articles on plants, animals, chemical elements, scientific theories, diseases, and particular technological developments (the computer, gas turbine engine, telephone, television, transistor, xerography, X-ray). The editors estimate that approximately 20 percent or more of the set's coverage is devoted to science and technology. The humanities and social sciences, while not neglected, receive proportionately less coverage, but it is a reasonable distribution given current knowledge trends. In some instances, however, topics that ought to be treated in a general encyclopedia are neglected or only mentioned superficially. EXAMPLE: The article "Chinese Language" fails to discuss the various systems (Wade-Giles, Pinyin, etc.) employed to transliterate Chinese characters into the Roman alphabet. EXAMPLE: There is no article on cults, and the index furnishes only two references, both of which turn out to be insignificant. Such contemporary cult phenomena as the People's Temple and Hare Krishna are completely ignored.

Because the encyclopedia aims to be useful to the entire family, considerable attention is given to practical subjects, like boots and shoes, boatbuilding, consumer education and protection, fishing, gardening, life insurance, nutrition, philately and other hobbies, photography, sewing machines, social security, trading stamps, and various sports such as bowling, skiing, and swimming. The rules of games like backgammon, checkers, and handball are also explained. In addition, medical topics are usually well covered from the practical standpoint—for example, "Blood"; "Heart"; "Obstetrics."

As is the case with the other better intermediate adult encyclopedias currently on the U.S. market (namely the *Academic American Encyclopedia, The New Illustrated Columbia Encyclopedia, The New Standard Encyclopedia,* and the British-made *New Caxton Encyclopedia*), *Funk & Wagnalls* is broadly international in its coverage of historical, geographical, biographical, artistic, social, and technical topics. For instance, the article "Motion Pictures, History of" accords generous attention to European as well as U.S. developments. But like the sets produced in the

United States, *Funk & Wagnalls* emphasizes North American trends and attitudes. EXAMPLE: The seven-page article "Education" traces the history of the discipline from an international perspective, but it is followed by an equally long article entitled "Education in the United States." Likewise, the articles "Education, Medical" and "Education, Military" accentuate U.S. developments.

History and Authority

Long a familiar name in U.S. reference book publishing, Funk & Wagnalls, Inc., was founded in 1876 by two enterprising, education-minded clergymen, Isaac Kauffman Funk and Adam W. Wagnalls. Over the years, the Funk & Wagnalls imprint has appeared on numerous reference works, including the well-known "Standard" dictionary line. Indeed, "Look it up in your Funk & Wagnalls" became something of a national slogan in the 1960s, coined by the then-popular *Laugh-In* television show. At the present time in the area of general encyclopedias, the firm publishes *Funk & Wagnalls New Encyclopedia* (under review here) and *The Young Students Encyclopedia,* a work for children.

Funk & Wagnalls New Encyclopedia first appeared in 1972 with a 1971 copyright date. Not a completely new work, it represented an extensive revision of the 25-volume *Funk & Wagnalls Standard Reference Encyclopedia,* published between 1959 and 1971. Earlier versions of the set date back to 1912 (see "Facts in Brief" for titles and dates). Since 1953 the encyclopedia has been marketed principally through supermarkets, although in recent years the publisher has also offered the set to schools and libraries. The supermarket connection has doubtless been profitable for Funk & Wagnalls, Inc., but it has done the set's reputation little good. There is a tendency among encyclopedia critics, librarians, and those more sophisticated consumers to dismiss automatically any encyclopedia bearing the "supermarket" label. And, in point of fact, most supermarket sets in the past have been of relatively low quality. Happily, *Funk & Wagnalls New Encyclopedia* is an exception to the rule.

The 1980 edition of *Funk & Wagnalls* (copyright 1979) lists an editorial and production staff of 90, the same number as the 1977 edition (when the *Buying Guide* last reviewed the encyclopedia). Leon L. Bram continues to serve as the editorial director. Bram, who came to Funk & Wagnalls in 1974, brings good credentials to the work, having previously served as executive editor of *Compton's Encyclopedia.* Robert S. Phillips and Norma H. Dickey continue as editor and executive editor respectively. The front matter in Volume 1 includes a consulting and contributing board of 303 names, many of whom are instantly recognizable as authoritative people, such as Brooks Atkinson, Bruce Catton, David Daiches, Dr. Michael DeBakey, former Supreme Court Justice William O. Douglas, Rhodes Fairbridge, Senator Barry Goldwater, Walter Gropius, Senator S. I. Hayakawa, Bowie Kuhn, William Menninger, Reinhold Niebuhr, Mario Pei, Walter Reuther, W. W. Rostow, Glenn Seaborg, Lee Strasberg, Allen Tate, Lionel Trilling, and Roy Wilkins. Few changes have occurred on this board since 1977 (e.g., George Amberg has been dropped; Detlev W. Bronk has been added). As the sampling here suggests, quite a few members of the board are now deceased. A more extensive list of 581 contributors entitled "Key to Signed Articles" follows. This list, which includes many members of the aforementioned consulting and contributing board, is arranged alphabetically by contributors' initials. Both lists indicate the person's academic degrees, occupation and affiliations, and published works, if any, but not the article(s) written for the encyclopedia. About 25 new contributors have been added since 1977, most of them college and university professors. Overall, *Funk & Wagnalls'* authority is impressive, although exactly how much responsibility the consultants have for the set's contents is not clear. Also, the relatively large number of consultants and contributors who are dead (estimated to be nearly 15 percent of the total roster) raises doubts about the encyclopedia's currency.

Reliability

Funk & Wagnalls gives every indication of being a conscientiously researched and edited encyclopedia. The set is not error-free, however. Inaccuracies inevitably occur where material is dated (see "Recency"). The *Buying Guide* also found a number of minor misstatements and, occasionally, mistakes of serious magnitude. EXAMPLE: The article "American Indians" states that Native Americans "spoke at least 2000 mutually unintelligible languages," a figure that exceeds generally accepted estimates. The article also implies that the Ojibwa and Chippewa Indians are two distinct tribes, when in fact they are the same tribe (the name Ojibwa being preferred in Canada, Chippewa in the United States). The article also errs in referring to camas root as "cannas root." The article also errs in stating that the Algonquian group "cultivated wild rice, which was a grain of great importance along the southern border of the Great Lakes and down the Saint Lawrence R." Actually, the rice was gathered, not cultivated, and it was of no great importance in the Saint Lawrence River area. The article also errs by omitting the Creek Confederacy from a list of the "principal tribes" of the southeast. But such lapses are the exception rather than the rule. Ordinarily, *Funk & Wagnalls* can be relied upon as a reasonably trustworthy source of general information.

Recency

Like practically all multivolume U.S. encyclopedias, *Funk & Wagnalls* practices continuous revision, whereby a certain portion of the set is revised each year. At the present time, *Funk & Wagnalls* has an extremely vigorous revision program that entails changes, both major and minor, in nearly 2,000 of the set's approximately 13,000 pages annually. According to documentation provided by the encyclopedia's editors to the *Buying Guide,* 5,140 pages have been reset or revised between fall 1977 and spring 1980, for an annual continuous revision rate well in excess of the minimum 10 percent standard. Also between 1977 and 1980,

3,550 articles (of a total of 25,000) have been added, revised, or completely rewritten. Calculated in this manner, the encyclopedia's revision rate is less impressive (about 5 percent), but much of the revision effort during the past three years has centered on adding or revising substantive articles of considerable length, such as "Canadian Literature." The editors also report that current events, death dates, population statistics, and other similar areas of volatile knowledge are methodically updated twice a year with each new printing in the spring and the fall. The *Buying Guide*'s investigations support these claims. Examination of many diverse subjects treated in *Funk & Wagnalls*—American Indians, botany, Canada, child psychology, dinosaurs, evolution, homosexuality, hypnosis, Mao Tse-tung, motion pictures, women's rights, etc.—reveals a high degree of up-to-dateness and attention to revision.

This does not mean, however, that *Funk & Wagnalls* is completely current in all areas. Indeed, numerous articles require either major or minor revision, and some subjects (e.g., present-day cults) are not covered at all. A good example of an article in need of updating is "Nuclear Power," which implies the Atomic Energy Commission (abolished in 1974) is still in existence, and fails to mention the Three Mile Island disaster when discussing nuclear safety. "Paris" is another article that has slipped into obsolescence. For instance, there is no mention of the controversial Pompidou National Center of Art and Culture (or Beaubourg), a new tourist landmark. "Suicide" likewise is out-of-date. The article fails to note the recent upsurge in teenage suicide, and there is nothing on the current debate over the so-called right to suicide. "Greenland" provides no information about the island's recent home rule status.

Consumers should be aware that, contrary to established encyclopedia publishing practice, *Funk & Wagnalls* does *not* usually include the date of the latest revision on the verso of the title page. Since 1971, the publisher has obtained new copyrights only every four years, even though the encyclopedia is extensively revised every year. Hence, the 1980 revision under review here bears a 1979 copyright date in the front of each volume, along with the statement that "volumes are published subsequent to copyright dates to contain the latest updated information," but no indication that the set was updated as recently as the spring of 1980. This policy ensures users of *Funk & Wagnalls* that they will get information current as of the copyright date or beyond, which is commendable, but, on the other hand, it is confusing when attempting to determine the actual date of the set's most recent revision. In the future, the publisher would do well to include the date of the latest printing, or updating, on the title page (or verso).

Another effort to enhance the encyclopedia's currency is the publication of *Funk & Wagnalls New Encyclopedia Yearbook,* a modestly priced annual supplement that reviews the events of the preceding year and is said to conform "to the same alphabetical arrangement and style as the encyclopedia." In the broadest sense this statement is true, but the *Yearbook* is otherwise unrelated to the encyclopedia and is therefore of limited value as an updating device. The 1980 volume (covering the events of

This Recency Table compares selected topics in *Funk & Wagnalls* with those in other encyclopedias of similar size and intended usership.

Topic	Funk & Wagnalls	Academic American	New Illustrated Columbia	New Standard
Afghanistan	Fairly current	Very current	Not current	Fairly current
Dinosaurs	Very current	Very current	Fairly current	Very current
Greenland	Not current	Very current	Fairly current	Very current
Thomas Jefferson	Fairly current	Fairly current	Fairly current	Fairly current
Mass Transportation/Subways	Fairly current	Very current	Fairly current	Fairly current
Nuclear Power	Not current	Very current	Not current	Not current
Paris	Not current	Very current	Not current	Not current
Sharks	Not current	Fairly current	Fairly current	Very current
Shock Therapy	Not current	Very current	Fairly current	Not current
Suicide	Not current	Fairly current	Not current	Very current
Tuberculosis	Fairly current	Fairly current	Fairly current	Fairly current
Zimbabwe	Very current	Very current	Not current	Very current

1979), for instance, begins with three general articles ("Defining Mexamerica," "In the Forests of the Future," and "The Year of the Child"), then offers a brief chronology of the year, followed by approximately 350 alphabetically arranged articles on standard topics (e.g., "Algeria"; "Anthropology"; "Archeology"), and concludes with a 30-page feature "Statistics of the World" and a general index. The writing tends to be lively, but most of the visual material is in black-and-white. Considering its low price ($6.98 plus $1.50 mailing costs and any sales tax) and ample coverage, the *Yearbook* is an attractive buy. Consumers should understand, however, that it does not directly update the encyclopedia.

Objectivity

The encyclopedia stresses facts, not debate of issues. In most instances, controversial material is simply ignored. EXAMPLE: The articles "Nuclear Energy" and "Nuclear Power" never once mention the worldwide controversy over the use of nuclear power. Radiation hazards are discussed, but only in terms of a waste disposal problem. EXAMPLE: The articles covering U.S. presidents Thomas Jefferson and Warren Harding do not include negative information about the private lives of the two men. In Jefferson's case, it is noted that "although he himself was a slave-owner, he proposed the emancipation of slaves," but nowhere are his black concubine and slave children mentioned. EXAMPLE: The brief, half-page article "Sex Education" concisely summarizes the purpose and content of sex education programs in the schools, but it fails to note the strong opposition to such programs in some quarters or what form the opposing arguments take. EXAMPLE: "Abortion" deals largely with medical and legal definitions, as opposed to the moral issues. The article does, however, point out that "opponents of the 1973 Supreme Court ruling, arguing for the rights of the unborn, sought to restrict its application and began a campaign for a constitutional amendment to prohibit or severely restrict abortion." As this example indicates, when polemical questions are treated, the encyclopedia is scrupulously fair. The problem is they are usually avoided.

Clarity and Reader Suitability

In keeping with its basic aim to be useful to the whole family, *Funk & Wagnalls* is clearly written in nontechnical, everyday language. The style is straightforward and normally nondescript, or flat. The article on the Olympic Games, for instance, is competently written but fails to convey a sense of the competitive zest and excitement that mark the international games. Although unfamiliar or technical terms are usually defined in context, the encyclopedia is not written to grade level, nor is it written in pyramid style (wherein articles become more complex as they progress). In most instances, the material will be understandable to those reading at the middle school level and up. A typical example of *Funk & Wagnalls'* style is found in the article "Psychiatry": "Several organic therapies, for example, have been used over the years in treating schizophrenia, either alone or in association with psychotherapy. Shock therapy consists of inducing coma by administering massive doses of insulin or inducing convulsions by application of electric shock through the brain with electrodes placed over the temples. Psychosurgery, as conventionally used, consists of cutting the nerve pathways between the frontal lobes and the lower centers of the brain. In recent years, the use of shock therapies and psychosurgery has declined, and treatment with drugs has become the most widely used organic therapy."

Arrangement and Accessibility

Funk & Wagnalls is arranged alphabetically, letter-by-letter ("Indiana" precedes "Indian Ocean"). Numerous external cross-references appear in the main A–Z sequence, such as "*Cathode Ray Tube.* See ELECTRONICS." Internal *See* and *See also* references likewise appear frequently within and at the end of many articles. The abbreviation *q.v.* (for the Latin *quod vide,* meaning "which see") is also used extensively within the body of articles to refer readers to other related entries in the set. All together, *Funk & Wagnalls* contains 80,000 cross-references by actual count. Usually the cross-reference system functions very well, but on occasion it fails. EXAMPLE: The nation of Zimbabwe, formerly Southern Rhodesia, is covered in the article "Rhodesia," but there is no cross-reference from "Zimbabwe" to "Rhodesia" (although there is one from "Southern Rhodesia" to "Rhodesia").

A detailed and accurate general index appears in the final two volumes. The index provides access to even the most specific information in the set. EXAMPLE: Readers seeking information on twins will be cross-referenced from "Twins" to "Multiple Birth," which fully describes the biological phenomenon of twinning. But only through the index will the reader learn that the article "Child Psychology" contains additional information on the subject. Note that *Funk & Wagnalls'* ratio of index entries (193,000) to total words (9 million) is excellent. By comparison, only the *Academic American Encyclopedia* has a better ratio (250,000 entries; 9 million words) in the intermediate adult class. *Funk & Wagnalls'* index could be improved, however, with the addition of more analytical references, or subentries. EXAMPLE: The index entry "Marijuana (drugs)" includes the following volume-page references: 16–24b; 8–179a, –181b; 12–153a; 16–184b; 17–120a; 19–418a; illus. 8–179. It would be helpful to users if, for instance, 12–153a were identified as dealing with hallucination, 16–184b with personality disorders, etc. But overall, *Funk & Wagnalls* is a well-arranged encyclopedia that most adults and students will find simple and easy to use.

One odd feature of the encyclopedia is that information on how to use the set is not at the very front of Volume 1 where it logically should be, but back on pages 81–84 of the book. The editors would do well to move this material forward, making it easier for readers to find when they first begin using the set.

Bibliographies

Volume 27 concludes with a 200-page bibliography printed on light blue paper. Carefully selected by some 20 librarians under the direction of Patricia Senn Breivik (director, Auraria Libraries, Denver), the 8,000 annotated titles are fairly up-to-date (but aging fast) and many are currently in print. Standard bibliographic information is provided to facilitate purchase or interlibrary loan. The titles are arranged by subject under about 150 headings, which are subdivided as necessary.

The bibliography, though useful to students and librarians alike, is open to criticism on two counts. First, only very minimal updating has occurred since 1974. For instance, the general reference section still lists *Social Sciences and Humanities Index,* when in fact it became two separate indexes some years ago. And second, the bibliographic references are not related to the encyclopedia's articles in any manner. Hence, the reader who consults any of the various articles on drugs in the set ("Drugs"; "Drugs, Addiction to"; "Heroin"; "Marijuana"; "Narcotics"; "Psychedelic Drugs") has no idea that the bibliography in the last volume lists eight titles recommended for further reading, including Brian Wells's

Psychedelic Drugs (Aronson, 1974), described as "various aspects objectively presented." A fairly detailed, two-page subject index prefaces the bibliography. Although this index is useful, a much better approach would have been to include subject references in the set's general index, as does *Collier's Encyclopedia,* which also groups its bibliographies in the final volume. For a brief discussion of the pros and cons of segregating bibliographies in a single volume, as opposed to listing them with individual articles throughout the set (as most encyclopedias do), see the *Collier's* review under "Bibliographies."

Graphics

The set's 7,500 illustrations account for about 20 percent of its total contents. An increasing number of graphics are in color (1,800; up from 1,365 in 1977), but the large majority remain in black-and-white. Unfortunately, the latter tend to be excessively dark and sometimes insufficiently detailed or clear. For instance, the photographs of moths accompanying the article "Evolution," intended to illustrate the concept of natural selection, are so poorly reproduced that their effectiveness is diminished. The preface notes that "the selection of pictures, illustrations, drawings, charts, diagrams, and maps was considered of special importance for the inclusion of information most suitably presented in pictorial and graphic terms." Although this statement is generally true, some articles that need them lack useful illustrations (e.g., "Subway"; "Sunflower"; "Surfing"; "Swastika") whereas others seem overly and perhaps unnecessarily endowed. Does the article on Shakespeare, for example, really need four full pages of color photographs (courtesy of the British Tourist Authority) when such articles as "Shadow Mountain National Recreation Area," "Shallot," "Shamanism," and "Shamrock" have none? In other instances, black-and-white reproduction is used where color obviously would have enhanced the graphic's informational value. EXAMPLE: The article on Georgia O'Keeffe, the American painter, includes a black-and-white reproduction of her *Cow's Skull: Red, White, and Blue.* On the positive side, the illustrations are all indexed in the set's general index. EXAMPLE: O'Keeffe's *Deer's Skull with Pedernale,* reproduced (in color) in the article "American Painting," is quickly and easily found through the index under "O'Keeffe, Georgia."

Among the intermediate adult encyclopedias currently on the market, *Funk & Wagnalls'* graphics are roughly comparable in number and quality to those in *The New American Encyclopedia, The New Illustrated Columbia Encyclopedia,* and *The New Standard Encyclopedia. Harver World Encyclopedia* is much superior to *Funk & Wagnalls* in this area, and the new *Academic American Encyclopedia* and British *New Caxton Encyclopedia* are visually outstanding.

Maps and gazetteer-indexes are distributed throughout the set, accompanying articles on continents, countries, U.S. states, and Canadian provinces. Prepared by C. S. Hammond & Company, the two-color maps are reasonably up-to-date and include political boundaries and place-names of any consequence. They are clearly drawn and easy to use. But physical information is lacking, and often the two-page maps bleed into the gutters, or inside margins. Small inset maps are also provided in some instances, depicting heavily populated areas in greater detail. A few historical maps appear here and there, but special-purpose maps are not abundant. At the beginning of Volume 1, some brief gazetteer-type information appears, including population data for the world's major cities, size (in square miles) of principal lakes and islands, length of the longest rivers, elevation of the highest mountains, etc. The world atlas that previously appeared in Volume 1 has been discontinued.

Physical Format

Only one binding is currently available, that being the Regency Edition bound in a maroon and gray Sturdite with black end panels and gold lettering and stamping. A distinctive FW monogram appears on the front of each volume. The volumes are not sewn but have a "perfect," or adhesive, binding. Although this type of binding will not withstand constant rugged use, it will hold up well enough under average conditions. The Sturdite binding is sold to consumers in both supermarkets and schools and libraries.

It should be noted here that *Funk & Wagnalls* employs the split-letter system of volume arrangement. Volume 1, for instance, contains the letters A–AMERI, Volume 2 AMERI–AUSTR, Volume 3 AUSTR–BLIZZ, and so on. The advantage is that each volume is approximately the same size (an important consideration in selling on the book-a-week basis). The disadvantage, however, is that in some instances the user might become confused. EXAMPLE: Volume 16 covers MAP–MOTIO and Volume 17 MOTIO–NORWE. A reader looking for material on motion pictures would presumably turn to Volume 17 (MOTIO–NORWE), where indeed the article "Motion Pictures, History of" is found. What might not be apparent to the user is that Volume 16 (MAP–MOTIO) also contains pertinent articles—"Motion Picture" and "Motion Picture Arts and Sciences, Academy of."

Inside the encyclopedia, the page layout is uninspiring. The Zenith typeface is small but legible. Because the paper is of indifferent quality, the print is occasionally smudged. Entry headings are large, dark, and bold, but in some cases subheadings are equally large, dark, and bold, thus making them practically indistinguishable from main headings. This sort of typography is not only frustrating for the reader but aesthetically unattractive. Most pages, but not all, include guide words at the top, another annoying feature. The volumes, which are light and easy to handle, lie flat when open. Considering *Funk & Wagnalls'* economy price, the set's physical construction and design are as good as can be expected. But in terms of quality alone, the set's physical format leaves much to be desired.

Special Features

Preceding the bibliography in Volume 27 (see "Bibliographies"), there are several pages devoted to "How to Use the Library" and "How to Write a Term Paper," useful features for students. Volume 1 includes several special features: "On the Origins and Purposes of Thinking," a stimulating 16-page essay by Dr. Marvin Bram of Hobart and William Smith Colleges; "World Statistics," a 6-page tabulation of population data for major world cities, elevations of principal mountains, lengths of rivers, and so on; and "Political and Social Data of the World," a 10-page country-by-country listing that gives each nation's capital city, political system, monetary unit, languages, and major religions. Following this material is the oddly placed "Guide to the Use of the *Funk & Wagnalls New Encyclopedia*" (see "Arrangement and Accessibility"). The set's outstanding special features, however, are its affordable price and supermarket method of distribution.

Sales Information

The maroon and gray Sturdite binding already described (see "Physical Format") is sold in supermarkets on the familiar book-a-week plan. As an inducement, Volume 1 is offered at only 9¢. The remaining 26 volumes sell for $2.99 each, or $77.83 for the set. Despite inflation, this price represents only a small increase over the past few years (in 1977 the total price of the set was $65.23). Also, with the purchase of Volumes 2 and 3, the customer receives the *Funk & Wagnalls Standard Desk Dictionary* (in two volumes) as a premium. It should also be pointed out that customers who miss or lose a particular volume can acquire it directly from Funk & Wagnalls, Inc. With the purchase of Volume 1, the consumer receives an owner's registration card and guarantee, stating, "Should you decide to collect the remaining volumes and then accidentally miss a Volume in the NEW ENCYCLOPEDIA series on sale at your supermarket, *we guarantee* that if you send in this card, you will be able to purchase that Volume direct from the publisher—*at the original price* plus 50¢ postage and handling. This guarantee goes into effect *immediately after* your supermarket has completed its sale of the entire encyclopedia and will continue in effect for 3 years to assure your set will be complete and perfect."

Advertising literature for *Funk & Wagnalls* is quick to point out that "as far as price is concerned, we know there is no comparable encyclopedia in existence that offers so much for so little cost. Our encyclopedia is sold through supermarkets instead of through door-to-door salesmen working on commission. So first, you save the commission. Then because we sell in great volume through these supermarkets, we can afford to charge less per volume. So you save again. The *Funk & Wagnalls New Encyclopedia* is an incredible bargain." These statements are true. High volume coupled with low markup has resulted in an encyclopedia of modestly high quality at a very low price. One nationally known consumer advocate, Herbert Denenberg, has called *Funk & Wagnalls* "dollar for dollar the best encyclopedia" (see *Caveat Emptor,* August–September 1979, p. 19). Note also that the publisher's marketing system has the added advantage of reaching many smaller communities in the more remote areas of the country that rarely, if ever, encounter a door-to-door encyclopedia sales representative.

In recent years, the Sturdite binding has also been sold directly to schools and libraries, a reflection of the set's considerable improvement in quality since 1971. Quality Books, Inc., currently handles institutional sales (see Appendix E for directory information). The school-and-library price tag of $139.50 includes three years' worth of the annual *Funk & Wagnalls New Encyclopedia Yearbook* (see "Recency"), which normally sells for $6.98 per volume. Aside from the *Yearbook,* the publisher offers no optional publications, research services, bookcases, or package deals with the purchase of the encyclopedia.

Summary

Funk & Wagnalls New Encyclopedia can be quickly summed up in this manner:

Scope: Good	Accessibility: Good
Authority: Good	Bibliographies: Fair
Reliability: Good	Graphics: Fair
Recency: Good	Physical Format: Fair
Objectivity: Good	Special Features: Few
Clarity: Good	Price: Very reasonable

To elaborate briefly, *Funk & Wagnalls* is an inexpensive, well-maintained multivolume encyclopedia in the intermediate adult category. Marketed at the retail level only through supermarkets, the set is now also distributed to educational institutions by Quality Books, Inc. The current title, first published in 1972 (copyright 1971), is a great improvement over its immediate forebear, *Funk & Wagnalls Standard Reference Encyclopedia* (1959–1971) and earlier versions of the set. Brief, factual articles on specific topics predominate, particularly in the areas of biography, geography, and the natural and technical sciences. *Funk & Wagnalls'* strongest features are its low price and relatively high degree of currency. The set's weakest features are an unappealing format, drab and poorly reproduced graphics, and aging and remote bibliographies. Overall, the encyclopedia delivers very good value for the consumer dollar.

As an adult encyclopedia, *Funk & Wagnalls* cannot compare with the largest adult sets. *The New Encyclopaedia Britannica, The Encyclopedia Americana,* and *Collier's Encyclopedia* provide a range and depth of coverage and treatment well beyond the limited capabilities of *Funk & Wagnalls.* Nor can it successfully compete with the several excellent young adult sets on the market, namely *Compton's Encyclopedia, Merit Students Encyclopedia,* and *The World Book Encyclopedia,* which are specifically and quite carefully designed for secondary student use. They provide a curriculum orientation, graduated readability, and vocabulary control that *Funk & Wagnalls* does not even attempt. But in the category of middle-sized, middle-priced adult encyclopedias, *Funk & Wagnalls* is clearly one of the two best buys, depending on how much the consumer has or wants to spend. From the standpoint of quality alone, the new *Academic American Encyclopedia* is far and away the best choice in this category. From the standpoint of price alone, *Funk & Wagnalls* is the best selection (it retails for $77.83 as opposed to $400 for the *Academic American*). In comparison with *The New Illustrated Columbia Encyclopedia,* the other major supermarket set currently being sold, *Funk & Wagnalls* has the advantage of being more up-to-date, more accessible, more readable, and better illustrated. *The New Standard Encyclopedia* compares well with *Funk & Wagnalls* in most respects, but it lacks an index and costs nearly $350. The British-made *New Caxton Encyclopedia,* although beautifully illustrated, is not as current nor as well indexed as *Funk & Wagnalls.* Also, the *New Caxton* has a natural British emphasis, and it costs a startling $599.50 plus the usual extras. The remaining two sets in the intermediate adult class—the *Harver World Encyclopedia* and *The New American Encyclopedia*—are aging relics that should be avoided at any price. In short, *Funk & Wagnalls New Encyclopedia* is unquestionably the best bargain among the middle-sized, middle-priced adult encyclopedias currently on the market. In terms of quality alone, however, it cannot begin to match the new *Academic American Encyclopedia.*

Other Critical Opinions

Booklist, January 15, 1979, pp. 830–832. Part of a series of reviews by the ALA Reference and Subscription Books Review Committee (RSBRC) entitled "Encyclopedias: A Survey and Buying Guide," this evaluation of *Funk & Wagnalls* (1975 edition) comes to no real conclusions about the encyclopedia. In its last regular review of *Funk & Wagnalls* (*Booklist,* January 15, 1975, pp. 512–515), RSBRC "recommended" the set to consumers and educational institutions "with limited budgets."

Katz, William A. *Basic Information Sources* (Vol. 1 of *Introduction to Reference Work,* 3rd ed., New York: McGraw-Hill, 1978), pp. 162–163. Katz, a professor of reference service, agrees with most critics that *Funk & Wagnalls* is a good buy "for the family with budget problems." He does not recommend the set for libraries, however.

Littlefield, Janet H. *American Reference Books Annual,* 1980, pp. 28–29. This reviewer notes that *Funk & Wagnalls* "proves to be a pleasant exception to the stereotype of the supermarket encyclopedia," and that the set is best suited for the "budget-conscious" consumer.

Harver World Encyclopedia

Facts in Brief

Full Title: **Harver World Encyclopedia: Alphabetical Encyclopedia in 20 Volumes.** *Editor:* Martin Self, Editor in Chief. *Publisher:* Harver Educational Services, Inc., New York; also copyright by Elsevier International Projects, Ltd., London, England. *Distributor:* Marshall Cavendish, 147 W. Merrick Rd., Freeport NY 11520. *Edition Reviewed:* Second Edition, 1975 copyright.

Volumes: 20. *Pages:* 5,855. *Articles:* 20,000. *Words:* 7,500,000. *Illustrations:* 16,000. *Maps:* 470. *Index Entries:* None. *Cross-references:* 30,000. *Contributors:* 135.

User Classification: Adult (Multivolume). *Reader Suitability:* Age 12 through General Adult. *Physical Size:* 8½ × 11 in.; 28 cm. *LC:* 74-21700. *ISBN:* 0-88346-050-5. *Lowest Retail Price:* Not sold at retail; to schools & libraries $375.50.

Purpose and Scope

The *Harver World Encyclopedia,* an entirely new general encyclopedia first issued in 1973, is said to be "new and modern in every sense." The preface cites two basic aims: "to provide the most up-to-date reference information that a family might require, lavishly illustrated, and to link that information together so that the entire set may serve as a kind of system of knowledge." Moreover, *Harver World* "is designed primarily as a reference book to supply answers to specific questions." Its facts are "accurate and concise," thus enabling the reader to "avoid the clumsiness of the larger encyclopedias that require you to read thousands of words before you find what you want." The writers of the preface make it sound as if *Harver World* is the first or the only encyclopedia to stress specific facts briefly presented in specific entries. But, of course, as the history of encyclopedias shows, this is not the case.

Harver World's articles are indeed quite specific and usually brief. Some are no more than two or three sentences long, and the average article comprises only about 200 words, or a third of a page. EXAMPLES: The articles "O" (the letter of the alphabet), "Oahu," "Oak," and "Oakland" (the city in California) are covered on one page. The following page covers seven short articles ("Oakley, Annie"; "Oak Ridge"; "Oakum"; "Oarfish"; "Oasis"; "Oates, Titus"; "Oats"), and the next page includes ten articles ("Oaxaca"; "Obadiah, Book of"; "Obelisk"; "Oberammergau"; "Oberhausen"; "Oberth, Hermann"; "Obesity"; "Oboe"; "Obregon, Alvaro"; "Ob River"). Major topics receive more space, however. The article "Ocean," for instance, comprises two pages. Typically, the article includes a color illustration, a shaded information box called "Facts about the Ocean," a chart indicating oceanic depths, and a marginal note of about 150 words that offers interesting snippets of information on the subject, in this case on sea serpents. Approximately 2,000 of the set's 20,000 articles are in the form of marginal notes similar to the one with "Ocean."

The preface states that *Harver World*'s emphasis is "on science, technology, history, religion, geography and the events, movements and personalities of the modern world." This description fairly accurately summarizes the set's subject strengths. Biographical and geographical topics predominate, with approximately 70 percent of the total written text devoted to people and places. Biographical entries include persons both living and dead. Examples of contemporary personalities covered, albeit very briefly, are Arthur Ashe, Leonard Bernstein, Stokely Carmichael (his first name is incorrectly given as "Stokeley"), Wilt Chamberlain, Charlie Chaplin, Maurice Chevalier, Noam Chomsky, Agatha Christie, John Kenneth Galbraith, Jacob Javits, Martin Luther King, Henry Kissinger, Jack Nicklaus, Birgit Nilsson, Floyd Patterson, Shirley Temple, and Kurt Vonnegut, Jr. But because the set has not been revised since 1975, readers will not find information about newer faces like Jimmy Carter, Ronald Reagan, Ayatollah Khomeini, Margaret Thatcher, Pope John Paul II, Alexander Haig, and Reggie Jackson. Biographical coverage is international, although Americans, Britons, and Europeans receive the most attention, in that order. Especially useful to students interested in science are the many biographies (albeit usually very brief ones) of engineers, chemists, physicists, mathematicians, biologists, and physicians.

Major countries and continents are accorded more than average space. EXAMPLES: "Africa" receives 19 pages, including two full-page maps (one political, the other showing vegetation distribution) and many illustrations. "Canada" is covered in over 12 pages. The article includes a shaded information box entitled "Canada at a Glance" (all countries have such boxes), a full-page map of the country, a color reproduction of the Canadian flag, several marginal notes, and numerous photographs. Smaller or less prominent nations receive proportionately less coverage. EXAMPLE: "Afghanistan" is accorded four pages, including the usual "Afghanistan at a Glance" box, color reproduction of the country's flag (which is now out-of-date), and photographs. Major world cities and natural features are also covered; for instance, the article on Paris is two pages in length, Philadelphia a page and a half, the Himalayas a single page. As might be expected, the U.S. states and Canadian provinces receive relatively generous attention. EXAMPLE: "Florida," a six-page article, provides a general survey of the state's land, climate, people, economy, education, government, and history. A full-page political map, a county locator map, a color reproduction of the state flag, and the customary illustrations accompany the printed text. Secondary place-names, such as smaller U.S. and Canadian cities, are covered very briefly, if at all. EXAMPLES: Miami and Jacksonville (the largest cities in Florida) receive several paragraphs, or about 200 words each. Tampa and St. Petersburg receive about half that coverage, and places like Orlando and Key West are not covered at all. Secondary place-names throughout the rest of the world receive little if any attention.

Subject coverage in *Harver World* is not well balanced. Scientific and technical topics—plants, animals, chemical elements, theories, diseases, and the various fields of study—are stressed. In some instances, articles in the area of science and technology are substantial. "Nuclear Energy," for example, runs to three pages. "Nuclear Reactor" covers half a page, "Nucleic Acids" the same, and "Number" nearly a whole page. Such articles tend to be tightly written and well illustrated. Ordinarily, however, coverage of the natural and physical sciences is exceedingly brief and often superficial, sometimes providing less information than a good one-volume encyclopedia. EXAMPLE: The 17-line article "Hydrochloric Acid" includes a succinct definition of the solution but practically nothing about its history, present-day manufacture, or acid concentrations. By way of comparison, the one-volume *New Columbia Encyclopedia* offers considerably more information, and *The Random House Encyclopedia*, also a small-volume work, puts the topic into better perspective, chemically speaking. Coverage of the social and behavioral sciences also suffers from excessive brevity, and in certain instances important topics (e.g., cults) are not covered at all. Coverage of the arts and humanities is particularly weak. Fewer entries are devoted to this general area than the others, and although some major topics like architecture and sculpture receive substantial articles, others such as the dance, drama, jazz, opera, painting, and most aspects of the decorative and graphic arts receive short shrift. Contemporary artists are often ignored. EXAMPLES: Balthus (pseudonym of Count Balthazar Klossowski), Giorgio de Chirico, Jim Dine, R. B. Kitaj, Georgia O'Keeffe, Alexander Rodchenko, and Clyfford Still are not found in *Harver World*. Hobbies also receive indifferent coverage. The encyclopedia lacks entries, for example, for gardening, leather work, models or model building, needlework, or sewing (although "Sewing Machine" is included).

Augmenting the approximately 20,000 encyclopedic articles in *Harver World* is a strange creation called the "Instant Reference Supplement." Appended to each volume in the set, the supplement is in fact nothing more than an antiquated British-made general dictionary—the *Universal Dictionary of the English Language* (edited by Henry Cecil Wyld and Eric Partridge, 1934)—which has been split into 20 parts to correspond with the number of volumes in the encyclopedia, and jazzed up with some contemporary illustrations (which accounts for the 1975 copyright). The dictionary's letter division roughly corresponds with that of the encyclopedia. EXAMPLE: Volume 1 of the encyclopedia covers the letters A—ANI, whereas the dictionary portion at the end of the volume covers A–ARM. (Both sets of letters appear on the spine of the volume, a potential source of confusion for users; see "Physical Format.") The publisher claims that the Instant Reference Supplement expands the encyclopedia's scope by "no less than 285,000 additional 'quick' entries, words, and technical and scientific terms." Literally this statement is true, but in the broadest sense the supplement adds little if anything to *Harver World*'s value as a reference source claiming to be "new and modern in every sense." Indeed, in some cases the supplement is an informational liability (see "Objectivity"). The supplement does, however, add approximately three million words and 4,000 illustrations to the encyclopedia's statistical profile (see "Facts in Brief"). The so-called Instant Reference Supplement, which was added to the set with this edition, is further discussed under "Recency," "Arrangement and Accessibility," and "Special Features."

History and Authority

Harver World was conceived as a completely new adult encyclopedia in 1969 and was first published in mid-1973. The set was produced abroad by the Elsevier Company of Amsterdam exclusively for an American audience. Elsevier has long been known throughout the world for its outstanding reference publications in many languages. Although *Harver World*'s text is original, some of the graphics have been reprinted from other Elsevier encyclopedias, such as the *Grote Winkler Prins Encyclopedie* and the *Visum Encyclopedia,* both well known to European readers. The encyclopedia was commissioned by the U.S. publisher, Harver Educational Services, Inc., originally of New York City. Harver Educational has no standing among U.S. encyclopedia publishers, and appears at present to be out of business. *Harver World* is currently distributed to schools and libraries by Marshall Cavendish, a well-known purveyor of large reference sets, mostly of a specialized variety, to educational institutions. Other independent encyclopedia distributors may also offer *Harver World* to institutional buyers. Maxwell Scientific International division of Pergamon Press, for instance, recently listed the encyclopedia in a catalog for librarians.

Harver World last appeared in 1975 in its second edition, which is under review here. The set was originally edited by Martin Self, formerly a senior editor at Encyclopaedia Britannica, Inc. Self, however, has long since disassociated himself from the work and the original publisher. *Harver World* lists an editorial and production staff of 34, including seven advisory editors, most of whom are respected authorities in their areas of specialization, such as Ian Ridpath (astronomy and space science). In addition, 135 contributors and advisers are indicated in the front of Volume 1. The qualifications of the staff and contributors are not provided, nor do their names appear in standard biographical reference sources. Most of these people are apparently British (Alan Blackwood, David Clutterbuck, Judith Cooke-Simmons, Colin P. L. Groves, et al.), but beyond this supposition nothing is known about them. As might be expected, all articles are unsigned. Overall, the set's authority is weak.

Reliability

Harver World is not entirely reliable. Factual errors, misspellings, and the like, occur just frequently enough to cast a shadow over the set's general dependability. EXAMPLE: The article "Florida" states that "the Governor serves a four-year term but may not directly succeed himself." Florida's governor does serve a four-year term, but under the provisions of the state's present constitution (revised in 1968), the governor may indeed serve two consecutive terms. The same article says that the state's county commissioners and administrative officials are elected. The statement is only partially correct, as most administrative officials are appointed, not elected. EXAMPLE: "Eritrea" gives the Ethiopian province's population as 1.5 million. In fact, Eritrea's current population is 3.5 million. EXAMPLE: "Indians, North American" cites the U.S. Supreme Court case *Worcestor* v. *Georgia [sic]*, misspelling *Worcester*. EXAMPLE: The short article "Sharks" contains at least three factual errors, including the length of the white shark. In many other instances, out-of-date information renders the encyclopedia unreliable. The color flag with "Afghanistan," for instance, has been superseded by a new flag. The article "Atomic Energy Commission" incorrectly informs that the commission is "responsible for controlling and supervising the production and use of atomic energy in the United States." In fact, the Atomic Energy Commission no longer exists, having been abolished in 1974. The longer *Harver World* goes without being revised, the more unreliable it will become (see "Recency").

Recency

The encyclopedia has not been revised at all since 1975 and obviously is no longer "admirably up-to-date," as reported in an earlier edition of the *Buying Guide.* The set's preface notes that "very few encyclopedias take you right up to the present in all areas—not just in a few articles that have been updated for the sake of appearances," and indeed in 1975 *Harver World* was as contemporary in coverage, treatment, and outlook as a general encyclopedia could possibly be. But, although the set is not yet grossly dated, its lack of currency is now quite apparent. EXAMPLES: According to *Harver World*, Hannah Arendt is still alive (she died in 1975), Saul Bellow has not won the Nobel Prize for literature (which he did in 1976), Benjamin Britten is neither dead nor titled (he received a life peerage before he died in 1976), Mao is still running China, Gerald Ford is the U.S. president, Pope John Paul II does not exist, nuclear power is the wave of the future, and the Afghan "government's growing awareness that massive aid from any great power may tend to restrict its independence and affect its neutrality has recently led to some reduction in the dependence on foreign assistance."

If *Harver World* were continuously revised (as are all multivolume sets of any consequence), such omissions and obsolete facts and impressions would be systematically updated each year. But the set's revision program has always been vague. In 1975, the publisher informed the *Buying Guide*

This Recency Table compares selected topics in *Harver World* with those in other encyclopedias of similar size and intended usership.

Topic	Harver World	Academic American	Funk & Wagnalls	New Caxton
Afghanistan	Not current	Very current	Fairly current	Fairly current
Dinosaurs	Fairly current	Very current	Very current	Fairly current
Greenland	Not current	Very current	Not current	Not current
Thomas Jefferson	Not current	Fairly current	Fairly current	Not current
Mass Transportation/Subways	Fairly current	Very current	Fairly current	Very current
Nuclear Power	Not current	Very current	Not current	Fairly current
Paris	Not current	Very current	Not current	Very current
Sharks	Fairly current	Fairly current	Not current	Fairly current
Shock Therapy	Not current	Very current	Not current	Fairly current
Suicide	Not current	Fairly current	Not current	Not current
Tuberculosis	Fairly current	Fairly current	Fairly current	Fairly current
Zimbabwe	Not current	Very current	Very current	Very current

that the set would be revised "with each major printing" but failed to indicate how frequently major printings might occur. At the same time, the publisher also indicated that an "annual updating yearbook is now being planned and will be available in 1976." Thus far such a yearbook has yet to appear. Note also that the so-called Instant Reference Supplement (see "Purpose and Scope") is well over 40 years old, being nothing more than a dictionary published in 1934. It seems clear that those who currently own the rights to *Harver World* either lack the will or the resources, or both, to maintain the set adequately.

Objectivity

Articles on controversial or sensitive subjects are usually unbiased. The emphasis is on facts, not opinion. For instance, treatment of sexual matters (e.g., "Abortion," "Birth Control," "Homosexuality," and "Reproduction") are straightforward and objective. The same is true of such diverse but polemical articles as "Drug Abuse," "Suicide," and "Women's Liberation Movement." Once in a while, however, editorial lapses occur. EXAMPLE: The article "Oswald, Lee Harvey" describes the subject as the "left-wing assassin of President John F. Kennedy." Actually, at this time Oswald's political affiliations are open to debate. More often the encyclopedia simply ignores controversial matters. EXAMPLES: The article "Evolution" states that "today the publication of the *Origin of Species* is regarded as a turning point in scientific thought, although at the time its ideas met with great resistance from both the Church and the public," but nowhere are the objections to the book or the ideas contained therein identified. Likewise, there is no indication that resistance to Darwinism continues to this day, or what form that resistance takes. The articles on presidents Thomas Jefferson and Warren Harding fail to mention unwelcome information about their personal lives, such as Harding's illegitimate child or Jefferson's black concubine. The article "Nuclear Energy" makes no mention of the growing political opposition to nuclear power (although this might be due more to the encyclopedia's lack of recency than any effort to gloss over the current controversy).

Clarity and Reader Suitability

The preface states that the encyclopedia is written in "everyday language," and that an effort has been made to "translate the specialists' jargon into a form intelligible to the average person." Here *Harver World* succeeds quite well. The writing style is almost always clear and to the point. Students with average reading abilities at the junior high or middle school level and up will have little difficulty understanding the text. When difficult or technical terms are used, they often appear in italics and are defined in the text. EXAMPLE: The article "Psychiatry," in a discussion of various medical treatments of mental illness, explains that "*sleep therapy*, in which the patient is kept asleep for long periods by the administration of a sedative drug, is effective only in that it tends to shorten the duration of manic-depressive attacks. *Hydrotherapy*, or the use of prolonged warm baths, has been found useful in controlling noisy, overactive patients. *Physiotherapy* (including heat and massage) also has a tonic and relaxing effect; and *occupational therapy* is now an important part of treatment of hospitalized patients. It distracts, stimulates and maintains contact with reality, as do planned recreation and social activities." This example also serves as a representative guide to the encyclopedia's overall writing style.

Advertisements for *Harver World* in the past have claimed that "care has been exercised . . . to correlate the subject material with current school curricula." No such claim, however, is made in the preface and there is no evidence whatsoever that the encyclopedia's topic selection and coverage were influenced by present-day school curricula, nor are its contents organized along curriculum lines. *Harver World* aims to be a source of quick factual information for both students and adults. It cannot compare, however, with such young adult sets as *Compton's Encyclopedia* and *The World Book Encyclopedia,* which are curriculum oriented, vocabulary controlled, written to grade level, and written in the so-called pyramid (simple to complex) style. On the other hand, *Harver World*'s style and readability are very similar to those of its major competitors, namely the *Academic American Encyclopedia, Funk & Wagnalls New*

Encyclopedia, The New Caxton Encyclopedia, and *The New Standard Encyclopedia.*

Arrangement and Accessibility

Harver World is arranged alphabetically, letter-by-letter ("Indiana" precedes "Indian Ocean"). An estimated 30,000 cross-references appear throughout the set. Many external *See* references are included among the main entries in the A–Z sequence (e.g., "*Handicapped.* See REHABILITA-TION"). But the large majority appear as internal *See* and *See also* references within or at the end of articles. Many of the internal references are printed in SMALL CAPITAL LETTERS. EXAMPLE: In the article "Diabetes," the reader is referred to a related topic in this manner: "Diabetes insipidus occurs when the PITUITARY GLAND fails to produce enough of a hormone called *anti-diuretic hormone,* or ADH." Note, however, that *Harver World* lacks a general index.

The preface extols the set's accessibility, citing the cross-references as "the marvellously complex web that links different pieces of knowledge together." The cross-references are indeed adequate, but they cannot and do not replace the need for a detailed analytical index. An encyclopedia the size of *Harver World,* to be fully accessible to the user, requires *both* cross-references and a detailed index. For instance, the topic phenomenology is discussed in the article "Existentialism," but the user seeking information about phenomenology does not know that because (1) there is no *See* reference in the A–Z listing from "Phenomenology" to "Existentialism" and (2) there is no general index to point the user to the "Existentialism" article. Significantly, the publisher is aware of the need for an index. In 1973, Harver Educational reported that an index of some 80,000 entries was in preparation. In 1974, 1975, and 1976, it was again reported that the long-awaited index volume would be forthcoming shortly. Like the promised yearbook (see "Recency"), the index has never appeared. And until such time as an index does appear and can be properly evaluated, *Harver World* remains an incomplete encyclopedia that fails to provide adequate access to its contents.

The so-called Instant Reference Supplement (see "Purpose and Scope") is in no way connected to the rest of the encyclopedia. Specifically, there are no cross-references linking the encyclopedic contents of *Harver World* with those of the supplement, which is actually a dictionary. In fact, many contemporary words used in the encyclopedia (e.g., *antihero*) do not appear in the dictionary supplement. This lack of any connection between these two distinct parts further diminishes any value the Instant Reference Supplement might have.

Bibliographies

None. In the past the publisher has stated that bibliographies will be included in the index volume said to be in preparation. But until that volume appears (and chances of that now seem remote), *Harver World*'s lack of bibliographies constitutes a serious weakness in the set.

Graphics

The set's illustrations are its best feature. Many of them have been drawn from two heavily illustrated Dutch encyclopedias, *Grote Winkler Prins* and the popular *Visum Encyclopedia*. Although neither as plentiful nor as handsomely reproduced as those found in the new *Academic American Encyclopedia* or the British *New Caxton Encyclopedia*, *Harver World*'s graphics justify the publisher's claim that "the many thousands of beautiful color illustrations are not merely decorations. They fulfill a function of their own in clarifying the ideas and description in the text. . . . The color photographs which accompany entries in history, geography, art and zoology have been carefully chosen to highlight the entries and add to the text" (preface). In point of fact, visual matter accounts for an estimated 35 percent of the encyclopedia's total text. Approximately 9,000 (or 75 percent) of the 16,000 illustrations are in full color. They are sometimes rather small (particularly those in the Instant Reference Supplement), but always clear and complementary to the printed text. The diagrams with articles on technical subjects are especially valuable. EXAMPLE: The article "Nuclear Energy" includes an informative cutaway drawing of a nuclear reactor.

Nearly 500 maps are included in the set. Of these about 130 are full-page in four-color. The maps are mainly political and physical, indicating prominent place-names, boundaries, and natural features. Also, some historical and distribution maps accompany articles on the major countries and important geographical topics, but more often than not needed special-purpose maps are lacking. EXAMPLE: The article "Indians, North American" contains no maps, historical or otherwise. Except for a few produced by staff cartographers, the maps originally appeared in various atlases published by Elsevier, internationally known for its cartographic excellence. The maps are deficient, however, in several respects. They are not indexed. They sometimes bleed off the page. And some countries have no maps. EXAMPLE: The article "Argentina" lacks a map of the country. The only map of Argentina in *Harver World* is found in "South America." A map of the continent is hardly adequate for a country as large and important as Argentina. Moreover, there is no cross-reference from "Argentina" to "South America."

Physical Format

Harver World is an attractively designed work. The preface suggests that an encyclopedia should be "not only a source of knowledge but an advertisement for knowledge." *Harver World* accomplishes this through an appealing dark blue buckram binding with gold lettering, a colorful and inviting two-column page layout that makes creative use of the wide margin space (see "Special Features"), and use of pleasing modern typefaces. The binding, however, is not sturdy and may crack under normal use. Called "perfect" binding, it is not sewn but held together by adhesive applied to the inside of the spine. Guide words appear at the top of most pages; the volumes, though tightly bound, lie fairly flat when open.

Aside from the inferior perfect binding, the only complaint about the set's format concerns the letter division. In order to make the volumes uniform in size, the letters are arbitrarily split so that they sometimes overlap. In some instances, the user does not know which volume to consult. EXAMPLE: Volume 8 covers ELE–FOR and Volume 9 FOR–GRA. The reader looking for the entry on Gerald Ford, for instance, might have to look in both volumes. Another problem with the letter division concerns the Instant Reference Supplement. Its letter divisions, which differ from those for the general encyclopedia, are printed on the spine of each volume directly below those for the encyclopedia; for example, Volume 8 has two sets of letters on its spine: ELE–FOR and ENR–FOX. This procedure will confuse many users.

Special Features

Some 2,000 boxed notes or "informative capsules" appear throughout the set in the wide outer margins. Printed in colored boxes, these informational snippets include interesting or useful facts on various topics. The preface refers to them as "unique," but other encyclopedias, including *The New Caxton Encyclopedia* and the *Young Students Encyclopedia*, use a similar information box technique. In *Harver World*, these information capsules or nuggets (as *Young Students* calls them) appear to be more for aesthetic than informational purposes.

The encyclopedia's other special feature is the curious Instant Reference Supplement. As already explained (see "Purpose and Scope"), the supplement is actually a 1934 general dictionary of British origin entitled *Universal Dictionary of the English Language*. The dictionary, which contains 285,000 entries and three million words, has been divided into 20 equal parts and appended to the encyclopedia. In 1975, the publisher reported that the Instant Reference Supplement was attracting "a great deal of attention." Little wonder. Exactly why anyone would tack an outdated dictionary onto an encyclopedia that claims to be thoroughly up-to-date and "modern in every sense" is a puzzlement. The supplement's chief value appears to be to inflate the encyclopedia's statistical profile (see "Facts in Brief").

Sales Information

Harver World is currently available to schools and libraries in the blue and gold binding already described (see "Physical Format") from Marshall Cavendish, a distributor of large reference sets to educational institutions. The school-and-library price is $375.50, plus $8 shipping and handling. This price is extremely high for an encyclopedia of *Harver World*'s size and quality. Consumers should be aware that *Harver World* might also be distributed by firms or representatives other than Marshall Cavendish. Pergamon Press, for instance, recently listed the set in a catalog for the library trade. It is the *Buying Guide*'s understanding that *Harver World* is not available at retail at the present time. This situation may change, of course, at any time in the future.

Summary

The *Harver World Encyclopedia* (1975 edition) can be quickly summed up in this manner:

Scope: Fair	Accessibility: Poor
Authority: Poor	Bibliographies: Poor (none)
Reliability: Fair	Graphics: Good
Recency: Poor	Physical Format: Fair
Objectivity: Good	Special Features: Few
Clarity: Excellent	Price: High

To elaborate briefly, *Harver World* is an intermediate adult work intended to be "a really useful family encyclopedia" (preface). First published in 1973 and issued in a second revised edition in 1975 by the U.S. firm Harver Educational Services, Inc., of New York, the set was actually produced by the internationally famous Elsevier Company of Amsterdam, London, and other major world cities. Although it was made in London and printed in the Netherlands, *Harver World* is intended primarily for a North American audience. The brief, factual articles emphasize biographical and geographical topics, along with contemporary social issues and general scientific and technical subjects. Unfortunately, the coverage sometimes suffers from excessive brevity (articles average only 200 words in length), and many topics in the social sciences and humanities are either inadequately covered or ignored altogether. Although clearly written and abundantly illustrated, *Harver World* is not always reliable, the contents are now quite dated, and access to the material is limited due to the lack of an index. Moreover, the set lacks bibliographies, is poorly bound, and has an outdated and practically worthless dictionary supplement. In sum, *Harver World* is an inferior encyclopedia, priced much too high for what it delivers.

Obviously, *Harver World* cannot successfully compete with the large comprehensive adult sets, namely *Collier's Encyclopedia, The Encyclopedia Americana,* and *The New Encyclopaedia Britannica*. It simply lacks the range and depth of coverage provided by these sets. On the other hand, it does have some features that might make the set attractive to young adults. Its good illustrations and visually appealing format, plus its brevity and general readability, are characteristics of the better young adult encyclopedias, like *Compton's Encyclopedia, Merit Students Encyclopedia,* and *The World Book Encyclopedia*. All things considered, however, *Harver World* cannot be preferred over any of the fine young adult sets, all of which possess indexes, have useful bibliographies and maps, and are curriculum oriented and vocabulary controlled.

In the intermediate adult category, *Harver World* is completely outclassed by the new *Academic American Encyclopedia,* which is superior in every respect. *Funk & Wagnalls New Encyclopedia* is also preferable to *Harver World* on all counts, except visual appeal. Likewise, *Harver World* suffers in comparison with the British-made *New Caxton Encyclopedia,* except in terms of price and, for U.S. and Canadian readers, audience suitability. *The New Standard Encyclopedia* offers bibliographies and is more current and reliable than *Harver World,* although both sets lack an index and fine graphics. *The New Illustrated Columbia Encyclopedia,* which has a somewhat more advanced reading level, also lacks an index, currency, and quality illustrations, but it is more reliable and much less expensive than *Harver World.* Indeed, the only set in the middle-sized adult class that *Harver World* clearly outranks is *The New American Encyclopedia,* an inferior work of little value.

Other Critical Opinions

Booklist, April 1, 1974, pp. 830–835. This unsigned review by the ALA Reference and Subscription Books Review Committee evaluates the first edition of *Harver World* (1973). The review criticizes the encyclopedia's uneven coverage, uncertain authority, and lack of bibliographies and an index. No final recommendation is offered, and the second edition (1975) has never been reviewed by this group.

New American Encyclopedia

Facts in Brief

Full Title: **The New American Encyclopedia: A Treasury of Information on the Sciences, the Arts, Literature, and General Knowledge.** *Editors:* John B. Phelps, Editor in Chief; Leonard Klingsberg, Managing Director. *Publisher:* The Publishers Agency, Inc., 3399 Forrest Rd., Cornwells Heights, PA 19020. *Distributor:* The Webster Publishing Company, Ltd., 1644 Bayview Ave., Toronto, Ontario M4G 3C2 Canada. *Former Titles: Standard International Encyclopedia* (2-volume abridged ed., 1970–1973); *World Educator Encyclopedia* (1964–1972); *World University Encyclopedia* (1964–1972); *World Scope Encyclopedia* (1945–1963); *New World Family Encyclopedia* (1953–1957); *Standard International Encyclopedia* (1953–1957). *Edition Reviewed:* Unabridged Edition, 1973 copyright (1974 printing).

Volumes: 20. *Pages:* 7,570. *Articles:* 27,000. *Words:* 5,500,000. *Illustrations:* 9,000. *Maps:* 420. *Index Entries:* None. *Cross-references:* 6,000. *Contributors:* 500.

User Classification: Adult (Multivolume). *Reader Suitability:* Age 12 through General Adult. *Physical Size:* 6½ × 9½ in.; 24 cm. *LC:* 72-86722. *ISBN:* 0-87781-235-7. *Lowest Retail Price:* $133.

Purpose and Scope

The New American Encyclopedia claims to cover "the range of accumulated human knowledge as it is of interest to both the student and the adult" (foreword). The publisher's foreword further notes that "in scope and utility it [the encyclopedia] aims to lead rather than follow previous encyclopedias; it makes available to the reader, for example, numerous articles filled with *practical* information, carefully selected and written for the entire family." It is also claimed that the set will "provide the educational advantage needed for today's student, from grade school to college, to compete in this increasingly technological world."

These statements considerably exaggerate *New American*'s worth as a general encyclopedia. Like most of the other intermediate adult encyclopedias currently on the market (such as *Funk & Wagnalls New Encyclopedia, The New Illustrated Columbia Encyclopedia, The New Standard Encyclopedia,* and *Harver World Encyclopedia*), the majority of the set's entries are devoted to biographical and geographical topics. Coverage is normally quite brief and often sketchy, limited to basic factual information with little or no historical or interpretative content. Articles average approximately a quarter of a page (or 175 words) in length. Many are much shorter, sometimes only a paragraph or two long. Major places such as countries and continents receive more extensive coverage. EXAMPLES: "Africa" is a 19-page article that includes numerous photographs (many in color), a one-page political map, and a lengthy bibliography. "China" is accorded 24 pages, again including many graphics and a sizable bibliography. The article, however, contains only a spot map of the country, although the caption notes that a "detailed map of China and its neighboring countries is included with the entry Japan." "Afghanistan," seven pages in length, offers the usual illustrative material and bibliography, but only a spot map. As in other articles on countries, the Afghan flag is described rather than pictured. Important historical personages also receive better than average coverage. EXAMPLES: Winston Churchill is accorded a page and a half, whereas Queen Elizabeth I is covered in about a page. Sir Francis Drake, of lesser importance historically, receives the average quarter of a page. Thomas Jefferson, one of the United States' more illustrious presidents, is covered in a page, whereas Warren Harding receives half a page. The late Justice William O. Douglas, on the other hand, is dispensed with in 11 lines (or about 120 words). The shorter articles tend to be of little value, except for vital statistics. The piece on Harding, for instance, fails to note that he died in office and Calvin Coolidge was his successor.

Again, like most of the other intermediate adult sets (including the new *Academic American Encyclopedia*), *New American* emphasizes scientific and technical subjects. The encyclopedia's dedication—to "the youth of the world"—stresses *New American*'s desire to be "the most up-to-date encyclopedia on the market—especially in the areas of science, math, and world events." Coverage of these knowledge areas is relatively comprehensive, but treatment tends to be overly brief and frequently superficial. EXAMPLE: The article "Semiconductor" is only a fourth of a page long and fails even to mention various electronic devices like integrated circuits made possible by semiconductors. EXAMPLE: "Oceans and Oceanography" is disappointingly brief and incomplete. The two-page article contains many facts, but the presentation is disjointed and choppy. EXAMPLE: "Nuclear Energy," covered in only half a page, is woefully inadequate. Current social trends are also emphasized. The foreword states that *New American* devotes more space "proportionately . . . to minority groups—their biographies, achievements, status and role in our society—than is found in other encyclopedias." This might be true. There are lengthy articles on anti-Semitism, black history and accomplishments, civil rights, and segregation. Nothing apparently is included on Mexican-Americans or Chicanos, but Cesar Chavez receives a page-long article. The arts and humanities receive proportionately less attention, and the treatment is usually very cursory.

Practical subjects like gardening and cookery are covered, but the articles are often too cursory or dated to be of much practical use. For instance, the foreword notes that "helpful articles have been prepared on a multitude of topics of great importance to the family," and cites plumbing as an example. The article "Plumbing," however, consists of two short paragraphs that inform the reader that plumbing "includes the pipes, fittings, connections, regulators, together with all the usage-hardware such as washbowls, showers, toilets, bidets, sinks, laundry tubs, and outlets." The remaining few words of the article are equally "helpful" to the person seeking practical information about plumbing. On the other hand, sometimes articles on practical topics are excessively long. "First Aid," for example, comprises 37 pages of text. Any encyclopedia that disposes of subjects like nuclear energy, Thomas Jefferson, and plumbing in a page or less but lavishes 37 pages on first aid cannot be said to possess balanced coverage. Perhaps *New American*'s curious approach to subject coverage stems from the fact that the 1973 edition (under review here) attempts to imitate the contents of seven competing sets (see "History and Authority" for more on this subject).

History and Authority

New American has a complex and at times perplexing history. Its oldest known ancestor appears to be the *Teacher's and Pupil's Cyclopaedia*, a four-volume work published in 1902. The work was expanded and retitled the *New Teacher's and Pupil's Cyclopaedia* in 1910. Later, in 1928, it became the ten-volume *Progressive Reference Library*, which in turn became the *World Scope Encyclopedia* in 1945. *World Scope* continued in existence until 1963, but in the interim it appeared under the titles *New World Family Encyclopedia* and *Standard International Encyclopedia*, both supermarket items.

In 1964, *World Scope* was acquired by Publishers Company, Inc., now the Publishers Agency, Inc. With practically no revision, *World Scope* was immediately retitled and sold variously as *The New American Encyclopedia*, the *World Educator Encyclopedia*, and the *World University Encyclopedia*. A two-volume abridgment also appeared under the old supermarket title *Standard International Encyclopedia*. All of these variant titles appear to be defunct, save *The New American Encyclopedia*. (For further information about the recently discontinued titles, see Appendix A.)

In 1968 the Publishers Company decided to concentrate its efforts on improving *New American*, so that it might be competitive with such better known and more highly regarded sets as *Compton's Encyclopedia*, *The World Book Encyclopedia*, and the now departed *American Peoples Encyclopedia* (see Appendix A). In an attempt to expand the set's coverage and provide better subject balance, the editors undertook an analysis of seven competing encyclopedias. If at least four of the seven covered a topic, it was automatically included in the new and expanded edition of *New American* that appeared in 1973. It is that set which is under review here.

The 1973 edition (1974 printing) of *New American* is indeed a much-improved encyclopedia over its various disreputable ancestors. Although some material that previously appeared in the pre-1973 editions has been retained, the present revision represents an almost entirely new work. The set is copyrighted by the New American Corporation, S.A., Brussels, Belgium (1973), and is printed by the firm of Arnoldo Mondadori Editore in Verona, Italy. The editor is John B. Phelps and Leonard Klingsberg is listed as publisher and managing director. Neither person has any standing among U.S. encyclopedia editors, nor is either man known to the *Buying Guide.* Phelps, however, is listed in the front matter of the encyclopedia as being a physicist and having a Ph.D. The editorial staff listed in Volume 1 numbers over 100, ranging from the editor in chief to six proofreaders. The publisher claims 500 contributors, but only 353 are included in the "partial list of contributors, consultants and sources of information" printed in the initial volume. Overall, the contributors are undistinguished. Also, many of them are either dead or retired. Their qualifications are indicated, but frequently they no longer hold the positions attributed to them. For instance, Dorothy Dodd is not the state librarian of Florida, nor has she been for many years. There is no indication of which articles the contributors wrote, nor are the articles themselves signed. It would appear that most of the text of the 1973 edition was staff written.

It should also be noted here that both the publisher and the current distributor of *New American* are held in questionable regard by the reference book community. The publisher has produced reference works of indifferent quality, and the Webster Publishing Company, Ltd., the distributor, has recently been fined on several occasions for advertising and selling imitations of G. & C. Merriam Company's *Webster's Third New International Dictionary.* In addition, Webster Publishing has in the past claimed that *Encyclopedia Buying Guide* rates *The New American Encyclopedia* "among the top encyclopedias in the world," when in fact the *Buying Guide* has consistently given the encyclopedia a poor rating.

Reliability

The foreword states, "The first criterion established for the NEW AMERICAN was *accuracy."* Unfortunately, the set does not live up to this claim. The text contains many factual errors and misspellings. EXAMPLE: The game lacrosse is entered in the encyclopedia as "La Crosse." EXAMPLE: "Florida" notes that the state's governor "can be reelected, but can not serve two terms in a row." This is incorrect. EXAMPLE: The article on C. P. Snow, the British scientist and writer, gives 1940 as the date of his famous Strangers and Brothers series of novels. In fact, the series was written over a 30-year period, beginning in 1940 and ending with *Last Things* in 1970. EXAMPLE: The article "Trucial Shaikdoms" refers to the "Federation of Arab Amirates." Actually the term is "Emirates." Moreover, the word in the title of the article is spelled *sheikhdom* or *sheikdom,* but not *shaikdom.* EXAMPLE: The article "Indians" has no fewer than nine misspellings and other typographical errors (e.g., "sandles with heels"), as well as numerous minor factual errors and misleading statements. EX-

AMPLE: The short article "Shark" contains at least four factual inaccuracies; for example, the statement "All species [of sharks] are more or less destructive of food fishes and do immense damage to the fisheries" is incorrect. Of all the encyclopedias reviewed in the *Buying Guide, New American* is by far the least reliable. Indeed, the number and variety of errors in *New American* must be some sort of record.

Recency

New American is now badly dated. Although the 1973 editorial overhaul greatly improved the set's recency, *New American* has not been revised since. Any multivolume encyclopedia that does not practice continuous revision on an annual basis cannot remain up-to-date for long, given today's rapidly growing and changing knowledge. The encyclopedia's coverage in certain areas gives the appearance of being contemporary, as articles on Carol Channing, drug abuse, folk music, Janis Joplin, and the women's movement attest. But an unacceptable number of articles are now hopelessly out-of-date. EXAMPLE: "Oceans and Oceanography" appears to have been written in the early or mid-1960s. In this field, recency is essential, as the state of knowledge about oceans has undergone revolutionary change during the past decade. EXAMPLE: According to *New American*, the current minimum wage is $1.60. EXAMPLE: According to *New American*, Saul Bellow's "most recently published" book is *Mr. Sammler's Planet.* EXAMPLE: "Abortion" fails to mention the landmark Supreme Court decision of 1973 that radically altered the legal status of abortion in the United States. EXAMPLE: The article "Refrigeration" is woefully dated. EXAMPLE: "Subway" informs that "Washington D.C. is the only major city now engaged in a subway building program." Actually, the Washington Metro is now operational and a number of other cities here and abroad are currently involved in subway projects. EXAMPLE: "Dinosaur" states, "Like all reptiles, the dinosaurs must have been coldblooded animals," a conjecture that fails to take into account the latest research on dinosaurs. EXAMPLE: In *New American*, Mao Tse-tung still lives, the so-called Gang of Four does not exist, and U.S. recognition of the People's Republic of China has not occurred. EXAMPLE: In *New American*, the Atomic Energy Commission, abolished in 1974, is still regulating the nuclear power business.

Several yearbook volumes designed to help keep *New American* current have been issued in recent years. The yearbook, however, has no true relationship to the encyclopedia, and therefore serves no real purpose as an updating tool. Consumers should be aware that the distributor, Webster Publishing Company, has advertised *New American* as having 23 volumes instead of 20, 8,590 pages instead of 7,570, 29,000 articles instead of 27,000, six million words instead of five and a half million, and being "up-dated to 1978" (see, for example, the *Los Angeles Times,* February 4, 1979). In reality, these statistics describe the 1973 20-volume set plus several yearbook volumes.

This Recency Table compares selected topics in *New American* with those in other encyclopedias of similar size and intended usership.

Topic	New American	Academic American	Funk & Wagnalls	New Caxton
Afghanistan	Not current	Very current	Fairly current	Fairly current
Dinosaurs	Not current	Very current	Very current	Fairly current
Greenland	Not current	Very current	Not current	Not current
Thomas Jefferson	Not current	Fairly current	Fairly current	Not current
Mass Transportation/Subways	Not current	Very current	Fairly current	Very current
Nuclear Power	Not current	Very current	Not current	Fairly current
Paris	Not current	Very current	Not current	Very current
Sharks	Fairly current	Fairly current	Not current	Fairly current
Shock Therapy	Not current	Very current	Not current	Fairly current
Suicide	Not current	Fairly current	Not current	Not current
Tuberculosis	Not current	Fairly current	Fairly current	Fairly current
Zimbabwe	Not current	Very current	Very current	Very current

Objectivity

Like the other intermediate adult sets with which it competes, *New American* is generally free from bias. Facts as opposed to opinions are emphasized. The treatment of the human reproductive system, for example, is straightforward and objective. The same is true of such controversial topics as abortion, fluoridation, flying saucers, homosexuality, I.Q. tests, the origins of race, and women's liberation. The article on homosexuality, for instance, notes that "today there is a great deal of controversy concerning the causes of homosexuality. While some regard it as innate, others consider it a learned response that becomes systematized into the personality." The whole tone of the article is dispassionate and relies upon available scientific reports. But also like its competitors, *New American* sometimes ignores unwelcome facts about historical personages. The article on Thomas Jefferson, for instance, gives no hint that the great man was a slave owner and fathered a number of slave children.

Clarity and Reader Suitability

The foreword speaks of *New American*'s "easy-to-read style" and suggests that reader suitability ranges from "all students from the primary grades to college." Many of the set's articles will be comprehensible to readers at the junior high or middle school level, but the set is definitely not for elementary students. In addition, some of the material, particularly on technical subjects, presumes considerable background knowledge and a specialist's vocabulary on the part of the reader. EXAMPLE: The article "Matrix" immediately launches into the algebraic behavior of matrices. Most of the article consists of mathematical examples. EXAMPLE: "Anthropology" reads like a college text and is occasionally difficult to follow. The subtopic "Physical Anthropology," for instance, rather awkwardly concludes that anthropologists "have also found that man himself helped to create the conditions for the spread of sickle cell anemia, a genetic defect which at the same time provides resistance to malaria, by helping to spread the conditions in which malarial mosquitoes breed."

Although difficult or technical terms are sometimes defined in the text, this is not done consistently. Articles such as "Architecture" and "Geophysics" use a specialized vocabulary, as indeed they must, but glossaries are not provided. The writing is sometimes choppy and disjointed. And in some instances the style is downright embarrassing. EXAMPLE: The article "Children, Adoption of" goes on for four pages in this manner:

> Remember, he will not stay a baby very long. And keep this in mind always: a child coming to your home will mean one of the biggest changes your life ever had. That you will want to cuddle him is fine. But never forget that the little blue or pink bundle you hold is a human being. You will have a great part in what he makes of his life. Maybe so, you say, but does not almost everything have risks? Yes, they do. Marriage, your own children, friendships, business, all, like adoption, have risks. You can never be sure that they will be perfect. There is a bit of a gamble in all of them. But in all of them, you can cut down on the odds. It takes thinking and planning and weighing, however, to get rid of most of the risks of adoption. So when you take your first step, do not leap into the dark. Move slowly in as much light as you can.

Certainly, in terms of readability and stylistic evenness, *New American* is no match for its chief competitors—that is, the *Academic American Encyclopedia, Funk & Wagnalls New Encyclopedia*, the British *New Caxton Encyclopedia, The New Illustrated Columbia Encyclopedia*, and *The New Standard Encyclopedia*. Moreover, *New American* cannot compete with the better young adult sets (which it resembles in size only) such as *Compton's Encyclopedia, Merit Students Encyclopedia*, and *The World Book Encyclopedia* because, unlike these sets, *New American* is not written to grade level, nor is its vocabulary controlled, nor is it written in pyramid fashion (from simple to complex).

Arrangement and Accessibility

New American is arranged alphabetically, letter-by-letter ("Indiana" precedes "Indian Ocean"). External cross-references (e.g., *"Child Development.* See GROWTH AND MATURATION") appear occasionally as entries in the A–Z sequence. But the bulk of the set's 6,000 cross-references are internal *See* references indicated by either *q.v.* (for the Latin *quod vide,* meaning "which see") or SMALL CAPITAL LETTERS. EXAMPLE: The article "Genetics" notes, "A number of observers noticed certain striking parallels in the behavior of genes and of chromosomes (*q.v.*)." Later in the article the reader learns that "a similar effect is seen in the inheritance of A-B-O blood types in man (see BLOOD: BLOOD TYPES)." *See* and *See also* references sometimes appear at the end of articles as well.

Significantly, *New American* lacks a general index. Cross-references, no matter how abundant they might be, are not an adequate substitute for a detailed general index. In the case of *New American* this is especially true, as the system of cross-references is not consistently well developed. EXAMPLE: The article "Trucial Shaikdoms" [*sic*] includes a *See* reference to "Federation of Arab Amirates" [*sic*], but there is no article in the set under "Federation of Arab Amirates" (or, for that matter, "Emirates"). EXAMPLE: There is an external reference from "Housing" to "Shelter," but again there is no article under "Shelter." EXAMPLE: "Sex" furnishes a *See also* reference to "Mating and Courtship Behavior," but the reference turns out to be an article entitled "Mating and Courtship of Animals." The article "Sex," however, fails to refer to the long and useful article "Anatomy and Physiology," which discusses the human reproductive system. EXAMPLE: There is no external entry for the topic "Race." The user must discover either through intelligent browsing or plain luck that the subject of race is treated in the article "Man." In addition, aspects of race are discussed in "Asia" and "Anthropology," but "Man" provides no references to them. EXAMPLE: "Anti-Semitism" includes a *See also* reference to "Prejudice: Intergroup Relations," but the article turns out to be one sentence long and adds absolutely nothing to the reader's knowledge of anti-Semitism.

New American is both a difficult and a frustrating encyclopedia to use, due not only to the lack of a general index but a grossly inadequate system of cross-references. It is often troublesome and sometimes practically impossible to find specific information in the set. The set's very poor accessibility is one of its greatest deficiencies.

Bibliographies

Most major or longer articles include bibliographies ranging from a single entry to 25 or more. The lists tend to be current as of the late 1960s or early 1970s. Obviously, important titles published during the past ten years are not included, but all too frequently significant or indispensable works published prior to the 1970s are omitted. The article "Nuclear Energy," for instance, provides two bibliographic entries, one from 1949 and the other 1963. The article on Warren Harding fails to include Francis Russell's *The Shadow of Blooming Grove* (1968). Like the general text, the bibliographies also contain an inordinate number of typographical or editing errors; for instance, the bibliography for "Indians," which has only five titles, manages to misspell one author's name and give the incorrect publication date for another entry. Moreover, not all major articles have bibliographies. EXAMPLES: "Oceans and Oceanography" lacks a bibliography, as does "Architecture," "Gestalt Psychology," "Pregnancy," and "Unions." Also, inconsistency in the provision of bibliographies is not uncommon. "Archives," for instance, a two-paragraph article, has a bibliography of three entries, whereas the 13-page "Architecture" has none. In comparison with *New American*'s competition in the area of bibliographies, the encyclopedia ranks last. The *Academic American Encyclopedia, Funk & Wagnalls New Encyclopedia, The New Illustrated Columbia Encyclopedia,* and *The New Standard Encyclopedia* all furnish better bibliographies. Only *Harver World Encyclopedia* and the British *New Caxton Encyclopedia,* which omit bibliographies altogether, are less impressive than *New American* in this area.

Graphics

The 1973 revision of *New American* greatly improved the set's illustrations. Approximately 4,000 are now in full color, 2,000 in two color, and the remaining 3,000 in black-and-white. Mondadori, the Italian firm that printed the set, has provided the illustrations. They include photographs, line drawings, diagrams, reproductions of art works, and charts. Color transparencies of the human anatomy are also furnished. The illustrations are usually sharp and sufficiently detailed, but they are not nearly as plentiful or well reproduced as the graphics in the *Academic American Encyclopedia, The New Caxton Encyclopedia,* and *Harver World Encyclopedia,* the best illustrated sets in the intermediate adult class (in that order). Of course, *New American*'s graphics are not indexed (see "Arrangement and Accessibility"). They do, however, add to the informational value of the set and are placed reasonably close to the text they are complementing, although many exceptions can be found. EXAMPLE: There seems to be little point to the photograph of a plate of spaghetti (captioned "Macaroni"), especially when the article "Macaroni" is on the next page. Another annoying feature of the set's illustrations is that representative sizes of plant and animal life are not indicated. EXAMPLE: A large, quarter-page color drawing of an aphid accompanies the article "Homoptera." The illustration makes the aphid, a very tiny plant pest, look like a gigantic monster, yet all the caption says is "an aphid, insect of the Homoptera order."

Various types of maps are provided. Those accompanying articles on major places are usually full-page, full-color political maps from the Rand McNally *Cosmo* series. They are quite detailed, but lack indexes. In addition, there are smaller, black-and-white maps found throughout the set. Drawn by staff cartographers, they usually show special features or simple locations. On the negative side, many countries of the world (e.g., Afghanistan) have only small spot maps, and some of the larger, more substantial maps are now considerably dated.

Physical Format

The volumes are adequately bound in a washable blue and white Kivar binding with gold lettering. A small blue and gold logo featuring the lamp of knowledge appears on the front cover of each volume. The letters on the spine are much too small to read at any distance. Otherwise the set's outward construction is both functional and attractive. Inside, a heavy-duty, glare-free paper has been used. The print, though undistinguished, is bold and clear. The page layout is inoffensive, and guide words normally appear at the top of each page. The volumes lie perfectly flat when open, thus facilitating easy consultation. An irritating feature, however, is the set's letter division. In order to make the volumes a uniform size, the letters are arbitrarily split so that they overlap. For instance, Volume 17 covers the letters RHINITIS–SNOW, and Volume 18 SNOW–TOPAZ. The user seeking C. P. Snow's biography, for example, has no idea which of the volumes contains the desired entry.

Special Features

The set boasts no outstanding special features, although it might be mentioned that the final 50 pages of Volume 20 are called the "Statistical Section." A hodgepodge of material, this section includes the text of the U.S. Constitution and its amendments, population data (1970) for selected U.S. cities, and lists of U.S. colleges and universities, Nobel Prize winners, and sports records.

Sales Information

New American is sold to individual consumers both through direct mail order and door-to-door canvassing on the subscription basis. There is only one edition available, that being the so-called Unabridged and Deluxe edition bound in blue and white Kivar already described (see "Physical Format"). The publisher's retail price is $249.50, but the set can be acquired via mail order for $133 plus $15 shipping and handling from the distributor, the Webster Publishing Company. The mail order price includes several volumes of the encyclopedia's yearbook (see "Recency") and a premium (a very bad dictionary entitled the *Webster Encyclopedic Dictionary*). Purchasers must, however, allow their names to be used for testimonial purposes on behalf of the encyclopedia. This deal is said to be "the most incredible encyclopedia bargain on the market today." Unfortunately, *New American* is not a bargain at any price, and anyone who agrees to give a testimonial for the set is doing the cause of consumerism no good. It should also be noted that potentially deceptive and misleading advertising has been employed in recent years to promote the encyclopedia (see "History and Authority" for details).

Consumers should be aware that earlier editions of this encyclopedia— variously titled *Standard International Encyclopedia, World Educator Encyclopedia, World Scope Encyclopedia, World University Encyclopedia,* and *The New American Encyclopedia* (pre-1973)—have presumably been discontinued but may be encountered as remainder stock or on the secondhand market. All of these titles are vastly inferior to the encyclopedia that currently bears the name *New American Encyclopedia.* (For further information about these defunct sets, see Appendix A.)

Summary

The New American Encyclopedia (1973 edition) can be quickly summed up in this manner:

Scope: Fair	Accessibility: Poor
Authority: Poor	Bibliographies: Poor
Reliability: Poor	Graphics: Fair
Recency: Poor	Physical Format: Fair
Objectivity: Good	Special Features: None
Clarity: Fair	Price: High

To elaborate briefly, *New American* was extensively revised and considerably improved in 1973. It is now at least a modestly respectable intermediate adult encyclopedia, its many glaring faults notwithstanding. The encyclopedia's purpose and scope are comparable to those of other smaller adult sets. Brief, factual articles predominate, emphasizing biographical, geographical, scientific, and social topics. Coverage, however, tends to be erratic and imbalanced. Treatment is often sketchy and devoid of any depth, and the articles are not always well written, nor are they always up-to-date. The encyclopedia contains many errors, ranging from typographical mistakes to major factual inaccuracies. Another serious liability is the set's muddled cross-reference system, a problem compounded by the lack of a general index. Attempting to access specific information in *New American* is often a difficult and frustrating business. Overall, comparatively speaking, the encyclopedia is inferior and not worth even its current "bargain" price. Consumers are advised to be on the alert for possibly misleading or deceptive advertising where *New American* is concerned.

Obviously, *New American* lacks the size and depth to compete with the three large comprehensive adult sets on the market, namely *Collier's Encyclopedia, The Encyclopedia Americana,* and *The New Encyclopaedia Britannica.* Likewise, although it claims to be for students "from grade school to college," *New American* lacks the curriculum orientation and careful attention to readability that distinguish the better young adult sets, such as *Compton's Encyclopedia, Merit Students Encyclopedia,* and *The World Book Encyclopedia.* In comparison with the various other intermediate adult sets, *New American* has nothing to offer the discriminating consumer. In practically every respect, the new *Academic American Encyclopedia, Funk & Wagnalls New Encyclopedia,* the British-made

New Caxton Encyclopedia, The New Illustrated Columbia Encyclopedia, and *The New Standard Encyclopedia* are preferable to *New American.* Even the fast-deteriorating *Harver World Encyclopedia* outperforms *New American* in all areas except price.

Other Critical Opinions

Booklist, January 15, 1979, pp. 832–833. Part of a series of reviews by the ALA Reference and Subscription Books Review Committee (RSBRC) entitled "Encyclopedias: A Survey and Buying Guide," this unsigned evaluation of *New American* (1973 edition) is negative about most aspects of the set, including its lack of recency, "sparseness" of cross-references, frequent inaccuracies, and inconsistent writing style. No overall recommendation, pro or con, is offered, however.

New Caxton Encyclopedia

Facts in Brief

Full Title: **The New Caxton Encyclopedia.** *Editors:* Graham Clarke, Editor; Bernard Workman, Associate Editor. *Publisher:* Caxton Publications, Ltd. (a member company of the British Printing Corporation), London, England; also copyright by Istituto Geografico de Agostini, Novara, Italy. *U.S. Distributor:* Purnell Reference Books (a division of Macdonald-Raintree, Inc.), 205 W. Highland Ave., Milwaukee, WI 53203. *Former Title: Purnell's New English Encyclopedia. Edition Reviewed:* Fifth Edition, 1979 copyright.

Volumes: 20. *Pages:* 6,500. *Articles:* 13,000. *Words:* 6,000,000. *Illustrations:* 17,300. *Maps:* 600. *Index Entries:* 50,000. *Cross-references:* None. *Contributors:* 83.

User Classification: Adult (Multivolume). *Reader Suitability:* Age 12 through General Adult. *Physical Size:* 9¼ × 12 in.; 31 cm. *ISBN:* 070-1400-560. *Lowest Retail Price:* Not sold at retail; to schools & libraries $599.50.

Purpose and Scope

The New Caxton Encyclopedia, a heavily illustrated British work, intends to be "a working guide to almost any subject imaginable." The brief introductory note in Volume 1 entitled "How to Use the Encyclopedia" also states that *New Caxton* "is not just a compilation of facts. It is a simple scheme of universal knowledge which, taken as a whole, presents a panoramic view of the world around us—its geography, its problems, its famous people, its discoveries, its arts, and its manner of living." A related goal of the encyclopedia is presentation of knowledge in an attractive and exciting manner. As Lord Wolfenden observes in his introduction to the set, "This encyclopedia can never be dull or heavy or forbidding. The pictures and the text are not only a source of knowledge but make it all come to life."

New Caxton, now in its fifth edition (1979), comprises some 13,000 articles accompanied by 17,300 color illustrations. Indeed, graphics account for approximately 50 percent of the set's total text. Most of the articles are concise, averaging half a page in length, or about 500 words. EXAMPLES: The article "Parthenogenesis" consists of roughly 250 words, plus a small illustration, covering a fourth of a page; "Parthians" (an ancient Iranian people) consists of 400 words, plus a small historical map;

"Particle" consists of 750 words, plus a sizable diagram; "Partnership" consists of 500 words; "Partridge" consists of 500 words, plus a photograph of the French, or red-legged, partridge commonly found in England; "Pascal, Blaise" consists of 1,000 words, plus a drawing of the philosopher and a reproduction of the title page of the first edition of his *Pensées;* "Pascal's Theorem" consists of 500 words, plus a line drawing; "Paschal" (the name of several popes) consists of 300 words, plus a color reproduction of a mosaic in the church of San Prassede in Rome; "Pascoli, Giovanni" (an Italian poet) consists of 300 words; "Pasolini, Pier Paolo" (an Italian writer and film director) consists of 300 words; "Passeriformes" (a bird classification) consists of 200 words, plus three fairly large photographs.

As these examples tend to show, *New Caxton*'s scope is international, with a distinct European emphasis. Not surprisingly, British topics and points of reference predominate. Subjects relating directly to the United States and the Americas are sometimes covered, sometimes not. EXAMPLE: The article "Abortion" defines the term, notes that the procedure "used to be a criminal offence in all Western countries, and still is in many," describes the legal situation in the United States in one sentence, and concludes with a full paragraph on the current scene in Great Britain. EXAMPLE: The U.S. Atomic Energy Commission, or its successor, the Nuclear Regulatory Commission, are nowhere mentioned in the encyclopedia. EXAMPLE: The article "Nucleus of the Atom," which partially covers nuclear energy and reactors, describes developments in Britain in considerable detail, then concludes with comparative data on various countries, including the United States. EXAMPLE: The article "Childhood" provides a lengthy general discussion of the topic, followed by a section on the legal status of children, of which all but a few sentences are devoted to the situation under British law. Most of the many photographs accompanying the article have a British context. EXAMPLE: The article on Warren Harding, the U.S president, consists of about 250 words, or less space than that devoted to Keir Hardie, the British Socialist leader. EXAMPLE: Georgia O'Keeffe, an important contemporary American artist, and William Styron, a living American writer of increasing stature, are among a number of notable Americans not found in *New Caxton*.

Many of the encyclopedia's 13,000 articles, however, do deal with biographical subjects. Here again, the coverage, which includes pronunciations, is international with a general European and specific British accent. A typical sample drawn from Volume 17 reveals entries for these people: James Clark Ross (a British explorer), John Ross (uncle of James Clark Ross and also an explorer), Ronald Ross (a British medical scientist), Roberto Rossellini (the Italian film director), Bernardo and Antonio Rossellino (Florentine sculptors), Christina and Dante Gabriel Rossetti (English poets), Giovanni Battista de' Rossi (an Italian Renaissance painter), Gioacchino Rossini (the composer), Edmond Rostand (the French dramatist), and Paul Rotha (a British filmmaker). American encyclopedias of comparable size and intended readership (like the *Academic American Encyclopedia, Funk & Wagnalls New Encyclopedia, Harver*

World Encyclopedia, The New Illustrated Columbia Encyclopedia, and *The New Standard Encyclopedia*) usually include entries for Betsy Ross (the flagmaker), Harold Ross (founding editor of *The New Yorker* magazine), John Ross (a famous chief of the Cherokee Indians), and Theodore Roszak (a modern American sculptor).

Geographical topics also account for a large number of entries. Countries and continents of the world receive adequate coverage, considering *New Caxton's* limited size. Africa, for example, is covered in 13 pages; China is accorded 25 pages, Canada 10 pages, and the smaller, less powerful Afghanistan just over a page. All such articles include the nation's flag (in color) and a small map showing physical features. Unfortunately, *New Caxton's* map coverage is now deficient, as the 128-page world atlas hitherto part of Volume 20 has been dropped from this edition (see "Graphics"). The U.S. states and Canadian provinces receive considerably less attention in *New Caxton* than they do in such competing sets as the *Academic American Encyclopedia, Funk & Wagnalls New Encyclopedia,* and *The New Standard Encyclopedia.* On the other hand, *New Caxton* provides strong coverage of British counties, cities, rivers, and other place-names of any consequence. EXAMPLE: Whereas the *Academic American Encyclopedia* accords Norfolk County in England only 150 words, *New Caxton* has a substantial article of nearly 1,000 words, accompanied by a map and two large photographs.

As noted in previous editions of the *Buying Guide,* subject coverage in *New Caxton* is reasonably well balanced among the humanities, social and behavioral sciences, and natural and technical sciences. Because of the encyclopedia's heavy emphasis on illustrative material, the fine arts in general and British and European cultural history in particular are well covered. Substantial and handsomely illustrated articles are included on such subjects as canopic jars, cave paintings, rock engravings, ceramic vases, the French Impressionists, op art, the opera, the Renaissance, and Joshua Reynolds and other important English artists. In point of fact, the set contains some 3,000 art reproductions, all in color.

In the sciences, articles on medicine, biology, genetics, geology, mining, navigation, atomic energy, solar power, surveying, dinosaurs, marine life, and the like provide generally satisfactory coverage. The article "Evolution," for instance, is an excellent survey of a complex subject. The scientific names of all plants and animals are given, and informative diagrams and photographs accompany most articles in the natural sciences. Metric measurements have replaced English (or customary) units throughout the set in this edition. This change might pose some difficulties for U.S. users, in that customary equivalents are *not* provided. EXAMPLE: The article "Shark" notes that "the basking shark (*Cetorhinus maximus*) which grows to a length of 12 metres or more, is found in most temperate seas." How many U.S. readers will know offhand that 12 meters equals 40 feet is questionable. It should be noted that many encyclopedias produced in the United States provide both customary units and metric equivalents (or, in the case of the new *Academic American Encyclopedia,* the other way around).

New Caxton's weakest subject coverage is in the area of social and political topics, especially those concerned with U.S. developments, problems, peoples, and institutions. EXAMPLE: The article "Indians, American, or Amerindians," which consists of barely 1,000 words, presumes to cover the entire hemisphere. The article is grossly inadequate to the task. EXAMPLE: The article "Supreme Court of the United States" makes no effort to explain how the court works, from where it derives its powers, its relationship to the other branches of the U.S. federal government, or who its major justices have been. EXAMPLE: "Women, Equality of" furnishes only superficial coverage of contemporary issues concerning women. Historical information regarding the British experience is relatively generous, but the article fails even to mention the proposed Equal Rights Amendment to the U.S. Constitution. EXAMPLE: The encyclopedia lacks coverage of cults and cult behavior in general, nor are specific cults covered (e.g., the People's Temple). EXAMPLE: The subject of suicide is completely ignored by *New Caxton.*

Volumes 19 and 20 of the fifth edition of *New Caxton* (under review here) are quite different from those of previous editions. In earlier editions, Volume 19 was entitled "Man, Earth and Space," a series of topically arranged essays entirely unrelated to the rest of the encyclopedia. In the fifth edition, alphabetical entries run through Volume 19 (which covers the letters TWAN–ZWIN), and the "Man, Earth and Space" feature has been dropped. Volume 20 in previous editions comprised a 128-page world atlas and gazetteer, a few pages of last-minute facts called "Recent Events, Personalities, and Changes," a general and a subject index, and a list of artists and their works represented in the set. In the fifth edition, the atlas and gazetteer, the update section, and the subject index have been dropped. Replacing them are a 133-page chronology of world events entitled "The Book of Key Facts" and a 48-page "Study Guide" arranged by broad topic (e.g., biology, computers and calculators, language, physics, tools, war), which points the reader to pertinent articles in the encyclopedia as well as further readings on the subject. The chronology, which covers 30,000 B.C. to A. D. 1978, lists 30,000 facts in such areas as politics and war, science and technology, religion and philosophy, and literature and the arts. There is an alphabetical index, but "The Book of Key Facts," like "Man, Earth and Space" before it, is unconnected to the rest of the set, thus diminishing its usefulness. Note that Volume 20 of the current fifth edition still includes the general index and list of artists and their works.

History and Authority

New Caxton first appeared in Great Britain in 1965 in weekly parts (called a part-work) under the title *Purnell's New English Encyclopedia.* This work was not a revision of, nor was it connected with, an older, now defunct six-volume item entitled *Caxton Encyclopedia* (London: Caxton Publishing Company, 1960). The initial edition of the bound work (now entitled *The New Caxton Encyclopedia*) came out in 1966 in 18 volumes.

Volumes 19 and 20 were added later (see "Purpose and Scope" for recent developments concerning these volumes). The second edition was published in 1969, followed by the third edition in 1972, the fourth edition in 1977, and the current fifth edition in 1979. The set actually originated in Italy as a publication of the Istituto Geografico de Agostini, a firm internationally respected for the high quality of its graphics and particularly its cartographic work. It has also been published in France under the title *Alpha: La Grande Encyclopédie Universelle en Couleurs.* A Spanish version called *Monitor* has also been produced. These national editions contain much the same text (print and visual) as *New Caxton*, although there are some differences in emphasis, particularly in biographical entries. Like the more recent *Random House Encyclopedia* (published abroad in various languages and titles, including *The Joy of Knowledge* in England), *New Caxton* is a good example of what the publishing industry calls "coproduction"—when firms in two or more countries jointly share the financing and editing of an expensive reference work that can be readily adapted for individual national markets.

New Caxton is published in England by Caxton Publications, Ltd., a member company of the giant British Printing Corporation (BPC). The set is distributed in the United States by Purnell Reference Books, a division of Macdonald-Raintree, Inc., of Milwaukee, an American company partly owned by BPC. The same British group also owns the rights to the once highly regarded but now defunct *Chambers's Encyclopaedia,* the largest British-made encyclopedia since *Encyclopaedia Britannica* (now *The New Encyclopaedia Britannica*) passed into U.S. hands in 1901. Recent revisions of *New Caxton* have reputedly cost the publisher millions of pounds, an investment that has apparently crimped any plans for resuscitating *Chambers's,* a job estimated to require at least $10 million if it is to be done right.

Graham Clarke, a contributor to previous editions of the encyclopedia, is now editor in chief. He replaces Bernard Workman, who edited the first four editions (1965–1977). Workman, now retired, however, is listed as associate editor. These men are supported by an Editorial Advisory Board of five distinguished scholars, four of whom are British, including Lord Wolfenden, the Countess of Longford (known better to Americans as Elizabeth Longford), and Sir Bernard Lovell. There is a small editorial staff of eight, identified by name and academic degrees only. None of these people is known to the *Buying Guide.* The front matter of Volume 1 also lists 26 contributors to the fifth edition. These contributors, who are identified by name, degrees, specialization, and publications, bring good credentials to the work. Some are well-known authorities in their field, such as Roger Clare (earth sciences), Ian Hogg (weapons), P. M. Kalla-Bishop (railroads), and Ian Ridpath (astronomy). All are British. In addition, 57 contributors to previous editions are listed (by name and degrees only). Most or all of these contributors are British, and those known to the *Buying Guide* (e.g., David Diringer, Walter Bradley Shepherd, and Jack Clifford Wright) are authoritative. It should also be noted that the informational core of this coproduced encyclopedia was prepared by more persons than those listed in Volume 1 as editors and contributors. Perhaps for this reason, the articles are not signed. Overall, *New Caxton* is an authoritative work.

Reliability

The encyclopedia is reasonably reliable. Auberon Waugh, writing in *Books and Bookmen* (July 1977, pp. 20–21), says "*New Caxton* generally gives most of the essential facts on every subject and gets them right." Likewise, the *Buying Guide* discovered no horrendous errors of fact or interpretation, although minor inaccuracies occasionally intrude. EXAMPLE: The article "Shark" contains several misstatements, such as identifying the so-called elephant shark (*Callorhynchus milii*) as a member of the shark family; it is not. EXAMPLE: "Tuberculosis" incorrectly informs, "In modern industrialized countries the incidence of tuberculosis is continually decreasing"; in fact, the disease has staged a comeback in recent years in the United States, where 30,000 cases are now reported each year. Earlier editions of *New Caxton* were plagued by such errors and typographical mistakes. Most, however, have since been corrected. For instance, former Arkansas governor Orval Faubus is no longer George Faubus in *New Caxton*'s article on Dwight Eisenhower (as he was during the first four editions). But, as the examples above show, the set is still not entirely free of error. A bigger problem concerning the encyclopedia's reliability involves articles like "Abortion" and "Canada" that are not up-to-date and, hence, not completely trustworthy. To say, for instance, that abortion "is legally allowable in the United States either by specific legislation or by judicial construction when practised to preserve life" is inaccurate. Likewise, to say that "French interests [in Canada] have been partially placated by the severance of nearly all the remaining official ties with Britain, the adoption of a new flag in 1964, and the succession of a French-Canadian, Pierre Trudeau, as prime minister" is misleading. This question of currency of information in *New Caxton* is discussed further in the next section.

Recency

New Caxton, originally published in weekly parts and then in bound form, has been updated by new editions that heretofore have appeared at irregular intervals: the second edition in 1969, the third in 1972, the fourth in 1977, and the current fifth in 1979. According to the U.S. distributor, Purnell Reference Books, the sixth edition is tentatively scheduled for 1982. Note that, unlike most American multivolume general encyclopedias, *New Caxton* is not continuously revised on an annual basis.

How thorough are *New Caxton*'s periodic revisions? The publisher reported that some $2 million was spent on updating the fourth edition in 1977, and most likely a similar or even larger amount was required for the 1979 revision. According to the publisher, 80 new articles and 300 color illustrations have been added to the current edition. Other articles have

This Recency Table compares selected topics in *New Caxton* with those in other encyclopedias of similar size and intended usership.

Topic	New Caxton	Academic American	Funk & Wagnalls	New Standard
Afghanistan	Fairly current	Very current	Fairly current	Fairly current
Dinosaurs	Fairly current	Very current	Very current	Very current
Greenland	Not current	Very current	Not current	Very current
Thomas Jefferson	Not current	Fairly current	Fairly current	Fairly current
Mass Transportation/Subways	Very current	Very current	Fairly current	Fairly current
Nuclear Power	Fairly current	Very current	Not current	Not current
Paris	Very current	Very current	Not current	Not current
Sharks	Fairly current	Fairly current	Not current	Very current
Shock Therapy	Fairly current	Very current	Not current	Not current
Suicide	Not current*	Fairly current	Not current	Very current
Tuberculosis	Fairly current	Fairly current	Fairly current	Fairly current
Zimbabwe	Very current	Very current	Very current	Very current

*Topic not covered in encyclopedia.

been substantially reworked, but in most cases only minor alterations have occurred, such as changing a statistic or adding a new fact. As indicated previously, all measurements have now been changed from customary to metric units. Also, a number of graphics have been dropped or cropped. The *Buying Guide* randomly compared the 1977 and 1979 editions of *New Caxton* for evidence of revision. This sampling of consecutive entries in Volume 17 is representative: "Skalkottas, Nicos" (no revision); "Skara Brae" (no revision); "Skating" (substantial revision, especially in the area of free skating); "Skeleton" (minor revision indicating that the human skeleton has 206 bones "plus a variable number of tiny 'sesamoid' bones"); "Skelton, John" (no revision); "Skiing" (substantial revision, particularly on Olympic skiing); "Skin" (no revision); "Skinner, Burrhas Frederic" (no revision); "Skinner, Cornelia Otis" (no revision); "Skittles" (no revision); "Skua" (minor revision in which the phrase "from the German for 'hunters' " was dropped); "Skull" (no revision); "Skunk" (minor revision in which the sentence "It sometimes transmits rabies" has been added, and the sentence "The male striped skunk grows to 24 inches, plus an 8-inch tail" in the 1977 edition now reads "The male striped skunk grows to 60 cm, plus a 20 cm tail"); "Skye" (minor revision involving change to metric units); "Skyscraper" (minor revision involving change to metric units and the addition of this sentence: "The tallest solid structure in London is the National Westminster Tower"); "Slander" (no revision); "Slang" (no revision); "Slate" (no revision); "Slauerhoff, Jan Jacob" (no revision); "Slav Languages" (no revision); "Slavery" (no revision).

As this sampling suggests, considerable revision has occurred between the 1977 and 1979 editions, although much of it is minor in nature. Unfortunately, some articles throughout the set are less than models of recency. EXAMPLE: The article "Indians, American, or Amerindians" provides no factual information on contemporary events, including recent Indian protest movements and land claims. EXAMPLE: "Afghanistan" is reasonably current, except for the flag (black, red, and green), which has been superseded by a new flag. EXAMPLE: "Nucleus of the Atom," which includes information about nuclear energy, is much out-of-date concerning the widespread disenchantment with nuclear power. The accident at Harrisburg's Three Mile Island facility is not mentioned. Instead, the article states that "in many countries there has been opposition to the increasing use of nuclear power, due mainly to its unfortunate association with nuclear weapons and fears of radiation hazards. Much scientific evidence discounts these fears and stresses the safety measures adopted in applying nuclear power, which are far more stringent than in any other industrial process." EXAMPLE: "Dinosaur" fails to note recent theories concerning why the dinosaurs vanished, the possibility that they were warm-blooded, and that today's birds may be descended from dinosaurs.

Again, unlike most U.S. multivolume general encyclopedias, *New Caxton* does not offer an annual supplement designed to keep the set up-to-date. An annual volume entitled *International Yearbook* is sold in Great Britain and Europe, but it is not available in the United States or Canada.

Objectivity

New Caxton strives to be as fair and unbiased as possible in its treatment of controversial or sensitive subject matter. EXAMPLE: The article "Unidentified Flying Objects" impartially describes the phenomenon, pointing out that "as most sightings have been made by individuals without witnesses, who have varied enormously in their description, it is difficult for scientists or psychologists to suggest any single cause." EXAMPLE: "Homosexuality" notes that historically the behavior "has sometimes been extolled; at other times it has been condemned as a heinous crime." The brief article also cites the authoritative Kinsey Report concerning the incidence of homosexuality among men, and states, "It is quite untrue that male homosexuals are necessarily effeminate in appearance or behaviour."

The encyclopedia, however, does not shrink from offering strong, albeit reasonable opinions. EXAMPLE: The article "Drugs, Addictive" objectively discusses the possible harmful effects of such drugs as cocaine and heroin, and offers this sensible advice to parents and others who would instruct the young: "Young people are likely simply to laugh at information which they know to be incorrect. In particular, every kind of opprobrium has (often inaccurately) been heaped on marijuana, which is probably the least harmful of the psychotropic drugs. When the parent tells the child that marijuana is a 'killer drug' that drives the user to homicidal frenzy, and the young person, by experience, knows this to be an exaggeration, the result is that subsequent warnings as to the genuinely lethal potential of drugs like heroin and cocaine are likely to be also laughed away."

Clarity and Reader Suitability

In an introductory note on how to use the encyclopedia, the editors state, "However abstruse the topic, the information is presented in a simple and straightforward way so that the puzzled or enquiring reader living in an increasingly complex and specialized world can consult the Encyclopedia with confidence." And Auberon Waugh, in his *Books and Bookmen* review (July 1977), calls the set's articles "models of lucidity." In most instances, *New Caxton* lives up to these words. The text, which will be comprehensible in most cases to readers at the high school level and beyond, is normally concise, direct, and interesting. Clarity is frequently enhanced by accompanying photographs, diagrams, graphs, and other visuals. Some articles in the sciences are especially notable for their clear explanations of complicated theories or processes. EXAMPLE: The article "Evolution" discusses negative reactions to Darwinism in this manner: "The chief obstacle to the general acceptance of evolution lay in the then common belief that inherited characters are carried in the blood and are 'mixed' in cross-breeding, which is the general rule between families. The mixture of bloods would thus tend to reduce all varieties to a single type, no matter how superior some varieties might appear to be. Every new advantage would thus be watered down and nullified long before it had a chance to make its mark on a species." EXAMPLE: Efforts to produce a "clean" nuclear bomb is explained in "Atomic Bomb":

> An attempt was then made to find a type of bomb which did not yield radioactive products. The ordinary A-bomb was designated "dirty," and war departments set to work to devise a "clean" bomb. In this they failed, for though the simple H-bomb is clean in the sense that none of its products is radioactive, it emits enormous quantities of neutrons which set up radioactivity as a secondary effect. An increase in the neutron yield, relative to the explosive power, is contemplated in the neutron bomb, designed to cause more deaths than damage to buildings. The most serious reaction which occurs is the conversion of the carbon-12 atoms in atmospheric carbon dioxide into carbon-14, which is radioactive and has a "half-life" of 5,570 years. Carbon dioxide, being a gas, never settles on the ground as "fall-out," but is absorbed from the air by all green plants and thus passes into the world's food.

There are instances, however, when a dictionary and some tolerance of unfamiliar scientific terminology will be required by the reader. EXAMPLE: The article "Nucleic Acids" begins "Complex biochemical macromolecules present in all living organisms and ultimately concerned in the everyday control of cellular functions and in the process of genetics." The *Buying Guide* doubts that this statement is even a complete sentence, and is still wondering what "macromolecules" are. Further on, the article informs that "complete chemical or enzymatic hydrolysis of a nucleic acid yields a mixture of simpler compounds: a pentose sugar, either ribose or deoxyribose: four out of five possible nitrogenous bases, the purine-derived adenine and guanine, and the pyrimidine-derived cytosine (rarely methyl cytosine), thymine and uracil, and phosphoric acid."

Technical terms, as the above example shows, are not normally defined in context, nor are the articles written to grade level, nor are they written in the so-called pyramid style (i.e., from simple to complex). Moreover, British spelling and terminology are used throughout. This should not pose any great difficulty for most U.S. readers, however. Efforts have been made in the fifth edition to improve the writing style of articles on U.S subjects (e.g., American football; baseball), and cross-references are ordinarily provided in the index from typically U.S. terms (e.g., *installment buying*) to their British counterparts (*hire-purchase*).

Arrangement and Accessibility

New Caxton is arranged alphabetically, word-by-word ("Indian Ocean" precedes "Indiana"). Oddly, the encyclopedia lacks both internal and external cross-references. This means, for instance, that the reader consulting the article "Atom" is *not* directed to related articles, such as "Nucleus of the Atom." The lack of cross-references is a glaring deficiency in the set. Fortunately, there is an analytical index of 50,000 entries in Volume 20. The index, which has been improved in recent editions, usually provides access to specific information in the encyclopedia, and it contains many *See* and *See also* references; for instance, under the index entry "Atom" are such *See* references as "Escape Velocity," "Neutron," "Nucleus of the Atom," and "Quantum Theory." On a number of occasions, however, the index fails to deliver. EXAMPLE: The index has no entry under "Shock Therapy" (nor is there an article in the set under that heading). Unless the reader knows enough to look under "Electroconvulsive Therapy" in the index, which leads to the article "Depression (Psychological)," information on shock therapy will be missed. Additional information on shock treatment is available in the article "Mental Health," but that is something the reader can only discover through browsing, not through the index. EXAMPLE: The reader seeking information on cults will find no article under that heading in *New Caxton* and only one likely entry in the index, "Cult Object," said to be in Volume 3 on page 124. Upon checking, however, the reader will find no material on cults or cult objects on that page. Actually, the reference should have been Volume 3, page 224. Such errors were encountered several times during the *Buying Guide's* examination of *New Caxton*.

It should also be noted that Volume 20 of *New Caxton* contains a separate index of "Artists and Their Works" represented in the encyclopedia. Limited to architects, painters, and sculptors, the index cites the artist, the work, and the volume and page where a reproduction of the work can be found. EXAMPLE: "Chagall, Marc; *The Anniversary;* 4:269." Although "Artists and Their Works" serves to call attention to *New Caxton's* most striking feature (its high-quality graphics, especially in the fine arts), the index merely duplicates information readily available in the general index, where, for instance, the reader can find *The Anniversary* reproduction under the title or under "Chagall, Marc."

Another finding device offered by the encyclopedia is the aforementioned "Study Guide" in Volume 20 (see "Purpose and Scope"). According to the editors, the principal purpose of the guide "is to help students of all ages who are interested in a particular subject to find without trouble all articles in the ENCYCLOPEDIA which will be useful in the study of that subject. In compiling the guide, emphasis has been placed on the needs of General Certificate of Education students in Britain." Listed under each of the 83 broad topics covered in the guide (e.g., art, chemistry, glass, insurance, medicine, religion, textiles, zoology) are articles in the encyclopedia on various aspects of the subject. Under aeronautics, for instance, the reader is referred to the articles "Parachute," "Shock-wave," "Unidentified Flying Objects," and "Wind-tunnel," along with articles on aviation pioneers, aircraft designers and builders, and specific aircraft, such as "Helicopter." This type of guide is not unique (compare, for example, the similar guide in Volume 24 of *Collier's Encyclopedia* or the much more extensive *Propaedia* volume of *The New Encyclopaedia Britannica*), but it will be useful to students and teachers alike, particularly in Great Britain.

Both the 1977 and 1979 editions of *New Caxton* have shown small improvements in the set's accessibility. Specifically, several annoying eccentricities in the index have been eliminated. Nevertheless, access to information in *New Caxton* could be improved by (1) provision of a more detailed analytical index and (2) addition of cross-references to the set itself. All too often important relationships between articles will be missed because of index failure or lack of cross-references. For instance, the articles "Genetics" and "Nucleic Acids" both deal with aspects of genetic research, yet no connection is made between these articles in the index or through cross-references. This is a serious weakness in the set.

Bibliographies

Prior to the 1979 edition (under review here), *New Caxton* offered no bibliographies. In this edition, bibliographies are included in the "Study Guide" in Volume 20 (see "Purpose and Scope"; "Arrangement and Accessibility"). Regrettably, the bibliographies are small in number, unrelated to articles in the encyclopedia, sometimes not as current as they might be, and very much oriented to a British readership. EXAMPLE: The subject of tele-communications includes this five-title bibliography: *History of Broadcasting in the United Kingdom* by Asa Briggs (1961–1979); *Book of Telecommunications* by Leonard de Vries (1962); *Understanding Television* by John R. Davies (1963); *SOS: Story of Radio Communication* by G. E. C. Wedlake (1973); and *Beginner's Guide to Colour Television* by G. C. King (1973). The current editors of *New Caxton* are to be commended for recognizing the need for bibliographies in their set. But the quality and quantity of these lists of further readings leave much to be desired.

Graphics

New Caxton's accessibility and bibliographies may not be up to snuff, but the graphics are fine in most respects. Indeed, the illustrations are the set's outstanding feature. They are practically all in color and include photographs, reproductions of works of art, schematic diagrams, and other instructive visual aids. Auberon Waugh remarks in his *Books and Bookmen* review (July 1977), "It may seem frivolous to harp on about the pictures when reviewing a reference book, but excellence should always be applauded and in presentation, the pictures are far the best I have seen and compare favourably with the most expensive art books." This observation is not an exaggeration. Along with the new *Academic American Encyclopedia* and the small-volume *Random House Encyclopedia,* the set is the most profusely illustrated adult encyclopedia on the market today, and its graphics are among the best found in any general encyclopedia anywhere.

Approximately 50 percent of *New Caxton*'s total text is given over to visual material. No page in the encyclopedia is without at least one color illustration. The quality of color reproduction, found wanting on occasion when the *Buying Guide* last reviewed the set in 1977, is now uniformly excellent. According to Graham Clarke, the new editor, in his preface to the fifth edition, "The technique of printing on layers of clear film has been constructively exploited in educational publications, and it is now being used for the first time in *The New Caxton Encyclopedia* to provide visual aids on various subjects, complementing the text and the text illustrations." Of special note are the transvision overlays (or transparent color drawings superimposed on one another to depict various aspects of structural development) that accompany the articles "Body, Human"; "Ecology"; "Oil, Petroleum"; and "Volcano." In numerous cases, *New Caxton*'s graphics are much more informative than the printed text.

There are instances, however, where the visual text could be improved. Nicholas Tucker, writing in the British newspaper *The Guardian* (May 29, 1979) touches on the two major criticisms. After praising *New Caxton* as "truly beautiful to look at," he notes that "the availability of such splendid colour resources sometimes leads to distortions; it is not really necessary, for example, to have such a large photograph of Robert Graves for the article on English literature, and it is noticeable that more space is often given to subjects like Periwinkle, which lend themselves well to illustration, than to subjects like Thinking, which do not." The *Buying Guide* made similar criticisms of the 1977 edition, pointing to an "unnecessarily large and not terribly vital reproduction of a Supreme Court brief" and "a large two-column photograph of a uniformed Red Cross worker helping up a woman who has fallen" as examples of such distortions. These particular instances have been corrected in the 1979 edition, but the general complaint remains valid. Is it necessary, for instance, to devote nearly half a page to an aerial photograph of the atomic research center at Oak Ridge, Tennessee, in the article "Atom"?

The set's map coverage is not satisfactory. As already noted (see "Purpose and Scope"), the 128-page color world atlas found in Volume 20 of the 1977 edition has been dropped. All that is left are small physical, political, and thematics maps accompanying place-name entries throughout the set. Countries of the world are customarily limited to a physical map and one or two distribution maps. EXAMPLE: "Canada" has a half-page physical map, plus three special-purpose maps showing vegetation, mineral, and industrial distribution in the country. The physical map naturally lacks political detail. Newfoundland, for instance, fails to include Goose Bay, Rigolet, Cartwright, St. Anthony, and Port Saunders. One bright note concerning *New Caxton*'s map coverage is the small but clear political maps of all British counties and some major cities. Few U.S. encyclopedias will include a map of Nottinghamshire, for example.

Physical Format

New Caxton is smartly bound in Balacron, a vinyl bookbinding material that looks and feels like leather. Tan in color with red and blue panels and gold lettering, the reinforced library binding is Smythe-sewn and will stand up well under normal use. The encyclopedia's outward appearance is attractive, but the lettering on the spine is too small to be read easily at a distance. The letter division, previously carried out to only three units, has been expanded to four units (e.g., Volume 1 covers the letters A–ARCH; Volume 2 ARCH–BELG). Each volume, which contains 320 pages, is under one inch in thickness, and the entire set requires only 17 inches of shelf space. Nevertheless, because of the weight of the paper used, the volumes, though thin, are actually quite heavy, weighing roughly three pounds apiece. Inside, the encyclopedia's three-column page layout is very pleasing to the eye, enhanced considerably by the profusion of full-color illustrations on every page. The margins are ample and the print, though rather small, is clear and readable. A heavy grade of coated art paper has been used to achieve good color reproduction. Guide words now appear at the top of each page, though occasionally they are cut off by uncropped illustrations. Finally, the volumes lie perfectly flat when open for easy consultation.

Special Features

New Caxton has several special or different features worth noting. First, of course, is the set's numerous and generally excellent graphics, including 3,000 full-color reproductions of great paintings, sculpture, and architecture (see "Graphics"). Second, throughout Volumes 1–19, readers will find colored boxes containing interesting snippets of information or arresting quotations. The long and illuminating survey article "House," for instance, includes a quotation from Bacon ("Houses are built to live in and not to look upon") and the boxed fact that "during the two world wars, ¾ million houses in Britain were damaged or destroyed." Third, pronunciations are furnished for biographical and geographical entries. The pronunciations are simple and reasonably easy to understand. EXAMPLE: *"Gielgud, John* [gēl´good]." Fourth, Volume 20 includes a 133-page world chronology entitled "The Book of Key Facts." Already described (see "Purpose and Scope"), this self-contained reference item adds little substance to the encyclopedia, but if readers remember it is there, it might come in handy on occasion for the quick date or historical overview. Fifth, and finally, Volume 20 also includes a 48-page "Study Guide" (see "Arrangement and Accessibility") that might be useful to students, particularly in the United Kingdom.

Sales Information

New Caxton is available in one binding only, that being the tan Balacron already described (see "Physical Format"). The U.S. distributor, Purnell Reference Books (a division of Macdonald-Raintree), normally sells only to schools and libraries. The current institutional price is $599.50, which represents the net price after a 25 percent discount off list. The international retail price is roughly $800. Schools and libraries ordering *New Caxton* should also figure on shipping and handling charges of about $25. Institutions that buy two or more sets at the same time receive $50 off the cumulative price. *New Caxton*, it should be understood, is not sold in-home on the subscription basis in the United States or Canada (as it is abroad). Schools and libraries serving a sizable Spanish-speaking population might also want to consider the Spanish version of *New Caxton*, called *Monitor*. Inquiries about the price and availability of the 13-volume *Monitor* should be directed to Purnell Reference Books.

Summary

The *New Caxton Encyclopedia* (1979 edition) can be quickly summed up in this manner:

Scope: Good	Accessibility: Fair
Authority: Good	Bibliographies: Poor
Reliability: Good	Graphics: Excellent
Recency: Fair	Physical Format: Good
Objectivity: Good	Special Features: Many
Clarity: Good	Price: High

To elaborate briefly, *New Caxton*, a profusely illustrated British import of recent vintage, is international in scope, with a general European and specific English emphasis. The set's subject coverage is strongest in cultural and historical areas, weakest in areas of contemporary social and political concern, particularly from the U.S. perspective. Major deficiencies include lack of currency in some articles, lack of adequate bibliographies, lack of any cross-references, and generally weak map coverage (the atlas in previous editions has been dropped). *New Caxton* is an adult encyclopedia, but ordinarily the text will be comprehensible to readers at the high school level and beyond. The style, while not condescending, is usually clear and direct. Indeed, some articles on scientific topics are notable for their lucid explanations of complicated theories or processes. On occasion, however, the vocabulary becomes overly technical or erudite. Lack of customary equivalents for metric measurements might be a problem for some U.S. readers. The set's outstanding feature is its graphics, which, though not perfect in all instances, are simply much better than one expects to find in a general encyclopedia. The many handsome art reproductions are particularly impressive, rendering the encyclopedia a browsing item as well as an information resource. In sum, *New Caxton* succeeds extraordinarily well as a visual production but is much less successful as a complete encyclopedia.

New Caxton is the only British-made encyclopedia of any consequence currently on the U.S market now that *Chambers's Encyclopaedia* (see Appendix A) is defunct, at least for the time being. Libraries that want and can afford a reasonably good British encyclopedia will not go wrong with *New Caxton*. In the context of library use, where a number of different encyclopedias are normally available, the set's emphasis on European and British people, places, and cultural history can be a decided plus. Perhaps the greatest barrier to selling U.S. consumers on *New Caxton* is not the set's several liabilities (like lack of cross-references), but its very high price (obviously the result of the set's high-quality graphics). Compared with U.S. encyclopedias of similar size and usership currently on the market, *New Caxton* is generally inferior to the new *Academic American Encyclopedia*, except in the area of graphics, where both sets are superb. Compared with *Funk & Wagnalls New Encyclopedia*, an inexpensive supermarket set, *New Caxton* offers vastly superior graphics and design, but it is not as current nor as well accessed. *The New Illustrated Columbia Encyclopedia*, another low-cost item, is inferior to *New Caxton* in most respects except in the areas of authority, reliability, and price. The *New Standard Encyclopedia* has little to offer when compared with *New Caxton* except a better record on revision and a considerably lower price tag. The remaining two sets in the intermediate adult class, the *Harver World Encyclopedia* and the *New American Encyclopedia*, are inferior to *New Caxton* in all respects except price.

Other Critical Opinions

Booklist, October 1, 1979, pp. 299–303. This unsigned review by the ALA Reference and Subscription Books Review Committee evaluates the fourth edition of *New Caxton* (1977). The review faults the encyclopedia for questionable authority, lack of signed articles, and occasional errors of fact and interpretation, but praises its illustrations and notes the value for U. S. readers of having the British point of view. At the end, the set is "not recommended" for "most" libraries. (Note that portions of this review no longer apply because the fourth edition of *New Caxton* differs in a number of ways from the fifth edition, e.g., Volume 19 is entirely changed.)

Cheney, Frances Neel. *American Reference Books Annual,* 1979, pp. 36–37. Cheney, a well-known reference book critic, provides few examples in this abbreviated review of the fourth edition (1977). She finds the illustrations "well-chosen" and "well-reproduced," but concludes that readers "will find the subject matter more fully covered in the standard American encyclopedias." Exactly what subject matter she means is not clear. (Note that portions of this review no longer apply because the fourth edition of *New Caxton* differs in a number of ways from the fifth.)

Kennerly, Sarah Law. *School Library Journal,* September 1971, pp. 98–100. Although very dated, this substantial review of the second edition of *New Caxton* (1969) is still useful for its incisive analysis and historical background. Many of Kennerly's criticisms have been acted upon by the editors over the years.

Waugh, Auberon. "Not Scholarly but Useful," *Books and Bookmen,* July 1977, pp. 20–21. The author of this favorable evaluation of the fourth edition (1977) compares *New Caxton* with *The New Encyclopaedia Britannica,* hence the title of the review. Users of the *Buying Guide* should be aware that only larger or more affluent libraries will carry the periodical *Books and Bookmen.* It is worth going to some lengths to obtain a copy of the review, however, if only for Waugh's conversational approach to encyclopedia criticism.

New Encyclopaedia Britannica

Facts in Brief

Full Title: **The New Encyclopaedia Britannica in 30 Volumes.** *Editors:* Philip W. Goetz, Editor in Chief; Bruce L. Felknor, Executive Editor; Mortimer J. Adler, Chairman, Board of Editors. *Publisher:* Encyclopaedia Britannica, Inc., 425 N. Michigan Ave., Chicago, IL 60611. *Distributor to Schools & Libraries:* Encyclopaedia Britannica Educational Corporation, 425 N. Michigan Ave., Chicago, IL 60611. *Former Title: Encyclopaedia Britannica* (1768–1973). *Edition Reviewed:* Fifteenth Edition, 1980 copyright.

Volumes: 30. *Pages:* 33,414. *Articles:* 106,800. *Words:* 43,000,000. *Illustrations:* 23,300. *Maps:* 1,080. *Index Entries:* 225,000. *Cross-references:* 83,100. *Contributors:* 4,300.

User Classification: Adult (Multivolume). *Reader Suitability:* Age 15 through Advanced Adult. *Physical Size:* 8¾ × 11¼ in.; 29 cm. *LC:* 78-75143. *ISBN:* 0-85229-360-7. *Lowest Retail Price:* $899; to schools & libraries $629.

Purpose and Scope

The New Encyclopaedia Britannica—the retitled and radically revised fifteenth edition of *Encyclopaedia Britannica*— is the oldest, largest, and best-known English-language encyclopedia. The fifteenth edition, first issued in 1974, intends to be a comprehensive, authoritative summary of the world's most important knowledge written for "the curious, intelligent" layperson. Known informally as *Britannica 3,* the fifteenth edition of this famous encyclopedia aims to be "both informational and educational," and toward that end the set is divided into three distinct parts: the single-volume *Propaedia* (Outline of Knowledge), the 10-volume *Micropaedia* (Ready Reference and Index), and the 19-volume *Macropaedia* (Knowledge in Depth). This tripartite arrangement (hence *Britannica 3*) represents a radical departure from the straight alphabetical organization that characterized all previous editions of the *Britannica.* To fully understand *Britannica 3*'s scope and purpose, the user must grasp the unique and interrelated functions of each of the parts.

The one-volume *Propaedia* is both an elaborate classification of knowledge and a topical index to the contents of the *Macropaedia.* It divides knowledge into ten main categories: Matter and Energy; The Earth; Life on Earth; Human Life; Human Society; Art; Technology;

Religion; The History of Mankind; and The Branches of Knowledge. These broad divisions are further subdivided into more specific topics and subtopics. Throughout, index references are provided to articles in the *Macropaedia*. The point of this volume is twofold. First, it serves to demonstrate what the editors of *Britannica 3* believe is the essential unity or interrelatedness of all knowledge. The encyclopedia's makers ardently embrace the concept of the "Circle of Learning," defined in the introduction to the *Propaedia* as "the faith that the whole world of knowledge is a single universe of discourse." Second, the *Propaedia* aims to provide topical access to the "Knowledge in Depth" contained in the *Macropaedia*, the heart of the encyclopedia. In the eyes of the editors, this approach facilitates the set's usefulness as an "educational" (as opposed to "informational") work, particularly for those concerned with self-education. On the other hand, some critics have dismissed the *Propaedia* volume as superfluous or intimidating (or both). For instance, Joseph Rosenblum, writing in *Wilson Library Bulletin* (December 1977, p. 300), put it this way: "Consider the 'Propaedia' of the *New Encyclopaedia Britannica*, labeled the 'Guide to the Britannica.' If the American pioneers had had such guides, this country would still be hugging the Atlantic seaboard. While the encyclopedia itself is not without merit, its supposed guide is so complex as to be worse than useless—worse, because anyone beginning an examination of the set with that volume must conclude that if the guide is so complicated, the remaining volumes must be inscrutable indeed."

The ten-volume *Micropaedia* also has a dual purpose. First, it serves as a source of quick reference information. This information is contained in some 102,000 brief articles of 750 words or less. These articles are heavily factual, limited to "look-it-up" type information, such as population figures, birth and death dates, concise historical summaries, and the like. In this regard, the *Micropaedia* functions as a self-contained, short-entry multivolume encyclopedia of approximately 14 million words. At least one critic has forcefully charged that much of the *Micropaedia* is simply an abridgment of the contents of the previous fourteenth edition of *Britannica* (see Samuel McCracken's *Commentary* article "The Scandal of 'Britannica 3' " cited under "Other Critical Opinions" at the end of this review). Second, the *Micropaedia* serves as an analytical index to the *Macropaedia* (just as the *Propaedia* serves as a topical index to the *Macropaedia*). Exactly how well the *Micropaedia* functions as an index is perhaps the most controversial question about *Britannica 3*. The issue is explored in detail under "Arrangement and Accessibility."

The 19-volume *Macropaedia* is the main part of the set. The *Propaedia* and *Micropaedia* are both subordinate to it, serving to make its contents accessible. It is in the *Macropaedia* that the great *Britannica* tradition lives. It is here that the reader encounters long scholarly articles reminiscent of those found in earlier editions of the *Britannica*, which established the encyclopedia's enduring reputation as a reference work of preeminent and even final authority. The *Macropaedia* contains 4,207 articles, all of them over 1,000 words and at least a dozen of them the length of a book. The articles average about 7,000 words, or five double-column pages.

The late Robert M. Hutchins, one of the moving forces behind the new *Britannica,* wrote in his foreword to the set: "These three—the *Propaedia,* the *Micropaedia,* and the *Macropaedia*— are designed to meet the encyclopaedic needs of the reader, whatever they may be." This is an exaggeration, typical of many of the sweeping claims made in the name of *Britannica 3.* But the set's coverage of the so-called Circle of Knowledge is indeed impressive. Most striking is the encyclopedia's truly broad international coverage. Considerably more attention is given to non-Western languages, cultures, and social systems than has ever been attempted by a general encyclopedia. EXAMPLE: The article "Visual Arts, East Asian" (in the *Macropaedia*) is textbook length. It comprehensively reviews the stylistic and historical development of Chinese, Korean, and Japanese painting, pottery, sculpture, architecture, etc. EXAMPLE: The *Macropaedia* articles "Motion-Picture Industry," "Motion Pictures, Art of," and "Motion Pictures, History of" not only devote considerable attention to developments abroad but provide an international perspective. "Motion-Picture Industry," for instance, immediately informs the reader, "Although the industry was once associated primarily with Hollywood, theatrical film production there had come to a virtual standstill in the late 1960s. Asian nations produced more films, especially Japan, which made some 700 films a year, and India, which made about half that many. American-financed and produced films, however, continued to dominate the screens of most of the world." EXAMPLE: Of 83 *Macropaedia* biographies in the area of philosophy, 17 are devoted to non-Western philosophers, including the eleventh-century Indian Rāmānuja and the contemporary Japanese Nishida Kitarō.

At one time, the *Britannica* naturally had a pronounced British orientation. (To this day the editors affect the British spelling of words like "behaviour" and "centre.") When the set's ownership passed into U.S. hands at the beginning of this century, the orientation became increasingly Western. And now, with the publication of the fifteenth edition (*Britannica 3*), the set has managed to become international, at least in a historical and comparative sense. In the area of international coverage, *Britannica 3* is far ahead of its chief competitors, *Collier's Encyclopedia* and *The Encyclopedia Americana.*

The *Britannica*'s traditional subject strength has heretofore been in the humanities. *Britannica 3* continues to cover the fine arts, language, literature, and philosophy and religion adequately, but science and technology now account for roughly 40 percent of the total coverage. It should be pointed out that, even if the ten-volume *Micropaedia* is merely an abridged version of the previous edition of *Britannica* (1929–1973) as alleged by Samuel McCracken (see "Other Critical Opinions"), *Britannica 3* is a new work, in terms both of organization and of content. The original editor of *Britannica 3,* Warren Preece, has estimated that "it is unlikely that more than 10 per cent of the new set was taken word for word from the previous edition," a comparatively small percentage when contrasted with the usual carry-over of 40 or 45 percent between other editions of the *Britannica.* Preece has also indicated that the most significant changes in the *Britannica* have occurred in the area of the sciences. "In 1929 nobody had gone into space. Nobody had transplanted a heart when I joined the company in 1957."

Like *Collier's Encyclopedia* (the newest of the advanced adult sets, produced from scratch in the late 1940s), *Britannica 3* provides reasonably well-balanced coverage of the basic knowledge areas in light of contemporary scholarship. The biological and medical sciences are especially well covered. The *Micropaedia,* for instance, includes brief but informative articles on practically all common illnesses and diseases, such as diabetes and tuberculosis. Such *Macropaedia* articles as the 17-page "Evolution" and the ten-page "Human Behaviour, Development of" exemplify the excellent survey coverage of the natural sciences. Emerging fields of study are also identified and summarized. The interdisciplinary field of psycholinguistics, for example, is treated briefly in the *Micropaedia* and more extensively in the *Macropaedia* article "Linguistics." Not covered, however, is the new and controversial field of sociobiology, which concerns the biology of human behavior and draws upon not only biology and sociology but psychology and philosophy as well. Also neglected by *Britannica 3* is the powerful movement known as scientific creationism, a theological challenge to the Darwinian theory of evolution.

Geography, traditionally well covered by the *Britannica,* accounts for roughly 15 percent of the encyclopedia's total printed text (or 6 million of 43 million words). The continents and major countries of the world receive exceptionally generous coverage. EXAMPLE: The *Micropaedia* article "Africa," nearly a page in length, furnishes a brief summary of the 50-page *Macropaedia* article, along with numerous cross-references to other *Macropaedia* articles, such as "Grasslands." The lengthy *Macropaedia* article "Africa" is followed by the articles "African Languages" (14 pages), "African Peoples, Arts of" (44 pages), "African Peoples and Cultures" (7 pages), and "Africans, Prehistoric" (4 pages). EXAMPLE: The *Micropaedia* article "China" offers the usual summary of the *Macropaedia* article and many cross-references to other *Macropaedia* articles, along with almost a page of quick reference information in a large shaded box. The box includes the country's official name, language, and religion, a color flag, a spot map, and much data on such topics as demography, economy, communications, and education and health. The *Macropaedia* article "China" (48 pages) includes an outline of the article at the beginning, a two-page physical map, and a sizable bibliography at the end. This article is followed by "China, History of," which, at 109 pages, is one of the longest in the set. Smaller countries naturally receive less coverage (e.g., the *Macropaedia* article "Afghanistan" runs to eight pages, including a full-page map and lengthy bibliography). The U.S. states and Canadian provinces are all covered in both the *Micropaedia* and *Macropaedia,* the latter articles averaging five pages in length. Oddly, there are no maps for these states and provinces in either the *Micropaedia* or *Macropaedia.* Smaller places and natural features (cities, towns, rivers, mountains, etc.) receive proportionately less coverage; for example, the Florida cities of Miami, Tampa, St. Petersburg, and Jacksonville are limited to entries in the *Micropaedia*. Major world cities, however, are covered at length in the *Macropaedia;* for instance, "Paris" covers nearly 15 pages, including a full-page map of the central city and several black-and-white photographs.

Biography also accounts for a large share of the total coverage in both the *Micropaedia* and the *Macropaedia*. Important figures are included in both (e.g., Thomas Jefferson), whereas less notable personalities (Warren Harding) appear in the *Micropaedia* only. Some critics have questioned why *Britannica 3* includes certain people while excluding others who are generally considered to be more important. EXAMPLES: Hank Aaron, Clara Bow, James Brown (the soul singer), Jim Brown (the ex-football player turned movie star), Joan Crawford, Jimmy Foxx, Mel Ott, and Stuart Roosa (of Apollo XIV fame) are included in the *Micropaedia* while Zbigniew Brzezinski, Richard Hofstadter, R. D. Laing, and Dwight Macdonald are ignored. The Abominable Snowman receives a brief entry but not the Loch Ness Monster. Also, in some instances biographees are merely identified by dates and occupation. EXAMPLE: The *Micropaedia* entry for William Styron simply informs that he was born in 1925 and is a "U.S. novelist." This information is followed by a reference to the *Macropaedia* article "Literature, Western," in which there are two sentences about Styron's novels.

Any reasonably informed critic who spends a little time with *Britannica 3* can readily point to imbalances or idiosyncrasies in the set's coverage. As the examples in the preceding paragraph suggest, the editors' topic selection in the area of biography is sometimes whimsical or uneven. The set can also be criticized for going overboard on its coverage of games, sports, and leisure activities. Not only are many contemporary athletes covered, but the *Micropaedia* contains a 56-page entry entitled "Sporting Record," which provides championship data on sports from archery to bobsledding to horse racing to roller-skating. And the *Macropaedia* has a 20-page article, "Athletic Games and Contests," which concludes with tables indicating various Olympic champions from 1896 to 1976. Unlike its enthusiastic coverage of sports, the encyclopedia has little to offer by way of practical, or how-to, information. For instance, students will look in vain for material on such subjects as how to write a business letter, how to prepare a research paper, how to study, or how to use the dictionary. The final volume of the *Micropaedia* (Volume 10) contains a 152-page Addenda, a catchall for various social data on countries, educational institutions, and national parks of the world. The Addenda section also includes the full text of six "Great Charters of the Western World" (the Magna Carta, the Bill of Rights, the Declaration of Independence, etc.), as well as color reproductions of the flags of the world (which duplicate similar reproductions with each country article in the *Micropaedia*) and a list of map terms and abbreviations. Unfortunately, this wealth of material is lost for most readers. They rarely think to turn to a volume in the middle of the set for such information, and in most cases cross-references are not provided (see "Arrangement and Accessibility").

But overall, despite these anomalies, *Britannica 3*'s coverage of the world's essential knowledge as perceived ten years ago is simply outstanding. No other general encyclopedia available in English can touch *Britannica 3*'s enormous range and depth of coverage. The *Micropaedia* alone comprises some 14 million words and is larger than most adult sets. And the *Macropaedia,* the intellectual guts of the encyclopedia, is twice the size of the *Micropaedia.* The great regret concerning the set's coverage is that it is now almost a decade out-of-date (see "Recency").

History and Authority

The name *Britannica* is practically synonymous with the word *encyclopedia.* The first *Britannica* appeared over 200 years ago, a three-volume set produced in Edinburgh between 1768 and 1771 by three enterprising Scots who were impressed by the success of Diderot's now famous French *Encyclopédie.* Issued serially in alphabetical format, the set emphasized ease of use. "Utility ought to be the principal intention of every publication," wrote William Smellie, *Britannica*'s first editor. "Wherever this intention does not plainly appear, neither the books nor their authors have the smallest claim to the approbation of mankind." It is these words that must haunt the editors and planners of the newest edition of the *Britannica.*

During the nineteenth century, new and successively larger editions of the encyclopedia appeared, the most famous being the ninth, called the "Scholars' Edition" in recognition of its long, erudite articles. Issued in 1889 after 14 years in the making, the ninth edition included numerous prominent contributors, and many of its articles continued to appear in subsequent editions. In 1901 the set was acquired by a group of Americans. Ten years later the greatest edition of the *Britannica,* the eleventh, appeared. Geoffrey Wolff, in his article "Britannica 3, History of" in the *Atlantic* (see "Other Critical Opinions" for complete reference), notes that "this edition, with its leisurely and elegant essays, brought alphabetical reference books to their highest level of quality, before or since. It has stood as a lion blocking the path against later encyclopedists." In 1920, Sears, Roebuck and Company bought the *Britannica* and under that company's ownership the twelfth, thirteenth, and fourteenth editions were produced, the latter in 1929. In 1936, the editors initiated a program of continuous revision designed to keep the set forever current.

In 1943, the late William Benton—a former United States Senator, advertising millionaire, and vice-president of the University of Chicago—acquired the *Britannica* from Sears after the university declined it as a gift. At the time of his death in 1973, Benton had served as *Britannica*'s publisher for 30 years, longer than anyone else in the encyclopedia's long history. From the beginning of Benton's ownership, however, the University of Chicago has received royalty benefits (3 percent) from the set in exchange for use of the university's name and editorial advice. By the 1960s it became apparent that the continuous revision program, designed to keep the *Britannica* relatively current, was not a complete success. Early in the decade, a physicist named Harvey Einbinder began questioning the fourteenth edition's recency and hence its reliability. Dr. Einbinder's investigations culminated in the publication of an explosive indictment of the set, *The Myth of the Britannica,* in 1964.

As early as the late 1950s, however, William Benton and two prominent colleagues from the University of Chicago, Robert Maynard Hutchins (former president of the university who died in 1977 at age 78) and Mortimer J. Adler (creator of the *Syntopicon,* an index to the major ideas found in *Great Books of the Western World,* edited by Hutchins), were laying plans to scrap the fourteenth edition and make, in Benton's words, the "best possible encyclopedia for people who read English."

Thus *Britannica 3* was born, the result of 15 years of hard intellectual labor, ten spent in planning the set and the last five writing and editing it. Dr. Einbinder, the unrelenting critic of the fourteenth edition, hailed the new *Britannica* as "unmatched for convenience, freshness, and accuracy." The set, said Einbinder, "maintains a standard of excellence that renders other adult encyclopedias obsolete." The normally circumspect Reference and Subscription Books Review Committee of the American Library Association called *Britannica 3* "a landmark" in the history of reference book publishing, although the committee did express reservations about the set's innovative arrangement. Most, though not all, other critics were equally awed by the set's magnitude (see "Other Critical Opinions" for a partial list of reviews), and for good reason. Over a 15-year period Benton spent some $32 million to produce *Britannica 3,* said to be the largest private publishing venture in history. The project involved more than 4,000 scholars from 134 countries, plus almost 400 editors and staff workers. It is estimated that some 2½ million staff-hours were required to produce the set, and that excludes the contributors' time and the typesetting and printing process.

No other general encyclopedia on the market today comes close to matching the rich array of human talent, historical tradition, and financial resources that went into the making of *Britannica 3.* The editorial staff, board of editors, advisers, and contributors are identified in the *Propaedia* volume. In 1979, Warren E. Preece, the original editor of the fifteenth edition, retired. He is succeeded by Philip W. Goetz, formerly the executive editor. In 1980, ownership of the *Britannica* passed from the Benton Foundation (established after William Benton's death in 1973) to a tax-exempt "supporting organization" that will pay out yearly grants to the University of Chicago, in addition to the school's standard annual royalty. This maneuver presumably will keep the encyclopedia in private hands, as well as avoid recently enacted tax restrictions on private foundations. (See "University of Chicago to Get Stock of Britannica to Support Institute" in the *New York Times,* October 2, 1980, p. 1+, for additional information on this transaction.) Also noteworthy are plans announced in 1980 to produce a Chinese-language version of the *Micropaedia* portion of *Britannica 3.* The encyclopedia, which will be prepared by Chinese editors and translators in Peking, is scheduled for publication in eight volumes in the mid-1980s by the state-owned China Publishing Company. Significantly, the *Britannica* will be the first modern English-language encyclopedia to be available in Chinese.

Reliability

Like its major competitors (*Collier's Encyclopedia* and *Encyclopedia Americana*), *Britannica 3* is a generally reliable reference work. Contributors like Kenneth Boulding (capital and interest), Sir Arthur Bryant (Samuel Pepys), Anthony Burgess (the novel), Barnaby Conrad (bullfighting), Malcolm Cowley (William Faulkner), Richard Dorson (folklore), Theodosius Dobzhansky (heredity), Frank Freidel (Franklin D. Roosevelt), Andrew Hacker (corporations), Arthur Koestler (wit and humor), Arthur Mizener (F. Scott Fitzgerald), John Scarne (roulette), Glenn T. Seaborg (transuranium elements), A. J. P. Taylor (Bismarck), and the late Arnold J. Toynbee (Julius Caesar) ensure a high degree of reliability. All articles in the *Macropaedia* are signed by the author's initials, following the standard *Britannica* practice. The initials are identified, along with a brief description of each contributor, in the back of the *Propaedia* volume. Also listed there are the authorities for the *Micropaedia*, although none of the *Micropaedia* articles is signed.

But like the first edition of the *Britannica*, which two centuries ago described California as "a large country of the West Indies," *Britannica 3* is not entirely free from error. Since the set was first published in 1974, several critics have discovered some rather alarming misstatements of fact and interpretation. Most diligent in this regard has been Samuel McCracken, whose article "The Scandal of 'Britannica 3' " in *Commentary* (see "Other Critical Opinions" for the complete citation) reels off numerous large and small inaccuracies, including mislabeled illustrations and distortions in the area of recent French history. *Britannica 3*, says McCracken, is "like a clock that strikes thirteen: by committing a preposterous and blatant mistake, it puts all that it says into doubt." In addition, numerous articles are now dated (see "Recency"), which also affects the set's reliability. EXAMPLE: The *Micropaedia* article "Greenland" erroneously gives Danish as the country's official language. With the advent of home rule in 1979, Greenlandic, an Eskimo tongue, became the official language. EXAMPLE: The *Micropaedia* article "Afghanistan" depicts the country's old flag (black, red, and green), not the new one (all red). The Addenda section (in Volume 10 of the *Micropaedia*) offers the same misinformation.

Recency

Britannica 3 is reasonably contemporary in its treatment of material, although the set no longer provides up-to-date information in many areas. As noted earlier (see "Purpose and Scope"), only approximately 10 percent of the encyclopedia's text was carried over word for word from the previous edition. The remaining 90 percent was prepared between 1969 and 1974. But since its publication in 1974, *Britannica 3* has not maintained even a minimally acceptable rate of continuous annual revision. Not a single new article has been added to the 19-volume *Macropaedia* in all that time. Moreover, relatively few of the *Macropaedia*'s 21,850 pages show any change since 1974, and more often than not changes that have been made involve only the insertion of an obituary date or the like. The ten-volume *Micropaedia,* which unlike the *Macropaedia* is on computer tape and thus easier and less costly to revise, shows a greater degree of revision activity. Almost 2,000 of its 10,500 pages were revised in some manner between 1975 and 1977 (when the *Buying Guide* last examined the set). Approximately the same amount of revision has occurred between 1978 and 1980 (the edition under review here). Again, most of these revisions entailed only the change of a statistic, word, or sentence or two, or the addition of a death date. The Addenda section in the final volume of the *Micropaedia,* which is heavily statistical, shows evidence of extensive revision. In addition, *Micropaedia* biographies of prominent political figures like Gerald Ford, Jimmy Carter, Walter Mondale, and Henry Kissinger have been revised, as have a number of articles on countries, including all those covering Communist-bloc nations (see "Objectivity").

Overall, the publisher estimates that some 4,000 of *Britannica 3*'s 106,800 articles are revised in some manner each year. This amounts to a revision rate of less than 4 percent a year. Most of the revisions, moreover, are quite routine, involving only the change of a statistic or addition of a date. At this rate, much of the encyclopedia will be badly dated by the mid-1980s. Already *Britannica 3* is out-of-date in numerous instances. EXAMPLE: The *Macropaedia* article "Petroleum Refining" informs the reader that "a major pipeline project was planned for the 1970s to bring crude oil from the newly discovered fields on the North Slope of Alaska." EXAMPLE: The *Micropaedia* and *Macropaedia* articles on Saudi Arabia both neglect to mention the country's role in the Organization of Petroleum Exporting Countries (OPEC). Indeed, OPEC simply does not exist in *Britannica 3*'s universe. EXAMPLE: The discussion of abortion in the *Macropaedia* article "Birth Control" notes that "some states of the United States liberalized the laws during the late 1960s," but makes no mention of the 1973 Supreme Court ruling, which completely altered the legal status of abortion in the country. EXAMPLE: There appears to be no mention of the Pentagon Papers case in the encyclopedia, despite its importance as a political *cause célèbre* during the Nixon years and its even more significant position as a landmark court case in the area of press freedom. EXAMPLE: The *Macropaedia* article "Censorship" deals with the question of "classified information in government" but never once notes the existence of the Freedom of Information Act, which has done much to change the rules in this area in the United States in recent years. Likewise, the article "Publishing, History of" deals with the same issue in a discussion of press freedom, but again there is no mention of the Freedom of Information Act. EXAMPLE: The final paragraph of the *Macropaedia* article "Afghanistan" observes, "The overthrow of the monarchy in 1973, however, casts some doubt on the nation's future; at the same time, the fact that the country has been able to combine a measure of democracy with political stability, indicates that it may also find, in due course, peaceful solutions to its economic and social problems." In view of the recent Soviet domination of Afghanistan, this commentary is woefully

This Recency Table compares selected topics in *Britannica 3* with those in other encyclopedias of similar size and intended usership.

Topic	New Encyclopaedia Britannica	Collier's	Encyclopedia Americana
Afghanistan	Not current	Fairly current	Fairly current
Dinosaurs	Fairly current	Very current	Fairly current
Greenland	Not current	Not current	Not current
Thomas Jefferson	Not current	Not current	Not current
Mass Transportation/Subways	Not current	Very current	Fairly current
Nuclear Power	Not current	Fairly current	Not current
Paris	Not current	Very current	Fairly current
Sharks	Fairly current	Fairly current	Fairly current
Shock Therapy	Fairly current	Fairly current	Fairly current
Suicide	Not current	Not current	Not current
Tuberculosis	Fairly current	Very current	Not current
Zimbabwe	Not current	Very current	Very current

out-of-date. EXAMPLE: Although the encyclopedia does note that the Atomic Energy Commission was disbanded in the mid-1970s, there is no mention of the U.S. Department of Energy, created in 1977. EXAMPLE: The *Macropaedia* article "China" is current as of 1973, reporting that "quasi-diplomatic liaison offices" have been established by the U.S. and Chinese governments. Of course, the two nations established diplomatic relations in 1979, a fact unreported by *Britannica 3*. EXAMPLE: The *Macropaedia* article "Nuclear Reactor" offers no information about the accident at Harrisburg's Three Mile Island plant several years ago, nor is the possibility of such accidents acknowledged. Rather, the article notes that "in the early 1970s nuclear production of electric power was becoming competitive in many areas and promised certain advantages, such as less air pollution, and a large number of nuclear installations were in the planning or construction stage all over the world."

The makers of *Britannica 3* have stated their belief that the set is designed to accommodate the knowledge explosion well into the twenty-first century. At least Mortimer Adler, *Britannica 3*'s guiding genius, has been quoted as saying that the encyclopedia will handle "all the expansions and alterations in human knowledge for at least fifty years." (See the *Newsweek* article cited under "Other Critical Opinions.") This is an extremely rosy view of *Britannica 3*'s future revision requirements. It is also an extraordinarily complacent and/or possibly self-deluding attitude toward continuous revision. Doubtless the *Micropaedia* will require the most revision on an annual basis, but much of the *Macropaedia* is also subject to knowledge changes and fluctuations, as several of the examples in the preceding paragraph indicate. The editors appear to believe that most if not all of the *Macropaedia*'s text is static, or not subject to rapid change. This notion is simply not true, and if they continue under that assumption for much longer, *Britannica 3* will cease to be competitive in the area of recency with the other two sets in the advanced adult category, *Collier's Encyclopedia* and *The Encyclopedia Americana. Collier's,* it should be noted, has an aggressive continuous revision program, but the *Americana* is badly dated in places.

In point of fact, *Britannica 3*'s poor performance in the area of revision is beginning to be noticed by librarians—professionals who work with reference materials day in and day out. The following letter, which appeared in the Summer 1980 issue of *RQ* (p. 407), epitomizes the feelings of disillusionment some librarians are experiencing regarding the lack of adequate revision of *Britannica 3.*

We have lost all faith in the long-relied-upon integrity of Encyclopaedia Britannica since the publication of the 1979 edition. We wonder how many others have noticed they paid some $300+ for revisions so minor and unimportant they are almost impossible to find. I have taken time to check pages in the 1974 and 1979 editions for changes and updates. In volume after volume no revisions show; in a couple which I did find the changes are simply rewording of the same information. Changes advertised in the brochure note such items as world population data and full-color illustrations of flags of the world—information readily located in a $4.00 almanac. It is no wonder the new Collier's Encyclopedia was included in a purchase package deal to help sell E.B.; it could hardly stand alone. As I pointed out to our book dealer, two subjects of intense world-wide research were totally unchanged. It does seem users have a right to expect some scholarly research to have been reported in a five year period on Cancer or Energy sources. Neither of these subjects was touched. . . .

We have had a costly lesson. No publication can stand on its reputation in today's world. Acquisitions librarians must take time to be sure of positive reviews; it appears they must also instruct business offices to issue on-approval orders, and processing branches to do no property stamping until given the word. What a sorry state we are in!

Rosalie Elespuru-Murphy
Reference Librarian, Learning Resources Center
Tompkins Cortland Community College
Dryden, New York

Like *Americana* and *Collier's,* as well as other major multivolume encyclopedias, *Britannica 3* is supplemented by a yearbook. Entitled *Britan-*

nica Book of the Year, it has been published continuously since 1938 and is one of the more informative and better produced yearbooks of this kind. Nonetheless, there is no direct relationship between *Britannica Book of the Year* and *Britannica 3.* The yearbook is useful as a record of the year's events, but its value as an updating supplement is slight. The publisher also issues two other handsomely produced and similarly useful annuals, the *Britannica Yearbook of Science and the Future* (1969–   ) and the new *Medical and Health Annual* (1976–   ).

Objectivity

In a preface to *Britannica 3,* Warren Preece, the set's original editor, assures users of the encyclopedia that every effort was made to "avoid expressions of bias or prejudice on any matter about which a respectable and reasonable difference of opinion exists," and that "in all areas in which the scholarly world acknowledges significant and reputable differences of opinion, diverse views concerning such differences [are] fairly presented, though the majority or accepted view may be so designated." This policy is in keeping with the universally accepted standards that have governed U.S. encyclopedia-making in modern times.

In most controversial areas, *Britannica 3* is free from blatant bias. Efforts are made to present opposing points of view. EXAMPLE: Treatment of the subject of abortion in the *Macropaedia* article "Birth Control" is entirely impartial, emphasizing the medical and legal aspects of the topic. Religious objections to abortion are noted but not discussed. The writer of the article, Ellinor Elizabeth Nancy Draper, identified as the author of a book called *Birth Control in the Modern World,* points out the potentially harmful effects of the operation, noting that "after abortion the likelihood of abnormal pregnancies, premature births, illness in the woman, or even sterility is increased." But she also notes that "in cases in which legal abortion has been denied, on the other hand, the children may suffer." The discussion concludes with the statement, "For purposes of birth control, medical opinion strongly favours contraception over abortion."

There are instances of bias in the encyclopedia, however. EXAMPLE: Both the *Micropaedia* and *Macropaedia* articles on Thomas Jefferson fail to mention his several illegitimate black children. Likewise, the Fawn Brodie book *Thomas Jefferson: An Intimate History* (1974), which documents Jefferson's controversial private life, is ignored, both in the articles and the bibliography that accompanies the *Macropaedia* article. The article, however, does include a forthright discussion of Jefferson's views on race (coverage not found in most adult encyclopedias) and the fact that he was a slave owner. EXAMPLE: The *Macropaedia* article "Evolution" states that "Charles Darwin established evolution as an inescapable fact," a view not accepted by proponents of scientific creationism, a Christian movement that opposes Darwinism. The so-called creationist arguments are not represented in *Britannica 3.*

Other critics have also found evidence of bias in the encyclopedia.

Robert Wood, writing in the *Review of Metaphysics* (June 1977, p. 750), points out that the article on the philosopher Martin Heidegger "is written by Arne Haess, who is not one of the most outstanding Heidegger scholars; the article contains many careless misrepresentations; it employs a kind of mock hyphenation of terms not employed by Heidegger himself; it suggests 'specific pretension,' 'grandiose illusion' and 'mystification' by way of evaluation. One suspects, in allowing such an article and even in commissioning no Heidegger scholar of note for it, that the editors are participating deliberately in a prejudice against Heidegger, widely shared in the Anglo-American *Kreis,* that alternates between ignoring and vilifying a serious and influential thinker." In another instance, Robert Gorham Davis, writing in the *New York Times Book Review,* asks, "Was a French Jesuit [Rev. Henri Chambre, S.J., author of *De Karl Marx à Mao Tsé-tung: Introduction Critique au Marxisme-Léninisme*] the right choice to write on Marxism, or William Manchester on the Kennedy family? Should Dr. Johnson receive more space than Sigmund Freud, or the Greek tyrant Pisistratus than Herbert Hoover? Is the full detailed horror of the Nazi extermination camps anywhere sufficiently faced? Why is there no reference to such deviant psychoanalysts as Wilhelm Reich and R. D. Laing, or to such dominant figures in the French intellectual scene as Roland Barthes, Michel Foucault, Jacques Lacan, Louis Althusser and Jacques Derrida?" But Davis concludes with "on the whole" praise for the "magnificent job" *Britannica 3* and its editors have done in covering and fairly treating the world's knowledge.

A far more serious charge of political bias is contained in both a review of *Britannica 3* in the scholarly journal *Slavic Review* (June 1975, pp. 411–412) by Romauld J. Misiunas, and in Samuel McCracken's broadside entitled "The Scandal of 'Britannica 3' " in *Commentary* (see "Other Critical Opinions"). Both writers accuse the encyclopedia of a pro-Soviet bias. As an example, the *Slavic Review* article points out that the Communist party is described in *Britannica* as "the leading political organization" in the Soviet Union, when in fact it is the only one permitted to exist. References to suppression of religion and internal dissent are also said to be omitted. And indeed, *Britannica* 3's articles on Moscow and the 15 Soviet republics were prepared by Soviet government employees and supplied to the encyclopedia through Novosti, the official Soviet press agency. As McCracken observes, "These *Britannica* articles have, perforce, been passed through the crystalline lattices of Soviet censorship."

Responding to these criticisms, the editors of *Britannica 3* promised that "the Soviet articles are being reviewed by committees of specialists and that suggested alterations will be incorporated into the regular periodic revision of the Britannica" (*New York Times,* September 21, 1975). By the late 1970s, the offending articles were revised. A ten-page booklet issued by the publisher in 1979 entitled *What's New in Britannica 3* describes the revision process in this way: "In 1974 we were criticized in the press for having commissioned local scholars as authors for many of the geographical articles on Communist countries (even though all the history articles of those countries were authored by Western scholars). Subsequent reexamination of those geographical articles under the most critical analysis did reveal some areas where improvements should be made. All of these articles (20 on countries and cities in eastern Europe, plus Cuba and Havana) were therefore re-assigned to Western scholars for revision, and all of the revised versions have now replaced the earlier articles in the set." Both Misiunas in the *Slavic Review* and McCracken in *Commentary* imply that *Britannica 3*'s original articles on Communist places were part of a plot to brainwash Western readers. A less conspiratorial view is that *Britannica*'s editors' efforts to be "international" in authority and authorship simply backfired.

The booklet called *What's New in Britannica 3* also notes that the encyclopedia's major articles on Mormonism and the Jehovah's Witnesses "drew numerous complaints from the followers of those religious creeds. . . . With the help of highly-qualified advisers and consultants, both of these articles have been rewritten and we believe they will now not only be acceptable to the former critics but will also provide a better understanding for the general reader."

Yet another allegation of bias has been made by the intrepid encyclopedia critic Harvey Einbinder (who, in 1964, published *Myth of the Britannica,* a strong indictment of the previous edition). In an article entitled "Politics and the New Britannica" in *The Nation* (March 22, 1975, pp. 342–344), Einbinder charges that *Britannica 3* deliberately soft-pedals negative or unflattering information about various countries so as not to jeopardize sales abroad: "Dr. Pangloss is alive and well in the new edition. Foreign countries are portrayed in glowing terms. An insistent optimism that is reminiscent of the *National Geographic* infuses the pages of the *Encyclopaedia*. Positive developments are emphasized: negative factors are slighted. Growth and progress are stressed; inertia and stagnation are minimized. No matter how impoverished a nation may be, hope is held out for a brighter, better future. Even when the facts presented are bleak and forbidding, contributors manage to find something hopeful to say about the future." The *Buying Guide*'s own investigations substantiate this criticism. The *Macropaedia* article "Afghanistan," for instance, concludes with the rosy forecast (now quite remote) that "the fact that the country has been able to combine a measure of democracy with political stability, indicates that it may also find, in due course, peaceful solutions to its economic and social problems." Likewise, the *Macropaedia* article "Canada" finds a silver lining in the cultural and political tensions between English- and French-speaking Canadians. Commenting on the Official Languages Act of 1969, the article points out, "Not only has this increased opportunities throughout the country for Canadians of French origin, but also it may increase the desire of other Canadians to speak French and interest themselves in French culture."

Clarity and Reader Suitability

Britannica 3 is written to be comprehensible to "the curious, intelligent" layperson. In most instances, the set achieves this goal, although some articles in the natural sciences and technical fields are well beyond the comprehension of nonspecialists. The *Choice* review (see "Other Critical Opinions" for complete reference) notes that *Britannica 3*'s article on atomic structure is less understandable to the lay reader than the comparable article in the *McGraw-Hill Encyclopedia of Science and Technology,* a specialized work. Other critics have pointed out that *Britannica 3*'s articles in the area of mathematics are entirely too difficult for the mythical "curious, intelligent" layperson.

It is practically impossible to generalize about the style of such a large and varied work as *Britannica 3*. Some articles are written in a very personal manner. EXAMPLE: Anthony Burgess on the novel is, by turns, informative, amusing, and cutting. Consider, for instance, his comments on the novelist as critic: "Novelists who achieve very large success are possibly not to be trusted as critics: obsessed by their own individual aims and attainments, shorn of self-doubt by the literary world's acclaim or their royalty statements, they bring to other men's novels a kind of magisterial blindness." Other articles are models of clarity on imposing or difficult subjects. EXAMPLE: Philip N. Powers on safety problems affecting nuclear reactors could hardly be more lucid: "A nuclear reactor is not a bomb and thus does not present a bomb-type hazard; nevertheless, the problem of safety is critical. It is simplified by certain self-controlling features of reactors; e.g., the fact that any increase in temperature in a boiling-water or pressurized-water reactor reduces the reactivity—that is, tends to shut down the reactor, thus providing an inherent stability. The possibility of a nuclear excursion, involving a substantial release of radioactive materials, nevertheless remains. A loss of coolant is conceivable. The loss would immediately stop the chain reaction, but the heat residue could melt the fuel, releasing a large volume of radioactivity." And other articles, as already noted, are excessively technical and complicated. EXAMPLE: J. N. Mohanty on the philosophies of India frequently presents the many concepts, schools, and works in transliterated rather than translated form; for example, "Mandana attempted to integrate this linguistic philosophy into his own form of *advaitavāda,* though later followers of Sankara did not accept the doctrine of *sphota.*" As Robert Wood notes in his review in the *Review of Metaphysics* (see "Other Critical Opinions"), "The wealth of detail under each of his [Mohanty's] basic headings is overwhelming enough without expecting the reader to deal with numerous Indian terms as well." Most articles, however, are written in a scholarly though readable fashion and will be intelligible to bright juniors and seniors in high school, college students, and adults with a twelfth-grade reading level or better.

Encyclopaedia Britannica, Inc., advertising, however, suggests that the set will be useful to children. From the beginning, advertisements have proclaimed the encyclopedia to be "ideal for homework. It is written in clear, readable language . . . the language of today . . . so that even the most complex subjects become much easier for your children to understand." As documentation for these claims, the firm points to favorable evaluative comments received from numerous junior high school librarians and media specialists around the country. A typical comment reads:

"I am very pleased with the number of students using the new *Encyclopaedia Britannica*. They are finding the material they need in most cases. I particularly like the *Micropaedia* with the Ready Reference and Index. It is real handy and many students get the information they need without going farther. If they need more information the references are right there, easy to use."

Thus far, however, knowledgeable encyclopedia critics have debunked the notion that *Britannica 3* might be useful for young readers. Robert Gorham Davis, writing in the *New York Times Book Review* (see "Other Critical Opinions"), states that "the editors' repeated insistence that the articles are accessible [comprehensible] to the curious non-expert or bright high-school student is frequently not true. Some of the technicians seem to be writing for their peers, and even the most brilliant expositor cannot make understandable the equivalent of a graduate course in structural linguistics or Husserl's phenomenology." The Reference and Subscription Books Review Committee quite correctly notes that *Britannica 3* lacks the vocabulary control and curriculum orientation of the better children's and young adult sets. And as Geoffrey Wolff says of *Britannica* salespeople in one of his *Atlantic* articles, "Anyone who claims . . . that the set is suitable for schoolchildren too young to drive an automobile should be had up for perjury."

The *Buying Guide* believes that *Britannica 3* is an advanced adult encyclopedia that normally requires a twelfth-grade or higher level of reading comprehension and that younger readers would be best advised to use encyclopedias that are more compatible with their reading skills and grade levels.

Arrangement and Accessibility

As already pointed out, the new *Britannica*'s arrangement is a radical departure from the straight alphabetical organization used by all previous editions. More than that, *Britannica 3*'s tripartite arrangement represents the first significant innovation in general encyclopedia organization since the alphabetical approach was introduced some three centuries ago. It has already been explained that the one-volume *Propaedia* is a topical guide and index to the *Macropaedia;* that the ten-volume *Micropaedia* is both a source of quick reference information and an alphabetical index to the *Macropaedia;* and that the *Macropaedia*, the heart of *Britannica 3*, provides lengthy articles that summarize the world's vital knowledge. Both the *Micropaedia* and the *Macropaedia* are arranged alphabetically, letter-by-letter ("Indiana" precedes "Indian Ocean"). The *Micropaedia*'s volumes are numbered with roman numerals I–X, whereas the *Macropaedia* has arabic numbers 1–19. Different colored panels on the spine of each volume keep the three parts from being confused. In the 1980 edition, the *Propaedia* is orange, the *Micropaedia* red, and the *Macropaedia* blue.

So much for the arrangement, which is different, certainly innovative, and possibly confusing. The key question is: how accessible is the material in the set, particularly the contents of the *Macropaedia?* It was, remember, the *Britannica*'s first editor, William Smellie, who proclaimed *utility* as the basic principle of encyclopedia-making. If an encyclopedia is overly complicated in arrangement or design, or if the knowledge and information it contains cannot be easily retrieved, then the encyclopedia lacks utility, at least in the sense Smellie was using the term.

Perhaps the best way to demonstrate how *Britannica 3*'s arrangement works and how accessible its contents are is through two relatively simple but representative step-by-step examples, with comparative references to *Britannica*'s chief rivals, *Collier's Encyclopedia* and *Encyclopedia Americana*. Note that the editors of *Britannica 3* recommend that most searches begin with the *Micropaedia*.

Example 1: Find information on the subject of abortion.

The Search in *Britannica 3*

Micropaedia consulted under "Abortion." Entry found. It includes a one-sentence definition of abortion, a *See also* reference to "Fetus," and six *See* references to the *Macropaedia*, as follows:

*attitudes, practices, and legal history 2:1069b (the "b" indicates the quarter of the column where the reference begins; a, b, c, and d are used for column one, and e, f, g, and h for column two).

*horse diseases and prevention 10:1284h.

*Listeria monocytogenes spread theory 9:543f.

*medical and legal aspects 11:851f.

*pregnancy termination factors 14:977f.

*Soviet Union legalization of abortion 14:821h.

Macropaedia consulted under each of the above references. The first reference (2:1069) contains a substantial three-quarter page discussion of the scientific and legal aspects of abortion in the article "Birth Control" (the same article cited under both "Objectivity" and "Recency"). The fourth reference (11:851) contains a lengthy paragraph on the legal situation in the article "Medicine and Surgery, Practice of." The discussion is international and generally duplicates the information found in "Birth Control." The fifth reference (14:977) contains an excellent one-page technical summary of the medical definition of abortion in the article "Pregnancy." The last reference (14:821) contains very brief information in the article "Population," which again duplicates that found in "Birth Control." It is interesting to note that this article provides current information on the legal status of abortion in the Soviet Union, whereas similar information is not available for the United States (see "Recency"). The two remaining references (9:543 and 10:1284) are marginal.

The Search in *Collier's Encyclopedia*

Consulted Volume 1 (A to AMELAND). Found two-and-a-half-page article, "Abortion." The article covers the history of abortion, its legal status in major countries around the world, an up-to-date discussion of the legal and ethical situation in the United States, and a lengthy section on various medical procedures. The article concludes with a short but very informative bibliographic essay on abortion that will be helpful to students seeking additional sources of information. The article is signed by Christopher Tietze, who is Senior Consultant to the Population Council in New York City. The article provides no cross-references. Also consulted *Collier's* general index (in Volume 24). Thirteen references found, including one to the article "Abortion" already located in Volume 1. The remaining 12 references lead the reader to pertinent but incidental information on the topic, for example, to the article on U.S. Supreme Court Justice Harry Blackmun, who wrote the majority opinion in *Roe* v. *Wade,* the case that legalized abortion in the United States. Comparatively speaking, the information found in *Collier's* is more extensive, somewhat less technical, and decidedly more current than that found in *Britannica 3.* In terms of accessibility, there is not a great deal of difference between the two encyclopedias in this instance. Both the *Micropaedia* (*Britannica*'s index) and the index to *Collier's* lead the reader to all relevant information on the subject in their respective sets, although *Collier's* furnishes twice as many references as *Britannica 3.* On the other hand, all of *Britannica 3*'s references are analytical, whereas only five of the *Collier's* references are analytical (that is, indicate the subject matter of the reference, e.g., "Abortion— attitudes, practices, and legal history 2:1069b").

The Search in *The Encyclopedia Americana*

Consulted Volume 1 (A to ANJOU). Found two-page article, "Abortion." The first part of the article, which emphasizes the legal and moral aspects of abortion, is signed by Glanville L. Williams, a professor of English law at Jesus College, Cambridge University, in England. The second part, which discusses medical procedures, is signed by Dr. Denis Cavanagh, a professor of obstetrics and gynecology at the University of South Florida in Tampa. There is no bibliography, and no cross-references. Also consulted *Americana*'s general index (Volume 30). Fourteen references found, including one to the article "Abortion" already located in Volume 1. The 13 remaining references (entailing use of eight other volumes) lead the reader to a variety of information, some of it directly related to abortion (e.g., forms of population control), some of it peripheral in nature (e.g., as related to the question of privacy), and some of it duplicatory. Comparatively speaking, *Americana*'s treatment of the topic is, like *Collier's,* more extensive, somewhat less technical, and decidedly more current than that found in *Britannica 3.* In terms of accessibility, there is not a great deal of difference between the two encyclopedias in this instance. Both the *Micropaedia* and the *Americana* index lead directly to the information being sought, although (again like *Collier's*) *Americana* furnishes twice as many references as *Britannica 3.* Both the *Americana* index and *Micropaedia* references are fully analytical.

Example 2: Find information about the court cases involving leaders of the American Communist Party during the 1950s. Specifically, how many people were tried, what was the basis of the charges, and what was the legal outcome?

The Search in *Britannica 3*

Micropaedia consulted under "American Communist Party." No entry found.

Micropaedia consulted under "Communist Party, U.S." and "Communist Party, American." No entries found.

Micropaedia consulted under "Communism." Entry found. It includes a brief one-paragraph definition of communism, a reference to a major article in the *Macropaedia* (4:1020), and 113 additional references scattered throughout the remaining 18 volumes of the *Macropaedia*. Twenty-six of these references are grouped under the subheading "Communist parties."

Micropaedia subheading "Communist parties" (under "Communism") consulted. No reference to American Communist Party found. Subheading "National Communism" (which includes 22 references) also consulted. No reference to American Communist Party found.

Macropaedia article "Communism" (4:1020) scanned for reference to American Communist Party. No mention found in the seven-page article.

Micropaedia consulted under "United States." Entry found. It includes a brief description of the geographical makeup of the country, a reference to a major article in the *Macropaedia* (18:905), a concise outline of what that article covers, and 441 additional references to other articles in the *Macropaedia*. These additional references are listed alphabetically by topic under subheadings like "agriculture," "communications," and "military affairs."

Micropaedia subheadings "constitution and law" and "government" consulted. No reference to American Communist Party found.

Micropaedia consulted under "United States, History of the." Entry found. It is similar in organization to the entry "United States." A similar search was conducted for references to American Communist Party. None found.

Micropaedia consulted under "Loyalty." No entry found. Frustrated, the user thinks for a moment. *Britannica 3* must have *something* on the subject. The Smith Act is pulled from memory. As the user recalls, the Act was a piece of legislation passed by the U.S. Congress during the McCarthy era designed to repress communist activity in the country.

Micropaedia consulted under "Smith Act." Entry found. The one-paragraph article describes the Smith Act as a "U.S. federal law passed in 1940 that made it a criminal offense to advocate violent overthrow of the government or to organize or be a member of any group of [sic] society devoted to such advocacy." The article continues by noting that after World War II this legislation "was made the basis of a series of prosecutions against leaders of the Communist Party. The conviction of the principal officers was sustained, and the constitutionality of the 'advocacy' provision upheld, by the Supreme Court in *Dennis v. United States* (1951); but in a later case (*Yates v. United States*, 1957) the court offset this position somewhat by a strict reading of the language of the Smith Act." The article is followed by two references to additional information in the *Macropaedia*. The first reference is to the article "United States, History of the" and informs the reader that 11 American Communist leaders were sent to jail in 1949 under the provisions of the Smith Act. The other reference (to the article "Constitutional Law") merely repeats some of the information found in the *Micropaedia* article "Smith Act."

The Search in *Collier's Encyclopedia*

Index volume consulted under "American Communist Party." No entry found. Under "Communist Party, United States," however, the index provides six references to the topic, four of which are analytical. The first refers to a two-page article entitled "Communist Party, United States," which offers a detailed historical summary of the American Communist Party. The article includes a section on "Communists and the Courts," which concisely answers the original question. The remaining references provide additional information in articles on Senator Joseph McCarthy, who vigorously opposed Communism in the 1950s, the AFL-CIO, civil liberties in the United States, Tom Clark (a former U.S. attorney general and Supreme Court justice), and presidential election data. Unlike the *Micropaedia*, the *Collier's* index leads the user directly to the information being sought.

The Search in *Encyclopedia Americana*

Index volume consulted under "American Communist Party." Cross-reference entry found, referring to "Communist Party (U.S.)." This entry provides 13 analytical references to the topic, including a basic review article entitled "Communist Parties." This article, unlike the more specific "Communist Party, United States" in *Collier's*, does not include information about court cases involving American Communist Party members in the 1950s. Rather, this information is found by pursuing references to such articles as "Civil Rights and Liberties," "Smith Act," "Supreme Court of the United States," and "United States." Although the needed information is scattered among a number of volumes in the *Americana*, the set's analytical index makes the material readily accessible.

At this point, six specific observations are in order concerning *Britannica 3*'s accessibility:

1. The *Micropaedia* as a source of ready reference information is not indexed at all, save for some *See* and *See also* references. The difficulties encountered by the user because of this are amply demonstrated in Ex-

ample 2 above. If the Smith Act had not been remembered by the user or if the Act had been unknown to the user, no information on the American Communist Party would have been found in either the *Micropaedia* or the *Macropaedia*. In another example, the *Micropaedia* has an article called "Secret Speech." It deals with Nikita Khrushchev's famous destalinization speech in 1956. But how are readers expected to find this article? There are no cross-references from either the *Micropaedia* or *Macropaedia* articles on Khrushchev, and, of course, there is no index to the *Micropaedia*. Hundreds of similar examples could be cited. At 14 million words, the *Micropaedia* alone is larger than most adult encyclopedias on the market today. Yet its contents are not accessible through a general index. Put another way, approximately one-third of the contents of *Britannica 3* are not indexed.

2. The *Micropaedia* as an analytical index to the *Macropaedia* is not as comprehensive nor as effective as *Collier's* and *Americana*'s single-volume alphabetical indexes. Sometimes the *Micropaedia* works well as an index, as Example 1 illustrates. Sometimes it fails completely, as Example 2 shows. The reason for the *Micropaedia*'s erratic performance as an index is not difficult to figure out. In its dual role as reference source and index, the *Micropaedia* includes about 102,000 entries, but only some 44,000 of these provide references to the *Macropaedia*. Counting analytical references, the *Micropaedia* provides only about 185,000 references to the *Macropaedia*, the heart of *Britannica 3*, and the *Propaedia* volume adds another 40,000 references, but not in alphabetical sequence (the *Propaedia* is arranged topically). It must be said that 225,000 index references to an encyclopedia containing 43 million words is an abominable indexing ratio. By comparison, *Collier's* index provides over 400,000 analytical references to a set only half the size of *Britannica 3*. The *Americana* index has 353,000 references.

3. Although the makers of *Britannica 3* claim the set's unique arrangement minimizes fragmentation of knowledge, this is not true. As both Examples 1 and 2 indicate, information on even the simplest topics is scattered throughout the set. The same, of course, is true of *Collier's* and the *Americana*.

4. The *Propaedia*, which contains approximately 40,000 references to the *Macropaedia*, is useless as an index when specific information is required. Topically arranged, the *Propaedia* is only a very selective index to the contents of the *Macropaedia*. As such, it is only useful to those who want to study a broad topic (like weaponry or political theory), and even then its complex design will discourage most readers.

5. Many illustrations in *Britannica 3* are not indexed, including all those in the *Micropaedia*. The *Macropaedia* article "Caricature, Cartoon, and Comic Strip," for example, includes a reproduction of an engraving by William Hogarth, but the *Micropaedia* entry on Hogarth fails to refer the reader to it.

6. *Britannica 3* is a treasury of information—factual, theoretical, and pictorial—but because the set is woefully underindexed, much of this information is inaccessible to even the most determined or skillful user.

What *Britannica 3* needs most of all is a detailed general index. Most likely such an index would encompass two volumes and run upwards of a million analytical entries.

It should be noted that practically all responsible critics have found fault with the encyclopedia on the same grounds. The *RQ* review by Nat Josel (see "Other Critical Opinions" for complete citation) observed that "neither the *Micropaedia* nor the *Propaedia* nor their combination obviates the need for the unity an index provides." Dorothy Ethlyn Cole, a library science professor, said in *Wilson Library Bulletin*, "The conclusion reached by this reviewer is that *Britannica 3* contains much excellent material, but is difficult to use. There are several reasons. The very division of content between *Micropaedia* and *Macropaedia* makes it necessary to consult another volume in the majority of cases; indeed, it was our experience that even simple searches might involve eight or nine volumes. This is not an unhappy experience for the leisurely reader; it can in fact often be a serendipitous one. The reader who wants to 'get it all together' in a short time may feel annoyed and frustrated. . . . By far the greatest source of difficulty in the use of *Britannica 3* is the indexing, and in this encyclopedia the use of the index is absolutely essential." Robert G. Hazo, writing in the *New York Times Book Review*, noted that "reader access to subject matter could just as easily have been achieved by shuffling the smaller articles of the 'Micropaedia' together with the larger articles of the 'Macropaedia.' (Both are alphabetically arranged.) Indeed, such an arrangement would be more convenient since it would eliminate the present duplication of the 4,000-plus larger articles by the matching summary pieces in the 'Micropaedia.' It would also eliminate the multiplication of exertions involved in using a 10-volume index which requires pulling different volumes rather than merely flipping pages in a single-volume index." Samuel McCracken in *Commentary* put it this way: "This arrangement has nothing to recommend it except commercial novelty." Bill Katz, always a perceptive observer, says that this is "the one major weakness of all these volumes: There is no separate index to the *Macropaedia*. The fourteenth edition of the *Britannica* had one of the finest indexes of any encyclopedia. No more." Finally, the reactions of U.S. and Canadian reference librarians participating in the encyclopedia surveys published as Part II of the *Buying Guide* ("Special Reports") are very negative, and sometimes outright vituperative, about *Britannica 3*'s accessibility.

The makers of the encyclopedia are well aware of this general unhappiness on the part of critics and librarians with the set's indexing. Thus far, there has been no hint that an effective index will someday be prepared, although that possibility always exists. Two efforts to deflect criticism of the set's accessibility (or inaccessibility), however, have been undertaken by Encyclopaedia Britannica Educational Corporation (EBEC), a sister company of Encyclopaedia Britannica, Inc., which distributes *Britannica 3* to schools and libraries. First, in 1977, EBEC developed a sound filmstrip entitled *How to Use Britannica 3*. The filmstrip, available free to schools and libraries owning the encyclopedia, offers an informative but quite elementary introduction to *Britannica 3*'s three-part arrangement and how the parts relate to one another. And second, in 1981 the company issued the *Library Guide to Encyclopaedia Britannica*, a one-volume compilation which consists of approximately 155,000 main entries plus 235,000 subentries derived from the 10-volume *Micropaedia* and 19-volume *Macropaedia* listed in a single alphabetical sequence. The foreword to the *Library Guide* stresses that the volume "is not a new work; it is not a reindexing of *Encyclopaedia Britannica.*" The chief purpose of the guide is to bring together all indexed entries in the *Micropaedia* and *Macropaedia* into one volume, thus resulting in "a considerable convenience to many readers" (foreword). *The Library Guide,* which sells for $35, is available only to schools and libraries. Unfortunately, the volume does little to improve accessibility to *Britannica 3*'s contents. Librarians who do order the *Library Guide* may return it if not satisfied.

Bibliographies

Virtually every article in the *Macropaedia* concludes with a lengthy bibliography (the *Micropaedia* and *Propaedia,* however, do not include bibliographies). Almost without exception, the bibliographies are carefully selected and concisely annotated. The annotations provide the reader with a helpful description of what each title listed contains and how it might be useful for further study. Indeed, the lists are authoritative reviews of the literature on a particular subject, resembling miniature bibliographic essays. Unlike previous editions of the *Britannica,* the bibliographies in the *Macropaedia* do not, as a rule, include obscure or inaccessible works. Likewise, the lists are generally limited to English-language titles. Two negative criticisms concerning the bibliographies are in order: (1) the lists fail to include the name of the publisher of the book being cited, and (2) some of the lists are now dated. The *Buying Guide* estimates that only 10 percent of the titles listed were published during the 1970s (and none during the 1980s); 50 percent were published in the 1960s, with the remaining 40 percent prior to 1960. Unfortunately, many important recently published titles are ignored, such as the aforementioned Fawn Brodie book *Thomas Jefferson: An Intimate History* (1974).

Graphics

Considering its size, *Britannica 3* is not a heavily illustrated encyclopedia. The *Propaedia* contains no illustrations whatsoever. The *Micropaedia* includes some 16,000 illustrations, mostly black-and-white photographs of people, places, and flora and fauna. These graphics are quite small, usually no larger than a good-sized postage stamp. In many instances, they lack sufficient detail and are poorly reproduced. See, for instance, the dim illustration of a sandbar shark with the *Micropaedia* article "Shark." The larger *Macropaedia* has even fewer illustrations, about 7,000, of which a thousand or so are in color (most contained in 160 color plates distributed throughout the *Macropaedia*). Here utilitarian diagrams and photographs predominate. These illustrations are normally larger than those found in the *Micropaedia*. They almost always enhance or clarify the written text. Those accompanying scientific and technical material are especially noteworthy. Although the use of color is quite limited, the quality of color reproduction is uniformly good throughout the set. Regrettably, most of the graphics in the *Macropaedia* are not indexed (see "Arrangement and Accessibility").

There are almost 300 maps in the *Micropaedia*. Small and in black-and-white, they emphasize historical developments. EXAMPLE: The entry "Inca Road System" is accompanied by a simple map showing the main portions of the Inca's remarkable highway system. In the *Macropaedia* there are 800 maps, of which 400 are in color. The continents and major countries of the world each have a physical-political map produced by Rand McNally & Company, accompanied by a detailed map index that includes references to cities and towns as well as physical features and points of interest. In addition, there are a variety of special-purpose maps for some larger places. EXAMPLE: The article on Australia includes maps showing geological structure, physiographic regions, rainfall patterns, average temperatures, soil analyses, vegetation zones, mineral resources, and population density. In other instances, there are few special-purpose maps. EXAMPLE: The article on Canada contains only one distribution map, that showing population density in the several provinces. Even more odd is the lack of map coverage for the U.S. states and Canadian provinces. This is a serious omission. On the other hand, major cities of the world like Chicago, Delhi, London, Mexico City, New York, Paris, and Tokyo have detailed and very useful maps showing major features, streets, attractions, etc. Unfortunately, these maps have not been revised since their initial publication in 1974, and some are beginning to show their age. EXAMPLE: The Paris map fails to include the Pompidou Center, the city's sensational and controversial art museum opened in 1977. Overall, the encyclopedia's map coverage is eccentric, spotty, and, for a general reference work as large as *Britannica 3*, very disappointing.

Physical Format

Britannica 3's most popular binding, called the Standard binding, is now regency red with gold lettering. Different colored panels on the spine of each volume visually identify the three parts of the set: the *Propaedia* has an orange panel, the *Micropaedia* bright red panels, and the *Macropaedia* blue panels. The pyroxylin-coated binding is as durable as any on the market today. Under heavy use, however, the gold lettering on the spine wears off quickly.

Inside, befitting the set's image as a serious work of scholarship, *Britannica 3* is dignified rather than inviting. The page layout is formal, sensible, predictable, orderly, and pleasing in a refined sort of way. The 9-point Times Roman type conveys the sense that this is a *real* encyclopedia, the final word. The *Micropaedia* has three columns of text whereas the *Macropaedia* and the *Propaedia* have two. Guide words appear at the top of each page in all three parts. In addition, the *Macropaedia* includes marginal notes, or sideheads, that aid the reader in locating specific material in the longer articles.

Special Features

The set's outstanding special feature, of course, is its new and radically different organization, discussed fully under "Arrangement and Accessibility." Indeed, *Britannica 3*'s original editor, Warren Preece, has written that "its appearance called forth adjectives such as monumental, revolutionary, fabulous, fantastic, extraordinary." Another significant special feature is the encyclopedia's extensive international coverage and authorship (see "Purpose and Scope"; "History and Authority"; and "Objectivity"). Another special feature, though not unique, is the inclusion of substantial information boxes for each country of the world in the *Micropaedia*. The boxes bring together an enormous amount of statistical data on population, religion, the economy, communication, transportation, education, health, and the like. Each box also includes the country's flag and a small locator map. Finally, users of *Britannica 3* should be aware of the 152-page Addenda section in Volume X of the *Micropaedia*. As already noted (see "Purpose and Scope"), this feature is a hodgepodge of information on countries, cities, educational institutions, national parks, and flags of the world. National life expectancy figures, for instance, are included in the country-by-country "World Population and Area" table. Unfortunately, because of its placement in the middle of the set and lack of adequate cross-referencing (e.g., the *Micropaedia* entry "China" fails to direct the reader to the Addenda section for additional data on the country), the Addenda section is overlooked by most users of *Britannica 3*.

Sales Information

The principal method of selling *Britannica 3* is in-home on the subscription, or installment, basis. Selected retail bookstores do occasionally carry the set, but experience has shown that this is not a productive sales approach. Charles E. Swanson, president of Encyclopaedia Britannica, Inc., has noted, "We are selling a few encyclopedia sets in bookstores. But most of them don't do well there. The problem: how do you get a bookstore clerk to explain the Britannica?" (*Publishers Weekly*, June 21, 1976, pp. 44–45). Nevertheless, the 1980s will very likely see renewed efforts on the part of the company to sell *Britannica 3* in stores, partly because of the Aretê challenge (see the *Academic American Encyclopedia* review under "Sales Information") and partly because in-home selling is no longer as lucrative as it once was due to increased regulation by the Federal Trade Commission (see "Selling Encyclopedias" in Part I of the *Buying Guide*). In 1980, for example, the firm opened its first permanent kiosk in a shopping mall (in Phoenix, Ariz.). Britannica is also experimenting with selling its products in such stores as Walden bookstores and Montgomery Wards in selected market areas.

Britannica 3 is currently available in several bindings, the most popular and least expensive being the Standard in regency red already described (see "Physical Format"). At present, this binding retails for $899, plus a whopping $50 shipping and handling, plus any state or local tax. The Heirloom binding, more decorative than the Standard, retails for $999, plus the usual added charges. Even more exotic bindings are available (e.g., Morocco), but these are for the very rich. The great majority of purchasers of *Britannica 3* will find the Standard binding quite adequate. The Standard binding is also available to schools and libraries at the discount rate of $629 delivered. Educators who wish to acquire the encyclopedia for their personal use receive $150 off the retail price (or a purchase price of $749).

Retail customers who wish to trade in an old edition of the *Britannica* for the current copyright will receive a $100 allowance on the old set, no matter when the old set was published or purchased. The company also offers a flat $50 trade-in allowance on major encyclopedias from other publishers. Smaller or less substantial sets used to bring $25 if traded on a new *Britannica 3*, but this offer has been discontinued. *Note that trade-in allowances do not apply to schools and libraries*, a point about which the *Buying Guide* was confused in the past.

Note also that *Britannica 3* may be available to individual consumers through such credit organizations as Visa, American Express, and Master Charge. These companies handle the financing and usually advertise reduced prices. For instance, recent Master Card literature offers "THE *new* ENCYCLOPAEDIA BRITANNICA PROGRAM at a *substantially reduced price!*" The advertising material refers to this as a "Group Discount Offer." This offer is said to "automatically" include a "full 10-year membership in the Britannica Library Research Service" that entitles the consumer to "receive up to 100 research reports on almost any subject— professionally prepared at Britannica's expense." Consumers are advised not to pay more than the current retail price for *Britannica 3* when purchased via a credit organization.

The publisher currently issues three yearbooks available as optional purchases to *Britannica 3* owners at $15.95 each, plus $1 shipping and handling. The yearbooks, which are available to nonowners of the encyclopedia at a slightly higher rate, are the *Britannica Book of the Year*, the *Britannica Yearbook of Science and the Future*, and the recently inaugurated *Medical and Health Annual* (first published in 1976 and dated 1977). These yearbooks are briefly described under "Recency." Consumers should be aware that none is a true updating supplement to the encyclopedia, despite advertising and sales pitches to the contrary. Also available to school and library consumers is the new *Library Guide to Encyclopaedia Britannica* (see "Arrangement and Accessibility"). Prepared and sold by Encyclopaedia Britannica Educational Corporation, the guide is priced at $35.

The firm reports that no combination deals or package offers are available in connection with the purchase of *Britannica 3*. It should be noted, however, that in the past many of the company's other reference publications were so offered, including *Compton's Encyclopedia, Britannica Jun-*

ior Encyclopaedia, the *Britannica Atlas,* the 20-volume *Annals of America* (a collection of some 2,000 original documents from American history), and *Webster's Third New International Dictionary* (the publisher, G. & C. Merriam Company, is a Britannica subsidiary). Moreover, the Wolff article about the history of *Britannica 3* in the *Atlantic* (see "Other Critical Opinions") states that "it is rarely possible to buy the *Britannica* without investing in a bookcase or a pair of dictionaries or some study guides or *Britannica Junior.* As the salesmen see it, this extra stuff is thrown in free with the set. As I see it, the buyer is forced to buy extra stuff." The *Buying Guide* advises consumers who want only *Britannica 3* to resist, firmly if necessary, any and all blandishments to put money into unneeded extras. If unwanted "gifts" are offered, insist that their retail price be deducted from the price of the encyclopedia. In recent times, for instance, the firm has offered a pecan-finished bookcase valued at $49.50 as a "free" inducement to preview the set. Any problems concerning the price of *Britannica 3* should be promptly referred to the company's home office (425 North Michigan Ave., Chicago, IL 60611; 312-321-7000). Moreover, any sales irregularities should be reported to the nearest regional office of the Federal Trade Commission (see the concluding pages of "Selling Encyclopedias" in Part I of the *Buying Guide* for addresses and telephone numbers).

Summary

The New Encyclopaedia Britannica can be quickly summed up in this manner:

Scope: Excellent	Accessibility: Poor
Authority: Excellent	Bibliographies: Good
Reliability: Good	Graphics: Fair
Recency: Poor	Physical Format: Excellent
Objectivity: Good	Special Features: Many
Clarity: Good	Price: High

To elaborate briefly, the fifteenth edition of *Encyclopaedia Britannica*—now officially *The New Encyclopaedia Britannica*—is in many respects worthy of its great name, a leader among encyclopedias for over two centuries. First published in 1974 and informally known as *Britannica 3* because of its three-part arrangement (*Propaedia, Micropaedia, Macropaedia*), the set is not only an entirely new version of the *Britannica* but a radically different kind of general encyclopedia. Of course, it will be years before the final critical verdict is in on *Britannica 3.* Will other encyclopedias follow its innovative lead, or will the set eventually be thought of as an oddity? For now, this much can be said with some confidence: *Britannica 3* provides a greater range and depth of coverage than any other general English-language encyclopedia on the market today. Further, it is more international in scope and authorship than any other general encyclopedia ever made anywhere. The set's authority is impeccable, its outlook contemporary, and its physical construction stately. Yet, despite these impressive strengths, *Britannica 3* is a flawed encyclopedia.

The set's greatest defect is its arrangement. In an effort to unify the so-called Circle of Knowledge, while at the same time preserving the encyclopedia's latter-day function as a source of quick reference information, the makers of *Britannica 3* split the set into small knowledge (the *Micropaedia*), large knowledge (the *Macropaedia*), and outline of knowledge (the *Propaedia*). The casual user is likely to find these artificial divisions confusing and hence the set difficult to use. But this is not the only problem with the tripartite arrangement. The ten-volume *Micropaedia* also serves as an index to the larger 19-volume *Macropaedia*. Unfortunately, as an index the *Micropaedia* is a failure. Numbers tell the story: the *Micropaedia* provides only about 185,000 index references to the 28-million-word *Macropaedia*, called by one knowledgeable critic "the intellectual matrix of *Britannica 3*." The *Buying Guide* estimates that at least 500,000 references are necessary to index the *Macropaedia* adequately. Moreover, the *Micropaedia*, as a 14-million-word source of factual information, is not indexed at all, save for cross-references. What *Britannica 3* needs to be fully accessible is a detailed general index of approximately one million references.

Britannica 3's other serious weakness—one that grows more evident with each passing year—is lack of currency. Because it was extensively revised at the beginning of the 1970s, the set is reasonably contemporary in its coverage and treatment of knowledge. But the current pace of revision is grossly inadequate, as it has been ever since publication of the fifteenth edition in 1974. In the last edition of the *Buying Guide* (1978), it was noted that unless revision activity accelerated considerably over the next several years, *Britannica 3* would soon cease to be useful as a source of current information and knowledge. That time is now very close at hand.

Other negative criticisms include many mediocre graphics, eccentric map coverage (there are no maps of U.S. states and Canadian provinces, for example), lack of much practical (or how-to) information, sugarcoated treatment of problems facing many countries of the world (e.g., racism in South Africa), overly technical writing in certain areas clearly too difficult for the "curious, intelligent" layperson (the intended reader), and the marginal value of the *Propaedia* volume for the large majority of users.

Obviously, whatever its strong and weak points, *Britannica 3* is a "must" for libraries of almost any size or mission. (Librarians, however, are advised not to replace the set at regular intervals without first carefully checking to see that the amount of revision warrants expenditure of over $600 for the new copyright edition.) But is *Britannica 3* a good buy for home or office use? How well does it meet individual consumer needs and interests?

An advanced adult encyclopedia is not for everyone. Adults with modest informational needs will ordinarily be better off with a smaller, less expensive adult set (such as the new and very attractive *Academic American Encyclopedia* or the bargain-priced *Funk & Wagnalls New Encyclopedia*) or one of the three fine young adult sets available

(*Compton's Encyclopedia, Merit Students Encyclopedia,* and *The World Book Encyclopedia*). Consumers with relatively young children will, again, find the young adult or larger children's sets more appropriate. But for those people who seriously need access to as wide a range of reliable general knowledge and information as possible (high school students planning to attend college, college students, professional people, inquisitive laypeople, and so on), only the advanced adult encyclopedia will fully meet their needs. Here the choice is limited to three sets: *Collier's Encyclopedia, The Encyclopedia Americana,* and *The New Encyclopaedia Britannica (Britannica 3).*

Each of these three large encyclopedias has its own particular strengths and weaknesses, and which is "best" is a matter of individual consumer needs and taste. Libraries of any consequence will stock all three. From the comparative standpoint, *Britannica 3* is the largest, followed by *Americana* and then *Collier's,* which is only half the size of the *Britannica.* Likewise, *Britannica* costs the most, again followed by *Americana* and *Collier's* in that order. *Collier's* is most readable and best indexed, although *Americana* is not far behind in both these areas. *Britannica 3*'s style is normally clear, but more scholarly than the other two. It is not well indexed, and its arrangement may well confuse many users. Each encyclopedia satisfactorily covers the major knowledge areas, but *Britannica* provides the greatest depth. Its international perspective is a strong feature. Visually, *Collier's* is superior to *Britannica,* which has many mediocre graphics and devotes most of its space to printed matter, and to *Americana,* which is dark and dreary. *Collier's* is also now clearly the most up-to-date of the three sets, due to its aggressive continuous revision program. *Britannica,* which revitalized itself with a completely new edition in 1974, has skimped on revision since that time, and *Americana* is often badly dated, especially in those volumes that have not been thoroughly and systematically revised in many years. *Britannica*'s authoritative contributors, international scope and authorship, great depth of coverage and treatment, and stately format are its best features, comparatively speaking. But when all is said and done, the *Buying Guide* believes *Collier's* represents the best consumer value in the advanced adult class.

Other Critical Opinions

The appearance of *Britannica 3* in 1974 was a major publishing event. As a result, the work was reviewed and described in many journals that ordinarily do not comment on encyclopedias. Listed below are annotated citations to those reviews and informative articles which should be readily available in most public and academic libraries. The one exception is the remarkable review by Harvey Einbinder in the now defunct biweekly newsletter *Bookletter,* issued by Harper's Magazine Company until it ceased publication in 1977. The review itself is not especially vital to consumers, but Einbinder's glowing appreciation of *Britannica 3* will interest those who are familiar with his book-length attack on the fourteenth edition, *Myth of the Britannica* (Grove Press, 1964).

Baker, John F. "A New Britannica Is Born," *Publishers Weekly,* January 14, 1974, pp. 64–65. Not a review, this informative report covers the how and who of the making of *Britannica 3.*

Booklist, February 1, 1979, pp. 889–891. Part of a series of reviews by the ALA Reference and Subscription Books Review Committee (RSBRC) entitled "Encyclopedias: A Survey and Buying Guide," this unsigned evaluation of *Britannica 3* (1974 copyright) is critical of the encyclopedia's performance in the areas of accessibility, objectivity, recency, and graphics. No final conclusions are offered, however. In its last regular review of the *Britannica* (*Booklist,* June 1, 1975, pp. 1021–1028), which also covered the 1974 copyright, RSBRC hailed the fifteenth edition as "a landmark in the history of reference book publishing," although reservations were expressed about the set's "difficult" arrangement.

Broyard, Anatole. "An Orgy of Serendipity," *New York Times,* June 10, 1974, p. 29. Broyard, a *Times* daily critic, calls the set "a browser's paradise."

Choice, October 1974, pp. 1086, 1088–1090. This unsigned review says the "new 15th edition is a better *Britannica,*" citing such features as international coverage and broad treatment of knowledge as the reason why.

Cole, Dorothy Ethlyn. "Britannica 3 as a Reference Tool: A Review," *Wilson Library Bulletin,* June 1974, pp. 821–825. A professor of library science provides one of the better early reviews of *Britannica 3,* concluding that it "contains much excellent material, but is difficult to use."

Davis, Robert Gorham. "Subject: The Universe," *New York Times Book Review,* December 1, 1974, pp. 98, 100. Although "the new Britannica is just about as good as it possibly could be," literary critic Davis does question the editors' claims that the encyclopedia can be read and understood by high school students, et al. He also finds some bias in the set.

Einbinder, Harvey. "Old Salesmanship and New Scholarship," *Bookletter,* September 16, 1974, pp. 1–3. As noted at the outset of "Other Critical Opinions," the periodical *Bookletter* is now defunct, having ceased publication after only two-and-a-half years. Tracking down this article, therefore, may be difficult, and most users of the *Buying Guide* can skip it without missing much. But serious students of *Britannica 3* should read it as an extraordinary apologia. Einbinder here acclaims *Britannica 3* as "a standard of excellence that renders other adult encyclopedias obsolete," apparently viewing publication of the new edition as vindication of his caustic attack on the previous (fourteenth) edition in *Myth of the Britannica.*

———. "Politics and the New *Britannica,*" *The Nation,* March 22, 1975, pp. 342–344. Here Einbinder returns to the attack, charging that the makers of *Britannica 3* have sugarcoated harsh truths about various countries (e.g., South Africa) so as not to jeopardize sales abroad.

Evans, G. Edward. *American Reference Books Annual,* 1979, p. 37–39. *ARBA*'s original review of *Britannica 3* (1975, pp. 34–37, by Richard A. Gray) lavishly praised the set. Evans's review is definitely revisionist in tone and substance. He criticizes the encyclopedia for lack of currency and especially inaccessibility ("Accessibility is *not* a hallmark of the new version of Britannica").

Fadiman, Clifton. "Must Encyclopedia Writing Be Stodgy?" *Saturday Review/World,* July 13, 1974, pp. 22, 26–27. Fadiman, a member of *Britannica*'s Board of Editors, not unexpectedly finds the encyclopedia to be without fault.

Fremont-Smith, Eliot. "Knowledge by the 30-Pack," *New York* magazine, December 23, 1974, p. 64. A well-known book reviewer, Fremont-Smith asks two questions: "How good is the new *Britannica?* And, should one buy it?" The answers are "excellent" and a "qualified no" (only libraries should buy it).

Hazo, Robert G. "The Guest Word," *New York Times Book Review,* March 9, 1975, p. 31. A hard, critical look at *Britannica 3*'s grand plan for encircling knowledge.

Josel, Nat. *RQ (Reference Quarterly),* Summer 1974, pp. 352–354. Josel, a librarian, emphasizes *Britannica 3*'s lack of adequate indexing.

Katz, William A. *Basic Information Sources* (Vol. 1 of *Introduction to Reference Work,* 3rd ed. New York: McGraw-Hill, 1978), pp. 153–155. An excellent summary of the set's basic strengths and weaknesses. Like many critics, Katz is highly critical of its poor accessibility: "The lack of proper indexing for the *Macropaedia* may be remedied in future revisions, but as of this writing it is a major drawback."

McCracken, Samuel. "The Scandal of 'Britannica 3,'" *Commentary,* February 1976, pp. 63–68. McCracken, who is identified as assistant to the president of Boston University, cites many errors of fact and interpretation in the encyclopedia. He also documents evidence of political bias concerning treatment of Communist nations (a problem since corrected). But his main point is what he calls the "equivocal" relationship between the encyclopedia and the University of Chicago. The school, says McCracken, "whether wittingly or not, allows its name, and the prestige that it confers, to serve as a kind of trademark for a commercial enterprise which consistently fails to live up to its own intellectual standards, and to the university's as well."

McDonald, Donald. "The New Britannica," *Center Magazine,* November—December 1975, pp. 66–70. Although the author finds some "anomalies" in *Britannica 3,* overall the encyclopedia "succeeds in meeting the editors' own demanding standards."

Misiunas, Romauld J. "The New Encyclopaedia Britannica," *Slavic Review,* June 1975, pp. 411–412. Articles on the Communist-bloc nations are exposed as "a rehash of the official [Soviet] point of view." All these articles have since been rewritten by Western scholars, but the Misiunas piece remains a good reminder of how easy it is for an encyclopedia to fall into the swamp of bias.

Prescott, Peter S. *Newsweek,* January 21, 1974, pp. 71–72. A useful summary of *Britannica 3*'s origins, makers, and statistics.

Schroth, Raymond A. "The Subversive Encyclopedia," *Commonweal,* October 25, 1974, pp. 81–84. The term "subversive" here does not pertain to the set's Communist-bloc articles (see Misiunas above), but rather *Britannica 3*'s "attempt to influence the curriculum of American secondary and higher education. Used creatively, it could be subversive in that it would subvert some of the university's more inhibiting structures." An interesting view of the encyclopedia.

Sheehy, Eugene. *College and Research Libraries*, July 1974, pp. 244–245. More descriptive than critical, this short review concentrates on explaining *Britannica 3*'s tripartite arrangement.

Shields, Gerald. "The Fifteenth Britannica: A Thirty-Volume University??" *Library Journal*, April 15, 1974, pp. 1101–1103. Shields, a library educator, describes the set's history and parts, but offers no judgments ("only usage will tell" how good the encyclopedia is).

Time, January 21, 1974, p. 47+. A slick, readable overview of *Britannica 3*'s creators and dimensions. The piece is notable for its anecdotal material regarding editors Preece and Goetz.

Waite, Dennis V. "Encyclopaedia Britannica: EB 3, Two Years Later," *Publishers Weekly*, June 21, 1976, pp. 44–45. An informative follow-up on John Baker's earlier *Publishers Weekly* article (see above), Waite's article emphasizes the sales picture, warts and all.

Wolff, Geoffrey. "Britannica 3, History of," *Atlantic*, June 1974, pp. 37–47.

———. "Britannica 3, Failures of," *Atlantic*, November 1976, pp. 107–110. Wolff, a novelist and former *Britannica* sales representative (summer vacation, 1959), has little good to say about the encyclopedia, but he says it in such a charming manner that even *Britannica 3* defenders will not be too annoyed by these companion pieces.

Wood, Robert E. "Philosophy in the New Encyclopaedia Britannica: Critical Study," *Review of Metaphysics*, June 1977, pp. 715–752. Wood, a teacher of philosophy, objectively analyzes all the encyclopedia's articles dealing with that subject (a little less than 3 percent of the total text). His long study, which is quite positive about *Britannica 3*, will be of interest only to serious students of the encyclopedia.

New Illustrated Columbia Encyclopedia

Facts in Brief

Full Title: **The New Illustrated Columbia Encyclopedia.** *Editors:* William H. Harris and Judith S. Levey. *Publisher:* Rockville House Publishers, Inc. (a division of Sigma Marketing Systems, Inc.), 615 South St., Garden City, NY 11530. *Distributor:* Time-Life Books, Inc., 777 Duke St., Alexandria, VA 22314. *Based on: The New Columbia Encyclopedia. Edition Reviewed:* 1978 copyright.

Volumes: 24. *Pages:* 7,522. *Articles:* 50,515. *Words:* 6,600,000. *Illustrations:* 5,000. *Maps:* 252. *Index Entries:* None. *Cross-references:* 66,000. *Contributors:* 119.

User Classification: Adult (Multivolume). *Reader Suitability:* Age 15 through Advanced Adult. *Physical Size:* 7¼ × 9½ in.; 24 cm. *LC:* 78-56359. *Lowest Retail Price:* Volume 1, $0.99; Volumes 2–24, $2.99 each = $69.76 the set; also available via mail order, $69.96.

Purpose and Scope

The New Illustrated Columbia Encyclopedia, a 24-volume set sold in supermarkets on the book-a-week plan and via direct mail order, is an expanded (but not updated) version of the one-volume *New Columbia Encyclopedia,* published in 1975 and currently sold in retail stores (see Part IV of the *Buying Guide* for a review of *New Columbia*). The multivolume *New Illustrated Columbia* and single-volume *New Columbia* have essentially the same printed text. The principal difference between the two encyclopedias, aside from their names and number of volumes, is that *New Illustrated Columbia* contains many more illustrations (5,000) than *New Columbia* (407). In addition, *New Illustrated Columbia*'s type size is slightly larger than *New Columbia*'s, and its page size is considerably smaller (7 × 9¼ inches as opposed to 9 × 12 inches).

The New Illustrated Columbia (like *New Columbia*) aims to provide "authentic and accurate information in a condensed form" on "a wide-ranging variety of subjects that fall within the province of a general reference work" (preface). Whereas the one-volume *New Columbia* is intended for "instant reference" use by adults and serious students in senior high school and up, *New Illustrated Columbia* aims to meet the needs of families and younger children. Advertising for the set makes this clear: "Best of all, the New Illustrated Columbia Encyclopedia is designed for everyone in your family. For your children as well as yourself. . . . Plan now to collect the entire set. It's the right thing to do for your children. Because it's the right encyclopedia." Apparently the editors believe that by adding thousands of graphics to the printed text of *New Columbia,* they have created a work suitable for a much younger and less sophisticated audience. Unfortunately, this is a mistaken belief (see "Clarity and Reader Suitability").

New Illustrated Columbia comprises more than 50,000 articles, most of which are very brief, averaging roughly 150 words in length, or seven articles per page. About 15,000 articles (30 percent of the total) concern geographical topics, including the continents, countries, and major cities and natural features of the world. In addition, the U.S. states, Canadian provinces, and about 2,000 North American cities and towns (some quite small) are covered. As might be expected, the larger or more prominent the place, the more coverage it normally receives. U.S. places, however, are accorded proportionately more coverage than their counterparts abroad. EXAMPLE: The article on Africa runs to nine pages, with over half the space consumed by large photographs and a map. EXAMPLE: The article on Afghanistan consists of two and half pages, most of it printed text. EXAMPLE: The article on Arkansas (the U.S. state) comprises two and half pages, including two large photographs, which account for a full page. EXAMPLE: The article on Arnhem (the German city) consists of nine lines. EXAMPLE: The article on Atlantic City, N.J. (a city much smaller than Arnhem), covers 26 lines.

Even a greater number of the articles (45 percent) deal with people, both living and dead. Emphasis has been placed on important political leaders in the United States, Great Britain, and the world, roughly in that order. In addition to famous leaders of the past like Clement Attlee, Charles de Gaulle, Gandhi, and the Roosevelts, *New Illustrated Columbia* includes such contemporary notables as Arthur Burns, Cesar Chavez, Betty Friedan, Edward Heath, Park Chung Hee, Ralph Nader, Yitzhak Rabin, and Anwar el-Sadat. Numerous writers, artists, musicians, scientists, theologians, philosophers, athletes, and the like are also covered. Biographical articles provide a thumbnail description of the person's career, major contributions, and important dates.

Although biographical and geographical articles predominate, most essential areas of knowledge are adequately covered, given the encyclopedia's space limitations. The 12,000 or so entries devoted to subjects other than people and places include concepts such as continental drift, empiricism, fraud, kinship, laissez-faire, parody, socialism, time, and viscosity. There are also succinct articles on things like cemeteries, the funny bone, gasoline, iron, milk, ohmmeters, parachutes, tobacco, and vitamins. Scientific and technical subjects are usually well covered, especially basic topics like the brain, cells, neutrons, nucleic acid, numeration, periodic law, photosynthesis, protein, and sources of energy. Flora and fauna receive concise coverage. EXAMPLES: "Snapper" (18 lines); "Snapping Turtle" (28 lines); "Sneezeweed" (13 lines); "Snipe" (17 lines); "Snowberry" (5 lines). Major disciplines in the sciences are accorded short survey treatment. EXAMPLES: "Biochemistry" (50 lines); "Biology" (42 lines); "Biophysics" (31 lines). The arts and humanities are likewise well covered. Particularly noteworthy are articles on national or regional cultural developments (e.g., "African Art"; "African Languages"; "African Negro Literature"; "African Negro Music") and individual genres (e.g., "Architecture"; "Ballet"; "Drama"; "Motion Pictures"; "Painting"). Coverage also includes an entry for every proper name in the Authorized (King James) Version of the Bible. The social and behavioral sciences, however, tend to receive less attention than the arts and natural sciences. The article "Opera," for instance, is nearly four times as long as "Psychoanalysis." The article "Child Abuse" is only 13 lines long, and the subjects of child development and human growth are completely ignored.

No adult encyclopedia limited to six and half million words can hope to achieve comprehensive coverage. Inevitably, *New Illustrated Columbia* omits some places, people, ideas, and things that logically or properly should be included. EXAMPLE: Ripon, Wisconsin, so-called birthplace of the Republican Party, has no entry but probably should. EXAMPLE: Eric Erikson, author of the provocative *Young Man Luther* and influential psychohistorian, is among the missing, as is novelist John Gardner, but Walter Cronkite and Bella Abzug are there. EXAMPLE: Also among the missing are Ronald Reagan, Jimmy Carter, Walter Mondale, Margaret Thatcher, Ayatollah Khomeini, Menachim Begin, and other national political leaders who emerged since 1975, omissions due to the encyclopedia's age rather than any editorial oversight (see "Recency"). EXAMPLE: The subject of condominium housing is ignored altogether, despite the fact that millions of people now live in one form or another of this type of housing. Failure to cover such topics as condominium housing, child development and human growth, and current political leaders is a serious deficiency in an encyclopedia that advertises itself as a reference work for the family. Also, when social and political subjects are covered, there is a tendency to emphasize historical aspects of the topic at the expense of contemporary developments (e.g., "Academic Freedom"; "Drug Addiction and Drug Abuse"; "Housing"; "Maritime Law"; "Police"; "Prison"; "Suicide"). And there is a dearth of practical, or how-to, information in the encyclopedia on such topics as letter writing, gardening, preparing a research paper, and caring for pets—all subjects that should be covered in a family encyclopedia.

Nevertheless, despite bad gaps, *New Illustrated Columbia* customarily provides clear, precise coverage of that knowledge and information considered most important or useful to North American readers as of the early 1970s (when the set's articles were prepared). As already noted, the encyclopedia is particularly strong in the areas of biography and geography. Although U.S. and Canadian people and places are emphasized, *New Illustrated Columbia*'s outlook is international. EXAMPLE: The article "Funeral Customs" mentions Islamic burial rituals and, at the end of the discussion, refers the reader to several books for further information, including *Funeral Customs the World Over*. In addition, metric equivalents are given throughout the volume. Overall, the encyclopedia's scope and coverage are best suited for serious students and adults, and not younger children and general family use, as advertisements for the set would have one believe. (See "Clarity and Reader Suitability" for more on the best potential audience for *New Illustrated Columbia*.)

History and Authority

As noted at the outset, *New Illustrated Columbia* is actually the one-volume *New Columbia Encyclopedia* (1975) expanded to 24 volumes by the addition of numerous illustrations and reduction of the page size. The set, intended chiefly for the supermarket trade, is published by Rockville House Publishers "by arrangement with Columbia University Press" (title page) and distributed by Time-Life Books. Hence, *New Illustrated Columbia* derives its authority entirely from *New Columbia*, except in the area of graphics (see "Graphics"). Exactly the same editors, consultants, and editorial staff are cited in the front matter of both encyclopedias.

New Columbia, which dates back to 1935 when it first appeared as the *Columbia Encyclopedia* (revised in 1950 and 1963), is universally acknowledged as an outstanding small-volume encyclopedia. Although it is not an official publication of Columbia University, the editors concede that "without Columbia University this book would not have been possible" (preface). Of the 90 or so academic consultants listed in the front matter, two-thirds are associated with the school. The list is impressive, including such renowned professors as Joseph L. Blau (religion), Robert Gorham Davis (literature), Theodosius Dobzhansky (genetics), Mark J. Kesselman (government), Lawrence C. Kolb (psychiatry), William E. Leuchtenburg (history), Robert McClintock (education), and Richard B. Morris (American history). In addition, an editorial staff of about 50 is indicated, headed by William H. Harris and Judith S. Levey, both of whom possess sound qualifications for making an encyclopedia. Harris was formerly managing editor of both *Collier's Encyclopedia* and *Merit Students Encyclopedia*, and Levey, who in 1976 was named as editor in chief of *New Columbia*, has also worked at Macmillan as an encyclopedia editor. A total of 119 contributing editors are listed, one of whom is Harris and another is William Jaber, who served as managing editor of the now defunct *Cadillac Modern Encyclopedia* (see Appendix A). All of *New Columbia*'s (and therefore *New Illustrated Columbia*'s) articles are unsigned, and therefore responsibility for specific articles cannot be determined. Articles in previous editions were also unsigned. But given its history of excellence since 1935, the high quality of the people associated with the project, and its indirect but very real affiliation with Columbia University, *New Columbia* stands as one of the most authoritative one-volume encyclopedias available today. And consequently the same judgment applies to *New Illustrated Columbia*.

A direct forebear of *New Illustrated Columbia* is the *Illustrated Columbia Encyclopedia*. A 22-volume supermarket set published in 1970 by Rockville, *Illustrated Columbia* was an expanded version of the one-volume *Columbia Encyclopedia* (1963). Now long out of print, *Illustrated Columbia* (see Appendix A) was modestly priced and presumably did well enough in the sales department, but reviewers were generally disappointed by the set's mediocre illustrations. Interested readers might want to consult *Booklist,* July 1, 1970, pp. 1299–1300; *Library Journal,* March 1, 1971, pp. 819–820; and *RQ,* Spring 1971, p. 270.

Reliability

As might be expected from the foregoing, the encyclopedia can be relied upon as a source of accurate information. Authority and reliability go hand-in-hand, and *New Illustrated Columbia* (out of *New Columbia*) very rarely slips up in either respect. There are occasional errors of fact, however. EXAMPLE: The article "Shark" contains several minor points of misinformation about shark anatomy and reproduction. The statement that sharks have "large deposits of fat," for instance, is incorrect. EXAMPLE: "Marine Biology" errs in defining the topic as the "study of ocean plants and animals." In fact, marine biologists study coastal and estuary forms of life, as well as those found in oceans. The article also gives the impression that all plankton are microorganisms, which is not true. EXAMPLE: The generally informative article "Abortion" states that "on Jan. 22, 1973, the Supreme Court ruled that a state may not prevent a woman from having an abortion during the first six months of pregnancy," without further explaining that the state is permitted to regulate abortion procedures in ways related to health during the second trimester. Such minor errors, while they detract from *New Illustrated Columbia*'s high standard of reliability, are not encountered frequently enough to diminish the book's overall usefulness as an authoritative source of quick reference information.

There are also occasional questionable interpretations or subject judgments. EXAMPLE: The article on Western drama includes a short discussion of the Theater of the Absurd, in which it is stated, "Probably the most famous plays of the theater of the absurd are Eugene Ionesco's *Bald Soprano* (1950) and Samuel Beckett's *Waiting for Godot* (1953)." *Godot,* yes. But *Bald Soprano?* EXAMPLE: "Homosexuality," an 800-word survey article that stresses causal relationships, states that "many Western men have pseudohomosexual longings toward other men at times of crisis in their cultural roles, such as an occupational failure." Such an assertion is questionable at best. But again, such examples are not serious or frequent enough to undermine the solid dependability of *New Illustrated Columbia.* The encyclopedia's reliability is vulnerable, however, in those instances where information is out-of-date, as in the case of "Copyright," where the law changed effective January 1978 (see "Recency" for more on this problem).

Recency

As already pointed out, the printed text of the encyclopedia is the same as that of the one-volume *New Columbia Encyclopedia* published in 1975. (Note that *New Illustrated Columbia*'s 1978 copyright pertains to the set's publication date, not the currency of its contents.) Age spots are naturally

This Recency Table compares selected topics in *New Illustrated Columbia* with those in other encyclopedias of similar size and intended usership.

Topic	New Illustrated Columbia	Academic American	Funk & Wagnalls	New Standard
Afghanistan	Not current	Very current	Fairly current	Fairly current
Dinosaurs	Fairly current	Very current	Very current	Very current
Greenland	Fairly current	Very current	Not current	Very curent
Thomas Jefferson	Fairly current	Fairly current	Fairly current	Fairly current
Mass Transportation/ Subways	Fairly current	Very current	Fairly current	Fairly current
Nuclear Power	Not current	Very current	Not current	Not current
Paris	Not current	Very current	Not current	Not current
Sharks	Fairly current	Fairly current	Not current	Very current
Shock Therapy	Fairly current	Very current	Not current	Not current
Suicide	Not current	Fairly current	Not current	Very current
Tuberculosis	Fairly current	Fairly current	Fairly current	Fairly current
Zimbabwe	Not current	Very current	Very current	Very current

beginning to show. For instance, Hannah Arendt and Mao Tse-tung are still alive, according to *New Illustrated Columbia*. Saul Bellow has not yet received the Nobel Prize, nor has the controversial Pompidou Center yet opened in Paris. Genetic research has yet to discover recombinant DNA and gene splicing. According to *New Illustrated Columbia*, the Soviet Union has never invaded Afghanistan, the nation of Zimbabwe does not exist, and Greenland has not achieved home rule. Hundreds of such examples could be cited. Unfortunately, *New Illustrated Columbia*, like *New Columbia*, is not continuously revised, as are most U.S. encyclopedias of any substance. Instead, new editions are occasionally—very occasionally—prepared (see "History and Authority"). It is not possible, therefore, for *New Illustrated Columbia* to compete successfully with its main rivals in the area of recency. As the Recency Table here indicates, the set lags well behind the new *Academic American Encyclopedia, Funk & Wagnalls New Encyclopedia,* and *The New Standard Encyclopedia* as far as currency of material is concerned.

Like most other multivolume general encyclopedias, *New Illustrated Columbia* is supplemented by an annual publication that claims to "update" the encyclopedia. This 300-page volume, entitled the *New Illustrated Encyclopedia Yearbook,* digests the preceding year's events, but its relationship to the encyclopedia is nil. In fact, the yearbook is not even prepared by the makers of *New Illustrated Columbia.* Consumers are advised to save their $7.95 per volume and invest in an annual like *World Almanac* or *Information Please,* if such information is desired.

Objectivity

In almost all cases, material found in *New Illustrated Columbia* is admirably free from bias. When polemical topics are treated, all legitimate viewpoints are normally covered. The article "Smoking" is a case in point. Both sides of the health question are discussed within the context of a historical survey, but the article concludes that "in 1964 definite proof that cigarette smoking is a serious health hazard was contained in a report by the Surgeon General's Advisory Committee on Health." Likewise, "Marijuana" impartially summarizes current evidence on the drug's effect: "Although the possibility that marijuana, like other perception-altering drugs, produces psychosis has not been entirely disproved, the drug is probably most dangerous to persons with already existing psychotic tendencies." And the magazine *Christianity Today* (January 16, 1976, p. 31) has noted that in its treatment of religious matters the encyclopedia "maintains about as consistent a stance of detachment as one could expect. . . . Biological evolution, while presented sympathetically, is labeled as belief and theory, not fact. So also the papacy's succession from Peter is presented as Catholic belief rather than historical truth."

Ordinarily, *New Illustrated Columbia* does not avoid controversial subject matter, as articles on such topics as homosexuality and abortion attest. But occasionally contentious topics and unpalatable information that should be covered in any adult encyclopedia are ignored. EXAMPLE: The encyclopedia's article "Woman Suffrage" fails to mention the pending Equal Rights Amendment to the U.S. Constitution, nor is there a separate article on the amendment. EXAMPLE: The article on Thomas Jefferson studiously avoids any reference to his views on race, his ownership of slaves, or his illegitimate slave children. Likewise, the bibliography accompanying the article fails to include Fawn Brodie's book *Thomas Jefferson: An Intimate History* (1974), which introduced contemporary readers to Jefferson's controversial private life. Some encyclopedists might argue that such information lies outside the purview of a general reference work, but is it not pertinent to a better understanding of the man, his public policies, and his times? After all, it was none other than John Quincy Adams who wondered if Sally Hemings was the reason Jefferson, once a staunch abolitionist, suddenly lost his distaste for slavery after 1790. If nothing else, mature students have a right to the facts, pleasant or not.

Clarity and Reader Suitability

New Illustrated Columbia is clearly intended for literate adults and students at the senior high school or college level. Ordinarily, it will not be comprehensible to younger students, as advertisements for the set suggest. For the intended audience, the writing style is clear and direct. Articles on complex subjects, particularly in the sciences, have been written with "initial readability" in mind, meaning that the articles become more advanced and technical as they progress. EXAMPLE: The article "Nucleic Acid" begins with a simply stated definition of the subject, then proceeds to discuss the two main types of nucleic acids, DNA and RNA. For instance, DNA is described in this manner: "Each DNA molecule is a long two-stranded chain. The chains are made up of subunits called nucleotides, each containing a sugar (deoxyribose), a phosphate group, and one of four nitrogenous bases, adenine, guanine, thymine, and cytosine, denoted A, G, T, and C respectively. The information carried by genes is coded in sequences of nucleotides, which correspond to sequences of amino acids in the polypeptide chains of proteins." After this admirably clear and straightforward discussion, the article moves on to an even more detailed description of DNA replication and the double helix model.

Arrangement and Accessibility

New Illustrated Columbia is arranged alphabetically, letter-by-letter ("Indiana" precedes "Indian Ocean"). When two or more articles have the same heading, the order of entry goes from person to place and then thing. For example, "Jefferson, Thomas" is entered before "Jefferson" the city, which is followed by "Jefferson Memorial." Places with the same name are included in multiple entries, arranged A–Z by state. A good understanding of the mechanics of arrangement is especially important in the case of a specific-entry encyclopedia like *New Illustrated Columbia.*

The encyclopedia has no general index. Instead, the set is said to be self-indexed via an elaborate system of 66,000 cross-references. In this respect, *New Illustrated Columbia* resembles *Harver World Encyclopedia, The New American Encyclopedia,* and *The New Standard Encyclopedia,* all multivolume adult works of similar size that rely on cross-references rather than an index to guide the reader to the set's contents. Like most of its competitors, *New Illustrated Columbia* provides numerous external *See* references, e.g., "Goiter. See THYROID GLAND." Even more plentiful are cross-references within the articles themselves, designated by terms printed in SMALL CAPITAL LETTERS, a system of internal cross-referencing used by several other adult encyclopedias (the *Academic American Encyclopedia, Harver World Encyclopedia,* and *The New American Encyclopedia*). EXAMPLE: The article on Thomas Jefferson informs, "Despite his contention that the Constitution must be interpreted strictly, he pushed through the LOUISIANA PURCHASE, even though such an action was nowhere expressly authorized. His eager interest in the West and in exploration had led him to plan and organize the LEWIS AND CLARK EXPEDITION," thus signaling the reader that additional information can be obtained in the articles "Louisiana Purchase" and "Lewis and Clark Expedition." The entire Jefferson article contains 17 such references.

Extensive as it is, the cross-reference system is not without its flaws and frustrations. EXAMPLE: The article "Cancer" quite appropriately discusses cells and tissue, but there are no references to the articles "Cell" and "Tissue," where these terms are fully explained. EXAMPLE: The article on Anne Hutchinson notes that some Puritan leaders viewed her "as an antinomian heretic," but there is no reference to the article "Antinomianism" (where indeed Hutchinson is mentioned, but again no reference is given to the article "Hutchinson, Anne"). EXAMPLE: The Freedom of Information Act (FIA) is discussed in the article "Censorship" in the context of the Pentagon Papers, but there is no external cross-reference directing the reader to this article (nor is there a separate article on FIA). EXAMPLE: The article "Federal Communications Commission" provides no reference to the article "Censorship," wherein the FCC's licensing and regulatory roles are succinctly explained. EXAMPLE: The article "Indians, North American" offers no clue that the encyclopedia also contains related material in the article "American Indian Movement."

The editors, in "How to Use the New Illustrated Columbia Encyclopedia" at the beginning of Volume 1, flatly state that "cross-referencing makes an index in *The New Illustrated Columbia Encyclopedia* unnecessary." This assumption is incorrect, as the examples in the preceding paragraph indicate. In most instances, information can be retrieved from the encyclopedia quickly and efficiently. But in a work as large as this—nearly seven million words—no system of self-indexing, no matter how extensive or clever, can completely replace the need for a detailed analytical index. How else, for instance, can the user locate the reference to the Freedom of Information Act in the article "Censorship," except through serendipity? Moreover, the 5,000 illustrations in the set lack both indexing and cross-referencing. The article "Motion Picture Photography or Cinematography," for example, includes a large graphic showing a scene from D. W. Griffith's famous picture *Birth of a Nation*, but the article "Griffith, D. W.," which briefly discusses the film ("a landmark in the history of the cinema"), gives no hint that a scene from the work can be found elsewhere in the encyclopedia. *New Illustrated Columbia*'s lack of an index is a serious deficiency.

Bibliographies

More than 44,000 bibliographic citations are included at the end of articles in *New Illustrated Columbia*. Limited to English-language titles, the citations are usually recent or represent the most useful works available on the subject. Not every article, however, has a bibliography. Why, for example, the article on vasectomy fails to cite even one of the many practical books available on the topic is puzzling. There are other omissions, perhaps more understandable. EXAMPLE: "Existentialism" cites Walter Kaufmann's useful collection *Existentialism from Dostoevsky to Sartre* (1956) but fails to note William Barrett's *Irrational Man* (1958), quite possibly the best analysis of the controversial philosophy yet to appear.

Most exasperating, however, is the encyclopedia's tendency to cite bibliographic references simply by author and date. EXAMPLE: The biographical entry for Roscoe Conkling, a nineteenth-century American politician, concludes: "See biography by his nephew, A. R. Conkling (1889); study by David M. Jordan (1971)." Obviously this abbreviated style is meant to conserve space, but the problems it will sometimes cause students, teachers, and librarians who might want access to the works cited are hardly worth the space saved. Future editions of *New Illustrated Columbia* should systematically provide author, title, publisher, date, and edition information for each bibliographic citation.

Graphics

The multivolume *New Illustrated Columbia* has the same printed text as the one-volume *New Columbia Encyclopedia,* but (as its title suggests) the set is also heavily illustrated. *New Illustrated Columbia*'s graphics, which number roughly 5,000 (3,000 in color), were selected and added to the printed text by Fratelli Fabbri Editori of Italy, which drew on its own extensive illustration files for the material. Practically all Fabbri's graphics are photographs or art reproductions. In the final volume (WAL–ZYR), for instance, a color photo of the Library of Congress accompanies the article on Thomas Ustick Walter (who designed the library's interior); a black-and-white photo of a scene from the opera *Troilus and Cressida* accompanies the article on Sir William Walton (who composed the opera); a black-and-white photo of a Huron Indian wampum belt accompanies the article "Wampum"; a color photo of a herd of wapiti (a deer found in North America) accompanies the article "Wapiti"; a black-and-white photo of Nazi leaders on trial at Nuremberg accompanies the article "War Crimes"; a color reproduction of Andy Warhol's silk-screen portrait of Marilyn Monroe accompanies the article on Warhol; a black-and-white photo of Earl Warren accompanies the article on the late chief justice; a color photo of an aerial view of Warsaw accompanies the article on that city; a black-and-white reproduction of a portrait of George Washington accompanies the article on the first U.S. president; a small black-and-white map and three large photos (two aerial views and an interior shot of a Boeing aircraft plant) accompany the article on Washington state.

Regrettably, both the aesthetic and informational quality of the Fabbri graphics in *New Illustrated Columbia* leaves much to be desired. Some of the graphics are very poorly reproduced, being either muddy (if in color) or excessively dark (if black-and-white). The photo of Earl Warren, for instance, renders the man unrecognizable. In too many instances, the illustrations serve little purpose other than to fill space, such as the photo of the aircraft plant with the Washington state article. Frequently, the illustrations are much larger than they need to be, again serving a space-filling rather than an informational function. The reproduction of the Andy Warhol silkscreen of Marilyn Monroe, for example, covers two-thirds of a page, which seems excessive. Likewise, the photo of the wapiti herd consumes nearly half a page. Some of the graphics are not placed with or adjacent to the article they are complementing. For example, the article on Andy Warhol is on page 7219 of Volume 24, but the silk screen of Marilyn Monroe, which exemplifies his work, is on the next page. In the case of the French artist Jean-Antoine Watteau, the article is on page 7255 and a reproduction of his painting *Gilles* on page 7253. Some graphics are reproduced in black-and-white that would be more useful from an informational standpoint if they were in color, such as the wampum belt. The previous edition of *New Illustrated Columbia,* entitled the *Illustrated Columbia Encyclopedia* (see "History and Authority"), was generally criticized for its lackluster graphics. The *Library Journal* review, for instance, called the encyclopedia's illustrations "extravagant rather than necessary, and many of them are atrociously reproduced. Some of them pretty up the page; some are fun to look at; but that they significantly aid understanding is doubtful" (March 1, 1971, p. 820). The same comments can be applied to the current edition.

New Illustrated Columbia has retained the 400 or so black-and-white line drawings included in *The New Columbia Encyclopedia.* These drawings, which usually accompany scientific topics, tend to be simple but instructive. Maps from *New Columbia* are also reproduced in *New Illustrated Columbia.* The maps are very elementary and quite small, except for a few large ones covering prominent places like Africa, China, Great Britain, the Soviet Union, and the United States. The U.S. state maps lack any substantive detail; for instance, the map of Alabama is limited to eight cities and five rivers, with no physical detail at all. Altogether, there are 252 maps, of which 111 are simple locator maps. Compared with its major competitors (the *Academic American Encyclopedia, Funk & Wagnalls New Encyclopedia,* and *The New Standard Encyclopedia*), *New Illustrated Columbia* provides very limited map coverage.

Physical Format

Only one binding is available, that being a washable deep blue Kivar with gold lettering and stamping. Each volume has a gilded top edge and is side-sewn. Though sturdy, the volumes do not lie flat when open, thus hindering easy physical use. Another annoying feature is the encyclopedia's split-letter system of volume arrangement. Each volume is approximately the same size (an important consideration in selling on the book-a-week basis), but the letter division can lead to confusion. For instance, Volume 14 ends with the letters MEX and Volume 15 begins with MEX. Which volume contains the article on the country of Mexico? The Gulf of Mexico? As it turns out, one is in Volume 14 and the other in Volume 15.

Inside the encyclopedia, the two-column page layout is uninviting and the type rather small. The preface points out that the printed text "was set by a computer, an innovation that enabled us to include more information on a page than in previous editions, and a new, modern typeface makes this edition easier to read." These observations are true. The print is indeed clear and attractive, and a remarkable amount of text is provided on each page. But the computer-assisted composition (which produces camera-ready pages from a master computer tape) does have one glaring drawback—lack of paragraphing. The article "Drama, Western," for example, consists of about 4,000 words and covers more than a full page of the encyclopedia, but it does not have even a single paragraph break. In this sense, *New Illustrated Columbia* is not easier but more difficult to read. It should be noted that the printed text of *New Illustrated Columbia* is a slightly enlarged photographic reproduction of the *New Columbia Encyclopedia*'s text. But whereas the latter has a large three-column 9 × 12 inch page, *New Illustrated Columbia* has a two-column 7 × 9¼ inch page.

Special Features

Several useful if unspectacular special features might be noted. As already mentioned, every proper name in the King James Version of the Bible is accorded an entry in the encyclopedia, with references to biblical passages where the name can be found. Pronunciations are provided for scientific, foreign, and unfamiliar entries. And metric equivalents are included for most measurements.

Sales Information

The blue and gold Kivar binding already described (see "Physical Format") is sold in supermarkets on the familiar book-a-week plan. Although prices may vary from place to place, Volume 1 normally sells at the introductory price of $0.99, with the remaining volumes at $2.99, or $69.76 for the set. Also, with the purchase of Volume 2, the customer receives the *Webster's New World Dictionary* (School and Office edition) as a premium. It should also be noted that customers who miss or lose a particular volume of the encyclopedia can acquire it directly from the publisher. With the purchase of Volume 1, the consumer receives an owner's registration card and guarantee, stating that "the publishers of The New Illustrated Columbia Encyclopedia guarantee that you and your family, as the owners of Volume One, are entitled to a full and complete set of 24 volumes. If you do not purchase one or more of the remaining volumes at your store, or if a volume in your set is lost or damaged, you can obtain the volume(s) you need by ordering directly from the publisher. This guarantee becomes effective after your supermarket has completed its sale of all volumes in the set. It will remain in effect for three years from that time. . . . For each volume, send check or money order for $2.99, plus 50¢ for shipping and handling" (to New Illustrated Columbia Encyclopedia, Box 1003, Radio City Station, New York, NY 10019).

The set can also be acquired as a unit via direct mail order from the distributor, Time-Life Books, for $69.96, plus a modest shipping and handling charge. As in the case of the supermarket distribution, *Webster's New World Dictionary* (School and Office edition) is offered free upon purchase of the encyclopedia. Aside from an annual supplement called the *New Illustrated Encyclopedia Yearbook* (see "Recency"), which sells for $7.95 per volume, the publisher or distributor offers no optional publications, research services, bookcases, or packages deals with the purchase of the set.

Like *Funk & Wagnalls New Encyclopedia* (the other adult supermarket encyclopedia currently available), *New Illustrated Columbia* can be, despite its several limitations, a real bargain, whether purchased as a complete set via direct mail or a volume a week at the local supermarket. Consumers should be aware, however, that *New Illustrated Columbia*, advertising claims to the contrary, will not be a bargain for younger children, who ordinarily will not be able to comprehend the articles.

Summary

The New Illustrated Columbia Encyclopedia can be quickly summed up in this manner:

Scope: Good	Accessibility: Poor
Authority: Excellent	Bibliographies: Good
Reliability: Good	Graphics: Poor
Recency: Poor	Physical Format: Fair
Objectivity: Good	Special Features: Few
Clarity: Excellent	Price: Very reasonable

To elaborate briefly, *New Illustrated Columbia,* a 24-volume set sold in supermarkets and by direct mail, is an illustrated version of the one-volume *New Columbia Encyclopedia* published in 1975. *New Illustrated Columbia* (like *New Columbia*) is best suited for literate adults and serious students at the senior high school level and beyond. Contrary to advertising claims, the encyclopedia ordinarily will not be useful to younger readers. The set's strong points include extensive coverage of biographical and geographical topics (which account for approximately 75 percent of the 50,000 articles), an experienced editorial staff and well-qualified consultants, a clear and precise writing style, and a very reasonable price tag. On the negative side, the encyclopedia's contents reflect the state of knowledge and information as of the early 1970s. Unfortunately, *New Illustrated Columbia* is not continuously revised as are most other multivolume adult encyclopedias. Also, the set lacks an index, relying rather on a network of 66,000 cross-references to furnish access to the contents. Although the cross-reference system sometimes works well, it fails too often to be considered effective. And the graphics, added to the set by the Italian firm of Fratelli Fabbri, are of poor quality from both the aesthetic and informational standpoint.

Obviously, *New Illustrated Columbia* cannot compare with the largest adult sets. *Collier's Encyclopedia, The Encyclopedia Americana,* and *The New Encyclopaedia Britannica* provide a range and depth of coverage and treatment well beyond the limited capabilities of *New Illustrated Columbia.* Nor can it successfully compete with the several excellent young adult sets on the market, namely *Compton's Encyclopedia, Merit Students Encyclopedia,* and *The World Book Encyclopedia,* which are specifically and quite carefully designed for student use. They offer a curriculum orientation, graduated readability, and vocabulary control that *New Illustrated Columbia* does not even attempt. But in the category of modestly priced, intermediate adult encyclopedias, *New Illustrated Columbia* represents a potentially good investment. From the standpoint of quality alone, the new *Academic American Encyclopedia* is far and away the best choice in this category. From the standpoint of price alone, *Funk & Wagnalls New Encyclopedia* (the other adult supermarket set currently available) is the best selection (it retails for $77.83 as opposed to $400 for the *Academic American*). *New Illustrated Columbia*, which costs roughly the same as *Funk & Wagnalls*, is more authoritative, but it lacks *Funk & Wagnalls'* recency, accessibility, popular readability, and editorial attention to graphics. *New Illustrated Columbia* is superior to *The New Standard Encyclopedia* in terms of price, authority, and accessibility, but it lacks *New Standard*'s aggressive revision program, and hence its currency. In comparison with the handsome British-made *New Caxton Encyclopedia*, *New Illustrated Columbia* costs much less ($69.76 as opposed to $599.50), is more authoritative, and has better bibliographies, but *New Caxton* has the edge in the areas of recency, accessibility, physical format, and of course graphics. The two remaining sets in the intermediate adult class—the *Harver World Encyclopedia* and *The New American Encyclopedia*—are aging relics that should be avoided at any price. In short, *New Illustrated Columbia* is a reasonably attractive buy for serious students and adults, but dollar-for-dollar the set does not offer as much as *Funk & Wagnalls New Encyclopedia*, nor can it begin to match the overall quality of the much higher priced *Academic American Encyclopedia*.

Other Critical Opinions

None.

New Standard Encyclopedia

Facts in Brief

Full Title: **New Standard Encyclopedia.** *Editor:* Douglas W. Downey, Editor in Chief. *Publisher:* Standard Educational Corporation, 200 W. Monroe St., Chicago, IL 60606. *Distributors:* Various independent local distributors throughout the United States & Canada. *Former Titles: Standard Reference Work for the Home, School and Library* (1912–1922; 1927–1929); *National Encyclopedia for the Home, School and Library* (1923–1926); *Aiton's Encyclopedia* (1910–1911). *Edition Reviewed:* 85th Printing, 1980 copyright.

Volumes: 14. *Pages:* 9,878. *Articles:* 17,623. *Words:* 6,300,000. *Illustrations:* 12,200. *Maps:* 935. *Index Entries:* None. *Cross-references:* 53,000. *Contributors:* 700.

User Classification: Adult (Multivolume). *Reader Suitability:* Age 12 through General Adult. *Physical Size:* 7 × 9½ in.; 24 cm. *LC:* 79-19849. *ISBN:* 0-87392-185-2. *Lowest Suggested Retail Price:* $349.50; to schools & libraries $279.50.

Purpose and Scope

The New Standard Encyclopedia "is designed to provide as much information of interest to the general reader as is possible within an illustrated set selling for a moderate price" (preface). It is further suggested that "although children as young as nine or ten can understand much of the material, the content is not juvenile and the level of detail is sufficient for basic reference use by persons of any age." Hence, like most multivolume encyclopedias in the intermediate adult and young adult categories, *New Standard* attempts to appeal to as wide a potential readership as possible. The encyclopedia's main thrust, however, is aimed at users in their teens and adults with modest educational attainments who are seeking simple (but not simplistic) treatment of general knowledge and information. Sometimes *New Standard* accomplishes this difficult goal quite well, sometimes not so well. (The question of the encyclopedia's most appropriate audience is discussed further under "Clarity and Reader Suitability.")

New Standard's 17,623 articles are normally very brief, averaging 375 words in length, or roughly half a page. Most often the articles simply provide basic factual information on specific subjects, such as biographical and geographical topics, associations and societies, and general terms and processes relating to the major areas of knowledge and their fields of study. The encyclopedia accords botanical, zoological, and fundamental scientific subjects especially good coverage. The article "Evolution," for example, concisely covers the essential principles, history, and terminology of the topic in about two pages. "Photosynthesis" achieves much the same results in a single page. North American subjects—people, places, organizations, history—are naturally emphasized, but the articles rarely provide more than the rudimentary facts and figures. Considerable information is presented in tabular form. The article "Cheese," for instance, furnishes an alphabetical list of major varieties of cheese that indicates their appearance, ingredients, origin, and customary use.

Given its relatively small size, *New Standard* covers many subjects quite well. The major countries and continents of the world, the U.S. states and Canadian provinces, and persons of first historical importance receive extended coverage. EXAMPLE: The article on Thomas Jefferson runs to six pages. It includes a full-page portrait, two useful tables (one summarizing Jefferson's biographical data and the other devoted to his presidential administrations), a sampling of Jefferson quotations, and a bibliography of books for further reading. EXAMPLE: "China" consists of 22 pages, including numerous photographs, a full-page physical map, a full-page political map, and a lengthy bibliography. Some areas of the humanities, social and behavioral sciences, and science and technology are also well covered. *New Standard* covers the subject of women's rights as thoroughly as or more thoroughly than its major competitors (namely, the *Academic American Encyclopedia, Funk & Wagnalls New Encyclopedia, Harver World Encyclopedia, The New Caxton Encyclopedia,* and *The New Illustrated Columbia Encyclopedia*). The long survey article "Architecture" concisely but accurately discusses the principal elements and terminology of the subject, both historically and in the modern period. The brief article "Electronic Music" provides a reasonably useful overview, accompanied by a photograph of a Moog synthesizer. The three-page entry "Refrigeration" describes the subject in readable, nontechnical terms. The heavily illustrated 14-page article "Ocean" adequately surveys the topic, again providing as much as or more information than comparable articles in *New Standard*'s competitors. "Biology" offers a reasonably good introduction to the discipline's history, trends, and concerns. Many useful, albeit very brief, opera plot summaries are included for famous works like *Carmen, The Girl of the Golden West,* and *La Traviata.* Familiar novels, however, are not digested. Also, as in most other intermediate adult encyclopedias, *New Standard* includes much practical, or how-to, information (on such topics as canning, civil defense, checking accounts, first aid, games, and insurance).

In other instances, coverage is quite superficial or lacking altogether. EXAMPLE: The article "Birth Control" succinctly defines the various known methods but makes no mention of how effective each is. Nor does the article note the risks to health associated with oral contraceptives and intrauterine devices. Approximately half the text is devoted to the history of birth control, which seems excessive under the circumstances. EXAMPLE: The subject of genetics (covered in "Heredity") receives only a few paragraphs. The coverage, though clear, mentions nothing about such recent developments as gene mapping and genetic counseling. EXAMPLE: Information about cults, ancient or modern, is totally lacking in the encyclopedia. There is no mention, for instance, of the People's Temple, Hare Krishna, or the Unification Church of the Reverend Sun Myung Moon. EXAMPLE: The three-page article "Child Development" is so simplified that it can properly be called oversimplified. For instance, the article fails to cite any child development theorists or researchers, including Jean Piaget or even Sigmund Freud. EXAMPLE: The subject of shock therapy, or electroconvulsive therapy, receives two sentences in the article "Psychiatry." There is no explanation of the effectiveness of the treatment, nor of the controversy concerning its application. EXAMPLE: Metric equivalents are normally not furnished.

New Standard's editors make a conscientious effort to cover all areas of general knowledge likely to be needed by or of interest to potential users, chiefly students and adults of modest intellectual means. Obviously, however, the editors are not always successful. The coverage is reasonably well balanced, with biographical, geographical, and scientific subjects predominating. But in some instances, the encyclopedia's text is so compressed or so elementary that it is either too sketchy or too simple to be of much use to anyone. And in other cases, topics that ought to be covered in an adult set are ignored or overlooked.

History and Authority

The Standard Educational Corporation (formerly the Standard Educational Society, Inc.) has published *New Standard* since 1930. The set originated from the five-volume *Aiton's Encyclopedia* (1910–1911), a popular work that was expanded to six volumes and retitled the *Standard Reference Work for the Home, School and Library* in 1912. Ten years later it became the *National Encyclopedia for the Home, School and Library* in ten volumes. In 1927 it reverted to the title *Standard Reference Work* and so remained until the Standard Educational Society acquired it in 1930.

New Standard has never been considered an encyclopedia of first importance by knowledgeable critics. During the past 25 years, however, the publisher has made substantial efforts to improve and modernize the set. A thoroughgoing revision program was initiated in the mid-1950s. Following its completion in 1965, a similar ten-year effort was launched, being completed in 1975. Ever since that time *New Standard* has consistently maintained a high degree of up-to-dateness.

Douglas W. Downey, the editor in chief, has held that position since 1964. In addition to Downey, the encyclopedia lists an editorial staff of 85, including 30 contributing editors (i.e., writers) and 23 artists. Practically all *New Standard*'s articles are staff written. The foreword notes that "staff members are qualified in their fields by education and experience and are trained in the techniques of encyclopedia writing." Almost all of these people are identified as holding a college degree, and some have advanced degrees. The encyclopedia's editorial advisory board consists of two well-qualified educators (both affiliated with schools of education in the University of California system) and three librarians, one of whom is the prominent Robert B. Downs. This group is said to be responsible for broad policy concerning the encyclopedia's content, style, and approach. Next, there is a list of 35 persons called authenticators and advisers. Their job is to review new and revised articles prepared by staff writers. All the authenticators and advisers are academicians, most from Southern and Midwestern schools. Finally, there is a long list of about 700 contributors, consultants, and special authenticators. These people, it is explained, also review staff-prepared articles and sometimes "assist in preparing material outside the fields covered by the regular Authenticators and Advisers, or specialized material within these fields." This list contains some readily recognizable names—Neil Armstrong, J. Edgar Hoover, Mario Pei—but most of them are associated with a particular national organization or government agency. For instance, Mrs. Fred J. Tooze, identified as president of the national Woman's Christian Temperance Union, verified the brief article on the WCTU in Volume 14. Many of the contributors, consultants, and special authenticators are now either retired or dead. The *Buying Guide* has been informed that *New Standard*'s advisory board and list of authenticators will be expanded over the next several years.

Reliability

The foreword states that "since each article is the work of several persons, the articles are not signed." But, again according to the foreword, "Each article published has been reviewed by seven or more persons. At least one of these is a recognized authority in the field being covered." Although the authority of the people associated with *New Standard* is not as a general rule impressive (see "History and Authority"), the editors appear to have created a workable system for ensuring factual reliability of material. Inevitably there are a few errors. The article "Indians, American," for instance, erroneously states that "no Indians had a written language," which ignores the Mayans and others. The article "Shark" errs by stating that "one species is landlocked in a freshwater lake, Lake Nicaragua in Central America." But when considered in proportion to the amount of factual information included in *New Standard*, such errors are not quantitatively significant. On the other hand, oversimplified or sketchy treatment sometimes may prompt the reader to mistaken conclusions. EXAMPLE: "Indians, American" informs that "when the white man arrived in America, the Indian was living in a Stone Age type of culture. His principal business was to get enough food to keep from starving," which is a gross overgeneralization. For additional examples of this problem, see "Purpose and Scope."

Recency

New Standard maintains a commendable level of up-to-dateness. The comprehensive ten-year revision projects carried out between 1955 and 1975 brought the set up to a reasonable standard of recency, and since

This Recency Table compares selected topics in *New Standard* with those in other encyclopedias of similar size and intended usership.

Topic	New Standard	Academic American	Funk & Wagnalls	New Caxton
Afghanistan	Fairly current	Very current	Fairly current	Fairly current
Dinosaurs	Very current	Very curent	Very current	Fairly current
Greenland	Very current	Very current	Not current	Not current
Thomas Jefferson	Fairly current	Fairly current	Fairly current	Not current
Mass Transportation/Subways	Fairly current	Very current	Fairly current	Very current
Nuclear Power	Not current	Very current	Not current	Fairly current
Paris	Not current	Very current	Not current	Very current
Sharks	Very current	Fairly current	Not current	Fairly current
Shock Therapy	Not current	Very current	Not current	Fairly current
Suicide	Very current	Fairly current	Not current	Not current*
Tuberculosis	Fairly current	Fairly current	Fairly current	Fairly current
Zimbabwe	Very current	Very current	Very current	Very current

*Topic not covered in encyclopedia.

that time the editors have apparently worked hard to keep the set as current as an encyclopedia can possibly be. In the early 1970s, an innovative computerized revision system was established to assist the staff in keeping track of areas of information that require "permanent" revision (e.g., census data), those areas that are becoming dated and might require revision, and new areas for possible inclusion. The company's IBM 360 computer is said to keep track of 10,000 to 15,000 data changes each year. The set is revised with each new printing. New printings normally occur once a year (the 1977 copyright was the 82nd printing and the 1980 copyright, under review here, is the 85th printing).

Since 1977, when the *Buying Guide* last reviewed *New Standard*, approximately 3,000 of the set's more than 17,000 articles have been revised in some manner, 58 new articles have been added, and over 100 dropped. In addition, nearly 400 new illustrations have been added during this period. All articles on the U.S. states, for example, are systematically being revised at the present time. New articles cover such diverse subjects as affirmative action, U.S. Department of Energy, gasohol, health foods, liquid crystal, OPEC, plastic surgery, racket and paddle games, rock

music, SALT, and whiplash. New biographees include Sir John Betjeman, John Cage, Joe Clark, Patricia Harris, Rod McKuen, Marshall
McLuhan, Margaret Thatcher, and Cyrus Vance. Editor Downey also
informs the *Buying Guide* that *New Standard*'s 1981 copyright (86th printing) will represent a major revision effort, involving some 1,500 new or
revised articles. Overall, *New Standard*'s rate of annual revision in recent
times has been in the neighborhood of 10 percent, a highly satisfactory
figure for a consistently well-maintained adult encyclopedia.

Another method of attempting to keep the encyclopedia current is by
means of an updating supplement entitled *World Progress: The Standard
Quarterly Review*. A three-ring publication that comes with its own
binder, *World Progress* is quite different from other encyclopedia updating services in that it appears every three months. It is written in a
reasonably lively style. The articles cover recent events, with an emphasis
on the countries of the world and such broad topics as agriculture, business and finance, literature, medicine, race relations, sports and athletics,
and the theater. It is like an encyclopedic *Time* magazine. The final issue
of the year contains a cumulated index for all four issues. Purchasers of
New Standard should be aware that *World Progress* articles are in no way
correlated with the encyclopedia.

Objectivity

New Standard usually presents its material in a fair and balanced manner. Evidence of intentional bias or prejudice is absent from the encyclopedia. Such controversial subjects as abortion, fluoridation, marijuana,
Ralph Nader, and race are treated objectively. Differing opinions are
usually presented in a straightforward, unemotional style. EXAMPLE: The
brief biographical sketch of Nader factually reports his consumer protection activities, noting at one point that "some of his recommendations led
to stricter controls by governmental regulatory agencies." The article
concludes, however, with the statement: "Nader's critics charge that he
relies on inexperienced researchers and releases reports based on superficial investigation," which is certainly true. EXAMPLE: The article "Homosexuality" provides a carefully balanced overview of the subject: "In the
United States, for example, most states have laws declaring sexual acts
between members of the same sex as criminal offenses. Beginning in the
mid-1960's a movement arose (called the Gay Liberation Movement) to
gain legal and social acceptance for homosexuals." EXAMPLE: The article
"Evolution" succinctly explains the tenets of Darwinian theory, but concludes with this note: "Most religious denominations now accept the theory, but in varying degrees. Some accept it as an unproved hypothesis.
Others accept only those parts that do not apply to man. Still others see
no conflict between evolution and theology."

In some instances, however, controversial subject matter is simply ignored. EXAMPLE: The article on Thomas Jefferson mentions that he inherited "several slaves" (a gross understatement), but ignores his various
slave children. Likewise, the Fawn Brodie book *Thomas Jefferson: An*

Intimate History (1974), which introduced contemporary readers to Jefferson's controversial private life, is excluded from the bibliography accompanying the article. EXAMPLE: The article "Chile" reports the death of Salvador Allende in a military coup in 1973, but the cause of the former Chilean president's demise is not mentioned (strong evidence now exists that Allende, a Marxist, was murdered by the right-wing generals who seized power). In the past, *New Standard* has been criticized by the *Buying Guide* and others for its conservative tone toward the political left. The encyclopedia has tended to extol the virtues of democratic government while painting Socialism and Communism as unmitigated evils, and sometimes unwelcome information about the so-called Free World has been avoided or downplayed, as in the case of Allende's death. Happily, the editors are aware of the need for a more evenhanded approach to such topics, and during the past few years efforts have been made to correct the problem; for instance, the article "Communism" has been revised to reflect a more objective point of view.

Clarity and Reader Suitability

New Standard is written in a simple, direct, economical style that normally will be comprehensible to young people in their teens and adults with at least seventh-grade reading skills. The goal is to provide basic information in a straightforward manner that will not intimidate or overwhelm the reader. *New Standard* succeeds quite well in this effort. As already noted (see "History and Authority"), members of the editorial staff trained in encyclopedia writing prepare the articles, thus ensuring a certain degree of stylistic consistency. A good example of the encyclopedia's style is found in the article on Warren Harding: "Harding proved to be well-meaning and hard-working as president but a bad judge of character. His brief administration (he died in mid-term) was badly tarnished by the corruption of a number of close associates, and he has been considered one of the worst Presidents in the nation's history." The encyclopedia's articles on scientific theories and processes are especially noteworthy for their clarity. EXAMPLE: The article "Atomic Energy" begins by describing the subject as "energy released in large amounts by the splitting or formation of atomic nuclei. The light and heat of the sun and other stars is an example of naturally occurring atomic energy. Artificially produced atomic energy can be released either in a steady, controllable manner, as in devices called *nuclear reactors*, or in the form of a violent explosion, as in *nuclear weapons*." Students and adults of above average intelligence and reading comprehension, however, may at times find *New Standard*'s style a bit too simple or bland for their taste.

Unlike most encyclopedias in the intermediate adult category, *New Standard* utilizes the technique of pyramid writing, or initial readability (proceeding from the simple to the complex), thus expanding the set's potential readership to include fairly young children. In addition, although the articles are not formally or systematically written to grade level, there is an attempt to write them on a level compatible with the sophistication of the subject matter. EXAMPLES: "Nature Study" is written at a fourth or fifth grade level. "National Convention" is written at a ninth or tenth grade level. "Naturalism" is written at an eleventh or twelfth grade level. In each case, the level of writing is determined by the complexity of the subject, not the grade at which the subject is presumably taught. Yet another aid to clarity and readability is accomplished by defining difficult or technical terms in context; for instance, the article "Dinosaur" notes that "most paleontologists (scientists who study fossils) agree that the extinction of the dinosaurs was a complex phenomenon that cannot be explained by a single theory." As this discussion indicates, *New Standard* is an adult encyclopedia that employs writing techniques characteristic of young adult encyclopedias. In a very real sense, *New Standard* is an encyclopedia for adults written at the young adult level.

Arrangement and Accessibility

New Standard is arranged alphabetically, word-by-word ("Indian Ocean" precedes "Indiana"). The set has no index. Instead, access to the contents is facilitated by some 13,000 external cross-references (e.g., "*Nuclear Energy*. See ATOMIC ENERGY") and approximately 40,000 internal *See* and *See also* references within and at the end of the articles. Like *The New American Encyclopedia* and *The New Illustrated Columbia Encyclopedia* (the only other multivolume adult sets that lack an index), *New Standard* is said to be self-indexing by virtue of its extensive cross-reference system.

Since as early as 1968, independent authorities on general encyclopedias have been saying that *New Standard*'s "lack of an index is a serious fault and a deterrent to the use" of the set. The *Buying Guide* repeats that point in the hope that future editions of *New Standard* will include an analytical index. It is sorely needed. Thousands of bits of information are buried, inaccessible except through luck or browsing. Hundreds of examples could be readily cited. For instance, the article "Motion Pictures" contains nearly a full-page discussion of the documentary, but there is no external cross-reference from "Documentary" to "Motion Pictures." It could be argued that most readers seeking information about documentaries would think to look under "Motion Pictures," which may or may not be true. The real issue is that a well-designed general encyclopedia will furnish all the modes of access—alphabetical or logical arrangement of entries, subheadings, cross-references, guide words, an analytical index—necessary to render its contents as accessible as possible. It should also be noted that accessibility of *New Standard*'s graphics is limited for want of an index. There is no way, for instance, for the reader of the unillustrated article "Pony Express" to know that the article on St. Joseph, Missouri, contains a photograph of a monument entitled *The Pony Express*. In a reviewing aid furnished by the publisher, *New Standard* editors concede that "there *is* buried information in NEW STANDARD. However, the information not already made available through our 'See' entries and 'See also' references is of such marginal value that it is not worth the added cost—which would have to be passed on to the customer—to publish a separate index." The *Buying Guide* cannot agree.

Bibliographies

Over 1,000 of *New Standard*'s articles (about 5 percent) include bibliographies, or lists of books for further study. Nonprint materials such as films and filmstrips are not cited, but in many instances books designated "For Younger Readers" are indicated. EXAMPLE: The article "Atomic Energy" has a bibliography of 19 titles, of which 7 are singled out as being suitable for younger readers, or students. Prepared by David E. King, *New Standard*'s librarian, the bibliographies normally contain several entries for shorter articles (e.g., "Dickinson, Emily") and up to 25 for major articles (e.g., "Canada"; "China"). Many of the bibliographies include quite recent titles, although sometimes important works are overlooked. As already noted (see "Objectivity"), Fawn Brodie's controversial but essential *Thomas Jefferson: An Intimate History* (1974) is not among the nine-item bibliography accompanying the Jefferson article. In the case of the article on Warren Harding, Francis Russell's *The Shadow of Blooming Grove* (1968) and Eugene Trani's *The Presidency of Warren G. Harding* (1977) are not included in the two-item bibliography.

Graphics

Graphics have never been one of *New Standard*'s stronger features, but there has been considerable improvement in this area over the past decade. The set now includes over 12,200 illustrations, of which 1,700 are in full color and another 2,800 in two color. Photographs predominate, although there are also many art reproductions, cartoons, diagrams, and maps. Some of the drawings accompanying articles on scientific and technical subjects are quite informative, such as the black-and-white graphic showing how a spring-wound clock works with the article "Clock." Practically all such drawings are produced or adapted by *New Standard*'s own art department. Another useful aspect of *New Standard*'s graphics is the inclusion of portraits of U.S. presidents' wives.

Often, however, the diagrams and photographs are irritatingly small and lack sufficient detail. Illustrations are usually placed to complement the text, but sometimes their informational value is nil. EXAMPLE: A tiny snapshot of a pyramid and some blurry figures by a strip of water accompanies the article "Climate," intended to illustrate "Desert Climate." In other instances, black-and-white reproduction is used where color obviously would have enhanced the graphic's informational value. EXAMPLE: The article "Cobra" includes a picture of the snake. The article informs that the cobra "may be yellowish to dark brown in color. The back of the hood is marked by a blotch shaped like a pair of eyeglasses." Unfortunately, the illustration is in black-and-white. EXAMPLE: The article on Georgia O'Keeffe, the contemporary American artist, includes a reproduction of her painting *Cow's Skull with Red*. Unfortunately, the illustration is in black-and-white. Most of the art reproductions found throughout the set, however, are in color. The color reproduction tends to be poor, largely because of the indifferent quality of paper used. As pointed out earlier (see "Arrangement and Accessibility"), the graphics in *New Standard* are not indexed, nor are they always accessible via cross-references. Users should be aware, however, that all reproductions of paintings in *New Standard* are separately indexed in the article "Painting."

Approximately 120 of the set's 935 maps are full-page, four-color works prepared by the noted cartographic firm, C. S. Hammond, Inc. These maps accompany articles on major continents, countries, and cities, as well as the U.S. states (but not Canadian provinces). Most of the rest of the maps are staff-drawn. They are usually small and lack sufficient detail for any serious geographical study (270 are simply locator maps). As might be expected, the encyclopedia also includes various historical and special-purpose maps scattered throughout, such as with the article "Crusades."

Among the intermediate adult encyclopedias currently on the market, *New Standard*'s graphics are roughly comparable in number and quality to those found in *Funk & Wagnalls New Encyclopedia, The New American Encyclopedia,* and *The New Illustrated Columbia Encyclopedia. Harver World Encyclopedia* is much superior to *New Standard* in this area, and the new *Academic American Encyclopedia* and British *New Caxton Encyclopedia* are in a league by themselves.

Physical Format

The bright red Sturdite binding with black panels and gold lettering is both attractive and sturdy. Each volume contains all of one or more letters of the alphabet (e.g., Volume 3 covers the letter C; Volume 4 the letters D and E), a system known as unit-letter arrangement. Inside, the format is less successful. The two-column page layout tends to be crowded, and the inside margins are very narrow. The many small, dark photographs found throughout (see "Graphics") give the contents an overall uninviting appearance. The typefaces used, however, tend to be bold and legible. The paper is of fair quality, although it does not reproduce color well. Guide words appear at the top of every page, and the volumes normally lie flat when open.

Special Features

New Standard has no unique features, but there are several items designed to assist readers that might be mentioned. First, the encyclopedia provides pronunciation information for difficult or unfamiliar names and terms—for instance "*Gielgud, John* [gĭl´go͝od]." The pronunciations are simple and reasonably easy to understand. Second, selected articles include glossaries of specialized terminology; for example, "Electronics" furnishes definitions of about 50 terms used in the field, such as *cathode, grid, integrated circuit,* and *semiconductor*. Third, much information is presented in tables or shaded boxes; for example, "Child Development" includes an information box labeled "Some of the Things a Child Must Learn." Fourth, the article "Painting" provides an index to all reproductions of paintings in the encyclopedia. Oddly, this fact is not pointed out in Volume 1 in the section called "Suggestions on How to Use New Standard Encyclopedia." And fifth and finally, the set's unit-letter arrangement constitutes a useful special feature (see "Physical Format"). In point of fact, *New Standard* is the only multivolume encyclopedia currently on the market that offers the unit-letter feature.

Sales Information

Standard Educational Corporation, *New Standard*'s publisher, does not maintain a direct sales organization. Instead, the encyclopedia is sold at the retail level through independent distributors in the United States, Canada, and abroad. These distributors buy *New Standard* from Standard Educational Corporation and then sell the set in-home on the subscription basis. Consumers should be aware that some distributors arrange to have their own special bindings. For example, Consolidated Book Publishers, Inc. (1727 S. Indiana Ave., Chicago, IL 60616) offers the "Universal Edition" of *The New Standard Encyclopedia*. The content is the same, only the binding is different. Such special bindings or "editions" may not adhere to the $349.50 retail price suggested by Standard Educational. Consumers are warned *not* to pay more than this price for *New Standard* under any circumstances, fancy binding or not. The encyclopedia is also available to schools and libraries either from an independent representative or directly from the publisher. The set sells to educational institutions for $279.50, or 20 percent off the suggested retail price. Combination offers vary from distributor to distributor. Many of them include all or some of the volumes of *Child Horizons*, a ten-volume series of books for young people also published by Standard Educational.

Summary

The New Standard Encyclopedia can be quickly summed up in this manner:

Scope: Good   Accessibility: Poor
Authority: Fair   Bibliographies: Good
Reliability: Good   Graphics: Fair
Recency: Excellent   Physical Format: Good
Objectivity: Good   Special Features: Few
Clarity: Excellent   Price: Reasonable

To elaborate briefly, *New Standard* is a compact, normally reliable source of brief factual information and knowledge on basic subjects. Biographical, geographical, and scientific and technical topics tend to be emphasized, as are subjects of particular interest or relating to North Americans. The encyclopedia is intended to serve "persons of any age," but its style and treatment is most suitable for students and adults with a limited intellectual and/or educational background. In a very real sense, *New Standard* is an adult encyclopedia written on a young adult level. The set's most impressive features are its conscientious attention to revision and the clarity of its articles. The set's greatest limitation is the lack of an analytical index. Until this deficiency is corrected, *New Standard* will remain a second-rate source of information.

As an adult encyclopedia, *New Standard* cannot begin to compare with the largest adult sets, namely *Collier's Encyclopedia, The Encyclopedia Americana,* and *The New Encyclopaedia Britannica.* They provide a range and depth of coverage and treatment well beyond the limited capabilities of *New Standard.* Nor can it successfully compete with the several excellent young adult encyclopedias on the market. *Compton's Encyclopedia, Merit Students Encyclopedia,* and *The World Book Encyclopedia* are specifically and quite carefully designed for use by young adults. They furnish a structured curriculum orientation and systematic vocabulary control based on readability testing which *New Standard* does not even attempt. But in the intermediate adult category, *New Standard* represents a viable and competitive source of general knowledge and information, particularly for unsophisticated or undereducated users. From the standpoint of quality alone, the new *Academic American Encyclopedia* is far and away the best choice in this category. In addition, the *Academic American* only costs a few dollars more than *New Standard.* But from the standpoint of price alone, *Funk & Wagnalls New Encyclopedia* is the best selection (it retails in supermarkets for $77.83 as opposed to $400 for the *Academic American* and $349.50 for *New Standard*). In comparison with *The New Illustrated Columbia Encyclopedia,* another inexpensive supermarket set, *New Standard* has the advantage of being much more up-to-date and more readable, although *New Illustrated Columbia* is more authoritative and much less costly. The British-made *New Caxton Encyclopedia,* although handsomely illustrated (which *New Standard* is not), is not as current nor as readable as *New Standard.* In addition, the *New Caxton* has a natural British emphasis and it costs a whopping $599.50. The two remaining sets in the intermediate adult class—the *Harver World Encyclopedia* and *The New American Encyclopedia*—are aging relics that should be avoided at any price. In short, *New Standard* is a decent but not outstanding encyclopedia that can adequately serve the needs of students and adults, especially those with a limited educational and intellectual background. But dollar-for-dollar, it does not offer as much as *Funk & Wagnalls New Encyclopedia,* nor can it begin to match the overall quality of the new *Academic American Encyclopedia.*

Other Critical Opinions

Booklist, December 15, 1978, pp. 712–714. Part of a series of reviews by the ALA Reference and Subscription Books Review Committee (RSBRC) entitled "Encyclopedias: A Survey and Buying Guide," this evaluation of *New Standard* (80th printing, 1975) criticizes the set's authority, sometimes overly simplistic coverage, and conservative political tone. Remarkably, the review suggests that *New Standard*'s cross-references are "almost an adequate substitute" for an index. No final conclusions are offered on the set, however. In its last regular review of

New Standard (*Booklist,* November 1, 1977, pp. 494–497), which covered the 1976 copyright, RSBRC conditionally "recommended" the encyclopedia "for home use only with reservation," citing a number of objections, including the opinion that "*New Standard*'s cross-reference structure is inconsistent and does not take the place of a good index."

Cheney, Frances Neel. *American Reference Books Annual*, 1980, pp. 29–30. This superficial review offers little substantive criticism, although *New Standard*'s cross-references are said to be "probably . . . an adequate substitute" for an index.

Katz, William A. *Basic Information Sources* (Vol. 1 of *Introduction to Reference Work*, 3rd ed. New York: McGraw-Hill, 1978), pp. 163–164. Katz, a well-known authority on reference work, offers a succinct but valuable critical assessment of *New Standard*, calling it "of real benefit to young adults and to older people with less than strong reading habits," while warning consumers about the set's mediocre graphics and lack of an index.

IV. SMALL-VOLUME ADULT ENCYCLOPEDIAS

New Columbia Encyclopedia

Facts in Brief

Full Title: **The New Columbia Encyclopedia.** *Editors:* William H. Harris and Judith S. Levey. *Publisher:* Columbia University Press, 562 W. 113 St., New York, NY 10025. *Distributor:* Barnes & Noble Bookstores, Inc., Mail Order Dept., 105 Fifth Ave., New York, NY 10003. *Former Title: The Columbia Encyclopedia* (First–Third Editions, 1935–1963). *Edition Reviewed:* Fourth Edition, 1975 copyright.

Volumes: One. *Pages:* 3,068. *Articles:* 50,515. *Words:* 6,600,000. *Illustrations:* 407. *Maps:* 252. *Index Entries:* None. *Cross-references:* 66,000. *Contributors:* 119.

User Classification: Adult (Small-volume). *Reader Suitability:* Age 15 through Advanced Adult. *Physical Size:* 9½ × 12¼ in.; 31 cm. *LC:* 74-26686. *ISBN:* 0-231-03572-1 (Standard Edition). *Lowest Retail Price:* $79.50 (from publisher); $29.50 (from distributor); to schools & libraries a substantial discount (from publisher).

Purpose and Scope

The New Columbia Encyclopedia, a revised edition of the highly regarded *Columbia Encyclopedia,* is a one-volume work said to offer "authentic and accurate information in condensed form" on "a wide-ranging variety of subjects that fall within the province of a general reference work." Intended for home, office, and library "instant reference," *New Columbia* is nevertheless primarily aimed at a literate adult usership, although high school students might find it helpful as a reliable source for general knowledge and basic information. *New Columbia* is also published in an expanded (but not updated) multivolume version entitled *The New Illustrated Columbia Encyclopedia.* The 24-volume *New Illustrated Columbia,* which is sold principally in supermarkets, adds some 5,000 illustrations to *New Columbia*'s printed text (see Part III of the *Buying Guide* for a review of *New Illustrated Columbia*).

New Columbia appeared in 1975 as the fourth edition of an encyclopedia that dates back to 1935. The new and retitled edition covers 7,000 subjects not included in the third edition (1963), such as "American Indian Movement," "Continental Drift," "Immunosuppressive Drug," "No-fault Insurance," "Pulsar," "Space Law," "Vasectomy," and "Watergate Affair." For the most part, articles in the previous edition have been rewritten, updated, or dropped. Many geographical topics, especially small American towns, which were included in the 1963 edition, are no longer covered. Indeed, the earlier edition attempted to cover "all populated places of one thousand or more" in the United States. Understandably, this policy is no longer possible, given the demographics of American society in the 1970s, but *New Columbia* does claim to treat all places of historical or cultural significance regardless of size. Of the encyclopedia's 50,000 entries, approximately 15,000 (or 30 percent) cover geographical topics, including all the countries of the world, the U.S. states, and some 2,000 U.S. cities and towns. As might be expected, the larger or more prominent the place, the more coverage it normally receives. U.S. places, however, are accorded proportionately more coverage than their counterparts abroad. EXAMPLE: The article on Africa comprises nearly two pages, including a large black-and-white map. EXAMPLE: "Afghanistan" takes up just under a full page, including a small locator map. EXAMPLE: The article on Arkansas (the U.S. state) covers two-thirds of a page, or nearly the same amount of space accorded Afghanistan. EXAMPLE: The article on Arnhem, a German city of over 130,000 population, consists of nine lines. EXAMPLE: The article on Atlantic City, N.J. (a city much smaller than Arnhem), covers 26 lines.

Even a greater number of the articles (45 percent) deal with people, both living and dead. Emphasis has been placed on important political leaders in the United States, Great Britain, and the world, roughly in that order. In addition to famous leaders of the past like Clement Attlee, Charles de Gaulle, Gandhi, and the Roosevelts, *New Columbia* covers such current notables as Arthur Burns, Cesar Chavez, Betty Friedan, Edward Heath, Park Chung Hee, Ralph Nader, Yitzhak Rabin, and Anwar el-Sadat. Numerous writers, artists, musicians, scientists, theologians, philosophers, athletes, and the like are also covered. Biographical articles provide a thumbnail description of the person's career, major contributions, and important dates.

New Columbia averages 15 to 16 articles per page of 150–175 words each. Although biographical and geographical articles predominate, all essential areas of knowledge are adequately covered. The 12,000 or so entries devoted to subjects other than people and places include coverage of such concepts as empiricism, fraud, kinship, laissez-faire, parody, socialism, time, and viscosity. There are also articles on things like cemeteries, the funny bone, gasoline, iron, milk, ohmmeters, parachutes, tobacco, and vitamins. Scientific and technical subjects are usually well covered, especially basic topics like the brain, cells, neutrons, nucleic acid, numeration, periodic law, photosynthesis, protein, and sources of energy. Flora and fauna receive concise coverage. EXAMPLES: "Snapper" (9 lines); "Snapping Turtle" (28 lines); "Sneezeweed" (13 lines); "Snipe" (17 lines); "Snowberry" (5 lines). Major disciplines in the sciences are accorded short survey treatment. EXAMPLES: "Biochemistry" (50 lines); "Biology" (42 lines); "Biophysics" (31 lines). The arts and humanities are likewise well covered. Particularly noteworthy are articles on national or regional cultural developments (e.g., "African Art"; "African Languages"; "African Negro Literature"; "African Negro Music") and individual genres (e.g., "Architecture"; "Ballet"; "Drama"; "Motion Pictures"; "Painting"). Coverage also includes an entry for every proper name in the Authorized (King James) Version of the Bible, a carry-over from previous editions of the encyclopedia. The social and behavioral sciences, however, tend to receive less attention than the arts and natural sciences. The article "Opera," for instance, is nearly four times as long as "Psychoanalysis." The article "Child Abuse" is only 13 lines long, and the subjects of child development and human growth are completely ignored.

No small-volume encyclopedia can hope to achieve comprehensive coverage. Inevitably, *New Columbia* overlooks some places, people, ideas, and things that logically or properly should be included. EXAMPLE: Ripon, Wisconsin, reputed to be the birthplace of the Republican Party, has no entry but probably should. EXAMPLE: Eric Erikson, author of the provocative *Young Man Luther* and influential psychohistorian, is among the missing, as is novelist John Gardner, but Walter Cronkite and Bella Abzug are there. EXAMPLE: Also among the missing are Ronald Reagan, Jimmy Carter, Walter Mondale, Margaret Thatcher, Ayatollah Khomeini, Menachim Begin, and other national political leaders who emerged since 1975, omissions due to the encyclopedia's age rather than any editorial oversight (see "Recency"). EXAMPLE: The subject of condominium housing is ignored altogether, despite the fact that millions of people now live in one form or another of this type of housing. Failure to cover such topics as condominium housing, child development and human growth, and current political leaders is a serious deficiency in an encyclopedia intended for "instant reference." Also, when social and political subjects are covered, there is a tendency to emphasize historical aspects of the topic at the expense of contemporary developments (e.g., "Academic Freedom"; "Drug Addiction and Drug Abuse"; "Housing"; "Maritime Law"; "Police"; "Prison"; "Suicide").

Nevertheless, despite some glaring gaps, *New Columbia* usually provides clear, precise coverage of that knowledge and information considered most important or useful to North American readers as of the early 1970s (when the encyclopedia's articles were prepared). In an amusing article in the *New York Times* (August 3, 1975) about *New Columbia* when it first appeared, Israel Shenker wrote that "making a one-volume encyclopedia is like taking the broth of the universe and condensing it into a bouillon cube." On balance, *New Columbia*'s makers have produced quite a good bouillon cube, though it has become stale over the years. As already noted, the encyclopedia is particularly strong in the areas of biography and geography. Although U.S. and Canadian people and places are emphasized, *New Columbia*'s outlook is international. EXAMPLE: The article "Funeral Customs" mentions Islamic burial rituals and, at the end of the discussion, refers the reader to several books for further information, including *Funeral Customs the World Over*. In addition, metric equivalents are given throughout the volume. And a good deal of statistical and enumerative information that was presented in essay form in the 1963 edition has now "been organized into charts for easy reference; for example, there are tables listing Shakespeare's plays, constellations, popes, U.S. Presidents and Supreme Court justices, British and Canadian prime ministers, and French, Spanish, and Russian rulers" (preface).

History and Authority

New Columbia is built on a long tradition of encyclopedic excellence. The initial edition of the *Columbia Encyclopedia* (see Appendix A) appeared in 1935, followed by major revisions in 1950 and 1963. According to the publisher, these three editions together sold approximately a million copies in their time. In 1975, a fourth major revision appeared as *The New Columbia Encyclopedia* (under review here). The 1963 edition spawned the fine *Columbia-Viking Desk Encyclopedia* and the less impressive *Illustrated Columbia Encyclopedia,* a multivolume supermarket item. Both these titles are now out of print (see Appendix A), but in 1978 a 24-volume set derived from *New Columbia* entitled *The New Illustrated Columbia Encyclopedia* appeared. Like its predecessor (the *Illustrated Columbia*), the *New Illustrated Columbia* is aimed principally at the supermarket trade. (For a review of *New Illustrated Columbia,* see Part III of the *Buying Guide.*) Another spin-off of the single-volume *New Columbia* is the *International Geographic Encyclopedia and Atlas* (Houghton Mifflin, 1979), a 1,005-page reference work that consists of the geographical entries in *New Columbia* plus maps taken from *Goode's World Atlas* (Rand McNally, 15th edition, 1978).

New Columbia was seven years in the making. Although it is not an official publication of Columbia University, the editors acknowledge that "without Columbia University this book would not have been possible." Of the 90 or so academic consultants listed in the front matter, two-thirds are associated with the school. The list is impressive, including such renowned professors as Joseph L. Blau (religion), Robert Gorham Davis (literature), Theodosius Dobzhansky (genetics), Mark J. Kesselman (government), Lawrence C. Kolb (psychiatry), William E. Leuchtenburg (history), Robert McClintock (education), and Richard B. Morris (American history). In addition, there is an editorial staff of about 50, headed by William H. Harris and Judith S. Levey, both of whom possess sound qualifications for making an encyclopedia. Harris was formerly managing editor of both *Collier's Encyclopedia* and *Merit Students Encyclopedia,* and Levey, who in 1976 was named as editor in chief of *New Columbia,* has also worked at Macmillan as an encyclopedia editor. A total of 119 contributing editors are listed, one of whom is Harris and another William Jaber, who served as managing editor of the now defunct *Cadillac Modern Encyclopedia* (see Appendix A). All of *New Columbia*'s articles are unsigned, and therefore responsibility for specific articles cannot be determined. Articles in previous editions were also unsigned. But given its history of excellence since 1935, the high quality of the people associated with the project, and its indirect but very real affiliation with Columbia University, *New Columbia* stands as one of the most authoritative one-volume encyclopedias available today.

Reliability

As might be expected from the foregoing, the encyclopedia can be relied upon as a source of accurate information. Authority and reliability go hand-in-hand, and *New Columbia* very rarely slips up in either department. There are occasional errors of fact, however. EXAMPLE: The article "Shark" contains several minor points of misinformation about shark anatomy and reproduction. The statement that sharks have "large deposits of fat," for instance, is incorrect. EXAMPLE: "Marine Biology" errs in defining the topic as the "study of ocean plants and animals." In fact, marine biologists study coastal and estuary forms of life, as well as those found in oceans. The article also gives the erroneous impression that all plankton are microorganisms. EXAMPLE: The generally informative article "Abortion" states that "on Jan. 22, 1973, the Supreme Court ruled that a state may not prevent a woman from having an abortion during the first six months of pregnancy," without further explaining that the state is permitted to regulate abortion procedures in ways related to health during the second trimester. Such minor errors, while they detract from *New Columbia*'s high standard of reliability, are not encountered frequently enough to diminish the book's overall usefulness as an authoritative source of quick reference information.

There are also occasional questionable interpretations or subject judgments. EXAMPLE: The article on Western drama includes a short discussion of the Theater of the Absurd, in which it is stated, "Probably the most famous plays of the theater of the absurd are Eugene Ionesco's *Bald Soprano* (1950) and Samuel Beckett's *Waiting for Godot* (1953)." *Godot*, yes. But *Bald Soprano?* EXAMPLE: *Homosexuality*, an 800-word survey article that stresses causal relationships, states that "many Western men have pseudohomosexual longings toward other men at times of crisis in their cultural roles, such as an occupational failure." Such an assertion is questionable at best. But again, such examples are not serious or frequent enough to undermine the solid dependability of *New Columbia*. The encyclopedia's reliability is vulnerable, however, in those instances where information is out-of-date, as in the case of "Copyright," where the law changed effective January 1978 (see "Recency" for more on the problem).

Recency

As already pointed out, the encyclopedia is a revised and retitled edition of the old *Columbia Encyclopedia* (see Appendix A), which first appeared in 1935 and was thoroughly overhauled in 1950 and again in 1963. Despite the issuance of periodic updating supplements (bound into new printings as addenda), the 1963 edition became increasingly dated by the late 1960s, and the publisher began planning a new edition in 1968. That work eventually appeared in 1975 under the title *The New Columbia Encyclopedia* and, according to its preface, is "as up to date as humanly possible as of January, 1975." At the present time, there are no plans for a new edition or the issuance of updating supplements. But, in 1977, an official of Columbia University Press did indicate to the *Buying Guide*

This Recency Table compares selected topics in *New Columbia* with those in other encyclopedias of similar size and intended usership.

Topic	New Columbia	New Lincoln Library	Random House	University Desk
Afghanistan	Not current	Not current	Not current	Not current
Dinosaurs	Fairly current	Not current	Very current	Not current
Greenland	Fairly current	Not current	Fairly current	Not current
Thomas Jefferson	Fairly current	Not current	Fairly current	Fairly current
Mass Transportation/Subways	Fairly current	Not current	Very current	Fairly current
Nuclear Power	Not current	Not current	Very current	Not current
Paris	Not current	Not current	Fairly current	Not curent
Sharks	Fairly current	Fairly current	Fairly current	Fairly current
Shock Therapy	Fairly current	Not current	Fairly current	Not current
Suicide	Not current	Not current*	Fairly current	Not current
Tuberculosis	Fairly current	Not current	Very current	Fairly current
Zimbabwe	Not current	Fairly current	Fairly current	Fairly current

*Topic not covered in encyclopedia.

that there will be "some updating in our next printing, when that comes along." And upon inquiry in 1980, Judith Levey, *New Columbia*'s editor, informed the *Buying Guide* that "we had indeed hoped to revise the Encyclopedia more frequently than in the past, but so far that has not been possible. At the moment we cannot make any commitment as to a possible revision date, but hope to be able to do so within the near future."

Fortunately, *New Columbia* was set by computer, a development that will facilitate faster and more economical textual revisions. In a statement about the encyclopedia's computer-assisted revision capabilities, editor William Harris said in 1975 that "overshadowing all other advantages and most relevant to the adoption of a computer-assisted composition program for the NCE is the superiority of a master computer tape to metal or offset plates as a means of storing the text of a reference book. Once a text is stored, it can be modified—to any extent desired—by instructing the computer to delete obsolete material, make minor corrections in otherwise acceptable material, or add new material. Any change may be as small or large as desired: a word or a sentence can be added to or deleted from an article, a wholly new article introduced or a complete article deleted. The time and cost involved are those required to make the changes in the computer tape by keyboarding any new material, giving instructions for deletions, and producing a new master tape." What this means, of course, is that *New Columbia* has the capability of being revised and updated easily and frequently. Therefore, the *Buying Guide* again urges the publisher to adopt a regular revision schedule and make it known to the public.

The 1976 *Buying Guide* praised *New Columbia*'s high level of currency. The 1978 *Buying Guide* observed that "the encyclopedia remains relatively current, although slight wrinkles of age are beginning to appear." At the present time, age spots have definitely begun to appear in some profusion. For instance, Hannah Arendt and Mao Tse-tung are still alive, according to *New Columbia*. Saul Bellow has not yet received the Nobel Prize, nor has the controversial Pompidou Center yet opened in Paris. Genetic research has yet to discover recombinant DNA and gene splicing. According to *New Columbia*, the Soviet Union has never invaded Afghanistan, the nation of Zimbabwe does not exist, and Greenland has not achieved home rule. Hundreds of similar examples could be cited. Nevertheless, as the Recency Table here indicates, *New Columbia* is usually as or more current than its major competitors, save *The Random House Encyclopedia*, which appeared in 1977 (or two years after *New Columbia*).

Objectivity

In almost all cases, material found in *New Columbia* is admirably free from objectionable bias. When polemical topics are treated, all legitimate viewpoints are normally covered. The article "Smoking" is a case in point. Both sides of the health question are discussed within the context of a historical survey, but the article concludes, "In 1964 definite proof that cigarette smoking is a serious health hazard was contained in a report by the Surgeon General's Advisory Committee on Health." Likewise, "Marijuana" impartially summarizes current evidence on the drug's effect: "Although the possibility that marijuana, like other perception-altering drugs, produces psychosis has not been entirely disproved, the drug is probably most dangerous to persons with already existing psychotic tendencies." In a brief review of *New Columbia*, the magazine *Christianity Today* (January 16, 1976, pp. 30–31) noted, "Happily, we can report that in its handling of religious matters the *New Columbia* maintains about as consistent a stance of detachment as one could expect. . . . Biological evolution, while presented sympathetically, is labeled as belief and theory, not fact. So also the papacy's succession from Peter is presented as Catholic belief rather than historical truth."

Also worth noting is the fact that *New Columbia*, unlike some encyclopedias in the small-volume adult category (e.g., the *New Lincoln Library Encyclopedia* and *The Volume Library*), usually does not avoid controversial subject matter, as articles on such topics as homosexuality and abortion attest. But the encyclopedia can be criticized for some of the people it has excluded from coverage. EXAMPLE: Why is Angela Davis, a black leader of considerable sociopolitical importance (and controversy), excluded while Benjamin Davis, Jr. (military leader), Bette Davis (film star), Colin Davis (British conductor), Miles Davis (jazz musician), and Rebecca Harding Davis (minor nineteenth-century novelist) are included?

Clarity and Reader Suitability

New Columbia is clearly intended for literate adults and students at the advanced high school or college level. The writing style is clear and direct. Earlier editions of *New Columbia* stressed the notion that the work is written in "language as intelligible as that of a newspaper." This edition still adheres to that concept—if one's newspaper is the *New York Times* or *Wall Street Journal*. Articles on complex subjects, particularly in the sciences, have been written with "initial readability" in mind, meaning that the articles become more advanced and technical as they progress. EXAMPLE: The article "Nucleic Acid" begins with a simply stated definition of the subject, then proceeds to discuss the two main types of nucleic acids, DNA and RNA. For instance, DNA is described in this manner: "Each DNA molecule is a long two-stranded chain. The chains are made up of subunits called nucleotides, each containing a sugar (deoxyribose), a phosphate group, and one of four nitrogenous bases, adenine, guanine, thymine, and cytosine, denoted A, G, T, and C respectively. The information carried by genes is coded in sequences of nucleotides, which correspond to sequences of amino acids in the polypeptide chains of proteins." After this admirably clear and straightforward discussion, the article moves on to an even more detailed description of DNA replication and the double helix model.

Arrangement and Accessibility

New Columbia is arranged alphabetically, letter-by-letter ("Indiana" precedes "Indian Ocean"). When two or more articles have the same heading, the order of entry goes from person to place and then thing. For example, "Jefferson, Thomas" is entered before "Jefferson" the city, which is followed by "Jefferson Memorial." Places with the same name are included in multiple entries, arranged A–Z by state. A good understanding of the mechanics of arrangement is especially important in the case of a specific-entry encyclopedia like *New Columbia*.

Like the previous editions, *New Columbia* has no general index. Instead, the work is said to be self-indexed via an elaborate system of more than 66,000 cross-references. As editor Harris once described it, "Major articles in TNCE have cross-references to other articles, until, like an interlocking highway system, with ramps, straightaways, overhead passes, and bypasses, a network of information unfolds—the total sum is there ready to be used." The metaphor might be exaggerated, but the idea is essentially correct. Numerous external *See* references are furnished, such as "*Goiter:* See THYROID GLAND." Even more plentiful are internal cross-references within the articles themselves, designated by terms printed in

SMALL CAPITAL LETTERS, a system of internal cross-referencing used by a number of encyclopedias, including the *University Desk Encyclopedia*. EXAMPLE: The article on Thomas Jefferson informs, "Despite his contention that the Constitution must be interpreted strictly, he pushed through the LOUISIANA PURCHASE, even though such an action was nowhere expressly authorized. His eager interest in the West and in exploration had led him to plan and organize the LEWIS AND CLARK EXPEDITION," thus signaling the reader that additional information can be obtained in the articles "Louisiana Purchase" and "Lewis and Clark Expedition." The entire Jefferson article contains 17 such references.

Extensive as it is, the cross-reference system is not without its flaws and frustrations. EXAMPLE: The article "Cancer" quite appropriately discusses cells and tissue, but there are no references to the articles "Cell" and "Tissue," where these terms are fully explained. EXAMPLE: The article on Anne Hutchinson notes that some Puritan leaders viewed her "as an antinomian heretic," but there is no reference to the article "Antinomianism" (where indeed Hutchinson is mentioned, but again no reference is given to the article "Hutchinson, Anne"). EXAMPLE: The Freedom of Information Act (FIA) is discussed in the article "Censorship" in the context of the Pentagon Papers, but there is no external cross-reference directing the reader to this article (nor is there a separate article on FIA). EXAMPLE: The article "Federal Communications Commission" provides no reference to the article "Censorship," wherein the FCC's licensing and regulatory roles are succinctly explained. EXAMPLE: The article "Indians, North American" offers no clue that the encyclopedia also contains related material in the article "American Indian Movement."

The editors, in "How to Use the New Columbia Encyclopedia" at the beginning of Volume 1, flatly state that "cross-referencing makes an index in *The New Columbia Encyclopedia* unnecessary." This assumption is incorrect, as the examples in the preceding paragraph indicate. In most instances, information can be retrieved from the encyclopedia quickly and efficiently. But in a work as large as this—nearly seven million words—no system of self-indexing, no matter how extensive or clever, can completely replace the need for a detailed analytical index. How else, for instance, can the user locate the reference to the Freedom of Information Act in the article "Censorship," except through serendipity? Suffice it to say that *New Columbia*'s lack of an index is a serious deficiency.

Bibliographies

More than 40,000 bibliographic citations are included in *New Columbia*. Limited to English-language titles, they are usually up-to-date or represent the most significant works available on the subject. Not every article, however, includes such citations. Why, for example, the article on vasectomy fails to cite even one of the many practical books available on the topic is puzzling. There are other omissions, perhaps more understandable. EXAMPLE: "Existentialism" cites Walter Kaufmann's useful collection *Existentialism from Dostoevsky to Sartre* (1956) but fails to note

William Barrett's *Irrational Man* (1958), quite possibly the best analysis of the controversial philosophy yet to appear.

Most exasperating, however, is *New Columbia*'s tendency to cite bibliographic references simply by author and date. EXAMPLE: The biographical entry for Roscoe Conkling, a nineteenth-century American politician, concludes: "See biography by his nephew, A. R. Conkling (1889); study by David M. Jordan (1971)." Obviously this abbreviated style is meant to conserve space (always of great concern to the editors of a small encyclopedia), but the problems it will sometimes cause students, teachers, and librarians who might want access to the works cited are hardly worth the space saved. Future editions of *New Columbia* should systematically provide author, title, publisher, date, and edition information for each bibliographic citation.

Graphics

New Columbia has comparatively few illustrations, certainly nothing to match the graphic wealth and color of its chief competitor, *The Random House Encyclopedia*. Except for the maps, practically all of *New Columbia*'s graphics are black-and-white line drawings. All 400 or so illustrations were newly made for this edition, and most illustrate scientific subjects. Examples include a rough sketch of the nitrogen cycle, a rather confusing representation of the dulcimer (a musical instrument), and an elementary drawing of how a generator works. Most of the drawings are simple but instructive. To their credit, the editors did not succumb to the temptation, so prevalent among encyclopedists today, to dazzle the reader with full-page plates of dogs and cats in flaming color. (Interestingly, however, the illustrated version of *New Columbia*—the multivolume *New Illustrated Columbia Encyclopedia*—is very much in the tradition of colorful dogs and cats.) Also, *New Columbia*'s illustrations have been placed on the same page as the topic they complement, a departure from the procedure in previous editions.

The encyclopedia's maps are very elementary and quite small, except for a few large ones covering prominent places like Africa, China, Great Britain, the Soviet Union, and the United States. The U.S. state maps lack any substantive detail; for instance, the map of Alabama is limited to eight cities and five rivers, with no physical detail at all. Compared with most of its major competitors (the *New Lincoln Library Encyclopedia, The Random House Encyclopedia,* and *The Volume Library,* all of which include an extensive atlas supplement), *New Columbia* offers very limited map coverage. Only when compared with the *University Desk Encyclopedia* is *New Columbia* preferable in the area of maps. Even the British *Pears Cyclopaedia* provides a 36-page world atlas.

Physical Format

The preface points out that *New Columbia* "was set by a computer, an innovation that enabled us to include more information on a page than in previous editions. The type of this edition is also easier to read." These observations are true. The print is indeed clear and attractive, and a remarkable amount of text is provided on each page. But the computer-assisted composition (which produces camera-ready pages from a master computer tape) does have one glaring drawback—lack of paragraphing. The article "Drama, Western," for example, consists of about 4,000 words and covers more than a full page of the encyclopedia, but it does not have even a single paragraph break. In this sense, *New Columbia* is not easier but more difficult to read.

Otherwise, the book's physical format is satisfactory. The binding is a sturdy D grade buckram with a blue vellum finish and gold lettering. The volume lies flat when open. Inside, the three-column page layout lacks the appeal of *The Random House Encyclopedia*'s two-page spreads in the *Colorpedia,* but it is not offensive. Guide words always appear at the top of the page, and the volume is thumb-indexed. The offset Bible paper is of the highest quality (Allied Solitude Opaque). The volume, which was printed and bound by Rand McNally, is quite heavy, weighing a bit more than ten pounds.

Special Features

Several useful if unspectacular special features might be noted. As already mentioned, every proper name in the King James Version of the Bible is accorded an entry in the encyclopedia, with references to biblical passages where the name can be found. Pronunciations are provided for scientific, foreign, and unfamiliar entries. And metric equivalents are included for most measurements.

Sales Information

An advertisement for *New Columbia* when it first appeared in 1975 started out, "BARBARA WALTERS INSTEAD OF DOOR-TO-DOOR SALESMEN" (See *Publishers Weekly,* May 5, 1975). Capitalizing on the public's wariness of in-home selling and high-pressure sales tactics, as well as the encyclopedia's convenient one-volume format and affordable price, Columbia University Press merchandises *New Columbia* in retail bookstores, via direct mail order, and through sales representatives to schools and libraries. Two editions are available, the blue and gold Standard Edition, which sells for $79.50 (or lower, depending on the store), and a leather-bound Deluxe Edition priced at $135. Educational institutions and government agencies receive a publisher's discount of 22 to 33⅓ percent, depending on the number of copies ordered. *New Columbia* is also distributed by Barnes & Noble of New York, said to be the world's largest bargain bookstore, at the discount price of $29.50, plus $3 shipping and handling for orders by mail. The Book-of-the-Month Club likewise offers the encyclopedia at a much reduced rate ($15). *New Columbia* is distributed in Canada by the firm of McClelland & Stewart. Finally, consumers should be aware that there is currently on the market a multivolume version of *New Columbia* entitled *The New Illustrated Columbia Encyclopedia.* This 24-volume set, sold in supermarkets and via mail order for around $70, expands the contents of the one-volume *New Columbia* by adding some 5,000 graphics and photographically enlarging the printed text. (See Part III of the *Buying Guide* for a review of *The New Illustrated Columbia Encyclopedia.*)

Summary

The New Columbia Encyclopedia can be quickly summed up in this manner:

Scope: Good   Accessibility: Poor
Authority: Excellent   Bibliographies: Good
Reliability: Good   Graphics: Fair
Recency: Poor   Physical Format: Good
Objectivity: Excellent   Special Features: Few
Clarity: Excellent   Price: Reasonable

To elaborate briefly, *New Columbia* was published in 1975 to replace the excellent but dated 1963 edition of the *Columbia Encyclopedia.* The encyclopedia's strong points include extensive coverage of biographical and geographical topics (which account for approximately 75 percent of the 50,000 articles), an experienced editorial staff and well-qualified consultants, and a clear and precise writing style. *New Columbia* is best suited for literate adults and serious students at the senior high school level and beyond. On the negative side, the encyclopedia's contents reflect the state of knowledge and information as of the early 1970s. Unfortunately, the editors have not been able to update *New Columbia* even once since it appeared in 1975, despite early expectations that its computer-assisted composition would lead to frequent revisions. Also, the encyclopedia lacks an index, relying rather on a network of 66,000 cross-references to furnish access to the contents. Although the cross-reference system sometimes works well, it fails too often to be considered effective.

Comparatively speaking, there are six small-volume adult encyclopedias currently on the market. Among these, *The Random House Encyclopedia* and the *University Desk Encyclopedia* are *New Columbia*'s most formidable competition, along with the older and well-known three-volume *New Lincoln Library Encyclopedia* (formerly *The Lincoln Library of Essential Information*). All four of these small-volume encyclopedias are priced in the same general range ($69.95–$99.98), and each possesses unique strengths and weaknesses. As the raw data indicate, *New Columbia* is the largest small-volume encyclopedia available. Moreover, it is twice the size of any of its major competitors in terms of written text. On the other hand, *University Desk* and especially *Random House* are superior in terms of graphics and design. Note also that *New Columbia,* though very clearly written, is more scholarly and technical in its presentation of material than either *Random House* or *University Desk.*

As a general proposition, without taking individual reference needs into account, the *Buying Guide* believes that *The New Columbia Encyclopedia* and *The Random House Encyclopedia* are the best small-volume adult encyclopedias on the market today. The two works could not possibly be more different in their design or presentation of information. *New Columbia* is a sober, erudite, print-oriented work of stately scholarship. The smaller *Random House* is a splashy, spirited, and at times exhilarating work of great visual appeal. Actually, the two works complement one another rather well, and some consumers (certainly many libraries) will want both titles. Others who need just one small-volume encyclopedia will have the happy task of choosing between two highly regarded works. Despite its increasingly dated text, *New Columbia* remains an outstanding one-volume encyclopedia.

Other Critical Opinions

Booklist, January 1, 1979, pp. 769–771. Part of a series of reviews by the ALA Reference and Subscription Books Review Committee (RSBRC) entitled "Encyclopedias: A Survey and Buying Guide," this evaluation of *New Columbia* generally praises the encyclopedia, although no final conclusions are offered, nor are any comparisons made with works of similar size and intended readership. In its last regular review of *New Columbia* (*Booklist,* December 15, 1976, pp. 628–629), RSBRC "recommended" the encyclopedia for homes, offices, and "all types of libraries."

Bunge, Charles A. "Current Reference Books," *Wilson Library Bulletin,* November 1975, p. 263. Bunge, an experienced and thoughtful reference book critic, views *New Columbia* as "a welcome revision and improvement of the third (1963) edition of the *Columbia Encyclopedia.*"

Choice, December 1975, p. 1292. This unsigned review finds *New Columbia* "an exceptionally attractively designed, easily read yet authoritative reference work of great scope, essential for all reference collections."

Gray, Richard A. *American Reference Books Annual,* 1976, p. 59. A short, favorable review noting that this edition has substantially increased the encyclopedia's coverage of scientific and technical subjects. Overall, "an excellent home reference work, but it is important as a library reference tool as well."

Johnston, W. T. *Consumers' Research Magazine,* February 1977, p. 13. Johnston, a Georgia librarian, briefly describes the encyclopedia and wisely advises prospective purchasers "to visit a library and look over, put to actual use, and compare the *New Columbia* and other encyclopedias before making a final choice."

Katz, William A. *Basic Information Sources* (Vol. 1 of *Introduction to Reference Work,* 3rd ed. New York: McGraw-Hill, 1978), pp. 166–169. Katz, a highly respected authority on reference work and sources, comparatively reviews four small-volume encyclopedias, namely *New Columbia, The Lincoln Library of Essential Information, The Random House Encyclopedia,* and the now defunct *Cadillac Modern Encyclopedia.* At least for libraries, Katz rates *New Columbia* Number One.

Sheehy, Eugene S. *College and Research Libraries,* January 1976, p. 61. This short, descriptive review concludes on a positive note: *New Co-*

lumbia "is sure to retain favor as a useful home encyclopedia and as a source for quick reference in libraries of all sizes."

Shenker, Israel. "Columbia Encyclopedia: Instant Universe Again," *New York Times,* August 3, 1975, p. 40. More a news article than a review, this piece furnishes a useful overview of the encyclopedia's fourth edition. It also includes the wonderful observation that "making a one-volume encyclopedia is like taking the broth of the universe and condensing it into a bouillon cube."

New Lincoln Library Encyclopedia

Facts in Brief

Full Title: **The New Lincoln Library Encyclopedia.** *Editor:* William H. Seibert, Editor in Chief. *Publisher:* Frontier Press Company, Box 1098, Columbus, OH 43216. *Former and Future Title: Lincoln Library of Essential Information. Edition Reviewed:* Fortieth Edition, 1980 copyright.

Volumes: Three. *Pages:* 2,323. *Articles:* 25,000 topics in 12 sections or "departments." *Words:* 3,500,000. *Illustrations:* 1,200. *Maps:* 140 (including a 48-page color Atlas of the World). *Index Entries:* 26,000. *Cross-references:* 8,800. *Contributors:* 122.

User Classification: Adult (Small-volume). *Reader Suitability:* Age 12 through General Adult. *Physical Size:* 9 ×11½ in.; 29 cm. *LC:* 24-14708. *ISBN:* 0-912168-00-5. *Lowest Retail Price:* $99.98.

Purpose and Scope

The New Lincoln Library Encyclopedia, a small-volume encyclopedia that has been on the U.S. market for nearly 60 years, is better known as *The Lincoln Library of Essential Information*, its title from 1924 through 1977. Apparently in recognition of this fact, the publisher has announced that the set's title will revert to *The Lincoln Library of Essential Information* in 1981. Despite these title changes and an expansion from two to three volumes in 1978, the encyclopedia's purpose and scope have not changed in the least. According to the preface, *New Lincoln Library* has two overriding aims: "One has been to embody in three volumes the greatest amount of useful information for the average reader that could reasonably be placed in one work. The other aim has been to select, condense, arrange, and verify the material with a thoroughness and accuracy greater than that attained in any comparable work." The preface further notes that "this information has been adapted to the needs of those who, following in the steps of Abraham Lincoln, will welcome every means of self-education." Of course the set is named in honor of Lincoln, "whose inspiring example demonstrated the possibilities of self-education."

New Lincoln Library intends to cover all areas of knowledge in 12 broad topical sections, called "departments." Volume 1 begins with a 48-page world atlas and contains these departments: Geography, Economics, and History; Volume 2 contains these departments: Government and Politics, Education, English Language, Literature, and Fine Arts;

and Volume 3 these departments: Mathematics, Science, Biography, and Miscellany. A 26,000-entry index to the entire set appears at the end of each volume.

Each department is subdivided into numerous logical topics presented in essay form, in A–Z dictionary fashion, or in tabular arrangement. EXAMPLE: History begins with a two-page general essay divided into paragraph-length subtopics like "The Task of the Historian" and "Divisions of History." Such headings are printed in dark bold type. Next, American history is covered chronologically in 38 pages, again with specific subtopics set off in bold type (e.g., "Colonization," "The Constitutional Convention," "The Marshall Plan," "New States and Slaves," "The New West," "Nixon and Watergate"). Much information in this section is in chart form, such as lists of presidents and vice-presidents, data on major American wars, and historical statistics concerning the states. Next, there is a 23-page dictionary of American history terms (e.g., "Compromise of 1850," "Dark Horse," "Dred Scott Case," "Embargo Act"), followed by a 14-page American history time chart from 1492 to 1979. The rest of the History department covers other countries and various aspects of world history in similar fashion. Four pages of test questions (e.g., "What were the two great issues of Jackson's administration?") and a lengthy bibliography conclude the department.

New Lincoln Library's most apparent strengths in terms of coverage are in the areas of historical and factual material. The history of such subjects as art, music, literature, government, economics, transportation, oceanography, and education are more than adequately covered, especially in light of the set's limited size. In addition, the encyclopedia provides an enormous amount of factual and statistical information, covering a wide variety of discrete topics and often presented in tabular form. In fact, *New Lincoln Library* includes approximately 200 tabulations on such subjects as air pollution, U.S. banking, important canals, U.S. coal production, bacterial diseases, the U.S. Federal Reserve System, U.S. forests, common logarithms, U.S. motor vehicle laws, Nobel Prize winners, world ports, rulers of major European powers, treaties, important tunnels, U.S. vice presidents, major world wars, and weights and measures. The encyclopedia also includes numerous dictionaries of specialized terms in such areas as abbreviations, geography, music, and science.

The encyclopedia is, above all else, a compact reference work. As the editors claim, "every available centimeter of space" (preface) is utilized, and the point is repeatedly made in the front matter that *New Lincoln Library* offers more information in three volumes than do "many more expensive encyclopedias of six to thirty volumes." As if to verify the editors' boast, *New Lincoln Library* was once available in 14 volumes (albeit slim ones) under the title *Encyclopedia of World Knowledge*, a supermarket set now defunct (see Appendix A). Moreover, in the past various sections of *Lincoln Library* (*New Lincoln Library*'s previous title) have been separately published as specialized encyclopedias, such as the *Lincoln Library of Language Arts* (Frontier Press, 2nd ed., 1972). But despite the braggadocio about the set's extensive scope, *New Lincoln Library* is remarkably deficient in many important areas. EXAMPLES: The subject of philosophy (often of considerable interest to those engaged in self-education) is almost completely ignored. The several pages covering religion provide superficial coverage at best. The social and behavioral sciences are very badly covered. The encyclopedia contains nothing, for instance, on child development and human growth. The subjects of sociology, anthropology, and psychology are practically ignored. Nowhere in *New Lincoln Library* are such important contemporary behavioral scientists as B. F. Skinner and Abraham Maslow even mentioned. The entire department called Education never once refers to Jean Piaget, a major figure in contemporary educational psychology. The subject of housing is treated in three cursory and dated paragraphs. At no point is condominium housing even mentioned. In the entire three volumes there is little or no information on such important social issues as the Equal Rights Amendment, race relations, drug use and abuse, human sexuality (homosexuality is ignored), abortion, and birth control. Other contemporary topics that are sensitive or controversial are likewise neglected, such as suicide. The U.S. states are not covered individually (except for Alaska and Hawaii), although major U.S. cities are. Such scientific topics as the Atomic Energy Commission and continental drift are not adequately covered.

The set's new editor, William H. Seibert, has informed the *Buying Guide* that *New Lincoln Library* will be thoroughly overhauled in 1981. Present plans call for extensive revision or complete rewriting of each department. For instance, the Geography department will add separate articles on each of the U.S. states. Education will be completely new and retitled the department of Education and Human Studies. A 27-page dictionary of political terms in the department of Government and Politics will be entirely rewritten. As already noted, the set's title will revert to *The Lincoln Library of Essential Information* in 1981. Also, the current three volumes will be reduced to two volumes, the size of the set prior to 1978. This major revision will be evaluated in the next edition of the *Buying Guide,* scheduled for 1984.

History and Authority

New Lincoln Library has been published continuously since 1924. Prior to 1978, the set was entitled *The Lincoln Library of Essential Information.* Along with *The Volume Library* (1911–) and *The New Columbia Encyclopedia* (first published in 1935 as the *Columbia Encyclopedia*), *New Lincoln Library* is among the oldest surviving small-volume encyclopedias produced in the United States. The work originated from an information base supplied by the topically arranged *Standard Dictionary of Facts* (1908–1927), a single-volume item published by Frontier Press and first edited by Henry Woldmar Ruoff, who was also founding editor of *The Volume Library.* Many editions and editors later, *New Lincoln Library* and *Volume Library* still closely resemble one another in terms of scope, arrangement, and style (although *New Lincoln Library* is a far better encyclopedia).

Over the years, *New Lincoln Library* and its predecessors have achieved general acceptance as a standard home and library reference source. It is found in most public libraries of any consequence as well as many academic libraries. In 1980, William H. Seibert became the set's editor in chief, replacing William J. Redding, who held that post throughout the 1970s. Seibert is also president of Frontier Press, the publisher of *New Lincoln Library*. The editor in chief is supported by an editorial staff of 13, all of whom are new since 1977 (when the *Buying Guide* last reviewed the set), except for two editors. None of these people is identified beyond name and title, and none is known to the *Buying Guide* as having previous experience at encyclopedia-making. In addition to the editor in chief, three members of the editorial staff bear the surname Seibert, thus making *New Lincoln Library* something of a family enterprise. Volume 1 also includes a list of contributors. This list, which differs only slightly from the one in 1977, contains a few notable names, such as the late Robert MacIver, the social scientist, and Peggy Sullivan, a well-known librarian. Generally speaking, however, the list of contributors is unimpressive. Many are now deceased, while others are retired and represent an earlier generation of scholarship. In most instances, their contributions were to previous editions of the encyclopedia. All contributors are identified by name and professional affiliation, but often this information is sadly out-of-date. Likewise, contributors' areas of subject responsibility are indicated but no articles are signed.

In 1981, *New Lincoln Library* will return to its original name, *The Lincoln Library of Essential Information,* and reduce its volumes from three to two. As already noted (see "Purpose and Scope"), the 1981 version (41st ed.) will be extensively revised, with some sections completely reworked. Editor Seibert informs the *Buying Guide* that a number of new contributors will be added in 1981, including Anthony J. Celebrezze (Secretary of State in Ohio and former Secretary of the U.S. Department of Health, Education, and Welfare) and Leonard Silk (a *New York Times* writer on economic matters).

Reliability

For the most part, *New Lincoln Library* is a reliable source of information, living up to its claim that "care has been taken that the material should be based on primary sources and be as consistently accurate as possible" (preface). Instances of factual error do occur occasionally, however. EXAMPLE: The article "American Indians" in the History department erroneously distinguishes between the Six Nations (or Iroquois Confederacy) and the Iroquois. The article also assigns the Winnebago to the wrong linguistic stock. EXAMPLE: The article "Shark" in the department of Science contains several misstatements, such as "sharks often turn upon their backs to seize their prey."

A much greater problem concerning reliability occurs in those areas where the treatment is out-of-date. Unfortunately, lack of currency does render the encyclopedia inaccurate in many cases. The Education department, for example, has not been thoroughly revised for at least a decade. As a result, the reader encounters such questionable statements as "the people of the United States have become the most avid readers in the world" (but nothing about the current alarm over diminishing reading skills), and such outright misinformation as the American Textbook Publishers Institute being "an organization of publishers representing a high percentage of all publishers, which has the aim of improving all procedures which go into the making of modern textbooks," when, in fact, the American Textbook Publishers Institute has been defunct for years. For further information about this problem, see the next section ("Recency").

Recency

Unlike most small-volume encyclopedias, *New Lincoln Library* practices continuous revision. "At each new printing, those portions which are affected by the passage of events are thoroughly revised," according to the editors. In the past, the set has been revised every two years, sometimes more frequently. The last edition of the *Buying Guide,* for instance, reviewed the thirty-eighth edition (1977) of the encyclopedia, whereas the fortieth edition (1980) is under review here. Evidence of some revision between 1977 and 1980 is not difficult to find. EXAMPLE: All the tabular information in the History department, such as the table showing prime ministers of Great Britain, has been brought up-to-date.

Unfortunately, not all articles and departments that need revision are actually revised. The editors state in the preface that "for each new edition, the contents are systematically tested and revised. Not only facts, but also the perspective of the work, are kept abreast of a world constantly changing in aspect, interests, and viewpoint. On the whole, this work generally will be found to surpass larger encyclopedias in up-to-dateness, just as it goes beyond other compact works in completeness." These claims are grossly exaggerated. EXAMPLE: Treatment of the country of Afghanistan is current only as of 1973. EXAMPLE: The material on American Indians includes nothing concerning the Native American movement of the 1960s and 1970s. In fact, the latest events recorded are establishment of the Indian Claims Commission in the 1940s and Canada's Indian Act of 1950. EXAMPLE: The article "Motion Pictures" in the department of Economics is unbelievably out-of-date. The camera, for instance, is said to be "equipped with a very fast, high grade lens of 2 to 3 inch focus. The shutter is a revolving, perforated disk driven by a crank which the operator usually turns at the rate of two revolutions per second." Notably, the encyclopedia has no information on Hollywood or the cinema as an art or entertainment form. EXAMPLE: A discussion of the U.S. public school system in the Education department suggests that the junior high school is "a new institution" and "a radical reform."

It should be reiterated here (see "Purpose and Scope"; "History and Authority") that the 1981 edition of the encyclopedia will be heavily revised, with some portions entirely redone. Editor Seibert has informed

This Recency Table compares selected topics in *New Lincoln Library* (1980 copyright) with those in other encyclopedias of similar size and intended usership.

Topic	New Lincoln Library	New Columbia	Random House	University Desk
Afghanistan	Not current	Not current	Not current	Not current
Dinosaurs	Not current	Fairly current	Very current	Not current
Greenland	Not current	Fairly current	Fairly current	Not current
Thomas Jefferson	Not current	Fairly current	Fairly current	Fairly current
Mass Transportation/Subways	Not current	Fairly current	Very current	Fairly current
Nuclear Power	Not current	Not current	Very current	Not current
Paris	Not current	Not current	Fairly curent	Not current
Sharks	Fairly current	Fairly current	Fairly current	Fairly current
Shock Therapy	Not current	Fairly current	Fairly current	Not current
Suicide	Not currrent*	Not current	Fairly current	Not current
Tuberculosis	Not current	Fairly current	Very current	Fairly current
Zimbabwe	Fairly current	Not current	Fairly current	Fairly current

*Topic not covered in encyclopedia.

the *Buying Guide* that the 1981 version (41st ed.) will be "the most extensive revision in the history of the *Lincoln Library*," and that he expects approximately 75 percent of the text to be revised in some manner or other. The entire encyclopedia will be reset and its contents stored on magnetic tape (in similar fashion, for instance, to *The New Columbia Encyclopedia*), thus holding out the possibility of speedier and more economical textual revision in the future. All departments in the 1981 edition will be affected, according to Seibert. The History department will have a major new article on the Vietnam War, for example, and Economics will add a new article entitled "Economic Theory." In other cases, the entire department will be revamped; for instance, the sadly out-of-date department of Education will be totally rewritten and retitled Education and Human Studies. The *Buying Guide* will assess both the quantity and quality of these in-progress revisions in its next edition.

Like most small-volume encyclopedias, *New Lincoln Library* does not issue an annual supplement, or yearbook. The publisher, however, does offer its customers an annual item called *Encyclopedia Yearbook* at $9.45 per volume. Prepared by Grolier, the yearbook obviously has no relationship whatsoever to *New Lincoln Library*, and therefore no real value as an updating tool.

Objectivity

With few exceptions, *New Lincoln Library* is painstakingly impartial in its presentation of material open to biased opinion or propaganda. The department of Government and Politics, for instance, includes detailed definitions of standard political terminology, among which are the terms *Bolshevism, Collectivism, Communism,* and *Socialism.* Such terms are defined accurately and without distortion or Cold War rhetoric. It should be noted again, however, that the encyclopedia completely ignores most sensitive or controversial subjects (see "Purpose and Scope"). How an encyclopedia can cover Northern Ireland and avoid any mention of the current troubles in that divided country is mindboggling, but *New Lincoln Library* does just that. Likewise, polemical information about birth control, abortion, drug abuse, race relations, the Equal Rights Amendment, shock therapy, and homosexuality is excluded.

Clarity and Reader Suitability

The writing style is normally clear, direct, and textbookish throughout. The material will be comprehensible to students and adults reading at the high school level and beyond. Because much information is presented in tabular form, *New Lincoln Library* might be useful on occasion to young people at the middle school and even elementary levels. Moreover, the many specialized glossaries (see "Special Features") contribute to textual clarity. EXAMPLE: The article "Investments" in the Economics department discusses the two main types of securities, "owner obligations (preferred and common stocks) and creditor obligations (bonds, notes, debentures, etc.)." In the dictionary accompanying that department, such terms as *bond, common stock, debentures, notes,* and *preferred stock* are succinctly defined. A typical example of *New Lincoln Library*'s style is found at the beginning of Economics: "Economics is the study of the means by which people obtain their livelihood and satisfy their wants. Many thinkers maintain that the economic system under which a people lives largely determines the form of all its institutions, including its morality, family life, religion, and art. Whether or not this view is entirely correct, there can be no doubt that, along with political government, economic conditions constitute a factor of supreme importance in the life of man."

Arrangement and Accessibility

New Lincoln Library's topical, or departmental, arrangement has already been described in considerable detail (see "Purpose and Scope"). Access to specific information in the set is facilitated by (1) an extended table of contents in the front of Volume 1; (2) brief, alphabetically arranged "Subject Guides" at the beginning of each department; (3) occasional cross-references within a department; and (4) an extensive "Master

Index" that contains some 26,000 entries in 65 pages. For user convenience, the index is printed in full at the end of all three volumes.

The encyclopedia is principally arranged for those interested in browsing or involved in self-education. Location of specific material depends almost solely on the index. The editors say that the index "enables the reader to obtain information with speed and precision" (preface). In most instances this claim is justified. The index is both exhaustive and analytical. Occasionally, however, the index fails. EXAMPLE: Brief information about Abu Dhabi, an oil-rich sheikhdom on the Persian Gulf, is found in the Government and Politics department under "United Arab Emirates," but there is no index entry for *Abu Dhabi*. Unless the user knows enough to look under "United Arab Emirates," the information about Abu Dhabi will not be found. EXAMPLE: A brief discussion of drug therapy as used in the treatment of mental illness is included in "Psychiatry" (in the Miscellany department, of all places), but the index includes no entry under the term *drugs*. EXAMPLE: The article "Rhodesia" in the Government and Politics department concludes with the statement that "all nationalists had agreed that the new country would be renamed Zimbabwe, after an ancient African civilization that once thrived in the area," but the index contains no entry under *Zimbabwe* (which, of course, is now the country's official name). Another complaint about the index is that it does not always provide necessary cross-references; for instance, the entry "Northern Ireland" (which provides one reference to the country) does not cross-reference the reader to the entry "Ireland, Northern" (which offers three references).

New Lincoln Library's arrangement is necessarily more complicated than the more common alphabetical arrangement. The editors defend their approach as more unitary (or less fragmentary) than the A–Z approach: "Our study has shown also that the alphabetical arrangement followed in most encyclopedias is not suitable for a single work designed to contain the fullest possible information. When unrelated subjects are ranked next to each other in an A-to-Z arrangement, a large amount of information is unavoidably repeated" (preface). Perhaps in theory this is true, but in fact *New Lincoln Library* fragments and duplicates an enormous amount of information. For example, information about Afghanistan is found in six different places (pages 201, 208, 231, 548, 766, and 2222) scattered throughout all three volumes. Moreover, some of the information is redundant. Although the set's index is reasonably satisfactory as a finding device, readers will still find *New Lincoln Library* sometimes difficult and frustrating to use, especially in comparison with an alphabetically arranged encyclopedia like *The New Columbia Encyclopedia* or the *University Desk Encyclopedia*.

The massive overhaul of the encyclopedia scheduled to occur in 1981 (see "Purpose and Scope"; "History and Authority"; "Recency") will not affect the set's basic arrangement, although some material will be transferred from one department to another (e.g., the Miscellany department will be reduced to 64 pages and much of its information updated and integrated into other departments). Plans also call for greatly expanding the present index of 26,000 entries to one of approximately 100,000 entries.

Bibliographies

Substantial lists of further readings usually appear at the end of each department. Carefully selected, they are classified and include both general and reference works. In most instances, the citations are to books published in the mid-1960s or before. The bibliographies on economics, education, and literature are especially dated. The 27 items on ecology include no publications since 1969. On the other hand, the list accompanying the section on American history is admirably up-to-date. Like *New Lincoln Library*'s general text, the encyclopedia's bibliographies are quite uneven in terms of currency.

Graphics

New Lincoln Library contains approximately 1,200 illustrations—mostly black-and-white photographs—that contribute only marginally to the set's informational value. "Following the concept of presenting essential information," explain the editors, "it has not been the aim to provide a heavily illustrated reference work. Rather, the intent is to provide a limited but useful array of photographs, maps, selected works of art, line drawings, graphs, and diagrams in locations where they will provide effective help and guidance" (preface). It is fair to say that *New Lincoln Library*'s illustrations have improved in recent editions, but the quality remains unimpressive in most instances. The illustrations often fail to complement the text directly, and rarely do they impart essential information. In addition, many of the black-and-white photographs lack sufficient detail and are dingy and lifeless. Others are out-of-date. Increasingly, color plates (unpaged) are being inserted throughout the set. The color reproduction is usually of good quality, but sometimes the plates are more visually effective than informative. There are exceptions, however. EXAMPLE: The color drawings illustrating the role of DNA and RNA in hereditary transmission are very informative. All illustrative matter is indexed.

Aside from a 48-page color world atlas at the beginning of Volume 1, there are few maps in the set. For instance, *New Lincoln Library* lacks map coverage of the U.S. states and Canadian provinces. The atlas, pepared by C. S. Hammond & Company, contains maps of major countries and continents. The maps show physical and political features, as well as economic and industrial distributions. Current as of the mid-1970s, the maps are small but sufficiently detailed for general student and home use. Regrettably, there is no gazetteer-index.

Physical Format

The set's burgundy Kivar binding with white lettering is both attractive and durable. Pagination, which is consecutive, appears on the spine of each book: Volume 1 (Pages 1–726); Volume 2 (Pages 727–1476); Volume 3 (Pages 1477–2323). Though tightly sewn, the volumes lie flat when open. Thumb-indexed, the volumes weigh just under five pounds apiece and are physically easy to handle. Inside, the two-column page layout is uninviting and cramped. Crowded pages and small print are typical of small-volume encyclopedias, and *New Lincoln Library* is certainly no exception. In 1978, the type was slightly enlarged, but the print still remains uncomfortably small. Also, the typeface used has an old-fashioned look about it. The paper, a heavier weight than that used prior to 1978, is of good quality. In 1981, *New Lincoln Library*—to be retitled *The Lincoln Library of Essential Information*—will revert to a two-volume format and thinner paper.

Special Features

New Lincoln Library possesses a number of noteworthy special features. Perhaps most important is the encyclopedia's practice of continuous revision. Unlike its major competitors (*The New Columbia Encyclopedia, The Random House Encyclopedia,* and the *University Desk Encyclopedia*), *New Lincoln Library* is revised every year or two (see "Recency" for additional information on this feature). Another important feature is the inclusion of specialized dictionaries, or glossaries, in most departments. The English Language department, for instance, provides dictionaries of good usage, synonyms and antonyms, foreign words and phrases, and abbreviations. Fine Arts has separate dictionaries of art and music terms. In all, there are some 65 such lists that define 8,500 expressions. Another useful feature is the provision of test or review questions at the end of each department. Users involved in self-education will especially welcome these questions, which total some 10,000. Possibly *New Lincoln Library*'s most conspicuous special feature is the enormous amount of information conveyed via charts and tables. The editors correctly note that "as a base of condensed information, there is no superior to a well-constructed tabulation" (preface). The encyclopedia contains more than 200 such tabulations, ranging from lists of band instruments to a chart showing the production of farm crops and meat in major countries of the world. Unfortunately, many of these tabulations are sadly out-of-date.

Sales Information

The encyclopedia is sold in-home by both door-to-door canvassing and appointment. Independent representatives do the selling, as Frontier Press (the publisher) does not maintain a sales organization in the field. There is only one edition available, that being the thumb-indexed burgundy Kivar binding already described (see "Physical Format"). The set retails for $99.98, plus shipping, handling, and any tax. Schools and libraries can acquire the set for $99.95 delivered. The same edition with gilt-edged top can be purchased for an additional dollar.

Summary

The New Lincoln Library Encyclopedia can be quickly summed up in this manner:

Scope: Fair   Accessibility: Fair
Authority: Fair   Bibliographies: Fair
Reliability: Fair Graphics: Fair
Recency: Poor   Physical Format: Fair
Objectivity: Fair Special Features: Many
Clarity: Good   Price: High

To elaborate briefly, *New Lincoln Library* (formerly *The Lincoln Library of Essential Information*) is a three-volume encyclopedia for home and library that has been part of the English-language reference landscape for nearly 60 years. Named in honor of Abraham Lincoln ("whose inspiring example demonstrated the possibilities of self-education"), the set is topically arranged in 12 sections, called departments, and offers an enormous quantity of general information and miscellany, much of it in tabular and dictionary form. Unfortunately, *New Lincoln Library* has many deficiencies, some of them quite serious. Although revised every year or two with each new edition, the encyclopedia is woefully out-of-date in many areas. Moreover, the set consistently fails to cover controversial or sensitive subject matter, offers mediocre graphics and bibliographies, and, though reasonably well indexed, may be cumbersome or frustrating for the average person to use.

In 1981, the encyclopedia will reduce its size to two volumes and return to its original name, *The Lincoln Library of Essential Information.* The *Buying Guide* has been informed that the 1981 (41st) edition will be completely reset and overhauled from top to bottom, comprising what the editor has called "the most extensive revision in the history of the *Lincoln Library.*" Certainly the encyclopedia needs this kind of attention. The *Buying Guide* will evaluate the results of this major revision in its next edition.

Comparatively speaking, there are six small-volume adult encyclopedias currently on the market. Among these, *The New Columbia Encyclopedia, The Random House Encyclopedia,* and the *University Desk Encyclopedia* are *New Lincoln Library*'s most formidable competition, along with the older and familiar *Volume Library* (1911–), which greatly resembles *New Lincoln Library* in scope and organization. All of these titles are priced in the same general range ($69.95—$99.98), and each possesses unique strengths and weaknesses. As the raw data indicate, *New Columbia* is the largest small-volume encyclopedia available. On the other hand, *Random House* and *University Desk* are superior in terms of graphics and design. *New Lincoln Library,* despite its many flaws, offers much information in condensed form. *Volume Library,* which possesses the longest history of any of these encyclopedias, is an inferior work in most respects.

As a general proposition, without taking individual reference tastes and needs into account, the *Buying Guide* believes that *The New Columbia Encyclopedia* and *The Random House Encyclopedia* are the best small-volume adult encyclopedias on the market today. *The New Lincoln Library Encyclopedia* (which will revert to its original title of *The Lincoln*

Library of Essential Information in 1981) is a worthy encyclopedia in some respects, but it simply is not as authoritative, current, reliable, accessible, or physically appealing as *New Columbia* or *Random House*.

Other Critical Opinions

Booklist, January 1, 1979, pp. 768–769. Part of a series of reviews by the ALA Reference and Subscription Books Review Committee (RSBRC) entitled "Encyclopedias: A Survey and Buying Guide," this evaluation covers the 1974 (36th) edition of *The Lincoln Library of Essential Information*. Why the 1974 edition is reviewed in 1979 is not explained. The review faults the encyclopedia for poor coverage in certain areas (e.g., controversial topics), lack of adequate currency, and weak bibliographies. No final conclusions are offered, however. In its last regular review of the encyclopedia (*Booklist,* June 15, 1972, pp. 865–866), RSBRC "recommended" *Lincoln Library*.

Katz, William A. *Basic Information Sources* (Vol. 1 of *Introduction to Reference Work,* 3rd ed. New York: McGraw-Hill, 1978), pp. 166–169. Katz, a highly respected authority on reference work and sources, comparatively reviews four small-volume encyclopedias, namely *Lincoln Library, The New Columbia Encyclopedia, The Random House Encyclopedia,* and the now defunct *Cadillac Modern Encyclopedia*. "If one had to rank for library purchase, the *Columbia* would be first, with *The Lincoln Library* and the *Random House Encyclopedia* tied for second."

Wynar, Bohdan S. *American Reference Books Annual,* 1973, p. 106. This brief, favorable review offers few critical and no comparative remarks. The review covers the 1972 (35th) edition.

Pears Cyclopaedia

Facts in Brief

Full Title: **Pears Cyclopaedia, 1980–81: A Book of Background Information and Reference for Everyday Use.** *Editors:* Christopher Cook, Editor; L. Mary Barker, Consultant Editor. *Publisher:* Pelham Books, Ltd., London, England. *U. S. Distributor:* Merrimack Book Service, Inc., 99 Main St., Salem, NH 03079. *Edition Reviewed:* 89th Edition, 1980 copyright.

Volumes: One. *Pages:* 1,056. *Articles:* 22 topical sections. *Words:* 1,250,000. *Illustrations:* 50. *Maps:* 36. *Index Entries:* 900. *Cross-references:* 150. *Contributors:* Staff produced.

User Classification: Adult (Small-volume). *Reader Suitability:* Age 12 through General Adult. *Physical Size:* 5¼ x 8 in.; 21 cm. *ISBN:* 0-7207-1264-5. *Lowest Retail Price:* $13.95; 20 percent discount to schools & libraries.

Purpose and Scope

Pears Cyclopaedia, a popular British compendium of basic reference information and miscellaneous facts, has been published annually since 1897. Material is presented in 22 topical sections: Events—Historical and Contemporary, Prominent People, Background to Public Affairs, Political Compendium, The World of Music, The World of Science, Background to Economic Events, Money Matters, The Contemporary Theatre, Ideas and Beliefs, Gazetteer of the World, General Information, Literary Companion, General Compendium, Medical Matters, Introduction to Psychology, Sporting Records, Biblical Glossary, Collecting Antiques, The Cinema, Gardening, and Atlas of the World. An eight-page general index concludes the volume.

Pears at least touches on all major areas of knowledge within these 22 sections, but systematic coverage is not attempted. Many specific topics receive either very superficial coverage or none at all. EXAMPLE: Information about most countries is contained in Gazetteer of the World, which accords each nation at most 20 lines; Greenland, for example, is dispensed with in nine lines. Smaller geographical units such as cities and states receive three to five lines. EXAMPLE: Prominent People covers only "some of the famous people in the history of the world," thus omitting many important contemporary figures, such as Georgia O'Keeffe (U.S. artist) and William Styron (U.S. writer). EXAMPLE: Coverage of philosophy is limited to brief articles on major schools and terms in Ideas and

Beliefs, such as "Cynics"; "Determinism and Free-Will"; "Dialectical Materialism"; "Empiricism"; "Existentialism"; "Good and Evil"; "Logical Positivism." Arranged alphabetically within the section, these articles average roughly 350–400 words in length. There are no entries, however, for such relevant topics as epistemology, ethics, logic, and Neoplatonism. EXAMPLE: Introduction to Psychology surveys the discipline in 30 pages without once mentioning Sigmund Freud, Jean Piaget, or B. F. Skinner. EXAMPLE: Many significant topics in the social and behavioral sciences are ignored, such as homosexuality, hypnosis, mass transportation, North American Indians, shock therapy, and suicide.

Pears is not only prepared and published in England but it has a strong British emphasis in terms of coverage. The section Political Compendium, for instance, deals exclusively with the British political system. Background to Economic Events concerns only the British economy. Sporting Records centers on popular British sports, such as bowls, cricket, rowing and sculling, and rugby. Between Keir Hardie and Thomas Hardy in Prominent People, one does *not* find Warren Harding. The article "Conservatism" in Ideas and Beliefs is limited to a discussion of the British Conservative Party. Brief information about abortion in Medical Matters is entirely from the British legal and medical point of view. The subject of copyright, explained in General Information, is treated strictly in terms of the 1956 British Copyright Act; the U.S. law, completely revised in 1976 (effective 1978), is not mentioned.

Its lack of systematic coverage of knowledge and heavy British orientation limits *Pears*'s usefulness as a general one-volume encyclopedia, especially for North American readers. Actually, unlike its competitors in the adult small-volume category, *Pears* attempts to combine the qualities of an encyclopedia and a yearbook. As an encyclopedia, *Pears* provides much basic background information (as its subtitle suggests) in condensed form, which is carried over from year to year, but it also covers current international political events in each annual revision (in Background to Public Affairs) and adds and drops articles and special features each year, like a yearbook. For instance, the section The Cinema in the 1980 edition replaced Wine in 1979.

History and Authority

Pears, first published in 1897 as *Pears' Shilling Cyclopaedia,* originated with A. & F. Pears, Ltd., a well-known London soap company that believed in progress through cleanliness and knowledge. An instant hit with the Victorian reading public, *Pears' Shilling Cyclopaedia* offered an intriguing combination of practical and exotic information, ranging from a "Dictionary of Medical Information for the Household" and cooking instructions with suggested menus for large dinner parties to the origin of flags and the eating habits of barnacles. In 1977, Pelham Books, Ltd., *Pears*'s current publisher, issued a facsimile edition of the 1897 *Shilling Cyclopaedia,* principally as an interesting historical document. For an amusing review of the *Shilling Cyclopaedia,* see Mary-Kay Wilmers's

"Onward and Upward with the Arts: Next to Godliness" in *The New Yorker* (October 8, 1979, pp. 145–163).

Today *Pears* is nearly 90 years old and, as Wilmers says, "still flourishing." The editor is Christopher Cook, holder of an array of degrees from English universities and compiler of several other reference works, including *British Historical Facts, 1830–1900* and *European Political Facts, 1918–1973.* Cook recently succeeded Lilian Mary Barker, who served as *Pears*'s editor for more than a quarter of a century and remains active in the capacity of consultant editor. Aside from Cook and Barker, no staff or contributors are identified, and of course none of the articles is signed. *Pears* is distributed in the United States by Merrimack Book Service, Inc., in Salem, N. H., for Michael Joseph, Inc. Merrimack also distributes the one-volume *Junior Pears Encyclopaedia,* a children's version of *Pears.* (See Part VII of the *Buying Guide* for a review of *Junior Pears.*)

Reliability

Pears is a generally reliable reference work. Inevitably, however, there are some factual errors and questionable interpretations. EXAMPLE: The six-line biography of Thomas Jefferson in the Prominent People section states: "He created the Republican Party, by which the federalists, led by Hamilton, were overthrown, and helped to draft the Declaration of Independence. He tried unsuccessfully to bring an end to slavery." The reference to the Republican Party is misleading, the statement that Jefferson "helped" to draft the Declaration of Independence is inaccurate, and the assertion that he tried to end slavery in the United States neglects to mention that Jefferson himself was a slave-owner and that any abolitionist sentiments he may have had were not expressed during his two terms as president.

Recency

Unlike most of its competitors in the small-volume adult class, *Pears* is revised annually with each new edition. Revision takes two forms. First, one or two major sections are completely changed every year. For example, the 1976 (85th) edition included Pets and Ponies among its 22 sections. In the 1979 (88th) edition, Wine replaced Pets and Ponies. And in the 1980 (89th) edition, under review here, Wine gave way to The Cinema. Each edition also includes several or more newly prepared "special topics," or articles on a particular subject. The 1980 edition, for instance, has added an eight-page article called "Twentieth-Century Popular Music" to The World of Music section. Likewise, "Plastics and Polymers," "Bats," and "Seeds and Seed Germination" have been added to The World of Science and "The Resurgence of Islam" to Public Affairs. The second method of revision employed by *Pears* entails continuous updating of each standard section (those that appear each year), particularly those concerned with political and economic matters, where change tends to be volatile. EXAMPLE: The initial section, Events—Historical and Contemporary, is revised and updated each year to include a

This Recency Table compares selected topics in *Pears* with those in other encyclopedias of similar size and intended usership.

Topic	Pears	New Columbia	Random House	University Desk
Afghanistan	Very current	Not current	Not current	Not current
Dinosaurs	Not current	Fairly current	Very current	Not current
Greenland	Very current	Fairly current	Fairly current	Not current
Thomas Jefferson	Not current	Fairly current	Fairly current	Fairly current
Mass Transportation/Subways	Not current*	Fairly current	Very current	Fairly current
Nuclear Power	Very current	Not current	Very current	Not current
Paris	Not current	Not current	Fairly current	Not current
Sharks	Fairly current	Fairly current	Fairly current	Fairly current
Shock Therapy	Not current*	Fairly current	Fairly current	Not current
Suicide	Not current*	Not current	Fairly current	Not current
Tuberculosis	Fairly current	Fairly current	Very current	Fairly current
Zimbabwe	Very current	Not current	Fairly current	Fairly current

*Topic not covered in encyclopedia.

chronicle of the world's major happenings from prehistory to the present. EXAMPLE: Public Affairs is revised and updated to include substantial reports on important recent political developments in the nations of the world. In the article "United States," for instance, the 1980 edition covers the Iran and Afghanistan crises and the early portions of the 1980 presidential election. "Canada" covers the Quebec separatist movement, the 1979 election of Joe Clark, and the 1980 return of Pierre Trudeau. Overall, *Pears* maintains a high degree of recency in those areas covered.

Objectivity

The first edition of *Pears* back in 1897 (see "History and Authority") was hardly a model of objectivity. Indeed, *Pears' Shilling Cyclopaedia*, as it was then called, unabashedly offered unsupported opinions on all manner of subjects, including writers (Kipling "is probably the most brilliant writer of short stories that the world has ever seen"), judges (who "were not allowed to wear gloves on the English bench for fear of bribes being dropped into them"), King Richard III (he "was *not* 'hunch-backed,' but he was a liar and a murderer"), Roman Catholics ("A 'Roman Catholic' is simply a gross contradiction in terms, for a person cannot be both Roman, i.e. a particular sect, and Catholic, i.e. universal"), and asthma ("The treatment of asthma should in every instance commence by clearing the bowels"). Nearly a century later in 1980, *Pears* is much more restrained and evenhanded in its treatment of knowledge and information. Articles in Ideas and Beliefs on such potentially polemical topics as Communism, Fascism, flying saucers, God, the Jehovah's Witnesses, the Ku Klux Klan, Marxism, papal infallibility, and parapsychology, for instance, are normally treated in a completely impartial manner. Yet remnants of the exuberant disregard for objectivity that characterized the early *Pears* can be found in the 1980 edition. EXAMPLE: In a subsection of the article "Physics—The Fundamental Science of Matter" in The World of Science on the applications of nuclear energy, the reader learns that "both uses represent epoch-making technical achievements, but mankind has yet to show itself capable of bearing sanely the burden of responsibility which nuclear physicists have laid upon it. . . . It is difficult to write even briefly about contemporary nuclear physics without feeling keenly the ambiguity of its powerful promises." EXAMPLE: In the article "Learning and Memory" in Introduction to Psychology, there is a brief discussion of J. B. Watson and his contribution to behavioral theory. The discussion concludes with this loaded sentence: "He ended his brilliant career in, of all things, the advertising profession."

Clarity and Reader Suitability

In most cases, *Pears*'s text will be comprehensible to students at the high school level and beyond, as well as adults with normal reading skills. The material is presented as tersely but clearly as possible. Difficult and technical terms are not defined in context, nor are glossaries usually provided. EXAMPLE: The article "Nuclear Power Stations" in General Information reads in part like this: "Environmental considerations are likely to be increasingly topical. Most of the products of the fission process are of necessity radioactive isotopes: they could be gaseous, like krypton, xenon and tritium or solid like strontium, caesium, zirconium and ruthenium. These are also present in the new radioactive elements plutonium, curium, actinium, etc. Further, in both the nuclear reactor and in the plant which is used to chemically treat and reprocess the nuclear fuel, radioactivity will be induced in associated structural materials, to varying degrees. In this case, unlike the former, the radioactive waste with which one is left can to a great extent be selected and is largely overshadowed in importance by the wastes arising from the fission and breeding processes."

Arrangement and Accessibility

As already noted (see "Purpose and Scope"), *Pears* is topically arranged in 22 broad sections, such as Prominent People, Background to Public Affairs, and The World of Science. Arrangement within these sections varies according to the nature of the topic involved. EXAMPLES: Prominent People is arranged alphabetically by biographee, from Sir Frederick Abel to Ernst Friedrich Zwirner. Background to Public Affairs is arranged both chronologically and geographically, with a detailed table of contents at the front of the section. The World of Science is arranged by major fields of study, such as astronomy, physics, chemistry, biology, and anthropology. This section also has a detailed table of contents at the front. Each section is designated by a letter of the alphabet; for instance, Prominent People is B and The World of Science is F. Pagination is inclusive for each section; for example, Prominent People covers pages B1–66.

Pears has comparatively few finding devices. Cross-references are limited to approximately 150 internal *See* and *See also* references. EXAMPLE: The article "Behaviourism" in Ideas and Beliefs furnishes two *See also* references, one to "Gestalt Psychology" (an article in the same section) and one to "Q18–20," which turns out to be a discussion of behaviorism in the Introduction to Psychology section. In most instances, however, needed cross-references are *not* provided. For example, no cross-reference is given from the article "Islam" in Ideas and Beliefs to "The Resurgence of Islam" in Background to Public Affairs, nor vice versa. Numerous similar examples could be cited. *Pears* does have a small general index of approximately 900 entries, but it is grossly inadequate. EXAMPLE: Dinosaurs are briefly covered in the General Information section, but there is no entry in the index under *Dinosaur*. EXAMPLE: In the article "Personality and Thinking" in Introduction to Psychology the reader learns that "the great British psychologist, Sir Cyril Burt, also produced what seemed to be striking evidence of the inheritability of intelligence with studies made of school children in the 1930s and the 1940s," but there is no mention of Burt in the index. EXAMPLE: None of the approximately 2,000 persons described in Prominent People is listed in the index. EXAMPLE: None of the approximately 9,000 place-names described in Gazetteer of the World is listed in the index. Two sections, however—The World of Music and Medical Matters—have their own indexes. Tuberculosis, for instance, is not found in the general index in the back of the book, but it is included in the index that concludes Medical Matters.

Finding specific information in *Pears* is frequently a frustrating business. Compared with the other topically arranged small-volume adult encyclopedias currently on the market (namely, *The New Lincoln Library Encyclopedia*, *The Random House Encyclopedia*, and *The Volume Library*), *Pears* is the most difficult to use and the most poorly accessed.

Bibliographies

None.

Graphics

Pears provides very little by way of graphics. In point of fact, aside from maps, the entire volume contains only about 50 black-and-white line drawings. Moreover, these drawings are limited to three sections: The World of Science, Collecting Antiques, and Gardening. What illustrations there are (e.g., drawings showing the types of trees and how to plant a tree or shrub) are useful, but numerous topics that would be more fully or better explained by the addition of an illustration lack them. The maps, 25 in all and all in color, are found in the Atlas of the World located in the middle of the volume. Prepared by George Philip & Son, Ltd., a respected British cartographic firm, the maps cover the major continents and countries of the world, with emphasis on the nations of Europe and the United Kingdom. The maps include both physical and political information, and are sufficiently detailed for general reference purposes.

Physical Format

Bound in thin red boards with gold lettering, *Pears* is quite small as one-volume encyclopedias go (only 5¼ × 8 inches), but it is reasonably well constructed for normal reference use. Consumers will initially encounter the book in a bright jacket with colorful photographs on the front. Inside, *Pears*'s very small print and unvarying double-column page layout will dishearten all but the most eager readers. As mentioned previously (see "Graphics"), there are few visuals and, aside from the atlas in the center, no color. Guide words appear at the top of each page, and the volume lies flat when open for easy consultation.

Special Features

Pears has three notable special features. First, it is the only small-volume encyclopedia currently available that is revised annually without fail. (*The New Lincoln Library Encyclopedia*—also known as *The Lincoln Library of Essential Information*—is also continuously revised, but it does not always appear every year.) Second, *Pears* combines the best qualities of encyclopedic and yearbook coverage of knowledge and information (see "Purpose and Scope"). And third, *Pears* is the only small-volume adult encyclopedia on the market that provides coverage and treatment from the British perspective, a useful feature particularly for library reference work.

Sales Information

Like practically all small-volume encyclopedias, *Pears* is sold in bookstores and similar retail outlets. There are no in-home sales. The book is distributed in the United States by the Merrimack Book Service, Inc., in Salem, N.H., for Michael Joseph, Inc. Educational institutions receive 20 percent off the current retail price of $13.95.

Summary

Pears Cyclopedia can be quickly summed up in this manner:

Scope: Poor   Accessibility: Poor
Authority: Fair   Bibliographies: Poor (none)

Reliability: Good	Graphics: Poor
Recency: Good	Physical Format: Fair
Objectivity: Good	Special Features: Few
Clarity: Good	Price: Very reasonable

To elaborate briefly, *Pears* is a popular British annual first published in 1897 by a London soap manufacturer, A. & F. Pears, Ltd. Part encyclopedia and part yearbook, *Pears* does not attempt to cover basic knowledge and information in a systematic fashion, and therefore many important topics receive short shrift or are completely ignored, although most major fields of study are touched on in one way or another. Quite naturally, much of the text centers on British interests and developments, which limits *Pears*'s potential for home use in the United States and Canada, but increases its appeal to libraries as a complement to small-volume encyclopedias with a U.S. orientation. The articles, which are tersely but clearly written, will ordinarily be comprehensible to students and adults with high school reading skills. Arranged in 22 topical sections, *Pears* is poorly indexed and furnishes far too few cross-references to render its contents readily or fully accessible. Other negative features include sparse graphics, lack of bibliographies, and excessively small print. In sum, *Pears* is generally ineffective as a single-volume source of information, although it contains much useful and interesting material.

Comparatively speaking, there are six small-volume adult encyclopedias currently on the U.S. market. Among these, *The New Columbia Encyclopedia, The Random House Encyclopedia,* and *The University Desk Encyclopedia* are *Pears*'s most formidable competition. *Pears,* which retails for only $13.95, has a decided price advantage over the others, which sell for between $69.95 and $79.50. But in practically all other respects, the larger and costlier encyclopedias are preferable to *Pears,* which is simply too small, too sketchy, too British, too inaccessible, and physically too drab to compete.

Other Critical Opinions

Booklist, July 15, 1977, pp. 1750–1751. This unsigned review by the ALA Reference and Subscription Books Review Committee is mainly descriptive. In the final paragraph of the review, *Pears* is "recommended" for individuals and libraries that have "a more than casual interest in British affairs."

Cheney, Frances Neel. *American Reference Books Annual,* 1979, p. 39. Cheney, a well-known reference book reviewer, suggests that, although *Pears* is principally for a British audience, Americans will find that "it contains a great deal of practical and useful information, conveniently arranged and easy to locate."

Random House Encyclopedia

Facts in Brief

Full Title: **The Random House Encyclopedia.** *Editors:* James Mitchell, Editor in Chief; Jess Stein, Editorial Director. *Publisher:* Random House, Inc., 201 E. 50 St., New York, NY 10022. *Distributor* (Special Two-Volume School & Library Edition): Encyclopaedia Britannica Educational Corporation, 425 N. Michigan Ave., Chicago, IL 60611. *British Title: The Joy of Knowledge* (10 Volumes). *Edition Reviewed:* One-Volume Trade Edition, 1977 copyright.

Volumes: One (also Special Two-Volume School & Library Edition available). *Pages:* 2,856. *Articles:* 25,875 (875 long articles in *Colorpedia;* 25,000 short articles in *Alphapedia*). *Words:* 3,000,000. *Illustrations:* 13,800. *Maps:* 100 (including 80-page Color Atlas). *Index Entries:* None. *Cross-references:* 20,000. *Contributors:* 500.

User Classification: Adult (Small-volume). *Reader Suitability:* Age 12 through General Adult. *Physical Size:* 8½ × 11¼ in.; 29 cm. *LC:* 77-3447. *ISBN:* 0-394-40730-X. *Lowest Retail Price:* $69.95 (One-Volume Trade Edition); to schools & libraries $71.45 (Special Two-Volume School & Library Edition).

Purpose and Scope

The Random House Encyclopedia is said to contain "the World's Basic Knowledge Illuminated with Thousands of Color Illustrations" (jacket cover). In his preface, editor James Mitchell calls *Random House* a " 'family bible' of knowledge for our time . . . its function is to provide access to information and to be a guide to general knowledge." The volume attempts to achieve its purpose in approximately three million words comprising (1) the *Colorpedia*—875 heavily illustrated two-page articles covering broad topics in thematic arrangement, and (2) the *Alphapedia*—25,000 short factual A-to-Z entries covering most names, places, and things mentioned in the *Colorpedia.*

The jacket cover also proclaims *Random House* to be "revolutionary in concept." Here, for the first time in a general adult encyclopedia, the illustrations are said to have "equal importance" with the written text. Other adult encyclopedias use graphics to supplement the text, but the makers of *Random House* employ them as an integral part of the encyclopedia text. Mitchell explains: "For a new generation brought up with television, words alone are no longer enough, and so in our *Colorpedia* section we have tried to make a new type of compact pictorial encyclopedia for a visually oriented age."

The 1,792-page *Colorpedia* contains roughly the same number of words as the 822-page *Alphapedia,* but is physically twice the size due to the many illustrations. The *Colorpedia* divides knowledge into seven main categories: The Universe, The Earth, Life on Earth, Man, History and Culture, Man and Science, and Man and Machines. Each of these categories is in turn broken down into narrower subjects, which are covered in the aforementioned two-page articles. For instance, the category Man includes such articles as "Adolescence," "Behavior Therapy," "Emotional Development," "The Growing Child," "Human Development," "Language Development," "Moral Development," "Psychotherapy," "Social Development," and "Thinking and Understanding." Note that the *Colorpedia* articles, though each is complete in itself, are thematically related. Thus, for example, "Life and Its Origins" (pp. 406–407), "Evolution of Life" (pp. 408–409), "The World before Man" (pp. 410–411), "The Cell in Action" (pp. 412–413), "The Genetic Code" (pp. 414–415), "Principles of Heredity" (pp. 416–417), "Evolution: Classical Theories" (pp. 418–419), "Evolution in Action" (pp. 420–421), etc., build one upon the other, continuously adding to the reader's understanding of a large and complex subject like Life on Earth.

Subject coverage in the *Colorpedia* is most extensive in the fine arts and the natural, technical, and medical sciences—areas that lend themselves to visual treatment. Conversely, coverage is less generous in those areas not particularly enhanced by illustrations, like history, literature, philosophy, and religion. Cells, electric current, and the digestive system, for example, are subjects best explained in both words and pictures, whereas one's understanding of socialism or logic or poetry is not necessarily improved by visual aids. Hence, birds receive no less than six double-page spreads, whereas the religions of Judaism and Buddhism are covered much less thoroughly in a couple of articles. The subject of wine, enhanced by illustrations of varieties of grapes and diagrams of how it is made, receives three articles, whereas the American novel gets short shrift.

According to the editors, "every important person, place, or thing mentioned on a *Colorpedia* page has an *Alphapedia* entry." The *Alphapedia* consists of 25,000 ready-reference articles that average about 60–75 words in length, although some are as long as 1,500 words, particularly those covering major countries. The last column of each *Alphapedia* recto (or right-hand) page is devoted to black-and-white illustrations, usually portraits of people. Significant place-names are especially well covered, considering the limitations of space. Articles on the nations of the world include such standard information and data as current population, form of government, language(s), monetary unit, gross national product, and major trading partners. Similar coverage is afforded the U.S. states and Canadian provinces. Cities naturally receive less attention, but the principal municipalities are adequately covered. For instance, New York City's entry runs to 450 words, London's 325 words, and Miami's 125 words.

The *Alphapedia* has been vigorously criticized in the area of biographical coverage for who is included, who is excluded, and for how much space is given to particular biographies. The *Time* magazine review (see "Other Critical Opinions") asks, for instance, "Why is Joe Namath given ten lines of biography, while only seven are accorded to the late Vladimir Nabokov? Why Walter Cronkite but not David Brinkley? If Capote rates an entry, why not Vidal? Such quibbles will depend on whose Gore is being axed." And Walter Clemons in *Newsweek* (see "Other Critical Opinions") is concerned that "Lucille Ball gets a longer entry than John Dryden, 'U.S. playwright' Abe Burrows more space than George Bernard Shaw, Corneille, Racine or Sophocles. Ayn Rand outweighs George Eliot and Albert Camus."

Indeed, any small-volume encyclopedia can be attacked as having greater breadth than depth. And it is true that *Random House*'s coverage is often superficial, oversimplified, skimpy, and wanting in specific instances. EXAMPLES: The article on William Styron is too brief and fails to provide substantive information about his literary themes. Georgia O'Keeffe, who gets 24 lines in the competing *New Columbia Encyclopedia*, is dispensed with in eight cursory lines. The article "The American Experience: Voting" neglects even to mention the landmark 1962 Supreme Court decision *Baker* v. *Carr*, the reapportionment case popularly known as "one-man, one-vote," which radically altered American political representation at the grassroots level. There is nothing in the book about condominium housing, even though estimates say that half the U.S. population will live in some form of condominium within 20 years. The Organization of Petroleum Exporting Countries (OPEC) is mentioned but its member nations are not. African music is given short shrift, and the article on censorship deals only with the official variety. Proper names are not pronounced, even difficult ones like Romain Gary and Zimbabwe.

But the encyclopedia's failures in scope and coverage do not mean that it lacks value as a popular reference source for students and adults. *Random House*'s great strength in terms of coverage is not a great wealth of factual information but its thematic presentation of knowledge. The *Colorpedia*'s double-page spreads can spark reader curiosity, either through browsing or specific interest, and understanding is enhanced from article to article, especially in areas like the physical and technical sciences where discrete data and concepts tend to produce tangible results. *Random House* relates one bit of knowledge to another. It connects the part to the whole. The book will not give you, for example, the melting and boiling points of hydrochloric acid, but it does connect hydrochloric acid to the whole chemical process. In most encyclopedias, it is the other way around.

History and Authority

An entirely new encyclopedia published in 1977, *Random House* was conceived in England by James Mitchell and John Beazley, both experienced encyclopedia-makers, and ultimately required eight years (1969–1977) and $7 million to develop and produce. Although most of the editorial work on the *Colorpedia* was done in England, *Random House* is a joint international project sponsored by Mitchell Beazley Publishers, Ltd., and the American company Random House, Inc., the latter providing the bulk of the necessary capital ($4.4 million). As Harvey Einbinder put it in his *Chicago Tribune* review (September 25, 1977), "The brains behind this achievement come from Britain and the bucks come from America." In addition, the encyclopedia is available in a number of national editions. For instance, the respected Paris firm of Larousse has undertaken to publish a French version; in the Netherlands the well-known Spectrum, a Dutch edition; in Italy, Fabbri is handling the project. And in the United Kingdom, the encyclopedia has appeared in a ten-volume edition entitled *The Joy of Knowledge.*

The encyclopedia is perhaps the best current example of what the publishing community calls "coproduction," a growing trend among publishers in different countries to combine their editorial and financial resources to produce a costly reference work, like an art set or, in this case, a heavily illustrated encyclopedia. Such works can then be translated and adapted for various national markets. For instance, 25 new *Colorpedia* spreads were created especially for the North American edition, and numerous illustrations throughout were changed to reflect American interests. And the *Alphapedia* was produced entirely in the United States. In addition, all the material was reviewed by U.S. authorities prior to publication.

Many prominent people contributed to the *Random House* project. As mentioned, editor James Mitchell and the late John Beazley are well-known English encyclopedia-makers. They provided the artwork for the visually attractive 20-volume Dutch *Great Spectrum Encyclopedia*, for instance. Jess Stein, the editorial director of the American edition, recently retired as editor of the fine Random House dictionary line. Philip W. Goetz, now editor in chief of *The New Encyclopaedia Britannica*, served as a consultant. Each of the major sections of the *Colorpedia* is introduced by a highly regarded authority: Sir Bernard Lovell (The Universe), William A. Nierenberg (The Earth), Salvador E. Luria (Life on Earth), Loren Eiseley (Man), Christopher Hill (History and Culture), I. Bernard Cohen (Man and Science), and William O. Baker (Man and Machines). About 500 major contributors and consultants are listed in the front matter, many only by name. In some cases, however, academic affiliations are indicated and the overwhelming majority, as might be expected, are British. In all, the project involved 77 editors, 32 design and production people, 31 art editors and visual planners, 226 artists, and 461 consultants and contributors, or a total of 827 people. Aside from the aforementioned introductions to the seven sections of the *Colorpedia*, none of the material in *Random House* is signed.

Reliability

Random House is normally a reliable encyclopedia, given the book's limited size. Compression of information, however, can and sometimes does lead to inaccuracies or false impressions. In only a few instances are facts completely wrong. EXAMPLE: The *Alphapedia* article "Supreme Court of the United States" states that the court "has heard several hundred cases since it was established." Actually, the Supreme Court hears about that many cases each year. EXAMPLE: The *Alphapedia* article "Indians, North American" erroneously labels Southeastern Indian tribes as "Southwestern." In addition, there is a wide discrepancy between the period of first arrival of aboriginal people in North America given in the *Alphapedia* ("about 20,000 BC or earlier") and the *Colorpedia* ("at least 40,000 years ago"). Despite such editorial lapses, the encyclopedia can usually be relied upon for accurate factual information and interpretations in accord with the findings of responsible contemporary scholarship.

Recency

Although *Random House* has not been revised since its initial appearance in 1977, it is more up-to-date than any of its small-volume competitors. Both coverage and treatment of material are thoroughly contemporary. The series of related articles on energy and the environment in the *Colorpedia* exemplify the encyclopedia's currency: "Energy for the Future"; "Energy Resources: Coal"; "Energy Resources: Oil and Gas"; "Energy Supplies"; "Earth's Dwindling Resources"; "Land Uses"; "Mineral Resources of the Land"; "Mineral Resources of the Sea"; "Misuse of the Land"; "Pollution of the Air"; "Pollution of Rivers and Lakes"; and "Pollution of the Sea." Likewise, *Colorpedia* treatment of medical and sexual topics are quite up-to-date. EXAMPLE: The series of articles "Reproduction," "Pregnancy," "Giving Birth," and "Birth Control" provides an excellent overview of current knowledge and developments in the area of human reproduction.

Obviously, there are areas where *Random House* is not entirely current. For instance, the *Alphapedia* article covering Paris enumerates many significant buildings in the city but does not mention the new and controversial Pompidou Centre in the Beaubourg neighborhood. The *Colorpedia* coverage of deserts includes nothing about the alarming trend toward what scientists call "desertification," or the drying up of once productive land. The several articles dealing with genes and genetic developments fail to include material on recombinant DNA or gene splicing. Also obvious is the inescapable fact that each year the encyclopedia goes without revision, the more dated its contents become. Readers will not find Ronald Reagan in *Random House*, for example, nor Alexander Haig, Margaret Thatcher, Menachem Begin, or Ayatollah Khomeini. According to *Random House,* the country of Zimbabwe is still Rhodesia, the Soviet invasion of Afghanistan never occurred, and "Iran is a constitutional monarchy headed by the shah." In 1977, Jess Stein of Random House (the encyclopedia's editorial director) informed the *Buying Guide* that the publisher planned to maintain *Random House* "on a continuous basis (from printing to printing) and is now budgeted for such work." Thus far, however, no revision of any kind has occurred. Upon inquiry in 1980, the *Buying Guide* learned that

This Recency Table compares selected topics in *Random House* with those in other encyclopedias of similar size and intended usership.

Topic	Random House	New Columbia	New Lincoln Library	University Desk
Afghanistan	Not current	Not current	Not current	Not current
Dinosaurs	Very current	Fairly current	Not current	Not current
Greenland	Fairly current	Fairly current	Not current	Not current
Thomas Jefferson	Fairly current	Fairly current	Not current	Fairly current
Mass Transportation/Subways	Very current	Fairly current	Not current	Fairly current
Nuclear Power	Very current	Not current	Not current	Not current
Paris	Fairly current	Not current	Not current	Not current
Sharks	Fairly current	Fairly current	Fairly current	Fairly current
Shock Therapy	Fairly current	Fairly current	Not current	Not current
Suicide	Fairly current	Not current	Not current*	Not current
Tuberculosis	Very current	Fairly current	Not current	Fairly current
Zimbabwe	Fairly current	Not current	Fairly current	Fairly current

*Topic not covered in encyclopedia.

"we are planning to prepare a general revision for publication a few years from now, but no date is set. In the meantime we will either reprint the book as it stands or do only some essential updates." At present, *Random House* remains reasonably current in most areas, as the Recency Table here indicates. But too many more years without substantive revision will surely diminish the encyclopedia's value as a source of recent information.

Objectivity

The editors of *Random House* are aware of what James Mitchell calls "the danger areas"—those subjects susceptible to biased or prejudiced treatment. "We have done our best to be as balanced as we can," he says in the preface, adding that "where there is controversy we have tried to present both sides of a case; where there is uncertainty our contributors have been encouraged to say so; where there are questions we have asked them." All examples checked by the *Buying Guide* substantiate these claims. The question of abortion, for instance, is treated in the *Color-*

pedia article "Questions of Life and Death." The issue is discussed thoughtfully albeit briefly as one involving morality. "Humans are moral beings because they cannot evade choices," the article states at the outset. Later, the "conflicting moral arguments of the 'absolutists' and 'relativists' " are noted concerning not only abortion but war, birth control, capital punishment, and euthanasia. Likewise, the double-page spread on birth control is straightforward and impartial, as is the excellent coverage of human reproduction, pregnancy, and birth.

Clarity and Reader Suitability

Random House, informs the preface, "has been created for ordinary people, not specialists." Editor Mitchell goes on to point out that "the great and best-selling popular encyclopedias of the past have always had one thing in common—simplicity. The ability to make even complicated subjects clear, to distill, to extract the principles from behind the complicated formulas, the gift of getting to the heart of things: these are the elements that make popular encyclopedias really useful to the people who read them. We have done our best to follow these principles." The makers of *Random House* have succeeded well in this respect. The style is always clear and simple enough to be understood by those with reading skills at the middle school level and up. Of course the heavy reliance on illustrative material also enhances informational clarity.

A typical example of the encyclopedia's successful effort to present even complex subject matter in an understandable manner is found in the *Colorpedia* article "Power Direct from the Sun and Earth." Note that the number in brackets refers to a graphic contained in the article:

"Of these possibilities, only the humble solar collectors are so far used. They consist of panels, usually mounted on the roof of a building and angled so as to obtain the maximum amount of sunlight. Water is pumped through the panels, picking up heat from the Sun as it goes. The pump is controlled by a sensor so that it operates only when the collector is several degrees hotter than the water in the storage tank. Unfortunately, the Sun does not shine all the time, particularly in northern areas such as Great Britain and parts of the United States, but despite this it is estimated that a well-designed solar collector system could halve hot water and space heating costs. Systems for converting solar energy directly into electricity are less attractive. The solar cells used by spacecraft are expensive and typically have conversion efficiencies of only ten percent or less. In principle electricity could be generated by covering rooftops with solar cells [2] but this would depend on producing cheap cells on the order of a dollar per square foot; they now cost over $100 per square foot."

Arrangement and Accessibility

As already explained (see "Purpose and Scope"), *Random House* is divided into two distinct parts: (1) the *Colorpedia,* which contains 875 two-page survey articles grouped thematically within seven broad knowledge areas, and (2) the *Alphapedia,* which contains 25,000 brief articles on nearly all people, places, and key words covered in the *Colorpedia.* The *Alphapedia* is arranged alphabetically, letter-by-letter ("Indiana" precedes "Indian Ocean"). The reason for the two-part arrangement is explained as follows in editor Mitchell's preface: "The history of these works [encyclopedias] has shown that there are two principal concepts of an encyclopedia. The first is that of a comprehensive fact-book for easy quick-reference use. The second is the complete library—a collection of treatises on all subjects. In planning *The Random House Encyclopedia,* we examined these two approaches, considering the advantages and disadvantages of each type. The solution we reached—which was to take the two traditions and marry them—was made primarily with the user in mind." Mitchell also notes that the terms *Colorpedia* and *Alphapedia* originated as nicknames while the encyclopedia was being produced, but this explanation has not stopped critics such as Edmund Fuller ("deplorable") and Christopher Lehmann-Haupt ("awful words") from roundly condemning this "pedia" jargon.

Given its nontraditional arrangement, how accessible are the contents of *Random House?* There is no index to the book, not at least in the generally understood sense of that word. But the *Alphapedia,* which includes entries for all major names and terms in the *Colorpedia,* does provide approximately 15,000 cross-references to the *Colorpedia.* Such references usually appear at the end of *Alphapedia* entries and are designated by means of a delta sign (or small triangle). In addition, the *Alphapedia* includes some *See* and *See also* references to other *Alphapedia* articles. The *Colorpedia* can be said to be self-indexing, due to the aforementioned fact that all key words and names therein can be located in the *Alphapedia.* Also, each *Colorpedia* article provides cross-references called "connections," which refer the reader to related articles in the *Colorpedia.* Located at the top of each verso (left-hand) page, the "connections" are usually *See also* references, but occasionally there is a *read first* reference as well. Thus, by means of what editor Mitchell describes as "the simple system of cross-reference between and within the two sections," the user is usually able to locate specific information quickly and effectively.

In some instances, however, the cross-reference system breaks down. EXAMPLE: The *Alphapedia* entry for the U.S. Supreme Court fails to refer the user to the *Colorpedia* article "Law in Action," which contains, among other things, a diagram of the American court system. EXAMPLE: The reader who looks in the *Alphapedia* under *Organization of Petroleum Exporting Countries (OPEC)* will find nothing, although there are entries for "Organization for Economic Cooperation and Development (OECD)," "Organization of African Unity (OAU)," and "Organization of American States (OAS)." But if the reader is thoughtful enough or lucky enough to check under "OPEC," references to the *Colorpedia* will be found. EXAMPLE: The *Alphapedia* entry "Suicide" lacks cross-references to "Death, Grieving, and Loss" and "Questions of Life and

Death," related articles in the *Colorpedia*. EXAMPLE: A 48-page "Time Chart" follows the *Colorpedia,* but it is not related to the *Colorpedia* or *Alphapedia* in any way. Important Supreme Court decisions, for instance, are included in the "Time Chart," but the *Alphapedia* article provides no references.

In the final analysis, *Random House* is not as easy nor as efficient to use as an encyclopedia arranged in straight alphabetical fashion. On the other hand, *Random House*'s elaborate but easily understood system of cross-references gets the reader to the right place in the book most of the time. In comparison with its major competitors, *Random House* is somewhat more accessible than *The New Columbia Encyclopedia* and *The New Lincoln Library Encyclopedia,* but less so than *The University Desk Encyclopedia.*

Bibliographies

Unlike most encyclopedias, *Random House* does not include its bibliographies at the end of specific articles, but rather provides a special bibliography section in the back of the book, similar to the way the larger *Collier's Encyclopedia* handles its bibliographies. In the case of *Random House,* a nine-page bibliography follows the *Alphapedia* and consists of 1,500 citations grouped topically in the same order as the seven major sections of the *Colorpedia,* and then is subdivided into general categories. Under Man, for instance, are such subheadings as "The Human Body— Structure, Function, and Health," "Psychology," and "Religion and Mythology." The citations are arranged alphabetically by author within these subject categories.

Generally speaking, the bibliographies are relatively current (with older classics cited when appropriate) but not especially well selected. Why, for example, should Mario Pei's *The Story of Language* be listed under "Sociology" when that category neglects to include a single work by Peter Berger or C. Wright Mills? How can any basic list covering sociology leave out Alvin Gouldner's absolutely essential *The Coming Crisis of Western Sociology* (1970)? How can any instructive list in the area of American history totally ignore revisionist historians like William Appleman Williams and Gabriel Kolko? Another complaint about the bibliographies is lack of consistent bibliographic style. Normally author, title, place, and date of publication are given, along with number of volumes if more than one. But in the sociology list one finds a citation for the 17-volume *International Encyclopedia of the Social Sciences* with no indication that it is a multivolume work.

Graphics

The illustrations in the *Colorpedia* are as important informationally as the written text. This portion of the encyclopedia aims to integrate words and pictures, and it succeeds in this difficult task very well. The *Colorpedia* was mainly developed abroad by the firm of Mitchell Beazley, which utilized the contents of International Visual Resource, a large art bank.

The *Colorpedia* articles include 11,325 color illustrations of practically every variety—drawings, diagrams, photographs, reproductions of paintings and other art work, charts, tables, maps, etc. The color reproduction is usually quite good, and the graphics are almost always attractive, appropriate, clear, and informative. As shown in a previously cited example involving the article "Power Direct from the Sun and Earth" (see "Clarity and Reader Suitability"), the illustrations are related to the printed text by internal references in brackets. Note also that the captions accompanying the illustrations are unusually detailed and often convey more specific or factual information than the main text.

Technical, scientific, and medical information particularly lends itself to visual instruction. Hence, it comes as no surprise that such *Colorpedia* articles as "Bacteria and Viruses," "Ceramics and Glass," "Diseases of the Skin," "How Computers Work," "Metals and Their Uses," "Mosses and Liverworts," "Reproduction," and "Zoos and Botanic Gardens" very successfully blend the visual and the textual into an enlightening and enlivening information package. Also, the bright illustrations provide a contemporary tone. The article "Birth Control," for instance, is current both in content and temper, due in large part to the drawings showing the various types of contraception. There is nothing old-fashioned about *Random House.* Several critics, however, have carped about specific illustrations. David Elliott, in the *Chicago Daily News,* wrote that "a few of the illustrations seem too contrived or even silly (like that of ten different animal species copulating)." Walter Clemons in *Newsweek* picked on the same item: "Sometimes the artists go crazy: a very peppy drawing of 'Sex in the animal world' shows a Disney woodland run amok—bunnies and field mice humping, birds going at it in a tree while earthworms twine below." In truth, the illustration is in good taste and, more important, it conveys much information both visually and through the extensive captions.

The remaining illustrations are also of good quality, though not as remarkable as those found in the *Colorpedia.* As noted previously, the *Alphapedia* includes black-and-white graphics in the last column of the recto pages. They mainly cover people, but there are also small locator maps and photographs of places among these illustrations. The principal map coverage is provided in an 80-page color world atlas containing 46 maps found at the back of the book. Prepared by Rand McNally, the atlas is accompanied by a gazetteer-index of 21,000 place-names. The maps are drawn to scale and show major physical and political features. Twenty-two pages of physical maps also appear in The Universe section of the *Colorpedia.*

Physical Format

Time magazine's review of *Random House* (see "Other Critical Opinions" for citation) observed, "A one-volume encyclopedia should be bigger than a breadbox and smaller than the British Museum." By this informal standard *Random House* does rather well. The single-volume trade edition found in bookstores weighs nearly 12 pounds and is almost four inches thick. The two-volume edition for schools and libraries distributed by Encyclopaedia Britannica Educational Corporation tips the scales at over 13 pounds—or exactly 5.9 kilos in metric measurement. Obviously, the encyclopedia is heavy and use in the home will require a stand, shelf top, coffee table, or the like. The volume fortunately lies perfectly flat when open.

A large, weighty book like *Random House* must be well bound or it will soon fall apart. Again, fortunately, the volume passes the test. The one-volume edition is Smyth-sewn and bound in full-cloth light tan D-grade buckram with gold lettering and single red and blue stripes on the spine and front cover. Also, the bottom edges of the binding are almost flush with the pages, a feature designed to prevent sagging when the book is standing on a shelf or desk. A dust jacket accompanies the trade edition. The two-volume edition is equally well bound in a Pyroxlin-coated dark blue library buckram with gold lettering. The volumes are naturally divided into the larger 1,792-page *Colorpedia* and the smaller 822-page *Alphapedia,* which is thumb-indexed.

Inside, the *Colorpedia*'s visually appealing double-page spreads are varied in layout. Normally, the printed matter is toward the top half of the three-column page and the illustrations toward the bottom, although the key illustration is always in the top right-hand corner of the recto page. The *Alphapedia,* also using a three-column page, is completely text, except for the black-and-white illustrations in the last column of the recto page. The print size varies from small to smaller, but the typefaces used are always sufficiently clear and readable. Note that the *Alphapedia* text is on computer tape and was set by automated typesetting facilities. (Among other things, this production feature will make future revisions of the *Alphapedia* easier and faster.) The 40-pound coated paper, carefully chosen to aid color reproduction, is of very good quality. From the standpoint of design, *Random House* is an outstanding encyclopedia. By way of confirmation, *Random House* was cited by the American Institute of Graphic Arts as one of the best-made books of 1977.

Special Features

The book's two unmistakable special features have already been identified and explained in some detail. They are (1) the encyclopedia's unique arrangement in two distinct but interrelated parts, the *Colorpedia* and the *Alphapedia,* and (2) its "revolutionary" effort to integrate the textual and the visual into an informational whole. There are several other special features, albeit much less dramatic ones. A 48-page "Time Chart" (from 4000 B.C. to 1976) "places most of the significant events in human history in perspective." Arranged in tabular form by seven categories (e.g., Principal Events, Religion and Philosophy, Science and Technology), the chart is entirely unrelated to the rest of the encyclopedia, and is rather inconspicuously located between the *Colorpedia* and the *Alphapedia.* Students who remember it will find the "Time Chart" a helpful feature. An eight-page "Flags of the World" section is similarly buried toward the back, between the picture credits and the world atlas. The flags are in color and are grouped by areas of the world. Finally, both the *Colorpedia* and *Alphapedia* provide equivalent metric weights and measures in parentheses.

Sales Information

The one-volume trade edition retails for $69.95 in book and department stores, although some outlets like the Barnes & Noble Sales Annex in New York City have offered the book for as little as $49.95. The two-volume edition for schools and libraries available through Encyclopaedia Britannica Educational Corporation sells for $71.45 delivered. At the present time, *Random House* is not sold directly in the home nor is it available via mail order or through a book club. It is possible, however, that at some time in the future the encyclopedia will be sold by mail or in-home.

Random House first appeared in September 1977 with an initial printing of 175,000 copies. The encyclopedia was vigorously backed by a $1 million budget for advertising and promotion, including $500,000 for television spots. The president of Random House, Inc., hit the road as part of the promotional blitz, and even a professional psychologist was engaged to analyze the potential American market. As a result, *Random House* generated more public interest than new encyclopedias of any size normally do, as the excellent review coverage in the popular press attests (see "Other Critical Opinions"). According to a report in *Publishers Weekly* (March 6, 1978, p. 67), approximately 105,000 copies of *Random House* were sold at the outset, a figure said to be "disappointing" (industry sources estimated that 140,000 copies had to be sold by the end of 1977 for the publisher to break even). Be that as it may, the initial printing was eventually sold out, and the second printing (unrevised; see "Recency") is now in the bookstores.

Summary

The Random House Encyclopedia can be quickly summed up in this manner:

Scope: Good	Accessibility: Fair
Authority: Good	Bibliographies: Fair
Reliability: Good	Graphics: Excellent
Recency: Good	Physical Format: Excellent
Objectivity: Excellent	Special Features: Few
Clarity: Excellent	Price: Reasonable

To elaborate briefly, *Random House,* an entirely new small-volume encyclopedia in 1977 unrevised since that time, is an immensely attractive reference work for older students and adults, which, in the words of one reviewer, brings an "exuberant approach to knowledge." The encyclopedia is nontraditionally arranged in two distinct but related parts. The larger *Colorpedia* provides thematic treatment of basic knowledge in bright, heavily illustrated two-page spreads, whereas the *Alphapedia* covers essential factual information in brief A-to-Z articles. Aimed at "a new generation brought up with television" (preface), the encyclopedia makes a great effort—largely successful—to integrate the visual and the textual, to bring words and pictures together to form an informational whole. On the negative side, the elaborate system of cross-references that links the two parts is not always as effective as it might be, and hence accessibility to the encyclopedia's contents leaves something to be desired. Also, like any small encyclopedia, *Random House* is sometimes overly simple, too brief, or superficial. And, though still reasonably current, the encyclopedia has not been updated since its publication in 1977. The work's great strength is not provision of a wealth of isolated facts but rather its coherent and stimulating treatment of knowledge.

Comparatively speaking, there are six small-volume adult encyclopedias currently on the market. Among these, *The New Columbia Encyclopedia* and *The University Desk Encyclopedia* are *Random House*'s most formidable competition, along with the older and well-known three-volume *New Lincoln Library Encyclopedia* (formerly *The Lincoln Library of Essential Information*). All four of these small-volume encyclopedias are priced in the same general range ($69.95–$99.98), and each possesses unique strengths and weaknesses. As the raw data indicate, *New Columbia* is the largest small-volume encyclopedia available. On the other hand, *University Desk* and especially *Random House* are superior in terms of graphics and design. Note also that *New Columbia,* though very clearly written, is more scholarly and technical in its presentation of material than either *Random House* or *University Desk.*

As a general proposition, without taking individual reference needs into account, the *Buying Guide* believes that *The New Columbia Encyclopedia* and *The Random House Encyclopedia* are the best small-volume adult encyclopedias on the market today. The two works could not possibly be more different in their design or presentation of information. *New Columbia* is a sober, erudite, print-oriented work of stately scholarship. The smaller *Random House* is a splashy, spirited, and at times exhilarating work of great visual appeal. Actually, the two titles complement one another rather well, and some consumers (certainly many libraries) will want both titles. Others who need just one small-volume encyclopedia will have the happy task of choosing between two highly regarded works.

Other Critical Opinions

Due to the publisher's aggressive promotion and the fact that it is a trade book available in retail stores, *The Random House Encyclopedia* has received wide critical coverage in both the popular press and the reference review media. All the annotated reviews listed here should be available in most public and academic libraries. Detailed information about the making of the encyclopedia can be found in the article " 'The Random House Encyclopedia': Story behind the Project," *Publishers Weekly,* May 9, 1977, pp. 33–38.

Booklist, March 15, 1980, pp. 1075–1077. Published nearly three years after *Random House* appeared in 1977, this unsigned review by the

ALA Reference and Subscription Books Review Committee is awkwardly written and strangely silent on one of the encyclopedia's major achievements: the integration of printed and visual matter into an informational whole. In the final paragraph of the review, *Random House* is "recommended" for use in the home and all types of libraries (except special). The recommendation, however, is qualified by the odd concluding note that the encyclopedia "is best suited to readers who like concise, multifaceted presentations of information and who enjoy discovering entities, events, facts, and concepts within thematic contexts."

Bunge, Charles A. "Current Reference Books," *Wilson Library Bulletin*, January 1978, p. 428. Bunge, a seasoned reference book reviewer, offers a succinct, intelligently prepared evaluation, pointing out that the encyclopedia's "excellent" illustrations are "worth the purchase price," although the gutters (or inner margins) are too narrow. The work is recommended for libraries "serving users from junior-high-age up."

Business Week, October 3, 1977, p. 13. This short review calls *Random House* "heroic and largely successful" and recommends it over *The New Columbia Encyclopedia*.

Cheney, Frances Neel. *American Reference Books Annual*, 1978, p. 41. Generally favorable, this review suggests *Random House* will be "useful as a quick reference source and for pictorial representations of a wide range of subjects."

Choice, March 1978, p. 48. This unsigned review has much good to say about the encyclopedia, but rejects it as a suitable reference source for academic libraries. No real documentation is provided to support that view.

Clemons, Walter. "Sausages and Lucille Ball," *Newsweek*, October 10, 1977, pp. 105–106. A negative review that criticizes the encyclopedia's illustrations ("this is a sad, gaudy book") and coverage ("what you get is a smattering"). Clemons concludes with a strong endorsement of *The New Columbia Encyclopedia* over *Random House*.

George, Mary. *Library Journal*, November 1, 1977, pp. 2252–2253. George, a librarian at the University of Michigan, points out that "the most distinctive feature of *RHE* is the abundance (some would say 11,300 is an overabundance) of color illustrations . . . that dominate the 'Colorpedia'," and therefore suggests the encyclopedia might find its most suitable audience among those "who have always resisted education or have been deprived of it."

Katz, William A. *Basic Information Sources* (Vol. 1 of *Introduction to Reference Work*, 3rd ed. New York: McGraw-Hill, 1978), pp. 166–169. Katz, a highly respected authority on reference work and sources, comparatively reviews four small-volume encyclopedias, namely *Random House, The New Columbia Encyclopedia, The Lincoln Library of Essential Information,* and the now defunct *Cadillac Modern Encyclopedia*. Katz has a number of complimentary things to say about *Random House*, but in the final analysis rates it behind the *New Columbia* as an effective reference source for libraries.

Kenner, Hugh. "Images at Random," *Harper's*, December 1977, pp. 102–107. Literary critic Kenner finds much wrong with the encyclopedia, including its construction ("signs of haste are everywhere") and a number of factual errors. Kenner also is quite bothered by the promotional hype attending the work's publication. Students of encyclopedias should not miss this blistering review.

Lehmann-Haupt, Christopher. "Books of the Times: The Random House Encyclopedia," *New York Times*, September 29, 1977. Among the points made in this generally favorable review is the observation that *Random House* tends to treat the areas of science and technology more fully than other knowledge areas because scientific topics lend themselves to pictorial treatment more readily than do most other subjects.

Publishers Weekly, August 1, 1977, p. 110. This first review of the encyclopedia is upbeat: "There's crowding of course, but the volume's exuberant approach to knowledge is remarkably well organized."

Sokolov, Raymond A. "Reference Books: The Random House Encyclopedia," *New York Times Book Review*, October 2, 1977, p. 15. Sokolov, a novelist and former food editor of the *New York Times*, offers many negative comments about the encyclopedia, including its graphics ("cluttered together without elegance"), style ("almost never a pleasure to read"), and paper ("inferior"). Sokolov's opinions can be debated but his offhand evaluation of the paper is simply wrong.

Time, October 10, 1977, p. 106. Despite "quibbles" about *Random House*'s coverage and physical size, the encyclopedia "is a welcome invitation not only to the mind's eye but also to the eye's mind."

University Desk Encyclopedia

Facts in Brief

Full Title: **The University Desk Encyclopedia.** *Editors:* Herman Friedhoff and Ben Lenthall, Chief Editors. *Publisher:* Elsevier, Amsterdam, Netherlands; copyright by Elsevier Publishing Projects. *U.S. Publisher:* E. P. Dutton & Company, Inc., 201 Park Ave. S., New York, NY 10003. *U.S. Distributor:* Bookthrift, Inc., 45 W. 36 St., New York, NY 10018. *Edition Reviewed:* 1977 copyright.

Volumes: One. *Pages:* 1,055. *Articles:* 25,000. *Words:* 2,000,000. *Illustrations:* 3,000. *Maps:* 350. *Index Entries:* None. *Cross-references:* 35,000. *Contributors:* 68.

User Classification: Adult (Small-volume). *Reader Suitability:* Age 12 through General Adult. *Physical Size:* 8½ × 11¼ in.; 29 cm. *LC:* 76-51902. *ISBN:* 0-525-93001-9. *Lowest Retail Price:* $69.95.

Purpose and Scope

The University Desk Encyclopedia, a one-volume work that originated abroad and was published in early 1977, intends to condense "the vital facts from every field of knowledge with special emphasis on relevance for today and therefore a lot of space on science and technology." The preface, entitled "Letter from the Chief Editors," also stresses that *University Desk* is designed for "your family, your business, your classroom," and that the book is filled with "pictures that are not only beautiful to look at but also informative." Most of the 25,000 specific-entry articles adhere to what the editors call "our normally brief formula." Each page averages 25 articles of about 80 words each. But there are also 46 so-called full-scale articles of a page or more in length that "treat particularly interesting subjects in depth"—such as American Indians, biological clocks, consumer protection, criminal law, family planning, guerrilla warfare, and the polar regions.

University Desk's scope is international, with particular emphasis on North America, Great Britain, and Europe. Subject coverage is likewise fairly well balanced, although the natural and technical sciences are stressed. Flora, fauna, chemical elements and compounds, and natural phenomena are especially well covered. The great majority of articles, however, deal with biographical and geographical topics. EXAMPLE: Page 662 is a typical page. The people covered are George Marshall (U.S. general and statesman), John Marshall (chief justice of the U.S. Supreme

Court), Thomas Riley Marshall (U.S. vice-president under Woodrow Wilson), Thurgood Marshall (justice of the U.S. Supreme Court), Marsilius of Padua (Italian political philosopher), John Marston (English playwright), Martha (of the Bible), José Marti (Cuban patriot), Martial (Spanish-born Latin poet whose full name was Marcus Valerius Martialis), three popes named Martin, Archer Martin (British biochemist), Glenn Martin (U.S. aircraft designer and manufacturer), Joseph Martin (U.S. speaker of the House of Representatives), Mary Martin (U.S. musical comedy star), Pierre Martin (French engineer), and Simone Martini (Italian painter). Places covered include the Marshall Islands, Marshalltown (Iowa), Marshfield (Mass. and Wis.), and Martha's Vineyard. U.S. presidents receive relatively substantial coverage, including a color portrait. Likewise, countries of the world, U.S. states, and Canadian provinces are accorded extended coverage that features a flag, a spot map, and standard information (population, etc.) in a boxed panel.

The encyclopedia's coverage is broad but usually lacks depth. The editors say, "We didn't want to be annoyingly telegraphic or unrecognizably abbreviated," but that is exactly what happens in all too many instances. EXAMPLE: The U.S. city of Phoenix (Ariz.) is covered in five lines. EXAMPLE: The complete entry for Marshfield (Wis.) is "city in central Wis., a manufacturing center in a dairying area. Pop 15,169." EXAMPLE: The five-line article on Hannah Arendt fails to note her controversial study *Eichmann in Jerusalem.* EXAMPLE: The five-line "Condominium" merely states "in real estate, individual ownership in property, such as an apartment, which is part of a larger complex owned in common." There is nothing about the extraordinary recent growth in the condominium housing area, or the problems associated with it. EXAMPLE: The 18-line "Genetics" (including the subentry "Genetic Counseling") simply defines the terms. EXAMPLE: "Phosphates" covers the subject only from a chemical point of view, completely ignoring production and trade information. EXAMPLE: The 27-line (250-word) "Supreme Court" fails to explain how the court operates, and it neglects to list its current (and past) members.

Except for the 46 so-called full-scale articles, or special essays, *University Desk* provides quite superficial coverage, normally limited to essential facts and brief definitions, sometimes complemented by a colorful illustration. Even pronunciation information is omitted. The encyclopedia lacks the depth of coverage furnished by the larger specific-entry *New Columbia Encyclopedia,* and it cannot match the broad thematic coverage afforded by the attractive *Random House Encyclopedia. University Desk* unfortunately falls between two stools, neither deep enough nor expansive enough to be considered outstanding.

History and Authority

When *University Desk* initially appeared in 1977, E. P. Dutton, the publisher, advertised the book as "the first all-new one-volume encyclopedia in 41 years," which was playing a bit loose with the facts. Be that as it may, the encyclopedia was indeed "all-new." According to the editors, it was in preparation for five years and required in toto "34 editors, 172 writers, 12 production people and 39 consultants and advisors." Actually, *University Desk,* like its competitor *The Random House Encyclopedia,* is an example of what the book industry calls "coproduction," that is, when publishers from different countries develop and finance an expensive reference work like an art set or encyclopedia that can be adapted to various national markets. In this case, Elsevier (the well-known Dutch publisher), Wentworth (a British firm), and Dutton (an American publisher) combined their resources to produce the book. Specifically, much of the general information and illustrative matter is derived from Elsevier's *Grote Winkler Prins,* a revision of the internationally famous multivolume *Winkler Prins Encyclopaedie.* Wentworth apparently provided the editorial staff, and Dutton helped bankroll the project.

In addition to the two chief editors, Herman Friedhoff and Ben Lenthall, 29 subeditors are listed in the front matter. Following the British practice, they are identified only by name and academic degree. A distinguished 13-member advisory board includes such British and American notables as Lord Alan Bullock, Dr. Frederick Burkhardt, Betty Friedan, Professor Emrys Jones, Eric Larabee, and Harold D. Lasswell. There is also an impressive board of consultants comprised of 24 Americans and two Canadians, most of whom are college professors. The front matter also lists some of the authors of the 46 special articles, e.g., Isaac Asimov ("Science Fiction"), Courtlandt Canby ("Civil War, US"), and William J. Wilson ("Racial Minorities"). *University Desk* is an authoritative encyclopedia, although none of the material is signed.

Reliability

Examples of misinformation and editorial carelessness are encountered just frequently enough to cast doubt on the overall reliability of the encyclopedia. EXAMPLE: The full-scale article "American Indians: A Profusion of Different Cultures" contains several serious errors of fact; for example, the Nez Percé and Salish (plateau peoples) are erroneously ascribed to the Great Basin area and called "Digger Indians." There are also several misspellings and typographical errors; for example, *has* appears as *his* in the next-to-last paragraph of the article. EXAMPLE: The article "Deserts" conveys the impression that deserts are receding ("In recent years, IRRIGATION has enabled reclamation of much desert land"), when in fact desertlike conditions are increasing around the world at an alarming rate. (But it is true that some selected desert land has been reclaimed in the United States, the Middle East, and elsewhere.) EXAMPLE: The article "Sharks," only 15 lines long, contains three errors, such as the erroneous statement that "all [sharks] are extremely fast swimmers and active predators." In other instances, the encyclopedia's information is dated and hence incorrect; for instance, the old tricolor flag for Afghanistan is given instead of the new all-red one. (For more on this problem, see "Recency.")

Recency

As might be expected in the case of an encyclopedia newly created in the mid-1970s, *University Desk* is reasonably up-to-date in most areas. In

This Recency Table compares selected topics in *University Desk* with those in other encyclopedias of similar size and intended usership.

Topic	University Desk	New Columbia	New Lincoln Library	Random House
Afghanistan	Not current	Not current	Not current	Not current
Dinosaurs	Not current	Fairly current	Not current	Very current
Greenland	Not current	Fairly current	Not current	Fairly current
Thomas Jefferson	Fairly current	Fairly current	Not current	Fairly current
Mass Transportation/Subway	Fairly current	Fairly current	Not current	Very current
Nuclear Power	Not current	Not current	Not current	Very current
Paris	Not current	Not current	Not current	Fairly current
Sharks	Fairly current	Fairly current	Fairly current	Fairly current
Shock Therapy	Not current	Fairly current	Not current	Fairly current
Suicide	Not current	Not current	Not current*	Fairly current
Tuberculosis	Fairly current	Fairly current	Not current	Very current
Zimbabwe	Fairly current	Not current	Fairly current	Fairly current

*Topic not covered in encyclopedia.

addition, the 46 long special articles frequently deal with contemporary subjects sometimes neglected by encyclopedias, such as consumer protection, endangered species, fusion power, futurology, racial minorities, and women's rights. Regrettably, *University Desk* has not been revised since its initial publication in 1977, nor are there plans to update the work in the foreseeable future. And as the Recency Table here clearly indicates, the encyclopedia is rapidly becoming dated in those areas where knowledge is most volatile, such as political topics. For example, according to *University Desk,* Ronald Reagan (who is in the encyclopedia) has not yet won the U.S. presidency, Alexander Haig (not in the encyclopedia) is not the U.S. Secretary of State, people like Margaret Thatcher, Menachem Begin, and Ayatollah Khomeini do not exist, Saul Bellow has yet to achieve the Nobel Prize for literature, recombinant DNA has yet to burst onto the scientific scene, Zimbabwe has yet to join the family of nations, the Soviet invasion of Afghanistan has not yet occurred, and Iran's "internal political stability and success in maintaining good relations with both Western and Soviet countries have contributed to its recent advance."

Objectivity

Like all authoritative encyclopedias, *University Desk* conscientiously strives for impartial and balanced treatment of sensitive and controversial subject matter. EXAMPLE: The brief article "Marijuana" describes the drug and its effects as objectively as possible and, although its legal status is not discussed, marijuana is said to be "the subject of much medical and social debate." EXAMPLE: "Flying Saucer" notes that "most sightings are obviously erroneous but a number by reliable observers remain unexplained." EXAMPLE: The article on the Central Intelligence Agency (CIA) observes, "The CIA has done much to further the interests of the US and its allies, but such fiascos as the BAY OF PIGS invasion of Cuba and the capture of the U-2 spy-plane over Russia, in which it was involved, have not helped international relations." Occasionally, however, unsupported partisan opinions are expressed as fact. EXAMPLE: The garbled final sentence of the article "Indians, North American" accuses militant Indians today of sometimes engaging in "pointless violence." (The entire sentence reads, "Although occasionally expressed in pointless violence this, combined with respect for the Indian philosophy of life," which is just another example of the sloppy editorial work characteristic of the encyclopedia; see "Reliability.")

Clarity and Reader Suitability

The encyclopedia's style is normally clear, concise, plain, and dry. Users who possess reading skills at the junior or middle school level and up will usually encounter little difficulty with the text. A typical example of *University Desk*'s style can be found in the first few sentences of the article "Revolutionary War, American": "In which Britain's 13 colonies gained their independence. It was a minor war with immense consequences—the founding of the US, and the forging of a new, dynamic democratic ideology in an age of absolutism. Despite elements of civil war and of revolution, the conflict was above all a political, constitutional struggle, and as such began many years before the actual fighting." Articles on technical subjects, however, will sometimes require high school level reading comprehension. Unfamiliar or difficult terms are not always explained in the article. EXAMPLE: "Solar Energy" informs the reader that "solar heat energy may be used directly in several ways. Solar evaporation is used to convert brine to SALT and distilled water. Flat-plate collectors—matt black absorbing plates with attached tubes through which a fluid flows to collect the heat—are beginning to be used for domestic water heating, space heating, and to run air-conditioning systems. Focusing collectors, using a parabolic mirror, are used in solar furnaces, which can give high power absorption at high temperatures." The text is clear but most readers will be forced to consult the dictionary for the meaning of *parabolic*.

Arrangement and Accessibility

University Desk is arranged alphabetically, letter-by-letter ("Indiana" precedes "Indian Ocean"). As already noted (see "Purpose and Scope"),

University Desk is a specific-entry encyclopedia, a feature that will enhance the user's chances of readily finding discrete topics. In addition, like its two major rivals, *The New Columbia Encyclopedia* and *The Random House Encyclopedia,* the encyclopedia lacks a general index but facilitates access to related information and topics through an extensive system of cross-references. External *See* references appear in the A–Z sequence, such as *"House of Representatives.* See CONGRESS OF THE UNITED STATES." Internal cross-references are designated by words and phrases printed in SMALL CAPITAL LETTERS within the text of the articles. EXAMPLE: The article on Sigmund Freud contains the sentence "Dissatisfied with HYPNOSIS and electrotherapy as analytic techniques, he evolved the psychoanalytic method, founded on DREAM analysis and FREE ASSOCIATION," thus referring the reader to the articles "Dream," "Free Association," and "Hypnosis."

This system works reasonably well, with one glaring exception. The 46 special articles that provide extended treatment of such subjects as air transportation, the brain, consumer protection, criminal law, earthquakes, endangered species, integrated circuits, Latin America, polar regions, surgery, and viruses are not always linked to the rest of the text via cross-references. EXAMPLE: The short, regular article "Birth Control" (225 words) includes internal cross-references to CONTRACEPTION, ABORTION, STERILIZATION, WOMEN'S RIGHTS, Margaret SANGER, Marie STOPES, BIRTH RATE, and PLANNED PARENTHOOD—WORLD POPULATION, but no reference to the long, special article "Family Planning" (2,000 words, or a page-and-a-half of text), where the encyclopedia's most informative material regarding birth control is found, including a frank description of the various types of birth control methods and their effectiveness.

Bibliographies

None. The lack of citations to additional sources of information is a serious deficiency in a general, cursory work like *University Desk.*

Graphics

In their preface, the editors note that "we filled the U.D.E. with pictures—pictures that are not only beautiful to look at but also informative. Where a chart, a table or a diagram could tell you at a glance what it takes some other books a thousand words to explain, we included it. . . . We were not simply embellishing an attractive volume, but attempting to break through the communication barrier which encyclopedias often maintain, and so to bring the subjects to life." And, indeed, the encyclopedia is copiously illustrated with some 3,000 appealing and instructive photographs, art reproductions, diagrams, line drawings, and charts—all in full color. The graphics, however, are not always clearly or faithfully reproduced. EXAMPLE: John Trumbull's painting *Surrender of General Burgoyne,* which accompanies the article "Revolutionary War, American" is reproduced in sepia instead of its true colors. In addition, the artist, Trumbull, is not identified, nor is the correct title of the painting given. In other instances, the graphics are not well positioned to complement the printed text. EXAMPLE: The article "Keeshond" is on page 594, whereas a photograph of a keeshond is on page 593. Overall, the graphics enhance *University Desk*'s value as a source of quick reference information, but comparatively speaking the encyclopedia is not as profusely nor creatively illustrated as *The Random House Encyclopedia*, which stands out in this area among the small-volume adult works currently available.

The encyclopedia's map coverage is quite limited. Articles on major continents include full-page political and thematic maps in color, but most countries have only spot maps the size of a postage stamp. The same is true of the U.S. states and Canadian provinces. None of the maps is indexed, nor are their cartographers identified. A few special-purpose maps are included, such as a large full-color representation of the visible side of the moon, which shows the major craters, mountain ranges, and "seas." Among all its competitors in the small-volume adult class, *University Desk* offers the worst map coverage.

Physical Format

University Desk is a Dutton "Sequoia Book," a label that signifies a specially produced book. The red-grained buckram binding with gold lettering is both stoutly constructed and appealing to the eye. A big volume that weighs close to nine pounds, the encyclopedia lies perfectly flat when open. Home purchasers will probably want to keep the book open on a stand or tabletop. Inside, the page layout, varied by colorful illustrations of all sizes, is very inviting. Although small, the print is exceedingly clear and readable. The typefaces used are modern and serviceable. Color appears throughout the book, not only in the many illustrations but also in panels setting off the country and state information profiles. In addition, the 46 special articles are printed on colored backgrounds. A heavy coated paper has been used to achieve the best color reproduction. *University Desk* is a handsomely made book.

Special Features

The encyclopedia is principally comprised of 25,000 brief, specific entries averaging about 80 words apiece. But there are 46 long articles covering some 1,000–2,000 words, or a page or more of text, which treat contemporary subjects in a refreshing and informative fashion. These articles, or special essays, are written by subject specialists and deal with such topics as adaptive radiation, air transportation, astronomy and the black hole phenomenon, biological clocks, modern Canada, the China Mao has created, cities, consumer protection, criminal law, the living Declaration of Independence, ethology, fusion power, aboriginal American Indian culture, paleontology, pollution, the modern American presidency, science fiction, and heart surgery.

Sales Information

University Desk is strictly a trade item—that is, it is sold only in bookstores and other retail outlets that carry books. The volume currently retails for $69.95, the same price as the similar *Random House Encyclopedia*. The *Buying Guide* has been informed, however, that E. P. Dutton & Company, the U.S. publisher, will shortly allow *University Desk* to go out of stock. Whether it eventually will be reprinted or issued in a revised edition is not known at this point. In any event, the encyclopedia most likely will remain available (at least for a time) via independent distributors. In 1980, for instance, it was being sold at the discount price of $11 by Bookthrift, Inc., a remainder house.

Summary

The University Desk Encyclopedia can be quickly summed up in this manner:

Scope: Fair	Accessibility: Fair
Authority: Good	Bibliographies: Poor (none)
Reliability: Fair	Graphics: Good
Recency: Fair	Physical Format: Excellent
Objectivity: Good	Special Features: Few
Clarity: Good	Price: High

To elaborate briefly, *University Desk* is a hefty, attractively produced one-volume encyclopedia for students and adults which originated abroad. An entirely new work first published in 1977, the book is the result of an international collaboration involving the encyclopedic resources of the Dutch firm of Elsevier, the editorial talents of many British and American editors, writers, and consultants, and the financial backing of the New York publisher E. P. Dutton & Company. A specific-entry encyclopedia of some 25,000 very brief articles, supplemented by 46 longer special essays of a page or more on contemporary subjects, *University Desk* lacks an index but does provide numerous cross-references throughout the text which usually—but not always—link related topics and facilitate access to specific information. The encyclopedia's coverage, though broad, lacks depth, often leaving the reader with only a smattering of information. Also on the negative side, *University Desk* is rapidly becoming dated in those areas where knowledge is most volatile, and the work's factual accuracy and attention to editorial detail leave something to be desired.

Comparatively speaking, there are six small-volume adult encyclopedias currently on the market. Among these, *The New Columbia Encyclopedia* and *The Random House Encyclopedia* are *University Desk*'s most formidable competition, along with the older and well-known three-volume *New Lincoln Library Encyclopedia* (formerly *The Lincoln Library of Essential Information*). All four of these small-volume encyclopedias are priced in the same general range ($69.95–$99.98), and each possesses unique strengths and weaknesses. As the raw data indicate, *New Columbia* is the largest small-volume encyclopedia available. On the other hand, *Random House* and *University Desk* are superior in terms of graphics and design. As a general proposition, without taking individual reference tastes and needs into account, the *Buying Guide* believes that *The New Columbia Encyclo-*

pedia and *The Random House Encyclopedia* are the two best all-around small-volume adult encyclopedias on the market today. *The University Desk Encyclopedia,* though clearly written and attractive in appearance, is not large enough to compete successfully with *New Columbia*'s depth of coverage, nor can it match *Random House*'s broad thematic treatment and outstanding use of graphics, nor is it as reliable as either of its main competitors.

Other Critical Opinions

Booklist, September 15, 1978, pp. 249–251. This unsigned review, prepared by the ALA Reference and Subscription Books Review Committee, is critical of practically all aspects of the encyclopedia, including its coverage, graphics, cross-references, and accuracy. In the final analysis, *University Desk* is "not recommended."

Bunge, Charles A. "Current Reference Books," *Wilson Library Bulletin,* September 1977, p. 93. Bunge, a veteran reference book reviewer, gives a lukewarm recommendation to *University Desk,* but points out that *The New Columbia Encyclopedia* "will remain a first choice."

Campbell, John D. *Library Journal,* June 1, 1977, p. 1267. "The chief feature of this encyclopedia," says Campbell, "is the illustrations, lots of them and in high-quality color." He wisely advises prospective purchasers to "look before buying."

Cheney, Frances Neel. *American Reference Books Annual,* 1978, pp. 42–43. This review suggests that the encyclopedia is "convenient to use and well illustrated," but observes that *The Random House Encyclopedia* offers more for the same price.

Choice, April 1979, p. 208. Called a "sumptuous production," the encyclopedia is praised for its appealing format and many illustrations. The unnamed reviewer, however, is critical of *University Desk*'s authority, cross-references, and placement of graphics.

Katz, William A. *Basic Information Sources* (Vol. 1 of *Introduction to Reference Work,* 3rd ed. New York: McGraw-Hill, 1978), p. 168. Katz notes that the encyclopedia's outstanding feature is its 3,000 illustrations: "These illustrations, coupled with numerous charts and diagrams, make it particularly suitable for younger readers and for adults who would rather look than read." For libraries, however, it is a "luxury item."

Sokolov, Raymond A. "Reference Books: The University Desk Encyclopedia," *New York Times Book Review,* October 2, 1977, pp. 15; 18. Sokolov, a novelist and former food editor of the *New York Times,* dismisses *University Desk* as a "jumped-up dictionary with coated paper, color pictures on every page and definitions of slightly greater than dictionary length."

Volume Library

Facts in Brief

Full Title: **The Volume Library: A Modern, Authoritative Reference for Home and School Use.** *Editors:* Thomas Layman, Managing Editor; Christopher T. Hollihan & Paul B. Murry, Senior Editors. *Publisher:* The Southwestern Company, Box 810, Nashville, TN 37202. *Former Titles: Cowles Volume Library* (1968–1969); *Cowles Comprehensive Encyclopedia* (1963–1967). *Edition Reviewed:* 1979 copyright.

Volumes: One. *Pages:* 2,605. *Articles:* 8,500 survey articles in 25 chapters or "volumes." *Words:* 3,500,000. *Illustrations:* 2,000. *Maps:* 150 plus 64-page color atlas. *Index Entries:* 45,000. *Cross-references:* 500. *Contributors:* 250.

User Classification: Adult (Small-volume). *Reader Suitability:* Age 12 through General Adult. *Physical Size:* 9 × 11 in.; 29 cm. *LC:* 78-65736. *Lowest Retail Price:* $86.95.

Purpose and Scope

The Volume Library "is a convenient and comprehensive encyclopedia that covers the major fields of man's knowledge and study" (preface). It is further noted that the encyclopedia is not for specialists but "the average well-informed person—the student, the businessman or woman whose job requires instant access to information, the adult who needs a convenient reference book on his home bookshelf, the parents who want to keep up with the developments and subjects their children are studying in school."

The encyclopedia intends to accomplish these aims by dividing general knowledge into 25 topical chapters, called "volumes." The volumes, which average about 100 pages apiece, are not thematically related but arranged alphabetically by topic. The volumes are Animals, Arts, Biography, Careers, Child Development, Earth Sciences, Economics and Business, Education, Food and Agriculture, Geography, Government and Law, Health, History, Industry and Technology, Language and Grammar, Literature, Mathematics, Philosophy and Religion, Plants, Recreation, Science, Social Science, United States, World, and Atlas. Each volume is subdivided into discrete subjects. EXAMPLE: The volume Arts has these subsections: "Architecture," "Painting," "Sculpture," "Ceramics," "Glass," "Graphic Arts," "Printing," "Music," "Dance," and a two-page bibliography. At the end of the 25 volumes there is an extensive subject index.

As the various chapter headings suggest, *Volume Library* does cover the universe of knowledge in the broadest sense, but the coverage is quite uneven and often very superficial, even for a one-volume work. The encyclopedia's scope is very much U.S.-centered, except in the case of historical references. For instance, the volume Education deals entirely with developments in the United States, except for a brief subsection on the history of education. The natural and technical sciences are accorded the fullest coverage, whereas social issues and most humanities subjects, particularly art and music, receive short shrift. The only mention of the topic *abortion* in the entire book, for instance, occurs in a brief article discussing miscarriages. Information about child development (in Volume 5) is limited to articles on kindergarten methods, educational playthings, and children's literature. There is nothing concerning pediatrics, human growth and maturation, or child care. *Volume Library* almost totally ignores the history and culture of Native Americans. Such subjects as interior decoration and etiquette, which were covered in earlier editions, are no longer mentioned. The history of established fields of study (e.g., mathematics, psychology) are reasonably well covered, considering the book's limited space. Biographical coverage, which accounts for about 10 percent of the total text, is erratic at best, but geographical topics (roughly 20 percent of the text) normally receive adequate attention, except for the U.S. states and Canadian provinces. The states are limited to half a page of text or less, and the provinces receive no coverage at all (they are not even listed in the index).

In those areas that lend themselves to enumeration, *Volume Library* presents much information in chart and tabular form. Economics and Business, for example, provides a number of informative charts, as do Government and Law (e.g., a list of the signers of the Declaration of Independence; presidential cabinets; justices of the U.S. Supreme Court), Health (a chart briefly describing infectious diseases), Industry and Technology (an energy conversion chart), Science (an inventory of manned space flights), and United States (1970 census tabulations for cities of 10,000 or more population). Likewise, the 60-page "College Profile" in Education is in tabular form, in order "to provide as much pertinent factual information on each college as possible within a limited amount of space." In addition, many volumes contain glossaries of specialized terms. Information of this type is the book's greatest asset.

History and Authority

Volume Library, the oldest small-volume encyclopedia of U.S. origin currently on the market, has been around for nearly 70 years. First published in 1911 by the Educators Association and the W. E. Richardson Company as *The Volume Library*, the book was acquired by Cowles Communications, Inc., in 1963 and revised and retitled *Cowles Comprehensive Encyclopedia—The Volume Library*. Later the title was shortened to *Cowles Volume Library*, and when the Southwestern Company acquired the rights in 1970, the work reverted to its original title. A pertinent bit of encyclopedia history is that *Volume Library*'s original editor, Henry Woldmar Ruoff, also compiled an 800-page item entitled the *Standard Dictionary of Facts* (1908–1927), which evidently served as the information base for the first edition of *The Lincoln Library of Essential Information* (1924), a work that greatly resembles *Volume Library* in purpose, scope, arrangement, and format. (Note that *Lincoln Library* recently changed its name to *The New Lincoln Library Encyclopedia.*)

The current edition (1979) lists an editorial staff of five, including the managing editor, Thomas Layman, and senior editors Christopher T. Hoolihan and Paul B. Murry, none of whom is identified beyond his name and title, nor is known in encyclopedia circles. Hoolihan is new to the encyclopedia since 1977, when the *Buying Guide* last evaluated *Volume Library*. Exactly the same list of 11 advisers that appeared in the 1977 edition is given in the current version. The advisers include the noted historian Henry Steele Commager and a well-known librarian, Donald T. Clark. Eight new contributors have been added and three dropped since 1977. Among those added are Roger I. Abrams (professor of law, Case Western Reserve Law School), Thomas W. Dodge (professor of social science, Southern Maine Vocational Technical Institute), Rosalina Rovira (chairman of the Modern Language Department, Texas A & I University), and Luis Jorge Wong (lecturer, Hunter College of the City University of New York). Most of the 250 contributors are academicians or industry representatives. A few are well known (like Carleton Coon, Fred Hechinger, Charlton Laird, and Stewart Udall), but most are not. All contributors are identified by name and academic, business, or government affiliation, but only 75 percent of the articles are signed. The people associated with *Volume Library* bring reasonably good qualifications to the work. Many of these authorities, however, are conservative scholars and business executives, an emphasis which colors the encyclopedia's presentation of material (see "Objectivity").

Reliability

Volume Library has corrected many of the blatant factual errors that plagued it in the past. But because certain portions of the text are out-of-date (see "Recency") or biased (see "Objectivity"), the encyclopedia cannot be considered an entirely reliable source of information. EXAMPLE: The article "Nuclear Chemistry" in Science contains this misleading information: "In recent years, commercial applications of atomic energy have been growing. The nuclear industry has perfected a cycle of operation consisting of mining uranium and thorium ores, chemical processing, fabrication into fuels and other components of nuclear reactors, reprocessing of spent fuel, and disposal of by-product waste. Nuclear reactors are producing electricity that promises, within a few years, to become competitive in cost with conventional power sources in many areas." EXAMPLE: The article "Theory of Government" in Government and Law offers the questionable information that under a Communist form of government "the worker is enslaved."

Recency

The *Buying Guide* found earlier editions of *Volume Library* in 1973 and 1977 to be much out-of-date. Over the past several years, the editors have worked hard to improve the encyclopedia's performance in this area. Evidence of extensive revision in many articles is readily apparent. For instance, *Volume Library* no longer claims that petroleum is "a plentiful resource" as it did in 1973, nor does it suggest that "there is a nationwide shortage of trained librarians, and this shortage is expected to worsen" as it did in 1977. The entire Economics and Business volume has been overhauled from top to bottom within the last few years. The article "Copyright" in the glossary that concludes Government and Law reports on the new U.S. law that took effect in 1978. The 90-page "College Profile" at the end of Education has been completely revised since 1977 and now furnishes a current list of U. S. two-year and four-year institutions.

Nevertheless, despite considerable revision activity, *Volume Library* remains dated in numerous areas, as the Recency Table here indicates. Many other instances of stale or outmoded material can be cited. EXAMPLE: The long article "Psychology and Psychiatry" in the Social Science volume reflects professional attitudes and developments current in the mid-1960s. EXAMPLE: The article "Public Health" in Health informs that "nearly 300,000 persons are admitted to mental hospitals annually" in the United States, and that "this figure is expected to increase by 20,000 each year." Today, of course, both the annual admissions and the trend are down. EXAMPLE: Information on kindergarten methods and educational toys in Child Development is sadly dated. There is no mention of the contemporary day-care concept. EXAMPLE: A discussion of conservation in the glossary accompanying Government and Law concludes with the Civilian Conservation Corps (CCC) of the New Deal, said to be "a new conservation policy." EXAMPLE: The article "Impeachment" in Government and Law notes that Andrew Johnson was the only U.S. president to be impeached, but there is no mention of Richard Nixon, against whom such charges were brought. EXAMPLE: The article "Business and the Computer" in Economics and Business is reasonably current but fails to mention the current trend toward minicomputers and microcomputers.

Volume Library is revised with each new edition, which appears every two to four years. Obviously, the encyclopedia has a long way to go until it achieves an acceptable level of currency, but its present position is no worse than most of the small-volume adult works currently available. Only *The Random House Encyclopedia* is demonstrably more up-to-date than *Volume Library*.

Unlike any of its small-volume competitors, *Volume Library* has an annual supplement entitled the *Volume Library Yearbook*. Similar to most encyclopedia annuals (designed to update multivolume sets), *Volume Library Yearbook* consists of roughly 500 heavily illustrated pages that review the events of the previous year. Unfortunately, the book is completely unrelated to the encyclopedia by cross-references or in any other manner. The yearbook sells for $10.75 to owners of *Volume Library*.

This Recency Table compares selected topics in *Volume Library* with those in other encyclopedias of similar size and intended usership.

Topic	Volume Library	New Columbia	New Lincoln Library	Random House
Afghanistan	Not current	Not current	Not current	Not current
Dinosaurs	Not current	Fairly current	Not current	Very current
Greenland	Not current	Fairly current	Not current	Fairly current
Thomas Jefferson	Not current	Fairly current	Not current	Fairly current
Mass Transportation/Subways	Very current	Fairly current	Not current	Very current
Nuclear Power	Not current	Not current	Not current	Very current
Paris	Not current	Not current	Not current	Fairly current
Sharks	Fairly current	Fairly current	Fairly current	Fairly current
Shock Therapy	Not current	Fairly current	Not current	Fairly current
Suicide	Not current	Not current	Not current*	Fairly current
Tuberculosis	Not current	Fairly current	Not current	Very current
Zimbabwe	Not current	Not current	Fairly current	Fairly current

*Topic not covered in encyclopedia.

Objectivity

The overall tone of *Volume Library* is conservative, not only in terms of its contributors (many of whom are industry representatives; see "History and Authority"), but also because of what is and is not included. Controversial topics are often ignored entirely, such as abortion, birth control, drug abuse, and homosexuality. In some instances, political information either reflects a simplistic notion of modern government or is propagandistic. EXAMPLE: The definition of Communism in the glossary with Government and Law includes this comment: "Communism, of which Soviet Russia is a present-day exponent, aims at world-wide revolution. . . . Today idealogical [sic]differences have produced a serious rift between these two totalitarian regimes, and the monolithic character of international communism has been disrupted for the time being at least." In the same section there is an illustration accompanying "Censorship" that shows piles of mail received by Radio Free Europe; the caption reads: "Behind the Iron Curtain very little outside news is received. Letters to Radio Free Europe arrive daily. All are anonymous, and are identified by code name. Many are answered by supplying information on the air." EXAMPLE: The introduction to the Industry and Technology volume characterizes private enterprise in this way: "Experience indicates that the greatest success occurs in an open society with decentralized control, offering competitive opportunity for independent approaches to most suitable solutions." EXAMPLE: The article "Energy and Power Sources" in Industry and Technology describes nuclear power in completely positive terms, neglecting to mention that there is an ongoing national debate on the subject. But then the author of that article is Philip Sporn, identified as Director and Consultant, American Electric Power Company. It should also be noted that *Volume Library* constantly employs sexist language and graphics; for instance, the article "Sociology" in Social Science informs that "every man is born into a group of men and throughout his life will belong to many groups"; photographs always depict medical doctors as males, nurses as females.

Clarity and Reader Suitability

Most sections of *Volume Library* will be comprehensible to students and adults with high school level reading skills. But both the style and quality of writing are uneven. The article "Sociology" in Social Science, for example, reads like an introductory college text, whereas "Theory of Government" in Government and Law is embarrassingly like a grade school civics lesson: "What do we mean by *many* when we say government is for the benefit of many? Government for the good of all the people is the ideal objective. How can this be secured? By a government that represents all the people!" Instances of sloppy editing are also found with disconcerting frequency. EXAMPLE: The profile of Switzerland in the World volume observes that "neutral Switzerland is not a member of the United Nations." A few paragraphs later the same information is repeated: "In 1946, to maintain is [*sic*] neutrality, Switzerland decided not to join the United Nations." The *Buying Guide* made exactly the same criticism of the 1973 and 1977 editions of *Volume Library*.

Arrangement and Accessibility

As already explained in some detail (see "Purpose and Scope"), *Volume Library* is topically arranged in 25 chapters, or "volumes," which are in turn subdivided into discrete sections or articles. There is a general index at the back of the book. The editors justify the topical arrangement by noting in the preface that "the entries are not fragmented and arranged alphabetically, as in large multivolume encyclopedias. Rather, all the information about a broad topic—for instance, government or business or plants—is covered in one place." The intention to avoid fragmentation and duplication of knowledge is commendable, but in practice the encyclopedia sometimes scatters information on the same topic in several or more different places. Moreover, the same information may be repeated in different volumes. EXAMPLE: The earth's atmosphere and its various layers (troposhere, stratosphere, ozonosphere, and ionosphere) are described in the article "Meteorology" in the Earth Sciences volume and again in "Physical Geography" in the Geography volume. Often the language used is quite similar in both places; for example, in one article the troposphere "is characterized by a decrease in temperature with each increase in altitude" and in the other "the identifying characteristic of the troposphere is the decrease in temperature with altitude." No quality small-volume encyclopedia can afford to indulge in redundancy of this kind.

Because *Volume Library* is topically organized, and because it contains very few cross-references (only about 500 in the entire book), the general index is essential to locate specific references. Happily, the computer-produced index is substantial, comprising over 45,000 entries in nearly 150 pages. Furthermore, the index is analytical in nature. EXAMPLE: The index entry "Paris" has 24 subentries, such as "Arc de Triomphe," "Bastille," "Louvre," "medieval art," "medieval schools," "Sorbonne," and "subway." But the index is far from perfect and, as a result, finding specific information in the encyclopedia is sometimes quite frustrating. EXAMPLE: The index provides seven references for the entry "Federal Communications Commission," but only one (the third) leads to substantive treatment of the agency, the others merely referring to articles where the FCC is cursorily mentioned. EXAMPLE: The index entry "Mental Institutions" refers the reader to the article "Psychology and Psychiatry" in the Social Science volume, where there is really no substantive information on the subject, but not to "Public Health" in Health where there is at least some statistical material. EXAMPLE: The article "Psychology and Psychiatry" notes the use of shock therapy in some cases of schizophrenia, but there are no index entries under "Shock Therapy," "Electroshock Therapy," or "Electroconvulsive Therapy." *Volume Library* is akin to a vast textbook of general knowledge, and as such it does not always succeed in making its contents readily accessible to users. In this regard, the encyclopedia suffers from the same difficulty as *The New Lincoln Library Encyclopedia,* which has a very similar arrangement.

Bibliographies

Lengthy bibliographies normally appear at the end of each chapter, or volume. For instance, the list of further readings that accompanies the History volume comprises almost 200 entries. As a general rule, the bibliographies are quite dated. EXAMPLE: The short list of six titles at the end of Child Development contains nothing more recent than 1963. EXAMPLE: Industry and Technology, an area of knowledge that changes rapidly, has a bibliography in which no title is newer than 1966. One entry, "ABC's of Computers," was published in 1961. All bibliographies in *Volume Library* are limited to print materials.

Graphics

Many of the encyclopedia's illustrations are dark and drab. Black-and-white photographs, line drawings, and charts predominate. Some are vintage 1950 or thereabouts. Occasionally color plates appear, seemingly more out of duty than for any serious reference purpose. EXAMPLE: The Food and Agriculture volume contains no color illustrations (even a photograph of several mink captioned "Today, a good brown pelt may bring $75; a pastel mutation as much as $125" is in black-and-white), where Recreation sports eight pages of glossy but blurry color photos of the postcard variety, courtesy of various state and federal tourist departments. EXAMPLE: Cézanne's famous painting *The Card Players* is reproduced in the section on twentieth-century art. The reproduction, captioned "Cézanne reworked impressionism's atmospheric light and color to create dynamic relationships between all connected elements of the picture," is in black-and-white.

A few black-and-white special-purpose maps of indifferent quality appear in such volumes as Earth Sciences, Economics and Business, and History. Very simple spot maps, again in black-and-white, are found in the World volume accompanying the articles on nations. Volume 25, however, comprises a 64-page color world atlas prepared by Rand McNally & Company. Drawn to scale, the maps show major political features and are current as of the late 1970s. The atlas is of good quality and sufficiently detailed for normal student use. Each map in the atlas has its own index, but the encyclopedia's general index furnishes references to the maps of continents, countries, and U. S. states.

Physical Format

Volume Library is durably bound in a good-looking tan buckram material called Scottek with gold lettering on the cover and spine. The book lies flat when open, but it is so tightly bound that the gutters, or inside margins, are practically nonexistent, thus making the inner columns of type physically difficult to read. The three-column page layout is uninspired, although the print is quite legible. Stiff paper covers with colorful illustrations separate the various chapters, or volumes, which are thumb-indexed. The lightweight paper is of reasonably good quality. *Volume Library* weighs almost ten pounds and will most likely require a stand or tabletop for convenient consultation.

Special Features

Many of the encyclopedia's topical volumes include lists of specialized terminology, such as a dictionary of earth science terms. Although these glossaries are sometimes quite dated and are not intended to be comprehensive, they are a useful aid for the nonspecialist. Otherwise, *Volume Library* offers no special features of note.

Sales Information

Volume Library is sold in-home by the publisher and authorized independent distributors, as well as in bookstores and similar retail outlets. The current retail price is $86.95, plus a small charge for shipping and handling. No discount is offered to schools and libraries. Interested consumers may order *Volume Library* through a local bookstore or directly from the publisher. As already noted (see "Recency"), the publisher also sells an annual supplement to the encyclopedia entitled the *Volume Library Yearbook,* which retails for $10.75.

Summary

The Volume Library can be quickly summed up in this manner:

Scope: Fair	Accessibility: Fair
Authority: Fair	Bibliographies: Poor
Reliability: Poor	Graphics: Poor
Recency: Fair	Physical Format: Fair
Objectivity: Poor	Special Features: Few
Clarity: Fair	Price: High

To elaborate briefly, *Volume Library* is a one-volume work that first appeared about 70 years ago. Topically organized with much material presented in tabular form, the encyclopedia stresses the natural and particularly the technical sciences. There are, however, many gaps in coverage, and in politically sensitive areas a conservative bias is apparent. Overall, the quality of *Volume Library* is quite uneven, as is its writing style. In too many cases, the book is out-of-date and sloppily edited, lacks objectivity, and hence is unreliable. Considering that there are much better works available for about the same money (or less), *Volume Library* is overpriced.

Comparatively speaking, there are six small-volume adult encyclopedias currently on the U. S. market. Among these, *The New Columbia Encyclopedia* and *The Random House Encyclopedia* are *Volume Library*'s most formidable competition, along with *The New Lincoln Library Encyclopedia* (formerly *The Lincoln Library of Essential Information*), which closely resembles *Volume Library* in terms of purpose, scope, arrangement, format, and quality. All of these encyclopedias are priced in the same general range ($69.95–$99.98), and each possesses unique strengths and weaknesses. As a general proposition, without taking individual reference tastes and needs into account, the *Buying Guide* believes that *The New Columbia Encyclopedia* and *The Random House Encyclopedia* are the best small-volume adult encyclopedias on the market today. *Volume Library*, on the other hand, has too many limitations to justify its price.

Other Critical Opinions

Booklist, January 1, 1979, pp. 771–772. Part of a series of reviews by the ALA Reference and Subscription Books Review Committee (RSBRC) entitled "Encyclopedias: A Survey and Buying Guide," this unsigned evaluation covers the 1974 edition of *Volume Library.* Why the 1974 edition was reviewed in 1979 is not explained, but since the encyclopedia changed its contents significantly between those dates, this review is invalid. In its last regular review of *Volume Library* (*Booklist,* September 15, 1975, pp. 195–197), RSBRC found the encyclopedia to be inaccurate, uneven, and out-of-date—and "not recommended."

V. MULTIVOLUME YOUNG ADULT ENCYCLOPEDIAS

Compton's Encyclopedia

Facts in Brief

Full Title: **Compton's Encyclopedia and Fact-Index.** *Editors:* Audrey Mitchell, Managing Editor; Robert Rauch, Associate Editor. *Publisher:* F. E. Compton Company (a division of Encyclopaedia Britannica, Inc.), 425 N. Michigan Ave., Chicago, IL 60611. *Distributor to Schools & Libraries:* Encyclopaedia Britannica Educational Corporation, 425 N. Michigan Ave., Chicago, IL 60611. *Former Title: Compton's Pictured Encyclopedia. Edition Reviewed:* 1980 copyright.

Volumes: 26. *Pages:* 11,100. *Articles:* 45,000 (including 30,000 short entries in the Fact-Index). *Words:* 8,600,000. *Illustrations:* 28,500. *Maps:* 2,000. *Index Entries:* 200,000. *Cross-references:* 40,800. *Contributors:* 475.

User Classification: Young Adult (Multivolume). *Reader Suitability:* Age 9 through 18. *Physical Size:* 7 ¾ × 10 ¼ in.; 26 cm. *LC:* 78–67841. *ISBN:* 0–85229–350–X. *Lowest Retail Price:* $419; to schools & libraries $319.

Purpose and Scope

Compton's Encyclopedia and Fact-Index is a curriculum-oriented general encyclopedia for young people from upper elementary to high school, as well as all-purpose family use. According to the preface, *Compton's* continues to be guided by the statement of purpose that accompanied the first edition in 1922: "To inspire ambition, to stimulate the imagination, to provide the inquiring mind with accurate information told in an interesting style, and thus lead into broader fields of knowledge." An effort has been made, we are told, to maintain the encyclopedia as "an innovative, forward-looking reference work for young people." Like its major competitors (namely, *The World Book Encyclopedia* and *Merit Students Encyclopedia*), *Compton's* stresses those subjects currently taught in U. S. and Canadian schools, although many articles on practical topics like fire prevention and furniture-making will also interest adult readers.

The bulk of the encyclopedia's coverage is contained in nearly 15,000 broad-entry articles that range in length from less than half a page (e.g., "Dinosaur") to three pages ("Afghanistan") to 27 pages ("Motion Pictures") to 40 pages ("Birds") to 50 pages ("Painting") to 110 pages ("United States"). These broad entries are complemented by approximately 30,000 very brief specific-entry articles called "fact entries." Located in the back of each volume, these short dictionary-style entries form part of *Compton's* useful Fact-Index, an innovative device that not only provides quick reference information but serves as an exhaustive index to the material in the main text. For instance, the Fact-Index contains a brief entry entitled "Abortion." The term is concisely defined, and then the reader is referred to the article "Birth Control" in the main portion of the set, as well as three other articles ("Japan"; "United States History"; "Women and Women's Rights"). The Fact-Index and how it functions is fully explained under "Arrangement and Accessibility" in this review.

Within the Encyclopaedia Britannica, Inc., family of encyclopedias, *Compton's* stands between *The New Encyclopaedia Britannica,* designed for adults, and the *Britannica Junior,* a set specifically aimed at elementary school students. The baby of the family is *Compton's Precyclopedia,* a set for very young readers. Thus *Compton's* is a middle-sized encyclopedia with no pretensions to comprehensive coverage. But within its scope, the set provides a quite remarkable range and depth of coverage. Only the slightly larger *World Book Encyclopedia* offers the reader more in the young adult category. All knowledge areas receive substantial attention. The physical and biological sciences, however, are especially well covered, as such substantive articles as "Aerospace Medicine," "Biochemistry," "Bioengineering," "Biological Clocks," "Bionics," "Biophysics," "Calculus," "Ecology," "Fractions," "Frog," "Genetics," "Lasers and Masers," "Lens," "Light," "Magnets and Magnetism," "Mechanics," "Percentage," "Petroleum Technology," "Relativity," "Solar System," "Solids," "Solid State Physics," "Sound," and "Universe" attest. Famous people receive adequate coverage and, like all sets in the young adult category, important places such as countries and states are accorded lengthy articles with maps, many illustrations, and information digests. Indeed, the profiles of U. S. states and Canadian provinces are outstanding features of *Compton's.* The emphasis throughout is naturally on the United States and Canada. For instance, Chinese literature receives only several paragraphs in the article "China," whereas Canadian literature has its own article of more than six pages. Significant place-names of the world are satisfactorily covered, however, as are international aspects of such topics as atomic energy, the family, flags, language, libraries, literature, motion pictures, opera, transportation, women's rights, and general historical subjects. Material about particular careers and colleges and universities is provided by *Compton's,* but not as abundantly as in *Merit Students Encyclopedia.* Finally, some contemporary social issues receive short shrift or are ignored entirely, such as cults (like the People's Temple and Hare Krishna), homosexuality, and suicide.

History and Authority

Compton's first appeared in 1922 as *Compton's Pictured Encyclopedia,* a profusely illustrated eight-volume set for young people. It was published by the F. E. Compton Company and, as far as is known, was not based on any existing encyclopedia. By 1932, the set had expanded to 15 volumes. In 1961, Encyclopaedia Britannica acquired the set, which was increased to 24 volumes in 1968, reduced to 22 in 1972, and again enlarged in 1974, this time to its present size of 26 volumes. The word "pictured" was dropped from the title in 1969, although this signified no change in editorial policy. As in the past, *Compton's* is the most heavily illustrated encyclopedia in its class.

Compton's history is distinguished by a number of "firsts." It was, for instance, the first encyclopedia to have an illustrated index. According to Louis Shores, a noted reference authority and encyclopedia editor, it was also the first encyclopedia to include reproductions of color photographs. *Compton's* also pioneered the Fact-Index approach (see "Purpose and Scope"). In short, the name *Compton's* is synonymous with progressive and innovative encyclopedia-making.

The 1980 edition of *Compton's* lists a relatively small editorial staff of 24, down from 65 in 1977 (when the *Buying Guide* last reviewed the encyclopedia). None of the staff is identified beyond name and title, nor are any of its members well known within the reference book community. A list of 475 editorial consultants, contributors, and artists found in Volume 1 includes many distinguished librarians (Lester Asheim, Augusta Baker, Leon Carnovsky, David Clift, Richard Dougherty, to name a few), some important educators and scholars (e.g., Carl Carmer, Carleton Coon, Vine Deloria, Milton Mayer, Allen Nevins, Wilbur Schramm, Carl Van Doren, T. Harry Williams), and a sprinkling of non-Western authorities (e.g., Kwang-rin Lee, professor of history, Sogang University, Korea). Interestingly, this list has not changed at all since 1977. As might be expected, a large number of the consultants and contributors are now deceased or retired. *Compton's* continues to be a reasonably authoritative encyclopedia, but its much reduced editorial staff and lack of new contributors are not encouraging signs for the future. As explained elsewhere in the *Buying Guide* (see "Selling Encyclopedias" in Part I), often a sharp reduction in staff signals a decline in an encyclopedia's sales, which in turn means there is less money the following year for maintenance, which leads to further reductions in staff, and so on until the encyclopedia finally expires. *Compton's* gives every appearance of being on this sort of downward slide.

Reliability

Compton's is normally a reliable encyclopedia. Although most of the articles are not signed, including the longer ones, all have been edited by staff editors to ensure a responsible degree of accuracy as well as conformity to the encyclopedia's graded style (see "Clarity and Reader Suitability"). In 1971, however, *Compton's* began including the names of contributors and consultants at the beginning of the articles they drafted. EXAMPLE: The article "Bionics" contains the following boxed information: "This article was contributed by Jack E. Steele, bionicist-physician, coiner of the word *bionics*, and formerly Assistant Chief, Mathematics and Analysis Branch, Aerospace Medical Research Laboratories, Wright-Patterson Air Force Base, Ohio. The consultant for the article was Hans L. Oestreicher, Chief, Mathematics and Analysis Branch, Aerospace Medical Research

Laboratories, Wright-Patterson Air Force Base." This practice enhances the set's authority and helps maintain a high level of reliability. It must be noted, however, that few new articles have been added during the past decade, and that *Compton's* reliability is obviously not good in those articles that are not up-to-date, such as "Iran" (see the next section, "Recency," for more on this point).

Recency

Until recent times, *Compton's* was one of the most up-to-date and consistently revised encyclopedias in the young adult category. The set is still continuously revised on an annual basis, the revision program including both spot revision (updating population figures, adding death dates, and the like) and area revision (reviewing and rewriting numerous articles in a broad subject area, such as biology or medicine). During the past ten or so years, however, the pace of the revision effort has slowed noticeably. In 1980, for instance, less than 100 of the encyclopedia's 15,000 main articles were updated. Some material is quite current; for instance, the article "Copyright and Trademarks" describes the new U. S. copyright law, which became effective in 1978; the article "Atomic Energy Commission" in the Fact-Index reports that the commission was abolished in 1974 and its "functions transferred to Energy Research and Development Administration (now part of Department of Energy) and to Nuclear Regulatory Commission." But many other articles are either stale or badly dated. EXAMPLE: The article "Child Development " reflects the state of knowledge on the subject as of the 1950s. Photographs accompanying the article are likewise a generation out-of-date. EXAMPLE: "Indians, American" contains nothing on the militant Native American civil rights protests of the 1970s. EXAMPLE: "Street Railways" reads and looks like something out of an old magazine or history book. Obviously, the article has not been touched in years. EXAMPLE: "Iran" concludes on this reassuring note: "The economic and land-reform programs of the shah, whose official coronation took place in 1967, helped make Iran's economic growth rate one of the highest in the world in 1968." This sentence represents the most current information in the article.

As noted previously (see "History and Authority"), *Compton's* is suffering from editorial cutbacks and lack of new contributors. As a result, the encyclopedia's present state of recency is not good and is growing worse with each passing year. Comparatively speaking, *Compton's* is no longer competitive in this area with *Merit Students Encyclopedia* and *The World Book Encyclopedia,* both of which are well-maintained sets.

The publisher offers two annual supplements intended to help keep the encyclopedia current, *Compton's Yearbook* and the more specialized *Yearbook of Science and the Future.* Both are authoritative and handsomely illustrated works available to *Compton's* owners at fair prices. *Compton's Yearbook* provides *See* references to the encyclopedia, thus enhancing the volume's usefulness as an updating device. But in the final analysis, the yearbooks are at best of peripheral value as a means for keeping the set current.

This Recency Table compares selected topics in *Compton's* with those in other encyclopedias of similar size and intended usership.

Topic	Compton's	Encyclopedia International	Merit Students	World Book
Afghanistan	Fairly current	Fairly current	Very current	Very current
Dinosaurs	Fairly current	Not current	Very current	Very current
Greenland	Not current	Not current	Not current	Very current
Thomas Jefferson	Fairly current	Fairly current	Fairly current	Fairly current
Mass Transportation/Subways	Not current	Fairly current	Fairly current	Very current
Nuclear Power	Not current	Not current	Fairly current	Very current
Paris	Fairly current	Not current	Very current	Very current
Sharks	Not current	Fairly current	Fairly current	Very current
Shock Therapy	Not current	Not current	Fairly current	Very current
Suicide	Not current	Not current	Very current	Fairly current
Tuberculosis	Not current	Not current	Very current	Very current
Zimbabwe	Very current	Fairly current	Very current	Very current

Objectivity

In most instances, *Compton's* presents its material in a straightforward, impartial manner. Articles dealing with such sensitive or polemical topics as abortion, birth control, drugs and drug abuse, and race are generally free from bias or moralizing judgments. EXAMPLE: About marijuana, the encyclopedia states that "although the exhilarating effects of marijuana have been known since A.D. 200, very little reliable information about its long-term physical effects is available. It is not physically addictive. Susceptible people have been known to develop a psychological dependence on it, and there are reports that it impairs social functioning."

Some touchy subject matter, however, is entirely ignored. EXAMPLE: All a user of *Compton's* will learn about fluoridation is that "a correctly regulated amount of fluorides in water has been shown to be safe and to reduce dental decay in children." There is no indication that the subject is, or has been, fraught with controversy for many years. The encyclopedia also occasionally engages in subtle political bias, promoting a nationalistic attitude toward the United States and Western democracies while concurrently disparaging other systems. EXAMPLE: "Communism" states that "communists now rule not only Russia but vast mainland China and smaller countries, including Cuba. They have never come to power by democratic elections. It has always been by force. Once in power, they begin to take over all the factories, mines, and farms. Soon all the people are working for the government. This inevitably leads to loss of freedom." The whole article is written in this vein, and, of course, the assertion that a communist government has never achieved power via democratic elections is no longer accurate.

Nonetheless, *Compton's* is overall a fair and impartial reference source. One of its strong points, for instance, is its treatment of women. In her excellent article "Lost Herstory," which appeared in *Library Journal* (January 15, 1973), Linda Kraft analyzed the question of sexist bias in a number of children's and young adult sets. She found that *The World Book Encyclopedia* and especially *Compton's* provided the fullest and least biased treatment of women, both from the historical and contemporary points of view. For instance, she writes, "The description of the women's struggle ends with the passage of the 19th Amendment in most of the articles. Again, only *Compton's* mentions the Equal Rights Amendment and devotes attention to the scope and variety of the women's liberation movement in the main context of the article. Most of the others [*Britannica Junior, Merit Students Encyclopedia,* and *The New Book of Knowledge*] fail to note the passage of post-19th Amendment legislation which has affected the status of women."

Clarity and Reader Suitability

Like the other multivolume encyclopedias in the young adult class, *Compton's* is written in pyramid style—that is, the articles begin with the easiest or most elementary material and then gradually progress to the more difficult or complex. EXAMPLE: The article "Dog" begins: "The dog is one of the most popular pets in the world. It ordinarily remains loyal to a considerate master, and because of this the dog has been called man's best friend. Class distinctions between people have no part in a dog's life. It can be a faithful companion to either rich or poor." Toward the end of the article, however, the text becomes more sophisticated as well as more detailed: "Authorities agree that the dog was the first of man's domesticated animals. How and when this domestication took place, however, remains unknown. A 50,000-year-old cave painting in Europe seems to show a doglike animal hunting with man. But most experts believe the dog was domesticated only within the last 15,000 years. Moreover, fossil remains that would substantiate the presence of dogs with humans have not yet been unearthed for periods earlier than 10,000 B.C."

Advertising for *Compton's* stresses the set's lively writing style. One recent advertisement proclaims, "If you're getting an encyclopedia for *me* . . . please make it COMPTON'S, the one that's fun to read, too!" and another says the encyclopedia "is read more like a newspaper or magazine than a tome of knowledge." With few exceptions, these claims are true. The reader is normally kept interested by a skillful mixture of attention-getting examples, entertaining anecdotes, colorful adjectives, varied sentence structure, and carefully chosen graphics. A typical example is found in the article "Reptiles": "Imagine a reptile longer than a railroad car, or one so tall it could poke its nose into a third-story window. Imagine also teeth six inches long set in a yawning mouth half as large as a house door. Fortunately, creatures like these are not alive today. They did live long ago, however, and they are known as dinosaurs." New or potentially difficult terms, particularly technical ones, are usually defined in context, and when appropriate, the articles are written to grade level. Ordinarily, *Compton's* will be comprehensible to students and adults reading at the fifth grade level and up.

Arrangement and Accessibility

Compton's is arranged alphabetically, letter-by-letter ("Indiana" precedes "Indian Ocean"). As already noted (see "Purpose and Scope"), the main encyclopedia set contains approximately 15,000 articles, of which 4,000-plus are lengthy, well-developed treatments of such broad topics as algebra, U.S. literature, the brain, Canadian history, child development, fish, genetics, money, rubber, water, and women's rights. Specific aspects of a topic are covered under appropriate subheadings. EXAMPLE: The article "Water" includes such subtopics as "Water in Man's Daily Life," "How Water Originated," "The Composition and Three Physical States of Water," "The Density and Weight of Water," "How Water Freezes and Expands," "How Water Evaporates and Boils," and "The Water Cycle." Substantial articles are also devoted to famous people like the American presidents and other national leaders, as well as the 50 U.S. states, Canadian provinces, and major countries of the world. These articles are heavily illustrated and often include study guides, lists of technical terms, fact summaries, time-line charts, and the like.

Specific-entry information is found in the Fact-Index, an innovative device of some 200,000 entries that serves as both an analytical index to the set and a source of ready-reference facts about people, places, animals, plants, events, and things not included in the main A-to-Z sequence. There are over 30,000 so-called fact entries, which are normally very brief, averaging only nine or ten lines apiece. So that readers will not forget to consult the Fact-Index, these fact entries (for example, "Goatfish"; "Gobelin Tapestries"; "Goblins"; "Goddard College"; "Godden, Rumer"; "Godfrey, Arthur") are listed in the set's main alphabetical sequence with the cross-reference notation "These Articles are in the Fact-Index." The Fact-Index likewise provides cross-references to the main articles. It also contains and indexes illustrations.

In the 1980 edition (under review here), a portion of the Fact-Index appears at the end of each volume, covering that part of the alphabet corresponding with the volume itself. Volume 14, for instance, covers the letters K and L; the Fact-Index at the back of that volume accordingly contains all references and cross-references beginning with the letters K and L, although many of the referrals are to other volumes. EXAMPLE: The entry "Ligament" is as follows: "*Ligament* (from Latin *ligare*, 'to bind'), a tough, fibrous band which connects bones or supports viscera S-210." The term is thus defined, and the reader is also referred to the article "Skeleton" (in the S volume on page 210), which contains more information about ligaments under the subheading "Bone Movement Varies." Beginning in 1981, however, the Fact-Index will be cumulated into a single volume at the end of the encyclopedia. This move should be welcomed by most users, as a single index is obviously easier to consult than 26 separate indexes (see "Physical Format" for more on this change).

The Fact-Index, whether cumulated into a single volume or in parts, not only serves as a very detailed index to *Compton's* but also includes much thumbnail information not included in the main text. The Fact-Index is not difficult to master, *if* the user is at home with such devices. Younger users may well find the Fact-Index confusing or beyond their capabilities, as might some older students. The problem is compounded by a rather complicated symbol system that denotes subentries and sub-subentries in the index. Little black squares signify the division "of a main entry into the alphabetically arranged first-level subentries"; little white squares indicate the division "of a first-level subentry into alphabetically arranged second-level subentries"; and little white triangles represent the division "of a second-level subentry into alphabetically arranged third-level subentries." The system is logical, analytical, and effective, but inhibiting.

In the final analysis, *Compton's* is an extremely well-organized encyclopedia. Its material is equally accessible to those seeking an overview of a broad subject and those looking for a quite specific piece of information. The Fact-Index is an excellent finding device as well as a source of ready-reference information. But, fine as it is, the Fact-Index is a rather sophisticated tool, and young users especially might find it a bit overwhelming.

Bibliographies

Nearly 400 articles append bibliographies, or lists of materials that provide additional information on a particular subject. The lists are usually graded for younger readers and advanced students. In some cases, the bibliographies include films. In all instances noted by the *Buying Guide*, however, the films are products of Encyclopaedia Britannica Educational Corporation, which raises questions about just how scrupulously the bibliographies are prepared. Another problem with the bibliographies, which rarely exceed a dozen unannotated entries, is that they are not always up-to-date. The articles "Atom," "Atomic Energy," and "Atomic Theory," for example, have a combined bibliography of 18 items, of which half were published prior to 1970. How useful a book entitled *Atomic Energy* published in 1961 will be to readers of *Compton's* is questionable. Another criticism is that many articles that lack bibliographies clearly should have them. EXAMPLE: "Novel" does not furnish a single suggestion for further reading, although this topic, perhaps more than most, lends itself to independent study. The bibliographies in *Compton's* are certainly better than none at all, but many are becoming dated and in need of revision. Furthermore, there are not enough of them.

Graphics

From the beginning, *Compton's* has excelled in the graphics area, in terms both of quality and quantity. Indeed, the set was called *Compton's Pictured Encyclopedia* until 1968, and it pioneered the reproduction of color photographs. At the present time, practically every page in the encyclopedia contains graphic aids of one kind or another, including photographs, instructional diagrams, charts, graphs, and maps. Most are of fine quality, and about 20 percent are in full color, with the large majority of others reproduced in either two color or half-tone. Some 50 art contributors are noted in the front matter of the first volume. Like its main competitors (*Merit Students Encyclopedia* and *The World Book Encyclopedia*), *Compton's* provides index references to all illustrations and maps. The only negative criticism of *Compton's* in the area of graphics is that some photographs are badly dated (see "Recency" for examples).

The maps, most by C. S. Hammond Company, are updated frequently. They range from political and physical to special-purpose maps that indicate industrial development, weather patterns, land use, etc. Almost without exception, the maps are clear and easy to use. Kilometers are usually indicated as well as miles.

Physical Format

Compton's is a very attractive, well-designed encyclopedia. It boasts outstanding page layout, judicious use of topical headings that assist scanning, and a bold, readable typeface. The set is published in two bindings designed for different markets. The two-piece orange and brown Lexotone binding with gold lettering is sold exclusively to schools and libraries. For the home and international market, there is a less expensive Kivar binding. Both bindings appear to be durable. As might be expected, the volumes lie flat when open, the paper is of good quality, and there are guide words at the top of each page.

When possible, each volume contains all of one letter of the alphabet or a combination of letters (for instance, W–Z). Called the unit-letter arrangement, this was another *Compton's* "first." In some cases, however, more than one volume is required for a particular letter (e.g., the letter F comprises Volumes 9 and 10). Paging in such instances is consecutive—page F-225 being in Volume 9 and page F-250 in Volume 10. What is sometimes frustrating is a reference in the Fact-Index to, say, page F-239. Is it in Volume 9 or Volume 10? This is a petty annoyance, but it could be readily corrected by including pagination on the spine of those volumes with split letters. In fact, this was done until 1974, when it was inexplicably discontinued.

In 1981, the encyclopedia's format will change slightly. The first three volumes, which currently comprise the letter A, will be compressed into two volumes, and Volume 26, currently W–Z, will become a master index, or cumulated Fact-Index (see "Arrangement and Accessibility"). Each of the first 25 volumes will continue to have a portion of the Fact-

Index at the back; for instance, Volume 25 will cover the letters W–Z for both main articles and Fact-Index entries.

Special Features

As noted throughout this review, *Compton's* has pioneered a number of new editorial techniques and special features during its nearly 60 years of existence. Its editors have been responsible not only for creating the unique Fact-Index (now imitated by some sets, for instance *The New Book of Knowledge*), but for the first reproduction of color photographs, the introduction of the unit-letter system, and a number of other design features involving creative layout of material.

True to its distinguished heritage, the present *Compton's* provides several noteworthy special features, all designed to enhance the set's value and appeal as a general reference source. Substantial study guides—called Reference-Outlines—accompany 80 core articles, such as "Ancient History," "Botany," "Economics," "India," and "Psychology." These guides cite references to appropriate material in various volumes of the encyclopedia. Another interesting and useful feature is a browsing device at the beginning of each book. Entitled "Here and There in Volume . . . ," it loosely organizes the volume's contents into reader-interest topics. Following "Here and There" is a feature called "Exploring Compton's—Volume . . . ," which offers a page of intriguing questions with references to where the answers can be found. The set also makes generous use of information boxes highlighting important facts. Finally, following in the footsteps of its leading competitors (*Merit Students Encyclopedia* and *The World Book Encyclopedia*), *Compton's* will begin adding metric equivalents throughout the set in 1981.

Sales Information

Some years ago, *Business Week* (March 2, 1974, p. 22) reported that the door-to-door sales force for *Compton's* had been disbanded because of the profit squeeze then affecting Encyclopedia Britannica, Inc. (the owner of *Compton's*), and that *Compton's* "was converted to a mail-order operation last fall." This information is no longer correct. In recent years, the encyclopedia has been sold in-home by Britannica's professional sales force, as well as to schools and libraries by Encyclopaedia Britannica Educational Corporation (a sister company). The Kivar binding (see "Physical Format") is available to retail customers at $419. This price represents only a very small increase (from $379) since 1977. The tougher Lexotone binding is sold to educational institutions at the discount price of $319 delivered (or $294 per set when two or more sets are ordered at the same time). Various Britannica products are often offered as optional purchases, including *Compton's Yearbook* (see "Recency"), which sells for $12.95, the *Yearbook of Science and the Future* (also $12.95), and *Compton's Precyclopedia,* a 16-volume set for beginning readers (see Part VI of the *Buying Guide* for a review of the *Precyclopedia*). A Library Research Service may also be offered.

Summary

Compton's Encyclopedia can be quickly summed up in this manner:

Scope: Good
Authority: Fair
Reliability: Good
Recency: Poor
Objectivity: Good
Clarity: Excellent

Accessibility: Excellent
Bibliographies: Fair
Graphics: Excellent
Physical Format: Excellent
Special Features: Many
Price: Reasonable

To elaborate briefly, *Compton's* is one of the best-known names among English-language encyclopedias. The set has long been admired for its innovative visual design techniques, its many first-rate illustrations and maps, its comprehensive and analytical Fact-Index (an inventive device pioneered by *Compton's* that provides both quick reference information and detailed access to the set's contents), its impressive range and depth of coverage in many areas of knowledge (particularly scientific subjects), and its lively writing style and graded readability. Unfortunately, *Compton's* is an encyclopedia in decline. In recent years, editorial cutbacks and lack of new contributors have jeopardized the encyclopedia's reputation as a work of consistently high quality. The set's slide into mediocrity is most noticeable in the area of up-to-dateness. Even some of the fine graphics are sadly dated. Another negative criticism, albeit a smaller one, is the tendency of *Compton's* to avoid controversial subject matter. Also, again occasionally, there is evidence of political bias and nationalistic rhetoric. It is also possible that the Fact-Index, a generally excellent finding device, will be too sophisticated for younger users, as well as some older ones. Finally, too many important articles lack bibliographies, and when bibliographies do appear they are often not current.

Comparatively speaking, *Compton's* competes directly with three other encyclopedias in the multivolume young adult class, namely *Encyclopedia International, Merit Students Encyclopedia,* and *The World Book Encyclopedia.* Each of these encyclopedias is aimed at roughly the same audience, each provides balanced coverage geared to the North American school curriculum, and each is authoritative and useful in its way. *The World Book Encyclopedia,* however, stands out from the rest as a consistently superior work available at a comparatively modest price. *Merit Students Encyclopedia,* a very well-maintained set, has supplanted *Compton's* as the chief challenger to *World Book* for dominance in its class. *Compton's,* once the preeminent encyclopedia in the young adult group, has been living on its reputation and little else for too many years. It is only preferable when compared with *Encyclopedia International,* a drab set with little to offer the discerning consumer.

Other Critical Opinions

Booklist, December 15, 1978, pp. 708–709. Part of a series of reviews by the ALA Reference and Subscription Books Review Committee (RSBRC) entitled "Encyclopedias: A Survey and Buying Guide," this unsigned evaluation of *Compton's* (1975 copyright) offers few negative criticisms and no final conclusions. In its last regular review of *Compton's* (*Booklist,* January 1, 1975, pp. 466–467), RSBRC "recommended" the encyclopedia for both home and library purchase.

Katz, William A. *Basic Information Sources* (Vol. 1 of *Introduction to Reference Work,* 3rd ed. New York: McGraw-Hill, 1978), pp. 159–161. Katz, a highly respected authority on general reference works, comparatively reviews *Compton's, Merit Students Encyclopedia,* and *The World Book Encyclopedia,* the three leading sets for young adults. Katz calls *Compton's* "a good second" choice to *World Book.*

Wynkoop, Sally. *American Reference Books Annual,* 1975, pp. 32–33. A generally favorable review that provides little by way of comparative analysis.

Encyclopedia International

Facts in Brief

Full Title: **Encyclopedia International.** *Editors:* Edward Humphrey, Editor in Chief; Bernard S. Cayne, Editorial Director. *Publisher:* Lexicon Publications, Inc. (a subsidiary of Grolier, Inc.), Sherman Turnpike, Danbury, CT 06816. *Alternate Titles: New Age Encyclopedia; Webster's New Age Encyclopedia. Edition Reviewed:* 1980 copyright.

Volumes: 20. *Pages:* 11,935. *Articles:* 29,830. *Words:* 9,500,000. *Illustrations:* 12,780. *Maps:* 867. *Index Entries:* 120,000. *Cross-references:* 15,000. *Contributors:* 2,000.

User Classification: Young Adult (Multivolume). *Reader Suitability:* Age 9 through 18. *Physical Size:* 8 × 10¼ in.; 26 cm. *LC:* 79-67180. *ISBN:* 0-7172-0711-0. *Lowest Retail Price:* $288.80; to schools & libraries $279.50.

Purpose and Scope

Encyclopedia International, which is also sold under the titles of *New Age Encyclopedia* and *Webster's New Age Encyclopedia,* "is intended to serve both the cultural and practical interests of the whole family, and it is especially concerned with the needs of students on the various school levels" (preface). First published in 1963 as an entirely new multivolume general encyclopedia, the *International* emphasizes material of interest to secondary school students for both academic work and out-of-school activities, such as caring for pets. Topics covered in the encyclopedia were originally determined by means of a national school survey conducted by Dr. J. Harlan Shores, then an education professor at the University of Illinois. An intermediate encyclopedia, the *International* is not intended to be as comprehensive in coverage, nor as exhaustive or scholarly in treatment, as an adult encyclopedia. Within the Grolier family of general encyclopedias, the *International* stands between the much larger and more erudite *Encyclopedia Americana* and *The New Book of Knowledge,* a children's set.

Approximately half of the *International*'s articles concern biographical and geographical topics. Famous people both living and dead are included, along with a sprinkling of fictitious literary characters like the Bobbsey Twins. About a third of the 10,000 biographical entries cover notable Americans. Biblical figures are also well represented. In keeping with a long-standing practice in Grolier encyclopedias, place-names receive extensive coverage. All continents, countries, and important cities of the world are included, as are all major U.S. and Canadian places. Moreover, most North American towns of any appreciable population are accorded brief entries. EXAMPLE: The *International* is the only encyclopedia in the young adult category to include an article on Potsdam, N.Y., a town of less than 10,000. On the other hand, all sets have an entry for Potsdam, Germany. Broad coverage of biographical and geographical subjects is one of the *International*'s most attractive features.

All major areas of knowledge are covered, although specific topics normally receive quite cursory attention. For instance, the article "Oceanography" is disappointingly brief, although it touches all the essential bases, including continental drift. Unlike the other encyclopedias in the young adult class, the *International* furnishes no visual material with "Oceanography" that might enhance the reader's understanding. The encyclopedia's strongest coverage has been and still is in the area of the social sciences and particularly social problems, such as air pollution, divorce, and drug abuse. In recent times, material on blacks and Native Americans has been updated and improved, reflecting the changing sociopolitical attitudes of the past ten or so years. EXAMPLE: The article "Abolitionists" contains a discussion of black Abolitionists, noting not only the contributions of Frederick Douglass, who is now found in almost all encyclopedias, but also those of lesser-known figures like pamphleteer David Walker. Likewise, there is reasonably good coverage of women—historically, biographically, and internationally. EXAMPLE: "Women, Status of" compares the status of women in all countries, describing the educational, economic, and political conditions that prevail. In other instances, however, the *International*'s coverage is either lacking or deficient. The subject of homosexuality, for example, is ignored altogether, as are contemporary cults and cult behavior. The arts and humanities receive proportionately less attention than the social and physical sciences.

In keeping with the encyclopedia's aim to be useful to the entire family, many articles are devoted to practical, or how-to, subjects, such as camping, cooking, how to fight and prevent fires, first aid, how to buy stocks, and numerous medical topics (e.g., disorders of the feet). Articles on technical subjects are also geared to practical matters when appropriate. EXAMPLE: "Refrigeration" not only explains the theory but also gets down to basic home refrigerator mechanics and design. The article likewise discusses home freezers and provides straightforward instructional and consumer advice: "The usual temperature for home freezing and storing is 0°F. In refrigerators the temperature should be kept at about 37°F. The freezer should have a thermometer so that the controls can be adjusted to 0°F. Lower temperatures are not harmful to the stored food but result in higher operating costs."

The *International* averages almost three articles per page. Approximately 75 percent of the articles are of the specific-entry variety, limited to a few hundred words, or a dozen or so lines of text. In addition to the customarily brief biographical and geographical entries, there are very brief articles on various birds, fish, flowers, historical events, organizations, and the like. The rest of the articles (e.g., "Baseball," "Christianity," "Highway," "Home Economics," "Money and Monetary Systems," "Photography," "Shelter," "Warfare") are considerably longer, some running to as many as 12 pages. The article "United States," the longest in the set, covers 80 pages.

History and Authority

The publisher, Lexicon Publications, Inc., is a wholly-owned subsidiary of Grolier, Inc., one of the largest U. S. publishers of general encyclopedias. As previously mentioned, the firm publishes *The Encyclopedia Americana* (for adults) and *The New Book of Knowledge* (for children), as well as the *International* (for young adults). Grolier is also responsible for several major specialized reference sets, including the *Catholic Encyclopedia for School and Home* and *Encyclopedia Canadiana*. During the 1970s, Grolier suffered severe financial losses and is no longer the powerful publisher it once was. A gradual but unmistakable decline in the overall quality of Grolier products has been noticeable for some time now. For instance, *Encyclopedia Canadiana* (1957–1958) is sadly out-of-date, but Grolier recently informed the Canadian Library Association that the set will not be revised. (See "Selling Encyclopedias" in Part I of the *Buying Guide* for further information about Grolier.)

The *International,* first published in 1963, was designed as a replacement for the *Grolier Encyclopedia,* once a highly regarded work that eventually grew stale and unprofitable (see Appendix A for further information). An entirely new work, the *International* is aimed at the same audience (secondary school student and home) as the old *Grolier.* Its editors also retained the better features of the *Grolier,* such as specific entries and emphasis on people and place-names. In 1965, an inexpensive abridgment of the *International* appeared under the title *Grolier Universal Encyclopedia.* Short-lived, *Grolier Universal* disappeared in 1972 (see Appendix A). Also, as noted at the beginning of this review, the *International* is currently distributed under at least two other titles, namely *New Age Encyclopedia* and *Webster's New Age Encyclopedia.* In the latter case, the distributor is the Webster Publishing Company of Toronto, Canada, a firm that has been fined recently for false advertising. (For additional information about this company, see the review of *The New American Encyclopedia* under "History and Authority" in Part III of the *Buying Guide.*)

In its 17 years of existence, the *International* has achieved a reasonably good reputation as a solid encyclopedia for young people, although the competition is formidable (i.e., *Compton's Encyclopedia, Merit Students Encyclopedia,* and *The World Book Encyclopedia*). Unfortunately, like *Compton's,* the *International* is an encyclopedia in decline. The 1980 edition lists a very small editorial staff of 11, all of whom except the editor in chief are new to the encyclopedia since 1977 (when the *Buying Guide* last reviewed the *International*). None of the staff, again except for the editor, Edward Humphrey, is known within the reference book community. In

addition to a shrinking staff, the *International* has lost its advisory board
and subject advisers of editions past. The contributors' list, located in the
final volume, contains some impressive names, including such recognized
authorities as Ray A. Billington, Loren Eiseley, Arthur Gelb, Harry M.
Johnson, John H. Knowles, Ashley Montagu, Edwin A. Salk, and Howard Winger. The list, however, has not changed greatly since 1977, and in
a number of instances where new names do appear, they are actually old
contributors not previously listed, such as Robert J. Clements and Robert
P. Tristam Coffin. This technique of "updating" one's list of contributors
hardly represents approved editorial practice. The *International* remains
an authoritative encyclopedia, though only marginally so. The set's
shrinking editorial staff and lack of many new contributors is a bad omen
for the future. As explained elsewhere in the *Buying Guide* (see "Selling
Encyclopedias" in Part I), often a sharp reduction in staff signals a decline in an encyclopedia's sales, which in turn means there is less money
the following year for editorial maintenance, which leads to further reductions in staff, and so on until the encyclopedia finally expires. The
International gives every indication of being in this situation.

Reliability

The *International* can usually be relied upon for accurate information,
except in those instances where the material is very dated (see "Recency"). Quite obviously, factual material has been checked and double-
checked. In some instances, however, errors of fact and interpretation are
encountered in the set. EXAMPLE: The article "Cell" contains a number of
minor inaccuracies. For instance, it is stated that the leaf is "a plant organ
composed of several kinds of tissue, all of which contribute . . . to the
process of photosynthesis," but *all* leaf tissues do not contribute to photosynthesis. Likewise, the statement that "in the plant cell, the protoplasm
is contained within a rigid cell wall" is incorrect. EXAMPLE: The article
"Vasectomy" accurately notes that vasectomy "is generally regarded as a
permanent method of birth control," but inaccurately adds that "fertility
can be restored after vasectomy in a considerable number of cases."
Actually, the vasectomy reversibility rate remains discouragingly low, and
to imply otherwise is to mislead the reader.

Recency

During its first ten or so years of existence, the *International* maintained an acceptable level of currency. In recent years, however, the pace
of revision has slowed considerably. The preface states that the encyclopedia is "published under a program of continuous annual revision. New
subjects are added each year and old ones are rewritten where necessary
to present the latest information." This is an overly optimistic rendering
of the *International*'s actual performance in the area of revision. In 1978,
for instance, the editors managed only 950 "new, revised or replaced"
articles (quoted from an Editorial Preview of the *International* for 1978
issued by the publisher). Simple arithmetic shows that the encyclopedia,

This Recency Table compares selected topics in the *International* with those in other encyclopedias of similar size and intended usership.

Topic	Encyclopedia International	Compton's	Merit Students	World Book
Afghanistan	Fairly current	Fairly current	Very current	Very current
Dinosaurs	Not current	Fairly current	Very current	Very current
Greenland	Not current	Not current	Not current	Very current
Thomas Jefferson	Fairly current	Fairly current	Fairly current	Fairly current
Mass Transportation/Subways	Fairly current	Not current	Fairly current	Very current
Nuclear Power	Not current	Not current	Fairly current	Very current
Paris	Not current	Fairly current	Very current	Very current
Sharks	Fairly current	Not current	Fairly current	Very current
Shock Therapy	Not current	Not current	Fairly current	Very current
Suicide	Not current	Not current	Very current	Fairly current
Tuberculosis	Not current	Not current	Very current	Very current
Zimbabwe	Fairly current	Very current	Very current	Very current

which has nearly 30,000 articles, is being revised well below the annual 10 percent figure generally conceded to be necessary to keep a major multi-volume general encyclopedia reasonably current. In fact, since 1975 the *International*'s annual rate of revision has averaged less than 3 percent.

As might be expected, many of the encyclopedia's articles are either badly out-of-date or fast becoming stale. EXAMPLE: The article "Child Development" appears to have been written in the early 1960s and never revised. Certainly current thinking and research are absent from the article. EXAMPLE: "Greenland" fails to note the island's new home-rule status. Again, the article gives the appearance of never having been revised. EXAMPLE: "Indian Tribes, North American" lacks information about Native American militancy during the 1970s. A subsection of the article entitled "The Indians Today" is a decade out-of-date. EXAMPLE: The article "Central Intelligence Agency (CIA)" includes nothing about the agency's abuses of power revealed several years ago, nor recent efforts by the president to curb or correct those abuses. EXAMPLE: "Suicide" informs that "few children under 15 commit suicide, and the rate for later adolescence is low." Nowhere does the article note that suicide among teenagers has escalated dramatically since the 1960s. EXAMPLE: "Anthropology" contains nothing about recent trends in the field (which is a rapidly changing one at the present time). Quite obviously the article has not been revised since the encyclopedia was originally published in 1963. EXAMPLE: "Phonograph Recordings" is current as of the early 1960s. Although useful for its historical material, the article has no value for the reader seeking information about the subject today. EXAMPLE: "Iran" is nearly two decades out-of-date. The latest information in the article is this: "In Sept., 1962, a 23,000 sq. mi. area of mountainous northwestern Iran was devastated by the worst earthquake in the country's history."

As indicated earlier (see "History and Authority"), the *International* is experiencing bad times. Its editorial staff has been drastically reduced and completely turned over in recent years, it lacks an appreciable number of new contributors, and its publisher has suffered severe financial setbacks during the 1970s. As a result, the encyclopedia's efforts to keep abreast of new knowledge and information have been too little too late. Comparatively speaking, the *International* cannot compete in the area of recency with *Merit Students Encyclopedia* and *The World Book Encyclopedia,* both of which are well-maintained sets.

Grolier claims that the annual supplement entitled *Encyclopedia Yearbook* helps keep the *International* current. The yearbook, however, is not specifically related to the encyclopedia in any discernible manner, and hence its value as an updating source is marginal at best. Actually, the consumer will be just as well off with one of the inexpensive almanacs described in Appendix B of the *Buying Guide.*

Objectivity

Like all reputable modern Anglo-American general encyclopedias, the *International* makes a conscious effort to treat controversial and sensitive subject matter as fairly and objectively as possible. It succeeds admirably. EXAMPLE: "Fluoridation" notes, "Vigorous opposition to the fluoridation of public water supplies has been forthcoming from various groups, which contend that the safety of fluoridation is still in doubt." After describing other objections to fluoridation, the article presents the other side of the issue, including the fact that "both the American Dental Association and the American Medical Association have endorsed fluoridation." As Bill Katz points out in his comments on the *International* in *Basic Information Sources* (3rd edition, 1978, p. 158), the set's emphasis is "on data rather than on debate."

Clarity and Reader Suitability

The *International* stresses and usually achieves clarity of style. Earlier editions noted that the encyclopedia pays special attention to those topics "most often sought in reference works by junior and senior high school students." As a result, the *International* is (or was) a curriculum-oriented set designed for a readership that falls between *The Encyclopedia Americana* (Grolier's encyclopedia for advanced students and adults) and *The New Book of Knowledge* (Grolier's set designed specifically for elementary school students). Like the other young adult sets, the *International* makes an effort to use vocabulary that reading studies have determined to be comprehensible to secondary school students. When difficult or unfamiliar terms are introduced, they are customarily defined in context. EXAMPLE: "Atomic Energy" defines the subject as "the energy released from the nucleus of an atom, by radioactive decay (radioactivity), by splitting its components (fission), or by uniting them (fusion)." And, when appropriate, articles are written to grade level; for instance, the article "Novel" is geared to a more advanced readership than the article "Exploration." Unfortunately, much of the *International*'s text is dry and lifeless—quite unlike the appealing and lively writing found in *Compton's Encyclopedia* and *The World Book Encyclopedia*.

Arrangement and Accessibility

The encyclopedia is arranged alphabetically, letter-by-letter ("Indiana" precedes "Indian Ocean"). Extensive cross-references are provided, both external ones in the main alphabetical sequence (e.g., *"North American Indian Tribes.* See INDIAN TRIBES, NORTH AMERICAN") and the internal type at the end of articles in the form of *See also* references. For instance, at the end of "Child Development" there are 11 references to other articles in the set, including "Adolescence," "Discipline in Home and School," "Infant Care," "Pediatrics," and "Twins, Psychological Studies of." Finally, comprising most of the final volume, there is a detailed analytical index of some 120,000 entries. Designed and compiled under the general direction of the late Maurice F. Tauber, a library science professor at Columbia University, the index provides ready access to very specific factual information contained in the set. In addition, the index brings together related information "in classified arrangements." EXAMPLE: Under the heading "Canada" there are numerous subtopics, from "agriculture" to "transportation." The subtopic "history" is further subdivided by period. As Professor Tauber states in his introduction to the index, its main objective is "that the subtopics under a heading bring together the many areas in which subjects can be treated in a general encyclopedia." The *International*'s basic arrangement in A-to-Z sequence, its abundant and well-chosen cross-references, and its intelligently constructed index all mesh to provide the user with easy and fairly complete access to the material in the set.

Bibliographies

Bibliographic references to additional readings are provided at the end of roughly 2,000 of the nearly 30,000 articles, or about 7 percent of the articles, usually the longer ones. The bibliographies are not graded (as they are in *Compton's Encyclopedia* and *The World Book Encyclopedia*), nor do they include nonprint materials. And frequently the titles cited are embarrassingly out-of-date. EXAMPLE: The article "Biology" concludes with a six-item bibliography. None of the citations is more recent than 1969. EXAMPLE: "Cell" also lists six books for further information, the latest a 1961 imprint. EXAMPLE: "Child Development" has a bibliography of 12 items, all of which were published between 1943 and 1961. EXAMPLE: "Paris" has a bibliography of 12 items, all published between 1945 and 1962. Some of them are guidebooks and one is entitled *Paris Today* (1948). These are not isolated examples.

Graphics

The *International* includes nearly 13,000 graphics, such as photographs, charts, diagrams, and schematic drawings. Most of the illustrations are in black-and-white, although recently the editors have reillustrated approximately 100 articles using four-color graphics, including "Abstract Art," "Castle," "Expressionism," "Geography," "Olympic Games," and "Washington, George," as well as a number of countries ("Afghanistan"; "Egypt") and U.S. states ("Arizona"; "Pennsylvania"). In some instances, however, color illustrations included in the 1977 edition of the *International* (the last one reviewed by the *Buying Guide*) have been dropped from the 1980 edition, such as four pages of drawings and maps from the article "Oceanography." In any case, the graphic quality of the present edition is a modest improvement over earlier ones. Although the detail in some black-and-white photographs is poor, most of the illustrations enhance the informational value of the encyclopedia. All are captioned and placed in close proximity to the text they complement. Some illustrations that require color to be most effective are in black-and-white, however. EXAMPLE: A reproduction of Georgia O'Keeffe's painting *Hibiscus with Plumeria* is in black-and-white, although the article on O'Keeffe speaks of "her enlarged flower studies in bright, clear colors." Likewise, some articles that logically require illustrations lack them, such as "Op Art." Also, some illustrations are not indexed.

Almost 900 maps of varying sizes and types are found throughout the set, accompanying articles on countries, states, cities, and so forth. C. S. Hammond & Company prepared four-color maps, both topographical and political, covering the nations of the world, the 50 U. S. states, and the Canadian provinces. Other reputable map firms, as well as the encyclopedia's own staff, also contributed to the *International*. All major maps have their own index.

Physical Format

Bound in white Sturdite with either red or blue panels and gold lettering, the *International* is both outwardly attractive and capable of withstanding heavy reference use. The lettering on the spine, however, is small and difficult to read at any distance. Inside, the page layout and typography have been designed with one eye on aesthetics and the other on utility. A variety of typefaces are used to achieve both, but many pages appear dark and rather dreary. As a consultant to the *Buying Guide* put it, the overall impression is one of "grayness." Guide words are printed at the top of each page. A reasonably good quality of paper has been used. The volumes, however, are tightly sewn and do not always lie flat when open, nor are the inside margins wide enough.

Special Features

The *International* provides several useful special features. The first is provision of Study Guides for some 300 major articles. The Study Guides, which are found at the beginning of the articles, briefly outline the article's contents and also refer the reader to related topics. The second feature is inclusion of Career Guides, which accompany roughly 60 articles on various occupations and professions. These guides succinctly discuss necessary education and training, employment qualifications, prospects for employment, salary expectations, and various types of work available. Other sources of information are also indicated. The third feature worth mentioning is inclusion of glossaries that define technical terms found in some of the longer articles. Like the Study and Career Guides, the glossaries appear with the articles they complement. It should be noted that none of these features is unique. All of the multivolume young adult encyclopedias currently on the market offer similar features.

Sales Information

The *International* is available in only one edition in either a blue and white or red and white Sturdite binding (see "Physical Format"). The blue and white binding is for the home consumer market and the red and white for schools and libraries. The set is sold in-home on the subscription, or installment, basis, as well as to educational institutions. Grolier reports the current retail price as $288.80, plus shipping, handling, and any tax. In 1977, the set sold at retail for $350, meaning that the *International* is actually cheaper today than it was several years ago. In recent years, however, Grolier and its subsidiaries have tended to change prices willy-nilly. The *Buying Guide* advises retail consumers interested in purchasing the *International not* to pay more than $288.80. If the price situation is unclear, the *Buying Guide* advises holding off purchase until a satisfactory clarification can be received from an authoritative source, either at the company's headquarters in Danbury, Conn. (see Appendix E for complete directory information) or via an independent medium like the *Buying Guide* (c/o R. R. Bowker Company, 1180 Ave. of the Americas, New York, NY 10036; 212-746-5100). Schools and libraries can acquire the set at the slightly discounted price of $279.50 plus the usual extras.

Consumers should also be aware that the *International* is currently sold in-home and by mail order by independent operators under the titles *New Age Encyclopedia* and *Webster's New Age Encyclopedia*. The contents of these latter sets are exactly the same as those of *Encyclopedia International*—only the title and binding have been changed. Price information concerning *New Age* and *Webster's New Age* is murky and contradictory. In 1980, for example, the Webster Publishing Company, which sells *Webster's New Age* via mail order, advertised the set at "not 1,000—not $900—not $800—but an astonishingly low $500." This advertisement was immediately followed by "Webster's New Testimonial-Seeking Offer Slashes $500 Price To Only $169." As already noted, the Webster Publishing Company, located in Toronto, Canada, has recently been fined for false advertising. The *Buying Guide* strongly advises against purchasing the *New Age Encyclopedia* or *Webster's New Age Encyclopedia* from anyone at any price.

Summary

Encyclopedia International can be quickly summed up in this manner:

Scope: Good	Accessibility: Good
Authority: Fair	Bibliographies: Poor
Reliability: Good	Graphics: Fair
Recency: Poor	Physical Format: Fair
Objectivity: Excellent	Special Features: Few
Clarity: Good	Price: Reasonable

To elaborate briefly, the *International,* which is also sold as *New Age Encyclopedia* and *Webster's New Age Encyclopedia,* covers all areas of general knowledge, with particular emphasis on geographical and biographical topics. Articles on people and places, which tend to be very brief, constitute approximately 50 percent of the encyclopedia's total entries. Contemporary social issues and practical, or how-to, subjects of interest to families and home owners are also emphasized. In the Grolier hierarchy, the *International*'s intended readership falls between the adult *Encyclopedia Americana* and the elementary *New Book of Knowledge.* The set is well indexed, admirably objective, and clearly (if dully) written, but during the past six or seven years the rate of revision has slowed perceptibly. As a result, many articles are badly dated and others are growing stale. Some of the bibliographies are so timeworn and useless that they must be a source of embarrassment to the editors. In addition, the set's illustrations and page layout tend to be dark and drab. Anyone contemplating purchasing the *International* should not pay more than the current price of $288.80; beyond that the set is not worth the asking price. Consumers should also avoid *New Age Encyclopedia* and *Webster's New Age Encyclopedia* at any price.

Comparatively speaking, the *International* competes directly with three other encyclopedias in the multivolume young adult class, namely *Compton's Encyclopedia, Merit Students Encyclopedia,* and *The World Book Encyclopedia.* Each of these encyclopedias is aimed at roughly the same audience, each provides balanced coverage geared to the North American school curriculum, and each is authoritative and useful in its way. *The World Book Encyclopedia,* however, stands out from the rest as a consistently superior work available at a comparatively modest price. *Merit Students Encyclopedia,* a very well-maintained set, has supplanted *Compton's Encyclopedia* as the chief challenger to *World Book* for dominance in its class. *Compton's,* once the preeminent encyclopedia in the young adult group, has been living on its reputation and little else for too many years. Like *Compton's,* the *International* is an encyclopedia in decline. When compared head-to-head with the *World Book* and *Merit Students,* it has little to offer except its current bargain-basement price.

Other Critical Opinions

Booklist, December 15, 1978, pp. 709–711. Part of a series of reviews by the ALA Reference and Subscription Books Review Committee (RSBRC) entitled "Encyclopedias: A Survey and Buying Guide," this unsigned evaluation of the *International* (1975 copyright) is critical of the set's "uneven" currency, dated bibliographies, and occasionally "incomplete, unclear, and outdated" graphics. Otherwise the review is quite favorable, although no final conclusions are offered. In its last regular review of the *International (Booklist,* July 1, 1969, pp. 1185–1190), RSBRC "recommended" the encyclopedia for use in the home, public libraries, and middle and secondary schools.

Katz, William A. *Basic Information Sources* (Vol. 1 of *Introduction to Reference Work,* 3rd ed. New York: McGraw-Hill, 1978), pp. 157–159. Here Katz compares the *International* with *Collier's Encyclopedia,* a work for advanced students and adults. "Which one of these is best? Opinion differs, but one may say that *Collier's* is a good set for anyone with an average to above-average vocabulary who does not require a sophisticated or a detailed explanation of complex matters. The *International* is a better set for those with less education or with problems in reading."

Wynar, Christine L. *American Reference Books Annual,* 1977, pp. 44–47. This lengthy and informative review of the *International* (1976 copyright) is quite positive, concluding that the set "continues the high standards of the earlier editions and is recommended for secondary schools, public libraries, and home use."

Merit Students Encyclopedia

Facts in Brief

Full Title: **Merit Students Encyclopedia.** *Editors:* Emanuel Friedman, Editor in Chief; William D. Halsey, Editorial Director. *Publisher:* Macmillan Educational Corporation, 866 Third Ave., New York, NY 10022. *Edition Reviewed:* 1980 copyright.

Volumes: 20. *Pages:* 12,000. *Articles:* 21,800. *Words:* 9,000,000. *Illustrations:* 19,200. *Maps:* 1,570. *Index Entries:* 140,000. *Cross-references:* 10,600. *Contributors:* 2,300.

User Classification: Young Adult (Multivolume). *Reader Suitability:* Age 9 through 18. *Physical Size:* 8½ × 11 in.; 28 cm. *LC:* 79–89007. *Lowest Retail Price:* $579.50; to schools & libraries $286.

Purpose and Scope

The *Merit Students Encyclopedia,* issued in 1967 as an entirely new work, is "specifically designed to meet the new educational and informational demands brought about by the changes that have taken place in our society and our schools during the past decade" (preface). Based on an analysis of both U. S. and Canadian public school curricula, as well as those from parochial schools, *Merit* claims to serve "the student at the fifth grade, where the use of the encyclopedia begins in most schools, and continues to serve him as he moves through elementary school and secondary school." The point is also made in the preface that not all education occurs in the classroom, and consequently *Merit* "covers the complete range of interests of children in the elementary and secondary schools and supports their out-of-school education. The interests that are covered range from religion and the arts to pets and sports."

As the foregoing suggests, *Merit* comprehensively covers the major fields of knowledge, but it does not intend to provide the depth of coverage found in the large multivolume adult sets, such as *Collier's Encyclopedia* (also published by Macmillan) or *The New Encyclopaedia Britannica.* Most of *Merit*'s articles are brief, averaging 400 words each or roughly half a page in length. Like all the multivolume young adult encyclopedias currently available with the exception of *Compton's Encyclopedia, Merit* emphasizes specific entries covering people, places, plants and animals, organizations and associations, concepts and terms associated with the various fields of knowledge (e.g., "Freedom of the Press"; "Genetics"; "Pop

Art"), and so on. Books of the Bible (e.g., "John, Epistles of") and selected literary works (*"Streetcar Named Desire, A"*) are succinctly covered. Most accredited colleges and universities in the U. S. and Canada receive short write-ups. In this area, *Merit* provides more extensive coverage than any other general encyclopedia, including the large adult sets, with the possible exception of *The Encyclopedia Americana.* Unfortunately, the entries for academic institutions are short on specifics and not always as current as they might be (see "Recency"). Much quick reference information appears in some 750 bar graphs, tables, and lists. EXAMPLE: The article "Disasters" includes a classified list of major world disasters under such topics as "Aviation Disasters," "Explosions and Fires," and "Earthquakes and Volcanic Eruptions." These lists furnish facts and tend to be very current.

Merit's longer articles tend to cover the same subject matter that receives extensive treatment in comparable encyclopedias. EXAMPLES: Volume 7 (FERN–GERM) includes long articles on fire, firearms, first aid, fish, fishing, flower arranging, football, gardens, and geometry. When appropriate, these articles stress practical information, such as fire prevention rules, what to do in case of poisoning, and the equipment needed for various kinds of fishing. The article "Florida" is some 25 pages long. "France" totals 28 pages. Such articles are, as usual, accompanied by boxed information, many illustrations, several kinds of maps, charts, etc. Presidents and other historical notables also receive good coverage. Millard Fillmore, for instance, not one of our most illustrious chief executives, is accorded five pages, whereas Thomas Jefferson gets 15.

The encyclopedia's subject coverage is well balanced, with no particular area of knowledge especially emphasized. Indeed, one of *Merit*'s signal strengths, like that of its chief competitor, *The World Book Encyclopedia,* is its fairly even coverage of those topics of interest to young adults, either for academic or personal reasons. For instance, abundant career information on most occupations and professions is provided, with names and addresses of organizations where readers can obtain additional information. Biographical and geographical topics account for approximately half of the 21,800 entries. As might be expected, North American people and places are emphasized. For example, Pierre Trudeau of Canada receives more than twice as much space as China's Mao Tse-tung. Pronunciation information is given for practically all entries—for instance, "Pierre Elliott Trudeau [pyär el ē ət trü dō]." Also, metric equivalents have now been added throughout the set.

History and Authority

Since its publication in 1967, *Merit* has achieved a reputation among educators and librarians as a solid, trustworthy source of general information. Macmillan, the publisher, has been active in the encyclopedia-making business for a good number of years, most notably as the publisher of the well-known adult set, *Collier's Encyclopedia.* According to

Macmillan, *Merit* was seven years in the making and cost over $7 million to produce.

The editors and staff are people with considerable experience and good credentials. Emanuel Friedman has edited the set since 1970, succeeding the founding editor, Bernard S. Cayne, who is now editorial director at Grolier, Inc. William D. Halsey, *Merit*'s editorial director, is a senior man in the world of encyclopedias and dictionaries. In 1980, he retired as president of Macmillan Educational Corporation after 25 years with the firm, but he remains active in his emeritus status. The resident editorial staff, listed in the front of Volume 1, now numbers 20, up one since 1977, when the *Buying Guide* last reviewed *Merit*. Seven of the 20 are new since 1977, and practically all hold baccalaureate degrees and about half advanced degrees. In addition to the editorial staff, there is an advisory board of 19 librarians, many of them foreign, such as Sir Frank Francis, formerly head of the British Museum, and Takahisa Sawamoto, formerly director of the library school at Keio University in Japan. Next in the *Merit* hierarchy come nearly 200 working scholars who form an "editorial faculty," or board of special editors. This group is responsible for both writing and authenticating many articles in the set. The authority of these specialists—people like James Baird, Lynn M. Case, Charles F. Gosnell, Walter Rideout, and Whitney Smith—is incontestable. Some members of the board, however, are now retired or deceased, such as Mario Pei.

Almost all of *Merit*'s articles are signed, either by a contributor, a reviewer, or an authenticator. A reviewer, it is explained, "vouches for the accuracy and completeness of the article but did not write it." Reviewers' names are preceded by an asterisk. In the final volume some 2,300 contributors and reviewers are identified by name, degrees, professional affiliation, and published works (if any). The list, however, includes members of the aforementioned board of special editors and is further inflated by numerous college and university officials—usually presidents and deans—who have merely authenticated brief articles about their schools. In fact, almost 50 percent of the 2,300 contributors and reviewers falls into this category. The people responsible for producing *Merit* generally bring fine qualifications to the work, but the number of writers making a substantial contribution has been exaggerated through the technique described above. An impressive number of new contributors has been added to the list since 1977, including James Applegate (associate professor of wildlife biology, Rutgers University), Roswell Atwood (director of education, International Association of Fire Fighters), Keith W. Bennett (an editor with the journal *Iron Age*), Charles Feldberg (manager, International Food Regulations, CPC International, Inc.), Kenneth Frey (professor of agriculture, Iowa State University), Robert Malone (author of *Rocketship*), Irwin D. Mandel (professor of dentistry and director, Division of Preventive Dentistry, Columbia Dental School), Bernard Vonnegut (professor of physics, State University of New York at Albany), and William H. Webster (director of the Federal Bureau of Investigation), who replaces former FBI director Clarence Kelley on the list. Overall, *Merit* is a reasonably authoritative encyclopedia.

Reliability

Merit is a responsibly edited encyclopedia. All reasonable steps have been taken to ensure its factual accuracy. In those gray areas where facts are open to interpretation, the encyclopedia presents the material in a fair and forthright manner. EXAMPLE: The article "Florida" sums up current trends in the state by noting that, despite the recent influx of new residents from the North, "the state has remained conservative. Many of the new residents are retired persons or small businessmen who oppose the higher taxes required for progressive government programs. Conservatism has also been encouraged by resentment of the civil rights policies of the federal government and of increasing protest and violence in the nation." EXAMPLE: "Homosexuality" handles this sensitive subject in this manner: "Puberty is accompanied by a marked rise in the sex drive. Courtship behavior is established, or in modern terms, dating begins. Most adolescents establish a sexual preference for the opposite sex. If this becomes the pattern for their adult life, they are called heterosexuals. Many adolescents also experiment with sexual relationships with friends of their own sex. If this becomes an established pattern for their adult life, they are called homosexuals. Another term used to denote homosexuals is 'gay.' Female homosexuals are also sometimes called lesbians."

Recency

Like its competitors in the multivolume young adult class, *Merit* is continuously revised on an annual basis. The 1980 edition, for instance, has added 34 entirely new articles on such subjects as anorexia nervosa, Mikhail Baryshnikov, the big bang theory, Joe Clark, the Environmental Protection Agency, the Freedom of Information Act, health foods, laetrile, rape, SALT, sports medicine, and Margaret Thatcher. In addition, 18 articles were completely rewritten, such as "Abortion"; "Birth Control"; "Castro, Fidel"; "Death"; "Electron Microscope"; "Enzyme"; "Fishing Industry"; "Nuclear Physics"; "Suicide"; and "Tubman, Harriet." According to data furnished by the publisher, another 1,379 articles were more modestly revised or updated. In all, 2,270 pages of text (out of a total of 12,000) were changed in some manner during preparation of the 1980 copyright.

Each year *Merit*'s rate of revision is well above the minimum 10 percent level. This constant attention to keeping the set reasonably current is one of *Merit*'s most commendable features. Headline events—dramatic political and social happenings, spectacular scientific developments, the passing of famous people, the giving of prestigious literary awards—are likely to be as current as can be expected from any general encyclopedia. EXAMPLE: The ten-page article "Iran" concludes: "In November Tehran students seized the U.S. embassy and held its employees captive, demanding the return for trial of the ex-shah, who had entered the United States for medical care. When Khomeini and the revolutionary council, backed by a surge of national and religious feeling, sided with the students, the government resigned and the revolutionary council formally

This Recency Table compares selected topics in *Merit* with those in other encyclopedias of similar size and intended usership.

Topic	Merit Students	Compton's	Encyclopedia International	World Book
Afghanistan	Very current	Fairly current	Fairly current	Very current
Dinosaurs	Very current	Fairly current	Not current	Very current
Greenland	Not current	Not current	Not current	Very current
Thomas Jefferson	Fairly current	Fairly current	Fairly current	Fairly current
Mass Transportation/Subways	Fairly current	Not current	Fairly current	Very current
Nuclear Power	Fairly current	Not current	Not current	Very current
Paris	Very current	Fairly current	Not current	Very current
Sharks	Fairly current	Not current	Fairly current	Very current
Shock Therapy	Fairly current	Not current	Not current	Very current
Suicide	Very current	Not current	Not current	Fairly current
Tuberculosis	Very current	Not current	Not current	Very current
Zimbabwe	Very current	Very current	Fairly current	Very current

took power. The continued detention of many hostages created a serious international crisis." EXAMPLE: The brief sketch of William Styron, the American writer, includes a reference to his recent best-selling novel *Sophie's Choice* (1979). Nonheadline subjects are also normally up-to-date. The article "Dinosaur," for instance, discusses recent evidence that has led some paleontologists to the conclusion that dinosaurs (at least some of them) were warm-blooded creatures, like mammals rather than reptiles. Inevitably, however, there are instances where *Merit* is not as current as it might be. Some of the articles covering colleges and universities, for instance, are now dated. EXAMPLE: Davidson College in North Carolina is described as "a private accredited college for men," but actually Davidson has been coeducational for a number of years.

An annual updating supplement entitled the *Merit Students Year Book* is available, but it is practically the same as *Collier's Year Book* (described under "Recency" in the *Collier's Encyclopedia* review in Part III of the *Buying Guide*). Although this yearbook contains a reliable summary of the events of the preceding year, it is unrelated to the encyclopedia itself. In addition, the book is written at a level beyond the comprehension of much of *Merit*'s intended audience.

Objectivity

As previous examples indicate (see "Reliability"), *Merit* does not shrink from an honest presentation of the world as it is, warts and all. Likewise, controversial issues are treated in a responsible manner, not dodged or ignored, as is the case with some encyclopedias for young adults. "In every case where more than one point of view exists or where research has developed conflicting data," say the editors in the preface, "various points of view are given and the fact that differences of opinion exist is clearly pointed out." Well-balanced articles on such polemical subjects as abortion, drug use and abuse, fluoridation, fraternities, homosexuality, suicide, and women's rights attest to the editors' conscientious efforts to present all legitimate sides of an issue.

Clarity and Reader Suitability

One of *Merit*'s strongest features is its stylistic clarity and directness. Like its major competition, *Merit* employs the so-called pyramid style of writing—that is, articles begin at the simplest level of comprehension and gradually become more advanced. In addition, according to the editors, "individual articles were designed and written primarily at the grade level at which they are taught." In most instances, the encyclopedia admirably achieves this goal. EXAMPLE: The article "Farming" is written for a lower level of reading comprehension than the article "Atomic Bomb" or "Automation," which are principally aimed at high school level readers. *Merit*'s graded approach does not affect the set's overall stylistic consistency: whatever the grade level, the emphasis is on clear, uncomplicated text. The article "Evolution" furnishes a representative example of *Merit*'s style. Here is a random paragraph from that article: "Although the overall trend of life has been toward greater complication, that is not always so in detail. For example, some animals have changed hardly at all for several hundred million years. In some cases, descendants have become less complex than their ancestors. Tapeworms, for example, have lost sensory, digestive, and other special organs that their ancestors had. Usually the apparent degeneration has made the organisms better adapted for some special way of life. The tapeworm, for example, is better adapted for life as a parasite." Note, however, that *Merit* ordinarily does not attempt to define potentially difficult or unfamiliar terms in context (e.g., *degeneration*).

Arrangement and Accessibility

The encyclopedia is arranged alphabetically, letter-by-letter ("Indiana" precedes "Indian Ocean"). Cross-references, though found throughout the set, are not abundant, averaging less than one per page. They appear as external references in the main A–Z sequence, such as "Zimbabwe. See RHODESIA." Internal *See also* references are also provided at the end of some articles (e.g., "Stage Design" concludes with a *See also* reference to "Theater"), but these are few and far between. Quite obviously, additional cross-references would improve easy and effective access to material in the set. EXAMPLE: The article "Animal" contains a lengthy and informative section subtitled "Adaptations in Animals," but there is no cross-reference to the excellent article "Protective Coloration," which deals with animal adaptation to the natural environment through camouflage. By way of comparison, *The World Book Encyclopedia* (*Merit*'s chief competitor) contains 100,000 cross-references as opposed to *Merit*'s 10,600.

The bulk of the final volume is devoted to a general index. Comprising approximately 140,000 analytical entries (a figure that compares favorably with *The World Book Encyclopedia* and *Compton's Encyclopedia*), the index is quite reliable and goes a long way toward making the contents of *Merit* reasonably accessible to the user, no matter how specific the information sought. The index has been improved in recent years with the inclusion of references to the set's nearly 20,000 graphics. The index is not perfect, however. In some instances, subtopics within an article are not indexed. EXAMPLE: Information about condominium housing can be located in the article "Housing," but there is no index reference under "Condominium," nor is there a subentry under "Housing." Moreover, there is no external cross-reference from "Condominium" to "Housing" in the A–Z sequence. In other instances, index references are not useful. EXAMPLE: The index entry "Shock Therapy" provides four references, one of which (6–288) is merely to a cross-reference ("*Electric Shock Therapy*. See under SHOCK THERAPY"). These criticisms notwithstanding, access to material in *Merit* is fairly good, though the encyclopedia has a long way to go to meet the high standards of accessibility established by *The World Book Encyclopedia* and, to a lesser degree, *Compton's Encyclopedia*.

Bibliographies

"No encyclopedia can tell every reader everything he wants to know about a subject. *Merit Students Encyclopedia* solves this problem by including throughout the set sources of additional information. Most major articles are followed by a bibliography suggesting books for further information" (preface). Limited to about 20 percent of the articles (usually those of some length), the bibliographies are sometimes graded; for instance, "Evolution" concludes with an 11-item bibliography divided into three groups: "For Younger Readers," "For Senior High School Readers," and "For Advanced Students." The bibliographies, which include only books, have improved in quality and quantity in recent years. Many have been expanded and updated during the past several years, and more attention now appears to be paid to the selection of the titles listed. For instance, Fawn Brodie's *Thomas Jefferson: An Intimate History* (1974), the most significant work on Jefferson to appear in many years, is cited in the bibliography ("For Advanced Students") at the end of the Jefferson article. The editors of *Merit* are to be commended for this important improvement.

Graphics

Like all its competitors in the young adult category, *Merit* appropriately includes numerous illustrations, running the gamut from full-page color plates of birds and similar subjects to both color and black-and-white photographs, reproductions of paintings, wood engravings, schematic drawings, and so on. It is apparent that the makers of the set devoted considerable energy and skill to the selection and placement of these varied graphic aids. The editors note that "in each case the type of illustration was selected to provide the best visual communication. Trees are drawn in simple black and white to show the shape of the tree, leaf, flower, and fruit as aids to identification. Flowers and birds are shown in full color because color is of importance in identifying these subjects" (preface). These claims are justified in most instances. The illustrations normally amplify or clarify the printed text, helping to increase the reader's understanding of the subject matter. Of the nearly 20,000 graphics, some 5,000 are in full color and many others in two color. As the editors correctly point out in the preface, color is used "functionally" to direct the reader's eye to essential information rather than to dazzle or look pretty. Sometimes, however, the color quality is poor, due perhaps to the use of paper that does not reproduce color well. Likewise, some of the black-and-white photographs lack good contrast, being excessively dark, such as a shot of a brokerage firm accompanying the article "Investment." And in a few cases, the photographs are quite dated. EXAMPLE: The photo of a street scene in Tehran in the article "Iran" is vintage 1960s. Overall, however, *Merit*'s illustrations are abundant and well chosen, and serve to enhance the printed text. Students will particularly find the various color transparencies useful. (See, for example, the articles "Anatomy and Physiology"; "Color"; "Protective Coloration"; and "Rome, Ancient.")

The 1,500-plus maps are of excellent quality. Some were produced in conjunction with Rand McNally and Company, and others were developed by *Merit* staff cartographers. Similar to most other multivolume sets currently on the market, *Merit* includes full-page color maps of the major countries, 50 U.S. states and 10 Canadian provinces, and selected cities of the world, such as Paris. In addition, there are numerous political, physical, economic, historical, and locator maps throughout the set. Considerable attention is paid to map revision and, as a result, they are very much up-to-date.

Physical Format

Merit is an exceptionally well-made encyclopedia. It is the sort of set people instinctively turn to because of its appealing layout, attractive and legible typefaces, and clean, inviting design. The binding of the 1980 edition is red Fabrikoid with black panels and gold lettering and stamping. The off-white, nonglare paper is generally satisfactory, although as mentioned earlier (see "Graphics") it does not reproduce color well. Guide words appear at the top of every page, and the margins are sufficiently wide. The volumes are easy to handle and lie flat when open for easy consultation. In physical appearance and construction, *Merit* represents a high level of contemporary encyclopedia-making.

Special Features

The most distinctive special feature *Merit* provides is the italicizing of essential factual information at the beginning of articles concerning people, places, and mineral and chemical elements. This technique is intended to facilitate quick reference. EXAMPLE: Immediately following the title and pronunciation, the article "Garnierite" notes: "*a minor ore of nickel. Named for Jules Garnier, a French geologist who discovered it. Dull earthy luster. Apple green to white. Hardness 2 to 3. Specific gravity 2.2 to 2.8.*" The article then continues in standard type and prose.

Other special features are similar to those found in most competing sets. These features include Student Guides for some major articles (actually they are little more than tables of contents to the articles), pronunciations for almost all entries, and scientific classifications for all plant and animal topics.

Sales Information

Merit is available in only one binding, that being the red Fabrikoid already described (see "Physical Format"). The retail price of the set has risen sharply in recent years, going from $299 in 1975 to $579.50 in 1980. As such, *Merit* is the most expensive young adult encyclopedia currently on the North American market, with *Compton's Encyclopedia* next highest at $419. Schools and libraries, however, can acquire *Merit* for $286 plus $6 shipping and handling, a very sizable discount; if two or more sets are ordered at the same time, the price to educational institutions is reduced to $256 per set. As might be expected, the large majority of *Merit*'s sales are to libraries.

Merit is available as part of a package deal that includes the *Merit Students Year Book* (see "Recency") and such assorted items as *Junior Classics* (ten volumes), *Everyday Library for Men* (six volumes), *Everyday Library for Women* (six volumes), a four-volume medical encyclopedia, etc. For the grand total of $864.50 plus tax, the consumer can acquire *Merit Students Encyclopedia*, the yearbook, and four of the premium sets (selected from about 15 titles), plus a bookcase and a reference service.

Summary

Merit Students Encyclopedia can be quickly summed up in this manner:

Scope: Excellent	Accessibility: Good
Authority: Good	Bibliographies: Good
Reliability: Excellent	Graphics: Good
Recency: Excellent	Physical Format: Excellent
Objectivity: Excellent	Special Features: Few
Clarity: Excellent	Price: High (retail)
	Reasonable (school & library)

To elaborate briefly, *Merit* is a curriculum-oriented encyclopedia intended to serve both the in-school and out-of-school informational needs of young people from the fifth through the twelfth grades. Written to grade level in pyramid style, the set provides comprehensive, well-balanced (albeit succinct) subject coverage. Information about careers and U.S. and Canadian colleges and universities is extensive. *Merit,* which first appeared in 1967 as an all-new reference work, also contains much information of general use to the entire family. In recent years, the encyclopedia has benefited from a vigorous program of annual continuous revision. In addition, the bibliographies have been improved, the set's nearly 20,000 graphics are now indexed, and metric equivalents have been added throughout. On the negative side, some of the graphics are not of the highest quality, and an infusion of cross-references would improve the set's already satisfactory accessibility.

Comparatively speaking, *Merit* competes directly with three other encyclopedias in the multivolume young adult class, namely *Compton's Encyclopedia, Encyclopedia International,* and *The World Book Encyclopedia.* Each of these encyclopedias is aimed at roughly the same audience, each provides balanced coverage geared to the North American school curriculum, and each is authoritative and useful in its way. *The World Book Encyclopedia,* however, stands out from the rest as a consistently superior work available at a comparatively modest price. *Merit Students Encyclopedia,* a very well maintained and constantly improving set, has supplanted *Compton's Encyclopedia* as the chief challenger to *World Book* for dominance in its class. *Compton's,* once the preeminent encyclopedia in the young adult group, has been living on its reputation and little else for too many years. It is preferable only when compared with *Encyclopedia International,* a drab set with little to offer the discerning consumer.

Other Critical Opinions

Booklist, December 15, 1978, pp. 711–712. Part of a series of reviews by the ALA Reference and Subscription Books Review Committee (RSBRC) entitled "Encyclopedias: A Survey and Buying Guide," this unsigned evaluation of *Merit* (1975 copyright) criticizes the "disproportionate" number of entries for colleges and universities, the rate of revision (without indicating what the rate is), and the bibliographies (since improved). Otherwise the review is favorable, although no final conclusions are indicated. In its last regular review of *Merit* (*Booklist,* December 15, 1973, pp. 396–397), RSBRC "recommended" the encyclopedia for both home and library use.

Katz, William A. *Basic Information Sources* (Vol. 1 of *Introduction to Reference Work,* 3rd ed. New York: McGraw-Hill, 1978), pp. 159–161. Katz, a highly respected reference book reviewer, comparatively evaluates *Compton's Encyclopedia, The World Book Encyclopedia,* and *Merit,* the three leading sets for young adults. Katz calls *Merit* "strong" but concludes that it "has a number of weaknesses that put it in third place."

Wynar, Bohdan S. *American Reference Books Annual,* 1979, pp. 35–36. This superficial review is little more than a summary of the evaluation of *Merit* that appeared in the 1978 edition of *Encyclopedia Buying Guide.* Interestingly, Wynar provides no examples to substantiate any of his criticisms.

World Book Encyclopedia

Facts in Brief

Full Title: **The World Book Encyclopedia.** *Editors:* William H. Nault, Editorial Director; A. Richard Harmet, Executive Editor; Robert J. Janus, Managing Editor; William J. Dobias, Executive Art Director. *Publisher:* World Book-Childcraft International, Inc. (a subsidiary of the Scott & Fetzer Company), 510 Merchandise Mart Plaza, Chicago, IL 60654. *Edition Reviewed:* 1980 copyright.

Volumes: 22. *Pages:* 14,280. *Articles:* 20,000. *Words:* 10,000,000. *Illustrations:* 29,500. *Maps:* 2,350. *Index Entries:* 150,000. *Cross-references:* 100,000. *Contributors:* 3,300.

User Classification: Young Adult (Multivolume). *Reader Suitability:* Age 9 through 18. *Physical Size:* 7½ × 10 in.; 26 cm. *LC:* 79-84167. *ISBN:* 0-7166-0080-3. *Lowest Retail Price:* $399; to schools & libraries $336.75.

Purpose and Scope

The World Book Encyclopedia, longtime best-selling general encyclopedia in the world, is designed "especially to meet the reference and study needs of students in elementary school, junior high school, and high school" (preface). Moreover, *World Book* "also serves as a general family reference tool." The set's guiding purpose, also stated in the preface, is presentation of "information from the vast reservoir of knowledge in the most accessible and usable form." Over the years, the encyclopedia has succeeded admirably in achieving this goal.

World Book is a specific-entry encyclopedia that also includes many longer articles, some of them 50 pages or more in length. Substantial space is devoted to the continents and countries of the world, the U.S. states and Canadian provinces, important cities in North America and abroad, prominent historical figures such as Alexander the Great, Martin Luther King, Jr., Napoleon, and, of course, all the U.S. presidents and Canadian prime ministers. Broad topics like U.S. literature, animals, astronomy, cells, dentistry, drama, horses, housing, language, medicine, mountains, police, the Renaissance, the Roman Empire, rubber, space travel, and water are also accorded fairly extensive treatment. In Volume 15 (P), for instance, the article "Painting" covers more than 60 pages, "Pet" 5 pages, "Philosophy" 8 pages, "Photography" 26 pages, "Physics" 9 pages, "Pioneer Life in America" 17 pages, "Plant" 34 pages, "Post

Office" 10 pages, "Prehistoric People" 12 pages, and "President of the United States" 13 pages. Articles on these and similar subjects are copiously illustrated and often include a variety of study aids, such as outlines, review questions, and subject guides. Most articles in *World Book,* however, are less than a page in length and succinctly cover people, places, organizations, and specific events and terms in all major fields of study. Pronunciations are provided for unusual or potentially difficult terminology and proper names. The pronunciation system, which entails phonetic respelling, is both accurate and reasonably easy to understand. EXAMPLE: *"Tuberculosis: too BUR kyuh LOH sihs."* The encyclopedia also furnishes metric equivalents throughout.

Topics covered in *World Book*—and to some extent the amount of coverage provided—are determined in large part by an ongoing analysis of curriculum materials and courses of study from hundreds of schools in the United States and Canada. Called the *Nault-Caswell-Brain Curriculum Analysis* (in 61 loose-leaf volumes), the study encompasses all grade levels from kindergarten through high school and represents a fair sampling of what is currently being taught in North American classrooms. The analysis is also designed to alert *World Book* editors to new curriculum trends. In addition, the encyclopedia is continuously tested by users in more than 400 selected classrooms in the United States and Canada. Students in these schools fill out cards after consulting *World Book,* indicating their question, what headings they looked under, and whether or not they found sufficient information. Approximately 100,000 such cards are received and studied by the encyclopedia's editors each year. This information, along with the curriculum analysis, helps keep *World Book*'s contents pertinent to the reference needs of elementary and secondary students.

Traditionally, the encyclopedia's coverage of biographical and geographical topics, as well as history and the social sciences, has been outstanding. For instance, in 1980 *World Book* is the only encyclopedia reviewed in the *Buying Guide* that provides a color reproduction of the new flag of Afghanistan and explains the origin and meaning of the flag. Since the days of Sputnik, when the general science curriculum was upgraded to meet the Soviet challenge in space, the set's coverage of scientific and technical subjects has expanded accordingly. Today, *World Book*'s attention to science and technology is unequaled except by the largest multivolume adult sets, like *Collier's Encyclopedia* and *The New Encyclopaedia Britannica.* The humanities and arts are also well covered and frequently updated, as such articles as "Architecture," "Ballet," "Canadian Literature," "Motion Picture," "Museum," and "Opera" attest. Sports and recreation are likewise well covered. Coverage naturally emphasizes material of interest or concern to North American readers, but, when appropriate, international developments are summarized. The article "Transportation," for example, not only furnishes current information on the subject in the United States but also notes trends in Canada, Europe, the USSR, Asia, etc. Compared with the other multivolume young adult encyclopedias currently available (namely *Compton's Ency-*

clopedia, Encyclopedia International, and *Merit Students Encyclopedia*), *World Book* offers the broadest and deepest subject coverage in its class.

History and Authority

World Book is now over 60 years old. It first appeared in 1917 in eight volumes under the imprint of the Handson-Roach-Fowler Company, the same firm that produced the *New Practical Reference Library,* a forebear of the now defunct *American Educator Encyclopedia* (see Appendix A). An entirely new work, *World Book* was an immediate success, and over the years it grew in both size and reputation. In 1945, Marshall Field III acquired the set, and three years later Field Enterprises Educational Corporation (a subsidiary of Field Enterprises, Inc.) became the encyclopedia's official publisher. In 1977, the publisher's name was changed to World Book-Childcraft International, Inc. (WBCI), and a year later WBCI was sold to the Scott & Fetzer Company of Lakewood, Ohio, a firm that manufactures and sells the Kirby vacuum cleaner line, among other products.

WBCI also publishes *Childcraft: The How and Why Library,* a multivolume set for beginning readers (see Part VI of the *Buying Guide* for a review); the *World Book Dictionary,* a two-volume work prepared under the editorial direction of Clarence Barnhart and one of the finest general English-language dictionaries currently available; and two yearbooks, the *World Book Year Book* and *Science Year* (see "Recency"). Although WBCI has a relatively small list of titles, those it does publish are quality products.

During the last several decades, *World Book* has achieved recognition as an outstanding reference work by teachers, librarians, reviewers, and the general public. For example, the high regard librarians have for the encyclopedia is expressed in the two national surveys published in Part II of the *Buying Guide.* And the public's high regard has made *World Book* the best-selling encyclopedia on the market today. This enviable position is the result of progressive editorial leadership and innovative production techniques. In 1955, for example, the classroom research project already described (see "Purpose and Scope") was initiated. Feedback from this ongoing program permits the editors to study actual student use of the encyclopedia, with an eye toward constantly improving the set's performance. In 1961, *World Book* was published in braille in 145 volumes, the largest such printing venture ever undertaken. Three years later, a large-type edition in 30 volumes was prepared for the partially sighted. More recently, the encyclopedia has been issued on tape for the visually handicapped. Published by the American Printing House for the Blind in cooperation with WBCI, the recorded edition of *World Book* comprises 219 cassettes (six playing hours each) in 19 volumes. The contents of the tapes are easily accessed via indexes in both braille and large-print. In 1977, the publisher installed what was then the most advanced electronic composition system in the encyclopedia industry. The online system permits editors, writers, and artists to work on page revision directly at video editing computer terminals. The system is also designed to schedule and monitor revision needs. And in 1980, a Portuguese-language version of *World Book* entitled *Enciclopedia Delta Universal* was published in 15 volumes in Brazil by Editora Delta of Rio de Janeiro. These and similar developments over the years have made the name *World Book* synonymous with encyclopedia excellence throughout the world.

The 1980 edition of *World Book* continues this tradition. Dr. William H. Nault, the set's editorial director, has been *World Book*'s guiding force for over two decades. Previously he was a classroom teacher, school administrator, and college instructor. The advisory board, headed by Nault, and its various consultant committees (which cover the basic knowledge areas) are comprised of reputable authorities, mostly academicians from leading U.S. universities, such as Kempton E. Webb, professor and chairman, department of geography, Columbia University. The encyclopedia maintains a large permanent staff of editors, artists, cartographers, researchers, and production people. The staff, placed at 95 in 1977 (when the *Buying Guide* last reviewed *World Book*), now numbers 100. Finally, there are well over 3,000 contributors and consultants. The list (in Volume 1) includes both authors and authenticators of articles, as well as illustrators. The list reads like a who's who of college professors: Robert H. Abramovitz (Yale University), Richard Altick (Ohio State University), Harold Boom (Yale University), Kenneth E. Clark (University of Rochester), Frank Freidel (Harvard University), John A. Garraty (Columbia University), Eric Goldman (Princeton University), Frederick Karl (City University of New York), Walter Kaufmann (Princeton University), Harry T. Moore (Southern Illinois University), Russel B. Nye (Michigan State University), Arthur Schlesinger, Jr. (City University of New York), and T. Harry Williams (Louisiana State University) are representative of the impressive roster of academic contributors. Other names, like Isaac Asimov, Harry A. Blackmun, Bruce Catton, Michael E. DeBakey, J. William Fulbright, Walter Lord, Carl T. Rowan, and John Scarne are equally impressive. And since 1977 numerous new authorities have been added to the contributors' list, such as Peter C. English (assistant professor of pediatrics, Duke University), F. B. Evans (professor of advertising, Northwestern University), and Sandra M. Faber (associate professor of astronomy, Lick Observatory, University of California).

Almost every article in *World Book* is signed, either by the author or a critical reviewer who has authenticated the text. In the case of some longer articles, two or more authors are indicated. Only the briefest articles are unsigned, such as "Castillo de San Marcos National Monument" (seven lines); "Catgut" (nine lines). The set's authority is unquestionably sound. Indeed, *World Book*'s authority equals that of any general encyclopedia being published today, including *The New Encyclopaedia Britannica* and other large multivolume adult sets.

Reliability

World Book, as might be expected, is highly reliable. Factual information has been checked and checked again for accuracy by the authors and editors. Where fact and opinion merge, the interpretation is in accord with responsible contemporary thinking. EXAMPLE: The article "Races, Human" introduces the topic of racial classification with the following words: "The idea of race has often been misunderstood, and the term has sometimes been misused on purpose. Race has often been confused with culture, language, nationality, or religion. Differences in physical appearance have led some people to mistakenly conclude that members of some races are born with superior intelligence, talents, and moral standards."

This is not to suggest, however, that *World Book* is completely free of errors. Any undertaking as large and complex as a multivolume encyclopedia will inevitably contain some mistakes, no matter how careful or conscientious the editors. *World Book* is no exception. EXAMPLE: The article "Kansas" notes that in 1972 "terms for governor and other top state offices were increased from two years to four years, effective in 1974," but several pages later the reader learns that "in 1972, Kansas voters approved a constitutional amendment that increased the terms of the governor and other chief state offices from two years to four years. The amendment took effect in 1975." Which date is correct, 1974 or 1975?

Recency

World Book has been continuously revised each year since 1925. It has one of the most vigorous and successful revision programs of any encyclopedia published today. The publisher estimates that more than $2 million is expended annually on revision alone. The aforementioned electronic composition system (see "History and Authority"), instituted a few years ago, greatly assists the speed and efficiency of the revision process. An article in *Publishers Weekly* entitled "World Book Editors, Artists to Create, Revise Encyclopedia Pages on Terminals" (September 1, 1975, p. 47) explains: "The key to this system is the editorial work flow which it must serve. In encyclopedia publishing, as much as 80% of the editorial and composition work involves revision of existing material—material which is already in the form of made-up pages from the previous edition. Therefore, the new World Book system is designed primarily to handle made-up pages and to facilitate their revision." In the 1980 edition (under review here), the publisher reports that more than 1,650 articles (of a total of 20,000) are new or revised, and that 4,450 pages (of 14,280) have been revised in some manner. Similar revision data have been reported throughout the 1970s, indicating that *World Book*'s rate of annual revision during the past decade has been well above the recommended 10 percent figure.

Extensive analysis by the *Buying Guide* of numerous articles in the encyclopedia justifies these claims. *World Book* is admirably current, both in terms of topics in the headlines (e.g., Iran) and those that normally receive little publicity (e.g., dinosaurs). The article "Nuclear Energy," for instance, covers the accident at the Three Mile Island nuclear reactor at Harrisburg, Pa. in 1979. The article also informs that the Energy and Development Administration (ERDA) was abolished in 1977

This Recency Table compares selected topics in *World Book* with those in other encyclopedias of similar size and intended usership.

Topic	*World Book*	*Compton's*	*Encyclopedia International*	*Merit Students*
Afghanistan	Very current	Fairly current	Fairly current	Very current
Dinosaurs	Very current	Fairly current	Not current	Very current
Greenland	Very current	Not current	Not current	Very current
Thomas Jefferson	Fairly current	Fairly current	Fairly current	Fairly current
Mass Transportation/Subways	Very current	Not current	Fairly current	Fairly current
Nuclear Power	Very current	Not current	Not current	Fairly current
Paris	Very current	Fairly current	Not current	Very current
Sharks	Very current	Not current	Fairly current	Fairly current
Shock Therapy	Very current	Not current	Not current	Fairly current
Suicide	Fairly current	Not current	Not current	Very current
Tuberculosis	Very current	Not current	Not current	Very current
Zimbabwe	Very current	Very current	Fairly current	Very current

and its functions transferred to the newly created Department of Energy. The article "Indian, American" provides information about the American Indian Movement (AIM) and its protest activities during the 1970s. Also treated are recent Indian land claims in New England. Population data are usually the latest available, and five-year projections (or estimates) are given for most countries of the world. The editors correctly state in their preface that "every subject area is under continuing surveillance. The annual revision program is never confined to a single area or to certain volumes. Thousands of pages are revised or updated each year." Almost without exception, *World Book*'s contents are as current as or more current than those of any other encyclopedia, be it adult, young adult, or children's.

World Book is also updated by the annual *World Book Year Book*, a handsomely illustrated volume in eight sections. They are: Chronology, a nine-page month-by-month listing of major events of the preceding year; The Year in Focus, an analysis of the year's significant developments and trends by the *World Book Year Book* board of editors, which includes such well-known people as James J. Kilpatrick and Sylvia Porter; Special Reports, or articles on such current topics as science fiction, hypnosis, the

Voyager space program, and religious cults; A Year in Perspective, which provides a backward glance at events 100 years ago; The Year on File, an alphabetical review of the current year's happenings from "Advertising" to "Zoos and Aquariums"; *World Book Supplement,* or reprints of seven or eight new or revised articles from the current edition of *World Book;* Dictionary Supplement, a lexicon of new words and phrases that have recently entered the language; and a cumulative Index covering the most recent yearbooks.

World Book Year Book is available to owners of the encyclopedia for $12.95–$14.95, depending on the binding chosen ($17.95–$19.95 to non-owners). Unlike the vast majority of encyclopedia yearbooks, *World Book Year Book* is good investment. Efforts are made to relate its contents to those of the encyclopedia by using the same entry headings in both works. Moreover, cross-reference tabs are provided, which, when entered in the encyclopedia, link the contents of the two works. It is not difficult to understand why *World Book Year Book* is the most popular annual encyclopedia supplement on the market, with well over two million copies sold each year. The publisher also offers an attractive annual updating volume covering scientific and technical developments entitled *Science Year.* It has been published each year since 1965 and contains about 75 articles, a few of which are reprinted from the encyclopedia. *Science Year* sells for $10.95–$13.95 to owners of *World Book*, $11.95–$14.95 to others.

Objectivity

In those areas where the possibility of an emotional or biased presentation exists, *World Book* scrupulously adheres to the facts as they are known today. In those cases where legitimate differences of opinion or doubt exist, the articles attempt to present all responsible sides of the issue. EXAMPLE: The five-page article "Evolution" concludes with a subsection entitled "Objections to the Theory of Evolution." Included here is a summary of the position embraced by scientific creationists (who represent a fundamentalist Christian point of view). EXAMPLE: The 15-page article "Nuclear Energy" includes information about both the advantages and disadvantages of nuclear power. The article also has an extensive section on potential hazards and safeguards. EXAMPLE: "Homosexuality" avoids making value judgments. The article does note, however, that "the majority of people in most Western countries consider homosexuality immoral or unnatural" while the final paragraph points out that "today, many social scientists oppose laws that prohibit homosexuality and provide punishment for it. These scientists believe that homosexuals are treated unfairly for private acts that do not directly hurt others. Many nations, including Canada, England, France, The Netherlands, and Sweden, have no laws against homosexual actions between consenting adults."

Another area of potential bias where *World Book* scores high marks is the avoidance of sexism, including sexist language and sexual stereotyping in the set's illustrations. Some years ago an article in *School Library Journal* by Linda Kraft entitled "Lost Herstory" (January 1973, pp. 26–35) examined the question of sexism in five encyclopedias for young people. *World Book* and *Compton's Encyclopedia* were generally found to be more impartial than the other sets (*Britannica Junior Encyclopaedia, Merit Students Encyclopedia,* and *The New Book of Knowledge*). In the current edition of *World Book,* the articles "Woman" and "Woman Suffrage" provide excellent international coverage of women's struggle, both past and present, to end sex discrimination in education, employment, the political process, and under the law. In addition, during the late 1970s the editors made an extensive effort to weed out sexist language and assumptions from the encyclopedia. The results of this project, which entailed the revision of more than 3,500 pages of text, are readily apparent. For instance, the article "Prehistoric Man" is now called "Prehistoric People."

Clarity and Reader Suitability

The encyclopedia strives to "present information in a clear, direct style that meets the most exacting standards of readability" (preface). This is an accurate statement. For many years, *World Book* has paid stricter attention to vocabulary control and precise levels of readability than any other general encyclopedia on the market. Like many multivolume sets available today, *World Book* constructs its longer articles to read from the simple to the more complex. The article "Nuclear Energy" is a good example. At the beginning of the article, the reader learns that "scientists knew nothing about nuclear energy until the early 1900's. They then began to make important discoveries about matter and energy. They already knew that all matter consists of atoms. But scientists further learned that every atom consists mainly of its nucleus and that the nucleus is held together by an extremely powerful force. Their next challenge was to release the enormous energy bound in the nucleus." As the reader continues, however, the style, tone, vocabulary, and subject matter become somewhat more advanced: "Radioactive decay, or radioactivity, is the process by which a nucleus *spontaneously* (naturally) changes into the nucleus of another isotope or element. The process releases energy chiefly in the form of particles and rays called *nuclear radiation.* Uranium, thorium, and several other natural elements decay spontaneously and so add to the natural, or *background,* radiation that is always present in the earth's atmosphere. Nuclear reactors produce radioactive decay artificially. Nuclear radiation accounts for about 10 per cent of the energy produced in a reactor."

Note in the example above that not only is the article written in pyramid style (from simple to complex), but new and technical terms are italicized and defined in context. This approach to vocabulary is based on a 44,000-word graded list developed by Dr. Edgar Dale of Ohio State University, a leading authority on readability and special consultant to *World Book.* Dr. Dale and his staff review all new and heavily revised articles in each edition of *World Book* prior to publication to make sure that the vocabulary is geared to the encyclopedia's intended readership. This procedure ensures a high degree of comprehension of material as well as assisting in vocabulary development. In addition, when appropriate, articles are written to grade level. EXAMPLE: "Pet" is written for elementary readers whereas "Nuclear Energy" is geared to secondary school students. Prior to publication, such articles are tested for readability and comprehension by students at the appropriate grade levels.

Perhaps more than any other encyclopedia, *World Book* writers have what the review journal *Choice* has called "a knack for clarity on complicated subjects" (December 1968, p. 1280). The encyclopedia also takes pains to make its text as interesting as possible. EXAMPLE: The article on Thomas Jefferson describes the Burr Conspiracy in this way:

> Aaron Burr, already discredited in politics, had further damaged his reputation by killing Alexander Hamilton in a duel in July, 1804. He then became involved in a mysterious scheme, the purpose of which is still not clear. He may have wanted to take the West away from the United States, or perhaps to conquer the Spanish Southwest. In any case, Burr tried unsuccessfully to get support from the British, French, or Spanish against his own government. He then raised a small military force of his own. In 1806, Burr set off down the Ohio River for New Orleans, hoping to gather recruits along the way. General James Wilkinson, the governor of Louisiana, had encouraged Burr to expect his support. But he decided to expose Burr's plot, and write to Jefferson about a "deep, dark, wicked, and widespread conspiracy." Jefferson had Burr captured, taken to Richmond, and tried for treason. To the disgust of Jefferson and others, Chief Justice Marshall interpreted the charge of treason so narrowly that the jury had to acquit Burr.

Arrangement and Accessibility

World Book is a specific-entry encyclopedia arranged alphabetically, word-by-word ("Indian Ocean" precedes "Indiana"). More than 100,000 cross-references appear throughout the set. Many are external references entered in the A–Z sequence along with the entry headings. Sometimes these external references guide the reader to specific sections of a particular article. EXAMPLE: "*Gateway Arch.* See MISSOURI (PLACES TO VISIT); SAINT LOUIS (PICTURE)." Numerous *See* and *See also* references also appear within and at the end of articles. Often these internal references take the form of lists of "Related Articles" at the end of a particular entry. The article "Child," for instance, lists 50 related articles, including "Day-Care Center," "Early Childhood Education," "Kindergarten," "Parent Education," "Pediatrics," and "Sex Education."

For much of its life, *World Book* existed without an index, relying entirely on its extensive system of cross-references to provide access to specific information. In 1972, however, the editors issued an additional volume called the *Research Guide/Index*. It contains over 150,000 index entries, plus some 200 reading and study guides distributed throughout the volume. It also includes an essay entitled "How to Do Research."

Unlike *Compton's* Fact-Index, *World Book*'s *Research Guide/Index* is very easy to use and understand. The index closely analyzes the text, down to the most minute fact. EXAMPLE: The article "Naples" states under the subheading "The People" that the city is "the birthplace of pizza, which a baker at the royal court may have invented in the 1700s." In the index under "Pizza," there is a reference to "Naples" ("The People") with the appropriate volume and page number following. Computer-produced, *World Book*'s index is both thorough and accurate. Illustrations and tabular information are also indexed. Since the addition of the *Research Guide/Index,* one of *World Book*'s special strengths has been easy and comprehensive access to the information contained in the set.

Bibliographies

Major articles normally conclude with selected bibliographies that list anywhere from 3 to 40 titles; for instance, "Transportation" cites 21 titles and "Indian, American" 37 titles. These bibliographies, which are usually divided into two reader categories ("Books for Younger Readers" and "Books for Older Readers"), tend to be well selected and reasonably current. Many articles that need bibliographies, however, lack them. EXAMPLES: "Homosexuality"; "Horse Racing"; "Hospital"; "Hotel"; "House"; "Housing"; "Human Body"; "Hurricane"; "Hydraulics"; "Hypnotism."

The encyclopedia also includes 200 reading and study guides in the aforementioned *Research Guide/Index* (see "Arrangement and Accessibility"), the final volume in the set. These guides provide lists of "Books to Read" (ordinarily ten titles), which, like the bibliographies throughout the set, are classified by reading level. Most of the guides also cite "Other Resources," such as films, filmstrips, cassettes, records, and other non-print materials. Usually the guides end with "Other Sources of Information," which indicate a few reference sources and/or organizations. The reading and study guide on American Indians, for instance, notes the American Indian Historical Society, the Canadian Department of Indian Affairs and Northern Development, the U.S. Bureau of Indian Affairs, and the National Congress of American Indians as potential sources of information, along with the *Readers' Guide to Periodical Literature* (a well-known magazine index in almost all libraries). Addresses for all publishers and organizations cited in the guides are given in the back of the volume. In some cases these guides are not as up-to-date as they might be. EXAMPLE: The reading and study guide on Thomas Jefferson includes nothing more recent than 1969; if nothing else, the list should cite Fawn Brodie's indispensable *Thomas Jefferson: An Intimate History* (1974). Overall, *World Book*'s bibliographies, while quite useful, are not always as plentiful or as current as they might be.

Graphics

Like *Compton's Encyclopedia* (a principal competitor), *World Book* has traditionally been noted for outstanding graphics. The set is extensively illustrated with constantly updated photographs, cutaway drawings, diagrams, charts, reproductions of famous paintings and other art works, and the like, many of which have been commissioned by *World Book* for exclusive use in the encyclopedia. The illustrations are strategically placed to clarify or supplement the printed text. Almost half of the 29,500 graphics are in color, and the quality of color reproduction is superb, due at least in part to the special paper used by *World Book* (see "Physical Format"). The editors make a special point of noting that color is used to enhance the informational value of an article, and "not merely for decorative effect or eye appeal" (preface). The truth of this statement is seen in such articles as "Architecture," which includes many black-and-white photographs and line drawings quite suitable for comparing styles and tracing the transition from one period to another. Less confident or knowledgeable art editors have a tendency to dress up such articles with flashy but hardly more instructive pictures. On the other hand, the article "Dinosaur" contains a number of drawings in color in order to convey the bright and variegated appearance of dinosaurs (recent research has dispelled the notion that all dinosaurs were greenish-gray in color).

World Book's 2,350 maps are likewise of excellent quality. Both physical and political maps accompany all articles on the U.S. states and Canadian provinces, as well as many countries and continents. Rand McNally is responsible for the physical series and the encyclopedia's own full-time cartographic staff produces the political series. All these maps are in color, and the political ones have their own indexes. In addition, there are numerous historical, locator, and city maps, as well as those showing population trends, economic development, climatic conditions, vegetation distribution, and so forth. Practically all of these special-purpose maps are produced by *World Book* cartographers.

Physical Format

World Book is currently published in four different bindings: (1) the less expensive Standard, which sells for $399; (2) the Renaissance at $449; (3) the Classical at $499; and (4) the heavy-duty School & Library binding at $336.75 to educational institutions and $449 to retail customers. Each of these bindings is attractive and constructed to withstand heavy use. The individual volumes are sewn and lie flat when open. The School & Library binding has several special features designed to make it hold up even under the most punishing use, including Pyroxylin-coated cloth covers, side-wire stitching, and mercerized head and foot bands. The School & Library binding also includes the date of the edition on the spine of each volume. *World Book* employs the unit-letter system in all bindings, meaning that all entries for a particular letter (A) or letters (Q–R) are contained in one volume (two letters, C and S, require two volumes apiece). The volumes are therefore not of equal size; for example,

Volume 1 (A) contains 976 pages, whereas Volume 12 (L) contains only 470 pages. In the 1980 edition, Volumes 1 (A), 13 (M), 14 (N–O), 15 (P), and 22 (*Research Guide/Index*) are a bit bulky, and some users, especially younger readers, might find them cumbersome to handle. Perhaps *World Book* is at the point where it should expand to 26 or even 30 volumes.

Inside, the encyclopedia is very appealing. The two-column page layout is well designed, with adequate margins and good use of boldface headings and subheadings. The Baskerville and Futura typefaces used by *World Book* are both aesthetically pleasing and functional. The high-quality paper—50-pound, machine-coated, web offset—is manufactured especially to meet the encyclopedia's exacting standards for color reproduction. In almost all respects, *World Book* is physically the best-made encyclopedia in its class.

Special Features

The encyclopedia provides a number of special features, some unique. In 1975, *World Book* became the first major encyclopedia to go metric. Anticipating that the United States will eventually switch to the International Metric System (now used by all the important nations of the world except the United States), the encyclopedia has added metric equivalents to more than 30,000 measurements cited in the set. EXAMPLE: In the "Naples" article it is noted that "the newer western part of the city lies along the Riviera di Chiaia, a broad drive that runs 3 miles (5 kilometers) along the Bay of Naples." EXAMPLE: In the article on Carry Nation, the hatchet-wielding foe of liquor, the reader learns that she was nearly six feet tall—or 183 centimeters. When and if the United States goes metric, *World Book* will have helped to prepare the way by accustoming its users to the new system.

Another noteworthy special feature is *World Book*'s Science Projects. Accompanying about 18 articles, the Science Projects are practical how-to-do-it demonstrations of basic scientific principles (e.g., the effects of air pressure), which the reader can conduct. Step-by-step instructions are provided through both words and pictures. See "Biology" for an example.

The provision of review questions at the end of many longer articles is another useful special feature. EXAMPLE: At the conclusion of the article "Revolutionary War in America" there are ten questions designed to test the reader's comprehension of the article, such as "What did John Adams mean when he wrote: 'The Revolution was effected before the war commenced'?" Such questions will be of help particularly to students. Articles with review questions also include a study outline of the topic.

Other special features include easily understandable pronunciations for unusual or potentially difficult names and terms, glossaries of specialized vocabulary for certain topics (e.g., "Photography"), the 200 reading and study guides in the final volume (discussed in detail under "Bibliographies"), and an informative essay entitled "How to Do Research" (also in the final volume).

Sales Information

World Book is sold in-home on the subscription, or installment, plan. Sales personnel—mostly local people including housewives and school-teachers who sell the encyclopedia and related products on a part-time basis—use both door-to-door canvassing and selling by appointment. Many potential *World Book* customers are reached through the publisher's aggressive national and local advertising campaigns. The publisher estimates that more than $1 million is spent each year on promotion. Moreover, telephone directories for most larger places in the United States and Canada list a *World Book* representative in the Yellow Pages under "Encyclopedias."

As already noted (see "Physical Format"), there are four different bindings currently available, ranging in price from $399 to $499. Quoted prices include shipping and handling, but not state or local tax. The least expensive binding is the Standard, which retails for $399, followed by the Renaissance at $449 and the Classical at $499. Consumers should understand that the contents of the encyclopedia are the same no matter what the binding. The reinforced School & Library binding is available to educational institutions at the discount price of $336.75; retail customers who wish to buy the School & Library binding will pay $449. Consumers should also be aware of the publisher's current "trade-in" policy, which permits owners of the *World Book Year Book* (see "Recency") a $13 per volume allowance (up to $130, or ten volumes) against the price of the current edition of *World Book*. Note that this trade-in deal applies only to retail sales (hence excluding schools and libraries). The publisher—World Book-Childcraft International, Inc. (WBCI)—now also offers what is called an "exchange option." Again limited to retail customers, the exchange option allows those who purchased both *World Book* and *Childcraft: The How and Why Library* in combination at least five years ago to exchange their old set of *World Book* for the latest edition at half its current price. (Note that *Childcraft*, a 15-volume set for beginning readers, is also published by WBCI; see Part VI of the *Buying Guide* for a review.)

Other WBCI publications are normally available at substantial discounts as optional purchases when bought in combination with *World Book*. These include the aforementioned *World Book Year Book* and *Science Year*, annual updating supplements (see "Recency"), and of course *Childcraft*, which can be acquired for $129 if purchased with *World Book* (the set retails for $179). Also offered is the *World Book Dictionary*, a truly outstanding general English-language dictionary published in two volumes. The dictionary, which bears the prestigious Thorndike-Barnhart imprint, is available in three different bindings (Standard, Renaissance, and Classical), which are listed at $69, $74, and $79 respectively, but cost $55.20, $59.20, and $63.20 if purchased in combination with *World Book*. And *Cyclo-teacher Learning Aid*, a teaching machine with programmed materials designed to teach or review basic subjects and concepts, is priced at $139 if purchased separately, $111.20 if purchased with *World Book*.

Some consumers may also be interested in acquiring the previously mentioned recorded edition of *World Book* (see "History and Authority"), the first general encyclopedia published on tape for the blind and partially sighted. The set comprises 219 cassettes, each of which plays for six hours, plus indexes in both braille and large-print. The cassettes are housed in 19 volumes, or cases, which require approximately five and a half feet of shelf space. The recorded edition of *World Book* is distributed by the American Printing House for the Blind, Inc. (1839 Frankfort Ave., Box 6085, Louisville, KY 40206), and sells for $1175 (estimated).

Summary

The World Book Encyclopedia can be quickly summed up in this manner:

Scope: Excellent	Accessibility: Excellent
Authority: Excellent	Bibliographies: Good
Reliability: Excellent	Graphics: Excellent
Recency: Excellent	Physical Format: Excellent
Objectivity: Excellent	Special Features: Many
Clarity: Excellent	Price: Reasonable

To elaborate briefly, *World Book* continues to be one of the best designed and meticulously edited general encyclopedias ever made. As the digest above indicates, the encyclopedia passes practically every major critical test with flying colors. The set is constructed to serve a very broad readership, ranging from students in the upper elementary grades to adults seeking basic information or reliable overview material on both academic and practical subjects. The set's authority is unimpeachable, its contents thoroughly accessible, and its up-to-dateness and rate of annual continuous revision unexcelled. The text is clear, direct, and usually interesting, and, when appropriate, the articles are written in pyramid style (i.e., from simple to complex). In addition, the vocabulary is strictly controlled by means of readability testing, and, again when appropriate, articles are written to grade level. The illustrations, including maps, are impressive, both in terms of quality and quantity. Only in the area of bibliographies, which are not always as plentiful or as current as they might be, does the encyclopedia fail to meet the highest standard. In sum, *World Book,* the best-selling general encyclopedia in the world, is at once a highly functional and aesthetically appealing reference work.

The *Buying Guide* is not alone in proclaiming *World Book*'s overall excellence. In 1978, a study conducted by the Information Center of the Chicago Public Library found that *World Book* was at the top of its list of most heavily used reference sources. And the independent surveys of U.S. and Canadian public librarians published in this edition of the *Buying Guide* (see Part II) confirm that *World Book* is far and away the first choice of professionals who deal with knowledge and information day in and day out.

Comparatively speaking, *World Book* competes directly with three other encyclopedias in the multivolume young adult class, namely *Compton's Encyclopedia, Encyclopedia International,* and *Merit Students Encyclopedia.* Each of these encyclopedias is aimed at roughly the same audience, each provides balanced coverage geared to the North American school curriculum, and each is authoritative and useful in its way. *The World Book Encyclopedia,* however, stands out from the rest as a consistently superior work available at a comparatively modest price. *Merit Students Encyclopedia,* a very well maintained and constantly improving set, has supplanted *Compton's Encyclopedia* as the chief challenger to *World Book* for dominance in its class. *Compton's,* once the preeminent encyclopedia in the young adult group, has been living on its reputation and little else for too many years. It is preferable only when compared with *Encyclopedia International,* a drab set with little to offer the discerning consumer. To repeat, *World Book* is tops in its class. The set adeptly combines the most desirable qualities associated with adult and juvenile encyclopedia-making. *World Book* is, page-for-page, the best encyclopedia on the market today.

Other Critical Opinions

Booklist, May 1, 1979, pp. 1383–1385. This unsigned review by the ALA Reference and Subscription Books Review Committee (RSBRC) is generally favorable, and the encyclopedia is "recommended" for home and library purchase. The review, however, questions *World Book*'s accuracy ("Most of the material sampled in *World Book* seems to be accurate") but, interestingly, not one example of an inaccuracy is cited. This same group also reviewed *World Book* five months earlier as part of a series entitled "Encyclopedias: A Survey and Buying Guide" (*Booklist,* December 15, 1978, pp. 714–715), in which the encyclopedia was pronounced "remarkably reliable."

Depp, Roberta J. *American Reference Books Annual,* 1978, pp. 43–44. An entirely favorable review that commends *World Book* to both young people and adults.

Katz, William A. *Basic Information Sources* (Vol. 1 of *Introduction to Reference Work,* 3rd ed. New York: McGraw-Hill, 1978), pp. 159–161. Katz, a highly respected reference book critic, comparatively evaluates *Compton's Encyclopedia, Merit Students Encyclopedia,* and *The World Book Encyclopedia,* the three leading sets for young adults. Says Katz, "Thanks to its timeliness, organization, and illustrations, as well as its writing style, *World Book* is usually a first choice."

VI. MULTIVOLUME CHILDREN'S ENCYCLOPEDIAS

Britannica Junior Encyclopaedia

Facts in Brief

Full Title: **Britannica Junior Encyclopaedia for Boys and Girls.** *Editor:* Marvin Martin. *Publisher:* Encyclopaedia Britannica, Inc., 425 N. Michigan Ave., Chicago, IL 60611. *Original Title: Weedon's Modern Encyclopedia* (1931–1932). *Edition Reviewed:* 1980 copyright.

Volumes: 15. *Pages:* 8,000. *Articles:* 4,100. *Words:* 5,300,000. *Illustrations:* 12,700. *Maps:* 1,050. *Index Entries:* 57,000. *Cross-references:* 5,800. *Contributors:* 800.

User Classification: Children (Multivolume). *Reader Suitability:* Age 7 through 14. *Physical Size:* 7¾ x 9½ in.; 24 cm. *LC:* 78-75145. *ISBN:* 0-85229-361-5. *Lowest Retail Price:* $199.50.

Purpose and Scope

The *Britannica Junior Encyclopaedia,* in the words of the editor, "is designed and edited as a beginner's encyclopaedia—a first introduction to reference and research work." The set's fundamental purpose is "to provide a simple, accurate, and easy-to-use reference work for the elementary school student." Furthermore, *Britannica Junior* is said to be "oriented to elementary school curriculums," accomplished by studying curriculum guides from various school systems and closely relating the contents of the encyclopedia to these guides. An Editorial Advisory Committee composed of educators with experience at the elementary school level also provides input concerning article selection and presentation.

Britannica Junior is *not* a watered-down version of the old *Encyclopaedia Britannica* (1768–1973) and it bears no resemblance to *The New Encyclopaedia Britannica* (1974–   ). In point of fact, *Britannica Junior's* contents and design are much more akin to Grolier's *New Book of Knowledge* (its only substantial competitor) than to either *Encyclopaedia Britannica,* new or old. The only relationship between the junior and senior *Britannica*s is that they share the same famous name and are published by the same firm.

Britannica Junior's scope is generally limited to those subjects taught in U.S. and Canadian elementary schools, although some articles also cover young people's out-of-school interests, such as hobbies and recreational activities. The 4,000 or so articles are usually devoted to broad topics (fire, fire prevention, first aid, fish, flags, Florida, flowers, folklore, folk songs, food, football, forestry, France, French literature, French Revolution, fuel). These and similar entries ordinarily run from one or two pages in length to 20 or 25 pages, depending on the nature and importance of the subject matter. Some specific entries covering persons and places of comparatively lesser importance (John Galsworthy, William Lloyd Garrison, Gaul, Geneva, the Grand Canyon) are accorded a single page or less. Shorter articles also treat specific plants, animals, organizations, scientific and literary terms, and historical events.

These main entries are supplemented by about 25,000 very brief factual articles in the Ready Reference Index. Most of these articles deal with biographical and geographical topics, such as Le Corbusier (the French architect) and Narragansett Bay. The Ready Reference Index (described under "Arrangement and Accessibility") is similar in construction to *Compton's* Fact-Index, *New Book of Knowledge*'s Dictionary Index, and to some extent the *Micropaedia* portion of *The New Encyclopaedia Britannica*.

Britannica Junior's coverage of the principal areas of knowledge is reasonably well balanced, although scientific and technical topics customarily receive fuller and more current attention than the humanities. EXAMPLE: The rapidly developing study of oceanography is comprehensively treated for readers at the elementary level, whereas the encyclopedia's coverage of contemporary music is practically nonexistent, except for a couple of superficial entries in the Ready Reference Index. The health sciences are adequately covered at this level, as are biological subjects. EXAMPLE: The article "Heart and Blood Vessels" clearly reviews the functions, workings, and diseases of the human circulatory system. EXAMPLE: "Reproduction" is an intelligent, informative presentation of how plants and animals, including human beings, reproduce. There is, however, no information on birth control, except for a brief definitional entry of 45–50 words in the Ready Reference Index. At a time when teenage pregnancy has reach epidemic proportions, it would seem reasonable for encyclopedias for young people to provide at least rudimentary information about birth control and family planning.

Biographical, geographical, and historical topics are adequately covered, considering the intended readership. George Washington, for instance, receives a ten-page article that fully reviews his life and achievements. The article includes numerous informative black-and-white illustrations and a concise time chart showing important dates during Washington's lifetime. The U.S. states and major nations of the world receive especially impressive coverage; for instance, "China" comprises 25 pages, "Chile" 7 pages. Various sports are also well covered. Contemporary social questions are sometimes dealt with, sometimes not. EXAMPLE: The articles "Drug" and "Drug Abuse" provide a good overview of the pervasive problem of drug use in today's society. A chart showing some commonly abused drugs provides accurate information at a glance. On the other hand, the contemporary women's movement and the problem of sexism are virtually ignored, except for a short entry entitled "Women's Liberation" in the Ready Reference Index and a paragraph on women's rights in the article "Civil Rights." Also, recently a 13-line entry on the Equal Rights Amendment has been added to the Ready Reference Index.

History and Authority

Britannica Junior is published by Encyclopaedia Britannica, Inc., "with the editorial advice of the faculties of the University of Chicago and the University Laboratory Schools," according to a notation following the title page. *The New Encyclopaedia Britannica* carries a similar notation. As explained earlier, *Britannica Junior* is not actually a junior version of *Encyclopaedia Britannica* or its successor, *The New Encyclopaedia Britannica*. Instead, *Britannica Junior* derives directly from an eight-volume children's encyclopedia entitled *Weedon's Modern Encyclopedia,* which was published in 1931–1932 by the S. L. Weedon Company of Cleveland, Ohio. In 1934, Britannica acquired the rights, expanded the set to 12 volumes, and retitled it *Britannica Junior: An Encyclopaedia for Boys and Girls.* In 1947, the set was again enlarged, this time to its present size of 15 volumes. Despite its impressive name and favorable reputation for reliability, *Britannica Junior* has never achieved the sales success its makers had envisioned. Perhaps the reason for this is that *Compton's Encyclopedia,* now also published by Britannica, not only appeals to much the same readership, but is unquestionably a superior set.

Marvin Martin has edited *Britannica Junior* for many years. He is supported by an editorial and production staff of 25, the same number as when the *Buying Guide* last reviewed *Britannica Junior* in 1977. An Editorial Advisory Committee assists in relating the set's contents to elementary school curricula. Comprised of ten members, including four from the University of Chicago Laboratory Schools, this group is experienced in both classroom teaching and curriculum planning. Members of the advisory committee are the same as in 1975, except for the addition of Rebecca T. Bingham (director of media services, Jefferson County Public Schools, Louisville, Ky.), who replaces the well-known Sara Fenwick. There are also 11 editorial consultants listed. Mainly college and university professors, they represent a wide range of subject authority. In addition, approximately 800 contributing editors and writers are noted in the first volume. Their academic qualifications are indicated, along with the topics they contributed or reviewed. The list contains a few prominent names (for instance, Isaac Asimov and J. Edgar Hoover), but for the most part the contributors are lesser-known scholars, government officials, and industry representatives. The contributors' list has not changed greatly since 1977, although a few new names have been added, such as Charles M. Croner (chief, Technical Services Branch, National Center for Health Statistics) and Ernest Clark Griffin (associate professor and chairman, Latin American Studies Program, San Diego State University). J. Edgar Hoover continues to be identified as "Former Director, Federal Bureau of Investigation," instead of the late director. Some of the other contributors are now also deceased. All articles in *Britannica Junior* are unsigned.

Reliability

Britannica Junior is a responsibly edited encyclopedia. As might be expected, the set normally has its facts correct, although now and then misinformation does occur. EXAMPLE: The article "Shark" contains several small errors; for example, the statement that "the man-eating Lake Nicaragua shark lives only in fresh water" is erroneous. EXAMPLE: The article "Indians, North American" inaccurately refers to the Creek Confederacy as "an individual Indian state." It is also misleading to say that "Europeans were impressed by the Indian's sense of freedom and joy of living." Other errors are due to outdated information. The article "Typewriter," for instance, incorrectly notes that "the latest major development in the electric typewriter is the proportional spacing model. In this model carbon paper ribbon provides a continuous supply of fresh carbon deposit." (For additional information on this problem, see "Recency.")

Recency

The publisher estimates that 350 articles in *Britannica Junior* are revised each year. This figure suggests that the encyclopedia's rate of annual revision is below the suggested 10 percent minimum standard. Close examination of numerous articles confirms the set's mediocre performance in the area of recency. Relatively little new material has been added to *Britannica Junior* between 1977 (when the *Buying Guide* last examined the set) and 1980. For instance, the 1980 edition (under review here) includes only 11 new articles of any substance, such as "Antarctic Region"; "Dance"; "Prefix and Suffix"; "Steinbeck, John." Also, some new entries are added to the Ready Reference Index (Volume 1) each year, but they are merely brief dictionary-style definitions of such terms as *Equal Rights Amendment*. Likewise, relatively few major articles in Volumes 2–15 have been thoroughly revised during the 1977–1980 period. In the current edition, for example, only 17 such articles are evident, including "Athletics"; "China"; "Family"; "Iran"; "Marriage and Divorce"; "Piano"; "Stamp and Stamp Collecting." The rest of the revision in the 1980 set occurs in the Ready Reference Index at the front of the set.

Evidence of dated material is not difficult to find. The article "Housing" concludes with the establishment of the Department of Housing and Urban Development (HUD) nearly 20 years ago. The modest coverage of rock music—six lines in the Ready Reference Index—is hardly in tune with today's young people. The article "Asia" still refers to the country of North Vietnam (now Vietnam) and contains such ambiguous statements as "Before World War II, Burma, Thailand, and Indochina built up a surplus rice supply and were active in world trade. Since the war they have exported less rice because of poorer crops and trouble within the countries." "Atomic Energy" is at least a decade out-of-date, and according to *Britannica Junior,* the Atomic Energy Commission, abolished in 1974, still has "responsibility for directing government work with atomic material for war and peace." "Farming" has not been revised for at least ten years. "Football" is not current concerning the rules of the game. The same is true of "Basketball." "Ku Klux Klan" (in the Ready Reference

This Recency Table compares selected topics in *Britannica Junior* with those in other encyclopedias of similar size and intended usership.

Topic	Britannica Junior	New Book of Knowledge	Oxford Junior	Young Students
Africa	Very current	Very current	Not current	Fairly current
Babies/Children	Not current	Fairly current	Not current	Not current
Disease	Fairly current	Fairly current	Not current	Fairly current
North American Indians	Very current	Fairly current	Not current	Not current
Sharks	Fairly current	Very current	Fairly current	Fairly current
Television	Fairly current	Very current	Not current	Fairly current

Index) fails to note the recent resurgence of the KKK. "Greenland" provides 1960 population data and makes no mention of the fact that the island achieved home rule several years ago. "Telephone" is current only as of the mid-1960s.

The publisher offers an annual volume entitled the *Illustrated Encyclopedia Yearbook* as a supplementary means of updating *Britannica Junior*. The yearbook, which sells for $8.95 plus a small charge for shipping and handling, furnishes the usual review of the preceding year's events, but it is in no way related to the encyclopedia. Hence, its value as an updating tool is nil. Also, in the past, consumers purchasing *Britannica Junior* have sometimes been encouraged to buy the *Britannica Book of the Year,* an annual designed to help keep *The New Encyclopaedia Britannica* current. Consumers should reject such blandishments. The *Britannica Book of the Year* is far too advanced for younger readers, and it has absolutely no connection with *Britannica Junior*.

Objectivity

The encyclopedia makes every effort to present sensitive and controversial material as fairly and impartially as humanly possible. EXAMPLE: The article "Discrimination" points out that "the discrimination against Negroes in housing has caused overcrowding in the places they can live, which helps create slums. This condition in turn leads to an increase in fires, disease, delinquency, and crime. The effects are felt by the people who practice the discrimination as well as the victims." EXAMPLE: "Drug Abuse" does not rant and rave about the evils of excessive drug use, whether it be abuse of licit drugs (alcohol and tobacco) or the more controversial illicit ones (like marijuana or cocaine). Rather, the article unemotionally points up the dangers of abuse while at the same time explaining why it is so widespread at the present time: "People abuse drugs for various reasons. Some do it to change their feelings. They may feel lonely, depressed, or inadequate. They may believe that drugs can magically solve their problems. Some abuse drugs for excitement and pleasure, to relieve boredom, or to keep up with their friends. Others believe that drugs expand intelligence or understanding." On the negative side, however, certain polemical subjects like birth control, abortion, and homosexuality are ignored altogether.

Clarity and Reader Suitability

Britannica Junior is specifically geared to children in the elementary grades. The encyclopedia will also be useful and comprehensible to average middle school students, as well as to slow readers at the high school level. Although the set is "oriented to elementary school curriculums" (preface), there has apparently been no effort to control vocabulary by means of a readability formula such as those used by *The New Book of Knowledge* or *The World Book Encyclopedia*. Nonetheless, *Britannica Junior* is usually very readable, although occasionally the syntax, or sentence structure, may be too sophisticated for average readers in grades 3 through 6, the set's principal target group. EXAMPLE: The article "Force" discusses centrifugal force in this manner: "The inward leaning (banking) of roads, airplanes, and bicycles on a turn helps to balance centrifugal force, which tends to hurl the object outward. By leaning inward the tendency to move outward is balanced so that the turn can be completed properly. Otherwise there is a tendency to skid or topple." Normally, new or technical terms are defined in context. EXAMPLE: The article "Disease" explains the meaning of such potentially unfamiliar words and phrases as *pathology, bacteria, protozoa, metabolism,* and *filterable viruses,* as well as the suffix *-itis.* For instance, "Diseases of metabolism (building up and breaking down of living cells) include those caused when certain organs of the body do not do their jobs." Overall, the encyclopedia's style and reader suitability are quite comparable to those of *The New Book of Knowledge (Britannica Junior*'s chief competitor).

Arrangement and Accessibility

The 4,100 main articles in Volumes 2–15 are arranged alphabetically, letter-by-letter ("Indiana" precedes "Indian Ocean"). A limited number of internal *See* references are provided within and at the end of the longer, broad-entry articles; for instance, the 11-page "Fossil" includes *See* references to "Amber"; "Arthropoda"; "Echinoderm"; "Ecology"; "Evolution"; "Geology"; "Man"; "Mollusk"; and "Vertebrate." External cross-references are also used, though quite sparingly, such as "Dinosaur: See FOSSIL." The principal means of locating specific information, however, is through the Ready Reference Index, which comprises Volume 1 of the set. This rather unusual procedure is explained in the following manner: "Most indexes are found in the back of a book or set but this one has been made Volume 1 because it must be used first if you wish to find all of the information in the set about your topic." As mentioned earlier (see "Purpose and Scope"), the Ready Reference Index includes some 25,000 brief factual articles on specific people, places, and things not covered in the main portion of the encyclopedia. These entries are also arranged letter-by-letter. But the Ready Reference Index also contains approximately 57,000 analytical index references to the 4,100 main articles. Hence, the Ready Reference Index serves the dual function of a source of quick reference information and a general index to the set.

The Ready Reference Index has been revised and redesigned recently. It is uncomplicated and easy to use, unlike the Fact-Index of *Compton's Encyclopedia* and the *Micropaedia* portion of *The New Encyclopedia Britannica* (with which the Ready Reference Index shares a similar, albeit simpler, structure). And it is contained in a single volume, unlike *The New Book of Knowledge*'s Dictionary Index, also similar in purpose and design to the Ready Reference Index. The Ready Reference Index usually makes the set's contents readily accessible, including illustrations. There are, however, occasions when the indexing is not thorough enough. EXAMPLE: The article "Adolescence" contains considerable information about physical and sexual maturation, but the index entry "Sex" does not refer the user to that article. EXAMPLE: The musical instruments lyre and cithara are mentioned in the article "Orchestra," and although there is an index entry "Lyre," there is none for the cithara. As a rule, access to the material in *Britannica Junior* is efficient, quick, and easy. But the Ready Reference Index unfortunately is not as comprehensive as it might be.

Bibliographies

Only one article—"Children's Literature"—contains a bibliography. This list is graded (readers under five; five to seven; seven to nine; and so on), encompasses seven pages, and includes only the best literature. Other topics should have such lists. The lack of bibliographies limits *Britannica Junior*'s usefulness as a children's reference work. The publisher has informed the *Buying Guide,* however, that a "reading guide" will be added to the 1981 edition. This guide will be evaluated in the next edition of the *Buying Guide.*

Graphics

Britannica Junior is tastefully and colorfully illustrated with numerous photographs, drawings, and charts. They are usually clear, informative, and placed in good relationship to the text they complement. The publisher claims that approximately half the illustrations are in color. This estimate appears to be too high. In a number of instances, black-and-white graphics are used where color would obviously enhance the informational value of the material. EXAMPLE: The photograph of a copperhead snake accompanying the article "Copperhead" notes in the caption that "this brown and copper-colored snake is about three and one-half feet long." Regrettably, the photo is quite dark and in black-and-white. In any case, *Britannica Junior* is not as profusely nor as strikingly illustrated as its main rival, *The New Book of Knowledge.*

Britannica Junior's maps are excellent. The final volume contains an atlas that includes both political and physical maps of continents, countries, and states. These maps were prepared by the reputable C. S. Hammond & Company of New York. Following the 144-plate atlas is an index of place-names, which has 57,000 entries. In addition, many historical, locator, and special-purpose maps are included throughout the encyclopedia. These were produced by Rand McNally, the Jeppesen Company, and the Britannica cartographical staff. The publisher boasts that *Britannica Junior* is "probably the best mapped encyclopedia at its cost." This statement is probably correct. The maps are plentiful, clearly drawn, easy to use, and satisfactorily indexed, although the maps in the separate atlas are not cited in the Ready Reference Index. All maps are current as of the end of the 1970s.

Physical Format

Two similar bindings are available, each designed for a specific market. Individual consumers receive a blue Holliston Lexotone binding with orange panels and gold lettering. (Lexotone is a strong Pyroxylin-coated nonwoven material.) For schools and libraries, there is a Holliston Sturdite binding. Both bindings are attractive and well constructed. The individual volumes are easy to handle and lie flat when open. The popular unit-letter system is used—that is, there are no split letters among the volumes. Inside, the layout is functional rather than striking. The margins are rather narrow on all sides, including the gutters (inside margins), but this does not interfere with legibility. The 10-point and 12-point type is well leaded and easy on the eyes. In addition, nonglare paper is used. Guide words appear at the top of each page. Overall, the set's appearance and construction are satisfactory. *Britannica Junior*'s competitor, *The New Book of Knowledge,* however, is a much more attractively and creatively designed encyclopedia for young people.

Special Features

The encyclopedia's chief special feature is the Ready Reference Index (see "Purpose and Scope"; "Arrangement and Accessibility"). Introduced as an integral part of the set from the beginning (1934), the Ready Reference Index is not unique among encyclopedias. *Compton's Encyclopedia*'s Fact-Index, the *Micropaedia* of *The New Encyclopaedia Britannica,* and *The New Book of Knowledge*'s Dictionary Index are all similar in purpose and design. But *Britannica Junior* is the only general encyclopedia currently produced whose index is at the beginning of the set rather than the end. Another special feature is *Britannica Junior*'s extensive world atlas in Volume 15 (see "Graphics"). Finally, the school and library edition of the encyclopedia comes with a paperback booklet entitled *Discovering Britannica Junior.* The 42-page book will assist students in developing basic reference skills, particularly when searching for information in *Britannica Junior.*

Sales Information

Britannica Junior is sold in-home on the subscription, or installment, basis for $199.50 plus shipping and handling and any tax. Only the blue, orange, and gold Holliston Lexotone binding already described (see "Physical Format") is available at retail. The set is also sold directly to schools and libraries at the same price (but minus the shipping and handling charge), although the binding (Sturdite) is slightly different, being reinforced for heavy use. The inexpensive 25-volume supermarket edition available in 1977 has been discontinued, at least at the present time. *Britannica Junior* may be sold in combination with other Britannica reference products, including *The New Encyclopaedia Britannica* and the *Britannica Book of the Year*. As explained (see "Recency"), this yearbook does not serve as a satisfactory updating supplement to *Britannica Junior* and should not be purchased as such. More appropriate would be the *Illustrated Encyclopedia Yearbook* (also described under "Recency"), an annual volume available to owners of *Britannica Junior* at $8.95 plus a small charge for shipping and handling.

Summary

The *Britannica Junior Encyclopaedia for Boys and Girls* can be quickly summed up in this manner:

Scope: Good	Accessibility: Excellent
Authority: Good	Bibliographies: Poor
Reliability: Good	Graphics: Good
Recency: Fair	Physical Format: Good
Objectivity: Good	Special Features: Few
Clarity: Good	Price: Reasonable

To elaborate briefly, *Britannica Junior* is a broad-entry encyclopedia for young children at the upper elementary and middle school levels. According to the editor's preface, the set "is designed and edited as a beginner's encyclopedia—a first introduction to reference and research work. Its content is oriented to elementary school curriculums." The set's material is readily accessible via the Ready Reference Index, which comprises Volume 1. This volume also provides brief factual entries on specific topics, mainly people and places, not covered in the main encyclopedic volumes. *Britannica Junior* is well constructed and modestly attractive in design, offering fairly good illustrations, many in black-and-white. The set has a reasonably clear style and is usually reliable. On the debit side, *Britannica Junior* is not always as up-to-date as it might be, and the rate of annual revision has perceptibly slowed in recent years. The lack of bibliographies diminishes the set's usefulness as an encyclopedia for young people learning about rudimentary research techniques. The publisher informs the *Buying Guide,* however, that this deficiency will be corrected in future editions.

At the present time, there are five multivolume encyclopedias for children aged 7–14 on the North American market: *Britannica Junior Ency-clopaedia, The New Book of Knowledge, The Illustrated Encyclopedia for Learning, Oxford Junior Encyclopaedia,* and *The Young Students Ency-clopedia.* The last three sets will not interest most consumers in the United States. *Oxford Junior* is very much a British production, *Young Students* lacks substance, and *The Illustrated Encyclopedia for Learning* is a dreadfully dated work of low quality. Obviously, the best buy comes down to a choice between *The New Book of Knowledge* and *Britannica Junior.* In the *Buying Guide*'s opinion, *The New Book of Knowledge* has the qualitative edge. It does everything *Britannica Junior* does and more. In terms of price, however, *Britannica Junior* (at $199.50) is currently $160 cheaper than *The New Book of Knowledge* ($360). Hence, from the standpoint of quality alone, *The New Book of Knowledge* is undoubtedly the best multivolume encyclopedia buy for young people in the elemen-tary grades. But from the standpoint of price alone, *Britannica Junior* is the best buy.

Other Critical Opinions

Booklist, December 1, 1978, pp. 634–635. Part of a series of reviews by the ALA Reference and Subscription Books Review Committee (RSBRC) entitled "Encyclopedias: A Survey and Buying Guide," this unsigned evaluation offers few negative criticisms and no final conclu-sions. In its last regular review of *Britannica Junior (Booklist,* Septem-ber 1, 1973, pp. 1–4), RSBRC "recommended" the encyclopedia for home, school, and public libraries.

Katz, William A. *Basic Information Sources* (Vol. 1 of *Introduction to Reference Work,* 3rd ed. New York: McGraw-Hill, 1978), pp. 161–162. Katz comparatively reviews the three leading sets for children, namely *Britannica Junior, The New Book of Knowledge,* and *The Young Stu-dents Encyclopedia.* He likes *The New Book of Knowledge* best, with *Young Students* in second place, and "the much older and dated" *Bri-tannica Junior* a third choice.

Wynar, Christine L. *American Reference Books Annual,* 1978, pp. 37–39. Wynar's lengthy review emphasizes the encyclopedia's revision failures. She concludes that *Britannica Junior* is an accurate and reliable set but because of problems with currency and readability "it cannot be enthu-siastically endorsed."

Childcraft

Facts in Brief

Full Title: **Childcraft: The How and Why Library.** *Editors:* William H. Nault, Editorial Director; Robert O. Zeleny, Executive Editor; Harry R. Snowden, Jr., Managing Editor; William J. Dobias, Executive Art Director. *Publisher:* World Book-Childcraft International, Inc. (a subsidiary of the Scott & Fetzer Company), 510 Merchandise Mart Plaza, Chicago, IL 60654. *Edition Reviewed:* 1980 copyright.

Volumes: 15. *Pages:* 5,000. *Articles:* Topically arranged resource library of fiction and nonfiction. *Words:* 750,000. *Illustrations:* 6,700. *Maps:* None. *Index Entries:* 20,000. *Cross-references:* None. *Contributors:* Staff produced, with many specially commissioned contributors.

User Classification: Children (Multivolume). *Reader Suitability:* Age 4 through 10. *Physical Size:* 7½ × 10 in.; 26 cm. *LC:* 79-88042. *ISBN:* 0-7166-0180-X. *Lowest Retail Price:* $179 if purchased separately; $129 if purchased with *The World Book Encyclopedia;* to schools & libraries $134.25.

Purpose and Scope

Childcraft is not strictly a children's encyclopedia, although the set has many characteristics of an encyclopedia. The publisher prefers to call the set a "children's resource library." The preface states that *Childcraft* is "designed especially for preschool and primary-grade children and for the older child who needs high-interest, easy-to-read materials. *Childcraft* also serves as a resource for parents, teachers, and librarians." Publisher advertisements also characterize the set as a "learning link between home and school."

Childcraft is essentially a browsing set with each volume built around a theme. The volumes cover literature and the language arts, arts and crafts, social studies, the natural and technical sciences, and human health and development. Poems and Rhymes, Stories and Fables, and Children Everywhere (Volumes 1, 2, and 3) contain a variety of carefully selected readings for children, including many tales from around the world by both classical and contemporary authors. World and Space, About Animals, and The Green Kingdom (Volumes 4, 5, and 6) are informational in nature and concern the physical world. The articles vary in length, but are usually two or four pages long with illustrations accounting for half or more of the space. Longer articles (for instance, "The

World of the Sea") are subdivided into smaller topics (e.g., "A real sea monster—about the giant squid").

How Things Work and How We Get Things (Volumes 7 and 8) deal with technology and manufacture. The information is extremely elementary, but the writers have a knack for conveying essential points. EX-AMPLE: The article on computers ("Machines that Answer") briefly describes their basic function and then brings home the key point about computers in language any young reader can understand: "Of course, you could add up all the numbers in a telephone book, or even work out a problem with a million numbers. But it would take you from now till who knows when to come up with the right answers. That's what's so great about computers. They work fast—faster than you can snap your fingers, even faster than you can wink an eye."

Holidays and Customs and Places to Know (Volumes 9 and 10) provide social facts and geographical information about the peoples and places of the world. Make and Do (Volume 11) is a practical crafts book with easily understandable instructions for making bottle figures, wall hangings, wind chimes, costumes, dolls, and the like. Look and Learn (Volume 12) concerns visual communication, including art, architecture, advertising, clothing, and gestures. Mathemagic (Volume 13) is the newest volume of *Childcraft,* replacing Look Again, which was Volume 13 in the 1976 set (when the *Buying Guide* last examined *Childcraft).* Mathemagic, designed to stimulate young people's interest in mathematics, contains an assortment of interesting articles and projects, including instructions for making a homemade abacus. There is also a "New Words" section at the back of the volume that pronounces and briefly defines 42 specialized terms "you have met in this book," such as *avoirdupois, equilateral, parallelogram,* and *sequence.* About Me (Volume 14) is about the child's birth, personality development, physical growth, and health—from the child's perspective. It is a unique and exciting book. Guide for Parents (Volume 15), the only book in the set for adults, includes articles on the growth and development of children, a 145-page alphabetical medical guide that ranges from abscesses to whooping cough, and a guide and index to all the volumes of *Childcraft.* The special school version of Volume 15 that contained "Curriculum Enrichment Guides" is no longer published, but the curriculum guides are available in a 64-page paperback booklet distributed free of charge to schools and libraries purchasing the set. The publisher reports that in 1981 this material will be built into Volume 15. Covering such topics of study as accidents and accident prevention, games and sports, clocks and calendars, climate and weather, U.S. history, food, sculpture, physical and mental health, and the solar system, these guides are enormously useful to primary and kindergarten teachers.

History and Authority

The publisher of *Childcraft* is World Book-Childcraft International, Inc. (WBCI), a subsidiary of the Scott & Fetzer Company of Lakewood, Ohio, a firm that manufactures and sells the Kirby vacuum cleaner line, among other products. WBCI is known and respected around the world for its reference products, including *The World Book Encyclopedia,* considered by many to be the best all-around general encyclopedia currently available, and the excellent *World Book Dictionary* (a Thorndike-Barnhart production), as well as *Childcraft,* which has been on the market for nearly 50 years and has been published not only in English but at least six foreign-language editions (Spanish, Portuguese, French, Italian, German, and Japanese).

Childcraft first appeared in 1934 as "a set of books all about children and the craft of training them." Of the seven volumes that comprised the first edition, four were for parents and teachers. As the set evolved over the years, however, it became almost entirely a resource for children, rather than one about them (as noted under "Purpose and Scope," only Volume 15 is currently for adults). In 1964, *Childcraft* was enlarged when the six-volume *How and Why Library* (1912–1959) was incorporated into the set. At the present time, WBCI maintains a sizable permanent staff of editors, writers, and artists devoted exclusively to producing *Childcraft* and its annual supplement, the *Childcraft Annual.* In addition to the editorial and production staffs (listed in the front of Volume 1 and identified by title and academic degrees), there is an editorial advisory board composed of five educators and chaired by William H. Nault, who is also editorial director of *The World Book Encyclopedia.* A six-member library consultant committee is also listed. The committee is mainly comprised of media specialists, such as Rebecca T. Bingham, director of media services, Jefferson County (Ky.) Public Schools. All of the literary contributions—poetry, stories, fables, folk tales, and the like—included in the set are signed, such as a selection from *Winnie-the-Pooh* by A. A. Milne. Likewise, the articles in Volume 15 (Guide for Parents) are signed, including the brief entries in the medical guide. But most of the material in the first 14 volumes is unsigned, the work of staff writers. Special consultants who worked on particular volumes are noted in Volume 15. For instance, Dr. Paul Bigelow Sears, professor emeritus of conservation, Yale University, furnished technical assistance and advice during preparation of The Green Kingdom (Volume 6).

Treatment (Reliability, Recency, Objectivity)

The very elementary factual information is presented accurately, though sometimes the superficial treatment invites misleading assumptions or conclusions. EXAMPLE: "What is a Cell?" in Volume 14 (About Me) vaguely describes a cell as "the smallest living part of me it is possible to imagine. A cell can be long, short, thin, fat, square, or round." *Childcraft,* like its chief competitor, *Compton's Precyclopedia* (also called *The Young Children's Encyclopedia),* makes no attempt to treat topics comprehensively. EXAMPLE: The articles "Do Moving Pictures Move?," "It's Done with Dots," "How to Change Color without Changing It," "Movie Tricks," and "Characters Who Seem to Move" provide stimulating introductory information on cinematography, but the set offers nothing concerning the motion picture industry, Hollywood, famous films, or other aspects of the subject equally interesting to young children. Here again the point should be made that *Childcraft* is not intended to cover all aspects of knowledge. Rather, the set is quite specifically designed and sold as a browsing set for beginning readers.

Because of the general nature of the material, timeliness is not as critical a factor in such sets as *Childcraft* as it is in true encyclopedias. Nonetheless, in those areas where currency is a consideration, *Childcraft* is as up-to-date as can be expected. In fact, the set is constantly changing and evolving. It was completely revamped in 1949 and again in 1964 when the *How and Why Library* was acquired from the L. J. Bullard Company and incorporated into the set. In 1972, *Childcraft* again underwent a major change when four volumes of the *Childcraft Annual* were added to replace a like number of volumes that were dropped from the set. Also, new volumes are sometimes created. For instance, Mathemagic has recently replaced Look Again as Volume 13. And with each new edition, one or two volumes are thoroughly revised and rewritten, as is the case with Volumes 4 (World and Space) and 11 (Make and Do) in the 1980 set. The publisher has informed the *Buying Guide* that a number of changes are planned for the 1981 edition. How Things Work (Volume 7) will be revised from top to bottom; How We Get Things (Volume 8) will be replaced with About Us, an introduction to different cultures of the world; and Holidays and Customs (Volume 9) will be entirely rewritten and retitled Holidays and Birthdays. In addition, the editors intend to add more bibliographies and new word lists throughout the set in 1981.

Childcraft is supplemented by the *Childcraft Annual*, a volume published each year in May since 1965. Unlike other annual updating supplements, each volume of *Childcraft Annual* is built around a single theme. For instance, the 1970 annual was an anthology of stories about children from 30 different countries. Entitled *Children Everywhere,* the book was added to the 15-volume set of *Childcraft* in 1972 as Volume 3. Recent annuals include *Animals in Danger* (1974), the *Magic of Words* (1975), *About Dogs* (1977), and *Story of the Sea* (1979). The 1980 *Childcraft Annual* is called *The Indian Book.* Attractively illustrated with abundant color drawings, art reproductions, and photographs, the book covers the major American Indian peoples, including those of Mexico, the Andes, and the Caribbean Islands. There is a concluding chapter on contemporary Indian life that notes, "Many Indians believe the government has often treated them unfairly. They say that promises have been made and then broken. Many tribes now have their own tribal councils to direct the activities of the tribe and to represent it in dealings with the government. And some Indians are now demanding that old promises made to their people should be kept." Like the individual volumes of *Childcraft,* the annual is indexed. Prior to publication, the text of *The Indian Book* was reviewed for accuracy and currency by a special consultant, Dr. Merwyn S. Garbarino, professor of anthropology, University of Illinois at Chicago Circle.

There is no overt bias in *Childcraft.* Delicate subject matter, like sexuality, is treated fairly and sensitively. Minority children frequently appear in the illustrations. Likewise, sexual stereotyping has been avoided in most instances. EXAMPLE: "Getting the News" in How We Get Things shows a female reporter interviewing a black policeman. Nevertheless, *Childcraft* does convey some unintentional bias. The children in the illustrations almost always have a bright, scrubbed, middle-class look about them. The attitude of the set reflects the attitudes of suburban America. EXAMPLE: The prototypical little girl in About Me says, "I like little babies. One day, when I am a woman, I may get married and have a baby of my own to love and care for . . . . One day, when all of me is grown up, I will be able to have a baby. I will be able to take care of a baby. I think I will like that."

Clarity and Reader Suitability

Like most reference works for very young readers, *Childcraft* attempts to present its material in the most creative and imaginative manner possible, utilizing both interesting writing and eye-catching illustrations. In most instances, *Childcraft* accomplishes this goal with a high degree of success. Beginning readers at the preschool and early elementary levels will find the writing style not only easy to comprehend but engaging. The publisher has informed the *Buying Guide* that "wherever possible, words within the range of the child's listening vocabulary are used. At the same time, *important* technical or abstract words are not avoided. Of course, clues to meaning are provided in the remainder of the sentence." These statements are true. The publisher also notes, again correctly, that "sentence structure and syntax avoid ambiguities and give the writing a pleasing, rhythmic effect." Indeed, much of *Childcraft* is or borders on poetry. Teachers, day-care personnel, and parents seeking read-aloud material will find *Childcraft* particularly suitable.

The publisher claims that the set is equally appealing to "the older child who needs high-interest, easy-to-read materials." This claim is not entirely justified. Slow or reluctant readers will not be overwhelmed by the vocabulary, but the older youngster may be turned off by what is perceived to be infantile or excessively juvenile attitudes, language, and illustrations. It is difficult, for instance, to imagine a 12- or 15-year-old reading the following without feeling patronized: "I like to go shopping with my family. But sometimes I go to the store by myself. It's fun to choose and buy the different foods and the many other things my family needs. Most of all I like to shop for toys and books." Moreover, because the majority of backward readers come from less affluent homes and neighborhoods, the set's middle-class approach to the world in general will not appeal to many older students who need easy-to-read material.

Arrangement and Accessibílity

As already explained (see "Purpose and Scope"), *Childcraft* is topically arranged, each volume dealing with a broad subject or theme. Unlike *Compton's Precyclopedia, Childcraft* does not provide cross-references. Individual volumes, however, have their own indexes and Volume 15 provides a 110-page index to the set. To repeat, *Childcraft* does not pretend to be an encyclopedia in the true sense. It is first and foremost a browsing set, or resource library, designed to stimulate the child's imagination and natural curiosity about people, places, and things. But specific information is readily accessible through the individual volume indexes and the general analytical index in the final volume.

Bibliographies

Heretofore the editors of *Childcraft* have not felt it always necessary to include bibliographies, or lists of additional materials for further study. In the 1980 edition, only Volume 13 (Mathemagic), Volume 15 (Guide for Parents), and some of the *Childcraft Annual* volumes (e.g., *About Dogs* and *Story of the Sea*) furnish bibliographies. The *Buying Guide* has been informed, however, that "the 1981 *Childcraft* will see the addition of glossaries and bibliographies to more volumes of the set." The systematic addition of bibliographies will make *Childcraft* more useful as an educational tool.

Graphics

Childcraft's illustrations are generally excellent. Comprising approximately 60 percent of the set's total text, they handsomely complement the printed matter. EXAMPLE: The article on drilling for oil in the World and Space volume includes a diagram showing the various layers of rock that must be penetrated before striking "black gold." EXAMPLE: The article on plant roots in *The Green Kingdom* has six informative drawings that visually indicate how root systems function during different seasons. EXAMPLE: The tapestry-weaving section of Make and Do provides step-by-step instructions, clarified by several color illustrations.

The preface correctly observes that "nearly every graphic technique appears somewhere in *Childcraft*." Many well-known artists have contributed drawings, including most winners of the Caldecott Medal, awarded each year for the most distinguished picture book for children. Such illustrators include Maurice Sendak and Robert McCloskey. Volume 14 (About Me) includes numerous drawings illustrating aspects of the human anatomy. Both color and black-and-white graphics appear in most volumes. Color is used both as an interest-catching device and for informational purposes. The reproductions of famous art works, photographs of people and things, and instructional drawings in Look and Learn are outstanding, both in terms of selection and color reproduction. The single criticism that might be made of the illustrations is the persistent use of photographs revealing well-groomed, well-fed, ever-smiling children (see "Treatment"). But, generally speaking, there are few encyclopedic sets on the market today that can match the overall graphic excellence of *Childcraft*.

Physical Format

Childcraft is currently available in only one binding. Called the Heritage binding, the volumes are each a different color with bright graphics all around the lower half of the book. The volumes, which are bound in a washable Pyroxylin-coated cloth fabric, should hold up under fairly heavy use. Like *Compton's Precyclopedia (Childcraft's* main competition), the set is imaginatively designed inside. The page layout is often stunning and irresistible. Inquisitive children often become totally absorbed in any volume they pick up, drawn by the creative page design, attractive typography, and captivating illustrations. Like *The World Book Encyclopedia, Childcraft* is printed on high-quality offset paper specially manufactured to achieve the best color reproduction possible.

Special Features

There are several features that deserve notice. The first is the unique book About Me, which was originally published as the 1969 *Childcraft Annual* and is now Volume 14 of the set. In characteristically simple but carefully chosen terms, the book explores the child physically and psychologically. It encourages the child to think about his/her individuality, to consider "What does *Me* mean to Me?" Strongly supportive of the self-awareness concept, About Me is unquestionably the most popular and the most originally conceived volume in the set.

Another special feature worth noting is the glossaries, or lists of specialized vocabulary, found at the end of six volumes (Children Everywhere; World and Space; About Animals; The Green Kingdom; Mathemagic; and About Me). Called "New Words," these lists pronounce and define between 35 and 100 words used in the text of the volume, such as *conch* (in About Animals). The editors anticipate adding more "New Words" lists to the set in 1981.

Another useful special feature is the 145-page medical guide in Volume 15. Arranged alphabetically, the guide provides concise entries on such topics as adenoids, allergies, birthmarks, bleeding, conjuctivitis, farsightedness, hernias, hives, menstruation, mumps, nutrition, poison ivy, poisoning and poisons, posture, shots, sleep, swollen glands, vaginal discharges, vomiting, warts, and whooping cough. The approach is practical and the writing style nontechnical.

Finally, a special feature of particular interest to preschool and primary school teachers is the "Curriculum Enrichment Guides" designed to enhance *Childcraft's* instructional value and capabilities. The curriculum guides, which cover such areas as climate and weather, U.S. history, and the solar system, are currently available in a 64-page paperback publication distributed without charge to schools and libraries purchasing the set. Beginning in 1981, however, the curriculum guides will become part of Volume 15.

Sales Information

Childcraft is available in only one binding, that being the multicolored Heritage binding already described (see "Physical Format"). The set is sold in-home on the subscription, or installment, basis at $179, or $129 if purchased in combination with *The World Book Encyclopedia.* The same binding is available to schools and libraries at the discount price of $134.25. The *Childcraft Annual* (see "Treatment" for a description) sells for $9.95 to *Childcraft* and/or *World Book Encyclopedia* owners, $10.95 to nonowners. Also sold with *Childcraft* (or separately) is the *Childcraft Dictionary*. A special edition of the highly regarded 30,000-entry *Macmillan Dictionary for Children* (originally published in 1975), the *Childcraft Dictionary* sells for $16.95 to both retail customers and educational institutions. Note that all prices include shipping and handling charges, but not local or state taxes.

Various foreign-language editions of *Childcraft* have been published over the years (see "History and Authority"), but none is currently available in the United States. However, the Spanish edition, *El Mundo de los Niños,* is sold by World Book-Childcraft International, Inc. (WBCI), in Puerto Rico, and the French version, *Je veux savoir,* remains in stock in Canada. Consumers interested in the latest information about the sales status of foreign-language editions of *Childcraft* should contact WBCI's home office in Chicago.

Summary

Childcraft: The How and Why Library can be quickly summed up in this manner:

Scope: Good	Accessibility: Excellent
Authority: Excellent	Bibliographies: Fair
Reliability: Good	Graphics: Excellent
Recency: Excellent	Physical Format: Excellent
Objectivity: Good	Special Features: Many
Clarity: Excellent	Price: Reasonable

To elaborate briefly, *Childcraft* contains much useful information for young children, but it is principally a browsing or enrichment set as opposed to a children's encyclopedia. Nevertheless, the general analytical index in the final volume makes the contents readily accessible to users. Its creative design, excellent illustrations, easy-to-read style, inclusion of much contemporary and classical literature, and adept treatment of a wide variety of subjects of interest to preschoolers and beginning readers are outstanding features. The informational content is necessarily quite elementary and selective, but what there is is authoritative and reasonably up-to-date. Children overwhelmingly respond positively to *Childcraft,* particularly the self-discovery volume, About Me. The set scrupulously avoids overt bias and takes considerable pains to include minority children in stories and illustrations. Efforts have also been made to eliminate sex-role stereotyping, so prevalent in many children's works today. *Childcraft* does, however, convey a certain subconscious bias in favor of suburban U.S. values. Children who live in affluent homes with loving, attentive parents will be quite comfortable with *Childcraft*. The set is about and for them. Disadvantaged children, on the other hand, will find the set naively unrealistic. In like manner, older children who need easy-to-read material at the elementary level will feel patronized by the simplistic tone and many pictures of small, well-scrubbed boys and girls.

When the pros and cons are totaled up, *Childcraft* is the best set of its kind on the U.S. market today. *Compton's Precyclopedia*, comparable in many ways, is also an attractive browsing set for beginning readers, but it lacks the superior quality of *Childcraft*'s overall design. The *Talking Cassette Encyclopedia*, a unique item comprising 100 cassette tapes on various topics, is aimed at roughly the same audience as *Childcraft*, but it has little substance and costs much too much ($490). It should be pointed out, however, that any children's reference work geared to the ages four through ten is a luxury for individual consumers. This is not to say that such works as *Childcraft* and *Compton's Precyclopedia* are not useful—they are. The point is, such sets are normally outgrown so quickly that the investment cannot always be justified, particularly for families with little discretionary income. On the other hand, school and public libraries of any consequence (including kindergartens and day-care centers) should probably stock one of these titles, preferably *Childcraft*.

Other Critical Opinions

Booklist, June 15, 1975, pp. 1080–1083. This unsigned review by the ALA Reference and Subscription Books Review Committee offers little criticism, and at the end the set is "recommended" for both homes and libraries.

Katz, William A. *Basic Information Sources* (Vol. 1 of *Introduction to Reference Work,* 3rd ed. New York: McGraw-Hill, 1978), p. 162. Katz briefly compares *Childcraft* and *Compton's Precyclopedia*. The judgment on *Childcraft*: "Thanks to excellent illustrations and well thought-out texts, the volumes are useful for preschool and early grades."

Wehmeyer, Lillian Biermann. *American Reference Books Annual,* 1980, pp. 27–28. Mainly descriptive in nature, this review concludes that *Childcraft* "is a good starting place for primary-grade readers" because the set permits children to comprehend the subject matter on their own level.

Compton's Precyclopedia

Facts in Brief

Full Title: **Compton's Precyclopedia: Based on The Young Children's Encyclopedia, Published by Encyclopaedia Britannica, Inc.** *Editors:* Howard L. Goodkind, Editor in Chief; Margaret Sutton, Managing Editor; Marvin Martin, Supervisory Editor. *Publisher:* F. E. Compton Company (a division of Encyclopaedia Britannica, Inc.), 425 N. Michigan Ave., Chicago, IL 60611. *Distributor to Schools & Libraries:* Encyclopaedia Britannica Educational Corporation, 425 N. Michigan Ave., Chicago, IL 60611. *Alternate Title: The Young Children's Encyclopedia. Edition Reviewed:* 1977 copyright.

Volumes: 16 (plus the *Teaching Guide and Index to Compton's Precyclopedia*). *Pages:* 3,000. *Articles:* 650 (plus 16 activity or "Things to Do" sections). *Words:* 325,000. *Illustrations:* 2,800. *Maps:* 20. *Index Entries:* 800. *Cross-references:* 500. *Contributors:* 52 writers; 98 artists.

User Classification: Children (Multivolume). *Reader Suitability:* Age 4 through 10. *Physical Size:* 8 × 9½ in.; 24 cm. *LC:* 76-43083. *ISBN:* 0-85229-323-2. *Lowest Retail Price:* $179; to schools & libraries $149.50.

Purpose and Scope

Compton's Precyclopedia has a unique purpose. Called a "training" encyclopedia by the publisher, the set is designed to acquaint very young readers with the concept of an encyclopedia and how it works. The presumption is that by using the *Precyclopedia* at an early age, children will be better prepared to cope with larger and more complex encyclopedias and other reference works as they mature. Hence the material in the *Precyclopedia* is arranged alphabetically, and many articles include cross-references.

As might be expected, the articles cover quite broad topics. Volume 6, for instance, includes "Fables," "Factories," "Family," "Farming," "Fire," "Flowers," "Flying," "Food," "France," "Friends," "Frogs," and "Future," as well as a sketch of Benjamin Franklin. Frequently more than one article or story is included under a broad heading. EXAMPLE: "Family" includes a black father's explanation to his sons of their Afro-American heritage. Entitled "Where Did I Come From?" the information is conveyed in simple narrative form accompanied by interesting drawings. Also under the topic is the story of a family's adventures camping in the woods. Called "The Indian Way—Almost," the short piece is attractively illustrated and provides a *See also* reference at the end: *"If you like this story, you'll like* 'Let's Take a Trip Up a Mountain' *under* Mountains *in Volume 10."*

The material is ordinarily presented in storytelling fashion, although poems and straight informational writing are also used. Each volume contains about 25 broad articles and some 40 or more topics in all. Approximately 50 articles in the set are geographical in nature, with emphasis on foreign places. Some of these articles pose the question "Where Am I?" encouraging the child to guess the place being described. But the largest number of entries concern scientific subjects. EXAMPLE: "Flashlight" explains how the instrument works through both words and diagrams. A cross-reference directs the reader to "Electricity" in Volume 5. Other articles in that volume dealing with science include "Earth," "Earthworms," "Echoes," "Eclipses," "Eyes and Ears," and a biography of Albert Einstein. Approximately 75 of the 159 pages in this volume concern science in one way or another.

The initial 24 pages of each volume are devoted to an activities or "Things to Do" section. Utilizing rhymes, riddles, jokes, jingles, and look-and-find pictures, the activities revolve around the letter and number of the particular volume, or they are related to articles in the volume. EX AMPLE: In Volume 6 the child is instructed to read the article "World of the Future" and then organize a robot game: "Each child takes a turn being a robot. The others try to guess what he is doing." The game also calls for a "robot suit." Easy instructions are provided for making such a costume.

Topic selection, according to the publisher, was guided more by what would appeal to young readers than by any effort to provide inclusive or encyclopedic coverage. Indeed, the *Precyclopedia* has been advertised as "a kind of literary 'Sesame Street.' " Viewed from this perspective, the *Precyclopedia,* despite its alphabetical arrangement and cross-references, is clearly more a browsing set than an encyclopedia. As such it is quite similar in purpose and style (but not organization) to *Childcraft: The How and Why Library,* a topically organized enrichment set for preschoolers and beginning readers.

History and Authority

In 1970, Encyclopaedia Britannica, Inc., published a 16-volume, mail-order and supermarket item called *The Young Children's Encyclopedia.* The following year, F. E. Compton Company, a division of Britannica since 1961, issued practically the same encyclopedia under the title *Compton's Young Children's Precyclopedia,* also in 16 volumes. In 1973, Compton reissued the set as *Compton's Precyclopedia,* and in 1977 both the *Precyclopedia* and *Young Children's* appeared in modestly revised editions. The major difference between the two sets concerns their intended market. The *Precyclopedia,* which includes a supplementary volume entitled *Teaching Guide and Index to Compton's Precyclopedia* (described under "Special Features"), is primarily directed at the school and library market. *Young Children's,* on the other hand, which has a cheaper binding and comes with a supplementary volume entitled *Parents' Manual,* is mainly directed at the home market. All differences between the two titles are enumerated in the review of *Young Children's* that follows later on in this section of the *Buying Guide.*

The *Precyclopedia*'s 35-member editorial and production staff is headed by Howard L. Goodkind, the set's editor in chief. Donald E. Lawson served as a general consultant and adviser. At the time Lawson was editor of *Compton's Encyclopedia,* but he has since moved to United Educators, Inc., a Chicago firm that publishes an encyclopedia yearbook and, until recently, the *American Educator Encyclopedia* (see Appendix A). Clifton Fadiman, the author and critic, is listed as a consulting editor. Some of Fadiman's verse appears in the set. Since 1978 (when the *Buying Guide* last reviewed the *Precyclopedia*), Marvin Martin, editor of *Britannica Junior Encyclopaedia,* has been named supervisory editor of the *Precyclopedia.* A six-member advisory board is chaired by Alex Sareyan, identified as executive director of the Mental Health Materials Center, Inc. Other members of the board bring substantial professional credentials to a work of this nature, such as Josette Frank, a consultant to the Child Study Association of America. Gwendolyn Brooks, the prize-winning black poet, and Robert L. Hess, a specialist in African history at the University of Illinois (Chicago Circle), are listed as special advisers. The contributors, both writers and artists, are identified by name only in Volume 1. Although individual articles are not signed, the last page of each volume does indicate who was responsible for the text and the visual work on specific pages. With very few exceptions, the editors, advisers, and contributors have not changed since the original 1971 edition.

Treatment (Reliability, Recency, Objectivity)

In keeping with the set's purpose and intended usership, the factual content of the *Precyclopedia* is quite elementary. The simple facts are accurate and reasonably up-to-date in light of current knowledge. The article on the Viking Leif Ericsson, for instance, states that he "reached the shores of North America almost 500 years before Columbus!" The article also explains that "scientists and explorers were never sure where he had landed or when" until quite recently. The black heritage article mentioned earlier is another good example of the *Precyclopedia*'s concern with contemporary material and themes. But, in some instances, the addition of new information would improve the articles. EXAMPLE: The two-page article about the Panama Canal would benefit from a simple discussion of the current situation in light of the recent treaties between the United States and Panama concerning the Canal Zone. EXAMPLE: "Measurement" notes that there are two major systems of measurement and that "most of the world recognizes one or both of these systems as the standard of measurement." Actually, however, the United States is the only important country that has not yet adopted the metric system, although this difficult process is now underway. The next edition of the *Precyclopedia* might profitably revise "Measurement" to stress metrication.

The current edition of the *Precyclopedia* is dated 1977. When the set will again be revised is not known at this time. Consumers should note, however, that the customary standard of encyclopedia revision (at least 10 percent of the text annually) does not apply in the case of beginner sets like the *Precyclopedia* or its principal competitor, *Childcraft.*

Happily, there is little evidence of sex stereotyping in the set. The article "Jobs," in fact, tackles the issue of sexism directly: "Who sews and irons? Mother does. But some fathers know how to sew and iron. . . . Who jumps rope, and who plays baseball? . . . If you've wanted to try skipping rope but thought it was just for girls, try it! It's fun! And it's not so easy as it looks. . . . If you are a girl who would like to hit or catch a baseball, go ahead and try. Of course, you'll have to talk the boys into letting you play. But if you keep trying, they'll probably give in. And if you do well, they may argue over whose side you will play on." In addition, children representing various ethnic groups appear in drawings throughout the set.

Clarity and Reader Suitability

The writing style is breezy, conversational, and contemporary. The articles are designed to whet the child's curiosity in a positive manner. Most of the text will be comprehensible to beginning readers in kindergarten or day-care and the early elementary grades. Possibly some parents and teachers might object to the style as being ungrammatical or too informal (see "Treatment" for an example), but they would be objecting to trifles. The point is, children will enjoy reading and using the *Precyclopedia.* And like many sets for older children and young adults, the *Precyclopedia* defines potentially unfamiliar terms in context. EXAMPLE: The article "Television" italicizes 15 words and phrases that are defined in the text, such as *producer, control room, earphones, floor manager.*

Arrangement and Accessibility

The *Precyclopedia* is arranged alphabetically, letter-by-letter ("Newspapers" precedes "New Zealand"). A majority of the articles include interesting, nontraditional cross-references (see "Purpose and Scope" for an example). *The Teaching Guide and Index* volume provides a simple index to the set. The guide portion furnishes a topical approach to the contents around which a teacher can develop instructional units, e.g., "About Make-Believe," "Home, School, and Family," and "Our Earth." As previously noted, the *Precyclopedia* is intended as a training encyclopedia, but given its very selective coverage and treatment of knowledge, the set is best described as a browsing library for beginning readers, similar in many respects to *Childcraft.*

Bibliographies

None. The lack of bibliographies, or references to sources of additional information, is not a grievous deficiency in a beginner set like the *Precy-*

clopedia. Failure to include at least simple bibliographies, however, is not in keeping with the editors' intention to acquaint very young readers with the rudiments of encyclopedia use.

Graphics

The illustrations—most of which are color drawings—account for approximately half the *Precyclopedia*'s total contents. The drawings, which include cartoons and watercolors, are uniformly excellent, although on occasion colors are distorted; for instance, oranges are red. Children beginning to explore the world of knowledge will find the graphics visually appealing, intellectually stimulating, and usually instructive.

Physical Format

The *Precyclopedia* has a two-piece tan and orange cloth binding with gold lettering and delightful figure drawings on the spine and front cover of each volume. Each volume contains all of one or more letters of the alphabet (e.g., Volume 1 covers the letter A; Volume 7 the letters G and H), a system known as unit-letter arrangement. Inside, the set is equally enticing, the creative page layout enhanced by the original art work. The typefaces used are large, bold, and clear. Guide words, however, are needed at the top of each page, and some pages are not numbered, which is frustrating and possibly confusing for younger readers. The volumes, which are very tightly bound, do not lie flat when open, another frustrating feature.

Special Features

The activity or "Things to Do" sections found at the beginning of each volume are not unique among children's sets, but they are cleverly constructed as both teaching devices and sources of constructive entertainment. Volume 1 indicates that an expert in early childhood development critically reviewed most of this material. (Note that *The Young Children's Encyclopedia* does not contain the activity sections.)

Another special feature is the *Teaching Guide and Index* volume that accompanies the set. Bound in paper covers and slightly smaller in size than the other volumes, the 96-page *Teaching Guide and Index* contains an index to the set of some 800 entries (on white paper) and a breakdown of topics frequently taught in the primary grades with references to appropriate articles in the *Precyclopedia* (on green paper). For instance, the broad topic "Health and Safety" includes references to such articles as "How We Move" (in Volume 16), "Baby's First Year" (in Volume 2), and "What the Doctor Can Do" (in Volume 4). This feature will be useful to teachers in the primary grades, as well as to those in nursery schools, kindergartens, and day-care centers.

Sales Information

The *Precyclopedia* is sold in-home on the subscription, or installment, basis for $179 plus shipping and handling and any tax. Schools and libraries can acquire the set for $149.50 delivered. That price includes the paperbound *Teaching Guide and Index.* Also, schools and libraries ordering two or more sets of the *Precyclopedia* at the same time receive a discount ($139.50 per set). Only one edition of the *Precyclopedia* is currently available, that being the tan and orange cloth binding already described (see "Physical Format"). The *Precyclopedia* is sold in combination with *Compton's Encyclopedia.* It should be noted that *The Young Children's Encyclopedia,* which has practically the same contents as the *Precyclopedia,* is currently sold in-home in combination with *The New Encyclopaedia Britannica.* (*The Young Children's Encyclopedia* is briefly reviewed further on in this section of the *Buying Guide.*)

Summary

Compton's Precyclopedia can be quickly summed up in this manner:

Scope: Good	Accessibility: Excellent
Authority: Good	Bibliographies: Poor (none)
Reliability: Good	Graphics: Excellent
Recency: Fair	Physical Format: Good
Objectivity: Excellent	Special Features: Few
Clarity: Excellent	Price: Reasonable

To elaborate briefly, *Compton's Precyclopedia,* first published in 1971 and based on *The Young Children's Encyclopedia* (1970), purports to be a starter or trainer set, designed to introduce small children to the ways of encyclopedias at a very young age. Hence, the *Precyclopedia* is alphabetically arranged, includes some cross-references, and has a general index— all characteristics of the larger, more sophisticated encyclopedias children will encounter when they are older. But in all other respects the *Precyclopedia* is first and foremost a browsing set, similar in scope, purpose, and style (but not organization) to *Childcraft: The How and Why Library.* Viewed as a browsing item, the *Precyclopedia* is quite successful. The contents, which accentuate scientific topics, are well chosen to encourage the child's curiosity and imagination. Factual information, though minimal, is reliable, interestingly presented, and fairly current, although some articles are in need of revision. The *Precyclopedia* was last revised in 1977, and it is not known when the next revision will occur. The set's format is attractive, enhanced by generous use of bright color drawings throughout.

All things considered, *Childcraft* is preferable to the *Precyclopedia.* The latter is appealing in many respects, but *Childcraft* is overall a better designed and maintained set. The *Talking Cassette Encyclopedia,* a unique item comprising 100 cassette tapes on various topics, is aimed at roughly the same audience as *Childcraft* and the *Precyclopedia,* but it has little substance and costs much too much ($490). It should be noted, however, that any children's reference work geared to the ages four through ten is a luxury for individual consumers. This is not to say that such works as *Childcraft* and the *Precyclopedia,* both of which retail for

$179, are not useful—they are. The point is, such sets are normally outgrown so quickly that the investment cannot always be justified, particularly for families with little discretionary income. On the other hand, school and public libraries of any consequence (including nursery schools, kindergartens, and day-care centers) should probably stock one of these titles, preferably *Childcraft.*

Other Critical Opinions

Booklist, November 1, 1979, pp. 453–456. This long, unsigned review by the ALA Reference and Subscription Books Review Committee makes several useful, albeit minor, criticisms, such as the set's lack of guide words at the top of each page. The review also contains several glaring errors; for instance, the claim that "scientific materials are absent from this set" is not true. The *Precyclopedia* is "recommended" for home use and preschool libraries.

Katz, William A. *Basic Information Sources* (Vol. 1 of *Introduction to Reference Work,* 3rd ed. New York: McGraw-Hill, 1978), p. 162. Katz briefly compares the *Precyclopedia* and *Childcraft.* The judgment on the *Precyclopedia:* "The set is more of a collection of readings than a true encyclopedia."

Wynkoop, Sally. *American Reference Books Annual,* 1975, pp. 33–34. Wynkoop's assessment of the *Precyclopedia* is entirely negative. She finds fault with everything from the lack of a preface and the choice of headings to the set's writing style and binding. The *Precyclopedia* is "not recommended."

Illustrated Encyclopedia for Learning

Facts in Brief

Full Title: **The Illustrated Encyclopedia for Learning in 12 Fact-filled Accurate Volumes Illustrated with More than 6,000 Dramatic Full-color Pictures.** *Editor:* Ruth Dimond, Editor in Chief. *Publisher:* Comet Press, New York, N.Y. *Distributor and Present Publisher:* The Publishers Agency, Inc., 3399 Forrest Rd., Cornwells Heights, PA 19020. *Edition Reviewed:* 1969 copyright.

Volumes: 12. *Pages:* 1,536. *Articles:* 4,500. *Words:* 291,000. *Illustrations:* 6,000. *Maps:* 425. *Index Entries:* None. *Cross-references:* None. *Contributors:* 13.

User Classification: Children (Multivolume). *Reader Suitability:* Age 7 through 12. *Physical Size:* 7 × 10¼ in.; 26 cm. *Lowest Retail Price:* $49.95; to schools & libraries $39.95.

Purpose and Scope

The Illustrated Encyclopedia for Learning is remarkably similar to the now defunct *Golden Book Encyclopedia* (see Appendix A), as a quick comparison of subtitles and statistics will show. Moreover, both sets have practically the same purpose, scope, style, and format. Intended for elementary school children, *Illustrated Encyclopedia* claims to be "authoritative, comprehensive, and accurate," as well as "entertainingly written and completely illustrated to make learning an adventure." The set also bears a striking resemblance to *The Ladies' Home Journal Children's Illustrated Encyclopedia for Learning,* an 18-volume mail-order item that is no longer in print (see Appendix A).

Illustrated Encyclopedia's articles are extremely brief, rarely more than 50 or 60 words in length. They are also heavily illustrated with gaudy colored drawings. Actually, the set is as much a children's picture dictionary as it is an encyclopedia. EXAMPLE: The article "Engineering" is covered in 45 words accompanied by two pictures showing bridge and building construction. In its entirety, the article comprises only one column, or half a page. By way of contrast, *The New Book of Knowledge,* an outstanding children's encyclopedia, devotes five pages to the subject of engineering.

Topic selection emphasizes people, places, and tangible things. For instance, there are entries for such persons as Sir Arthur Eddington (English astronomer), Sir Anthony Eden, Gertrude Ederle (the first woman to swim the English Channel), Paul Ehrlich (German bacteriologist), John Ericsson (a nineteenth-century inventor), and John Erskine (a little-known American writer). But there are no entries for such subjects as adolescence, adoption, extrasensory perception, family life, marriage and divorce, and women's rights. Quite obviously, *Illustrated Encyclopedia*'s claim to be "comprehensive" is not justified.

History and Authority

As far as is known, the 1969 edition was the first and so far the only edition of *Illustrated Encyclopedia.* Initially published by the small Comet Press (200 Varick St. in New York City), it is now owned and distributed by the Publishers Agency, Inc., a firm that also publishes the adult *New American Encyclopedia.* The company is not highly regarded in encyclopedia publishing circles. *Illustrated Encyclopedia*'s editors are likewise unknown in the encyclopedia community. Ruth Dimond, the editor, is listed as having a Ph.D. from the University of Wisconsin. The associate editor, Eleanor Chancis Bassman, has a social work degree from Columbia University and is identified as a child guidance consultant and family counselor (facts that make it even stranger that the encyclopedia contains nothing on such topics as adolescence and family life). Thirteen consultants and reviewers are noted on the verso of the title page. They include reading specialists and elementary school educators and administrators based in the New York City area. None of the material is signed, nor are areas of subject responsibility indicated in the consultant and reviewer list.

Reliability

Illustrated Encyclopedia is, of course, over ten years old. It is sadly out-of-date and hence not reliable as a source of current information. In addition, most of the articles are so sketchy and vague that the material cannot be considered trustworthy. EXAMPLE: The Empire State Building is still "the tallest building in the world," according to *Illustrated Encyclopedia.* EXAMPLE: In the article on George Eliot, the nineteenth-century English novelist whose real name was Mary Ann Evans, the encyclopedia says, "She used the pen-name of George Eliot because she was very shy." This statement is a distortion of the facts. EXAMPLE: "Porpoise" informs the reader that the animal likes to eat fish and lives in the water, but nowhere does the brief article mention the most interesting information about the porpoise—its remarkable intelligence. Over and over again, the set's fundamental unreliability is found in articles covering all areas of knowledge.

Recency

As already mentioned, *Illustrated Encyclopedia* has not been revised since it first appeared in 1969. The set is now quite dated. It should be either overhauled or withdrawn from the market.

This Recency Table compares selected topics in *Illustrated Encyclopedia* with those in other encyclopedias of similar size and intended usership.

Topic	Illustrated Encyclopedia	Britannica Junior	New Book of Knowledge	Young Students
Africa	Not current	Very current	Very current	Very current
Babies/Children	Not current*	Not current	Fairly current	Not current
Disease	Not current	Fairly current	Fairly current	Fairly current
North American Indians	Not current	Very current	Fairly current	Not current
Sharks	Fairly current	Fairly current	Very current	Fairly current
Television	Not current	Fairly current	Very current	Fairly current

*Topic not covered in encyclopedia.

Objectivity

Illustrated Encyclopedia simply avoids most controversial topics. Drug abuse, sexuality, race, and death are not discussed, for instance. However, in those instances when a subject that is open to debate is covered, an effort is made to give both sides of the question. EXAMPLE: The article "Flying Saucer" points out that the U.S. Air Force has dismissed most sightings as "just plain mistakes." But the article continues by noting that "some sightings, however, have never been explained. Some people believe that flying saucers come from another planet."

Clarity and Reader Suitability

Despite a number of reading experts among the consultants and reviewers, there is no evidence of vocabulary control. For instance, the word *ethnology* appears as an entry in *Illustrated Encyclopedia*, but it is doubtful that the word is included in the reading vocabulary of very many children. Moreover, new, difficult, or technical terms are rarely defined in context. EXAMPLE: The article on Sigmund Freud identifies him as "an Austrian doctor who developed psychoanalysis." Several sentences later the article refers to the "subconscious mind." None of these terms is explained in the text, or treated as separate articles.

No effort has been made to relate the topics covered to grade school curricula or children's out-of-school interests. Rather, the encyclopedia is a hodgepodge of subjects with no particular relevance to the informational needs of young people or to their levels of reading comprehension. The heavily pictorial format suggests a set for preschoolers and beginning readers, but the vocabulary used sometimes requires high school level reading skills. Most of the articles are written in simple, declarative sentences, but the material is neither "entertainingly written" as claimed, nor does the style "make learning an adventure."

Arrangement and Accessibility

Illustrated Encyclopedia is arranged alphabetically, letter-by-letter ("Indiana" precedes "Indian Ocean"). The set provides absolutely no cross-references, nor is there a general index. As a result, much of the information—such as it is—remains inaccessible to the user, and relationships between related topics are not indicated. EXAMPLE: There is no entry for race or the races of humankind, but the 70-word article "Ethnology" does mention the three major racial groups. Unless the young reader is brilliant or ingenious enough to look for this information under "Ethnology," it will not be found.

Bibliographies

None. As in the case of *Britannica Junior Encyclopaedia*, the lack of bibliographies limits *Illustrated Encyclopedia*'s usefulness as a general reference work for children.

Graphics

As the set's title suggests, considerable space (roughly 50 percent of the total text) is devoted to illustrations. All of them are in color and are artists' drawings. Not only are the pictures garish, they rarely add to the informational content of the articles they accompany. Detail is frequently bad or lacking, color reproduction is sometimes out of register, and occasionally color is applied unevenly. The very simple maps—also staff produced—mainly serve to locate major places. They are too small and too elementary to serve any serious geographical reference purpose.

Physical Format

The set is bound in washable, padded, drab olive covers with blue and gold lettering. The binding is both sturdy and practical. A world globe motif appears on the front cover of each volume. The books lie flat when open, though they are rather tightly sewn. Inside, the print is large and clear. The two-column page layout, however, sometimes gives the impression of being cluttered and is unattractive. Illustrations frequently bleed into the margins. Guide words are not provided, either at the top or bottom of the page.

Special Features

None.

Sales Information

Illustrated Encyclopedia is sold to individual consumers and educational institutions by direct mail order only. In 1976, because the encyclopedia had become dated and most likely will not be revised in the future, the publisher reduced the price of the set to $49.95. Cash customers and schools and libraries can acquire the set at a 20 percent savings, or for $39.95. Note, however, that the publisher refuses to provide current price information to the *Buying Guide* and, therefore, these figures are estimates based on information supplied by the publisher several years ago. Consumers should also be aware that *Illustrated Encyclopedia* may be available from regional distributors at so-called bargain prices. For instance, the *Tampa Tribune-Times* (Tampa, Fla.) carried an advertisement for *Illustrated Encyclopedia* on Sunday, December 12, 1976. Said to be "a reference library and the first step on the road to a college education," the set was being sold by Southern Guild, Inc., for $18.88. No matter who distributes the work, there is only one edition of *Illustrated Encyclopedia* on the market, that being the olive binding already described (see "Physical Format").

Summary

The Illustrated Encyclopedia for Learning can be quickly summed up in this manner:

Scope: Poor	Accessibility: Poor
Authority: Poor	Bibliographies: Poor (none)
Reliability: Poor	Graphics: Fair
Recency: Poor	Physical Format: Fair
Objectivity: Fair	Special Features: None
Clarity: Fair	Price: High

To elaborate briefly, *Illustrated Encyclopedia* fails in almost every way as a general reference work for children. The set is badly dated, unreliable, poorly designed for access to material, and superficial in both coverage and treatment. Even at the reduced price of $18.88, *Illustrated Encyclopedia* is a poor bargain. Among the multivolume children's sets now on the market, *Illustrated Encyclopedia* ranks last. As one of the *Buying Guide*'s subject consultants commented, the set is "pitifully inadequate for any age level. It is difficult to understand how this encyclopedia was thought to merit publication." Comparatively speaking, *The Young Students Encyclopedia* is a generally commendable and reasonably priced small encyclopedia for elementary school students. The two best (but more costly) sets especially designed for young readers are *The New Book of Knowledge* and *Britannica Junior Encyclopaedia*. Unless price is an overriding consideration, one of these two encyclopedias will be the first choice of discerning consumers seeking a multivolume children's set.

Other Critical Opinions

None.

New Book of Knowledge

Facts in Brief

Full Title: **The New Book of Knowledge.** *Editors:* William E. Shapiro, Editor in Chief; Martha Glauber Shapp, Editorial Consultant; Sue R. Brandt & Cathleen FitzGerald, Executive Editors; Franklin N. Sayles, Art & Production Director; Bernard S. Cayne, Editorial Director. *Publisher:* Grolier, Inc., Sherman Turnpike, Danbury, CT 06816. *Former Title: The Book of Knowledge* (1912–1965). *Edition Reviewed:* 1980 copyright.

Volumes: 20 (plus a "Combined Index" for schools & libraries; also the *Home and School Reading and Study Guides to the New Book of Knowledge). Pages:* 10,500. *Articles:* 9,326. *Words:* 6,800,000. *Illustrations:* 21,400. *Maps:* 1,031. *Index Entries:* 90,000. *Cross-references:* 2,500. *Contributors:* 1,435.

User Classification: Children (Multivolume). *Reader Suitability:* Age 7 through 14. *Physical Size:* 8 × 10¼ in.; 26 cm. *LC:* 79-53915. *ISBN:* 0-7172-0511-8. *Lowest Retail Price:* $360; to schools & libraries $264.50.

Purpose and Scope

The New Book of Knowledge "will be useful to a wide range of readers, starting with preschool children and including students in school up to the age when they are ready for an adult encyclopedia" (preface). First published as an entirely new work in 1966, replacing the earlier *Book of Knowledge* (1912–1965), *The New Book of Knowledge* is specifically aimed at elementary school students. The emphasis is on children in grades three through six, although the set is equally useful for advanced students in the primary grades as well as slower readers in junior high school. Like *Britannica Junior Encyclopaedia,* its chief competitor among the multivolume children's encyclopedias, *The New Book of Knowledge* bases its coverage to a great extent on those topics that form the North American elementary school curriculum. As a recent advertisement for the encyclopedia puts it, "Students quickly discover that *The New Book of Knowledge* provides more than enough information needed to successfully complete their classroom assignments and research projects."

The New Book of Knowledge naturally includes material on basic subject matter in all areas of knowledge. Geography, which accounts for approximately 25 percent of all entries, is especially well covered. The continents and countries of the world receive extended treatment, the length of the article determined by the relative size and importance of the

388

place. The heavily illustrated article "Africa," for example, runs to 22 pages and covers the essential facts concerning the continent's physical features, plants and animals, natural resources, economy, history, people, and so on. "China" covers 18 pages of text, whereas "Afghanistan" is limited to four pages. The U.S. states and Canadian provinces are likewise accorded adequate coverage, with much factual information highlighted in boxes. Major world rivers, mountains, cities, and the like are also covered, normally in articles of one, two, or three pages. Biographical entries are not as extensive as those devoted to geographical topics, but important people are not neglected; for instance, Thomas Jefferson has an article of seven pages, Aristotle receives nearly a page, and John L. Lewis and Sinclair Lewis share a page.

Scientific and technical subjects are adequately covered, reflecting the current elementary school curriculum. The article "Computers," for instance, is an excellent nine-page introduction to the subject. The encyclopedia also offers such related articles as "Automation," "Electronic Communication," and "Electronics." The recently revised article "Nuclear Energy" (20 pages) also serves as a good introductory overview to a complex topic. "Dinosaurs" (ten pages) is both readable and creatively illustrated. The article "Birds as Pets" includes detailed instructions on how to build a birdhouse. A number of other articles in the area of science and technology provide similar practical projects and experiments for both in-school and out-of-school activities.

Coverage of social and behavioral science topics has been expanded in recent years, again reflecting changes in the elementary school classroom and among young people themselves. Recent editions of the encyclopedia, for instance, have added or upgraded material in the areas of careers, consumer education, drug abuse, death and dying, environmental pollution and ecology, ethnic studies, family living, and women. Coverage of human sexuality, criticized in previous editions of the *Buying Guide*, has been improved by the addition of a page-long subsection entitled "Human Reproduction" in the article "Reproduction." Written by Dr. Jean Pakter, identified as director, Bureau of Maternity Services and Family Planning, New York City Department of Health, the article clearly explains "the miracle of reproduction" in reasonably nontechnical and readable fashion. For instance, the article notes that "every human being has a belly button, which is a reminder of how each of us began life." The encyclopedia continues, however, to ignore such subjects as homosexuality and masturbation. Because these and other sex-related topics are of considerable interest, concern, and sometimes mystery to young people, *The New Book of Knowledge* is negligent for not covering them.

The humanities and arts are reasonably well covered. Such articles as "Books," "Country and Western Music," "Languages," "Olympic Games," "Painting," "Percussion Instruments," "Plays," "Pottery," and "Television" provide clear and comprehensive coverage of the subject for interested elementary school children. Artistic expression in different cultures or parts of the world is treated in survey articles, such as "African Art," "African Literature," "African Music." Literary topics are especially well covered. Such articles as "Fables," "Fairy Tales," and "Folklore" include examples of stories, tales, children's street rhymes, and the like. The Cinderella story, for example, is retold in its entirety, as is the folktale of Pecos Bill. Biographies of authors also include a portion of their works. EXAMPLE: The entry for Rudyard Kipling devotes a page and a half to the English author's life and then reprints his poem *If,* a song from the *Jungle Books* entitled "Mowgli's Song against People," and a short story from the *Just So Stories.* In all, the encyclopedia contains 170 stories, poems, and excerpts from children's literature. Music also receives excellent coverage. For instance, *The New Book of Knowledge* is the only set in its category that adequately covers rock music, a subject that enthralls many young people and should be treated in some depth in encyclopedias for them. *Britannica Junior* covers the subject in a couple of terse sentences; *The Young Students Encyclopedia* provides two paragraphs; *Oxford Junior Encyclopaedia,* produced in the land of the Beatles, ignores the subject altogether.

As the articles on rock and country and western music suggest, considerable material in the set is designed to appeal to children's out-of-school interests, as opposed to the curriculum-oriented subjects that comprise the bulk of the encyclopedia. Articles on games, hobbies, and leisure activities exemplify this type of material. Many articles also include practical, or how-to, information of interest to young people. EXAMPLES: The article "Baby" includes practical information about infant care and might be helpful to youngsters who baby-sit. "Bicycling" discusses the sport and includes an illustrated section on maintenance and safety. "Book Reports and Reviews" furnishes helpful tips on how to prepare different types of reports. "First Aid" contains practical advice about what to do when someone is choking, bleeding, drowning, etc. "Plays" provides excellent how-to information concerning choosing a play, determining all the various costs, how to produce different sound effects and props, and how to apply makeup.

History and Authority

The publisher, Grolier, Inc., is one of the largest U.S. publishers of general encyclopedias. The firm is responsible for *The Encyclopedia Americana* (for adults), *Encyclopedia International* (for young adults), and *The New Book of Knowledge* (for children). Grolier also publishes several major specialized reference sets, including the *Catholic Encyclopedia for School and Home, Encyclopedia Canadiana,* and the *Australian Encyclopedia.* Grolier likewise distributes numerous reference sets for children aimed at both the home and the school and library markets, such as the *Illustrated Encyclopedia of the Animal Kingdom* and *Peoples of the Earth.* During the 1970s, Grolier suffered severe financial losses and is no longer the powerful publisher it once was. A gradual but unmistakable decline in the overall quality of Grolier products has been noticeable for some time now. For instance, *Encyclopedia Canadiana* (1957–1958) is sadly out-of-date, but Grolier recently informed the Canadian Library

Association that the set will not be revised. (See "Selling Encyclopedias" in Part I of the *Buying Guide* for further information about Grolier.)

Between 1912 and 1965, Grolier published *The Book of Knowledge* (see Appendix A), a longtime favorite children's encyclopedia among librarians, teachers, and informed parents. In 1957, however, Grolier tentatively decided to scrap the set, apparently because much of the material was stale and its topical arrangement had become a liability. The plan that emerged called for a completely new work, which would be alphabetically arranged and closely related to the U.S. elementary school curriculum. Nine years and several million dollars later, *The New Book of Knowledge* was born. Over the past 15 years, it has achieved an excellent reputation and is generally considered the foremost encyclopedia for grade school children. Unlike Grolier's other two major multivolume sets (*The Encyclopedia Americana* and *Encyclopedia International*), the firm's weakened financial condition during the 1970s has not apparently affected the maintenance of *The New Book of Knowledge* (see "Recency"). Consumers may also be interested to know that there is a Spanish-language version of *The New Book of Knowledge* entitled *El Nuevo Tesoro de la Juventud.* Produced in Mexico City principally for a Latin American audience, *El Nuevo Tesoro de la Juventud* is distributed in the United States and Canada by Grolier Educational Corporation (a subsidiary of Grolier, Inc.).

Since 1977, when the *Buying Guide* last evaluated *The New Book of Knowledge,* the encyclopedia's editorial staff has changed markedly. William E. Shapiro is now listed as editor in chief, replacing Martha G. Shapp, who continues in the position of editorial consultant. Supporting Shapiro is an editorial and production staff of 40, down considerably since 1977. Also gone are the curriculum and library advisory boards and lengthy list of subject consultants. In their stead is a modest list of 31 advisers and consultants, one of whom is Lowell Martin, a well-known librarian and encyclopedist who played a key role in designing *The New Book of Knowledge.* For the most part, the advisers and consultants are academicians who bring good credentials to the work. The same can be said of the 1,435 contributors, consultants, and reviewers (or authenticators) listed in Volume 20. Included are such responsible authorities as Leonard Bernstein (the conductor and composer), Marchette Chute (an expert on Shakespeare), Nathan Glazer (professor of education and sociology, Harvard University), Eda LeShan (a noted author on child development), Robert Payne (a popular writer on the Orient), Fredrick J. Stare (professor of nutrition, Harvard University), and Irving Stone (author of *Lust for Life,* etc.). The list also includes a number of children's authors and school administrators. In addition, quite a few new contributors have been added to the list since 1977, such as Don M. Cregier (associate professor of history, University of Prince Edward Island), Alan T. King (deputy executive director, U.S. Parachute Association), and Deena Teitelbaum (Board of Examiners, Board of Education, New York City). Unlike all the major competing sets (*Britannica Junior Encyclopaedia, Oxford Junior Encyclopaedia,* and *The Young Students Encyclope-*

dia), nearly every article in *The New Book of Knowledge* is signed, sometimes by both the original author and a reviewer, the latter an authority who authenticates the material.

Reliability

The New Book of Knowledge has a well-deserved reputation for reliability. Not only is the set carefully checked for factual accuracy, but it is usually in accord with responsible contemporary thinking in those areas not subject to hard facts. EXAMPLE: The article "Drugs, Abuse of" (by Dr. Dana L. Farnsworth, recently retired as director of Harvard University's health services) very clearly discusses various aspects of the problem, often correcting misconceptions about the effects of certain drugs: "For a long time most people thought that if a person used marijuana he was almost certain to start using stronger drugs, such as heroin. This idea is not true. There is nothing in the chemical composition of marijuana that makes a person crave other drugs, and many people use marijuana but not other drugs. However, almost everyone who uses stronger, more dangerous drugs did start with marijuana."

Occasionally, material is not presented as clearly as it might be, thus leading to wrong impressions. For instance, the discussion of the absorption system in the article "Refrigeration" is not entirely clear. Likewise, occasional errors of fact do occur; for instance, "Sharks, Skates, and Rays" errs in claiming the dogfish is the smallest shark. Such errors, however, are not significant nor frequent enough to alter the basic judgment that *The New Book of Knowledge* is a trustworthy source of information.

Recency

The New Book of Knowledge is continuously revised on an annual basis. Articles are rewritten to reflect new facts and important new developments or trends. New material is added in response to curricular changes or to meet the changing informational needs of young people. The addition of the article "Country and Western Music" to the 1980 set is a good example of the effort to keep the encyclopedia in tune with the interests of its readers. Other new or thoroughly revised articles in the 1980 edition include "Antigua and Barbuda" (a new Caribbean nation), "Astronomy," "Balloons and Ballooning," "Children's Literature," "Crime and Criminology," "Dominica" (another new Caribbean nation), "First Aid," "Lasers," "Missiles," "Nuclear Energy," "Solar Energy," "Soccer," and "Tuvalu" (a new Pacific island nation). In all, the publisher reports more than 1,100 new or revised articles in the 1980 edition entailing changes of one sort or another in 2,776 text pages (of a total 10,500 pages). Moreover, approximately 1,150 new graphics were added to the set in 1980, and some 120 maps were updated. There are instances, of course, where *The New Book of Knowledge* is not entirely current. For example, the article "Indians of North America" fails to provide recent population statistics. But the encyclopedia's rate of revision shows significant improvement since 1977 (when the *Buying Guide* last examined the set), and on balance, *The New*

This Recency Table compares selected topics in *The New Book of Knowledge* with those in other encyclopedias of similar size and intended usership.

Topic	New Book of Knowledge	Britannica Junior	Oxford Junior	Young Students
Africa	Very current	Very current	Not current	Fairly current
Babies/Children	Fairly current	Not current	Not current	Not current
Disease	Fairly current	Fairly current	Not current	Fairly current
North American Indians	Fairly current	Very current	Not current	Not current
Sharks	Very current	Fairly current	Fairly current	Fairly current
Television	Very current	Fairly current	Not current	Fairly current

Book of Knowledge is currently doing a very good job of keeping abreast of new knowledge and information.

Like most major multivolume general encyclopedias on the North American market, *The New Book of Knowledge* is supplemented annually by a yearbook. Called the *New Book of Knowledge Annual* (with the subtitle *The Young People's Book of the Year),* the volume is heavily illustrated with both color and black-and-white photographs, but it lacks cross-references and bears little real relationship to the encyclopedia. The 1980 *Annual,* for instance, includes an informative article entitled "Nuclear Energy: Good or Bad?," but there is no effort to direct the interested reader to the basic article on nuclear energy in the encyclopedia. Toward the end of the 1980 volume, however, are reprints of 17 new articles from *The New Book of Knowledge.* According to a prefatory note, "They are included here to help you keep your encyclopedia up-to-date." The *Annual,* which sells for $12.75 and normally contains between 350 and 400 pages, is hardly an effective device for keeping the encyclopedia current, but it does contain some useful material.

Objectivity

The preface declares that "where authorities disagree or information is unknown, the reader is so informed. An underlying principle of editorial policy is the presentation of fact, not opinion." This statement fairly describes the editors' policy toward topics open to controversy. Likewise, in recent years there has been a strong effort to avoid sexist language and forms of sex stereotyping. Much work still remains to be done in this area, however. The article "Evolution," for instance, observes, "The most important result of the slow evolution of life is man. Man has been on earth only about 2,000,000 years. This is less than 1/1000 of the time that life has existed. Man is therefore a latecomer. But he has already had a greater influence on the face of the earth than any other form of life." Also, in some cases touchy or controversial subject matter is completely avoided. There is no coverage of birth control—not a single substantive mention of this subject, despite the fact that sex education is taught in many schools at the upper elementary and middle school levels. The aforementioned article "Evolution" contains nothing concerning the so-called creationist point of view; indeed Darwinism is presented as fact. The editors' commitment to impartial presentation of knowledge and information is evident throughout the set, but too often these good intentions have not been realized.

Clarity and Reader Suitability

The articles are written principally for readers in the upper elementary grades, although topics with special appeal to even younger students are written at a lower level. Some topics requiring a technical vocabulary are written at a higher level. In every instance, however, the articles have been tested against the Dale-Chall readability formula. (Dr. Edgar Dale, a readability expert, is a *World Book Encyclopedia* consultant; Dr. Jeanne S. Chall, also an authority on readability, is a *New Book of Knowledge* consultant; together they produced the *Dale–Chall Formula for Predicting Readability*). And when unfamiliar or technical terms are used, they are often printed in boldface and defined in context. EXAMPLE: The article "Drugs" naturally uses a number of technical terms. In one section, the reader learns that "duplicating natural substances in the laboratory is called **synthesizing** them; an artificially made drug is called a **synthetic drug**." As a result, the style and vocabulary of *The New Book of Knowledge* articles are quite precisely directed at the intended readership. There has been an honest effort, too, to make the articles interesting. Particularly noteworthy are the first sentences, which are frequently attention-getting. EXAMPLE: "Skunks" begins in this manner: "If you suddenly meet a skunk face to face—stand still."

Arrangement and Accessibility

The New Book of Knowledge is arranged alphabetically, letter-by-letter ("Indiana" precedes "Indian Ocean"). Access is facilitated by numerous cross-references, both external references entered in the main alphabetical sequence (e.g., "*Marijuana*. See DRUGS, ABUSE OF") and *See also* references at the end of articles. Finally, there is a detailed analytical index of some 90,000 entries divided among the 20 volumes.

The index is absolutely essential for finding specific information in *The New Book of Knowledge*. The reason is because many of the encyclopedia's articles are broad in scope. For instance, documentary films do not have their own entry, nor is there an external cross-reference to the topic in the A-to-Z sequence. The topic can be found, however, through the index under the heading "Documentary Motion Pictures," which refers the reader to two broad articles, "Motion Picture Industry" and "Television Production." The index—called a Dictionary Index—contains not only references to articles in the encyclopedia, but also includes some 5,000 very brief articles or fact summaries. EXAMPLE: There is no entry for Muhammad Ali in the main A–Z portion of the encyclopedia, but the boxer is briefly discussed in the Dictionary Index. Most of these fact summaries deal with people, places, organizations, and specialized terms (e.g., *meningitis*). In a few cases, the fact summaries probably should be expanded into full-scale articles and included in the main A–Z section of the set. EXAMPLES: "Bermuda Triangle"; "Biofeedback"; "Cayman Islands"; "Concentration Camps"; "Devil"; "Garvey, Marcus"; "Pentagon, The"; and "Political Science."

Like the Fact-Index found in *Compton's Encyclopedia*, the Dictionary Index is divided among the 20 volumes, the letters of the alphabet covered in the index corresponding to those covered in the volume. The index pages are printed on blue paper for easy identification. As pointed out in the case of *Compton's*, the divided-index approach does have the disadvantage of having to consult more than one—sometimes many—volumes to research a topic. EXAMPLE: A student using *The New Book of Knowledge* to find information about abortion would most likely first look in the "A" volume under that term. Not finding an entry, she might then look in the index to the "A" volume, again for the term "abortion." Finding nothing, she might then look in the index to the "B" volume under "Birth Control." Finding nothing, she might then (if she is persistent) look in the "P" volume ("Population Control"), the "S" volume ("Sex"), the "R" volume ("Reproduction"), and so on. A "Combined Index" to *The New Book of Knowledge* has been published, which brings together all 20 sections of the index in one letter-by-letter alphabetical sequence. This cumulated index is said to be "prepared especially for school and library use," but presumably it can also be acquired by individual consumers. A weakness of the Dictionary Index, whether published in 20 parts or in a single volume, is that it does not fully index the numerous illustrations found throughout the set. For example, there is a scene from the movie of Shakespeare's *Taming of the Shrew* in the article "Motion Picture Industry," but there is no reference to the graphic in the index under the heading "Taming of the Shrew, The" or "Shakespeare, William."

Bibliographies

There are no lists of recommended further readings included with the articles. Instead, bibliographies are found in the first half of a paperbound supplement entitled *Home and School Reading and Study Guides*, available to purchasers of the set at no additional charge. The bibliographies, which are limited to book titles, cover about 1,000 topics keyed to titles of articles in the encyclopedia. Approximately 6,000 book titles are listed. Reader suitability is indicated. Prepared by John T. Gillespie, a library science professor at C. W. Post Center of Long Island University, and Christine B. Gilbert, formerly at Post, the bibliographies are well selected and fairly up-to-date. These lists would be more useful, however, if they were printed with the articles themselves. As Christine Wynar notes in her review of *The New Book of Knowledge* in *American Reference Books Annual* (1977, p. 50), "It is hard to picture a third, fourth or even fifth grade reader turning to the Study Guide volume after reading one or more articles in the encyclopedia in order to find additional reading suggestions."

Graphics

No children's encyclopedia today can afford poor graphics. *The New Book of Knowledge* passes the test with flying colors. Indeed, nearly 75 percent of the 21,400 illustrations are in color, with more than 7,000 in full color. The set contains much art work commissioned exclusively for the encyclopedia. There are also many photographs, art reproductions, and functional drawings and diagrams. These illustrations are almost always placed in good relationship to the printed text they are meant to clarify or enhance. As already pointed out (see "Recency"), new graphics are constantly being added to the set to replace those that have become stale or outmoded.

The major maps are produced by Jeppesen & Company and the Diversified Map Corporation, both reputable cartographic firms. Other special-purpose maps (historical, distribution, etc.) are drawn by staff cartographers. Like the other graphics, the set's maps are of good quality, being attractive and simple enough for younger students. U.S. state maps are especially useful and varied. For most states there are six different maps: a locator map showing the state's position in the country; a small landform map; an equally small land map showing major topographical features; a full-page map (with index) showing key places and physical features; a three-quarter-page map showing important places of interest and major highways; and a small map outlining the state's counties.

Physical Format

The volumes are arranged by the unit-letter plan—that is, one or more letters is completely contained in a volume. The set is good-looking, bound in a washable red Sturdite binding with silver lettering. There is a gold and silver leaf motif stamped on the front of each volume (presumably representing the tree of knowledge). Inside, the page layout is both attractive and utilitarian. Boldface headings and subheadings are used to break up longer articles and to guide readers to specific topics. Fact boxes and similar devices are employed not only to convey information but to facilitate creative page composition. The typefaces used are legible and inviting to the eye. In the 1980 edition the type size of the Dictionary Index (and the Combined Index) has been enlarged to improve readability. Good use of white space gives the typical page a pleasing, uncluttered appearance. In a departure from customary procedure, guide words are printed at the bottom of the page, instead of at the top. Frequently, however, the guide words are eliminated by illustrations at the bottom of the page. The volumes usually lie flat when open for easy consultation.

Overall, *The New Book of Knowledge* is both visually appealing and physically well constructed.

Special Features

The encyclopedia has several special features of interest to consumers. The most obvious is the Dictionary Index, which not only furnishes comprehensive access to the encyclopedia's contents, but also includes about 5,000 brief articles, called fact summaries. Another special—or different—feature is that pronunciations are included in the index rather than with the articles in the main A–Z portion of the set. Why this procedure was adopted is understandable, but it is not helpful to the user. Another more valuable special feature is the inclusion of various how-to activities, designed to encourage independent study or projects. EXAMPLES: "Ship Models" provides a step-by-step plan for making a model Viking ship. "Recorder" explains how to play the musical instrument. "Recipes" instructs children in how to prepare Heavenly Hash and Television Nibbles, among other goodies. Finally, the paperbound booklet entitled *Home and School Reading and Study Guides* contains both lists of books for further reading (see "Bibliographies") and detailed suggestions to parents and teachers concerning how best to utilize the encyclopedia at various grade levels. Arranged by broad topics (such as Social Studies or Health and Safety), the guide portion of the booklet discusses learning activities appropriate for children in particular grades, with emphasis on articles to be read in the encyclopedia. Interested parents and teachers both will find the study guides valuable adjuncts to the encyclopedia.

Sales Information

The New Book of Knowledge is available to retail customers in a Lexotone binding at $360. The set is sold both in-home on the subscription, or installment, basis and via direct mail order. A reinforced library binding, the red Sturdite already described (see "Physical Format"), is sold to educational institutions at the discount price of $264.50. Consumers should be aware that the retail price of *The New Book of Knowledge* has fluctuated quite wildly during the past six or so years. In 1975, the publisher, Grolier, retailed the set for $280. The price eventually rose to $350 but, in 1978, a mail order campaign was introduced that reduced that figure to approximately $182 (including shipping and handling). Now the price has apparently returned to its level of several years ago ($360), which is about $160 more than the set's chief competitor, *Britannica Junior Encyclopaedia*. The *Buying Guide* advises retail consumers interested in purchasing *The New Book of Knowledge not* to pay more than $360. In all likelihood, the set can be acquired for less than that amount. If the price situation is unclear or confused, the *Buying Guide* advises consumers to hold off purchase until satisfactory clarification can be received from Grolier's headquarters in Danbury, Conn. (see Appendix E for complete directory information). When sold in-home, the encyclopedia may be offered in combination with the *New Book of Knowledge*

Annual, an updating supplement (see "Recency") that, according to the publisher, currently sells for $12.75 per volume.

North American consumers should also know that a Spanish-language version of *The New Book of Knowledge* can be acquired through Grolier Educational Corporation (a subsidiary of Grolier, Inc.). Entitled *El Nuevo Tesoro de la Juventud* and advertised as "The Book of Knowledge in Spanish," this 20-volume set lists at $350, with schools and libraries offered the discount price of $234.50.

Summary

The New Book of Knowledge can be quickly summed up in this manner:

Scope: Excellent	Accessibility: Excellent
Authority: Excellent	Bibliographies: Good
Reliability: Excellent	Graphics: Excellent
Recency: Excellent	Physical Format: Excellent
Objectivity: Good	Special Features: Many
Clarity: Excellent	Price: Reasonable

To elaborate briefly, *The New Book of Knowledge* is the outstanding encyclopedia for children aged 7–14. The set's coverage, based loosely on the North American elementary school curriculum, is quite broad and in some instances equal to that found in the multivolume sets for young adults, namely *Compton's Encyclopedia, Merit Students Encyclopedia, The World Book Encyclopedia,* and Grolier's own *Encyclopedia International.* The writing style and vocabulary, however, are carefully geared to readers at the elementary school level. Hence, *The New Book of Knowledge* can be very useful for slower junior high and even high school students. The encyclopedia is authoritative, reliable, well illustrated, and effectively organized for easy access of material. Moreover, the set's rate of revision has improved during the past several years, making *The New Book of Knowledge* one of the most up-to-date encyclopedias on the market today. On the negative side, the set's efforts to present knowledge and information in an impartial manner are not always successful.

At the present time, there are five multivolume encyclopedias for children aged 7–14 on the North American market: *Britannica Junior Encyclopaedia, The New Book of Knowledge, The Illustrated Encyclopedia for Learning, Oxford Junior Encyclopaedia,* and *The Young Students Encyclopedia.* The last three sets will not interest most consumers. *Oxford Junior* is very much a British production, *Young Students* lacks substance, and *The Illustrated Encyclopedia for Learning* is a dreadfully dated work of low quality. Obviously, the best buy comes down to a choice between *The New Book of Knowledge* and *Britannica Junior.* In the *Buying Guide*'s opinion, *The New Book of Knowledge* is the superior set. It does everything *Britannica Junior* does and more. In terms of price, however, *Britannica Junior* (at $199.50) is currently $160 cheaper than *The New Book of Knowledge* ($360). Hence, from the standpoint of quality alone, *The New Book of Knowledge* is unquestionably the best multivolume encyclopedia buy for young people in the elementary grades. But from the standpoint of price alone, *Britannica Junior* is the best buy. Consumers should be aware, however, that *The New Book of Knowledge* may be available in certain areas or during special promotions at a price much lower than $360.

Other Critical Opinions

Booklist, December 1, 1978, pp. 637–639. Part of a series of reviews by the ALA Reference and Subscription Books Review Committee (RSBRC) entitled "Encyclopedias: A Survey and Buying Guide," this unsigned evaluation is generally favorable, although the set is faulted for occasional "sweeping generalizations or contradictory language." In its last regular review of *The New Book of Knowledge* (*Booklist,* April 15, 1973, pp. 773–775), RSBRC "recommended" the encyclopedia for home, school, and public libraries.

Katz, William A. *Basic Information Sources* (Vol. 1 of *Introduction to Reference Work,* 3rd ed. New York: McGraw-Hill, 1978), pp. 161–162. Katz comparatively reviews the three leading sets for children, namely *The New Book of Knowledge, Britannica Junior Encyclopaedia,* and *The Young Students Encyclopedia.* He rates *The New Book of Knowledge* the best of the bunch, with *Young Students* in second place.

Wynar, Christine L. *American Reference Books Annual,* 1977, pp. 47–51. This long and informative review is mostly positive, citing the set's curriculum orientation, interesting writing style, and currency of material as outstanding features.

Oxford Junior Encyclopaedia

Facts in Brief

Full Title: **Oxford Junior Encyclopaedia.** *Editors:* Laura E. Salt, Geoffrey Boumphrey, and Robert Sinclair, General Editors. *Publisher:* Oxford University Press, Inc., 200 Madison Ave., New York, NY 10016. *Edition Reviewed:* 1971–1976 copyright.

Volumes: 13. *Pages:* 6,500. *Articles:* 3,600. *Words:* 3,750,000. *Illustrations:* 6,100. *Maps:* 150. *Index Entries:* 35,000. *Cross-references:* 2,000. *Contributors:* 1,050.

User Classification: Children (Multivolume). *Reader Suitability:* Age 7 through 14. *Physical Size:* 7½ × 10 in.; 26 cm. *ISBN:* 0-19-910020-9. *Lowest Retail Price:* $189.

Purpose and Scope

The *Oxford Junior Encyclopaedia,* widely known and used in Great Britain but much less so in the United States, is principally directed at school children in the elementary and junior grades. The set also attempts to serve a "far wider circle of readers . . . to whom the large, standard encyclopedias are too heavy and technical, and the popular alternatives for the most part neither sufficiently complete nor authoritative" (preface). Unlike the other "junior" reviewed in this part of the *Buying Guide* (that is, *Britannica Junior Encyclopaedia*), *Oxford Junior* is not curriculum-related. In addition, although the preface suggests that "treatment and vocabulary [are] suitable for the young reader," *Oxford Junior*'s readability level tends to be more suited to middle school students (aged 11–14), whereas its main North American competitors, *The New Book of Knowledge* and the aforementioned *Britannica Junior Encyclopaedia*, are chiefly geared to readers in grades three through six.

Oxford Junior covers the universe of knowledge in topical fashion (see "Arrangement and Accessibility"), and its scope is international. As might be expected, however, there is a decided British emphasis, not only in terms of coverage but also of tone, style, and spelling. EXAMPLE: The brief entry covering Santa Claus is entitled "Father Christmas." EXAMPLE: The article "Americans (U.S.A.)" notes that "each state has a parliament of its own which makes laws relating to local matters and raises taxes for the state's special needs. The people of each state also elect representatives to a national parliament called Congress." British readers, of course, will understand the term "parliament" and perhaps benefit from the analogy. American readers, on the other hand, may well be confused by the reference, especially since the United States does not have a parliamentary form of government in the strictest sense. EXAMPLE: The volume covering sports and games includes numerous articles of interest almost exclusively to British users, such as "Association Football," "Eton Football," "Hare Hunting," and "Pub Games." Other sports, like lacrosse, are treated entirely from the English point of view. This observation is true of many other subject areas as well.

The peoples and countries of the world are adequately covered, considering the limitations of space and the intended readership. The natural and technical sciences are also fairly well covered, with particular attention given to recent technological advances in such areas as space exploration, the use of computers, and electronics developments. Some important scientific topics, however, are dealt with too briefly or superficially, even for middle school readers. The coverage of oceans and oceanography, for instance, is largely limited to two pages of text with accompanying diagrams. Most significant aspects of the subject are touched upon, if only barely, although there is no mention at all of the recent—and vitally important—United Nations Conference on the Law of the Sea.

The humanities (literature, language, art, philosophy, and the like) are accorded much more cursory and certainly less satisfactory coverage than the physical and technical sciences. The same is true of smaller geographical units. For instance, none of the U.S. states receives a separate article, although most are mentioned (very fleetingly) in the article "United States of America." Only the largest or most prominent cities of the world receive individual entries—Boston, London, Los Angeles, Moscow, New York, etc. The newer social sciences also receive short shrift, and current political coverage is practically nil. In these areas, *Oxford Junior* is historical rather than contemporary in coverage. There is a lengthy article on women's suffrage, for example, but the present-day women's movement is ignored.

Consumers should also be aware that only metric measurements are given. Customary, or English, measurements (those used in the United States) are unfortunately omitted. EXAMPLE: "Jute is an annual plant, growing to a height of from 2 to 3 metres." Although the U.S. will most likely go metric someday, the lack of customary equivalents will pose a problem for most U.S. readers at this time. Such leading U.S. encyclopedias as the *Academic American Encyclopedia, Collier's Encyclopedia, Merit Students Encyclopedia, The New Columbia Encyclopedia, The New Encyclopaedia Britannica, The Random House Encyclopedia,* and *The World Book Encyclopedia* include both systems of measurement.

History and Authority

Oxford Junior, originally published in 1948, is generally regarded as the best encyclopedia for children produced in Great Britain. It is the only multivolume British encyclopedia for young people marketed in the United States, although it has never sold well here, obviously due to its strong British flavor. In 1963, the New York publisher Little and Ives, Inc., by arrangement with Oxford University Press, undertook to adapt the set for U.S. readers. Entitled the *American Oxford Encyclopedia,* only the first of a projected 14 volumes ever appeared (in 1965), the project being abandoned when the publisher encountered financial difficulties. (See Appendix A for additional information about *American Oxford.*)

Oxford Junior is currently produced under the general editorship of Laura E. Salt, Geoffrey Boumphrey (who worked on Volumes 1–3), and Robert Sinclair (Volumes 4–13), all experienced encyclopedists. Each of the topical volumes is edited by a specialist or two. In most instances, these people are outstanding authorities. Volume 9 (Recreations), for example, lists the late Cecil Day Lewis, former Oxford professor and noted poet, as the volume editor. Likewise, each volume has its own set of contributors, sometimes separated into "principal" and "other" contributors. Almost without exception, the contributors have excellent qualifications. Many of them are Oxford University scholars, and others are connected with equally impressive British academic institutions. It is rare indeed to find such prominent figures as A. J. P. Taylor, E. O. James, Lord Raglan, Jacquetta Hawkes, Asa Briggs, J. Bronowski, Robert Payne, and Max Beloff associated with an encyclopedic work principally for children. The articles, however, are unsigned.

Reliability

The encyclopedia has been carefully edited for factual accuracy. Nonetheless, errors, inconsistencies, and inexplicable omissions do occur now and then. EXAMPLE: The article "American Negroes" (in Volume 1) informs that "the position of the Negroes since then [after Reconstruction] has gradually improved, particularly since the end of the Second World War. The United States Supreme Court has banned the segregation of Negroes and whites on buses. In 1955 it banned similar segregation in state schools, and directed the University of Alabama to admit two Negro students." At no point in this article is the famous *Brown* v. *Board of Education* (1954) Supreme Court decision mentioned. Moreover, the 1955 date is misleading, since school desegregation was first ordered in 1954. Also, the statement about the University of Alabama is flatly wrong, as the incident referred to occurred in 1963. EXAMPLE: The article "United States of America" (Volume 3) erroneously states that "most of the Negro population of the United States lives in the South, many of them working on the plantations and farms." Interestingly, the article "American Negroes" (in Volume 1) says that "about two-fifths of them [blacks] still live in the southern states, compared with about two-thirds in 1950 and 90% in 1910." EXAMPLE: The article "American Indians, North" (in Volume 1) misleadingly terms the Southwest region "the Mexico area." Moreover, the article concerns itself exclusively with the Pueblos, completely ignoring the numerous Navajo, Apache, and other tribes of that area. Although such omissions and errors are infrequent, they occur just often enough to plant small seeds of doubt about the set's reliability in the discerning reader's mind. *Oxford Junior* is also sometimes unreliable due to lack of currency (see "Recency").

Recency

Unlike most multivolume encyclopedias, *Oxford Junior* is not continuously revised on an annual basis. Rather, the set is revised at infrequent intervals on a volume-by-volume basis. Initially, the first volume (entitled Mankind) appeared in 1948, the second (Natural History) and third (The Universe) in 1949, the fourth (Communications) in 1951, and so on until the final volume (Index and Ready Reference) was published in 1957. A revised edition appeared volume-by-volume between 1960 and 1965. Since that time, corrected and updated reprints of each volume have been published, bringing the set generally up-to-date as of 1974. Recent major revisions have occurred in Volumes 4 (Communications) and 10 (Law and Society). Such revisions entail changes in both the written text and illustrative matter. In some cases, for instance, old articles are revised and rewritten with new photographs or diagrams added. In other cases articles on new subjects appear for the first time.

The set as a whole is reasonably up-to-date in those areas covered, but as pointed out earlier, recent political events and personalities are not treated at all. Thus, the name of the present prime minister of England appears nowhere in the set, nor does the leader of the loyal opposition, nor does the U.S. president, the Israeli prime minister, and so forth. The Vietnam War is accorded one line in the article "Armies, War." John F. Kennedy is mentioned only in the article "Assassination." In the preface, the editors discuss the set's emphasis, noting that "in point of general balance the stress is laid rather on the modern world, though due space is given to the factors which have shaped it, no less than to those which are changing it." Generally speaking, this statement is an accurate reflection of *Oxford*

This Recency Table compares selected topics in *Oxford Junior* with those in other encyclopedias of similar size and intended usership.

Topic	Oxford Junior	Britannica Junior	New Book of Knowledge	Young Students
Africa	Not current	Very current	Very current	Fairly current
Babies/Children	Not current	Not current	Fairly current	Not current
Disease	Not current	Fairly current	Fairly current	Fairly current
North American Indians	Not current	Very current	Fairly current	Not current
Sharks	Fairly current	Fairly current	Very current	Fairly current
Television	Not current	Fairly current	Very current	Fairly current

Junior's approach to knowledge, if it is realized that the encyclopedia is mainly concerned with broad concepts and not specific facts and people. Hence, such articles as "Comets," "Earthquakes," "Flowers," "Heredity," "Hydraulics," "Magnets," "Radar," and "Sharks, Rays, and Chimaera" are reasonably modern in their emphases and perspective. On the other hand, articles like "Africa," "China," "Greenland," "Iran," and "Paris" are often sadly dated. Photographs and other graphics accompanying the articles are also frequently of antique vintage.

Objectivity

Like all reputable modern general encyclopedias, *Oxford Junior* makes every effort to present its material in an impartial manner. There is little evidence of religious, political, or racial bias in the set. Such topics as communism, Mormons, and race relations are treated evenhandedly. EX-AMPLE: The article "Race Relations" (Volume 10) notes that "in the United States of America, the people of European stock drove the native AMERICAN INDIANS (q.v. Vol. 1) westwards, taking their lands and killing many of them. Today the Indians are a tiny minority, but they are protected by the State and possess certain tribal lands; moreover, when they leave their 'reservations' they have equal status with all other citizens." The same article also states that Australia admits immigrants only if "they are of European race." This statement is no longer true. Immigration of non-whites into Australia was restricted until 1973, when official curbs were lifted. In addition, it is incorrect to speak of a "European" race. Such slips do not appear to be intentional bias, but simply errors of fact (see "Reliability"), sometimes due to lack of currency (see "Recency").

There is considerable evidence, however, that *Oxford Junior* is guilty of bias concerning certain controversial or sensitive subjects, such as sex and drugs. The bias is one of omission rather than commission. It is odd, to say the least, that an encyclopedia that purports to be for both younger and older children avoids topics like drug abuse and modern popular music. The Beatles, for instance, receive not one line of coverage in the entire encyclopedia. This sort of neglect of the facts of contemporary life is a deficiency in the encyclopedia.

Clarity and Reader Suitability

As already pointed out, *Oxford Junior* is chiefly aimed at students aged 11–14 in the middle grades. Slower readers at any level will find the set's style normally beyond their comprehension. Use of British terminology and spelling may add to the problem. For instance, the article "Afghanistan" (Volume 3) informs that "there is no railway in Afghanistan; but transport is gradually becoming quicker as better and more numerous roads are completed, allowing motor-lorries to replace camel caravans." It is doubtful if U.S. children will know the term *motor-lorries*. The guiding editorial principle regarding style is said to be "clear exposition and simple language" (preface), but unlike its major North American competitors (*Britannica Junior Encyclopaedia* and *The New Book of*

Knowledge), *Oxford Junior* is not vocabulary-controlled, nor are difficult or potentially unfamiliar words always defined in the text, nor is the set written to grade level.

Arrangement and Accessibility

Oxford Junior is arranged topically. Each volume covers a very broad area of knowledge: 1—Mankind (anthropology, archaeology, and religion); 2—Natural History (plants, animals, and other living things); 3—The Universe (astronomy, geology, weather, and geography); 4—Communications (language, printing, and modes of travel); 5—Great Lives (excludes living persons); 6—Farming and Fisheries (how people acquire their food); 7—Industry and Commerce (mining, manufacturing, business, and trade); 8—Engineering (power, machinery, and technology); 9—Recreations (games, sports, theater, and other entertainments); 10—Law and Society (political systems, methods of law enforcement, etc.); 11—Home and Health (the family, dress, furniture, cooking, and the human body and its disorders); and 12—The Arts (history of music, art, and literature). Volume 13—Index and Ready Reference—contains a general index to the other 12 volumes, as well as historical charts, brief factual summaries of the nations of the world, and other quick reference information.

Each of the first 12 volumes is, in turn, arranged alphabetically, letter-by-letter ("Easter" precedes "East Indies"). Each volume is also complete and independent in itself, although there are cross-references from one volume to another. Such references are printed in capital letters, followed by the abbreviation *q.v.* (meaning "which see") and the volume number in parentheses. EXAMPLE: The article "American Negroes" in Volume 1 contains the following sentence: "The 19th-century Negro leader, BOOKER WASHINGTON (q.v. Vol. V), urged his people to seek redress through education." *See also* references are also found at the end of many articles. In all, the set provides approximately 2,000 cross-references. Access to detailed information, however, is normally achieved through the general index in Volume 13, which comprises nearly 35,000 entries.

Oxford Junior is the only multivolume encyclopedia currently on the North American market that still retains a topical-alphabetical arrangement, although a number of small-volume sets are so arranged, including *The New Lincoln Library Encyclopedia, Pears Cyclopaedia, The Random House Encyclopedia,* and *The Volume Library*. The old *Book of Knowledge* was organized topically, but when the planners of *The New Book of Knowledge* considered arrangement, the topical approach was rejected. Research findings indicated that, although some young people can handle a topically arranged encyclopedia, many have difficulty locating specific material with that approach. Thus, *The New Book of Knowledge* opted for a straight A-to-Z arrangement, which is not only simple to understand but completely familiar. On the other hand, advertising literature for *Oxford Junior* points to these advantages of the set's topical arrangement: "Separate subject volumes mean that the encyclopaedia may be built up gradually [i.e., individual volumes can be purchased separately], and updated volumes incorporated into existing sets." In the final analysis, *Oxford Junior*'s arrangement, like some of its text (which emphasizes subjects of interest to British readers), will be foreign to many U.S. users, particularly young people. Brighter children should have little or no difficulty finding their way around the set, but others will be turned off by what appears to be an unnecessarily complicated arrangement.

Bibliographies

Bibliographies, or references to other sources of information, are not provided in the set. Because no encyclopedia—certainly not one so small as *Oxford Junior*—contains all the knowledge and information a student might need, the lack of bibliographies is a serious deficiency.

Graphics

Approximately a third of the total space in the set is devoted to illustrations, including maps. Many of the illustrations are black-and-white photographs, but there are also some excellent color reproductions in some of the volumes. EXAMPLE: In the first volume, a reproduction of Van Gogh's *A Gypsy Encampment* appears. The only problem is that the picture is placed within the article "Ghosts," or some 18 pages from "Gypsies." Unfortunately, this is not an isolated example; for instance, the color plate intended to accompany the article "Colour" (in Volume 3) is placed between the articles "Coasts" and "Colombia." As already noted (see "Recency"), many of the illustrations, especially photographs, are out-of-date. There are comparatively few charts and diagrams. The maps are of indifferent quality. All are black-and-white, small, and insufficiently detailed for any serious geographical study. The set's best maps, found in the Index and Ready Reference volume, are historical in nature, showing the political features of the world's great empires.

Physical Format

Oxford Junior is a solidly made encyclopedia. The red cloth binding with gold lettering is both sturdy and attractive, although the lettering is not legible from a distance. Each volume, which contains approximately 500 pages (except for the final volume of 278 pages), comes with an eye-catching, four-color jacket cover. Inside, the page layout is uncluttered but not especially inspiring. The typefaces used are bold and legible, and the heavy semigloss paper is of high quality. Guide words appear at the top of each page unless cut off by an illustration, which occasionally happens. The volumes lie flat when open for easy consultation. Overall, the physical design and construction of the encyclopedia reflect the fine workmanship customarily associated with the Oxford University

Press and its various reference publications, ranging from the *Oxford Concise Dictionary of Music* to the famous *Oxford English Dictionary*.

Special Features

As mentioned previously, the set's topical arrangement is now unique among general multivolume encyclopedias available to U.S. consumers. Another feature worth noting is the variety of quick reference information contained in the final volume. The 50 pages of historical charts and alphabetical "Guide to the Principal People and Places in the Old and New Testaments" are especially helpful student aids.

Sales Information

Sales campaigns to sell *Oxford Junior* in the United States have not been successful, and the set is no longer sold door-to-door on the subscription basis. Interested consumers can, however, order the encyclopedia directly from Oxford University Press in New York City. The only edition available is the red cloth binding already described (see "Physical Format"). The set currently lists for $189 plus shipping and handling and any tax. No discount is offered to educational institutions. *Oxford Junior* has no annual supplement or yearbook, and it is not sold in combination with other Oxford University Press publications.

Summary

The *Oxford Junior Encyclopaedia* can be quickly summed up in this manner:

Scope: Fair	Accessibility: Fair
Authority: Excellent	Bibliographies: Poor (none)
Reliability: Fair	Graphics: Fair
Recency: Fair	Physical Format: Excellent
Objectivity: Fair	Special Features: Few
Clarity: Good	Price: Reasonable

To elaborate briefly, *Oxford Junior* broadly covers all areas of knowledge in a reasonably reliable fashion. The set's subject strengths are clearly in the physical and technical sciences, whereas the humanities and particularly contemporary social and political topics get short shrift. Concepts tend to be emphasized over facts, and historical developments receive more attention than present-day activities in all areas except the harder sciences. The material is clearly written for students at the middle school level and beyond, and the set's outstanding authority and solid physical construction and design are excellent features. On the negative side, *Oxford Junior*'s British orientation and topical arrangement are decided disadvantages for U.S. users. The lack of current political information (for any country) is another drawback, as is the absence of bibliographies.

When compared with the two fine U.S. children's sets designed for roughly the same readership—*Britannica Junior Encyclopaedia* and *The*

New Book of Knowledge—Oxford Junior has very little to offer the discerning consumer. Even the superficial *Young Students Encyclopedia* is preferable. U.S. and Canadian families should not consider *Oxford Junior,* unless they are Anglophiles or have a special need for the British point of view. On the other hand, U.S. and Canadian school and public libraries might well supplement their stock of children's encyclopedias by acquiring the somewhat foreign and sometimes unique *Oxford Junior Encyclopaedia.*

Other Critical Opinions

Booklist, May 1, 1979, pp. 1395–1396. This unsigned review by the ALA Reference and Subscription Books Review Committee is generally negative, emphasizing the encyclopedia's British origins and perspective. This same group also reviewed *Oxford Junior* five months earlier as part of a series entitled "Encyclopedias: A Survey and Buying Guide" (*Booklist,* December 1, 1978, pp. 639–640). This review is also largely negative, although no final conclusions are offered.

Talking Cassette Encyclopedia

Facts in Brief

Full Title: **Talking Cassette Encyclopedia.** *Editor:* None listed. *Publisher:* Troll Associates, 320 Rte. 17, Mahwah, NJ 07430. *Edition Reviewed:* 1971 copyright.

Volumes: 10. *Pages:* Approximately 17 hours listening time. *Articles:* 100. *Words:* 100,000. *Illustrations:* None. *Maps:* None. *Index Entries:* 155. *Cross-references:* None. *Contributors:* Staff produced.

User Classification: Children (Multivolume). *Listener Suitability:* Age 4 through 10. *Physical Size:* 10 × 12 in.; 30 cm. *Lowest Retail Price:* $490.

Purpose and Scope

The *Talking Cassette Encyclopedia* is published, as its title suggests, in audio rather than print form. The ten volumes, or binders, comprise 100 alphabetically arranged cassette tapes (ten to a volume), each on a different subject. According to the publisher, an effort has been made to relate the topics covered to the U.S. elementary school curriculum. Included among the 100 topics, or articles, are "Airplanes," "Amelia Earhart," "Animal Habits," "Ants," "Betsy Ross," "Birds," "Clara Barton," "Columbus," "Computers," "Deserts," "The Fire Station," "Florence Nightingale," "Galaxies," "Indian Homes," "Indian Legends," "Indian Music," "Indian Tools," "Indian Weapons," "John Paul Jones," "Life in Ancient Egypt," "Life in Ancient Greece," "Life in Ancient Rome," "A Look at Brazil," "Mammals," "Oil," "Plastic," "Prehistoric Animals," "Radar," "Rivers," "Steel," "Story of Your Eyes," "Story of Your Teeth," "Supreme Court Justice," "Telephones and How They Work," "Television," "Thomas Jefferson," "Volcanoes," "Whales," and "What Is Geology."

Obviously, being limited to 100 such topics, the encyclopedia's coverage is highly selective. For instance, only three U.S. presidents are covered, namely Washington, Jefferson, and Theodore Roosevelt. Likewise, only three countries of the world have articles: Brazil, Japan, and Mexico. Each tape contains only about 1,000 words and runs 8–12 minutes, meaning that no single topic receives more than very limited coverage. EXAMPLE: Dinosaurs, which are included in "Prehistoric Animals," receive about 30 seconds worth of coverage. By no stretch of the imagination can the *Talking Cassette Encyclopedia* be considered a full-fledged reference encyclopedia for children. Rather, it is an introductory work designed to accustom preschoolers and beginning readers to the encyclopedic format while at the same time presenting new facts in an attention-catching manner. In purpose and scope, the encyclopedia is quite similar to both *Childcraft: The How and Why Library* and *Compton's Precyclopedia* (both of which are reviewed in this part of the *Buying Guide*).

History and Authority

The *Talking Cassette Encyclopedia* was published in 1971 by Troll Associates. Troll is well known to librarians and teachers as an educational publisher of quality audiovisual and read-along materials, including such items as the *Troll Talking Picture Dictionary* and the *Talking Encyclopedia of the New American Nation*. The *Talking Cassette Encyclopedia*'s editors and contributors are not identified, nor is any of the material signed in any manner. An advertisement for the set, however, does say the text is "written by experts in their fields [and] spoken by professional narrators."

Treatment (Reliability, Recency, Objectivity)

As previously noted (see "Purpose and Scope"), the encyclopedia's coverage is highly selective and lacks depth. But those topics that are covered receive reasonably good treatment, considering the set's elementary text. The many tapes reviewed by the *Buying Guide* revealed no glaring errors of fact, nor was any evidence of bias uncovered. The tape on Thomas Jefferson, for example, provides a clear albeit simple explanation of slavery at the time, and notes that although Jefferson opposed slavery, "he did not free his." The encyclopedia has not been revised since its original publication in 1971. Most of the tapes, however, are as timely as such rudimentary material need be, although some would doubtless benefit from revision where knowledge has changed greatly during the past decade, such as "Automobiles," "Computers," "Conservation," "A Look at Brazil," "A Look at Japan," "A Look at Mexico," "The Moon," "Observing the Universe," "Oceans," "Planets," "Supreme Court Justice," "Television," and "Volcanoes." The latter tape might add information about Mount St. Helens, for example. The publisher has informed the *Buying Guide* that *Talking Cassette Encyclopedia* will undergo a "major revision" in the near future.

Clarity and Listener Suitability

Children from the preschool level to the upper elementary grades will normally find *Talking Cassette Encyclopedia* comprehensible. Although there is no evidence of vocabulary control or readability testing, technical or potentially unfamiliar terms are defined in context. EXAMPLE: The word *ichthyology* (that branch of zoology concerned with fish) is introduced and defined in the tape "Fishes." The text also includes a brief note on the word's origin. The encyclopedia's style is consistently clear and interesting. The aforementioned "Fishes," for instance, uses the narrative approach of a mother and child visiting an aquarium. Along the way they encounter porpoises, sharks, and a variety of other marine life. The material is also clearly spoken, sometimes by more than one reader. In addition, most tapes are accompanied by sound effects and background music. Overall, the tapes are carefully produced to arouse and maintain the young listener's interest.

Arrangement and Accessibility

Talking Cassette Encyclopedia consists of 100 tapes arranged alphabetically by title, such as "Airplanes," "Amelia Earhart," "Animal Defense" and on through "Whales," "What Is Chemistry," "What Is Geology," and "Winter." There are no cross-references within the spoken text, but a printed index, or "Cross-Referenced Subject Guide," does come with the set. Here, for instance, the user can learn that the subject of dinosaurs is covered in the tape "Prehistoric Animals." The index is woefully incomplete, however. EXAMPLE: There is no indication in the index that sharks are covered in "Fishes." The publisher would do well to expand its system of finding devices when the set is revised.

Bibliographies

None. The lack of bibliographies, or references to sources of additional information, is not a grievous deficiency in a beginner set like *Talking Cassette Encyclopedia*. Failure to include at least some references, however, does nothing to acquaint young children with an important encyclopedia function that will be encountered in most sets for older children.

Graphics

None.

Physical Format

The encyclopedia's ten volumes, or binders, come in a sturdy dark blue slipcase. The binders, which are a lighter blue with gold lettering, hold ten cassette tapes each. In some instances the tapes are so tightly inserted in the binder that they are difficult to remove for use. A positive feature is that each topic, or article (e.g., "Thomas Jefferson"), is recorded in its entirety on both sides of the tape, thereby eliminating the need for rewinding.

Special Features

Talking Cassette Encyclopedia's only special feature is that its text is recorded on tape. The only other general encyclopedia currently available on tape is *The World Book Encyclopedia*. Published in 219 cassettes (six playing hours each) in 19 volumes, the recorded edition of *World Book* is designed especially for the visually handicapped.

Sales Information

The encyclopedia is available directly from Troll Associates, the publisher, for $490 delivered. The set can be ordered on approval and returned if the customer is not satisfied. A cassette player said to be valued at $35 is given free with each set ordered. Obviously, schools constitute the principal market for *Talking Cassette Encyclopedia.*

Summary

The *Talking Cassette Encyclopedia* can be quickly summed up in this manner:

Scope: Poor	Accessibility: Fair
Authority: Good	Bibliographies: Poor (none)
Reliability: Good	Graphics: None
Recency: Fair	Physical Format: Good
Objectivity: Good	Special Features: Few
Clarity: Excellent	Price: High

To elaborate briefly, *Talking Cassette Encyclopedia* is a beginning encyclopedia for preschoolers and primary school students published on cassette tape instead of in print form. The encyclopedia's scope is limited to 100 topics studied in U.S. elementary schools, such as animal life, North American Indians, famous people, early civilizations, and technical achievements. Each topic is covered in a single cassette tape with a playing time of 8–12 minutes (or roughly a thousand words). The text is normally clear and well spoken. But aside from this and its novelty as a "talking" encyclopedia, the set has little to offer children of any age. Its contents are highly selective and lack depth. Under no circumstances can *Talking Cassette Encyclopedia* be considered a full-fledged reference work. Rather, it is an introductory set designed to accustom young children to the encyclopedic format while at the same time presenting new facts in an interesting manner.

Comparatively speaking, there are only three multivolume sets currently produced for children aged 4–10. *Childcraft,* a topically arranged work, and *Compton's Precyclopedia,* alphabetically arranged, are both quality items, though *Childcraft* holds the edge as a better designed and maintained set. *Talking Cassette Encyclopedia,* unique because it is recorded instead of printed, has little substance and costs much too much ($490). Like *Childcraft* and *Compton's Precyclopedia, Talking Cassette Encyclopedia* will appeal chiefly to the educational (as opposed to the home) market—affluent elementary schools, kindergartens, nursery schools, day-care centers, and the like. In addition, the set could be useful in work with visually handicapped children.

Other Critical Opinions

None.

Young Children's Encyclopedia

Facts in Brief

Full Title: **The Young Children's Encyclopedia.** *Editors:* Howard L. Goodkind, Editor in Chief; Margaret Sutton, Managing Editor; Marvin Martin, Supervisory Editor. *Publisher:* Encyclopaedia Britannica, Inc., 425 N. Michigan Ave., Chicago, IL 60611. *Alternate Title: Compton's Precyclopedia. Edition Reviewed:* 1977 copyright.

Volumes: 16 (plus the *Parents' Manual*). *Pages:* 2,700. *Articles:* 650. *Words:* 300,000. *Illustrations:* 2,500. *Maps:* 20. *Index Entries:* None. *Cross-references:* 500. *Contributors:* 52 writers; 98 artists.

User Classification: Children (Multivolume). *Reader Suitability:* Age 4 through 10. *Physical Size:* 8 × 9½ in.; 24 cm. *LC:* 76-41025. *ISBN:* 0-85229-322-4. *Lowest Retail Price:* $74.50.

Purpose and Scope

The Young Children's Encyclopedia is described in the accompanying *Parents' Manual* as a "training" encyclopedia, or "a set of books, organized alphabetically, with enough of the flavor and features of an adult or teenage encyclopedia to prepare the child for the many hours he will spend with reference books during the critical school years that lie just ahead." It is also stated that "the emphasis is on stimulating curiosity, on building concepts, and on opening doors into the universe, and not solely on the acquisition of facts." *Young Children's* was first published in 1970, and in 1977 it appeared in a minimally revised edition.

According to the publisher, *Young Children's* contains the same editorial and pictorial content as *Compton's Precyclopedia.* The major difference between the two sets is how they are sold (see "Sales Information"). There are also several minor differences: (1) *Young Children's* has no index but does come with a 144-page paperbound *Parents' Manual,* which briefly indicates the "Big Idea" in each article as well as related articles; (2) the *Precyclopedia* lacks the *Parents' Manual* but does have a *Teaching Guide and Index,* which makes the set more useful in schools and libraries and as a so-called training encyclopedia; (3) each volume of the *Precyclopedia* is introduced by a 24-page activity or "Things to Do" section, a feature not included in *Young Children's;* and (4) *Young Children's* has a cheaper binding (Kivar) than the *Precyclopedia.*

Authority, Reliability, Recency, Etc.

See *Compton's Precyclopedia* review in this part of the *Buying Guide.*

Sales Information

In the past, *Young Children's* was sold through supermarkets and discount stores on a book-a-week basis, as well as via direct mail order. These methods of distribution have been discontinued, at least for the time being. At present, *Young Children's* is sold in-home in combination with *The New Encyclopaedia Britannica*, an advanced adult set. *Young Children's* currently retails for $74.50 plus shipping and handling and any tax. *Compton's Precyclopedia*, which is practically the same work as *Young Children's* (see "Purpose and Scope"), is sold in combination with *Compton's Encyclopedia*, a multivolume set for young adults. The *Precyclopedia*, which has a library reinforced binding, retails for $179, with schools and libraries able to acquire the set for $149.50. Hence *Young Children's* is a good bargain when compared with *Compton's Precyclopedia*.

Summary

The Young Children's Encyclopedia can be quickly summed up in this manner:

Scope: Good	Accessibility: Fair
Authority: Good	Bibliographies: Poor (none)
Reliability: Good	Graphics: Excellent
Recency: Fair	Physical Format: Fair
Objectivity: Excellent	Special Features: Few
Clarity: Excellent	Price: Reasonable

For additional information, see the review of *Compton's Precyclopedia* in this part of the *Buying Guide*.

Other Critical Opinions

Booklist, March 15, 1973, pp. 654–656. This unsigned review by the ALA Reference and Subscription Books Review Committee is mainly descriptive and offers no final conclusions.

Young Students Encyclopedia

Facts in Brief (Xerox Education Publications edition)

Full Title: **Young Students Encyclopedia.** Specially prepared with the staff of *My Weekly Reader. Editors* (Original Edition): George H. Wolfson, Editorial Director; Richard Harkins, Editor; Mary Lou Kennedy, Managing Editor. *Editors* (Revised Edition): Laurence Urdang, Editor in Chief; Robert B. Costello, Managing Editor. *Publisher:* Xerox Education Publications, 245 Long Hill Rd., Middletown, CT 06457. *Edition Reviewed:* Revised Edition, 1977 copyright.

Volumes: 21 (plus a one-volume *World Atlas* and a two-volume *Xerox Intermediate Dictionary*). *Pages:* 3,500. *Articles:* 2,400. *Words:* 1,500,000. *Illustrations:* 4,400 (plus 1,400 in the dictionary). *Maps:* 335. *Index Entries:* 15,000. *Cross-references:* 10,000. *Contributors:* 39.

User Classification: Children (Multivolume). *Reader Suitability:* Age 7 through 14. *Physical Size:* 8½ × 11¼ in.; 29 cm. *LC:* 76-43151. *Lowest Retail Price:* Volume 1, free; Volumes 2–21 plus *World Atlas* and two-volume *Xerox Intermediate Dictionary*, $6.50 each = $149.50 the set (by mail order); to schools & libraries $156.

Facts in Brief (Funk & Wagnalls edition)

Full Title: **Young Students Encyclopedia.** *Editors:* Harold J. Blum, Editorial Director; Jean F. Blashfield, Editor in Chief; Leonard Dal Negro, Project Director. *Publisher:* Funk & Wagnalls, Inc., 666 Fifth Ave., 9th Fl., New York, NY 10019. *Edition Reviewed:* 1972 copyright (1973 printing).

Volumes: 20. *Pages:* 3,124. *Articles:* 2,400. *Words:* 1,500,000. *Illustrations:* 3,600. *Maps:* 300. *Index Entries:* 15,000. *Cross-references:* 10,000. *Contributors:* 39.

User Classification: Children (Multivolume). *Reader Suitability:* Age 7 through 14. *Physical Size:* 7½ × 10 in.; 26 cm. *LC:* 76-179290. *Lowest Retail Price:* $69.50 (available to schools & libraries only).

Purpose and Scope

Two different editions of the *Young Students Encyclopedia* are currently available. There is a revised edition published by Xerox Education Publications dated 1977 (originally published 1972), and there is an edition published by Funk & Wagnalls, Inc., dated 1972. Aside from their different publishers and dates of publication, the two editions also differ in (1) number of volumes—the Xerox edition has 24 including an atlas and two-volume dictionary, whereas the Funk & Wagnalls edition has 20 volumes without the atlas and dictionary; (2) number of illustrations— Xerox has 4,400 plus 1,400 in the dictionary, whereas Funk & Wagnalls has 3,600; (3) physical size—Xerox is considerably larger (8½ × 11¼ in.) than Funk & Wagnalls (7½ × 10 in.); and (4) method of marketing— Xerox is now sold both via direct mail order and to schools and libraries, whereas Funk & Wagnalls, originally a supermarket item, is now sold only to schools and libraries.

From the consumer point of view, it is confusing, to say the least, to have two encyclopedias with the same title, one dated 1977 and the other 1972, competing for the same market. The *Buying Guide* strongly recommends that one of these editions be retitled in the future, in order to avoid possible consumer confusion over which set is which.

Despite the many differences between the two editions, the actual encyclopedic content of the two is quite similar, although obviously the Xerox revised edition (1977) is more current than the Funk & Wagnalls version (1972). When the Xerox edition was originally published in 1972, the content of both sets was identical, except for the amount of illustrative matter and the supplementary atlas and dictionary volumes. This review will deal principally with the Xerox revised edition, with comparative comments referring to the Funk & Wagnalls set when appropriate.

According to the introductory material, which is similar for both editions, *Young Students* is "designed for young people, for use as an early reference and activities source at home or at school." The encyclopedia aims "to provide a basic introduction to man's ideas, language and world." The scope of the encyclopedia was determined by three concerns: "coverage of those ideas most often included in school curriculums, variation in reading abilities, and encouragement of active reader participation." Approximately 100 "prime concepts," from ancient history to physics, were chosen for particular emphasis. They represent major topics taught in U.S. elementary schools as well as children's out-of-school interests. Moreover, these concepts "serve as a basic introduction and 'umbrella' for the more than 2,400 articles" included in the encyclopedia.

The articles cover the U.S. presidents and other historically significant people, major place-names including the 50 U.S. states and various Canadian provinces, sports and games, and specific subjects like agriculture, air, architecture, dancing, digestion, ice cream, nervous system, noun, novel, oxygen, sewing machine, snowmobile, and X-ray. The articles are usually very brief and, when compared with the larger children's sets like *The New Book of Knowledge* and *Britannica Junior Encyclopaedia*, they either lack factual depth or fail to cover all aspects of the topic. EXAMPLE: The article "Ocean" does not include a discussion of either continental drift or oceanic pollution, although both subjects are part of the school curricula for this age group. EXAMPLE: "Refrigeration" oversimplifies the principle behind the process; different refrigeration systems are not explained. EXAMPLE: "Forestry" treats the topic almost exclusively from the career standpoint, omitting discussion of the major forests of the world, the kinds of forests, and so forth. Also, in some instances basic concepts of concern to young children like seasonal changes, the process of growth and maturation, and the notion of time are either ignored or very sketchily covered. Likewise, normal adolescent questions about human sexuality and such specific concerns as menstruation and masturbation are not covered.

Although they are brief and sometimes quite superficial, the articles are often accompanied by various visual aids, usually photographs or charts. Occasionally colored boxes containing interesting facts or informational "nuggets" also accompany articles. For instance, the article "Fire Prevention" provides a nugget that informs the reader that "Fire Prevention Week is observed annually during the week of October 9. Many schools and communities have special clean-up projects and public information programs." Some articles are also accompanied by glossaries that list and define difficult or new terms. Portions of some articles are printed in light blue type, indicating a "learning by doing" activity. The second paragraph of the article "Fingerprint," for example, is in blue type and reads in part: "Sharpen a soft-leaded pencil and rub the side of the point across the balls of your fingers. Be careful not to stick yourself with the point. The raised parts, or ridges, on the skin of your fingertips will be covered with gray powder. Press your fingertips against the sticky side of transparent tape. Peel the tape away and stick it to a sheet of white paper. Examine your fingerprints—marks that can never be made by any other person."

In sum, *Young Students'* coverage is more concerned with stimulating the reader's imagination and presenting selected facts in an interesting manner than it is with providing relatively full summaries of knowledge or exhaustive factual information. Note also that the Xerox edition includes a 34,000-entry dictionary and a world atlas as supplements to the encyclopedia. Neither the dictionary nor the atlas is directly related to the main A–Z contents of the encyclopedia.

History and Authority

Young Students was originally published in 1972. Two editions of the set were jointly prepared by Xerox Education Publications (XEP) and Funk & Wagnalls, Inc. XEP, formerly American Education Publications, also publishes the well-known *My Weekly Reader, Current Events,* and numerous other classroom magazines as well as a variety of books for elementary and secondary students. Funk & Wagnalls is an established publisher of reference books, including dictionaries and *Funk & Wagnalls New Encyclopedia* (which is reviewed in Part III of the *Buying Guide*).

As already noted (see "Facts in Brief"), separate editorial staffs prepared the two editions, although both utilized the same authorities as curriculum consultants and contributors, and ultimately the encyclopedic text was the same in both editions. The 17 curriculum advisers, headed by John F. Fanning (Deputy Superintendent of Schools in Lower Merion

County, Pa.), are mainly college professors and educators, although four of the consultants are XEP staffers, including John Maynard, editor of *Current Events*. The 39 contributors are predominantly children's book authors. Although the articles in *Young Students* are not signed, the contributors' topics are identified under their names in the front of the first volume. It is apparent, however, that most of the material is staff written.

At some point after 1972, XEP and Funk & Wagnalls parted company insofar as *Young Students* is concerned. Hence, when XEP invested some $250,000 to produce a revised edition, Funk & Wagnalls was not involved. The XEP revision was prepared by Laurence Urdang, Inc., a freelance firm that specializes in producing various types of dictionaries. The front matter of the 1977 Revised Edition lists 13 people, headed by Laurence Urdang (editor in chief) and Robert B. Costello (managing editor), as being responsible for the revision project. George H. Wolfson, now retired, is listed as editorial director for XEP, a position he also held when the encyclopedia was initially published in 1972.

Reliability

Young Students is a generally reliable encyclopedia, although factual errors do occasionally appear. EXAMPLE: The article "Indians, American" erroneously speaks of "the Algonkian language." In fact, Algonkian is a language family, not a language. EXAMPLE: "Indian Wars" gives incorrect dates for the Seminole Wars, which began well before 1833 as reported by the encyclopedia and ended later than 1842, again as reported by *Young Students*. EXAMPLE: "Sharks and Rays" contains several minor factual errors, including the statement that sharks "can not see colors." They can. Also, some information in the encyclopedia is not accurate due to being out-of-date; for example, the article on Iran notes, "Today, the shah chooses the premier to head the elected members of parliament." This criticism is especially true of the Funk & Wagnalls edition of the encyclopedia (1972), which has never been revised.

Recency

When it first appeared in 1972, *Young Students* was an entirely new encyclopedia planned in the late 1960s. At the time its topic selection and treatment were quite fresh, including brief but up-to-date information on such contemporary subjects as rock music and drug abuse. In some respects, that judgment is still valid today, although most of the material in the encyclopedia is now nearly a decade old. Of course, in the case of Funk & Wagnalls' 1972 edition, all of the material is that old.

The XEP 1977 revised edition, prepared by Laurence Urdang, Inc. (see "History and Authority"), added a modest number of new articles (e.g., "British Empire," "Dadaism," "Plate Tectonics," "Spanish Main," "Transistor," "Vietnam War," and biographies of Presidents Ford and Carter), considerably lengthened others (e.g., "Central America," "Sikkim," "Vietnam"), significantly revised still others (e.g., "Angola," "Baroque

This Recency Table compares selected topics in *Young Students* (1977 XEP edition) with those in óther encyclopedias of similar size and intended usership.

Topic	Young Students	Britannica Junior	New Book of Knowledge	Oxford Junior
Africa	Fairly current	Very current	Very current	Not current
Babies/Children	Not current	Not current	Fairly current	Not current
Disease	Fairly current	Fairly current	Fairly current	Not current
North American Indians	Not current	Very current	Fairly current	Not current
Sharks	Fairly current	Fairly current	Very current	Fairly current
Television	Fairly current	Fairly current	Very current	Not current

Art," "Electricity," "Quicksand"), and simply changed a few words or a statistic in others (e.g., "Battery," "Evolution," "Genetics," "Milky Way," "Golf," "Radiation," "Space Research," "X-ray"). In addition, some of the information boxes, or so-called nuggets, were revised, metric equivalents were added throughout the set, and many illustrations were altered, added, or replaced. According to XEP in a memorandum to the *Buying Guide,* "Eighty percent of the entries had some revision, whether it was one word, one sentence, one paragraph, or was completely rewritten." In most instances, the extent of the revision was minimal, often involving only the addition of a metric equivalent. Overall, the 1977 revision was made to sound more impressive than it really was. In fact, XEP's 1977 revised edition of *Young Students* is not significantly different from the original 1972 edition. Many of the articles in both editions are now out-of-date or fast becoming dated. EXAMPLE: The article "China" informs, "Mao Tse-tung is the leader of the People's Republic of China." Moreover, the article contains nothing about the recent changes in Sino-American relations that culminated in an exchange of ambassadors and diplomatic recognition in 1979. EXAMPLE: There is no mention of the pending Equal Rights Amendment anywhere in the encyclopedia. EXAMPLE: "Indians, American" includes out-of-date population figures and neglects the Indian militancy of the 1970s.

When will *Young Students* be revised again? XEP informs the *Buying Guide* that a new revision is scheduled for 1982. This revision will entail a general updating of stale material as well as the addition of 1980 U.S. census data. Funk & Wagnalls is less clear about its revision plans. Earlier an extensive revision effort was planned for publication in 1981, but that has been dropped or postponed.

In an effort to keep the original 1972 edition current, Funk & Wagnalls, Inc., publishes the *Young Students Encyclopedia Yearbook,* an annual supplement to the encyclopedia that appears each year in the spring. The yearbook covers the headline events of the preceding year, with emphasis on subject matter of interest to young readers. Priced at a modest $4.98 plus shipping and handling, the yearbook is written in the same simple style as the encyclopedia, and new words are defined in context. But the yearbook is not directly related to the encyclopedia via cross-references, etc., and therefore is of only marginal value as an updating device. No yearbook is published for the XEP edition of *Young Students*.

Objectivity

A conscientious effort has been made to confront controversial topics as honestly and fairly as possible. The article on the Federal Bureau of Investigation, for instance, notes that "for reasons of national security, it [the FBI] keeps files on people and organizations important to the Federal Government. Because of these records, the FBI is often accused of 'snooping'—investigating people's private lives unnecessarily." In some instances, however, the encyclopedia appears to take a stand on important contemporary issues. EXAMPLE: "Water Pollution" concludes with the following balanced but overall liberal statement: "To have enough clean water, the dumping of industrial wastes and untreated sewage will have to be stopped. Although some businesses and cities are making efforts to halt water pollution, too many of them are not. It takes money to clean up pollution. But water is essential to life and health." It is worth remarking also that this brief article makes no mention of recent federal efforts in the pollution area. EXAMPLE: "Negro History" ends with several paragraphs on the status of blacks today in the United States. It is pointed out that "black leaders have different ideas about how the battle [for equality] can be won," and the final words are devoted to the Black Power movement: "This is frightening to many white people (as well as to many black people). But after more than 400 years of being denied rights that the Constitution promises to *all,* it is not surprising that blacks are no longer willing to wait for what they are legally entitled to." Implicitly this comment seems to condone the racial violence of the 1960s.

Clarity and Reader Suitability

Like so many children's encyclopedias that are curriculum-oriented, *Young Students'* articles are written so that the simplest or most basic information is at the beginning of the entry. The articles then become progressively more complex, depending on the nature of the subject matter. In addition, some articles are written at a higher reading level than others, again depending on the subject matter. John F. Fanning, chief curriculum consultant to the set, explains in the foreword: "A reader's ability to deal effectively with a given topic usually depends on the prior experiences he brings to the topic. As a result, those topics which are familiar to most children or deal with concrete ideas can be comprehended by students at lower reading levels. Unfamiliar or complicated topics are, by their nature, useful only at higher reading and comprehension levels."

In order to achieve desired reading levels, all articles were checked against standard *Weekly Reader* vocabulary and readability lists. In addition, new or difficult words are defined in the text. EXAMPLE: "The best way to prevent addiction is to keep people from getting drugs, except when a doctor *prescribes* (gives) them." The articles in *Young Students* are usually written in an interesting and readable style.

Arrangement and Accessibility

Young Students is alphabetically arranged, letter-by-letter ("Indiana" precedes "Indian Ocean"). A variety of cross-references are provided. They appear in the main A-to-Z sequence (e.g., *"Norsemen.* See VIKINGS"). They also appear frequently at the end of articles in the form of either *also read* references or *for further information on* citations. Cross-references total over 10,000 throughout the set.

Specific access is provided by a general index located in the final volume. The index is said to contain approximately 15,000 entries; it also includes pronunciations for unfamiliar or difficult terms, birth and death dates for biographical entries, and basic scientific classifications for plants and animals. Generally speaking, *Young Students* is well organized and comparatively simple to use. Access to specific information should pose no problem for even the youngest users.

Bibliographies

Bibliographies are not included with the articles in either the XEP or Funk & Wagnalls edition of *Young Students*. Like *Britannica Junior,* which also lacks bibliographies, this deficiency limits the usefulness of the encyclopedia as a children's reference work.

Graphics

Young Students is a heavily illustrated encyclopedia. Approximately 40 percent of the XEP edition is devoted to visual aids of one sort or another. The Funk & Wagnalls edition, which contains somewhat fewer illustrations (3,600 as opposed to 4,400), gives 30 percent of its total space to graphics. Most of the illustrative matter is in color. Photographs are emphasized over other types of graphics, although there are numerous drawings, charts, and diagrams. As Dr. Fanning explains in the foreword, "Photographs, rather than drawings, were chosen to illustrate the bulk of the material. Today's young readers, with their prior experience of visual media, demand photographic accuracy and realism." The illustrations are usually up-to-date, almost always directly complement the text and add to the informational value of the set, and are generally clear and sufficiently detailed. In a few instances, however, the quality of reproduction is poor or the photographs are faded or too dark or too small to be of more than marginal value from an informational standpoint. EXAMPLE: The tiny 2 × 2-inch photo of Le Corbusier's church of Notre-Dame-du-Haut at Ronchamp in the article on architecture is so little and drab that only the barest outline of the building can be determined. Yet the accompanying text asks: "Can you see in the photograph of the church at Ronchamp, that the mood is one of safety and trust?" This technique of relating the visual and textual is commendable, but only when the graphic involved is of satisfactory quality.

Color is used creatively throughout. Not only are a large majority of the illustrations reproduced in full color, but information contained in boxes is presented on a colored background, as are the charts, diagrams, and "nuggets" described above (see "Purpose and Scope"). Among the many children's sets, only *The New Book of Knowledge* uses color as inventively as *Young Students*.

Some 300 physical, historical, and special-purpose maps appear throughout the set in both editions. Produced by Pictograph Corporation, the maps are usually unsatisfactory, lacking clarity and detail. Unlike the larger children's sets such as *Britannica Junior* and *The New Book of Knowledge,* countries and U.S. states do not have full-page physical and/or political maps with the articles. There are no indexes or gazetteers with any of the maps. To help correct this situation, the XEP edition added a one-volume atlas to the set in 1974. It has not been revised since that time. Prepared especially for XEP by C. S. Hammond & Company, the atlas includes more than 40 political and physical maps of the major countries and all the continents of the world, about 20 historical maps, and assorted others showing population distributions and the world's oceans. Although the atlas does have a "Gazetteer Index of the World," it is not sufficiently detailed, omitting all place-names except the continents and major countries, the 50 states and Canadian provinces, and various colonial possessions. On the plus side, the volume provides excellent basic information about what maps do and how they are made. Like the encyclopedia, the maps and atlas text are designed for the elementary student.

Physical Format

As already pointed out (see "Facts in Brief" and "Purpose and Scope"), the XEP and Funk & Wagnalls editions of *Young Students* are outwardly quite different in format. XEP's 1977 Revised Edition contains a total of 24 tall, thin, lightweight volumes bound in a gray Permalin-coated buckram with lettering in blue and brown ink. A small blue ink drawing depicting the world appears on the front cover of each volume. The binding, which is held together with a strong adhesive applied to the inside of the spine (called "perfect" binding), seems to be reasonably durable. This binding represents a marked improvement over the XEP set's 1972 binding (also perfect) which tended to come apart under normal use. The individual volumes of the current edition usually lie flat when open, and they are light enough that even the youngest readers will have no problem handling them. The Permalin coating, however, is slippery and the volumes tend to slide off the shelf quite easily.

The Funk & Wagnalls edition, by contrast, comprises 20 smaller volumes bound in bright orange Pyroxylin-coated boards with multicolored lettering. A colorful collage of squares and pictures decorates the front cover of each volume. The binding is washable but not durable. Also perfect-bound, the volumes crack and split under normal use, and the pages may become loose. Initially, the volumes do not lie flat when open. Like the XEP binding, the Funk & Wagnalls binding is lightweight but slick.

Inside, the XEP edition is inviting. The varied two-column page layout, ample line spacing, creative use of color, and generous margins all contribute to a pleasing appearance. The typefaces used are large, legible, and modern. Guide words appear at the top of each page. The Funk & Wagnalls edition is similar, although it utilizes a one-column layout. Overall, both editions are aesthetically appealing but rather cheaply made, particularly the Funk & Wagnalls set.

Special Features

Both editions feature "learning by doing" activities and projects designed to stimulate the imagination of the young student. Printed in blue type, these "mind-stretching" exercises were developed by educators "who understand the nature of a child's curiosity, his ability to peruse experiments, his coordination, and his span of interest." An example of one of these activities is given above (see "Purpose and Scope").

Another interesting feature found in both editions is the presentation of tidbits of information—called nuggets—in brightly colored boxes printed in the margins. Many of the so-called nuggets are amusing or present fascinating facts. For instance, the nugget accompanying the article "Ocean" informs the reader that "the ocean contains about five to six million tons of gold, but men would have to filter about 250 million cubic feet of ocean water to get just one ounce of it."

The Funk & Wagnalls edition has a 33⅓ rpm record entitled *Crazy Fun Trip* attached to Volume 1. Made of plastic, the record is a "wild excursion that takes you from Africa to the South Pole," or on a complete tour of the contents of the first volume. This promotional device is successfully produced, but has limited informational value.

The XEP edition has three volumes of supplementary material that the Funk & Wagnalls set does not. In addition to the one-volume world atlas already described (see "Graphics"), there is a two-volume general English-language dictionary for children entitled *The Xerox Intermediate Dictionary*. Edited by William Morris, who also produced the highly regarded *American Heritage Dictionary*, this dictionary contains some 34,000 entries and 1,400 illustrations. A unique feature of the dictionary is that young students helped select the vocabulary covered, thus accounting for the inclusion of such informal terms as *loser, nitty-gritty,* and *pot shot.* Like the atlas, the dictionary is especially designed for use by children in grades three through six.

Sales Information

The XEP 1977 Revised Edition in the gray Permalin-coated buckram binding already described (see "Physical Format") is sold to individuals by direct mail order on a subscription basis. Volume 1 is free; the remaining 23 volumes cost $6.50 apiece (including postage and handling), or $149.50 for the set. The same binding is available to schools and libraries at $156 delivered. The XEP set carries this guarantee: "Once you receive the set, you may examine and use it for a full 30 days before deciding whether or not you wish to keep it. During this 30-day period you can compare *Young Students Encyclopedia*—feature for feature, price for price—with similar reference sets. If you don't agree that it is the finest children's encyclopedia value you've seen . . . that it is the most clearly written, best organized, and most interesting reference for children 7–13—return the entire set to us at the end of 30 days and owe nothing!"

The 1972 20-volume Funk & Wagnalls set was initially designed for the supermarket trade, but that method of distribution has been discontinued. The publisher now sells the set exclusively to schools and libraries at the reduced price of $69.50. Reports have reached the *Buying Guide* that the set has been discounted as low as $29.95 in certain areas of the country.

It bears repeating that only consumer confusion can result from having two different editions of the same encyclopedia—one revised and one not—competing for the same market. The *Buying Guide* urges both publishers to get together and resolve this problem in the near future.

Summary

The 1977 revised edition of the *Young Students Encyclopedia* published by Xerox Education Publications can be quickly summed up in this manner:

Scope: Fair   Accessibility: Excellent
Authority: Good   Bibliographies: Poor (none)
Reliability: Good   Graphics: Good
Recency: Fair   Physical Format: Good
Objectivity: Good   Special Features: Many
Clarity: Good   Price: Reasonable

The original 1972 version of the *Young Students Encyclopedia* published by Funk & Wagnalls, Inc. can be quickly summed up in this manner:

Scope: Fair   Accessibility: Excellent
Authority: Good   Bibliographies: Poor (none)
Reliability: Good   Graphics: Good
Recency: Poor   Physical Format: Fair
Objectivity: Good   Special Features: Many
Clarity: Good   Price: Reasonable

To elaborate briefly, *Young Students* is available in two different and distinct editions, one dated 1977 (published by Xerox Education Publications) and the other 1972 (published by Funk & Wagnalls, Inc.). Both editions were initially prepared in the early 1970s as a cooperative publishing venture between XEP and Funk & Wagnalls, but the firms have now gone their separate ways regarding *Young Students,* hence the anomaly of two different editions of the same encyclopedia competing with one another. The two editions have much the same encyclopedic content, but the XEP version is more up-to-date, contains more illustrations, is physically larger and better bound, and includes several features not offered by the Funk & Wagnalls set, such as metric equivalents, an atlas, and a dictionary. The encyclopedia intends to serve upper elementary school students and is curriculum oriented, vocabulary controlled, and written to grade level. Coverage, however, tends to be quite superficial, with the emphasis on captivating and stimulating the imagination of the young reader. Toward that end, the encyclopedia (both editions) contains many interesting activities, questions, visual aids, etc.

At the present time, there are five multivolume encyclopedias for children aged 7–14 on the North American market: *Britannica Junior Encyclopaedia, The New Book of Knowledge, The Illustrated Encyclopedia for Learning, Oxford Junior Encyclopaedia,* and the *Young Students Encyclopedia.* The first two sets are the leaders in almost every respect, and the best buy comes down to a choice between them. The last three sets will not interest most consumers. *Oxford Junior* is very much a British production, *The Illustrated Encyclopedia for Learning* is a dreadfully dated work of low quality, and *Young Students* lacks the fullness of coverage and timeliness to compete successfully with *Britannica Junior* and *The New Book of Knowledge.* If, however, a smaller and less costly multivolume children's encyclopedia is desired, *Young Students* should be given serious consideration. Although it lacks substance and currency (comparatively speaking), it is a creatively constructed set that many children will find appealing.

Other Critical Opinions

Booklist, July 15, 1980, pp. 1690; 1692. This unsigned review by the ALA Reference and Subscription Books Review Committee (RSBRC) is limited to the 1977 revision published by XEP. The review is basically favorable and the encyclopedia is "recommended as a supplementary resource" for children in the home and library. Unfortunately, the review is marred by a number of errors; for instance, XEP does not offer an "annual yearbook" as implied, and the text maps are provided by Pictograph Corporation, not Pictography Corporation. This same group also reviewed *Young Students* (the original Funk & Wagnalls edition, 1973 printing) earlier as part of a series entitled "Encyclopedias: A Survey and Buying Guide" (*Booklist,* December 1, 1978, pp. 640–641). The review contains a few negative comments, but no final conclusions are offered. Why the 1973 printing was reviewed in 1978 is not explained.

Katz, William A. *Basic Information Sources* (Vol. 1 of *Introduction to Reference Work,* 3rd ed. New York: McGraw-Hill, 1978), pp. 161–162. Katz, a well-known and highly respected reference book critic, comparatively reviews the three leading sets for children, namely *Britannica*

Junior Encyclopaedia, The New Book of Knowledge, and *Young Students.* He rates *The New Book of Knowledge* the best in its class, with *Young Students* in second place.

Wynar, Christine L. *American Reference Books Annual,* 1974, pp. 26–27. Wynar reviews the original Funk & Wagnalls edition (1973 printing), offering cautious praise tempered by warnings that *Young Students* "in no way approaches the comprehensive treatment provided in the major juvenile encyclopedias." The only comparative reference in the review is to *The World Book Encyclopedia,* which seems inappropriate (*World Book* is a much larger set, comprising 14,280 pages and 20,000 articles, whereas *Young Students* has 3,500 pages and 2,400 articles).

VII. SMALL-VOLUME YOUNG ADULT/CHILDREN'S ENCYCLOPEDIAS

Illustrated World Encyclopedia

Facts in Brief

Full Title: **Illustrated World Encyclopedia.** *Editors:* Roger Bobley, Editor in Chief; Doris Millspaugh, Associate Editor. *Publisher:* Bobley Publishing Corporation, 311 Crossways Park Dr., Woodbury, NY 11797; copyright by Mer-Fried Corporation. *Former Titles: Illustrated Home Library Encyclopedia* (1955–1957); *Illustrated Encyclopedia of Knowledge* (1954–1955). *Edition Reviewed:* One Volume Edition (also called Deluxe Edition on cover and spine), 1977 copyright.

Volumes: One. *Pages:* 1,619. *Articles:* 7,300. *Words:* 2,500,000. *Illustrations:* 2,000. *Maps:* 150 plus 8-page Color Atlas. *Index Entries:* None (*Index & Study Guide* volume said to be separately published @ $14.95). *Cross-references:* 2,500. *Contributors:* 105.

User Classification: Children (Small-volume). *Reader Suitability:* Age 7 through 14. *Physical Size:* 8½ × 11¼ in.; 29 cm. *Lowest Retail Price:* $19.95; to schools & libraries $16.95.

Purpose and Scope

Designed mainly for readers at the elementary and middle school levels but also intended for use by the whole family, the *Illustrated World Encyclopedia* attempts to cover all areas of knowledge, with emphasis on practical information. The editors rather grandiosely claim that "practically all the factual reference material you and your family will ever need can be found between the covers of this carefully cross-referenced one-volume compilation of over 7,300 articles on 15,000 subjects" (preface). Actually, the encyclopedia's coverage leaves something to be desired, being quite uneven and often superficial, especially when a topic is not discrete or lacks specificity, like art or energy.

Such everyday subjects as automobiles, beans, dressmaking, first aid, glands, locks, lumber, nutrition, obesity, photography, teeth, and sports and games are reasonably well covered, considering the encyclopedia's limited space and intended readership. For instance, the article "Backgammon" is a page in length (or about 1,500 words) and fully explains the rules of the game, with numerous helpful examples of different moves. The article "Baby-sitting" (500 words) provides much practical information on the subject, including a list of safety rules and a note concerning the requirement that "money paid to baby-sitters [must] be reported and

'Social Security' taxes paid on it." The article "Swimming and Diving" receives over a page (about 2,000 words) of coverage.

The broad and vital subject of energy, however, is dispensed with in 250 words. The article "Art" (half of which is devoted to commercial art) totals only 350 words. "Gene" receives only 175 words, as does "Genetics." The subject of death is not covered at all, nor is suicide, nor are drug laws—despite the fact that such subjects are of considerable interest to young people and parents. The only mention of the present-day women's movement comes at the end of the 250-word article "Feminism": "The year the war ended England gave women the right to vote, and the United States did the same thing two years later, in 1920. Now women are taking their places next to men as students, doctors, lawyers, scientists, and executives." "Women in the Armed Forces," a longer article, is equally uninformative and out-of-date. "Football" rambles on for over three pages but rock music is nowhere to be found in the encyclopedia.

Biographical and geographical topics account for approximately half of the entries. Historical notables are fairly well covered, with people like Descartes, Benjamin Franklin, Clark Gable, William Henry Harrison, Napoleon, Nero, Peter the Great, Adam Smith, and Harry Truman receiving anywhere from 200 words (Gable) to a full page (Truman). Literary and artistic personalities are particularly well covered—if they are dead. For instance, readers will find reasonably full sketches of James Barrie, Irving Berlin, Alexander Borodin, and Samuel Butler, but nothing about Saul Bellow or Benjamin Britten. The same is true of political and entertainment figures. Major countries like China and France receive two or more pages of coverage, whereas smaller nations (Chile, for instance) are covered in a single page or less. U.S. states normally receive a page or two, which includes a small spot map and several black-and-white photographs of the postcard variety. Only the largest U.S. and world cities are covered, usually in a few paragraphs. The same is true of natural features like rivers and mountains.

Note that the previous edition of *Illustrated World* (1973) was published in both 15 and 21 volumes. The 1977 single-volume edition under review here is an abridgment of the 1973 multivolume work. The editors explain in their preface, "By eliminating all but the best and most important illustrations and by making certain other changes in format, this remarkable one-volume edition was made possible. In fact, for the very first time, virtually the entire encyclopedic content of a well-known, 6,720-page, 21-volume encyclopedia has been republished in a single 1,600-page volume." Specifically, the contents of the 1973 multivolume work and the 1977 one-volume abridgment are very similar except in these respects: (1) the extensive plot summaries, or so-called Literary Treasures, included in the 1973 set are not reprinted in the 1977 volume, thus reducing the encyclopedia's contents by approximately two million words; (2) the 15,000 illustrations in the 1973 set have been reduced to 2,000 in the 1977 edition; and (3) occasionally—very occasionally—new articles have been added to the 1977 volume, such as those on Gerald Ford and Jimmy Carter. Otherwise the contents are practically the same. In terms of format, the page size has been increased (from 6¼ × 9¼ in. to 7¾ ×10¾ in.), the columns expanded from two to three, and the print size greatly reduced.

History and Authority

Illustrated World is not a well-known or especially reputable encyclopedia. It is rarely found in carefully selected school and public libraries. Knowledgeable critics over the years have dismissed the encyclopedia for its poor design (now even worse in the one-volume abridgment), inadequate accessibility, sometimes oversimplifed text, lack of strict standards concerning reliability, and poor performance in the area of recency. There is general agreement, however, that some improvement has occurred in recent years, although the 1977 abridgment does nothing to enchance *Illustrated World*'s reputation.

The encyclopedia first appeared in 1954 as the multivolume *Illustrated Encyclopedia of Knowledge* published by Premiumwares of Brooklyn, N.Y. It was reissued the following year as the *Illustrated Home Library Encyclopedia*. Both titles represented encyclopedia-making at its worst. In 1958, the Bobley Publishing Corporation acquired the set, improved and enlarged it, and retitled it the *Illustrated World Encyclopedia*. Since 1958, the set has appeared variously in 15 and 21 volumes, and now as a one-volume abridgment. When it first appeared in 1954, the encyclopedia was said to have been prepared by the impressive-sounding National Lexicographic Board, under the direction of Albert H. Morehead. Morehead, under the aegis of the board, produced a number of mediocre general dictionaries in the 1950s, but consumers should be aware that the National Lexicographic Board no longer exists.

The 1977 edition lists an editorial staff of six, headed by Roger Bobley, who has edited *Illustrated World* for the past ten years. Doris Millspaugh, the associate editor, was previously identified as the staff librarian. A list of 105 contributors and consultants also appears in the front matter. These are the same 105 names that were listed in the 1973 edition. As a rule, they are not distinguished names in their fields, and more than a few have been deceased for years. Their qualifications are briefly noted but their areas of subject responsibility are not. Since none of the articles in the volume is signed, it is not possible to determine who is responsible for which articles. It is apparent, however, that much of the encyclopedia is staff written. Overall, the volume's authority is poor.

Reliability

Illustrated World is not a reliable encyclopedia. Not only is it often grossly out-of-date (see "Recency"), but it is riddled with factual errors, distortions due to oversimplification, and articles that present incomplete and hence sometimes misleading information. EXAMPLE: The article "Florida" characterizes the city of Tampa as a "fishing resort in the western part of the state." Tampa is on the west coast of Florida but a fishing resort it is not. EXAMPLE: The article on factories states, "Factories are

built so that they are the most comfortable and healthful places possible."
EXAMPLE: The entry on fainting observes that "almost always doctors
consider that there is nothing serious, and nothing to worry about, in
fainting." EXAMPLE: The biographical sketch of the English author Henry
Fielding suggests, "He used everyday people who might be your next-
door neighbors as characters, and he used everyday events that could
happen to you." EXAMPLE: The article "Election" notes that "in most of
the states, people are allowed to vote when they reach the age of 21, but
in some states they can vote at 18." The 26th Amendment to the U.S.
Constitution lowering the voting age to 18 was ratified in 1971. The same
article erroneously reports that "every state requires a voter to be able to
read and write and to live in his voting district for some number of
months before the election." EXAMPLE: The article "Shark" contains at
least eight errors of fact, one for every paragraph. EXAMPLE: The article
"Indian" contains numerous erroneous statements, such as "the big
feathered headdress was worn only by the Sioux tribe of the western
plains." In addition, this article, like many others, has many typographical mistakes, such as, "If you visit the Southwest today you will see
Indians stil [sic] making beautiful rugs, jewelry, pottery, and baskets."

Recency

In the past, the publisher's promotional literature claimed that *Illustrated World* was "the only encyclopedia which is updated and revised
with every printing—sometimes two or three times in a single year." This
statement is blatantly untrue. No revision or new printing appeared between 1973 and 1977, until the set was reissued in the one-volume format
already described (see "Purpose and Scope"). Moreover, the amount of
revision evident in the 1977 work is so trivial that it could fit into the
proverbial thimble. Practically every article checked by the *Buying Guide*
in the 1977 volume appeared verbatim in the 1973 set. In a few instances,
new entries have been added (e.g., articles on presidents Ford and
Carter), and the profile of Richard Nixon has been updated to include his
resignation. But in all other cases, the text of the two editions is exactly
the same. To the *Buying Guide*'s best knowledge, no new edition of
Illustrated World has appeared since 1977. A letter from the editor in
1980 advised that "the current edition of the *Illustrated World Encyclopedia* is not sufficiently different from the last one to warrant another review." There is no indication when *Illustrated World* might again be
"revised."

Illustrated World was not a model of up-to-dateness in 1973. The article
"Ocean," for instance, was then so far out of touch with current facts and
theories as to be practically useless. "Refrigeration" was then 20 years
out-of-date, as was "Architecture." Because these same articles are reprinted in the 1977 edition, *Illustrated World* is now just that much more
out-of-date. Indeed, some of the material is scandalously old. EXAMPLE:
"Petroleum" provides 1965 oil production figures. EXAMPLE: "Marriage"
cites divorce statistics current in the 1950s. EXAMPLE: Earl Warren and

This Recency Table compares selected topics in *Illustrated World* with those in other encyclopedias of similar size and intended usership.

Topic	Illustrated World	Junior Pears	Nelson's Encyclopedia	Purnell's Pictorial
Africa	Not current	Very current	Very current	Fairly current
Babies/Children	Not current	Not current*	Not current*	Not current*
Disease	Not current	Not current*	Fairly current	Not current*
North American Indians	Not current	Not current*	Fairly current	Fairly current
Sharks	Fairly current	Not current*	Fairly current	Fairly current
Television	Not current	Very current	Very current	Very current

*Topic not covered in encyclopedia.

Francisco Franco live, according to *Illustrated World*. EXAMPLE: The latest information in "Civil Liberties and Civil Rights" informs the reader, "In 1964 Congress passed a Civil Rights Act admitting Negroes to parks, swimming pools, theaters, hotels, restaurants, and other public places." EXAMPLE: According to *Illustrated World,* there is not currently and never has been a natural gas shortage. EXAMPLE: In the article "Bill of Rights," the reader learns that "the Fifth Amendment is the one that is most often in the news. . . . Many people have used this right to refuse to say whether they have ever been Communists." EXAMPLE: The article "Motion Pictures" informs that "most movies are still made in black and white."

According to an advertisement in *Publishers Weekly* several years ago (March 7, 1977, p. 38), the publisher issues two yearbooks designed to help keep the encyclopedia current. Entitled *Book of the Year* and *Science Annual,* each volume was then priced at $14.95 if purchased directly from the publisher. The *Buying Guide* has not seen these yearbooks, but $14.95 per volume seems expensive for this sort of material. In any event, *Illustrated World* is sadly out-of-date at the present time, and it is very doubtful if any number of yearbooks could substantially improve the situation. What the encyclopedia needs—and has not had for years—is a thoroughgoing overhaul.

Objectivity

Some effort has been made to avoid outright bias, but the encyclopedia is not always objective. Comments about U.S. political leaders, for instance, sometimes include unwarranted editorial judgments. EXAMPLE: President Kennedy is said to have "acted with great bravery" during the 1962 missile crisis, whereas the incident is entirely ignored in Nikita

Khrushchev's biography. EXAMPLE: Pat Nixon, the former first lady, is described as "an attractive woman [who] radiates warmth and charm in public." In other instances, unsavory events are simply unreported. The Central Intelligence Agency, for example, merely "sends secret agents all over the world to learn the secrets of foreign governments," and naturally "all of its work must be kept secret from possible enemies." Nowhere, however, does the reader learn that many of the CIA's past field practices have been condemned by the American people. On the other hand, the Soviet Union is characterized as "a tyrannical communist government."

Clarity and Reader Suitability

Clarity and readability are the encyclopedia's best features. The articles are written in a very simple, usually clear style that will be comprehensible to readers at the third grade level and up. Difficult, unfamiliar, and technical words are normally defined within the context of the discussion. For instance, the article "Family" contains this sentence: "In nearly all civilized countries, the human family today is based on *monogamy*, a word meaning 'one marriage,' that is, one husband and one wife." In addition, new words are sometimes consciously introduced and explained to the reader. The article "Don Quixote," for example, concludes in this way: "In many ways the character of Don Quixote resembles that of his creator, CERVANTES, whom you can read about in another article. The word *quixotic* is applied to anyone who, like Don Quixote, is too romantic and unpractical." The article "Encyclopedia" notes that *Illustrated World* is a children's encyclopedia that "has been written to make each article understandable by those who knew nothing about the subject before." *Illustrated World* usually achieves this goal.

In some cases, however, the writing is choppy, casual, repetitive, and poorly constructed. EXAMPLE: The article "Childbirth" consists of three paragraphs, the last of which reads: "First, there must be a mother and father. In the mother's body there is everything needed for the birth of that baby when it is ready to come into the world. Without a father, however, the baby could not be conceived, which is the word for the beginning of a new baby's development. There must be a father as well as a mother, or there could never be any babies." Adults as well as children might find this explanation of childbirth confusing. On the opposite page, the article "Child" begins: "If you are a child, it means that your body and mind are growing and changing." Don't adult bodies and minds grow and change, too? The *Buying Guide* believes that there must be a more precise yet understandable definition of *child* available.

Arrangement and Accessibility

Illustrated World is arranged alphabetically, letter-by-letter ("Indiana" precedes "Indian Ocean"). Approximately 2,500 cross-references appear throughout the volume. They fall into two typical categories. First, there are several hundred external references entered in the main A–Z sequence. EXAMPLE: "*Chickasaw:* see MUSKHOGEAN." And second, there are over 2,000 internal references that appear within the text of the articles themselves, designated by capital letters. EXAMPLE: The article "Electrocution" notes that "until 1972, many states of the United States used electrocution as a means of CAPITAL PUNISHMENT," thus referring the reader to the article "Capital Punishment."

Unfortunately, the cross-reference system is neither extensive enough nor sufficiently well constructed to make the contents of a 2½-million-word encyclopedia readily accessible. EXAMPLE: There is no cross-reference from "Child" to "Baby-sitting" or vice versa. EXAMPLE: No reference is made from "Energy" to "Petroleum" or vice versa. EXAMPLE: No reference is made from "Conservation" to "Ecology" or vice versa. EXAMPLE: The one-sentence entry "Sex" refers the reader to "Reproduction," which concludes with this note: "To learn more about human reproduction, read the article on CHILDBIRTH." But none of these articles—"Sex," "Reproduction," or "Childbirth"—provides a reference to "Human Body," which, under the subheading "Reproductive System," contains the most straightforward and informative material on human reproduction to be found in the encyclopedia. EXAMPLE: The article "Grammar" includes a reference to SYNTAX but there is no entry for syntax in the volume.

An *Index & Study Guide* volume is said to be available for $14.95, which would bring the price of the encyclopedia to $34.90 plus tax. Although the *Buying Guide* has not seen the index, it is most likely very similar to the one that accompanied the 1973 multivolume edition of *Illustrated World.* If so, it is a very poor index, lacking specificity as well as analytical references.

Bibliographies

None. This omission is a serious deficiency.

Graphics

The encyclopedia is quite weak in terms of graphics. Many of the tiny, black-and-white photographs and line drawings are unclear and possess minimal informational value. In numerous instances where color would enhance understanding, it is lacking. EXAMPLE: The article "Byzantine Empire" includes a black-and-white reproduction of a Byzantine mosaic, which is captioned: "A mosaic looks like a painting, but it is made of many colored stones pasted together." The diagrams and charts are normally quite small and very elementary. The 150 maps included throughout the volume are merely locator devices that lack any other geographical information or value. At the end of the book there are eight color maps drawn by Hammond, which cover Africa, Asia, Canada, Europe, the Near and Middle East, India and China, South America, the United States, and the world. Obviously, only the most prominent physical and political features are indicated.

Physical Format

The outward appearance of the volume is attractive. The sturdy green binding with gold lettering and stamping is covered by a handsome silver and black dust jacket that features a color picture of the world on the cover. Inside the book, it is a different story. The three-column page layout is only occasionally relieved by drab black-and-white illustrations. The print is very small and not always legible. The use of subheadings is sometimes confusing. For instance, the article "Family" contains three subheadings printed in larger type than the main entry. As a result, the reader must look several times to determine the title of the article. Guide words at the top of each page help minimize this problem, however. The lightweight paper is of modestly good quality, and the volume lies flat when open. Actually, the volume is quite hefty, weighing over six pounds, and some owners will want to keep it open on a stand or tabletop.

Special Features

Aside from the fact that *Illustrated World* is a one-volume abridgment of what was previously a 15- and 21-volume encyclopedia, the only special feature is a 16-page pronunciation guide found in the back of the book, just before the atlas. The guide, according to the editors, provides pronunciations for all "difficult proper nouns found throughout the encyclopedia." Among its 4,650 entries, the guide includes such names as Addis Ababa, Faulkner, Io, Nazism, Sault Sainte Marie, and Vishinsky. Two pronunciations are given for each entry, one phonetic and the other simple respelling with accented syllables capitalized. The *Buying Guide* looked in vain for a pronunciation for Don Quixote.

Sales Information

Illustrated World is available in only one edition, that being the One Volume Edition (also called the Deluxe Edition) in the dark green binding already described (see "Physical Format"). The encyclopedia is not sold door-to-door on the subscription basis. Rather, like most one-volume items, it is marketed through various retail outlets (department stores, chain stores, and bookstores) or by direct mail order from the publisher or an authorized distributor. The current retail price as indicated by the publisher is $19.95, although the volume has been advertised variously at $39.95 and $49.95. Schools and libraries can obtain the encyclopedia at the discount price of $16.95. A Bobley executive has informed the *Buying Guide* that the company expects to sell 200,000 copies of *Illustrated World* each year.

Note that *Illustrated World* has several supplements which, if purchased, will increase the price of the encyclopedia considerably. As already pointed out (see "Arrangement and Accessibility"), there is an *Index & Study Guide* volume at $14.95. In addition, there are two updating yearbooks (see "Recency"), which also sell for $14.95 apiece. If all four of these volumes are acquired, the total bill will be $64.80 plus tax and any other charges. This figure seems exorbitant in light of the encyclopedia's poor quality.

Summary

The *Illustrated World Encyclopedia* can be quickly summed up in this manner:

Scope: Fair
Authority: Poor
Reliability: Poor
Recency: Poor
Objectivity: Fair
Clarity: Fair

Accessibility: Poor
Bibliographies: Poor (none)
Graphics: Poor
Physical Format: Fair
Special Features: Few
Price: High

To elaborate briefly, *Illustrated World* is a 1977 one-volume abridgment of the 1973 set, which appeared in both 15- and 21-volume editions. Actually, the text of the 1977 and 1973 works are practically the same, except for the deletion of numerous plot summaries (or Literary Treasures) that accompanied the 1973 set and some 13,000 illustrations. The encyclopedia has not been revised since 1977, and its contents are sadly out-of-date in many instances. Primarily intended for children in the upper elementary and middle school grades, *Illustrated World* covers most subjects studied at this level. In addition, coverage of practical topics like diseases, gardening, hobbies, and sports renders the volume potentially useful to all members of the family. But as the digest above indicates, *Illustrated World* is a grossly inadequate encyclopedia for readers of any age. Despite its seemingly low price, the encyclopedia is not a bargain; indeed, misinformation is no bargain at any price.

There are currently seven small-volume children's encyclopedias on the North American market, none of which can be enthusiastically recommended. The largest is the *Illustrated World Encyclopedia* (1,619 pages; 7,300 articles), but it is a highly inadequate work that discriminating consumers will avoid. The other large work, the new two-volume *Nelson's Encyclopedia for Young Readers* (973 pages; 2,000 articles), is far and away a better encyclopedia than *Illustrated World*, but it too has numerous deficiencies. The remaining five—*The Junior Encyclopedia of General Knowledge, Junior Pears Encyclopaedia, Purnell's First Encyclopedia in Colour, Purnell's Pictorial Encyclopedia,* and *Rand McNally's Children's Encyclopedia*—are all very slight works of British origin that qualify as encyclopedias in name only. Until such time as an enterprising publisher brings out a quality small-volume encyclopedia for young people, consumers will either have to go without or turn to the higher priced multivolume sets, of which *The New Book of Knowledge* and *Britannica Junior Encyclopaedia* are the best all-around for the age group 7–14.

Other Critical Opinions

Booklist, December 1, 1978, pp. 635–637. Part of a series of reviews by the

ALA Reference and Subscription Books Review Committee (RSBRC) entitled "Encyclopedias: A Survey and Buying Guide," this unsigned evaluation of the 21-volume 1973 edition has little good to say about the encyclopedia. Why the 1973 edition was reviewed in 1978 is not explained. In its last regular review of *Illustrated World* (*Booklist,* January 15, 1978, pp. 836–838), RSBRC found the encyclopedia unacceptable ("not recommended") because of "its many flaws."

Katz, William A. *Basic Information Sources* (Vol. 1 of *Introduction to Reference Work,* 3rd ed. New York: McGraw-Hill, 1978), p. 164. Katz warns against purchase of *Illustrated World,* noting that the encyclopedia is dated and has poor illustrations.

Junior Encyclopedia of General Knowledge

Facts in Brief

Full Title: **The Junior Encyclopedia of General Knowledge.** *Editors:* Theodore Rowland-Entwistle and Jean Cooke, Editors. *Publishers:* Octopus Books, Ltd., London, England. *U.S. Distributor:* Mayflower Books, Inc., 575 Lexington Ave., New York, NY 10022. *Edition Reviewed:* 1978 copyright.

Volumes: One. *Pages:* 224. *Articles:* 103. *Words:* 100,000. *Illustrations:* 400. *Maps:* 11. *Index Entries:* 1,100. *Cross-references:* None. *Contributors:* 13.

User Classification: Children (Small-volume). *Reader Suitability:* Age 7 through 12. *Physical Size:* 8 ¾ × 12 in.; 30 cm. *ISBN:* 0-7064-0737-7. *Lowest Retail Price:* $9.95.

Purpose and Scope

The Junior Encyclopedia of General Knowledge is a small British-made volume designed to introduce encyclopedic knowledge and information to young children. The foreword, written by Magnus Magnusson, puts the work's purpose in perspective: "You won't find all human knowledge in an encyclopedia; but in this one you will find all you want to know at first glance. . . . The Junior Encyclopedia of General Knowledge is both a doorway and a key, an Open Sesame to a new world of awareness." To accomplish its aims the encyclopedia divides knowledge into 11 broad sections that comprise 103 articles. The sections are The Earth in Space, Plants, Animals, Lands of the World, The Arts, Science and Technology, Transport and Communications, History of the World, Sports and Games, Emblems, and People at Work. A five-page index rounds out the encyclopedia's contents.

The articles within each section are normally two-page spreads, with half the text devoted to words and the other half to color illustrations, mostly photographs. Obviously, the subject coverage is highly selective. For instance, the section Animals contains ten articles: "Mammals"; "Mammals: The Carnivores"; "Mammals: The Herbivores"; "Birds"; "Perching Birds"; "Reptiles and Amphibians"; "Fishes"; "Invertebrates: The Arthropods"; "The Other Invertebrates"; and "Fingertip Facts." Many members of the animal kingdom are not even mentioned in these articles (e.g., such insects as bees, wasps, fleas, mosquitoes, and termites), and those that are covered usually receive very cursory treatment.

Sharks, for instance, are limited to five short paragraphs, plus a large photo of a great white. The volume provides practically no biographical information, and geographical coverage is quite superficial. EXAMPLE: The United States and Canada are covered in the two-page article "North America" (in Lands of the World). One-third of the article is consumed by a large photo of a wheat field in the United States. EXAMPLE: Iran and Afghanistan are each covered on the same page of "Western Asia." No political information is furnished. Entirely neglected by *Junior Encyclopedia* are the social and behavioral sciences, such as sociology, anthropology, economics, psychology, education, and political science. On the other hand, scientific and technical topics are emphasized.

Although prepared and published in Great Britain, the encyclopedia makes an effort to be international in its approach to knowledge. The article "The Postal Services" (in Transport and Communications), for example, follows a letter posted by Abdul in Marrakesh to his pen pal (or "pen-friend") George in Vancouver. The article "Football" (in Sports and Games) stresses the game as played in the United Kingdom, but American football is described. "Fingertip Facts on Sports" in the same section, however, is devoted to quick reference information on sports predominantly of interest to British readers, such as the English Channel swim, the British Commonwealth Games, and cricket records. Metric measurements with English equivalents are given throughout the volume.

History and Authority

Junior Encyclopedia was first published in 1978 by Octopus Books in London and has not been revised since that time. Octopus Books is not a major British publisher of encyclopedias, nor is the U.S. distributor, Mayflower Books, a known quantity in the reference book field. The volume's editors are Theodore Rowland-Entwistle and Jean Cooke, who have also edited *Purnell's Pictorial Encyclopedia*, a work quite similar in format, contents, and organization to *Junior Encyclopedia*. Five consultants and 13 contributors are noted in the front matter. Most of these people are identified only by name and academic degrees; none is known to the *Buying Guide* as experienced hands at encyclopedia-making. Also, none of the articles in *Junior Encyclopedia* is signed.

Reliability

No factual errors were uncovered during the course of the *Buying Guide*'s examination of the encyclopedia. It should be understood, however, that the material is quite elementary and only the most basic facts are provided. Information on sharks, for instance, in the article "Fishes" is limited to such general comments as "a shark constantly sheds its teeth, which are replaced by a succession of new teeth. However, the biggest of all the family, the so-called whale-shark, 13 metres (42 ft.) long, has feeble teeth. One of the strangest sharks is the hammerhead, unique among fishes: as its name suggests, its head sticks out on either side of the body, the eyes being situated on the ends."

Recency

In most instances, the information in *Junior Encyclopedia* is so general in nature that currency of material is not a major consideration. Where timeliness is important or imperative, however, the encyclopedia performs well. EXAMPLE: The article "World Wars and After" (in History of the World) concludes with this paragraph: "The United Nations, to which nearly all countries belong, has helped to keep the peace. It stopped Communist North Korea from conquering South Korea, but a similar attempt by the United States to stop the Communists of North Vietnam from taking over South Vietnam failed." An entirely new work in 1978, *Junior Encyclopedia* is current as of the late 1970s. The *Buying Guide* has no information at this time as to when or if the encyclopedia will be revised.

This Recency Table compares selected topics in *Junior Encyclopedia* with those in other encyclopedias of similar size and intended usership.

Topic	Junior Encyclopedia	Illustrated World	Nelson's Encyclopedia	Purnell's Pictorial
Africa	Very current	Not current	Very current	Fairly current
Babies/Children	Very current	Not current	Not current*	Not current*
Disease	Not current*	Not current	Fairly current	Not current*
North American Indians	Not current*	Not current	Fairly current	Fairly current
Sharks	Fairly current	Fairly current	Fairly current	Fairly current
Television	Very current	Not current	Very current	Very current

*Topic not covered in encyclopedia.

Objectivity

The encyclopedia does not ordinarily cover controversial or sensitive areas of knowledge, but when it does the topic is treated in a straightforward, evenhanded manner. EXAMPLE: The article "Creating a Family" (in Science and Technology) discusses human reproduction and sexual organs openly and factually: "At birth boys and girls have different reproductive organs, although they do not function until several years later. Apart from this, young boys and girls are very similar until a stage called puberty is reached. In girls this occurs at about the age of 11 or 12. Their hips grow wider and they begin to develop breasts. Hair begins to grow under the armpits and between the legs. At the same time they begin to have periods. These are normal events that occur in all women. Some bleeding usually occurs for a few days each month, when an unfertilized egg cell leaves the body." Occasionally, the encyclopedia's text is marred by sexist language. One article in Science and Technology, for instance, is entitled "The Feats of Man." Care appears to have been taken, however, to avoid sex stereotyping in the illustrations.

Clarity and Reader Suitabilty

Junior Encyclopedia's text normally will be comprehensible to children in the elementary and middle school grades. As the example above indicates (see "Objectivity"), new or potentially difficult terms (e.g., *puberty; periods*) are defined in context. The writing style is almost always clear and direct. Rarely do the writers attempt to be clever, cute, or creative. EXAMPLE: The article "Radio and Television" (in The Arts) notes that "the invention of television depended on finding a way to turn moving pictures into a series of electrical signals which could be sent by radio. Many people worked on it, including the Scotsman John Logie Baird, who built his first TV apparatus in 1925. Television broadcasting began in the 1930s, but it was only after World War II that it really became established."

Arrangement and Accessibility

As already noted (see "Purpose and Scope"), the encyclopedia is topically arranged by 11 broad sections covering a particular area of knowledge, such as The Arts. Each section contains from 2 to 18 articles, most of which are two-page spreads. All but the last two sections (Emblems and People at Work) conclude with a quick reference feature called "Fingertip Facts." All sections and articles are listed in the contents at the front of the volume. Specific topics (e.g., sharks) can be located via the simple index at the back. The index, which contains approximately 1,100 entries, is accurate and effective.

Bibliographies

None. The foreword states, "You won't find all human knowledge in an encyclopedia; but in this one you will find all you want to know at first glance—until your curiosity leads you further." It is unfortunate that the encyclopedia fails to provide any references as to where that curiosity might be satisfied.

Graphics

All in full color, the illustrations—mostly photographs—account for roughly half the encyclopedia's text. They usually clarify or enhance the printed text and are well placed in relationship to the material being illustrated. Picture captions also contain considerable information. The few maps in the Lands of the World section have no reference value whatsoever.

Physical Format

The red and yellow volume is sturdily bound in cloth-covered boards. Consumers will first encounter the book in a bright jacket cover with colorful photographs on the front. Inside, the two-page spreads comprised of equal amounts of printed text and pictorial material are appealing to the eye. The type is large and legible. Guide words indicating the section (not article) appear at the top of most pages; sometimes, however, they are eliminated by an illustration. The same is true of page numbers, which appear at the bottom of most pages. The volume lies flat when open for easy consultation. Overall, *Junior Encyclopedia* is a nicely made book.

Special Features

The only special feature offered by the encyclopedia is that each section concludes with fact panels on the subject called "Fingertip Facts." EX-AMPLE: The Earth in Space section ends with "Fingertip Facts on the Universe and the Earth," two pages of data that include the diameter of each planet, the speed of the moon's rotation, the length of the world's ten longest rivers, the height of the ten highest mountains, and the land area of each continent.

Sales Information

Junior Encyclopedia is sold in retail bookstores for $9.95. The volume can also be ordered directly from the distributor, Mayflower Books, Inc.

Summary

The Junior Encyclopedia of General Knowledge can be quickly summed up in this manner:

Scope: Poor	Accessibility: Excellent
Authority: Fair	Bibliographies: Poor (none)
Reliability: Excellent	Graphics: Excellent
Recency: Excellent	Physical Format: Good
Objectivity: Good	Special Features: Few
Clarity: Excellent	Price: Reasonable

To elaborate briefly, *Junior Encyclopedia* is a profusely illustrated, topically arranged one-volume item for children, prepared and published in Great Britain. Its coverage is highly selective and usually quite superficial, but what material the encyclopedia does contain is reliable, up-to-date, clearly written, and readily accessible. No one should consider *Junior Encyclopedia* to be a conprehensive reference work. It is not. On the other hand, the book does have the capability to stimulate the intellectual curiosity of young readers and answer at least some of their elementary questions.

There are currently seven small-volume children's encyclopedias on the North American market, none of which can be enthusiastically recommended. The largest is the *Illustrated World Encyclopedia* (1,619 pages; 7,300 articles), but it is a highly inadequate work that discriminating consumers will avoid. The other large work, the new two-volume *Nelson's Encyclopedia for Young Readers* (973 pages; 2,000 articles), is far and away a better encyclopedia than *Illustrated World*, but it too has numerous deficiencies. The remaining five—*The Junior Encyclopedia of General Knowledge, Junior Pears Encyclopaedia, Purnell's First Encyclopedia in Colour, Purnell's Pictorial Encyclopedia,* and *Rand McNally's Children's Encyclopedia*—are all very slight works of British origin that qualify as encyclopedias in name only. Until such time as an enterprising publisher brings out a quality small-volume encyclopedia for young people, consumers will either have to go without or turn to the higher priced multivolume sets, of which *The New Book of Knowledge* and *Britannica Junior Encyclopaedia* are the best all-around for the age group 7–14.

Other Critical Opinions

None.

Junior Pears Encyclopaedia

Facts in Brief

Full Title: **Junior Pears Encyclopaedia.** *Editor:* Edward Blishen. *Publisher:* Pelham Books, Ltd., London, England. *U.S. Distributor:* Merrimack Book Service, Inc., 99 Main St., Salem, NH 03079. *Edition Reviewed:* 20th Edition, 1980 copyright.

Volumes: One. *Pages:* 704. *Articles:* 18 topical sections. *Words:* 280,000. *Illustrations:* 150. *Maps:* 10. *Index Entries:* None. *Cross-references:* 100. *Contributors:* Staff produced.

User Classification: Children (Small-volume). *Reader Suitability:* Age 7 through 14. *Physical Size:* 4½ × 7¼ in.; 19 cm. *ISBN:* 0-7207-1263-7. *Lowest Retail Price:* $11.95; 20 percent discount to schools & libraries.

Purpose and Scope

Junior Pears Encyclopaedia is a children's version of *Pears Cyclopaedia,* a single-volume reference work for adults (see Part IV of the *Buying Guide* for a review). Like the senior *Pears, Junior Pears* is British in origin and flavor, is issued annually, and presents its contents in thematic rather than alphabetical fashion. Specifically, *Junior Pears* consists of 18 broad topical sections: The World—Its History; The World—Its Geography; The World—Its Famous People (Actual and Mythical); A Dictionary of Science and Mathematics; A Dictionary of Radio and Television; A Dictionary of Aircraft, Rockets and Missiles; Motor Cars, Motorcycles, Three-Wheelers, Scooters and Mopeds; Railways; Ships; The English Language; Music and the Arts; Sport; Conservation; Something to Join; The Armed Services, the Police and Fire Brigades; The Law; Natural History; and Miscellany. These topics are presented in a variety of ways (narrative form, alphabetical lists, etc.), depending on the nature of the subject; for instance, The World—Its History naturally lends itself to chronological treatment, whereas The World—Its Famous People is treated alphabetically.

Junior Pears is "for young people, and is intended to provide information on the main topics in which, as we judge, young people are likely to be interested" (preface). The editor recognizes, however, that "a single-volume encyclopedia is not and could not be a substitute for deeper reading"; that it can give only "the gleaming bare bones of information" (also quoted from the preface). Indeed, some readers and critics might question certain of the encyclopedia's omissions and enthusiasms. There is nothing, for instance, on motion pictures, a subject of considerable interest to many young people. Likewise, there is little in the encyclopedia on medicine, biology, sociology, and economics. The arts and humanities receive less than 80 pages of coverage, whereas various forms of transportation claim nearly 140 pages. *Junior Pears* also places heavy emphasis on technology, history, and political institutions (the law; the armed forces).

Coverage is almost entirely from the British perspective. EXAMPLE: The section A Dictionary of Radio and Television describes the British Broadcasting Corporation (BBC), briefly covering its functions and extent of operation, even to the point of providing the names and addresses of the BBC's local radio stations throughout England. No mention is made, however, of the major U.S. and Canadian broadcasting networks. EXAMPLE: The section Conservation concludes with a list of organizations (with addresses) active in the environmental movement, such as the Royal Society for the Protection of Birds. Unfortunately for U.S. and Canadian readers, the addresses (and most of the organizations) are British. EXAMPLE: The section The Armed Services, the Police and Fire Brigades gives information solely about the British army, navy, air force, police, etc. This strong emphasis on British events and institutions very much limits *Junior Pears*'s usefulness as a home reference source in the U.S. and Canada. On the other hand, it contains much information not found in similar works published in North America (such as the *Illustrated World Encyclopedia* and *Nelson's Encyclopedia for Young Readers),* and hence may be of value in library reference collections for children.

History and Authority

Junior Pears first appeared in 1961 and has been issued annually ever since. As already noted, *Junior Pears* is a children's version of the venerable *Pears Cyclopaedia,* a single-volume work for adults published each year since 1897. Both *Pears* volumes share the same publisher (Pelham Books, Ltd.), are quite alike in terms of treatment and organization of material, and enjoy great popularity and respect throughout the English-speaking world. Edward Blishen has been the editor of *Junior Pears* from the beginning. No other editors or contributors are identified, except for a list of 14 illustrators opposite the title page. None of the material in *Junior Pears* is signed.

Reliability

Over the years *Junior Pears* has gained a well-deserved reputation for factual accuracy. Only occasionally does an error intrude; for instance, in the world history section it is reported that in 1980 "Pierre Trudeau is returned to power in Canada nine months after his defeat by Jim Clark." Actually Clark's name is Charles Joseph Clark and he is familiarly known as Joe Clark.

Recency

The encyclopedia is updated annually. The flyleaf of the jacket cover asserts, "The book has been revised page by page and brought up-to-date fact by fact." Careful examination of many topics in the book tends to justify this claim. EXAMPLE: The recent accident at the Three Mile Island nuclear power plant at Harrisburg, Pa., is noted in the section Conservation. EXAMPLE: The section The World—Its History includes information about the return to power of Indira Gandhi in India, the election of Robert Mugabe as prime minister of the new state of Zimbabwe, and the aforementioned defeat of Joe Clark by Pierre Trudeau in Canada. EXAMPLE: According to the editor, the entire section The Law has been completely rewritten for the 1980 edition. Also, each year *Junior Pears* devotes one section to a topic of pressing importance. In 1979, for example, that topic was computers; in the current edition it is the environmental movement.

This Recency Table compares selected topics in *Junior Pears* with those in other encyclopedias of similar size and intended usership.

Topic	Junior Pears	Illustrated World	Nelson's Encyclopedia	Purnell's Pictorial
Africa	Very current	Not current	Very current	Fairly current
Babies/Children	Not current*	Not current	Not current*	Not current*
Disease	Not current*	Not current	Fairly current	Not current*
North American Indians	Not current*	Not current	Fairly current	Fairly current
Sharks	Not current*	Fairly current	Fairly current	Fairly current
Television	Very current	Not current	Very current	Very current

*Topic not covered in encyclopedia.

Objectivity

Generally speaking, *Junior Pears*, like most encyclopedias for young children, avoids controversial or sensitive subject matter in such areas as religion, politics, sexuality, and drugs. The section The World—Its History does include, however, a glossary of political terms that concisely defines words like *Communism, detente, Democracy, Imperialism, National Socialism,* and *Socialism.* The definitions are clear and free of political bias; for example, *Communism* is "the theory, as expounded by Marx and Engels, which aims at the creation of a society in which the private ownership of land, factories, banks, trading houses, etc., is abolished, and everyone receives what he needs and works according to his capacity. Communists believe that revolution and the use of force are justified to bring about the creation of such a society." On the other hand, the special section in this 1980 edition (under review here) entitled Conservation is quite polemical in tone. For instance: "As the slaughter of small birds that give great joy to many people is indeed a great pleasure to the killers, since they are passionately devoted to such slaughter, it is clear that alternative, non-destructive, forms of the same kind of pleasure must be devised: a moral equivalent of slaughter that will cause the killer's hearts to beat faster and their eyes to gleam." Such moral outrage is seldom encountered in modern encyclopedias.

Clarity and Reader Suitability

The editor's preface observes that efforts have been undertaken to make the encyclopedia "pleasant to read" and not merely a "dry assemblage of information." Most of the narrative material is clear and readable, though not especially entertaining. In a few instances, however, the text becomes quite informal and even personal. For example, the section Natural History begins in this way: "The first thing I do when I get up in the morning is to draw back the curtain and look out through the window at the garden and the new day. If it is a bright summer morning I cannot wait even to get dressed, but go straight downstairs in my dressing-gown. Then I unlock the door and step out into the garden to breathe the fresh morning air 'before many people have used it,' as somebody once said." Although *Junior Pears* is a reference work specifically prepared for children, no attempt has been made to control the vocabulary, nor are potentially new or difficult terms defined in context. Normally, young people in the upper elementary and middle school grades will not have great difficulty comprehending *Junior Pears*. In a few cases, however, the writing may be beyond average readers at the seventh and eighth grade level. In addition, British spelling and usage are used throughout, which might confuse or discourage some young readers in the United States and Canada.

Arrangement and Accessibility

As already explained (see "Purpose and Scope"), *Junior Pears* is arranged thematically in 18 broad sections, such as A Dictionary of Science and Mathematics, Railways, The English Language, and Sport. Arrangement within these sections varies according to the nature of the topic involved. EXAMPLES: The section The World—Its History is mainly chronological in arrangement. A Dictionary of Radio and Television is alphabetical in arrangement. Sport is arranged alphabetically by type of sport, for example, archery, badminton, basketball, boxing, cricket, fencing. The Law is arranged topically under such headings as "What is Law?" "The Branches of Law," "The Courts of England and Wales," and "Lawyers."

Finding specific information in *Junior Pears* can be a trying experience. The encyclopedia has a detailed table of contents, and some sections also have their own even more detailed contents pages. Beyond this, the reader is given very little assistance in locating particular events, people, facts, etc. There is no index, and the few cross-references are mostly limited to the section The World—Its Famous People. A reader looking for information about the weather, for instance, must be informed or lucky enough to consult the contents for the section The World—Its Geography, where it is revealed that there are six pages of material on meteorology. Otherwise there is no logical way of finding this material. What *Junior Pears* needs to make its contents reasonably accessible is a detailed general index. Until such time as an index is added, finding information in the encyclopedia will remain more a matter of luck than of logic.

Bibliographies

Seven of the 18 sections in the encyclopedia append short, selected lists of books for further reading. Unfortunately, the titles listed are not always appropriate for young readers, such as Sir John Betjeman's *First and Last Loves* in the bibliography at the end of Music and the Arts. Moreover, entries lack publication dates and are limited to works published in Great Britain.

Graphics

All 150 graphics in *Junior Pears* are black-and-white line drawings. The informational value of some sections would obviously be enhanced by the addition of color illustrations. Music and the Arts, for example, contains black-and-white drawings of the Bayeux tapestry, an illuminated manuscript, and a stained-glass window. In most instances, however, the simple diagrams are informative, such as the cutaway drawings in the section on automobiles. The few maps, also in black-and-white, have little reference value for students of any age.

Physical Format

Junior Pears, quite small as children's encyclopedias go (only 4½ × 7¼ inches), is bound in thin orange boards with gold lettering. The binding is glued instead of sewn, meaning the volume will not stand up to heavy or rough use. Consumers will initially encounter the book in a bright jacket with colorful photographs on the front. Inside, the encyclopedia's single-column page layout, small print, and lack of color will intimidate or turn off some readers, especially younger ones. The pagination, which is inclusive for each section (for example, Railways covers pages H1–H34), may also be confusing to younger users. Page numbers and guide words appear at the top of most pages. The paper is of reasonably good quality, but the volume does not usually lie flat when open.

Special Features

Junior Pears has three notable special features. First, it is the only small-volume children's encyclopedia currently on the North American market that is revised each year. Second, *Junior Pears* combines the best qualities of encyclopedic and yearbook coverage of knowledge and information. As an encyclopedia, *Junior Pears* provides much basic background information in condensed form that is carried over from year to year, but it also covers current events in each annual revision (in the section The World—Its History) and adds and drops articles and special sections each year, like a yearbook. For instance, the section Conservation in the 1980 edition replaced the 1979 section Computers. And third, *Junior Pears* provides strong coverage of British personalities, events, and institutions (including many addresses), a particularly useful feature for library reference work.

Sales Information

Like practically all small-volume encyclopedias, *Junior Pears* is sold in bookstores and similar retail outlets. There are no in-home sales. The book is distributed in the United States by the Merrimack Book Service, Inc., in Salem, N.H., for Michael Joseph, Inc. Educational institutions receive 20 percent off the current retail price of $11.95.

Summary

Junior Pears Encyclopaedia can be quickly summed up in this manner:

Scope: Poor	Accessibility: Poor
Authority: Fair	Bibliographies: Fair
Reliability: Good	Graphics: Fair
Recency: Excellent	Physical Format: Fair
Objectivity: Fair	Special Features: Few
Clarity: Fair	Price: Reasonable

To elaborate briefly, *Junior Pears,* published annually since 1961, is a juvenile version of *Pears Cyclopaedia,* a one-volume British reference work that dates its origins back to the nineteenth century. *Junior Pears* aims to cover those subjects in which "young people are likely to be interested" (preface), but in fact the coverage is erratic and imbalanced. British personalities, events, and institutions are emphasized, which limits the encyclopedia's value as a reference source for the home in North America, but may well increase its usefulness to libraries. *Junior Pears's* writing style tends to be uneven and, in some instances, will be beyond the reading capabilities of average students in the upper elementary and middle school grades. Arranged in 18 topical sections, the encyclopedia lacks an index and provides far too few cross-references to make its contents readily or fully accessible. Other negative features include dull graphics, small print, and a weak binding. Overall, *Junior Pears* is an eccentric albeit often informative British reference work for children that might be useful in library reference collections in the United States and Canada, but nowhere else.

There are currently seven small-volume children's encyclopedias on the North American market, none of which can be enthusiastically recommended. The largest is the *Illustrated World Encyclopedia* (1,619 pages;

7,300 articles), but it is a highly inadequate work that discriminating consumers will avoid. The other large work, the new two-volume *Nelson's Encyclopedia for Young Readers* (973 pages; 2,000 articles), is far and away a better encyclopedia than *Illustrated World*, but it too has numerous deficiencies. The remaining five—*The Junior Encyclopedia of General Knowledge, Junior Pears Encyclopaedia, Purnell's First Encyclopedia in Colour, Purnell's Pictorial Encyclopedia,* and *Rand McNally's Children's Encyclopedia*—are all very slight works of British origin that qualify as encyclopedias in name only. Until such time as an enterprising publisher brings out a quality small-volume encyclopedia for young people, consumers will either have to go without or turn to the higher priced multivolume sets, of which *The New Book of Knowledge* and *Britannica Junior Encyclopaedia* are the best all-around for the age group 7–14.

Other Critical Opinions

Booklist, January 1, 1981, p. 643. This short, unsigned review by the ALA Reference and Subscription Books Review Committee is mainly descriptive. At the end, however, the encyclopedia is dismissed because of "its British approach."

Roginski, Jim. *American Reference Books Annual,* 1979, pp. 34–35. Roginski dislikes everything about *Junior Pears:* its Britishness, its typeface, its glued binding, its pagination, its organization, its bibliographies, and its "pedantic and didactic" writing style.

Nelson's Encyclopedia for Young Readers

Facts in Brief

Full Title: **Nelson's Encyclopedia for Young Readers.** *Editors:* Laurence Urdang, Editor in Chief; George C. Kohn, Managing Editor. *Publisher:* Thomas Nelson Publishers, 407 Seventh Ave. S., Nashville, TN 37203. *Edition Reviewed:* 1980 copyright.

Volumes: Two. *Pages:* 973. *Articles:* 2,000. *Words:* 350,000. *Illustrations:* 1,300. *Maps:* 200. *Index Entries:* 5,700. *Cross-references:* 2,500. *Contributors:* Staff produced.

User Classification: Children (Small-volume). *Reader Suitability:* Age 7 through 14. *Physical Size:* 7½ × 10¼ in.; 26 cm. *LC:* 80-14522. *ISBN:* 0-8407-5184-2. *Lowest Retail Price:* $34.95.

Purpose and Scope

Nelson's Encyclopedia for Young Readers, published in 1980, is a completely new two-volume reference work for children in the elementary grades. The brief preface states that *Nelson's* "will answer many of your questions about the world in which you live. It will guide you from very early times through the present day and point you toward tomorrow. It will take you to every major country of the globe and let you explore the depths of outer space. It will tell you how machines work, why nature behaves as it does, and when the important events of history occurred." *Nelson's* 2,000 specific entries cover significant people, places, plants, animals, historical events, technological developments and inventions, holidays, sports, and the like. Articles average half a page in length, or roughly 175 words. As might be expected, the coverge is quite thin, even for a children's encyclopedia. Most articles contain only a few basic facts fleshed out by general, and often vague, statements. The half-page article "Chile," for example, notes that the country "gained its independence in 1818, driving out the Spanish rulers." The nation's recent history, however, is glossed over in the next sentence with this sweeping and essentially meaningless observation: "Since then, the country has developed into a modern, industrial republic, despite internal political wars and economic problems." At no point in the article is it mentioned, for instance, that Chile had the first elected Marxist president (Salvador Allende) in the western hemisphere. The article "Negroes" contains nothing about the contemporary civil rights struggle in the United States and abroad. The closest the article comes to that subject is the statement, "In the United States alone there are today about 23 million Negroes, who are usually referred to as Blacks." Likewise, "Panama Canal" completely ignores the recent treaty controversy.

Biographical and geographical topics are emphasized, accounting for approximately 30 percent of all the entries. Coverage is highly selective. For instance, Thomas Jefferson is included but Warren Harding is not. China is in but not Afghanistan. Religious subjects receive generous attention, relatively speaking. Important Christian figures like Jesus, John, Judas Iscariot, Luke, Mark, and Peter have individual entries, as do Christianity, the Catholic Church, the Orthodox Church, the Bible, and Protestantism. Other major religions such as Islam and Judaism are also covered. Scientific and technical subjects are accorded reasonably good coverage (again relatively speaking). Prominent members of the animal and plant kingdoms have individual entries, as do such topics as anesthetics, atoms, the bathyscaphe, decimals, germs, gravity, heat, the internal-combustion engine, lasers, nebula, ore, plastics, rubber, Sputnik, typhoons, and X-rays. On the other hand, the encyclopedia's coverage of social and behavioral topics is dreadfully inadequate. No information can be found in *Nelson's* on such pertinent subjects as adoption, marriage, divorce, human sexuality and maturation, babies and infant care, women's rights, rape, crime, death, suicide, IQ tests, psychology, and mental illness. Practical subjects of interest to children like book reports, babysitting, and cheerleading are also ignored. It is difficult to understand why *Nelson's* includes a two-page article on plows but completely ignores etiquette and manners, for example. Overall, the set's purpose is not well defined, and its coverage is both sketchy and imbalanced.

History and Authority

Nelson's is an entirely new children's encyclopedia published in September 1980 by Thomas Nelson Publishers. The encyclopedia was prepared by Laurence Urdang, Inc., of Essex, Connecticut, a firm that specializes in compiling and revising reference works, including dictionaries and encyclopedias. The set's editor in chief, Laurence Urdang (president of Laurence Urdang, Inc.), is well known in the reference book field as the editor of such titles as the *Collins Dictionary of the English Language,* the *Dictionary of Advertising Terms,* and *Twentieth Century American Nicknames.* Suffice it to say that Urdang is well qualified to edit a children's encyclopedia. He is supported by an editorial staff of 11, including 4 consulting editors: Clifton Fadiman, Millicent Selsam, R. J. Unstead, and William Worthy, all of whom bring good credentials to the project. All material in *Nelson's* is unsigned, having been written by members of the editorial staff.

Reliability

The encyclopedia provides only the most elementary facts. These facts are consistently accurate, although occasionally an error or two turns up. EXAMPLE: The article "American Indians" incorrectly places the Aztecs in

Central America, instead of in Mexico where they belong. EXAMPLE: "Prince of Wales" notes that "the present Prince of Wales is His Royal Highness, Prince Charles, who will become King of England when Queen Elizabeth II dies," erroneously implying that Charles can become king only upon the death of his mother. EXAMPLE: "Sharks" begins with the statement that "sharks are the flesh-eaters of the sea," suggesting that sharks are the only flesh-eaters in the sea, which of course is not true.

Recency

As already pointed out, *Nelson's* is a new encyclopedia published in 1980. Most of the material is fresh and reflects the current state of knowledge. The article "Nuclear Energy," for instance, emphasizes environmental concerns: "Great care must be taken in the operation of nuclear reactors, for they can be very dangerous. After use, their fuel remains radioactive for thousands of years. Radioactive materials can cause bad burns that lead to cancer and death in almost all living things. For that reason, nuclear waste must be buried deep underground to keep it away from people, animals and plants." In many instances, however, current information appears to be deliberately avoided. The aforementioned article "Panama Canal" (see "Purpose and Scope") contains nothing about the recent history of the waterway, including the controversial treaties concluded between the United States and Panama in 1978. Articles on Iran, Mexico, and other volatile countries also avoid contemporary issues and developments.

This Recency Table compares selected topics in *Nelson's* with those in other encyclopedias of similar size and intended usership.

Topic	Nelson's Encyclopedia	Illustrated World	Junior Pears	Purnell's Pictorial
Africa	Very current	Not current	Very current	Fairly current
Babies/Children	Not current*	Not current	Not current*	Not current*
Disease	Fairly current	Not current	Not current*	Not current*
North American Indians	Fairly current	Not current	Not current*	Fairly current
Sharks	Fairly current	Fairly current	Not current*	Fairly current
Television	Very current	Not current	Very current	Very current

*Topic not covered in encyclopedia.

Objectivity

Normally the encyclopedia avoids controversial subject matter. As previously noted (see "Purpose and Scope"), such topics as human sexuality, drugs, death, adoption, women's rights, and IQ tests are not covered.

When potentially controversial subjects are covered, *Nelson's* either ignores the controversy entirely or treats the topic in a strictly matter-of-
fact manner. EXAMPLE: The article "Federal Bureau of Investigation" fails
to mention the agency's recent problems with the law. EXAMPLE: "Cuba"
simply reports, "In the 1950s, Fidel Castro led a successful revolt against
Batista, who was a dictator in Cuba at that time. Castro took control in
1959 and has since made Cuba into a socialist state, with strong ties to the
U.S.S.R. and other Communist countries." EXAMPLE: "Evolution" points
out that Darwin's books "aroused much controversy because they seemed
to contradict Christian beliefs in the creation of the world by God."
EXAMPLE: "Vietnam War" dispassionately records the history of that conflict. EXAMPLE: "Flying Saucers" notes that "some scientists believe that
UFOs should be closely studied; others say they are explainable, scientific
phenomena."

Clarity and Reader Suitability

As the many examples quoted throughout this review indicate, *Nelson's*
is written in a clear, straightforward manner, usually without embellish-
ment or attempts to be cute or entertaining. Concepts are usually explained in terms that can be readily understood by children in the primary
and upper elementary grades. The article "Supreme Court," for example,
concisely describes what is meant by *judicial review*. Frequently, words
and phrases that might not be familiar to the encyclopedia's readers are
defined in context—for example, "Much of the Court's business concerns
appeals in cases affected by federal law. (An appeal is a request for a
rehearing of a case by a higher court.)" *Nelson's* attention to vocabulary
building is one of its most attractive features.

Arrangement and Accessibility

The encyclopedia is arranged alphabetically, letter-by-letter ("Easter"
precedes "East Indies"). Access to specific information is facilitated by
some 2,500 internal cross-references. These references most often appear
within the text of an article designated by CAPITAL LETTERS. For
example, the article "Africa" contains the following sentence: "These
eastern lakes feed three great rivers, the NILE, the Congo, and the
ZAMBEZI, on which the mighty VICTORIA FALLS are situated."
Thus the reader is alerted that the encyclopedia also has articles on the
Nile and Zambezi rivers, as well as the Victoria Falls. In addition, some
articles conclude with *See also* references. The article "Africa," for instance, has four *See also* references: "Arabs," "Negroes," "Sahara," and
"Tropics." *Nelson's* also furnishes a 5,700-entry index at the back of
Volume 2. Unfortunately, the main entries in the index are almost exactly
the same as the A–Z entries in the encyclopedia, which means the index
does little more than duplicate the alphabetical arrangement. The reader
seeking information on, say, motion pictures will not find an entry in the
encyclopedia under that term. In the index, there is also no entry for

motion pictures. Yet the encyclopedia does contain an article entitled "Movies." A carefully constructed index would include cross-reference entries under "Motion Pictures" and "Cinematography" directing the reader to the entry "Movies." Analytical references appear under most main entries in the index; for example, under the entry "Television" there are references to "Edison, Thomas Alva" and "Industry." Again unfortunately, the analytical references are not always complete. EX-AMPLE: The entry "Christianity" includes analytical references to articles on Jesus, John, Luke, Mark, Matthew, and Paul, but inexplicably omits Judas and Peter.

Bibliographies

None. This is a major deficiency in an elementary encyclopedia like *Nelson's*.

Graphics

The 1,500 illustrations—all simple line drawings—rarely add much of value to the set's contents. The drawings, of which over half are in color, tend to be small and lacking in detail, poorly reproduced, and more decorative than informative. According to a note on the verso of the title page, some of the illustrations first appeared in *Black's Children's Encyclopedia,* published in 1961 (with several later revisions) by A. & C. Black, Ltd., a British publisher.

Physical Format

Nelson's is bound in stiff boards covered with a brightly decorated washable material. The two-volume set comes in a flimsy cardboard slipcase. Inside, the single-column page layout is frequently broken up by graphics, which appear on practically every page. As befits a reference work for children, the text type is large and readable, and the entry headings are enormous. The paper is of indifferent quality, but the volumes do lie flat when open for easy consultation. Although the volumes are easy to handle and reasonably attractive to the eye, the set is cheaply made.

Special Features

None.

Sales Information

Nelson's is a trade item; that is, it is sold through retail outlets that handle books and related products. The encyclopedia can also be ordered direct from the publisher or, in the case of schools and libraries, through a book wholesaler. The set was introduced in 1980 at $29.95, but it currently sells for $34.95, which seems high considering the work's mediocre quality.

Summary

Nelson's Encyclopedia for Young Readers can be quickly summed up in this manner:

Scope: Poor   Accessibility: Good
Authority: Good   Bibliographies: Poor (none)
Reliability: Good   Graphics: Poor
Recency: Good   Physical Format: Fair
Objectivity: Good   Special Features: None
Clarity: Excellent   Price: High

To elaborate, *Nelson's* is a brand-new encyclopedia for children in the elementary grades. Edited by Laurence Urdang, a well-known lexicographer and maker of reference works, the two-volume set emphasizes coverage of biographical, geographical, religious, and scientific and technical subjects. Conversely, social and behavioral topics are almost completely ignored. In most instances, the set's articles are quite superficial, limited to a few facts surrounded by sweeping generalizations. What material there is is usually reliable, current, and clearly and impartially presented. Moreover, the set is reasonably well organized, although the index could be improved. The graphics, which lack detail and are poorly reproduced, add little to the informational value of the encyclopedia. The set's lack of bibliographies is another serious deficiency. On balance, *Nelson's* provides skimpy and imbalanced coverage of that knowledge and information likely to be of interest to elementary school children. The encyclopedia, which gives the impression of being cheaply made, seems overpriced for what it delivers.

There are currently seven small-volume children's encyclopedias on the North American market, none of which can be enthusiastically recommended. The largest is the *Illustrated World Encyclopedia* (1,619 pages; 7,300 articles), but it is a highly inadequate work that discriminating consumers will avoid. The other large work, the new two-volume *Nelson's Encyclopedia for Young Readers* (973 pages; 2,000 articles), is far and away a better encyclopedia than *Illustrated World*, but it too has numerous deficiencies. The remaining five—*The Junior Encyclopedia of General Knowledge, Junior Pears Encyclopaedia, Purnell's First Encyclopedia in Colour, Purnell's Pictorial Encyclopedia,* and *Rand McNally's Children's Encyclopedia*—are all very slight works of British origin that qualify as encyclopedias in name only. Until such time as an enterprising publisher brings out a quality small-volume encyclopedia for young people, consumers will either have to go without or turn to the higher priced multivolume sets, of which *The New Book of Knowledge* and *Britannica Junior Encyclopaedia* are the best all-around for the age group 7–14.

Other Critical Opinions

None.

Purnell's First Encyclopedia in Colour

Facts in Brief

Full Title: **Purnell's First Encyclopedia in Colour.** *Editor:* Michael W. Dempsey, Editor in Chief. *Publisher:* Purnell & Sons, Ltd., Maidenhead, Berkshire, England. *U.S. Distributor:* Pergamon Press, Inc., Maxwell House, Fairview Park, Elmsford, NY 10523. *Edition Reviewed:* 1974 copyright.

Volumes: One. *Pages:* 125. *Articles:* 300. *Words:* 50,000. *Illustrations:* 500. *Maps:* None. *Index Entries:* 550. *Cross-references:* None. *Contributors:* 5.

User Classification: Children (Small-volume). *Reader Suitability:* Age 7 through 12. *Physical Size:* 8½ × 11¾ in.; 30 cm. *ISBN:* 0-361-021089. *Lowest Retail Price:* $6.95.

Purpose and Scope

Purnell's First Encyclopedia in Colour is a very small one-volume British encyclopedia of inconsequential scope designed for young children. The book contains no introductory matter whatsoever, but it is clearly intended as a first or beginning reference book for readers in the elementary grades. The approximately 300 articles, which range from "Acid" to "Zoos," average two per page, or approximately 175 words each. A few articles like "Automobile," "North America," "Railways," and "Stars" cover a page or more and exceed 250 words. Many other articles ("Butter," "Camel," "Dodo," "Dragonfly," "Fox," "Gold," "Maps," "Panda," "Rodents," "Rose," "Shells," "Tides," "Wool," "Zebra") are limited to a paragraph or so, or about 100 words.

The encyclopedia's subject coverage concentrates heavily on the natural world and human technical accomplishments. Animals, plants, geographical places and features, the weather, machines, instruments, and means of transportation comprise the contents of *Purnell's First.* Not covered are such topics as art, babies, bicycles, death, drugs, games, human reproduction, marriage and the family, and sports. As a general encyclopedia, the volume obviously has minimal value. But, because the subjects covered are of interest to young readers and because the articles are brightly illustrated, *Purnell's First* has the potential to stimulate youthful curiosity about the natural world and recent technological developments.

History and Authority

As far as is known, the book first appeared in 1974 in England and has not been revised or reissued since that time. The publisher is Purnell & Sons, Ltd., a reputable British firm known internationally for its reference publications, and the book is distributed in the United States by Pergamon Press. Michael W. Dempsey, the editor, has written numerous books for children on scientific topics, which perhaps accounts for the encyclopedia's overwhelming emphasis on the natural and technical sciences. The five contributors are merely listed with their academic degrees. At least two of them, however, are experienced hands at preparing children's reference books: both Theodore Rowland-Entwistle and Jean Cooke have edited *The Junior Encyclopedia of General Knowledge* and *Purnell's Pictorial Encyclopedia* (both reviewed in this part of the *Buying Guide*).

Dempsey has also edited the now defunct 16-volume *Harver Junior World Encyclopedia* (see Appendix A), and a comparison of the two works reveals considerable similarity of style and content. EXAMPLE: The article "Africa" in *Purnell's First* begins: "Africa is the world's second largest land mass, or continent. It is almost three times the size of Europe." The same article in *Harver Junior,* which was adapted for U.S. readership in 1972, begins: "Africa is the world's second largest continent. With its area of 11,671,000 square miles, it is three and a half times as large as the United States." EXAMPLE: The article "Bats" in *Purnell's First* begins: "Bats are the only mammals that fly. They have small furry bodies rather like those of mice, and broad, thin wings made of skin." The same article in *Harver Junior* begins: "Bats are the only mammals that fly. They have small furry bodies, rather like those of mice, and broad, thin wings." Another small children's reference work entitled *Purnell's First Encyclopedia of Animals* (Purnell, 1974) contains very similar material; for example, the article on bats starts out, "Bats are the only mammals that can fly properly." (*Purnell's First Encyclopedia of Animals* is not reviewed in the *Buying Guide,* as it is a specialized encyclopedia.)

Reliability

Purnell's First is a trustworthy encyclopedia, as far as it goes, which is not far. Most factual information is limited to physical characteristics of plants, animals, places, etc. Several typographical errors occur; for instance, in a picture caption *Chinese temple* comes out *Chinese temble.*

Recency

Although now more than several years old, *Purnell's First* remains reasonably current due to the fact that its contents are so elementary and generalized. For example, the article on the computer asks, "How do the astronauts know the exact moment to fire the rockets? A computer tells them. Only a computer could work out all the calculations quickly enough. . . . Computers are used today for many things from working out people's wages to producing weather forecasts." This information, though simple, is current.

This Recency Table compares selected topics in *Purnell's First* with those in other encyclopedias of similar size and intended usership.

Topic	Purnell's First	Illustrated World	Nelson's Encyclopedia	Purnell's Pictorial
Africa	Fairly current	Not current	Very current	Fairly current
Babies/Children	Not current*	Not current	Not current*	Not current*
Disease	Not current*	Not current	Fairly current	Not current*
North American Indians	Not current*	Not current	Fairly current	Fairly current
Sharks	Fairly current	Fairly current	Fairly current	Fairly current
Television	Fairly current	Not current	Very current	Very current

*Topic not covered in encyclopedia.

Objectivity

Purnell's First presents its material in an impartial, straightforward manner. No religious, sexual, political, or racial bias exists in the book—if for no other reason than topics in these areas are not covered.

Clarity and Reader Suitability

The writing style, like the contents, is quite simple. Unfamiliar, difficult, or technical terms are normally explained in context. Descriptions of rather complicated processes are usually clear and will be comprehensible to readers at the third grade level and up. EXAMPLE: The article "Refrigerator" explains: "When a liquid turns to a gas it takes in, or absorbs, heat. A refrigerator works by sending a special liquid through pipes in the food compartment and making it turn to a gas. As the liquid turns to gas it absorbs heat from the food. In this way the food is cooled. The gas is turned back to a liquid in another part of the refrigerator."

Arrangement and Accessibility

The encyclopedia is arranged alphabetically, letter-by-letter ("Newts" precedes "New Zealand"). There are no cross-references, either external or internal. A simple A–Z index at the back of the book facilitates finding specific topics. In future editions, should there by any, some cross-references would be helpful, such as from "Rats and Mice" to "Rodents" and vice versa.

Bibliographies

None. Obviously such an elementary encyclopedia as *Purnell's First* would be enhanced by the inclusion of bibliographies, or lists of works to consult for additional information.

Graphics

There are approximately four color drawings on each page of the encyclopedia, or about 500 illustrations throughout the book. The drawings, like the text, are rudimentary and lack detail, but they usually contribute to the informational value of the encyclopedia. For example, several colorful pictures accompany the article "Flowers." One picture shows a simple cross section of a flower, with the stamens and carpels labeled. Another depicts three different types of flower heads. Another shows a bee in a flower with the legend, "Bees carry pollen from flower to flower as they feed on nectar at the bottom of the petals." Overall, the illustrations comprise approximately a third of the volume's entire text.

Physical Format

Purnell's First is bound in washable boards with drawings of a dinosaur, octopus, and assorted other items on the covers. The binding, which is glued instead of sewn, will not withstand heavy use. Inside, the large two-column page is fairly attractive and inviting, frequently broken up by the illustrations, which sometimes spread over both columns. The large print and wide margins help give the book an open, free appearance. The medium-grade paper should last for the life of the book. One defect in the format is lack of guide words at the top of each page. The encyclopedia lies perfectly flat when open.

Special Features

None.

Sales Information

Purnell's First can be purchased through retail bookstores or ordered directly from Pergamon Press, the U.S. distributor. The book can also be acquired through the British Book Centre (153 E. 78 St., New York, NY 10021), a division of Pergamon Press.

Summary

Purnell's First Encyclopedia in Colour can be quickly summed up in this manner:

Scope: Poor	Accessibility: Good
Authority: Good	Bibliographies: Poor (none)
Reliability: Good	Graphics: Good
Recency: Fair	Physical Format: Fair
Objectivity: Good	Special Features: None
Clarity: Excellent	Price: Reasonable

To elaborate very briefly, *Purnell's First* is a small, inconsequential British-made encyclopedia for children in the elementary grades. It heavily emphasizes the natural and technical sciences, and is profusely illustrated with colorful drawings. The work appears to be a spin-off of the now defunct *Harver Junior World Encyclopedia* (see Appendix A). The volume possesses little merit as an encyclopedic source of factual knowledge. It does have the potential, however, to motivate and, perhaps in some cases, satisfy the young child's inquiring mind.

There are currently seven small-volume children's encyclopedias on the North American market, none of which can be enthusiastically recommended. The largest is the *Illustrated World Encyclopedia* (1,619 pages; 7,300 articles), but it is a highly inadequate work that discriminating consumers will avoid. The other large work, the new two-volume *Nelson's Encyclopedia for Young Readers* (973 pages; 2,000 articles), is far and away a better encyclopedia than *Illustrated World*, but it too has numerous deficiencies. The remaining five—*The Junior Encyclopedia of General Knowledge, Junior Pears Encyclopaedia, Purnell's First Encyclopedia in Colour, Purnell's Pictorial Encyclopedia,* and *Rand McNally's Children's Encyclopedia*—are all very slight works of British origin that qualify as encyclopedias in name only. Until such time as an enterprising publisher brings out a quality small-volume encyclopedia for young people, consumers will either have to go without or turn to the higher priced multivolume sets, of which *The New Book of Knowledge* and *Britannica Junior Encyclopaedia* are the best all-around for the age group 7–14.

Other Critical Opinions

Boone, Peggy Clossey. *American Reference Books Annual,* 1978, p. 40. This short notice criticizes the binding as "unsuited to heavy library use" but is otherwise fairly favorable, concluding that *Purnell's First* may be "very handy for student reports and pleasure reading."

Purnell's Pictorial Encyclopedia

Facts in Brief

Full Title: **Purnell's Pictorial Encyclopedia.** *Editors:* Theodore Rowland-Entwistle and Jean Cooke. *Publisher:* Purnell & Sons, Ltd., Maidenhead, Berkshire, England. *U.S. Distributor:* Pergamon Press, Inc., Maxwell House, Fairview Park, Elmsford, NY 10523. *Edition Reviewed:* 1979 copyright.

Volumes: One. *Pages:* 192. *Articles:* 88. *Words:* 75,000. *Illustrations:* 550. *Maps:* None. *Index Entries:* 975. *Cross-references:* None. *Contributors:* 13.

User Classification: Children (Small-volume). *Reader Suitability:* Age 7 through 12. *Physical Size:* 8 ¾ × 12 in.; 30 cm. *ISBN:* 0-361-04416-X. *Lowest Retail Price:* $19.95.

Purpose and Scope

Purnell's Pictorial Encyclopedia, new in 1979, is a thematically arranged reference volume for children in the elementary grades. Although the book contains no preface or statement of purpose, it is clearly intended to introduce young readers to selected portions of knowledge via 88 two-page survey articles grouped within six broad sections. These sections are Earth and the Universe; The Living World; The World of Ideas; Sounds and Pictures; People and Places; and Science and Technology. The articles, which are heavily illustrated, emphasize overview information rather than factual data. For example, the article "The Great Religions" (in The World of Ideas) provides only a paragraph or two on each of the world's major faiths, the intention being to put them into a comparative perspective rather than to furnish hard facts like the number of followers each faith has, who its founders and early adherents were, and so forth. Other articles in The World of Ideas section include "The Great Philosophers," "Myths and Legends," "Sharing Ideas," "Producing a Book," "The Story of a Newspaper," and "Radio and Television."

All the essential knowledge and information of possible interest to children obviously cannot be covered in a profusely illustrated one-volume encyclopedia of 192 pages. *Purnell's Pictorial Encyclopedia*'s greatest deficiency is the selectivity and shallowness of its coverage. A seven-line paragraph on Christianity, for instance, is not sufficient coverage for readers of any age. In some cases, topics are merely mentioned in passing. The only information in the encyclopedia about sharks, for instance, is in the article "Plants and Animals of Oceans" (in The Living World), in which the reader learns that "sharks are big fish" and not much more. In yet other cases, prominent people, places, events, inventions, and the like are entirely ignored. What coverage there is tends to concentrate on scientific and technical subjects. The arts and humanities are also fairly well represented. The social and behavioral sciences, however, are grossly neglected, except for a smattering of historical and anthropological information in the People and Places section. A British-produced work, *Purnell's Pictorial* gives only metric measurements. Children in the United States may have difficulty with such text as "the Nilotes are extremely tall Negroes. They range from about 1.78 metres to 2.13 metres in height."

History and Authority

Issued as a new work in 1979, *Purnell's Pictorial* is published by Purnell & Sons in England, which also publishes *Purnell's First Encyclopedia in Colour,* another single-volume work for young children (reviewed in this section of the *Buying Guide*). The editors, Theodore Rowland-Entwistle and Jean Cooke (a husband-and-wife team), have produced a number of reference works for children, including *The Junior Encyclopedia of General Knowledge* (also reviewed in this section of the *Buying Guide*). The front matter lists 15 additional staff members and contributors, some of whom also worked on *The Junior Encyclopedia of General Knowledge,* a volume that greatly resembles *Purnell's Pictorial* in terms of purpose, scope, and organization but contains different material.

Reliability

As far as it goes, *Purnell's Pictorial* is usually reliable. The brief treatment of television in the article "Sharing Ideas" (in The World of Ideas section) accurately describes the medium's recent technical development: "Television's progress was slowed down by World War II (1939–1945), but developments came thick and fast in the 1950s. A snag with TV is that its waves travel in straight lines and do not follow the curve of the Earth, but the development of satellites in the 1960s and 1970s means that TV signals can now be 'bounced' off a satellite, enabling broadcasts to be seen simultaneously all over the world." In some instances, however, faulty generalizations or oversimplifications may lead to erroneous conclusions. EXAMPLE: The article "The Great Religions" informs, "Like Buddhism, Christianity split into sects," implying that Buddhism and Christianity are the only factional religions among the major faiths, which of course is not the case.

Recency

As previously noted, *Purnell's Pictorial* appeared as a new encyclopedia in 1979. Its contents are generally current as of the late 1970s, as the aforementioned example concerning television (see "Reliability") indicates.

This Recency Table compares selected topics in *Purnell's Pictorial* with those in other encyclopedias of similar size and intended usership.

Topic	Purnell's Pictorial	Illustrated World	Junior Pears	Nelson's Encyclopedia
Africa	Fairly current	Not current	Very current	Very current
Babies/Children	Not current*	Not current	Not current*	Not current*
Disease	Not current*	Not current	Not current*	Fairly current
North American Indians	Fairly current	Not current	Not current*	Fairly current
Sharks	Fairly current	Fairly current	Not current*	Fairly current
Television	Very current	Not current	Very current	Very current

*Topic not covered in encyclopedia.

Objectivity

Purnell's Pictorial is a reasonably impartial encyclopedia. The topic of evolution, for instance, is accorded fairly balanced treatment in the article "The Descent of Man" (in The Living World section). In most instances, however, potentially controversial subjects are simply ignored, like drugs, political ideology, and suicide. Also on the negative side is the encyclopedia's occasional use of sexist language; for example, in the article "The World of Ideas" the reader is left with the impression that only "men" have ideas: "Early men's thinking concentrated mainly on the practical day-to-day business of living. . . . Yet men's minds already brimmed with more abstract ideas long before they became civilised enough to build towns or raise crops from seeds. . . . One man's brilliant idea could then be communicated rapidly throughout an empire."

Clarity and Reader Suitability

Children with reading skills at the upper elementary school level will normally have little difficulty comprehending *Purnell's Pictorial Encyclopedia*. Although the spelling is British (e.g., *civilised* instead of *civilized*), peculiarly British terminology has been avoided. As the examples already cited in this review indicate (see "Reliability" and "Objectivity"), the style is clear and matter-of-fact. Little effort has been made to write lively or entertaining prose, although some articles do begin with questions designed to arouse interest in the topic, such as, "You may often have wondered 'Where did Mankind come from, and why are people so different from animals in some ways, and so like them in others?' "

Arrangement and Accessibility

The encyclopedia's thematic arrangement has already been described in some detail (see "Purpose and Scope"). Each article is included under one of the six broad sections, such as Earth and the Universe. All sections and their articles are listed in the table of contents at the front of the book. Because the text provides no cross-references, access to specific information must be obtained through the general index in the back. Unfortunately, this simple 975-entry index is neither comprehensive nor analytical nor accurate. EXAMPLE: The mythological Zeus is discussed at length in the article "Myths and Legends" but nowhere does an entry for Zeus appear in the index. EXAMPLE: The subject of television is covered in the two-page article "Radio and Television" (pages 80–81) and more briefly in "Sharing Ideas" (page 73), but the index entry "Television" directs the reader only to page 71 (which contains information about myths, not television). Many similar errors were noted during the *Buying Guide*'s examination of the encyclopedia. In addition, the graphics, which account for approximately half the text, are not indexed at all.

Bibliographies

None. The lack of bibliographies, or references to sources of additional information, is a serious deficiency in an elementary work like *Purnell's Pictorial*.

Graphics

The 550 illustrations comprise roughly 50 percent of the book's total text. Relatively few (about 60) of the illustrations are in color, the rest black-and-white. Photographs predominate although some drawings, diagrams, and art reproductions are also included. In most instances, the graphics add to the informational value of *Purnell's Pictorial*, but in some cases they seem unnecessarily large. The entirety of page 105, for example, is taken up by a photo of a youngster playing with clay. The caption reads: "Wedging clay is an important preliminary to successful pottery—and it's also great fun." Likewise, the whole of page 85 is devoted to a photo of a child playing the cello. The caption in this instance reads: "Big cello—small player; but it's never too soon to start finding out about instruments and how to play them." But is a full-page graphic required to convey this point, especially in a one-volume encyclopedia where space is severely limited?

Physical Format

The volume is durably bound in red cloth-covered boards with gold lettering. Consumers will most likely first see the book in its colorful jacket with various photographs on the front. Inside, the two-column layout is nicely varied due to the use of many different-sized graphics and the allowance of wide margins. The print is reasonably large and usually legible, although smudged copy occurs here and there, such as on page

77. Page numbers at the bottom of the page are frequently eliminated by illustrations, which can be a minor annoyance. The nonglare paper is of fair quality, and the volume lies flat when open for easy consultation.

Special Features

The encyclopedia's only special feature is the inclusion of "Inquiry Desk" articles in each section. For example, the Sounds and Pictures section includes the article "Arts Inquiry Desk," a two-page feature that poses about a dozen interesting questions and then provides the answers, such as "Why does a violin make a noise when it is rubbed with a bow?" and "How did the circus originate?"

Sales Information

Purnell's Pictorial retails for $19.95 and can be acquired directly from the U.S. distributor (Pergamon Press), through bookstores, or in the case of schools and libraries, through a book wholesaler.

Summary

Purnell's Pictorial Encyclopedia can be quickly summed up in this manner:

Scope: Poor	Accessibility: Poor
Authority: Good	Bibliographies: Poor (none)
Reliability: Good	Graphics: Fair
Recency: Good	Physical Format: Fair
Objectivity: Fair	Special Features: Few
Clarity: Excellent	Price: High

To elaborate briefly, *Purnell's Pictorial* is a single-volume British import of recent vintage aimed at children in elementary school. Thematically arranged, the volume's 88 two-page survey articles are clearly written but very shallow in content. Other limitations include an incomplete and inaccurate index, use of sexist language, lack of bibliographies, and unnecessarily large graphics in some instances. Overall, *Purnell's Pictorial* will be of only marginal value to young students as a source of encyclopedic knowledge and information.

There are currently seven small-volume children's encyclopedias on the North American market, none of which can be enthusiastically recommended. The largest is the *Illustrated World Encyclopedia* (1,619 pages; 7,300 articles), but it is a highly inadequate work that discriminating consumers will avoid. The other large work, the new two-volume *Nelson's Encyclopedia for Young Readers* (973 pages; 2,000 articles), is far and away a better encyclopedia than *Illustrated World*, but it too has numerous deficiencies. The remaining five—*The Junior Encyclopedia of General Knowledge, Junior Pears Encyclopaedia, Purnell's First Encyclopedia in Colour, Purnell's Pictorial Encyclopedia,* and *Rand McNally's Children's Encyclopedia*—are all very slight works of British origin that qualify as encyclopedias in name only. Until such time as an enterprising publisher brings out a quality small-volume encyclopedia for young people, consumers will either have to go without or turn to the higher priced multivolume sets, of which *The New Book of Knowledge* and *Britannica Junior Encyclopaedia* are the best all-around for the age group 7–14.

Other Critical Opinions

None.

Rand McNally's Children's Encyclopedia

Facts in Brief

Full Title: **Rand McNally's Children's Encyclopedia.** *Editor:* John Paton. *Publisher:* Rand McNally & Company, Box 7600, Chicago, IL 60680; copyright by Grisewood & Dempsey, Ltd. *British Title: Ward Lock's Children's Encyclopedia. Edition Reviewed:* 1976 copyright.

Volumes: One. *Pages:* 61. *Articles:* Five topical sections comprising 27 two-page spreads. *Words:* 15,000. *Illustrations:* 300. *Maps:* None. *Index Entries:* 350. *Cross-references:* None. *Contributors:* Staff produced.

User Classification: Children (Small-volume). *Reader Suitability:* Age 7 through 12. *Physical Size:* 9½ × 12¾ in.; 32 cm. *LC:* 77-70935. *ISBN:* 0-528-82101-6. *Lowest Retail Price:* $4.95; to schools & libraries $4.97.

Purpose and Scope

Rand McNally's Children's Encyclopedia, published in Great Britain in 1976 under the title *Ward Lock's Children's Encyclopedia* and brought out in the United States by Rand McNally & Company in 1977, provides very limited information on selected topics of interest to children in the elementary grades. The brief introduction states that the encyclopedia "gathers together a mass of information in a new way," and proceeds to explain that the book is divided into five broad sections (Our Wonderful World, Wonders of Life, Around the World, The Story of Man, and Here, There and Everywhere), which in turn contain two-page spreads on more specific topics like "The Air Around Us," "Your Body," "Deserts," "Food from the Soil," "Insects and Spiders," "Knights and Castles," "The Motor Car," "Power from the Sun," and "Trains and Railways." These two-page articles are profusely illustrated with four-color drawings. Actually, the encyclopedia is a midget version of the *Colorpedia* section of the new *Random House Encyclopedia,* a visually exciting one-volume work for adults that also utilizes topically arranged two-page spreads and, interestingly, also originated in England.

Rand McNally's coverage, like that found in *Purnell's First Encyclopedia in Colour, Purnell's Pictorial Encyclopedia,* and *The Junior Encyclopedia of General Knowledge* (other one-volume British imports for young readers), greatly emphasizes the natural and technical sciences. Plants, animals, jungles, mountains, farming, transportation, space exploration— these are the main concerns of *Rand McNally's Children's Encyclopedia.*

The scope of the coverage is generally international. Only the article "Knights and Castles" might be considered of special interest to British readers, but even in this case the perspective is European. Not covered at all are such topics as art, babies, death, divorce, drugs, family life, games and sports, marriage, and rock music. Obviously, this little book is of negligible consequence as an encyclopedic work, but it does possess some value as a browsing item for imaginative young readers.

History and Authority

As already noted, the encyclopedia is of recent British origin. The *Buying Guide* is not familiar with the name Ward Lock, which appears in the British title, nor with the editor John Paton, who is the sole person listed as having responsibility for the work. Grisewood & Dempsey, Ltd., holders of the copyright, also own the rights to the larger one-volume *Great World Encyclopedia* (now out-of-print; see Apendix A). Michael W. Dempsey (of Grisewood & Dempsey) is a well-known British writer of science books for children as well as an experienced children's encyclopedist. For instance, Dempsey has edited the now defunct 16-volume *Harver Junior World Encyclopedia* (see Appendix A) and the tiny *Purnell's First Encyclopedia in Colour,* which resembles *Rand McNally's* in terms of scope and coverage.

Reliability

Rand McNally's provides accurate information for children on the subjects it covers. Most of the text, of course, is very general and nonfactual. For example, the two-page spread "Mountains" contains a paragraph on skiing, which goes like this: "The first skis were probably made thousands of years ago from large animal bones. There is a pair of skis on show in a Swedish museum which are thought to be five thousand years old. Skis have often been used by troops in times of war. But it was not until the early 1800s that skiing first became a sport. Today, millions of holiday makers go each year to ski resorts all over the world." In some instances, however, specific facts are given, usually in picture captions. EXAMPLE: The article "Living in a City" informs the reader that "London today stretches over 18.6 miles." All such facts were checked and found to be accurate.

Recency

Because it is a fairly new work, *Rand McNally's* is quite current in both fact and tone. Such articles as "Into the Future," "The Motor Car," "The Story of Aircraft," and "Trains and Railways" include captioned illustrations of the latest kinds of transportation, such as the French Aerotrain, the electric car, the supersonic Concorde jet, and space-age monorails. Most of the treatment, however, is so general that currency of material is not a major consideration.

This Recency Table compares selected topics in *Rand McNally's* with those in other encyclopedias of similar size and intended usership.

Topic	Rand McNally's	Illustrated World	Nelson's Encyclopedia	Purnell's Pictorial
Africa	Not current*	Not current	Very current	Fairly current
Babies/Children	Not current*	Not current	Not current*	Not current*
Disease	Not current*	Not current	Fairly current	Not current*
North American Indians	Not current*	Not current	Fairly current	Fairly current
Sharks	Fairly current	Fairly current	Fairly current	Fairly current
Television	Not current*	Not current	Very current	Very current

*Topic not covered in encyclopedia.

Objectivity

The encyclopedia is usually objective, avoiding both bias and controversy. For example, the legend under the drawing of the Concorde in "The Story of Aircraft" notes that the airplane looks "like some strange bird" and that it "takes only 3½ hours to cross the Atlantic," but there is no hint of the dispute concerning the plane's noise and its landing problems in the United States. In a few cases, however, *Rand McNally's* is wittingly or unwittingly partial in the area of technological development. EXAMPLE: In the two-page spread "Power from the Sun," there is a boxed note labeled "Power from the Atom" wherein the reader learns that "there is only so much coal and oil in the world. After a while these precious substances will be all used up. When they are, we will have to rely much more on atomic power." At the present time, our use of atomic (or nuclear) energy is a matter of heated social and political debate.

Clarity and Reader Suitability

The text is simple enough that most elementary school students will have little difficulty understanding it. Technical or unfamiliar words are normally defined in context, and the many illustrations are an additional aid to comprehension. The style is admirably clear and straightforward.

Arrangement and Accessibility

As previously pointed out (see "Purpose and Scope"), *Rand McNally's* is topically arranged by five broad subject divisions: Our Wonderful World, Wonders of Life, Around the World, The Story of Man, and Here, There and Everywhere. Within these categories are a total of 27 general articles, all presented in two-page spreads except for the last one

("Into the Future"), which is limited to a single page. Although the articles are complete within themselves, their subject matter is often complementary. Around the World, for instance, contains these six somewhat related articles: "Cold Lands," "Deserts," "Food from the Soil," "Jungles and Forests," "Living in a City," and "Mountains." A contents page lists all of the subject categories and articles. In addition, there is a 350-entry index on the last page, so that readers can find the paragraph on skiing, for example, in the article "Mountains." Essentially, *Rand McNally's* aims to foster interest in knowledge rather than provide quick reference information. Viewed in this light, the encyclopedia is well arranged and access to its contents is satisfactory.

Bibliographies

None. The lack of bibliographies, or lists of materials for additional information, constitutes a serious deficiency in a beginning encyclopedia like *Rand McNally's*.

Graphics

Rand McNally's graphics are quite similar to those found in three other British one-volume encyclopedias for children currently available in the United States, namely *The Junior Encyclopedia of General Knowledge, Purnell's First Encyclopedia in Colour,* and *Purnell's Pictorial Encyclopedia.* All of the illustrations are colorful drawings that add to the informational value of the book. In most cases, the drawings include lengthy captions, which contain much useful and specific information. The pictures, which are abundant and on every page, sometimes have informative labels. EXAMPLE: The article "The World of Plants" has five distinct illustrations, one of which shows a cross section of a flower with its various parts labeled (petals, sepals, stamens, etc.). Illustrations comprise approximately 50 percent of the book's total text.

Physical Format

Although *Rand McNally's* has a large page size (9¼ × 12½ in.), the volume is light and easy to handle. It is bound in washable boards with bright drawings on the front cover. The binding is sturdy and will withstand very heavy use. Inside, the page layout is inviting, similar to that found in the innovative *Random House Encyclopedia* for adults. Printed text and illustrations are integrated to form an informational whole throughout the two-page spreads. Children will be drawn to the varied page designs. The nonglare paper is heavy and durable. The volume lies flat when open. The *Buying Guide's* only complaint about the book's format is the lack of page numbers on some two-page spreads.

Special Features

None.

Sales Information

Rand McNally's is sold as a trade book at $4.95 in bookstores and other retail outlets. It is also available to educational institutions in a reinforced library binding at $4.97.

Summary

Rand McNally's Children's Encyclopedia can be quickly summed up in this manner:

Scope: Poor
Authority: Good
Reliability: Good
Recency: Good
Objectivity: Good
Clarity: Excellent

Accessibility: Good
Bibliographies: Poor (none)
Graphics: Good
Physical Format: Good
Special Features: None
Price: Reasonable

To elaborate briefly, *Rand McNally's* is a slim but engaging one-volume item for young children. It initially appeared abroad as *Ward Lock's Children's Encyclopedia* in 1976, and the following year it was published in the United States as *Rand McNally's Children's Encyclopedia*. In arrangement, treatment, and design, this little encyclopedia very much resembles the *Colorpedia* section of the innovative *Random House Encyclopedia*, a one-volume work for adults. Specifically, *Rand McNally's* is topically arranged with subjects treated in two-page spreads that are heavily illustrated with colorful drawings. The printed and illustrative matter are integrated to form an informational whole. Nevertheless, *Rand McNally's* is only a 61-page book, and its coverage is obviously highly selective, limited in most instances to topics covering the natural world and technical developments. Essentially, the volume is meant to stimulate youthful interest in knowledge rather than provide comprehensive factual information.

There are currently seven small-volume children's encyclopedias on the North American market, none of which can be enthusiastically recommended. The largest is the *Illustrated World Encyclopedia* (1,619 pages; 7,300 articles), but it is a highly inadequate work that discriminating consumers will avoid. The other large work, the new two-volume *Nelson's Encyclopedia for Young Readers* (973 pages; 2,000 articles), is far and away a better encyclopedia than *Illustrated World*, but it too has numerous deficiencies. The remaining five—*The Junior Encyclopedia of General Knowledge, Junior Pears Encyclopedia, Purnell's First Encyclopedia in Colour, Purnell's Pictorial Encyclopedia*, and *Rand McNally's Children's Encyclopedia*—are all very slight works of British origin that qualify as encyclopedias in name only. Until such time as an enterprising publisher brings out a quality small-volume encyclopedia for young people, consumers will either have to go without or turn to the higher priced multivolume sets, of which *The New Book of Knowledge* and *Britannica Junior Encyclopaedia* are the best all-around for the age group 7–14.

Other Critical Opinions

Amdursky, Marion. *American Reference Books Annual*, 1978, p. 40. This nine-line review notes that *Rand McNally's* may be suitable for browsing but the "lack of detail in the text limits the usefulness of the book."

Appendix A
Discontinued Encyclopedias, 1960–1981

The following encyclopedias are out of print and therefore unavailable from the publishers, except in instances when a small stock may be on hand awaiting final closeout. These encyclopedias, however, will sometimes be encountered in secondhand bookstores, antique or junk shops, and in discount stores as remainder items. *For general information about purchasing a used encyclopedia,* see "Finding the Right Encyclopedia" in Part I of the *Buying Guide.* There is also the chance that a fly-by-night publisher will obtain the plates and reprint a defunct encyclopedia (obviously without permission from the original publisher) and attempt to pass it off as a new work. This disreputable practice is less prevalent today than in the past. It should be noted, too, that a few of these sets, while not available at the present time, have been reported as undergoing major revision and will perhaps reappear in the future, either under the original title or a new one. The *Buying Guide* includes such information in the descriptions that follow. Finally, for discontinued encyclopedias not found here, consult S. Padraig Walsh's *Anglo-American General Encyclopedias: A Historical Bibliography, 1703–1967* (R. R. Bowker Company, 1968).

American Educator Encyclopedia

A 20-volume set for young adults, the *American Educator* contained approximately 7,750 pages, 13,000 articles, and five million words when it was last published in the late 1970s. A product of United Educators, Inc., of Lake Bluff, Ill., the encyclopedia was unable to compete with such strong competitors as *Compton's Encyclopedia, Merit Students Encyclopedia,* and *The World Book Encyclopedia.*

The 1978 edition of the *Buying Guide* summarized the *American Educator* as follows:

American Educator was improved measurably by a thoroughgoing overhaul in 1972, but the set has not progressed since that time, except for minimal updating of material and occasional cosmetic gestures. Designed principally for middle and high school students, the encyclopedia provides concise, quite selective, and sometimes superficial coverage of basic subjects. Its fullest coverage is of botanical and zoological topics. *American Educator*'s greatest deficiency—and it has many— is its lack of a general index. Numerous cross-references simply are not sufficient to render the set's contents fully accessible, particularly when the cross-references themselves are not always reliable. Overall, the set has a dark, dull, drab, uninviting look about it.

American Educator is the smallest encyclopedia in the young adult category. It has little to recommend it over the better sets in this class—*Compton's Encyclopedia, Merit Students Encyclopedia,* and *The World Book Encyclopedia.* It is true that *American Educator* is less expensive than the other encyclopedias in its class. But when size and quality are also taken into account, *American Educator* is a bad buy.

Another critical opinion of *American Educator* can be found in *American Reference Books Annual,* 1973, pp. 103–104 (review by Christine L. Wynar).

American Family Encyclopedia

This work was published from 1938 to 1964 as *The New American Encyclopedia* (not to be confused with the 20-volume set of the same title, which is currently available from The Publishers Agency). In 1965, it became the *American Family Encyclopedia* and continued under that title until it was phased out in the early 1970s. Not a large work (1,500 pages, a million words, 20,000 entries, 800 illustrations, no maps), it was published by Books, Inc., in both one- and eight-volume editions. A set of poor quality, it conspicuously failed to live up to its claim as "a concise and comprehensive reference work, especially planned, compiled and written for school, college, office and home use."

American Oxford Encyclopedia

An effort to adapt the British *Oxford Junior Encyclopaedia* for a U.S. audience, this project never got off the ground. Of the planned 14 volumes, only the first was published (in 1965). Like the *Oxford Junior,* the set would have been topically arranged. Financial problems on the part of the publisher—the New York firm of Little and Ives, Inc.—caused the failure of this potentially worthwhile venture.

American Peoples Encyclopedia

The American Peoples Encyclopedia was a 20-volume set for adults that comprised over 11,000 pages, 35,000 articles, and ten million words. Initially published in 1948 by Spencer Press in Chicago, the set apparently derived from the old *Nelson's Encyclopedia* (1905–1940). In 1961 Grolier, Inc., one of the Big Four encyclopedia publishers, acquired the work and improved it considerably. *American Peoples* died in 1976. In no particular order, the causes of death were an inflated price ($325.50 in 1975), lack of distinctive purpose or personality, a laggardly revision program, and negative reviews.

Toward the end, some hucksterism was employed to sell the set, although Grolier was not directly involved. The 1975–1976 *Buying Guide* reported the situation this way:

Consumers should be aware that at least one distributor, removed from Grolier's direct control, has recently circulated misleading advertising literature about *American Peoples*. Individual consumers, as well as school and public librarians, should scrutinize all advertisements côncerning *American Peoples* with special care. The set should be thoroughly reviewed by the consumer prior to purchase.

Consumers should also be aware that *American Peoples* is currently being sold under the title of *University Society Encyclopedia* by the University Society, Inc., Midland Park, N.J. Again, prospective purchasers are advised to watch for misleading claims made on behalf of the *University Society Encyclopedia*.

The 1975–1976 *Buying Guide* summarized *American Peoples* as follows:

The *American Peoples Encyclopedia* is a middle-sized, middle-priced, modestly made adult encyclopedia. The set has considerable range but lacks depth. For instance, it contains more entries than *Collier's Encyclopedia* but is less than half *Collier's* size. The set stresses brief factual information presented in clear, relatively simple terms. Like other Grolier general encyclopedias (see especially *Encyclopedia Americana* and *Encyclopedia International*), *American Peoples* provides extensive coverage of biographical and geographical topics. Treatment of material is usually authoritative, reliable, and impartial. Access to material is good, facilitated by numerous cross-references throughout the set and a sufficiently detailed general index.

Illustrations, however, are not indexed. This limitation is perhaps offset somewhat by the criticism that the illustrations themselves are quite unremarkable. A more serious deficiency is the set's lack of up-to-dateness in some areas. If *American Peoples* is to remain competitive in the intermediate adult category, attention to revision will have to be increased in future editions. Another liability is the set's limited and dated bibliographies. And the writing style, while usually clear, is colorless and bland, as is the set's general appearance.

American Peoples must compete with the larger but more expensive advanced adult sets (like Grolier's own *Encyclopedia Americana*) as well as the smaller but less expensive young adult sets (like *Compton's Encyclopedia* and *The World Book Encyclopedia*). Moreover, it competes directly with several other middle-sized adult encyclopedias: *Funk & Wagnalls New Encyclopedia, The New American Encyclopedia, The New Caxton Encyclopedia,* and *Harver World Encyclopedia.*

American Peoples does not compete well. Not only is the set dull and unglamorous with no reputation to speak of among the encyclopedia-buying public, but it lacks any distinctive feature or outstanding quality which might make it attractive to the consumer. It is too adult for families with children, and it is too abbreviated for adults who want and can afford a truly adult encyclopedia. In comparison with the other intermediate adult sets, *American Peoples* lacks *Funk & Wagnalls New*

Encyclopedia's low-price advantage, it lacks *Harver World*'s currency and attractive design, and its lacks *New Caxton*'s brilliant illustrations. Only when compared with *New American* does *American Peoples* stand out as a clearly superior set.

Other critical opinions of *American Peoples* can be found in *American Reference Books Annual,* 1973, pp. 104–105 (review by Bohdan S. Wynar) and the *Booklist,* July 15, 1974, pp. 1206–1208. Finally, bear in mind that the set could be resurrected at any time under the title *American Peoples Encyclopedia, University Society Encyclopedia,* or any other pretentious name.

Basic Everyday Encyclopedia

A small, one-volume desk encyclopedia (574 pages, 900,000 words, 12,500 entries), this once-useful work was published by Random House, Inc., in 1954. Available in both hardcover and paperback editions, it went out of print in 1972. It was edited by Jess Stein, who later served as editor in chief of the well-received *Random House Dictionary of the English Language* and most recently as editorial director of *The Random House Encyclopedia.*

Book of Knowledge

One of the most popular children's encyclopedias of its time (1912–1965), this set was superseded by *The New Book of Knowledge,* essentially a new work that retained certain of the best features of the older set. The most striking difference between the two titles is arrangement, the older encyclopedia being topically arranged whereas the present set is alphabetical. Published by Grolier, Inc., *The Book of Knowledge* appeared in from 10 to 20 volumes during its long and successful history. When discontinued in 1966, the set had about four million words in nearly 8,000 pages.

Cadillac Modern Encyclopedia

The *Cadillac Modern Encyclopedia* was a single-volume general adult encyclopedia issued in 1973 and never subsequently revised. Edited by Max S. Shapiro and published by the Cadillac Publishing Company, Inc. (first located in New York City and later in St. Louis), the encyclopedia comprised 1,954 pages, 18,000 articles, and roughly 2.5 million words. It was reported out of print in 1980, but the possibility of encountering *Cadillac Modern* in a discount or secondhand bookstore is not unlikely. The possibility also exists that the encyclopedia might be revised at some time in the future.

The 1978 edition of the *Buying Guide* summarized *Cadillac Modern* as follows:

> To elaborate briefly, *Cadillac Modern* is a one-volume encyclopedia prepared from scratch in the early 1970s. Although now beginning to

show its age, the work still retains its contemporary treatment and perspective in most areas. Almost 4,000 biographies and a like number of geographical entries are included, but the encyclopedia's outstanding coverage is in the area of the natural sciences and particularly mathematics. Current social and political topics are not covered nearly so well. Overall, *Cadillac Modern* is a clear, concise, informative, and reasonably priced small encyclopedia best suited to the adult reader or student with an aptitude for science. A new edition is tentatively scheduled to appear in 1978 or 1979.

Despite its name, *Cadillac Modern* is not the top luxury small-volume encyclopedia on the market. At the present time, *The New Columbia Encyclopedia, The Random House Encyclopedia,* and *The University Desk Encyclopedia* are all preferable, unless cost is an overriding consideration. Among the rest of the small-volume competition, *Cadillac Modern* stands up rather well when compared with the older *Larousse Illustrated International Encyclopedia and Dictionary,* the two-volume *Lincoln Library,* and the definitely inferior *Volume Library.*

Other critical opinions of *Cadillac Modern* can be found in *American Reference Books Annual,* 1975, pp. 31–32; the *Booklist,* January 1, 1979, pp. 767–768; *Choice,* April 1975, p. 195; and *Library Journal,* March 1, 1974, pp. 642–643 (review by Annette Hirsch).

Chambers's Encyclopaedia

Chambers's Encyclopaedia, a 15-volume British work of considerable substance, is currently unavailable in the United States, but doubtless it will reappear some time in the future. When that might be will depend upon the present owner's ability to find the money required for a major revision, estimated to be at least $6 million and as high as $10 million. The encyclopedia is also "virtually unobtainable" in Britain at the present time, according to a report in the London *Observer* by Ken Creffield (dated April 10, 1977).

When last published in 1973 (a corrected reissue of the 1966 New Revised Edition), *Chambers's* comprised nearly 13,000 pages, 28,000 articles, and 14½ million words. *Chambers's* originated in the mid-nineteenth century as a part work published by the respected firm of W. & R. Chambers of Edinburgh (Scotland). Note that *Chambers's* was entirely unrelated to Ephraim Chambers's earlier and very influential *Cyclopaedia* (1728). By 1901, after *Encyclopaedia Britannica* passed into U.S. hands, *Chambers's* had become the largest and most prestigious general encyclopedia produced in Great Britain. Since 1945, the set has had several owners, most recently International Learning Systems Corporation, Ltd., a subsidiary of the mammoth British Printing Corporation. This same group owns *The New Caxton Encyclopedia,* a heavily illustrated 20-volume set of British make that is distributed in the United States by Purnell Reference Books, a division of Macdonald-Raintree, Inc., in Milwaukee. (See Part III of the *Buying Guide* for a review of *The New Caxton Encyclopedia.*)

The 1975–1976 *Buying Guide* summarized *Chambers's* as follows:

> *Chambers's Encyclopaedia* supplanted *Encyclopaedia Britannica* as the largest and most authoritative British-made adult set when the *Britannica* became an American production in the early 1900s. Today *Chambers's* reputation is maintained by its scholarly, literate treatment of historical subjects, particularly in the fields of biography, geography, and the humanities. Although the set's scope is international, its emphasis is entirely British, a fact which drastically limits its appeal on the American market.
>
> A greater limitation to the set's appeal anywhere is its lack of currency. Unlike most American multivolume encyclopedias, *Chambers's* is not kept up-to-date by continuous revision. Instead, revised editions are issued periodically. During the last ten years, however, no new revision has appeared (only reprints with "corrections"), and at the present time the encyclopedia is dreadfully dated. Much of the historical material remains useful, but unless *Chambers's* soon adopts a realistic revision policy, the set is unlikely to survive. Other deficiencies include unsatisfactory illustrations, inadequate bibliographies, and a generally dull format. In addition, the writing style, although impeccably correct, is simply too learned and academic for most American readers.
>
> American consumers interested in an adult encyclopedia with a British (or different) perspective would do well to look beyond *Chambers's* to *The New Caxton Encyclopedia*, a reasonably current and handsomely illustrated 20-volume set. The *New Caxton* decidedly lacks the depth and historical range of *Chambers's*, but its style and appearance are much more attractive.

Other critical opinions of *Chambers's Encyclopaedia* can be found in the *Booklist*, February 1, 1978, pp. 882–884; *Choice*, October 1967, pp. 793–795; and *Library Journal*, April 15, 1967, pp. 1601–1602 (review by Allan Angoff).

Child's World

The Child's World was an eight-volume topical series for children from the ages of 7 through 14. Not an encyclopedia per se, the set was intended as "supplementary and enrichment material for the home and classroom library." Each volume was devoted to a broad subject of interest to young readers, such as *People and Great Deeds*. In 1977, the publisher, Standard Educational Corporation, reported that *Child's World* "has been discontinued and there are no plans to revive it." It was noted, however, that three volumes of the set—*The World of the Arts, The World and Its Wonders*, and *Plant and Animal Ways*—have been given new covers and incorporated into a book series for young people called *Child Horizons*, also published by Standard Educational Corporation.

The 1975–1976 *Buying Guide* summarized *Child's World* as follows:

> *The Child's World*, designed to enrich and stimulate the intellectual curiosity of young readers, does not purport to be an encyclopedia. It

does, however, provide considerable factual material in the form of biographies, informal surveys of foreign countries, discussions of the arts, instructions for crafts, and descriptions of the natural world. Presentation of this material is not always satisfactory. The writing style varies from volume to volume, factual information is sometimes inaccurate due to error or oversimplification, and the social studies volumes—*People and Great Deeds* and *Countries and Their Children*—present a sugarcoated view of the world. Except for one volume, bibliographies are lacking in the set. The volumes are too tightly bound. On the plus side, *Child's World* is usually well illustrated, and it contains two useful subject guides in the *How to Live with Your Children* volume.

Although *Child's World* is designed for a somewhat more advanced reader than *Childcraft* (which is comparable in purpose and organization), it is not preferable. The consumer considering *Child's World* would be best advised to buy *Childcraft* (the outstanding nonencyclopedic set for children) or one of the better children's encyclopedias (*The New Book of Knowledge, Britannica Junior Encyclopaedia,* or *Young Students Encyclopedia*), depending on the main use to which the set will be put.

Other critical opinions of *Child's World* can be found in the *Booklist,* June 1, 1968, pp. 1101–1105, and *School Library Journal,* September 15, 1966, pp. 210–213 (review by Sarah Law Kennerly).

Columbia Encyclopedia

This highly respected title has been replaced by *The New Columbia Encyclopedia.* For many years regarded by most authorities as the best and unquestionably the most comprehensive one-volume encyclopedia in the English language, it was initially issued in 1935 by the Columbia University Press and underwent major revisions in 1950 and 1963. The 1963 (or third) edition, which comprised some 7½ million words and 75,000 articles in 2,400 pages, became noticeably dated by the early 1970s, and in 1975 *The New Columbia* (technically the fourth edition) appeared. *The Illustrated Columbia Encyclopedia* (see below) and the *Columbia-Viking Desk Encyclopedia* (see below), both of which derived from the 1963 edition, are now also out of print.

Columbia-Viking Desk Encyclopedia

A very carefully edited abridgment of the 1963 *Columbia Encyclopedia* (see above), this handy one-volume encyclopedia first appeared in 1968. It consisted of 1½ million words and some 33,000 concise entries in over 1,200 pages. The title was discontinued in 1974, most likely because the *Columbia* itself was passing from the scene. Whether there will be a similar condensed version of *The New Columbia* remains to be seen. Still in print, however, is the ten-volume *Large Type Columbia-Viking Desk Encyclopedia,* a special edition of the *Columbia-Viking* printed in 18-

point type for the partially sighted. It retails for $50 a set from Franklin Watts, Inc. (a subsidiary of Grolier, Inc.), 730 Fifth Ave., New York, NY 10019.

Complete Reference Handbook

A single-volume handbook of general information for home, school, and office use, this title was first published in 1964 and reported out of print in the early 1970s. It consisted of approximately 400,000 words, 5,400 entries, and 270 black-and-white illustrations in 720 pages. The articles were arranged alphabetically under broad topical headings like Philosophy, Religion, Art, and the United States. A work of unexceptional quality, the *Complete Reference Handbook* was revised and published in 1976 under the title *Quick Reference Encyclopedia,* but that work is also now out of print (see below).

Cultural Library

This multivolume children's set was on the market under various titles for over 50 years until it was discontinued in 1969. First published as *Our Wonder World* (1914–1930), it later became the *New Wonder World* (1932–1955), and, when acquired by the Parents Magazine Press in 1959, it was retitled the *New Wonder World Encyclopedia.* Three years later the set was again renamed, this time the *New Wonder World Cultural Library.* Finally in 1965 it became the *Cultural Library.* Designed chiefly for elementary and junior high school students, the set was topically arranged with each volume dealing with a different subject. In all, the ten volumes included 2½ million words, over 3,000 illustrations, and 4,500 pages. Although the set contained much encyclopedic information as well as recreational reading material, it was not considered an important reference work for young people. A lengthy review was published in the *Booklist,* November 1, 1965, pp. 225–234.

Disney's Wonderful World of Knowledge

A thematically arranged 20-volume set for children published by Grolier Educational Corporation in 1973, *Disney's Wonderful World of Knowledge* derived from a 16-volume work published in Italy in 1970 entitled *Enciclopedia Disney. Disney's,* which was aimed principally at the home mail order and school and library markets, sold for $129.50 several years ago. A work of poor quality, the set was criticized for imbalanced coverage, an inconsistent reading level, careless and inappropriate writing, and an inaccurate index. Although Grolier claims *Disney's* is or shortly will be out of print, consumers may well encounter advertising for the set in the future. A detailed analysis of *Disney's* can be found in the *Booklist,* July 15, 1975, pp. 1202–1203.

Dunlop Illustrated Encyclopedia of Facts

This single-volume book of miscellaneous information was issued by Doubleday in 1969 in a hardcover edition. Bantam Books also published a paperback edition in the same year. Containing 864 pages and 2,400 entries, *Dunlop* was a British publication prepared by the same people who produce the *Guinness Book of World Records*. Although well reviewed (see, for example, *Library Journal,* September 1, 1969, p. 2907), the encyclopedia was reported out of print in the early 1970s and has never been revised since that time.

Encyclopedia of World Knowledge

The *Encyclopedia of World Knowledge* was a brief effort (1969–1972) to develop a supermarket edition of the well-known *Lincoln Library of Essential Information.* Issued in 14 quite thin volumes, the set was an almost exact reprint of the material found in the two-volume *Lincoln Library.* It was sold on the book-a-week basis at a total cost of $39.73, which was about 20 percent less than the retail price of the *Lincoln Library* at the time. Why such a commendable project was phased out so quickly is not known for certain, but most likely the decision was influenced by the ruthlessly competitive nature of supermarket encyclopedia selling.

Everyday Reference Library

According to the publisher, J. G. Ferguson Publishing Company of Chicago, this three-volume work subtitled "an encyclopedia of useful information" is temporarily out of print. Intended for general student, office, and family use, the last edition was topically arranged and included about 1½ million words in 1,634 pages. It first appeared under the title *Everyday Reference Library* in a one-volume edition in 1951, although it was published somewhat earlier as *Austin's New Encyclopedia of Usable Information,* a work based on the *Handy Encyclopedia of Useful Information,* edited by Lewis Copeland, who also edited the *Everyday Reference Library* with Lawrence W. Lamm. In 1975 the publisher reported that "a major revision and updating of the set" was in the planning stages. As of late 1980, however, the anticipated revision had not yet appeared. See *Booklist,* March 15, 1966, pp. 669–671, for a review of the *Everyday Reference Library.*

Funk & Wagnalls Standard Reference Encyclopedia

Sold only in supermarkets and via direct mail, this 25-volume set served as the basis for *Funk & Wagnalls New Encyclopedia.* Like the present work, it offered a large quantity of information (9,660 pages, seven million words, 30,000 articles) in a clear, concise style designed to serve student and family needs. The set was published between 1959 and 1971. Prior to that it appeared as the *Universal Standard Encyclopedia* (1954–1958), the *New Funk & Wagnalls Encyclopedia* (1949–1952), and the *Funk & Wagnalls New Standard Encyclopedia of Universal Knowledge* (1931–1943). The latter set was based in part on a famous old work entitled the *New International Encyclopedia,* which Funk & Wagnalls acquired in 1930. The *Funk & Wagnalls Standard Reference Encyclopedia* was also published in a large three-volume edition called the *New Universal Standard Encyclopedia* (see below). Both titles were discontinued with the publication of *Funk & Wagnalls New Encyclopedia* in 1972.

Golden Book Encyclopedia

Published in 1960 and revised in 1969, the *Golden Book Encyclopedia* comprised 16 volumes, 1,536 pages, 1,375 articles, and roughly 600,000 words when it was retired in the late 1970s. The encyclopedia, published by the Golden Press (a division of Western Publishing Company), was written for children aged 7–12.

The 1978 edition of the *Buying Guide* summarized the *Golden Book Encyclopedia* as follows:

> *Golden Book,* a heavily illustrated encyclopedia for young children, has never been known as a work of quality. Topic selection and treatment are both erratic and often superficial, even considering the youngest reader's informational needs. The encyclopedia's usefulness is further diminished because it has not been revised for years. Also, some material in the set is inaccessible due to inadequate indexing and cross-referencing. Even the colored drawings, the set's best feature, are sometimes unsatisfactory in terms of both quality of reproduction and reference value. In practically every respect, *Golden Book* gives the impression of being a third-rate production.

Other critical opinions of *Golden Book* can be found in the *Booklist,* December 15, 1970, pp. 313–317, and *Library Journal,* January 15, 1960, pp. 360–361.

Golden Home and High School Encyclopedia

Principally a supermarket set, this inexpensive 20-volume encyclopedia for young people was published in 1961 by the Golden Press. Derived from the now defunct *Golden Book Encyclopedia* (see above), the set was never revised and went out of print in 1970. It was a small, mediocre work (1½ million words, 6,000 articles, 3,000 pages), distinguished by abundant colorful illustrations and unusually slim volumes. In addition to the supermarket edition, there was a school and library edition in the somewhat more sturdy and attractive Goldencraft binding. The set was also sold as *The Golden High School Encyclopedia* and *The Golden Junior High School Encyclopedia.*

Golden Treasury of Knowledge

Like *The Golden Home and High School Encyclopedia* (see above), this was a low-cost supermarket item from the Golden Press. Consisting of 16 small volumes of less than 100 pages each, it included both informational and recreational reading material for children in the 7-to-14 age group. It, too, was profusely illustrated with some 2,000 drawings in color. First published in 1958 and slightly revised in 1961, the set lacked the quality of the better children's resource libraries. It was reported out of print in the early 1970s.

Great World Encyclopedia

The *Great World Encyclopedia* was an inconsequential single-volume item for students and adults from Great Britain. It consisted of 278 pages, 70 articles, and about 200,000 words. It was distributed in the United States by Two Continents Publishing Group, which went out of business several years ago.

The 1978 edition of the *Buying Guide* summarized *Great World* as follows:

> *Great World* is a one-volume British import of recent vintage which has several agreeable features, namely textual clarity, instructive and attractive illustrations, an appealing format, and acceptable reliability. The problem with the book is that its coverage and treatment of material are very superficial. A general encyclopedia—even of the small one-volume variety—which does not even provide the most rudimentary biographical information about a historical figure like Mao Tse-tung is simply not worth much as a digest of the world's essential knowledge. Another grievous limitation is the encyclopedia's poor index, an absolutely necessary finding device because of the book's topical arrangement. Despite its reasonable price and certain good qualities, *Great World* is too deficient as a general source of encyclopedic knowledge to be of more than marginal value to students and adults.

Other critical opinions of *Great World* can be found in *American Reference Books Annual,* 1977, p. 47 (review by Roberta J. Depp); the *Booklist,* June 15, 1977, pp. 1602–1603; *Library Journal,* May 1, 1977, p. 1003 (review by Dortha H. Skelton); and *Wilson Library Bulletin,* May 1977, p. 782 (review by Charles A. Bunge).

Grolier Encyclopedia

Unrelated to the now also defunct *Grolier Universal Encyclopedia* (see below), the *Grolier Encyclopedia* was published between 1944 and 1963. A major encyclopedia of intermediate size (5½ million words, 28,000 brief entries, some 9,000 illustrations) intended for high school and home use, it first appeared in ten volumes but had grown to 20 by the time it was discontinued. The encyclopedia derived from the British *Harmsworth's Universal Encyclopedia* (1920–1923). In 1931, Doubleday, Doran and Company acquired the American publishing rights and produced a modified version of the set called *Doubleday's Encyclopedia.* A decade later, Grolier, Inc., obtained the rights, and in 1944 the *Grolier Encyclopedia* appeared, continuing for the next 20 years. Thereafter the rights were acquired by the New York firm of H. S. Stuttman Company, Inc., which folded the set into a shortlived project entitled the *Unified Encyclopedia* (see below).

Grolier Universal Encyclopedia

As noted above, this set had no relationship to the *Grolier Encyclopedia,* despite the similarity in titles. Instead, *Grolier Universal* was based directly on the *Encyclopedia International,* an entirely new set when first published in 1963. Indeed, some of the textual and illustrative material in *Grolier Universal* was identical to that found in the *International.* During its rather brief life (1965–1972), *Grolier Universal* also appeared under the titles *Modern Reference Encyclopedia* and the *New Age Encyclopedia.* Why exactly the same encyclopedia was marketed under three different titles was never made clear by the publisher. A set of some substance, *Grolier Universal* aimed to serve the reference needs of secondary school students and families. Toward this end, it was originally priced in the $100 bracket, although this figure had doubled by 1972 when it was withdrawn from the market. The set was first published in ten volumes and later increased to 20. It contained about five million words and 25,000 articles in some 6,500 pages. For a review, see the *Booklist,* June 15, 1965, pp. 961–965.

Hamlyn Younger Children's Encyclopedia

A single-volume item produced in Great Britain for children aged 7–14, the *Hamlyn Younger Children's Encyclopedia* contained only 255 pages and 80,000 words in 24 topically arranged sections. The encyclopedia, distributed in the United States by A & W Publishers, was reported out of print in 1980. The 1978 edition of the *Buying Guide* summarized *Hamlyn Younger* as follows:

> *Hamlyn Younger* is a small, topically arranged one-volume encyclopedia of British origin and flavor which possesses only marginal value as a reference work for children. Its coverage and treatment are frequently shallow, and many topics of interest to young readers are not covered at all. The abundant color drawings provide the encyclopedia with a somewhat enticing page layout, but they are not always useful from an informational standpoint. In sum, *Hamlyn Younger* is a superficial textbook of general knowledge which the inquiring child will find interesting to look at, but unsatisfactory as a source of specific information.

For another critical opinion of *Hamlyn Younger,* see the *Booklist,* March 15, 1977, p. 1121.

Harver Junior World Encyclopedia

Harver Junior World Encyclopedia, a set of 16 very thin volumes designed for children between the ages of 7 and 12, contained a total of 1,350 pages, 1,550 articles, and approximately a million words. A British import, *Harver Junior* initially appeared in 1960, produced by Purnell and Sons, Ltd. (now Macdonald Educational, Ltd.), a member company of the giant British Printing Corporation. The set, which bears no relationship to the adult *Harver World Encyclopedia,* was distributed in the United States by Harver Educational Services, Inc. Never revised, the encyclopedia was reported no longer available in 1977. Late that year, a representative of Macdonald Educational in London informed the *Buying Guide* that *Harver Junior* was in the early stages of being updated. In 1980, the same representative reported that "at present the work is undergoing up-dating and the current edition is going out of print. We do not have any firm dates at present to quote for the new edition." When (and if) the new edition does appear, it will be distributed by Purnell Reference Books, a division of Macdonald-Raintree, Inc., in Milwaukee.

The 1975–1976 *Buying Guide* summarized *Harver Junior* as follows:

> *Harver Junior World Encyclopedia,* a small multivolume set for students at the elementary level, has little to recommend it at this time. Although of British origin, it has been adapted for American and Canadian readers. The set's subject emphasis is clearly natural science, but its correspondingly weak coverage of topics in the humanities and social sciences makes the encyclopedia of little practical use to young students seeking general information in all areas of knowledge. Moreover, the articles are often ambiguous, superficial, or too sketchy. The material is also sometimes unreliable, frequently out-of-date, and poorly arranged for efficient access. The style of presentation, while usually simple, is not always clear. New or difficult vocabulary is not always defined. The set completely lacks bibliographies, and the graphics are merely passable. The physical format could be improved in several respects.
>
> *Harver Junior* should be avoided. Among the smaller children's encyclopedias, the *Young Students Encyclopedia* and the *Modern Century Illustrated Encyclopedia* [now out of print] are clearly superior in almost every respect to *Harver Junior.*
>
> Only the *Golden Book Encyclopedia* and *The Illustrated Encyclopedia for Learning* are of poorer quality than *Harver Junior.*

Other critical opinions of *Harver Junior* can be found in *American Reference Books Annual,* 1973, pp. 105–106 (review by Christine L. Wynar) and the *Booklist,* February 15, 1979, pp. 946–947.

Home University Encyclopedia

Initially published in 1941 and discontinued in 1972, this small and inconsequential multivolume set originated from the old *New York Post World Wide Illustrated Encyclopedia* (1935), which later became the *World Wide Illustrated Encyclopedia* (1937) and was also distributed as the *University Illustrated Encyclopedia.* It first appeared in 15 volumes, but was reduced to 12 when revised in 1961. Comprising four million words, 40,000 specific entries, and 5,000 illustrations in 5,000 pages, the set was published by Books, Inc., a subsidiary of the Publishers Company, Inc., now The Publishers Agency, Inc. In 1972 the publisher reported that the *Home University Encyclopedia* was defunct and would not be revised in the future, in order that the firm might concentrate on its major adult set, *The New American Encyclopedia.*

Illustrated Columbia Encyclopedia

This 22-volume work was a photographic reproduction of the 1963 one-volume *Columbia Encyclopedia* (see above), with some 7,000 new illustrations added. Reported out of print in 1975, it originally appeared in 1967 in both a supermarket edition published by the Rockville House Publishers, Inc., and a school and library edition by Columbia University Press. The illustrations—mostly black-and-white photographs—sometimes lacked clarity, but otherwise the set received high marks for quality (see the *Booklist,* July 1, 1970, pp. 1299–1300). In 1978 the *Illustrated Columbia Encyclopedia* was replaced by *The New Illustrated Columbia Encyclopedia* (see Part III of the *Buying Guide* for a review).

Illustrated Libraries of Human Knowledge

A topically arranged set of 18 volumes, *The Illustrated Libraries of Human Knowledge* was divided into three broad areas or "libraries": *Man in His World Library* (six volumes), *Creative Man Library* (six volumes), and *Man and Science Library* (five volumes). The final volume, a master index, was entitled the *Omni-Topika.* The set comprised nearly 3,000 pages and was handsomely illustrated throughout with resplendent colored photographs. It was intended for general student and adult use. Originally published in 1968 by the London firm of Aldus Books, Ltd., it was issued in a limited edition in this country by Charles E. Merrill Publishing Company. In 1975, Merrill reported the U.S. edition was out of print, noting that Aldus still holds all copyright and distribution rights. Although the set lacked adequate indexing and failed to provide bibliographies for further reading, its articles and illustrations were quite satisfactory. A detailed review appeared in the October 15, 1973, issue of the *Booklist* (pp. 182–184). Because of the fairly recent origin of the set, the possibility exists that it may reappear on the North American market in the future.

International Everyman's Encyclopedia

An English work of good quality published by J. M. Dent & Sons, Ltd., London, this multivolume adult encyclopedia is currently available in its sixth edition (1978) in the United Kingdom and other parts of the English-speaking world (except the United States) under the title *Everyman's Encyclopaedia* (see Appendix C for a brief descriptive note). The encyclopedia first appeared in 1913–1914, the second edition in 1931–1933, the third in 1949–1950, the fourth in 1958, and the fifth in 1967.

The fourth edition was published in the United States as the *Macmillan Everyman's Encyclopedia* and the fifth as the *International Everyman's Encyclopedia.* Neither of these U.S. adaptations of *Everyman's* apparently made much of an impression on the U.S. market. *International*

Everyman's, published here in 1970 in 20 volumes by a Washington, D.C., outfit called Encyclopedia Enterprises, Inc., contained about a million more words than its British parent, the result of an effort to add material that would make the set more relevant to a U.S. readership. Sold exclusively in supermarkets on the book-a-week basis, *International Everyman's* presumably disappeared from the U.S. market in the early 1970s. In 1975, a Dent representative reported that the " 'Americanised' edition of our *Everyman's Encyclopaedia* was indeed published by Encyclopedia Enterprises, Inc.—but this corporation ceased trading three or four years ago and our agreement with them terminated at that time. No new arrangements have been made for American publication of the *International Everyman's Encyclopedia*—although it is my understanding that a quantity of sheets of the existing edition was disposed of cheaply at the time of the demise of Encyclopedia Enterprises and that there may therefore be a few sets still available on the market—but I would think that the supply must be virtually dried up by now."

In all likelihood, this explains why the Reference and Subscription Books Review Committee listed Plaza Merchandising, Inc., as the encyclopedia's distributor in its May 1, 1972, review in the *Booklist.* It might also account for the Committee's erroneous assertion that it was reviewing the *sixth* edition of the set, when in fact it was the fifth.

Ladies' Home Journal Children's Illustrated Encyclopedia for Learning

This 18-volume, 2,124-page juvenile set more closely resembled a child's picture dictionary than an encyclopedia for young people. Garishly illustrated and blandly written, it was remarkably similar in text, design, and quality to the *Illustrated Encyclopedia for Learning,* a 12-volume set currently available from The Publishers Agency. The magazine *Ladies' Home Journal* sponsored the encyclopedia, which was published a volume at a time in the early 1970s by a New York firm called Books and Periodicals, Inc. In 1975, Downe Publishing, Inc., the publisher of *Ladies' Home Journal,* informed the *Buying Guide* that "Books and Periodicals, Inc., is no longer in existence and the encyclopedia itself is no longer in print. The few copies that were left were sold as remainders." See the *Booklist,* May 1, 1971, for a critical note.

Larousse Illustrated International Encyclopedia and Dictionary

A one-volume item for adults, *Larousse Illustrated International Encyclopedia and Dictionary* was a U.S. version of the British *Longmans English Larousse,* a work modeled along the lines of the French *Petit Larousse Illustré. Larousse Illustrated,* which first appeared in 1972 and was reported out of print in 1980, comprised 1,550 pages, 15,000 brief encyclopedic articles (plus 50,000 dictionary entries), and approximately three million words.

The 1978 edition of the *Buying Guide* summarized *Larousse Illustrated* as follows:

Larousse Illustrated is a fact-oriented volume divided into two related parts, a general encyclopedia and a general dictionary. The encyclopedic coverage, which is devoted almost exclusively to people, places, and historical events, is very brief and often superficial. All proper names mentioned in the work have entries in the encyclopedia, whereas all scientific and technical terms used in the text are defined in the dictionary. Thus the book is uniquely self-indexing. *Larousse Illustrated*'s greatest strengths are stylistic clarity and helpful graphics. Its greatest weaknesses are lack of currency and hence diminished reliability. Doubtless the volume would benefit from a thorough editorial overhaul.

Other critical opinions of *Larousse Illustrated* can be found in *American Reference Books Annual*, 1974, p. 24 (review by Christine L. Wynar); the *Booklist*, November 15, 1973, pp. 297–298; and *Wilson Library Bulletin*, February 1973, p. 521 (review by Charles A. Bunge).

Library of Universal Knowledge

Part dictionary, part book of miscellany, this one-volume potpourri was initially published as the *Library of Universal Knowledge* in 1942, although parts or all of it appeared under other titles as early as 1940. Sold by the Chicago firm of Consolidated Book Publishers (also Processing and Books, Inc.), the book was revised in 1961 and discontinued about a decade later. It appeared to be a scissors-and-paste job, actually four books published in a single volume, including *Webster's Comprehensive Encyclopedic Dictionary* (which was not *the* Webster's). The work contained some 1,700 pages, was clumsily arranged, and claimed to be a "practical self-educator."

Little and Ives Illustrated Ready Reference Encyclopedia

This supermarket set of 20 slim volumes (3,000 pages, two million words, 7,000 colored illustrations) first appeared in 1961. It was, however, almost certainly based on an earlier work entitled the *Illustrated Encyclopedia of the Modern World*. When the publisher, the New York firm of Little and Ives, faltered in the mid-1960s, the rights to the set that bore the company's name were acquired by Grosset and Dunlap, Inc. Grosset subsequently revised the set and reissued it in 1968 as a single-volume item called the *New University One-Volume Encyclopedia,* now also defunct (see below). Both works were of marginal quality.

McKay One-Volume International Encyclopedia

Similar in purpose and format to the *Columbia-Viking Desk Encyclopedia,* also discontinued some years ago (see above), this Americanized version of the British *Hutchinson's New 20th Century Encyclopedia* (1970) was reported out of print in 1975. Published by David McKay Co., Inc., the volume comprised over a million words and some 17,000 concise entries in 1,140 pages. It also provided an unusually large number of illustrations for a one-volume encyclopedia—over 1,500, mostly small black-and-white photographs and line drawings. The principal criticism of the book as a reference work for U.S. users was its distinct British orientation, although efforts had been made to revise it for use in the United States and Canada. See reviews in *American Reference Books Annual,* 1972, p. 76 (review by Bohdan S. Wynar); the *Booklist,* June 15, 1972, pp. 866–868; *Library Journal,* March 1, 1971, p. 820 (review by Louis Barron); and *RQ,* Fall 1971, p. 82. Consumers should note that the *New Hutchinson 20th Century Encyclopedia* appeared in 1977 and was briefly available in the United States (see below), but no attempt had been made to Americanize the work (as *McKay One-Volume International Encyclopedia* did for the 1970 edition of *Hutchinson's*).

Modern Century Illustrated Encyclopedia

The *Modern Century Illustrated Encyclopedia* was a 24-volume set for children between the ages of 7 and 14 that comprised some 2,300 pages, 2,000 articles, and over a million words. Published in 1972 by McGraw-Hill Far Eastern Publishers, Ltd., of Singapore, *Modern Century* appeared in both hardcover and paperbound editions. At various times, several U.S. distributors were involved, including Dell Publishing Company, Inc. (New York). Never revised, the encyclopedia was remaindered by Scholastic Book Services at the bargain price of $19.97 for the paperback set, which was boxed. Quite possibly, *Modern Century* will continue to be encountered in discount stores at cut-rate per volume prices for some time to come. As far as the *Buying Guide* can determine, there are no plans at present for an updated edition of *Modern Century*. Note, however, that the encyclopedia remains in print in England under the title *Encyclopedia Apollo* (see Appendix C for details).

The 1975–1976 *Buying Guide* summarized *Modern Century* as follows:

> The *Modern Century Illustrated Encyclopedia* is a competently produced set for young people. It provides balanced, reliable, impartial, and relatively current information on many topics covered in American and Canadian elementary and secondary schools, as well as subjects of extracurricular interest. Treatment is frequently as extensive as that found in the larger children's sets, such as *The New Book of Knowledge* and *Britannica Junior Encyclopaedia*. In other instances, treatment is very brief and lacks precise detail. There is also a dearth of how-to-do-it information, and little effort has been made to stimulate the reader's curiosity or challenge the reader to pursue a subject further. Indeed, the writing style, while comprehensible to average students in the upper elementary and junior high school grades, is quite dry and uninspiring. No bibliographies are provided to encourage further study.
>
> Other deficiencies include an inadequate general index, the lack of any revision since the set's initial publication in 1972, mediocre visual aids and graphic design, and the omission of pronunciation informa-

tion. Perhaps the most attractive feature of *Modern Century* is its bargain price. Unquestionably, the buyer receives value for his dollar.

The set obviously cannot compare in terms of scope and overall design with the two outstanding large children's sets (*The New Book of Knowledge* and *Britannica Junior*), nor is it as creatively made as the comparably sized *Young Students Encyclopedia*, the best all-around set in the small children's category. But money-conscious consumers would do well to compare *Modern Century* with these better (although more expensive) sets in terms of specific informational needs. If all that is required is an authoritative, matter-of-fact summary of basic general knowledge for young people, *Modern Century* is a good buy. If more is desired, *Modern Century* is not a good buy, even at its low price.

Another critical opinion of *Modern Century* can be found in the *Booklist*, April 1, 1974, pp. 835–836.

My First Golden Encyclopedia

This little single-volume work of 384 pages, 650 articles, and 70,000 words was published in 1969 by Golden Press, a division of Western Publishing Company, Inc. The encyclopedia, intended for very young children aged 4–8, was reported out of print in 1980.

The 1978 edition of the *Buying Guide* summarized *My First Golden Encyclopedia* as follows:

> *My First Golden Encyclopedia* is the peewee among general encyclopedias. It is included in the *Buying Guide* for those consumers who might be seeking a very small, very elementary, and very inexpensive beginning encyclopedia for their children. Obviously, as the book's statistical profile readily shows, its scope and coverage are quite limited and its actual value as a reference work in the literal sense is practically nil. It is more accurately a picture dictionary for children rather than an encyclopedia. Nevertheless, preschoolers and first graders just beginning to read will find *My First Golden* both stimulating and instructive. The foreword to the book observes that "Mrs. Watson has managed to present a great deal of basically complex information in a way that will fascinate children as much as their favorite bedtime story." This is an accurate description of the book and its potential value.

My First Golden Learning Library

This colorful young children's set appeared in 16 volumes. They were incredibly thin books containing only 24 pages each, or a total of 384 pages for the entire set. Designed for beginning readers in kindergarten or the early primary grades, the set provided about 600 very simply written entries printed in large type, accompanied by color illustrations throughout. While attractive to youngsters, the set had little or no true reference value. The publisher, Western Publishing Company, reported it out of print in 1970. *My First Golden Encyclopedia,* a one-volume reprint, is now also out of print (see above).

National Encyclopedia

An encyclopedia with a checkered history, this medium-sized set intended for student and family use was initially published in 11 volumes by P. F. Collier and Company in 1932. Modestly successful, it continued under the Collier imprint until 1950, at which time the firm replaced it with the larger and vastly superior *Collier's Encyclopedia.* The *National Encyclopedia*—now in 20 volumes comprising 7,800 pages, seven million words, and 33,000 articles—was subsequently acquired by an outfit named Educational Enterprises, Inc., then located in Washington, D.C.

All available evidence suggests that Educational Enterprises continued to sell the set for the next 20 years without revising it in any meaningful way, except to update the copyright page. Indeed, the set may still be on the market, although the publisher is no longer at its last known address (125 Ellison St., Paterson, N.J.). In the March 1, 1968, issue of the *Booklist,* it was reported that the *National Encyclopedia* at that time was sold only as part of a package deal that included, among other items, a yearbook, a research service, several children's sets, a dictionary, a medical encyclopedia, an atlas, and a bookcase. It is presumed that this combination offer is no longer available and that the *National Encyclopedia* is, as it should be, defunct. But if the set should surface again, or if it should be encountered on the secondhand market, encyclopedia consumers are herewith warned *not* to purchase it under any circumstances without first thoroughly checking the recency of its contents.

New Century Book of Facts

Similar in purpose and design to *The Lincoln Library of Essential Information,* this single-volume encyclopedic handbook compressed much miscellaneous information into its 1,800 pages. It first appeared in 1902 as the *Century Book of Facts,* was revised and retitled the *New Century Book of Facts* in 1909, and thereafter was published in periodic new editions until the early 1970s when it was discontinued, at least temporarily. The Continental Publishing Company, which acquired the book around 1963, scheduled a revised edition for 1972, but it never materialized.

New College Encyclopedia

Advertised in the September 1, 1978, issue of the *Booklist* (page 71) as "brand new," this one-volume encyclopedia for students and adults apparently came and went like a comet. Arranged alphabetically and illustrated with numerous full-color graphics, the 960-page *New College Encyclopedia* was published by Galahad Books and distributed by A & W Promotional Book Corporation. The volume listed for $39.95 but was widely remaindered at half that price by Quality Books, Inc., and other dealers. It is distinctly possible that consumers will continue to encounter the *New College Encyclopedia* in discount stores, secondhand bookstores, and the like for some time to come. The volume should be carefully examined prior to purchase for scope of coverage, quality of contributors, reliability, recency, accessibility, graphics, physical format, etc. To the best of the *Buying Guide*'s knowledge, the encyclopedia has never been submitted to anyone for review.

New Golden Encyclopedia

The word *Golden* in an encyclopedia title inevitably means a young people's set. It also signifies a Western Publishing Company product, Golden Press Division. This particular title—like *My First Golden Learning Library* (see above)—was a very small one-volume encyclopedia for beginning readers that consisted of 155 colorfully illustrated pages. Of minimal value as a child's reference resource, it was first issued in 1946, underwent a revision in 1963, and was phased out a decade or so later.

New Human Interest Library

A work of both limited quality and size (seven volumes, 2,800 pages, 1½ million words, 3,000 illustrations), this topically arranged set initially appeared in 1914 as the *Human Interest Library*. Fourteen years later it became the *New Human Interest Library*. In 1938 it was acquired by Books, Inc., which continued to publish the set until its demise in 1972. The last printings carried the imprint of the International Book Corporation, a Miami (Florida) distributor.

New Hutchinson 20th Century Encyclopedia

This single-volume encyclopedia for students and adults is a standard reference item in Great Britain, where it has been published for over 30 years by Hutchinson & Co. of London. The work originally appeared in 1948 as *Hutchinson's Twentieth Century Encyclopedia* and underwent minor revisions in 1951, 1956, and 1964. In 1970, the heavily revised fifth edition was retitled *Hutchinson's New 20th Century Encyclopedia,* and in 1977, the sixth edition, also fully revised, appeared as the *New Hutchinson 20th Century Encyclopedia.* For a brief time, the sixth edition was distributed in the United States by the Merrimack Book Service in Salem, N.H., but in 1980 it ceased to be available. For reviews of the sixth edition, see *American Reference Books Annual,* 1979, p. 34 (review by Frances Neel Cheney); the *Booklist,* April 1, 1979, pp. 1233–1234; and *Wilson Library Bulletin,* January 1979, p. 408. Note also that the fifth edition of *Hutchinson* (1970) was published in an Americanized version entitled the *McKay One-Volume International Encyclopedia,* which of course is no longer available (see above).

New Masters Pictorial Encyclopedia

This extremely poor-quality encyclopedia was published in various formats by an equally varied group of booksellers. As far as can be determined, it was first marketed as an eight-volume, chain-store set under the imprint of the Walton Educational Plan, an outfit in Chicago. Over the years the set turned up as part of several combination deals available through mail-order stores and supermarkets. One such package offered the *New Masters Pictorial Encyclopedia* along with a multivolume dictionary and history of civilization. The set also appeared at one point in an inexpensive paperbound edition. The last known printing was issued by the Publishers Company (also of Chicago) and a subsidiary, Books, Inc. The set contained approximately 20,000 short entries in 2,000 pages with about 1,000 illustrations. In almost every respect, the set conspicuously failed to meet even the minimum standards of quality expected of a general encyclopedia.

New Universal Standard Encyclopedia

Published in three excessively large and unwieldy volumes, this encyclopedia was identical in contents to the now discontinued 25-volume *Funk & Wagnalls Standard Reference Encyclopedia* (see above). There was only one known printing (1968), which bore Funk & Wagnalls' imprint and was originally sold by that company as a direct-mail special edition. Later, American Plantations, Inc. (Hialeah, Florida), became the distributor. According to American Plantations, the encyclopedia was discontinued some years ago when the remaining stock—some 6,500 copies—was sold to a secondhand bookstore in New York City.

New University One-Volume Encyclopedia

Newly published in 1968, this desk encyclopedia derived from an earlier work, the small 20-volume *Little and Ives Illustrated Ready Reference Encyclopedia,* a chain-store set now also discontinued (see above). The one-volume version contained approximately 20,000 concise articles in 830 pages; there were no illustrations. Not an outstanding encyclopedia but reasonably useful for quick reference, it appeared under the imprint of Grosset and Dunlap, Inc., a New York firm. Apparently, however, the rights have since been acquired by Ottenheimer Publishers, Inc., of Baltimore, Md., who reported the title out of print in 1975. It is entirely possible that the *New University One-Volume Encyclopedia* will be revised and reissued in the future.

Our Wonderful World

This unique 18-volume set of books for young people more closely resembled an encyclopedic anthology than a true encyclopedia. Organized by broad knowledge areas that were subdivided into nearly 400 thematic units, the set included much material excerpted from previously published books, periodical articles, pamphlets, and the like. A fairly sizable set (8,500 pages, 4½ million words, 4,000 basic articles), it was profusely illustrated with drawings specially commissioned for the set, as well as many color and black-and-white photographs. Indeed, the editors believed that it was the best and most heavily illustrated work of its kind.

The set was prepared under the editorial direction of Herbert Zim, a noted children's book author, and first published in 1955–1957 by the Spencer Press, then a Sears, Roebuck and Company affiliate. For a time, the set was sold exclusively through Sears, Roebuck's retail stores and mail-order division. In 1961 Grolier, Inc., acquired *Our Wonderful World*, publishing it until the set's unexpected demise in 1972. Unlike many works that have been discontinued over the past 21 years, *Our Wonderful World* was genuinely lamented by those who recognize quality reference works in the children's and young adult category. An unusual and sometimes fascinating set, it was included on many authoritative lists of recommended works. See the *Booklist,* April 1, 1964, pp. 711–716, for a lengthy critical assessment of *Our Wonderful World.* An informative review also appeared in *Library Journal,* September 15, 1964, pp. 3503–3504.

Quick Reference Encyclopedia

A revision of the *Complete Reference Handbook* (1964), the *Quick Reference Encyclopedia* was a one-volume item for students and adults published by Thomas Nelson, Inc., in 1976. The 880-page volume consisted of 29 topical sections plus a number of appendixes. Coverage emphasized English-language skills and business writing in particular, although much general encyclopedia information was included. The encyclopedia was reported out of print in 1980.

The 1978 edition of the *Buying Guide* summarized the work as follows:

> *Quick Reference* is a recent revision of *The Complete Reference Handbook,* a mediocre one-volume desk item originally published in 1964. The book's most distinctive quality is the large amount of space (35 percent of the total text) it devotes to various aspects of grammar and language usage, with particular emphasis on business English. The remainder of the book is heavily weighted toward humanities subjects, like art, philosophy, and religion. Except for U.S. history and government, the social and behavioral sciences are entirely ignored, as are most natural and technical science topics. The encyclopedia's best feature is its clear, straightforward style. Its worst feature is poor accessibility, due to a topical arrangement, a muddled index, and no cross-references. Overall, *Quick Reference* is simply too uneven and too awkwardly constructed to be of more than minimal value as a small general encyclopedia.

Another critical opinion of *Quick Reference* can be found in *American Reference Books Annual,* 1978, p. 54 (review by Donald G. Davis, Jr.).

Rand McNally Student Encyclopedia

The *Rand McNally Student Encyclopedia in Color,* a topically arranged one-volume item for young adults, initially appeared in a British version entitled *The Hamlyn Children's Encyclopedia in Colour,* published by the Hamlyn Publishing Group, Ltd. (London). This same firm produced the companion *Hamlyn Younger Children's Encyclopedia* (1972), which was distributed for a time in the United States by A & W Publishers, Inc., but is now out of print (see above). In 1972, Rand McNally & Company (Chicago) issued a U.S. adaptation of *Hamlyn Children's Encyclopedia* under the title *Rand McNally Student Encyclopedia in Color*. A work of minimal consequence, the book contained six topical sections in 544 pages and totaled approximately 300,000 words. Apparently there are no plans at present to revise the encyclopedia, and in 1977 Rand McNally reported that the title had been phased out.

The 1975–1976 *Buying Guide* summarized *Rand McNally Student Encyclopedia in Color* as follows:

> The *Rand McNally Student Encyclopedia* has very limited value as a reference work. It is attractive, reliable, reasonably objective, and relatively up-to-date for a 1972 publication. As a textbook or browsing item, it might be quite useful to young people. But, because its scope is largely restricted to summarizing elementary information readily available elsewhere, and because it is not successfully organized for maximum retrieval of that information which it does contain, the encyclopedia is a poor buy, despite its extremely low price. At the present time, there is no other one-volume work available in the young adult category. For this reason, consumers seeking an inexpensive encyclopedia for students in the 9-to-18 age group should either turn to a low-cost one-volume adult title, such as *The Cadillac Modern Encyclopedia*, or consider investing in one of the less expensive multivolume young adult sets, for instance, *Compton's Encyclopedia* or the *American Educator*.

Other critical opinions of *Rand McNally Student Encyclopedia in Color* can be found in *American Reference Books Annual*, 1973, p. 108 (review by Christine L. Wynar) and *Wilson Library Bulletin*, December 1972, p. 363 (review by Charles A. Bunge).

Richards Topical Encyclopedia

A topically arranged set for young children, this encyclopedia first appeared in 1933 as the *Richards Cyclopedia*, a 12-volume work published by J. A. Richards, Inc., of New York. Six years later it was revised, enlarged, and retitled *Richards Topical Encyclopedia*. In the mid-1940s, Grolier, Inc., acquired the Richards firm and continued to publish the encyclopedia until 1962. By that time the set, now expanded to 15 volumes comprising 8,664 pages and 4½ million words, had become largely dated. Instead of revising the set, Grolier arranged for the H. S. Stuttman Company to merge *Richards Topical Encyclopedia* with the defunct *Grolier Encyclopedia* (see above), creating the 30-volume *Unified Encyclopedia* (see below), a short-lived venture that petered out by the mid-1960s.

Standard International Encyclopedia

This title has a somewhat involved history. Issued in 1970 as a "new" work, the *Standard International Encyclopedia* in fact bore an unmistakable likeness to the 1964 edition of *The New American Encyclopedia,* which derived from the old *World Scope Encyclopedia* (see below). Both the *New American Encyclopedia* and the *Standard International* contained some five million words and 26,000 articles, although the *New American* had 16 volumes whereas the *Standard International* was compressed into two. The latter was published by the United Publishing Corporation, a subsidiary of the Publishers Company, Inc., a firm that owned and marketed the *World Educator Encyclopedia* (see below) and the *World University Encyclopedia* (see below), both verbatim reprints of the 1964 *New American Encyclopedia.* All of these titles are no longer in print. The *Standard International Encyclopedia* disappeared from the scene in 1972.

Unified Encyclopedia

The *Unified Encyclopedia* was an unfortunate blend of two outdated, mediocre encyclopedias. In 1960 by arrangement with Grolier, Inc., which held title to both sets, the New York firm of H. S. Stuttman Company, Inc., merged *Richards Topical Encyclopedia* (see above) with the alphabetically arranged *Grolier Encyclopedia* (see above). When completed, this hybrid reference work—the *Unified Encyclopedia*—comprised about six million words and 32,500 articles in 30 volumes. It came as no surprise when the set was phased out in 1964.

Universal World Reference Encyclopedia

A 16-volume set of very poor quality published by Consolidated Book Publishers, a Chicago firm, the *Universal World Reference Encyclopedia* first appeared in 1945 as "20 volumes in 10." Earlier the set had been published as the *Standard American Encyclopedia* (1937–1941), a 15-volume work. In 1942, this set was revised and issued as the *International World Reference Encyclopedia* in ten volumes. Three years later the set was again revised and retitled as the *Universal World Reference Encyclopedia,* a set comprising 16 volumes, 6,300 pages, 4½ million words, and some 40,000 entries (if cross-references are included). The set was revised only once (1958) between 1945 and 1975, and even that revision was not a thorough overhaul. In the late 1960s, Consolidated indicated that a major revision would occur in or around 1970, but the project fell through. Again, in 1972, the publisher announced the set would be substantially revised by 1974, but again this was never implemented. Finally, in 1975, Consolidated reported that the *Universal World Reference Encyclopedia* had been discontinued, with no immediate plans to rejuvenate the set. Other critical reviews of the encyclopedia can be found in *American Reference Books Annual,* 1971, p. 68 (review by Bohdan S. Wynar), and the *Booklist,* April 1, 1965, pp. 717–722.

University Society Encyclopedia

The *University Society Encyclopedia,* published in 20 volumes by the University Society, Inc., of Midland Park, N.J., is actually one and the same as the *American Peoples Encyclopedia,* a now defunct set once published by Grolier, Inc. (see above). The possibility exists that some independent encyclopedia representatives may still be selling the *University Society Encyclopedia* in certain parts of the country. Consumers are hereby warned to avoid the set, which was mediocre to begin with and is now very dated. See the critical notes on the set under *American Peoples Encyclopedia* above.

Wonderland of Knowledge

A clearly and simply written 12-volume encyclopedia for children, the *Wonderland of Knowledge* covered some 6,000 broad topics derived from elementary school curricula. It first appeared in 15 volumes in 1937, issued under the imprint of Publishers Productions, Inc., a subsidiary of the United Educators, Inc., publisher of the *American Educator Encyclopedia* (now also defunct; see above). Although it was not an outstanding work, *Wonderland* had steadily improved over the years, particularly under the editorship of Everett Edgar Sentman, who had also served as the *American Educator*'s editor in chief for many years. The set totaled 6,000 pages, over three million words, and about 7,500 illustrations. In 1975, *Wonderland* was discontinued. According to United Educators, it is now in the process of being completely reconstructed, both editorially and graphically. A new edition had been anticipated for sometime in the late 1970s, but as of the end of 1980 it had not appeared. If *Wonderland of Knowledge* does indeed reappear, it will most likely be retitled and geared to the supermarket trade.

World Educator Encyclopedia

This 12-volume set was identical in text to the 16-volume 1964 edition of *The New American Encyclopedia,* although the binding and, of course, the number of volumes differed. The *World Educator* also had the same text as the *World University Encyclopedia* (see below), another exact reprint of the 1964 *New American Encyclopedia.* All these sets were published by the Publishers Company, Inc., of Washington, D.C., or its subsidiary, Books, Inc. Likewise, all were virtually identical to an earlier work, the *World Scope Encyclopedia* (see below), which was published between 1945 and 1963 and possessed an equally labyrinthine ancestry. The *World Educator* and all its incestuous relatives were, at best, mediocre encyclopedias.

World Scope Encyclopedia

The *World Scope Encyclopedia*'s publishing history is quite involved and often unclear. As best as can be determined, the set's earliest forebear was the *Teacher's and Pupil's Cyclopaedia,* a four-volume work published in 1902. In 1910, this set became the *New Teacher's and Pupil's Cyclopaedia* in five volumes. Although it continued to appear under that title until 1927, it was also published variously as the *Practical American Encyclopedia* and the *Unrivalled Encyclopedia* in 1911 and as the ten-volume *International Reference Work* between 1923 and 1927. In 1928, the encyclopedia was revised and retitled as the *Progressive Reference Library,* which continued publication until 1939.

After the war, the *Progressive Reference Library* was acquired by the Universal Educational Guild (New York) and reissued, virtually without revision, under the title *World Scope Encyclopedia.* Consisting of 20 volumes in ten (the last two volumes being *Webster's New Illustrated Dictionary*), the set continued until 1963 when the publisher foundered. As pointed out above, *World Scope* was then acquired (in 1964) by a Washington-based firm, Publishers Company, Inc., which immediately reprinted the set under three different titles: *The New American Encyclopedia, The World Educator Encyclopedia,* and the *World University Encyclopedia.* All of these titles are now defunct, with the exception of *The New American Encyclopedia,* which now bears little resemblance to its ancestor, the *World Scope Encyclopedia.*

World University Encyclopedia

A 12-volume encyclopedia designed for student and family use, this set was an exact reprint of the 1964 edition of *The New American Encyclopedia,* which in turn was based on the *World Scope Encyclopedia* (see above). Both works appeared in 1964 under the imprint of the Publishers Company, Inc. While *The New American Encyclopedia* is still on the market, the *World University Encyclopedia* was discontinued in 1972. For a substantive critical review, see the *Booklist,* November 15, 1965, pp. 283–288.

World Wide Encyclopedia

Published in 1967 by Books, Inc., a subsidiary of the Publishers Company, Inc., the *World Wide Encyclopedia* was an inexpensive work of exceedingly poor quality. Relatively small in size (3,200 pages, two million words, 20,000 entries, 1,000 illustrations), it bore no relationship to the several other Publishers Company sets with similar titles, for instance the *World Educator Encyclopedia* (see above). It was, however, adulterated with material extracted from the *American Family Encyclopedia* and the *New Human Interest Library* (both described above). The set, which appeared in both hardcover and paperbound editions, was phased out in the early 1970s.

Young People's Illustrated Encyclopedia

New to the U.S. market in 1972, this inferior 20-volume set designed for elementary school students (particularly grades three through six) was discontinued, at least for the time being, in 1975. It appeared under the imprint of the McGraw-Hill Far Eastern Press (Singapore), was first published in Australia, and was distributed in the United States by the Children's Press in Chicago. A small, comparatively inexpensive set, it contained over 1,500 entries arranged in alphabetical fashion. It also contained numerous factual errors, and the articles were sometimes much too brief. Generally, the illustrations, which were profuse and mostly in color, lacked acceptable clarity or detail.

The *Young People's Illustrated Encyclopedia* was similar in some ways to the *Modern Century Illustrated Encyclopedia,* a 24-volume set now also out of print (see above). McGraw-Hill Far Eastern Press published both sets, both utilized some of the same editorial staff, and both used some of the same illustrative material. There is, however, little likeness between the text of the two encyclopedias, and *Modern Century* was clearly the superior work.

In 1975, Children's Press informed the *Buying Guide* that *Young People's* had been withdrawn from the market as "temporarily" out of print. In early 1976, however, the set was being sold via mail order by Parents' Magazine Book Clubs, Inc. (52 Vanderbilt Ave., New York, NY 10017). In response to an inquiry by the *Buying Guide,* an official of Parents' Magazine Book Clubs noted that "we have the mail order rights granted from Children's Press. However, it is our plan to sell off the remaining stock and not reprint." In 1977, the Children's Press catalog listed *Young People's* as being available for $69.95. The catalog included this information: "Enclosed with every set is our new instructional tape titled How to Use the YOUNG PEOPLE'S ILLUSTRATED ENCYCLOPEDIA." Upon inquiry, a Children's Press representative told the *Buying Guide* in late 1977 that *Young People's* is "definitely out of print and will not be reprinted or revised." The representative also indicated that the Parents' Magazine mail-order campaign had ended. As of late 1980 nothing more has been heard about the set. For other critical opinions of *Young People's,* see *American Reference Books Annual,* 1973, p. 109 (review by Christine L. Wynar), and the *Booklist,* June 15, 1974, pp. 1115–1116.

Appendix B
Encyclopedia Supplements: Almanacs and Yearbooks

The annuals described here contain a wide variety of reliable factual information frequently sought by encyclopedia users. Because they are inexpensive as well as up-to-date, any of these books can serve as an economical updating supplement to a general encyclopedia. All eight described here are recommended for home, library, or office, whether used in conjunction with an encyclopedia or not. Consumers should also be aware that most multivolume encyclopedias have their own annual supplements, or yearbooks. Sometimes overly expensive and often related to the encyclopedia in name only, these yearbooks are usually not a good buy. There are exceptions, however (such as the *Britannica Book of the Year* and the *World Book Year Book*). All such yearbooks currently on the market are briefly evaluated by the *Buying Guide* in the encyclopedia reviews (Parts III–VII) under the heading "Recency."

Hammond Almanac of a Million Facts, Records, Forecasts

Similar in coverage, style, and arrangement to *Information Please Almanac*, the *Reader's Digest Almanac and Yearbook*, and the *World Almanac and Book of Facts*, this 1,040-page annual provides over a million facts about sports, history, religion, government, the arts, countries of the world (with color maps), and the like. The 1980 edition includes such uncommon features as a Wall Street glossary and toll-free telephone numbers for hotels. Edited by Martin A. Bacheller, the *Hammond Almanac* is published each year in November (dated the following year) and sells for $3.95 in paperback (distributed by New American Library) and $6.95 in hardcover (Hammond Almanac, Inc.). It was initially published in 1969 as the *New York Times Encyclopedic Almanac*, then became the *Official Associated Press Almanac* in 1972, the *CBS News Almanac* in 1976, and acquired its present title in 1979.

Information Please Almanac

Published annually since 1947 as an outgrowth of the old-time radio show "Information Please," this popular almanac is now available from Simon & Schuster in both paperback ($3.95) and hardcover ($7.95). The book is sold at newsstands, bookstores, drugstores, etc. Like the other almanacs described here, *Information Please* includes a chronicle of the year's most significant events, emphasizing the national political scene and international developments. About a tenth of the text is given over to brief profiles of the countries of the world. The latest geographical changes are incorporated into each new edition. Beginning in 1978, color maps were added to the volume. The 1980 edition (issued in November of the preceding year) provides a number of new features, including a section on the "new" religions. Much space is devoted to sports, including many lists of record-holders and award-winners. There is also current information on postal rates, tax regulations, legal holidays, marriage and divorce laws, accredited colleges and universities (including tuition costs), religious denominations, the 50 states, the 50 largest U.S. cities, famous people, and much more. An extensive list of words frequently encountered in crossword puzzles is a special feature. Like all the almanacs here (except for *News Dictionary*), the arrangement is topical, with a subject index providing access to specific information.

News Dictionary: An Encyclopedic Summary of Contemporary History

Not as well known as, say, *Information Please* or the *World Almanac*, this excellent digest of the key news stories for a given year has been published by Facts on File under its present title since 1964 (prior to that time it was called *News Year*). The book is available in both a hardcover edition for $14.95 and a paperback edition for $9.95. Unlike the other books included in this section, *News Dictionary* is arranged alphabetically rather than by topic. Thus, to find current information about Africa, agriculture, Argentina, atomic energy, auto racing, or awards, the user consults the "A" section of the book. In this sense, *News Dictionary* is similar to most encyclopedia yearbooks, which are arranged in A-to-Z fashion. Although there is no index, the book contains numerous cross-references and, as the publisher says, is as easy to use "as looking up a word in *Webster's*." Clearly and concisely written, it provides more coverage of the year's news events than other almanacs, but it does not offer the broad range of information on standard subjects (e.g., lists of elected officials, societies and associations, holidays, or academic institutions) that the others do. Recent editions have added photographs.

Reader's Digest Almanac and Yearbook

The *Reader's Digest Almanac and Yearbook* first appeared in 1966 (covering the calendar year 1965) and since that time has become an increasingly popular home and library quick reference source. The book is published by the Reader's Digest Association and distributed to the book trade by W. W. Norton and Company. It still sells for $5.95 and is issued every February (covering the developments of the previous year). Containing over a million words and roughly 450 graphics (including maps) in 1,024 pages, the *Reader's Digest Almanac* begins with a survey article on news events and then covers a variety of broad topics—accidents and disasters, animals, arts, books, climate, Congress, crime, economy, elections, history, language, newspapers and magazines, people in the news, science, sports, travel, and so on—in alphabetical fashion. Population figures and zip codes are included for all U.S. cities and towns of 7,500 or more. The section on language provides helpful information about how to write better and how to build one's vocabulary, along with lists of words by grade level. Likewise, the section on medicine and health will be informative to the average person seeking nontechnical definitions of common diseases and the like. Most charts or tables of data are printed in alternating dark and light backgrounds to facilitate scanning across columns. An excellent 38-page index.

Statistical Abstract of the United States

The preface rightly notes that *Statistical Abstract* "is the standard summary of statistics on the social, political, and economic organization of the United States. It is designed to serve as a convenient volume for statistical reference and as a guide to other statistical publications and sources." Published by the Government Printing Office for the U.S. Bureau of the Census, *Statistical Abstract* has appeared annually since 1878, recently celebrating its centennial edition. Much of the data is presented in the form of charts and tables, many of which provide retrospective statistics for comparative purposes. New editions typically add 100 or so new tables, and there is now a Guide to Sources that lists over 1,000 statistical publications by subject for further reference. Available in both paperback ($9) and hardcover ($12), *Statistical Abstract* has recently added a pocket-sized insert entitled *USA Statistics in Brief,* which supplements the basic volume. The insert sells for 75¢.

Teacher Brothers' Modern-Day Almanac

The newest and least substantial of the annual almanacs described here, the 80-page *Teacher Brothers' Modern-Day Almanac* furnishes a miscellany of useful and entertaining facts on such topics as astronomy, astrology, the weather, medicine, nutrition, automobile fuel consumption, pets, personalities in the news, and holidays. Begun in 1979 and modestly priced at $1 for the paper edition and $5.90 for the hardcover edition, the almanac is sold in bookstores and can be ordered direct from the publisher, Running Press.

U.S. Fact Book: The American Almanac

The *U.S. Fact Book* is actually a verbatim reprint of *Statistical Abstract of the United States* (see above) with some original introductory material added; for example, Ben J. Wattenberg provided an introduction to the 1978 edition of *U.S. Fact Book.* Although both books contain exactly the same statistical material, the *U.S. Fact Book* is a better buy because it costs considerably less ($3.95 in paper; there is no hardcover edition) than *Statistical Abstract.* Also, the *U.S. Fact Book,* which is published by

Grosset & Dunlap, appears about two months prior to the U.S. government's edition. Note that Grosset is able to reprint and sell *Statistical Abstract* under a different title because the book is a government publication and therefore not protected by copyright.

World Almanac and Book of Facts

The oldest and best-known book of its kind, the *World Almanac* first appeared in 1868, a by-product of the *New York World*, then one of Manhattan's leading daily newspapers. Today the *World Almanac* is published by the Newspaper Enterprise Association and distributed to the book trade in paperback by Ballantine Books ($4.50) and in hardcover ($7.95) by Doubleday and Company. It may also be copublished under the name of local newspapers in larger cities. The *World Almanac* is a best-seller among reference books. In fact, it is now listed in the *Guinness Book of Records* as the largest selling single volume after the Bible. Each year roughly 1,500,000 copies are sold. The *World Almanac* is popular for good reason. It not only contains an enormous amount of new factual information in each edition, but also much standard material that is updated and repeated each year. For instance, users can always be assured of finding tables of weights and measures, lists of art galleries and museums, directions about how to apply for passports or patents, instructions for obtaining birth certificates and other vital records, and so forth. In addition, there is information about postal rates, income tax schedules and exemptions for both state and federal government, marriage and divorce laws, legal holidays, colleges and universities, mayors and city managers, the languages of the world, magazines and newspapers—basic information that people constantly need. A special feature is the listing of all U.S. places of 5,000 or more with zip codes. New features are added every year; for instance, the 1980 edition (published in November 1979) includes material on the safety of nuclear power plants, a glossary of Chinese names and places, and a review of the 1970s. A detailed 33-page index is found at the front of the almanac. Students interested in the history of the *World Almanac* should consult John Tebbel's informative article "A Century of 'The World Almanac' " in *Saturday Review*, December 9, 1967, pp. 62–63.

Appendix C
Encyclopedias in the United Kingdom

Appendix C of the *Buying Guide* identifies the principal general English-language encyclopedias, multivolume and small-volume, currently sold in the United Kingdom (England, Scotland, Wales, and Northern Ireland). In addition, most of the encyclopedias noted here are marketed in the Commonwealth nations (including Canada and Australia) as well as such English-speaking countries as Ireland and South Africa.

Prices quoted here are for the most part taken from *British Books in Print* (1981 edition). Normally, schools and libraries receive a substantial discount. Consumers are advised to check with individual publishers for current price information.

Of the 26 encyclopedias included in this section, 20 are evaluated in the *Buying Guide*, either in the review portion (Parts III–VII) or Appendix A (which covers discontinued titles). In the case of the six encyclopedias not treated elsewhere (e.g., *Arthur Mee's New Children's Encyclopedia*), a brief critical note is provided here. Concise reviews of many of the encyclopedias available in the United Kingdom can also be obtained in these publications: "Battling Hard from A to Z" by Ken Creffield in the London (England) *Observer*, April 10, 1977; "Checking the Facts" by Nicholas Tucker in the Manchester (England) *Guardian*, May 29, 1979; and *Encyclopedia Ratings 1981* (4th ed., 1981) by James P. Walsh. The latter publication is a 9½ × 14-inch folded chart that succinctly evaluates and rates 20 general encyclopedias on the British market. The chart sells for 80 pence (about $1.50) and can be acquired from Reference Books Research Publications, 51 High St., Croydon, England CRO 1QD.

Arthur Mee's New Children's Encyclopedia

This 20-volume encyclopedia for children aged 7–14 first appeared in 1910 as the *Children's Encyclopedia*, the British counterpart of the *Book of Knowledge* (now *The New Book of Knowledge;* see review in Part VI of the *Buying Guide*). The *Children's Encyclopedia*, widely recognized as the first modern encyclopedia for young people, was edited by Arthur Mee (1875–1943), and eventually the set became known as *Arthur Mee's Children's Encyclopedia*. In 1975, under the editorial direction of Grolier, Inc. (a U.S. firm with international holdings), a revamped and modernized edition appeared under the title *Arthur Mee's New Children's Encyclopedia*.

The set has not been revised since 1975. Topically arranged, it comprises some 4,000 pages, 7,500 illustrations, and roughly 1½ million words in 20 volumes. British in flavor and emphasis, *Arthur Mee's* has been criticized for its limited scope, unhandy arrangement, deficient index, lack of bibliographies, and lack of continuous revision. Priced at £140, the set is available from Franklin Watts Ltd., 8 Cork St., London, England W1X 2HA.

Chambers's Encyclopaedia

Currently the largest British-made encyclopedia available, *Chambers's* is an advanced adult set comprising nearly 13,000 pages, 28,000 articles, and 14½ million words in 15 volumes. Unfortunately, the encyclopedia has not been significantly revised since 1966. It has been withdrawn from the U.S. market and, according to Ken Creffield in the London *Observer* (April 10, 1977), the situation is not much better in Great Britain: "Chambers, once Britain's most prestigious encyclopaedia, is in sad decline. It is virtually unobtainable, although a few shops still have sets gathering dust." The encyclopedia is officially priced at £290 in the U.K., but apparently it has been remaindered for as low as £100. The set is now published by Caxton Publications Ltd., Holywell House, 72–90 Worship St., London, England EC2 2EN. See Appendix A of the *Buying Guide* for an evaluation of *Chambers's*.

Children's Britannica

Like *Arthur Mee's New Children's Encyclopedia* (see above), the *Children's Britannica* is a British-made set for young people aged 7–14. First published in 1960 in two volumes, the encyclopedia has now grown to 20 volumes comprising approximately 6,500 pages, 2,500 articles, and 6,000 illustrations. The set resembles the U.S.-made *Britannica Junior Encyclopaedia* (see Part VI of the *Buying Guide*), particularly in terms of layout and typography, but they are not the same encyclopedia. Nor is the *Children's Britannica* a "junior" version of *The New Encyclopaedia Britannica* (formerly *Encyclopaedia Britannica*). Overall, the *Children's Britannica* is not a work of high quality. Its scope is quite limited, the coverage sketchy, the indexing inadequate, the illustrations undistinguished, and revisions too occasional. Priced at £120, the set is published by Encyclopaedia Britannica International Ltd., 156 Oxford St., London, England W1N OHJ.

Collier's Encyclopedia

This U.S.-made multivolume encyclopedia for adults is fully described and evaluated in Part III of the *Buying Guide*. In the U.K. it is distributed by P. F. Collier Ltd., Rawplug House, 147 London Rd., Kingston, Surrey, England KT2 6BR. The current price is £592.

Compton's Encyclopedia

This U.S.-made multivolume encyclopedia for young adults is fully described and evaluated in Part V of the *Buying Guide*. In the U.K. it is distributed by Encyclopaedia Britannica International Ltd., 156 Oxford St., London, England W1N OHJ. The current price is £126.

Encyclopedia Americana

This U.S.-made multivolume encyclopedia for adults is fully described and evaluated in Part III of the *Buying Guide*. In the U.K. it is distributed by Franklin Watts Ltd., 8 Cork St., London, England W1X 2HA. The current price is £350.

Encyclopedia Apollo

An inconsequential 14-volume set for children aged 7–14, *Encyclopedia Apollo* was originally published in the early 1970s by McGraw-Hill Far Eastern Publishers Ltd. of Singapore. The encyclopedia, which contains some 2,300 pages, 2,000 articles, and over a million words, is currently available from Niles & Mackenzie Ltd., 43 Dover St., London, England W1X 3RE, at £56. For a time it was marketed in the United States as the *Modern Century Illustrated Encyclopedia* (in 24 volumes). For an evaluation, see Appendix A of the *Buying Guide* under that title.

Encyclopedia International

This U.S.-made multivolume encyclopedia for young adults is fully described and evaluated in Part V of the *Buying Guide*. In the U.K. it is distributed by Franklin Watts Ltd., 8 Cork St., London, England W1X 2HA. The current price is £250.

Everyman's Encyclopaedia

Along with the *New Caxton Encyclopedia* (see below), *Everyman's* is currently the best British-produced encyclopedia on the market. Written in scholarly prose suitable only for adults and advanced students, the 12-volume set comprises nearly 9,000 pages, 50,000 concise articles, 5,600 black-and-white graphics, and roughly eight million words. *Everyman's* was first published in 1913–1914 by J. M. Dent & Sons Ltd. Dent has subsequently issued revised editions in 1931–1933, 1949–1950, 1958, 1967, and, most recently, 1978. The 1978 sixth edition, which reputedly cost the publisher £1 million (about $2 million), constitutes a thorough revision of the text from top to bottom, including a larger format and new illustrations throughout. While recognized as a reliable and authoritative source of basic information (the 350 contributors are mostly British academics), *Everyman's* can be faulted for its omission of an index, staid appearance, and lack of annual continuous revision.

The fourth edition (1958) of the encyclopedia was sold in the United States as the *Macmillan Everyman's Encyclopedia* and the fifth (1967) as the *International Everyman's Encyclopedia,* both of which have long since disappeared from the market (see Appendix A). The new sixth edition (1978), however, is not generally available in the United States. According to a Dent representative (in *Publishers Weekly,* January 8, 1979, p.

44), "There are really too many American encyclopedias for us to publish an edition there." He also noted that "clearing the rights on pictures would add perhaps another £10,000 to £20,000 to the editorial bill." But the set, currently priced at £234, is sold in practically all other parts of the English-speaking world. In the U.K., consumers should contact J. M. Dent & Sons Ltd., 33 Welbeck St., London, England W1M 8LX; in Canada the address is J. M. Dent & Sons (Canada) Ltd., 100 Scarsdale Rd., Don Mills, Ontario M3B 2R8.

Joy of Knowledge Encyclopedia

Brand-new in 1977–1978, this heavily illustrated, topically arranged 10-volume set for students and adults contains approximately 3,000 pages, 26,000 articles, 14,000 graphics, and 3½ million words. The *Joy of Knowledge* is published in the U.K. by Mitchell Beazley Ltd., 14 Manette St., London, England W1V 5LB. Each volume retails for £14.95, or £149.50 the set. There is also a two-volume edition now available at £69.50. The *Joy of Knowledge* is published in the United States as *The Random House Encyclopedia* in a one-volume trade edition and a two-volume school and library edition. See Part IV of the *Buying Guide* for an evaluation.

Junior Pears Encyclopaedia

This British-made one-volume annual for elementary school children is fully described and evaluated in Part VII of the *Buying Guide. Junior Pears,* an offspring of the famous *Pears Cyclopaedia* (see below), is published by Pelham Books Ltd., 44 Bedford Sq., London, England WC1B 3DU, at £3.50.

Larousse Illustrated International Encyclopedia and Dictionary

According to the preface, this single-volume work for adults is "an American equivalent of *Petit Larousse Illustré.*" Priced at £10.75, *Larousse Illustrated* is distributed in the U.K. by McGraw-Hill Book Co. (U.K.) Ltd., McGraw-Hill House, Shoppenhangers Rd., Maidenhead, Berkshire, England SL6 2QL. No longer in print in the United States, the book is briefly evaluated in Appendix A of the *Buying Guide.*

Library of Knowledge Colour Encyclopedia

The *Library of Knowledge* (no relation to the *Joy of Knowledge* noted above) is a small, ineffective British-made encyclopedia for children aged 7–14. Last published in 1976, the nine-volume set comprises some 1,440 pages, 2,000 articles, 2,000 illustrations, and one million words. Aside from being colorful and sometimes interestingly written, the *Library of Knowledge* has little to offer the young reader. Specifically, its coverage is sketchy and uneven, the index is inadequate, there are no bibliographies, and revisions are infrequent. The set is published by Aldus Books Ltd., 17 Conway St., London, England W1P 6BS. It currently sells for £35.55.

Macmillan Children's Encyclopedia

Now in its second edition (1980), the *Macmillan Children's Encyclopedia* is a two-volume set totaling 993 pages published in Great Britain for children aged 6–12 (or a somewhat younger readership than that assumed for *Junior Pears Encyclopaedia* noted above). The set contains numerous color illustrations, but they are not always as informative as users might like. The printed text also leaves something to be desired, being superficial in coverage and given to sweeping generalizations. Priced at £14.95, the encyclopedia is published by Macmillan London Ltd., Little Essex St., London, England WC2R 3LF.

Macmillan Family Encyclopedia

This U.S.-made, Dutch-financed set—entitled the *Academic American Encyclopedia* in North America but the *Macmillan Family Encyclopedia* throughout the rest of the world—is the first entirely new large-scale multivolume general English-language encyclopedia to appear in over a decade. Published in 1980, it comprises 9,728 pages, 28,500 articles, and 15,000 illustrations in 21 volumes. The set, which is reputed to have cost over £10 million ($20 million) to launch, is admirably up-to-date, well accessed for easy and efficient retrieval of even the most specific bits of information, contains excellent bibliographies, and provides many colorful and informative visuals. Priced at £195, the *Macmillan Family Encyclopedia* is distributed in the U.K. by Macmillan London Ltd., Little Essex St., London, England WC2R 3LF. For a detailed review of the set, see the *Academic American Encyclopedia* at the beginning of Part III of the *Buying Guide*.

Merit Students Encyclopedia

This U.S.-made multivolume encyclopedia for young adults is fully described and evaluated in Part V of the *Buying Guide*. In the U.K. it is distributed by P. F. Collier Ltd., Rawplug House, 147 London Rd., Kingston, Surrey, England KT2 6BR. The current price is £592.

New Book of Knowledge

This U.S.-made multivolume encyclopedia for children aged 7–14 is fully described and evaluated in Part VI of the *Buying Guide*. In the U.K. it is distributed by Franklin Watts Ltd., 8 Cork St., London, England W1X 2HA. The current price is £175.

New Caxton Encyclopedia

Along with *Everyman's Encyclopaedia* (see above), *New Caxton* is currently the best British-produced encyclopedia on the market. The set is especially noteworthy for its handsome and plentiful illustrations, perhaps the finest of any general encyclopedia anywhere. *New Caxton* is published by Caxton Publications Ltd., Holywell House, 72–90 Worship St., London, England EC2 2EN. Currently priced at £485, the encyclopedia is very expensive for a work of only 6,500 pages, 13,000 articles, and six million words in 20 volumes. Comparatively speaking, *Everyman's,* which contains eight million words in 12 volumes, is priced at £234. *New Caxton* is distributed in the United States by Purnell Reference Books in Milwaukee. For a full evaluation of the encyclopedia, see Part III of the *Buying Guide.*

New Columbia Encyclopedia

This U.S.-made one-volume encyclopedia for advanced students and adults is fully described and evaluated in Part IV of the *Buying Guide.* In the U.K. *New Columbia* is distributed by Oxford University Press Ltd., 37 Dover St., London, England W1X 4AH. The current price is £45.

New Encyclopaedia Britannica

Although many people still think of the *Britannica*—the world's oldest, largest, and most famous English-language encyclopedia—as a British work, it has been owned and produced by Americans since the turn of the century. The "new" *Britannica* (the 15th edition, often called *Britannica 3*), which first appeared in 1974, is fully described and evaluated in Part III of the *Buying Guide.* In the U.K. it is distributed by Encyclopaedia Britannica International Ltd., 156 Oxford St., London, England W1N OHJ. The current price starts at £605.

New Hutchinson 20th Century Encyclopedia

The *New Hutchinson 20th Century Encyclopedia,* a single-volume work for adults produced in Great Britain, comprises roughly 1,300 pages, 15,000 concise articles, 1,600 black-and-white illustrations, and well over one million words. First published in 1948 as *Hutchinson's Twentieth Century Encyclopedia* and subsequently revised in 1951, 1956, and 1964 under that title, the encyclopedia was retitled *Hutchinson's New 20th Century Encyclopedia* in 1970 (fifth edition), and most recently it became the *New Hutchinson 20th Century Encyclopedia* in 1977 (sixth edition). *New Hutchinson* is published by the Hutchinson Publishing Group Ltd., 3 Fitzroy Sq., London, England W1P 6JD, at £12.50. For a time it was marketed in the United States by the Merrimack Book Service in Salem, N.H., but the book did not sell and was withdrawn from the market in 1980. See Appendix A of the *Buying Guide* for further information, including several review citations, concerning the *New Hutchinson 20th Century Encyclopedia.*

New Standard Encyclopedia

This U.S.-made multivolume encyclopedia for adults is fully described and evaluated in Part III of the *Buying Guide.* At the present time, *New Standard* is not distributed in the U.K., but it is sold abroad by independent representatives in a number of countries, including Canada, Australia, and Ireland. Foreign representatives are free to determine their own prices for the set. Such prices, however, should be in line with the current recommended U.S. retail price of $349.50 (or approximately £175).

Oxford Junior Encyclopaedia

Oxford Junior is a British-produced set for children aged 7–14. Thematically arranged, the encyclopedia comprises 6,500 pages, 3,600 articles, 6,100 illustrations, and over 3½ million words in 13 volumes. *Oxford Junior* is published by Oxford University Press Ltd., 37 Dover St., London, England W1X 4AH, at a price of £6.25 per volume (which can be purchased individually) or £75 for the set. The encyclopedia is also distributed in the United States by Oxford in New York. For a full evaluation of *Oxford Junior,* see Part VI of the *Buying Guide.*

Pears Cyclopaedia

This famous British title has been a reference standby since 1897, when A. & F. Pears Ltd., a London soap manufacturer, issued the first annual volume. Intended for adult use (there is the *Junior Pears Encyclopaedia* for the younger set; see above), *Pears* consists of 22 topical sections comprising over a thousand pages and a million words in a single volume. It is currently published by Pelham Books Ltd., 44 Bedford Sq., London, England WC1B 3DU, at £4.75. *Pears* is also distributed in North America by the Merrimack Book Service in Salem, N.H. See Part IV of the *Buying Guide* for a detailed description and evaluation of *Pears.*

Reader's Digest Library of Modern Knowledge

A brand-new work in 1977, this British-made set of three volumes is intended for students, adults, and general family use. Consisting of 1,408 pages, 2,400 graphics, and about one million words in 23 topically arranged sections, the *Reader's Digest Library of Modern Knowledge* is more a browsing set than a bona fide encyclopedia. Its virtues include clear explanations of complex subject matter, an effective index, and a reasonable price. On the other hand, the set's coverage is quite abbreviated, it lacks bibliographies, and the illustrations are undistinguished. Priced at £29.95, the set is published by the Reader's Digest Association Ltd., 25 Berkeley Sq., London, England W1X 6AB.

World Book Encyclopedia

This U.S.-made multivolume encyclopedia for young adults and the family is fully described and evaluated in Part V of the *Buying Guide.* British consumers should note, however, that the *World Book* edition sold in the U.K. has two additional volumes devoted entirely to the British Isles (hence the U.S. edition of *World Book* has 22 volumes, whereas the U.K. edition has 24). In the U.K. *World Book* is distributed by World Book-Childcraft International, Inc., Canterbury House, Sydenham Rd., Croydon, England CR9 2LR. The set currently sells for £324.

Appendix D
Encyclopedia Bibliography

Informative Books and Articles

Collison, Robert L. "Encyclopaedias," in *The New Encyclopaedia Britannica: Macropaedia,* Vol. 6. Chicago: Encyclopaedia Britannica, Inc., 1980, pp. 779–799. An outstanding encyclopedia article on encyclopedias. It has not been revised, however, since the new *Britannica* (15th edition) appeared in 1974. The article's bibliography particularly needs to be updated.

Collison, Robert L. *Encyclopedias: Their History Throughout the Ages.* 2nd ed. New York: Hafner Publishing Company, 1966. This standard work is subtitled "a bibliographical guide with extensive historical notes to the general encyclopedias issued throughout the world from 350 B.C. to the present day." The book is useful only for historical information about encyclopedias.

Darnton, Robert. *The Business of Enlightenment: A Publishing History of the Encyclopédie, 1775–1800.* Harvard University Press, 1979. Diderot's famous *Encyclopédie,* a best-seller in eighteenth-century France, helped create a cultural and political revolution. Darnton, a Princeton historian, tells the fascinating story of the *Encyclopédie*'s publishing history, including the economic and censorship problems.

Einbinder, Harvey. "Encyclopedias: Some Foreign and Domestic Developments," *Wilson Library Bulletin,* December 1980, pp. 257–261. Einbinder, a critic given to extremes, lavishly praises recent foreign developments while finding little to cheer about on the home front.

"Encyclopedia Sales Frauds," *Consumer Reports,* March 1971, pp. 172–174. Despite being a decade old, this detailed rendering of all the old door-to-door tricks still contains useful advice from one of our leading consumer magazines.

Graham, Beryl Caroline. "Treatment of Black American Women in Children's Encyclopedias," *Negro History Bulletin,* April 1976, pp. 596–598. Eight well-known encyclopedias are analyzed by Graham, a school librarian in Boston, Mass. The major finding: "There is an urgent need for the majority of children's encyclopedias to improve the image portrayals and content treatment of black American women."

Harmet, A. Richard. "Encyclopedia," in *The World Book Encyclopedia,* Vol. 6. Chicago: World Book-Childcraft International, Inc., 1980, pp. 216–222. Unlike Collison's article on encyclopedias in *The New Ency-*

clopaedia Britannica (see above), which is historical in emphasis, Harmet's article concentrates on the practical questions of how contemporary encyclopedias are made and used.

Johnston, W. T., and Trulock, Joy B. "Buying an Encyclopedia," *Consumers' Research Magazine,* February 1975, pp. 12–16. A short but helpful consumer article by two Georgia librarians.

Kister, Ken. "Encyclopedias and the Public Library: A National Survey," *Library Journal,* April 15, 1979, pp. 890–893. This questionnaire survey reports the opinions of U.S. public librarians regarding the effectiveness of each general encyclopedia currently on the North American market. Note that the survey is reprinted in Part II ("Special Reports") of the *Buying Guide,* along with Norman Horrocks's companion survey of Canadian librarians.

Kleinfield, N. R. "Encyclopedia with New Twist," *New York Times,* May 30, 1980, pp. 1-D; 9-D. Although this article deals principally with the new *Academic American Encyclopedia,* it contains valuable information on the state of the U.S. encyclopedia industry as a whole.

Kraft, Linda. "Lost Herstory: The Treatment of Women in Children's Encyclopedias," *School Library Journal,* January 1973, pp. 26–35. A well-documented analysis of sexist bias in five leading encyclopedias for young people. The specifics of Kraft's article are now dated but her basic concerns remain valid.

Machalaba, Daniel. "Coming Soon: Encyclopedias That Can Talk," *Wall Street Journal,* February 18, 1981, p. 29. A short, popularly written piece on the electronic encyclopedia that may be in your future.

SantaVicca, Edmund Frank. *The Treatment of Homosexuality in Current Encyclopedias.* Ph.D. dissertation, University of Michigan, 1977. Ann Arbor, Mich.: University Microfilms, 1979. SantaVicca's 323-page thesis objectively analyzes the scope and accessibility of information on homosexuality, male and female, in eight multivolume encyclopedias. A valuable study for editors, critics, and students of encyclopedias.

Walsh, S. Padraig. *Anglo-American General Encyclopedias: A Historical Bibliography, 1703–1967.* New York: R. R. Bowker Company, 1968. An A-to-Z listing with critical annotations. Serves as a useful complement to Collison's *Encyclopedias: Their History Throughout the Ages* (see above).

Whitelock, Otto V. St. "On the Making and Survival of Encyclopedias," *Choice,* June 1967, pp. 381–389. Though published nearly 15 years ago, this critical look at the editorial problems confronting general encyclopedias in the mid-1960s remains remarkably fresh. Whitelock, an experienced encyclopedia editor, explores such topics as what makes a great encyclopedist, the application of new technology to encyclopedia-making, and the relationship between general and specialized encyclopedias.

Additional Sources for Encyclopedia Reviews

American Reference Books Annual (ARBA). Littleton, Colo.: Libraries Unlimited, 1970–   . *ARBA* attempts to review all English-language reference works published or distributed each year in the United States, including encyclopedias. Continuously revised encyclopedias are said to be reevaluated every five years, but this schedule is not strictly followed. The encyclopedia reviews, which have grown quite lengthy in recent years, tend to be eccentric. Sometimes, for instance, the reviews are comparative, sometimes not. *ARBA*'s initial review of *Encyclopedia International* in 1971, for example, vaguely compared this young adult set with unnamed "other standard encyclopedias for the intended audience," whereas the latest review (1977) compares *Encyclopedia International* with *The Encyclopedia Americana,* a 30-volume set for an entirely different readership. *ARBA* reviews, however, are sometimes interesting and may provide an additional backup opinion if one is required.

Booklist. Chicago: American Library Association, 1905– . Semi-monthly. This periodical includes unsigned reviews produced by the ALA Reference and Subscription Books Review Committee (RSBRC). The 50-member committee, established in 1930, has as its goal to evaluate "reference books likely to be of general interest," a goal it does not attain. Continuously revised encyclopedias are said to be reexamined every five years, but this schedule is not strictly followed. At one time, RSBRC produced between 35 and 50 well-researched reviews each year. In recent times, however, while the number of reviews has increased greatly, the quality of RSBRC's criticism has noticeably deteriorated, including the encyclopedia reviews. This is exemplified by a group of reviews published under the collective title "Encyclopedias: A Survey and Buying Guide" in the *Booklist* between December 1, 1978 and February 15, 1979. These reviews were later reprinted in a pamphlet entitled *Purchasing an Encyclopedia* (see below for a detailed note on this publication).

RSBRC encyclopedia evaluations are open to the following criticisms: (1) the reviews are sometimes extremely late, as in the case of *The Random House Encyclopedia,* which was published in 1977 but not reviewed until 1980; (2) the reviews typically lack comparisons with encyclopedias of similar scope, usership, and price; (3) the reviews are quite uneven in treatment and fail to provide standard data about each encyclopedia; (4) the reviews tend to emphasize numerical counts at the expense of matters of substance; (5) the reviews are written in the sort of blank, undigestible prose associated with committees and bureaucracies; and (6) the reviews are unsigned, thus concealing individual responsibility for opinions expressed behind a roster of committee names.

Denenberg, Herbert S. "Consumers' Guide to Buying an Encyclopedia," *Caveat Emptor,* August–September 1979, pp. 19–20. In this very succinct article, Denenberg, a well-known consumer advocate, enunciates nine rules for buying an encyclopedia "that will protect you from the rip-offs and show you the way to go." He also provides thumbnail comments on nine major encyclopedias; for example, *Funk & Wagnalls New Encyclopedia* is "dollar for dollar the best encyclopedia."

Instructor. Dansville, N.Y.: Instructor Publications, Inc., 1891– . Monthly. Aimed at teachers and library media specialists, this magazine periodically comments on those encyclopedias especially appropriate for school use. While sometimes informative, these reviews lack the stringent critical standards required of authoritative evaluations. In some instances, the reviews amount to little more than publicity puffs. Under no circumstances should an encyclopedia be purchased solely on the basis of an *Instructor* review.

Katz, William A. *Basic Information Sources* (Vol. 1 of *Introduction to Reference Work,* 3rd ed. New York: McGraw-Hill, 1978), pp. 135–185. Bill Katz's brief critical comments on individual encyclopedias in Chapter 5 of this leading textbook are lucid, comparative, authoritative, and helpful to both librarians and general consumers. A new edition of *Introduction to Reference Work* is scheduled to appear early in 1982.

Purchasing an Encyclopedia: 12 Points to Consider. Chicago: American Library Association, 1979. This pamphlet reprints a series of reviews that originally appeared in the *Booklist* (see above) under the collective title "Encyclopedias: A Survey and Buying Guide." The following review of the 38-page pamphlet is reprinted from the "Professional Reading" section of *Library Journal,* December 15, 1979, p. 2632.

Published serially in *Booklist* between December 1, 1978 and February 1, 1979, this little publication includes 20 general encyclopedia reviews and 12 evaluative criteria prepared by the 60-member ALA Reference & Subscription Books Review Committee. Unfortunately, the reviews—in progress for five years (!)—are sadly deficient, and reference librarians who refer patrons to this pamphlet should be conversant with its most glaring limitations:

1) Many of the nearly 40 general encyclopedias currently in print, like the *Random House Encyclopedia,* are not reviewed nor even mentioned; 2) Quite old editions are reviewed (between 1973 and 1975) which may cause some consumer confusion, e.g., the now defunct 21-volume *Illustrated World Encyclopedia* (1973) is reviewed whereas the more recent one-volume abridgment (1977) is not covered; 3) In some instances bibliographic information is garbled, e.g., the Committee errs when it cites *Britannica Junior Encyclopaedia* as a closed entry [1935–1975] and misleads by describing *Compton's Encyclopedia* as first published in 1975; 4) Coverage of British sets distributed in this country is baffling, i.e., *Chambers's Encyclopaedia,* unrevised for years and now withdrawn from the market, is reviewed while the *New Caxton Encyclopedia,* the only British work of any consequence currently available in the U.S., is unaccountably ignored; 5) On occasion, reviews in this pamphlet directly contradict or call into question previous Committee judgments, e.g., a review of the *New Standard Encyclopedia* published in the November 1, 1977 issue of *Booklist* (p. 494–497) concludes that the set's "cross-reference structure is inconsistent and does not take the place of a good index," but the review in this pam-

phlet states, "Despite the lack of an index, the panel found the many cross-references to be almost an adequate substitute"; 6) Comparative references are skimpy and superficial, and summaries comparing encyclopedias of similar size, price, and usership are completely lacking; and 7) The writing style, always a problem for group reviewers, is uneven and soporific, except for the odd unintentionally humorous comment, e.g., one title is characterized as "fully ripened."

It is regrettable that the Committee has compromised its previous high standards of encyclopedia criticism with this inexcusably sloppy work.—KENNETH F. KISTER, EDITOR, ENCYCLOPEDIA BUYING GUIDE, TAMPA, FLA.

RQ. Chicago: Reference and Adult Services Division of the American Library Association, 1960– . Quarterly. *RQ (Reference Quarterly)* includes a review section in the back devoted to reference books. New small-volume encyclopedias and major new editions of multivolume encyclopedias are sometimes reviewed.

Sheehy, Eugene P., comp. *Guide to Reference Books*. 9th ed. Chicago: American Library Association, 1976; supplement 1980. This essential list, formerly prepared by Constance M. Winchell, includes a section on general encyclopedias. The annotations, or brief notes, normally provide only descriptive information.

Wilson Library Bulletin. New York: H. W. Wilson Company, 1914– . Monthly. This general library magazine carries a column by Charles Bunge entitled "Current Reference Books," which usually comments briefly on new small-volume encyclopedias. Large multivolume sets, however, are not reviewed.

Last but surely not least are *librarians,* indispensable sources of information about all types of reference materials, including general encyclopedias. Specifically, reference librarians can assist consumers by (1) explaining how to evaluate an encyclopedia properly, (2) providing access to critical reviews in the *Booklist, ARBA,* the Katz book, the *Buying Guide,* etc., and (3) offering advice about individual sets based on the librarian's professional experience. Note that Part II of the *Buying Guide* ("Special Reports") provides a cross section of librarian opinion in the United States and Canada regarding most encyclopedias currently on the North American market.

Appendix E
Directory of Publishers and Distributors

Distributors are designated here by an imprint note (in parentheses) following the title of an encyclopedia. Addresses of publishers and distributors of general encyclopedias in the United Kingdom are provided in Appendix C.

Americana Corporation (a subsidiary of Grolier, Inc.)
Sherman Tpke.
Danbury, CT 06816
203-797-3500
Encyclopedia Americana

Aretê Publishing Company, Inc. (a subsidiary of VNU America, Inc.)
Princeton Forrestal Center
101 College Rd. E.
Princeton, NJ 08540
609-452-8090; 800-257-5133 (toll-free)
Academic American Encyclopedia

Barnes & Noble Bookstores
Mail Order Dept.
105 Fifth Ave.
New York, NY 10003
212-924-9324
New Columbia Encyclopedia (Columbia University imprint)

Bobley Publishing Corporation
311 Crossways Park Dr.
Woodbury, NY 11797
516-364-1800
Illustrated World Encyclopedia

Bookthrift, Inc.
45 W. 36 St.
New York, NY 10018
212-947-0909; 800-223-0282 (toll-free)
University Desk Encyclopedia (Elsevier Publishing Projects imprint)

Cavendish, Marshall
See Marshall Cavendish

Caxton Publications Ltd.
See Purnell Reference Books

P. F. Collier, Inc.
See Macmillan Educational Corporation

Columbia University Press
562 W. 113 St.
New York, NY 10025
212-678-6777
New Columbia Encyclopedia

Comet Press
See The Publishers Agency, Inc.

F. E. Compton Company (a division of Encyclopaedia Britannica, Inc.)
425 N. Michigan Ave.
Chicago, IL 60611
312-321-6600
Compton's Encyclopedia and Fact-Index
Compton's Precyclopedia

Elsevier Dutton Publishing Company, Inc.
2 Park Ave.
New York, NY 10016
212-725-1818
University Desk Encyclopedia (Elsevier Publishing Projects imprint)

Elsevier International Projects Ltd.
See Marshall Cavendish

Elsevier Publishing Projects
See Elsevier Dutton Publishing Company, Inc.

Encyclopaedia Britannica, Inc.
425 N. Michigan Ave.
Chicago, IL 60611
312-321-7000
  Britannica Junior Encyclopaedia
  Compton's Encyclopedia and Fact-Index (Compton's imprint)
  Compton's Precyclopedia (Compton's imprint)
  New Encyclopaedia Britannica
  Young Children's Encyclopedia

Encyclopaedia Britannica Educational Corporation
425 N. Michigan Ave.
Chicago, IL 60611
800-621-3900 (toll-free)
  Britannica Junior Encyclopaedia (Encyclopaedia Britannica imprint)
  Compton's Encyclopedia and Fact-Index (Compton's imprint)
  Compton's Precyclopedia (Compton's imprint)
  New Encyclopaedia Britannica (Encyclopaedia Britannica imprint)
  Random House Encyclopedia (Special Two-Volume School & Library Edition; Random House imprint)

Field Enterprises Educational Corporation
See World Book-Childcraft International, Inc.

Frontier Press Company
Box 1098
Columbus, OH 43216
614-864-5278
  New Lincoln Library Encyclopedia (also known as *The Lincoln Library of Essential Information*)

Funk & Wagnalls, Inc.
666 Fifth Ave.

New York, NY 10019
212-974-0713
  Funk & Wagnalls New Encyclopedia
  Young Students Encyclopedia

Grolier, Inc.
Sherman Tpke.
Danbury, CT 06816
203-797-3500
  Encyclopedia Americana (Americana imprint)
  Encyclopedia International (Lexicon imprint)
  New Book of Knowledge

Harver Educational Services, Inc.
See Marshall Cavendish

Lexicon Publications, Inc. (a subsidiary of Grolier, Inc.)
Sherman Tpke.
Danbury, CT 06816
203-797-3500
  Encyclopedia International

Macdonald-Raintree, Inc.
See Purnell Reference Books

Macmillan Educational Corporation (a subsidiary of Macmillan, Inc.)
866 Third Ave.
New York, NY 10022
212-935-2000
  Collier's Encyclopedia
  Merit Students Encyclopedia

Marshall Cavendish
147 W. Merrick Rd.
Freeport, NY 11520
516-546-4200
  Harver World Encyclopedia (Harver Educational Services imprint; Elsevier International Projects imprint)

Mayflower Books, Inc.
575 Lexington Ave.
New York, NY 10022
212-888-9200
  Junior Encyclopedia of General Knowledge (Octopus imprint)

Merrimack Book Service, Inc.
99 Main St.
Salem, NH 03079
617-685-4636
  Junior Pears Encyclopaedia (Pelham
    Books imprint)
  Pears Cyclopaedia (Pelham Books
    imprint)

Thomas Nelson Publishers
405 Seventh Ave. S.
Nashville, TN 37203
615-244-3733; 800-251-1236 (toll-free)
  *Nelson's Encyclopedia for Young
    Readers*

Octopus Books Ltd.
See Mayflower Books, Inc.

Oxford University Press, Inc.
200 Madison Ave.
New York, NY 10016
212-679-7300
  Oxford Junior Encyclopaedia

Pelham Books Ltd.
See Merrimack Book Service, Inc.

Pergamon Press, Inc.
Maxwell House
Fairview Park
Elmsford, NY 10523
914-592-7700
  *Purnell's First Encyclopedia in Col-
    our* (Purnell & Sons imprint)
  Purnell's Pictorial Encyclopedia
    (Purnell & Sons imprint)

The Publishers Agency, Inc.
1411 Ford Rd.
Cornwell Heights, PA 19020
215-638-7000
  *Illustrated Encyclopedia for Learn-
    ing* (Comet imprint)
  New American Encyclopedia

Purnell & Sons Ltd.
See Pergamon Press, Inc.

Purnell Reference Books (a division of
  Macdonald-Raintree, Inc.)
205 W. Highland Ave.

Milwaukee, WI 53203
414-273-0873
  New Caxton Encyclopedia (Caxton
    imprint)

Quality Books, Inc.
400 Anthony Trail
Northbrook, IL 60062
800-323-4241 (toll-free)
  Funk & Wagnalls New Encyclopedia
    (Funk & Wagnalls imprint)

Rand McNally & Company
Box 7600
Chicago, IL 60680
312-673-9100
  *Rand McNally's Children's Encyclo-
    pedia*

Random House, Inc.
201 E. 50 St.
New York, NY 10022
212-751-2600
  Random House Encyclopedia

Rockville House Publishers, Inc. (a division of Sigma Marketing Systems, Inc.)
615 South St.
Garden City, NY 11530
516-827-2700
  *New Illustrated Columbia Encyclo-
    pedia*

Southwestern Company
Box 810
Nashville, TN 37202
615-790-4000
  Volume Library

Standard Educational Corporation
200 W. Monroe St.
Chicago, IL 60606
312-346-7440
  New Standard Encyclopedia

Time-Life Books, Inc.
777 Duke St.
Alexandria, VA 22314
703-960-5000
  *New Illustrated Columbia Encyclo-
    pedia* (Rockville House imprint)

Troll Associates
320 Rte. 17
Mahwah, NJ 07430
201-529-4000; 800-526-5289 (toll-free)
  Talking Cassette Encyclopedia

VNU America, Inc.
See Aretê Publishing Company, Inc.

Webster Publishing Company Ltd.
1644 Bay View Ave.
Toronto, Ontario M4G 3C2 Canada
416-484-6900; 800-268-6362 (toll-free)
  New American Encyclopedia (Publishers Agency imprint)
  Webster's New Age Encyclopedia (same as *Encyclopedia International;* Lexicon imprint)

World Book-Childcraft International, Inc. (a subsidiary of the Scott & Fetzer Company)
510 Merchandise Mart Plaza
Chicago, IL 60654
321-245-3456
  Childcraft: The How and Why Library
  World Book Encyclopedia

Xerox Education Publications
245 Long Hill Rd.
Middletown, CT 06457
203-347-7251
  Young Students Encyclopedia

Title and Subject Index

Encyclopedias fully reviewed in the *Buying Guide* are CAPITALIZED in the index. The word *encyclopaedia* is alphabetized as if it were spelled *encyclopedia*. Readers seeking information about encyclopedias as a type of reference work (as opposed to a specific title) should first consult the heading "Encyclopedias—general information" and its many analytical references.

public library surveys, 58, 66
See also *Funk & Wagnalls Standard Reference Encyclopedia,* 482–483
Funk & Wagnalls New Encyclopedia Yearbook, 127–128, 134
Funk & Wagnalls New Standard Encyclopedia of Universal Knowledge, 123
See also *Funk & Wagnalls Standard Reference Encyclopedia,* 482
Funk & Wagnalls Standard Desk Dictionary, 133
Funk & Wagnalls Standard Encyclopedia, 123
Funk & Wagnalls Standard Reference Encyclopedia, 482–483
See also *Funk & Wagnalls New Encyclopedia,* 123, 125, 134; *New Universal Standard Encyclopedia,* 494

Golden Book Encyclopedia, 483
public library survey, 58, 66
See also *Golden Home and High School Encyclopedia,* 483; *Illustrated Encyclopedia for Learning,* 383
Golden High School Encyclopedia, 483
Golden Home and High School Encyclopedia, 483
See also *Golden Treasury of Knowledge,* 483
Golden Junior High School Encyclopedia, 483
Golden Treasury of Knowledge, 483–484
Goode's World Atlas, 240
Great Books of the Western World, 182
Great Soviet Encyclopedia, 7, 99
Great Spectrum Encyclopedia, 79, 274
Great World Encyclopedia, 484
public library surveys, 58, 66
Grolier, Inc., 19–21, 112, 321, 327, 388, 390–391, 397, 518
Federal Trade Commission case (Von Brand decision), 25–26
Grolier Encyclopedia, 484
See also *Encyclopedia International,* 321; *Grolier Universal Encyclopedia,* 485; *Richards Topical Encyclopedia,* 496; *Unified Encyclopedia,* 497
Grolier Universal Encyclopedia, 485
See also *Encyclopedia International,* 321; *Grolier Encyclopedia,* 484
Grote Spectrum Encyclopedie, 79

Grote Winkler Prins Encyclopedie, 139, 144, 288
Guide to Reference Books (Sheehy), 36, 516
Guinness Book of World Records, 482

Hamlyn Children's Encyclopedia in Colour, 495–496
Hamlyn Younger Children's Encyclopedia, 485
public library surveys, 58, 66
See also *Rand McNally Student Encyclopedia,* 495
Hammond Almanac of a Million Facts, Records, Forecasts, 501
Handbook of Buying (Consumers' Research), 45
Handy Encyclopedia of Useful Information, 482
Harmsworth's Universal Encyclopedia, 484
Harvard Encyclopedia of American Ethnic Groups, 36
Harver Junior World Encyclopedia, 485–486
See also *Purnell's First Encyclopedia in Colour,* 459
HARVER WORLD ENCYCLOPEDIA, 136–147
chart, *see* insert
public library surveys, 58, 66
See also *Harver Junior World Encyclopedia,* 485–486
Historia Naturalis (Pliny), 5
Home University Encyclopedia, 486–487
How and Why Library, 369–370
How to Use Britannica 3, 197–198
Human Interest Library, 493
Hutchinson's New 20th Century Encyclopedia, 489–490, 493, 510
Hutchinson's Twentieth Century Encyclopedia, 493, 510

Illustrated Columbia Encyclopedia, 487
See also *Columbia Encyclopedia,* 480; *New Columbia Encyclopedia,* 240; *New Illustrated Columbia Encyclopedia,* 211–212, 218
ILLUSTRATED ENCYCLOPEDIA FOR LEARNING, 383–387
chart, *see* insert